Multimedia Literacy

Second Edition

Fred T. Hofstetter

University of Delaware

With Multimedia CD-ROM by

Patricia Fox

Trident Technical College

Irwin
McGraw-Hill

Boston, Massachusetts   Burr Ridge, Illinois   Dubuque, Iowa
Madison, Wisconsin   New York, New York   San Francisco, California   St. Louis, Missouri

DEDICATION

Throughout this project my wife, Laura, provided a constant source of inspiration and support. She was always eager to be the first beta tester of the tutorials in this book.

During our courtship in 1979, when Laura was head of the PLATO mainframe computer in Belgium and I directed one in the United States, we would log on during off-peak times and exercise our system privileges to use the intercontinental PLATO satellite link for two-way interactive conversations. My proposal that we marry filled 11 screens. This book is dedicated to the memory of the day she typed *y-e-s.*

Irwin/McGraw-Hill

*A Division of The **McGraw·Hill** Companies*

Multimedia Literacy, Second Edition

Copyright © 1997, 1995, by The McGraw-Hill Companies, Inc. All rights reserved. Printed in the United States of America. Except as permitted under the United States Copyright Act of 1976, no part of this publication may be reproduced or distributed in any form or by any means, or stored in a database or retrieval system, without the prior written permission of the publisher.

Disclaimer: This book and the accompanying optical disc are designed to help you improve your computer use. However, the author and publisher assume no responsibility whatsoever for the uses made of this material or for decisions based on their use, and make no warranties, either expressed or implied, regarding the contents of this book or any accompanying optical disc, its merchantability, or its fitness for any particular purpose.

Neither the publisher nor anyone else who has been involved in the creation, production, or delivery of this product shall be liable for any direct, incidental, or consequential damages, such as, but not limited to, loss of anticipated profits or benefits resulting from its use or from any breach of any warranty. Some states do not allow the exclusion or limitation of direct, incidental, or consequential damages, so the above disclaimer may not apply to you. No dealer, company, or person is authorized to alter this disclaimer. Any representation to the contrary will not bind the publisher or author.

This book is printed on acid-free paper.

2 3 4 5 6 7 8 9 0 VNH VNH 9 0 3 2 1 0 9 8 7

P/N 029389-9

ORDER INFORMATION
ISBN 0-07-913107-7

This book was set in Utopia and Gill Sans.
The editor was Rhonda Sands.
The production supervisor was Richard DeVitto.
The project manager was Gary Palmatier.
The copy editor was Elizabeth von Radics.
Illustrations were by Ideas to Images.
The cover and interior designs were by Gary Palmatier, Ideas to Images.
The compositor was Ideas to Images.
Von Hoffmann Press, Inc., was printer and binder.

The credits on page xxi are an extension of this copyright page.

Library of Congress Cataloging-in-Publication Data
Hofstetter, Fred T. (Fred Thomas), 1949–
    Multimedia literacy / by Fred T. Hofstetter ; with a multimedia CD-ROM
  produced by Pat Fox. — 2nd ed.3.
        p.   cm.
    Includes index.
    ISBN 0-07-913107-7
      1. Multimedia systems.   2. Computer literacy.   3. CD-ROMs.
  I. Fox, Patricia.
QA76.575.H645 1997
006.6 — dc20   96-43261
                                          CIP

http://www.mhcollege.com

Contents

HANDS-ON TUTORIAL

Part Five   Multimedia Tools and Techniques   199

CHAPTER **18**   **Screen Design Principles**   200

CHAPTER **19**   **WYSIWYG Text Editing**   207

CHAPTER **20**   **Graphics**   223

CHAPTER 5 7 **Multimedia and the Web**   456

HANDS-ON TUTORIAL

Part Eleven   Multimedia Front-Ending   459

CHAPTER 5 8 **Front-End Your PC**   460

CHAPTER 5 9 **Front-End Your Television Tuner**   465

CHAPTER 6 0 **Front-End the World Wide Web**   472

CHAPTER 6 1 **Front-End the Stock Market**   478

Introduction

AS CHAIRMAN of Chrysler Corporation, Lee Iacocca said, "Lead, follow, or get out of the way." So it is with multimedia. Never has an industry grown so quickly or had such an impact on the way we receive, process, and communicate ideas.

This book is designed to teach you about the world of multimedia—how multimedia is changing the world we live in, how to use it effectively, why it became a multibillion-dollar industry so quickly, and the impact it will have on your way of life. This book will also teach you how to tell when someone is using multimedia, how to see through the hype, and, most important, how to do it yourself—how to create your own multimedia applications and make them sizzle with effectiveness.

This book defines and teaches the basic skills of multimedia. Skills that will enable you to create beautifully typeset text, full-color pictures, animation, audio commentary, motion video clips, and stereo sound tracks. Skills that let you surf the Internet, download multimedia objects, and create multimedia Web pages. Skills that let you put any word or picture anyplace on your computer screen and make any part of the screen into a trigger that you can link to any object on your computer. When a user selects one of the triggers, the object of the link will appear. This object can be text, a picture, a sound, a movie, an animation, a Web page, or an application on your computer or network.

Think about the power this provides: Once you can display an object on your computer screen and link it to any other object on your computer, you have gained control over all your computer's capabilities. You can have your computer provide you with instant access to every note you ever took, every talk you ever gave, and every slide you ever photographed. You can create an effective presentation that includes instant access to all of your company's information when your boss asks you for a report. You can author a multimedia title and publish it on a CD-ROM or mount it on the World Wide Web (WWW). You can send multimedia e-mail messages to anyone with a multimedia PC connected to the Internet. If you would like to be able to do some of these things, this is the book for you.

Organization

This book and its accompanying CD-ROM have twelve parts. The first four are conceptual, dealing with definitions, principles, applications, hardware, future trends, and social issues; the rest of the book is a tutorial, which teaches you how to create multimedia applications and World Wide Web pages. The CD-ROM brings what you read to life through color pictures, stereo sound, animation, and full-motion video clips.

Part One defines multimedia, tells you who uses it for what, describes how it is changing the world, tells you who needs to know about it, and provides a taxonomy of multimedia objects that you can use when creating your own applications.

Part Two deals with multimedia applications. Dozens of full-color screen prints and photos illustrate how multimedia is being used in classrooms, boardrooms, homes, retail stores, just-in-time training, cinema, video arcades, government, and industry. The CD-ROM that comes with this book includes demonstrations of these applications that you can run on any multimedia PC with Windows 3.1, Windows 95, or Windows NT, or on the Macintosh with SoftWindows version 2.0 or higher. The CD also demonstrates several of the development packages that were used to create these applications.

Part Three focuses on multimedia hardware. Remember how the VHS and Beta videotape standards competed for market share when home VCRs were invented? There are even more competing multimedia standards today. Part Three tells you what the standards are, recommends the standard to follow, and provides a checklist of features to look for when buying a multimedia computer.

Part Four looks into the future of multimedia and discusses how it will impact us all. Acknowledging the rapid rate at which the technology is advancing, Part Four describes how you can keep up with this fascinating field, continue to increase your multimedia skills, and help influence future uses of multimedia.

Parts Five through Eight provide you with a multimedia toolkit. Step-by-step tutorials guide you through the creation of text, graphics, sound, and video, using the multimedia authoring software PODIUM, which is included on the CD-ROM. You will learn how to enter text, import clip art, digitize existing pictures, create new pictures, record sound, create MIDI sequences, make CD Audio clips, edit digital video, create buttons, and interact with the user. Then you will use these skills to create a multimedia application on the history of flight. In addition, the *Multiliteracy CD* contains resources for creating several advanced applications.

Part Nine teaches you how to send and receive multimedia e-mail. You will learn how to create a multimedia e-mail message, pack the message into an e-mail envelope, and send it to anyone on the Internet. You will be able to pack any combination of pictures, audio, video, software, and multimedia applications into your e-mail envelope.

Part Ten is a World Wide Web page tutorial, in which you will learn how to create a home page and a résumé and mount them on the Web. The home page will establish your presence on the Web, and your online résumé can help you get a job.

Part Eleven teaches multimedia front-ending, which makes computers and networks easier to use. For example, with a single mouse click, your users will be able to perform tasks that formerly required many complicated transactions with different servers on the network.

Part Twelve concludes the book with a tutorial on multimedia publishing, providing you with strategies and techniques for distributing your applications.

In addition to letting you complete the tutorials, the version of the authoring software PODIUM included on the CD-ROM lets you create small applications with up to seven original screens. To create longer applications, however, you will need to order a retail copy of the software. See Appendix A for ordering information.

Also included at the back of the book is a section called "For Further Information." This section contains contact information for many of the products (software, hardware, publications, and other resources) discussed in this book.

The book concludes with a glossary that defines the terms a multimedia-literate person should know. The author has coined a new term that combines the words *multimedia* and *literate* into the adjective **multiliterate**, which is what you will be when you finish this book:

> **mul·ti·lit·er·ate** \ ˌməl-tē-'li-tə-rət \ *adj* : understanding the principles of multimedia, its impact on the world, and how to use it for attaining business, professional, educational, and personal objectives.

Interactive CD-ROM Brings the Book to Life

The CD-ROM packaged with this book is known as the *Multiliteracy CD*. The CD is tied to each chapter in the book and includes:

- Hundreds of examples, vividly illustrated with pictures, animation, and full-motion video clips

- Demonstrations of many of the most popular commercial multimedia packages available today

- A step-by-step tutorial on how to build multimedia applications using PODIUM, which is included on the CD

- Clip art, clip music, and clip video for creating advanced multimedia applications

- Shareware versions of the graphics programs, video tools, multimedia utilities, e-mail client, and Web page creation tools used in the tutorials

- An electronic version of the index, with hypermedia links to the multimedia materials that were used to present it initially

The book and the CD are designed to serve either as a course of instruction that can be used in more-formal settings, or for self-study by those learning more informally. The reading level and computer skills required are appropriate for any business professional, teacher, executive, college student, marketing rep, audiovisual professional, or high-school student.

- Chapter 1 illustrates how multimedia impacts everyone's way of life, with charts and graphs that show why it's to anyone's advantage to become multiliterate.

- Chapter 2 provides a taxonomy of multimedia, and the CD-ROM brings the taxonomy to life with multimedia examples in full color with stereo sound, animation, and full-motion video clips.

- Chapters 3 through 8 survey multimedia applications in business, education, entertainment, government, health, and public information. The book provides a comprehensive overview of these applications, whereas the CD contains demonstrations of selected applications supplied by multimedia publishers. The demos allow you to take products for a "test drive" and consider whether you would like to purchase a retail copy.

- Chapter 9 profiles several of the development packages that were used to create these applications. The book explains the purposes of the different packages, and the CD demonstrates their features.

One of the most important issues in multimedia is deciding what hardware to buy.

- Chapter 10 reviews the competing multimedia standards and recommends the one to follow.

- Chapter 11 presents the components of a multimedia computer.

- Chapter 12 provides a checklist that will come in handy when you buy a multimedia computer.

- Chapter 13 shows you how to configure a multimedia computer so that all of the audio and video mixing can be done by your software, without the need for an external video or audio mixer.

- The CD illustrates all of this in full color, providing a multimedia hardware presentation that can be used to present and discuss these materials in class.

The next four chapters look into the future of multimedia:

- Chapter 14 explores the multimedia frontiers of electronic publishing, fiber-optic superhighways, rural datafication, and virtual reality.

- Chapter 15 reviews emerging video, voice, and datacommunication technologies and shows how they are creating a new form of multimedia called telecomputing.

- Chapter 16 addresses the issues raised by the impact multimedia is having on our sensibilities and moralities, questions who is in control, describes the problems multimedia is causing, and suggests what you can do to solve them.

- Chapter 17 offers suggestions for staying abreast of new developments in this fast-paced field, and how to contribute your own ideas to the continued evolution of multimedia.

- The CD contains a multimedia presentation that will not only help instructors present this material in class, but also provide individual readers with a quick online reference.

Hands-on Tutorial and Projects

The rest of the book is a hands-on tutorial you complete on your multimedia computer.

- Chapters 18 through 22 cover introductory multimedia tools and techniques. The book provides step-by-step instructions for the tools and techniques that you will use to create multimedia projects.

- The CD includes hypermedia software that lets you create these applications, along with an "answer section" that shows one correct way of completing them.

■ Chapters 23 through 28 contain a project in which you will create a simple multimedia application called the History of Flight. You will use multimedia on the CD to make the aircraft come to life with full-color slides, audio clips, and full-motion video.

■ Chapters 29 through 44 present more tools and techniques, and Chapters 45 and 46 show how to design and create advanced applications that use resources provided on the *Multiliteracy CD.* For students with Internet access, Chapter 47 teaches World Wide Web search strategies and shows how to download multimedia objects from the Internet.

■ Chapters 48 through 51 show how to create, send, and receive multimedia e-mail messages over the Internet.

■ Chapters 52 through 57 are a Web page creation tutorial that includes multimedia as well as more-traditional Web page elements.

■ Chapters 58 through 61 deal with multimedia front-ending. Tutorials demonstrate how to front-end your PC, television, Web sites, and the stock market.

■ The projects culminate in Chapters 62 through 66, where you learn how to distribute applications on CD, on diskettes, and on the World Wide Web.

World Wide Web References

Throughout this book you will find World Wide Web addresses listed as references you can visit to find out more about a given topic. The Web addresses begin with *http://.* When you want to go to a Web address, pull down your Web browser's File menu, choose Open Location, and type the Web address. On the *Multiliteracy CD,* the addresses are hotlinked to their corresponding Web sites: Clicking on a Web address makes the CD tell the browser to go to that Web page.

The World Wide Web is a dynamic technology with new Web sites getting created every day. Sometimes Web sites get removed. As this book goes to press, all of the Web addresses printed here are working perfectly. If you discover that a Web site no longer exists, just move on to the next sentence in the book.

Instructor's Guide

An *Instructor's Guide* accompanies *Multimedia Literacy.* The guide includes suggested course outlines, a test bank, teaching tips, hints for helping students when they encounter difficulties, and strategies for using the text and CD in class.

System Requirements

The software on the *Multiliteracy CD* will run on any computer that meets or exceeds the following specifications:

■ 4 megabytes of RAM

■ 386SX processor

■ hard disk drive with 4 megabytes of storage free

■ CD-ROM drive

■ 8-bit waveform audio

■ 640 × 480 display with 256 colors

In general, the faster your processor and the more RAM you have, the faster your software will run. More-detailed information about multimedia hardware selection is provided in Part Three of this book.

How to Install the Software on the CD-ROM

The CD that comes with this book is known as the *Multiliteracy CD.* The software on the CD is very easy to install on any computer that has Windows 3.1 or higher. Simply insert the CD into your CD-ROM drive and run the install program you will find in the root directory of the CD. Here are detailed instructions that show how to perform the installation:

▶ If your computer is not already running Windows, type **WIN** and press Enter.

If you have Windows 3.1 on a PC or SoftWindows on a Macintosh:

▶ Pull down the Program Manager's File menu and select Run. The Run dialog will appear.

If you have Windows 95:

▶ Click the Start button and select Run. The Run dialog will appear.

Then follow these steps to install the CD:

▶ In the Run dialog, you must tell the computer to run the install program from the root directory of the CD. Assuming the CD-ROM drive is D, here is the command to type: **D:\install**

▶ Click the OK button, and a PODIUM Installation dialog will appear. All of the software on the CD is accessed via PODIUM.

▶ The Installation dialog will ask you just one question: On what drive do you want to install PODIUM? You should respond by typing the letter of your hard drive, which will probably be C.

▶ The installation creates a very important directory called *wnpodium* to provide PODIUM with a read/write workspace on your hard drive.

▶ When the installation is done, you will find a PODIUM icon in the PODIUM group on your Windows desktop. The name of the icon is *Multimedia Literacy.* To start the CD, double-click this icon. You will find that much of this book is available in a multimedia format on the CD. The CD is self-explanatory; go ahead and explore it.

▶ If you have an Internet connection, you should tell PODIUM the name of your Web browser so the CD can launch Web sites when you click on Web resources. If PODIUM is full-screen, press F2 to put PODIUM into a window. Pull down the PODIUM Controls menu, choose Configuration, and enter the complete path\filename of your Web browser in the WWW Browser field. Do not change anything else in the configuration, which is set up automatically for you. Then click OK. Press F2 to make PODIUM go full-screen again.

Acknowledgments

Creating this book is one of the most exciting projects I have worked on. While researching it I made many new friends, and the brainstorming that ensued inspired new ideas and innovations.

I want to acknowledge and thank all of my students, who continue to teach me a lot.

Carl Jacobson, director of Management Information Services at the University of Delaware, inspired PODIUM's ability to front-end the World Wide Web. Thanks to Carl's insight and advice, it became possible for PODIUM users to access and repurpose Web data in a simple yet powerful way.

University of Delaware research professor L. Leon Campbell provided valuable service as the author's "intelligent agent" on the Internet. Almost daily, Leon sent the author information about new media and the Web from his extensive surfing of the network. Leon is a valued friend and colleague.

Caravel Academy teacher Judith Conway and University of Delaware professors Frank Murray, Al Cavalier, and Lou Mosberg contributed to the section on cognitive psychology in Chapter 4. I am grateful for their insight and collegiality.

Susan Brynteson, director of libraries at the University of Delaware, read and commented on the section on copyright and fair use of new media, as did Lisa Livingston, director of CUNY's Instructional Media Division and chair of the CCUMC Fair Use working committee. I am grateful for the guidance they provided. All educators owe a debt of gratitude to Lisa for her dedication to creating the CCUMC *Fair Use Guidelines for Educational Multimedia*.

Pat Fox, Trident Technical College's professor of computer graphics and CD-ROM designer par excellence, produced the *Multiliteracy CD*. She designed it so that users always realize where they are and how to navigate elsewhere. When you try the CD, you will surely agree that Pat is an expert in making hyper-media easy to use.

When Frank Ruggirello worked for McGraw-Hill, he managed the first edition of this book. Rhonda Sands of McGraw-Hill succeeded him and oversaw the production of the second edition. I am grateful to both Frank and Rhonda for many inspirations and contributions, especially for providing the resources for Pat Fox to create the *Multiliteracy CD*.

I want to thank the production crew at Ideas to Images. Copy editor Elizabeth von Radics, who became known affectionately as the "Serif of Style," not only improved my writing style, but she also made many contributions based on her knowledge of computer technology and multimedia techniques. Likewise, project manager Gary Palmatier not only did a superb job of designing the graphics and laying out the text so it would fit within the prescribed page count, but he also made many insightful suggestions and even wrote a few missing paragraphs. Every author should be so blessed as to have a production team that understands the subject matter so well.

At the University of Delaware, my assistant Denise Methven coordinated hundreds of contacts with the vendors who provided products for review and illustration. George Harding, who is one of the world's best multimedia hardware engineers, reviewed and commented on references to hardware. Pat Sine, who manages the Instructional Technology Center (ITC), read and commented on the entire document, especially the section on the World Wide Web. ITC network administrator George Mulford, a linguist, gave the manuscript a most careful reading, and I am grateful for his contributions. Student assistant Grahame Murray worked through the tutorial to verify its accuracy.

Many reviewers provided helpful suggestions, insights, and constructive criticisms of the manuscript and early versions of the CD-ROM. I would like to thank: John Anderson, Pamplin College of Business at Virginia Polytechnic Institute; Sultan Bhimjee, San Francisco State University; Pat Fox, Trident Technical College; Pat Harley, Howard Community College; Bill Hix, Motlow State Community College; Tom Oliver, Clark State Community College, Ohio; and Mark Workman, Frank Philips Community College.

Finally, the 1996 multimedia class of the National Computer Educator's Institute spent two weeks under the expert tutelage of Pat Fox, working with a rough draft of the manuscript and an early version of the CD-ROM. Many improvements to the text and CD resulted from their intense 12-hour-a-day sessions with the package. We will always be grateful to: Lila G. Adkins, Howard College; Donna M. Austin, Louisiana State University—Shreveport; Frank W. Averill, Judson College; Jack A. Bajema, Grand Rapids Community College; Sharon R. Bajema, Ottawa Hills Science & Math Academy; Fred W. Bounds, Dekalb College; Carlos Candelario, University del Este; Jaime F. Castillo, U.P.A.E.P.—Puebla, Mexico; Denise Duzan, Panola College; Lyn C. Emmons, Niagara College; Ann Eubanks, SUNY Plattsburgh; Donald F. Fama, Cayuga Community College; Carlos R. Figueroa, Universidad del Turabo; Kent W. Fockler, Tulsa Junior College; Thomas D. Hankins, West Virginia Graduate College; Van L. Jorgensen, Big Bend Community College; Gene R. Lundak, Winona State University; Bill J. Moon, Palm Beach Community College; Nancy L. Nelson, Conestoga College; Margaret G. Robinson, Lawson State Community College; Susan Sikina, Delaware Technical Community College; J. Marvin Walker, Blinn College; and Cathy Yang, University of the Ozarks.

Credits

Figure 1-2: Courtesy of Link Resource.

Figure 1-3: Courtesy of Market Vision.

Figure 1-4: Courtesy of Frost & Sullivan.

Figures 1-5, 29-1: Courtesy of Intel Corp.

Figure 1-6: Rendering by Donna Cox and Robert Patterson, National Center for Supercomputing Applications/University of Illinois; data collection by Merit Network, Inc.

Figure 2-1: © 1994 USA Today. Reprinted with permission.

Figures 2-2, 11-1, 11-2, 11-4, 11-5, 11-6, 11-7, 13-6, 15-2, 15-3: Photos by Jack Buxbaum.

Figures 2-4, 2-5: Courtesy of BeachWare.

Figures 2-5, 2-6, 31-9, 31-10, 37-2: Courtesy of Jasmine Multimedia Publishing, Inc.

Figure 2-7: Courtesy of K-Mart.

Figure 3-1: Courtesy of MusicWriter.

Figure 3-2: Courtesy of IBM Corporation.

Figure 3-3: Photo of Capitol by Roger Goldingay. © Aris Multimedia Entertainment, Inc. 1994.

Figure 3-4: Courtesy of Union Pacific Railroad.

Figures 3-5, 9-10, 9-11, 9-12, 9-13, 45-11: Courtesy of Allen Communication.

Figures 3-6, 3-7, 3-8: Courtesy of AT&T.

Figure 3-9: Courtesy of Industrial Training Corporation.

Figures 3-10, 3-11, 3-12, 3-13: Courtesy of Chrysler Corporation.

Figures 3-14, 3-15, 3-16: Courtesy of Styles on Video, Inc.

Figure 4-1: Courtesy of National Training Laboratories (NTL) Institute.

Figures 4-2, 4-3, 4-47: Courtesy of The Learning Company.

Figures 4-4, 4-5: Courtesy of National Geographic Society.

Figures 4-6, 4-7, 4-8: Courtesy of Amazing Media.

Figure 4-9: Courtesy of the National Association of Biology Teachers.

Figures 4-10, 4-11, 4-12: Courtesy of Falcon Software, Inc.

Figure 4-13: Courtesy of University of Delaware.

Figures 4-14, 4-15, 8-8, 8-9, 8-10, 8-11, 8-12: Courtesy of McGraw-Hill, Inc.

Figures 4-16, 4-17: Courtesy of Syracuse Language Systems.

Figures 4-18, 4-19: Courtesy of Heinle & Heinle, Inc.

Figures 4-20, 4-21, 4-45, 4-46, 5-8, 5-9, 18-5: Courtesy of Brøderbund Software, Inc.

Figures 4-22, 4-23, 4-24: Courtesy of Multicom Publishing, Inc.

Figures 4-25, 4-26: Courtesy of Environmental Systems Research Institute.

Figures 4-27, 4-28, 4-29, 4-30, 5-10, 5-11: Courtesy of Medio Multimedia, Inc.

Figure 4-31: Courtesy of Scott Foresman and American Broadcasting Corporation.

Figures 4-32, 4-33: Courtesy of MidiSoft Corporation.

Figure 4-34: © 1995 Play Music, Inc.

Figure 4-35: © 1995 Voyetra.

Figures 4-36, 8-4, 8-5, 8-6: Courtesy of Compton's NewMedia, Inc.

Figure 4-37: Courtesy of The Learning Team.

Figure 4-38: Courtesy of The Education Group, Inc.

Figures 4-39, 4-40: Courtesy of Videodiscovery, Inc.

Figures 4-41, 4-42: Courtesy of KidSoft, Inc.

Figures 4-43, 4-44: Courtesy of Macmillan New Media.

Figure 4-48: Courtesy of 7th Level, Inc.

Figures 4-49, 4-50, 18-3: Courtesy of Time Warner Interactive.

Figures 5-1, 5-2: Courtesy of Gryphon Software Corporation.

Figures 5-3, 5-4, 5-5: Courtesy of Drew Pictures.

Figures 5-6, 5-7: Courtesy of Phillips Interactive Media of America.

Figures 5-12, 5-13: Courtesy of Straylight Corp.

Figures 5-14, 5-15: Courtesy of StereoGraphics Corporation.

Figures 5-16, 5-17: Courtesy of Sports Sciences.

Figures 6-1, 6-2: Courtesy of CITY-INFO.

Figure 6-3: Courtesy of North Communications.

Figures 6-4, 6-5, 6-6: Courtesy of Oregon Department of Human Resources.

Figures 6-7, 6-8, 6-9, 6-10: Courtesy of Georgia Tech Multimedia Lab.

Figure 6-11: Courtesy of Quanta Press.

Figures 7-1, 7-2, 7-3, 7-4: Courtesy of The BOHLE Company.

Figure 7-5: The Dynamic Human: The 3d Visual Guide to Anatomy and Physiology. Copyright © 1996 Times Mirror Higher Education Group, Inc., Dubuque, Iowa. All rights reserved. Reprinted by permission.

Figures 7-6, 7-7: Courtesy of High Techsplanations, Inc.

Figures 8-1, 8-2, 8-3, 18-1: Courtesy of Grolier Electronic Publishing, Inc.

Figures 9-1, 9-2: Courtesy of Microsoft Corporation.

Figures 9-3, 9-4, 9-5, 9-6: Courtesy of Software Publishing Corporation.

Figures 9-7, 9-8, 9-9: Courtesy of Macromedia, Inc.

Figures 11-3, 13-3: Courtesy of Creative Labs, Inc.

Figure 13-4: Courtesy of Turtle Beach Systems, Inc.

Figure 14-2: © 1996 Len Bullard. Used by permission.

Figure 15-1: Courtesy of RCA.

Figures 23-1, 23-5, 24-1, 25-1, 26-1, 27-1, 28-1: Photos by David K. Brunn. © 1994 Aris Multimedia Entertainment, Inc.

Figures 31-4, 31-5, 31-6: Photos by Aris Entertainment. © 1994 Aris Multimedia Entertainment, Inc.

Figures 33-1, 33-2, 33-3, 33-4: Courtesy of PG Music, Inc.

Figure 44-2: Courtesy of Pat Fox.

Figures 47-1, 47-6: Courtesy of Yahoo.

Figures 47-2, 47-7: Courtesy of AltaVista.

Figure 47-3: Courtesy of Lycos.

Figure 47-4: Courtesy of WebCrawler.

Figure 47-4: Courtesy of Excite.

Chapter 48 Eudora screens courtesy of QUALCOMM Incorporated.

Chapter 60 screens of The Weather Channel courtesy of The Weather Channel Inc.

Chapter 61 Quick Quotes screens courtesy of Time Inc. New Media.

Logos in Chapter 17:

NewMedia: Courtesy of NewMedia.

Internet World: Courtesy of Mecklermedia Corporation.

T.H.E. Journal: Courtesy of T.H.E. Journal.

Technology & Learning: Courtesy of Peter Li Education Group.

Wired: Courtesy of Wired.

Syllabus: Courtesy of Syllabus Press.

Communications Industries Report: Courtesy of the International Communications Industries Association.

Cinefex: Courtesy of Cinefex.

Directory of Video, Multimedia & Audio-Visual Products, ICA, and *INFOCOMM International:* Courtesy of the International Communications Industries Association.

EDUCORP Online: Courtesy of EDUCORP Multimedia.

Multimedia and Videodisc Compendium for Education and Training: Courtesy of Emerging Technology Consultants.

CD-ROM Online: Courtesy of CD-ROM Online.

AECT: Courtesy of the Association for Education Communications and Technology.

SALT: Courtesy of Society for Applied Learning Technology.

SOFTBANK COMDEX: Courtesy of SOFTBANK COMDEX, Inc.

CeBIT: Courtesy of CeBIT.

AACE: Courtesy of the Association for the Advancement of Computing in Education.

NAB: Courtesy of the National Association of Broadcasters.

Interactive Healthcare: Courtesy of Stewart Publishing, Inc.

National Demonstration Laboratory: Courtesy of the National Demonstration Laboratory.

Part One

Understanding Multimedia

People retain only 20% of what they see and 30% of what they hear. But they remember 50% of what they see and hear, and as much as 80% of what they see, hear, and do simultaneously.

— Computer Technology Research, 1993

Multimedia is the buzzword of the decade. Like most buzzwords, it has been used in many contexts. You find it on the covers of books, magazines, CD-ROMs, video games, and movies. It is used in advertising shoes, hairstyles, drugs, cars, computers, soft drinks, beer, kitchen floors, vacations, airplanes, televisions, telephones, houses, museums, newspapers, arcades, theme parks, Olympic Games, and shopping malls. Sometimes the term is used to add hype to products that have nothing to do with multimedia. The many uses and abuses of the word *multimedia* have led to confusion over just what multimedia is. For this reason, a book on multimedia literacy must begin by defining it.

1 Definitions

After completing this chapter, you will be able to:

- **Define multimedia, describe why it is effective, and explain how it will be important to life in the twenty-first century**

- **Demonstrate how multimedia is changing the world through telecommuting, home shopping, electronic publishing, and computer-based education**

- **Show how fast multimedia is growing in business, industry, homes, online services, and education**

- **Identify and define the components of a Multimedia PC**

- **Define the Internet and the World Wide Web and understand how they provide access to multimedia resources on a worldwide basis**

O DEFINE multimedia properly, one must go beyond stating what it is and put the term in context. In this chapter you will not only get a standard "textbook" definition of multimedia, but also learn why it is important, how fast it is growing, how it is changing the world, and who needs to know about it. The term *Multimedia PC* will be defined, along with the nomenclature needed to understand the specifications of a multimedia computer. Then you will learn how the Internet and the World Wide Web are being used to distribute multimedia applications on a worldwide basis.

WHAT IS MULTIMEDIA?

Multimedia is the use of a computer to present and combine text, graphics, audio, and video with links and tools that let the user navigate, interact, create, and communicate.

As depicted in Figure 1-1, this definition contains four components essential to multimedia. First, there must be a computer to coordinate what you see and hear, and to interact with. Second, there must be links that connect the information. Third, there must be navigational tools that let you traverse the web of connected information. Finally, because multimedia is not a spectator sport, there must be ways for you to gather, process, and communicate your own information and ideas.

1-1

Multimedia is the use of a computer to present and combine text, graphics, audio, and video with links and tools that let the user navigate, interact, create, and communicate.

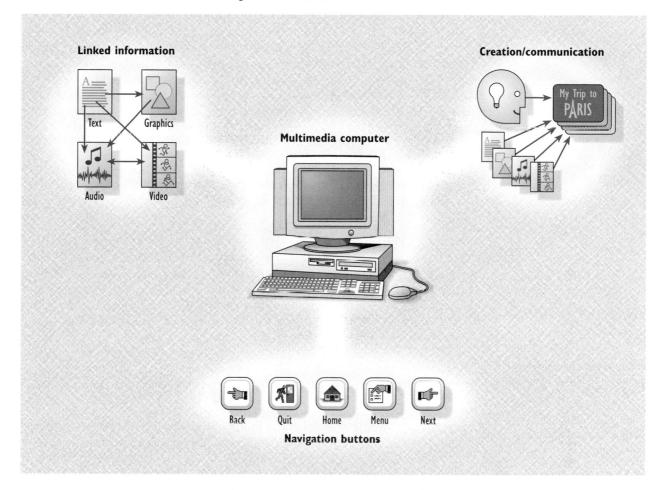

If one of these components is missing, you do not have multimedia. For example, if you have no computer to provide interactivity, you have mixed media, not multimedia. If there are no links to provide a sense of structure and dimension, you have a bookshelf, not multimedia. If there are no navigational tools to let you decide the course of action, you have a movie, not multimedia. If you cannot create and contribute your own ideas, you have a television, not multimedia.

WHY IS MULTIMEDIA IMPORTANT?

Multimedia is fast emerging as a basic skill that will be as important to life in the twenty-first century as reading is now. In fact, multimedia is changing the nature of reading itself. Instead of limiting you to the linear presentation of text as printed in books, multimedia makes reading dynamic by giving words an important new dimension. In addition to conveying meaning, words in multimedia serve as triggers that readers can use to expand the text in order to learn more about a topic. This is accomplished not only by providing more text but by bringing it to life with sound, pictures, music, and video.

The more you learn about multimedia, the more books pale by comparison. For example, suppose you read a lengthy document and want to refer back to the page on which a certain idea was mentioned. You check the index, but the topic you want is not listed. A multimedia document can be searched automatically to find any topic or combination of topics, whereas a printed book makes this almost impossible. In fact, a multimedia document can refer not only to information within itself, but also to all the other documents to which it has been linked, and to all the documents to which they have been linked. Multimedia uses links to let you navigate the universe of connected information at the speed of light. Comparing this global network of multimedia to our highway system that lets motorists travel almost anywhere, the U.S. government has named the network the **Information Superhighway**.

Multimedia is highly effective. As Computer Technology Research (CTR) reports, people retain only 20% of what they see and 30% of what they hear. But they remember 50% of what they see *and* hear, and as much as 80% of what they see, hear, and do *simultaneously*. That is why multimedia provides such a powerful tool for teaching and learning.

Multimedia will help spread the Information Age to millions of people who have not yet used a computer. A Roper survey sponsored by IBM found that more than half of the respondents did not want a computer that required a manual to use it (*Washington Post* 12/27/93 Business: 13). Multimedia provides the computer industry with the key to reaching this untouched market, which will cause computer use to skyrocket.

HOW FAST IS MULTIMEDIA GROWING?

As Figures 1-2 through 1-4 illustrate, multimedia is one of the fastest-growing markets in the world today. Freeman Associates predicts that the installed base of CD-ROM drives will grow to 161 million units by the year 2000. One-third of U.S. households already have home computers, a third of which are multimedia PCs. The Information Workstation Group forecasts that multimedia will be a $30 billion industry: The top three applications will be entertainment ($9.1 billion), publishing ($4.7 billion), and education and training ($4.3 billion).

Fueling this growth are advances in technology (see Figure 1-5) and price wars that have dramatically lowered the cost of multimedia computers. The growing number of consumers has created a larger market for multimedia titles, and new tools are enabling more people to become developers. Noting how multimedia enables individuals to create productions that once required teams of specialists, Frost & Sullivan (1993) forecast a 50% growth rate for desktop video during each of the next seven years. The home market for PCs is growing at a rate almost three times faster than the overall PC market.

Online multimedia services are booming. Forrester Research predicts that the service market will grow to $3 billion by 1998. Because only 13% of the 31 million home PC owners currently belong to a service, there is plenty of room for growth. And grow it will: Bell Atlantic plans to serve multimedia to more than 8 million homes by the end of the decade. You can see the latest Internet growth charts on the Web at http://www2.mids.org/growth/internet.

Educational use of multimedia is also skyrocketing. According to the Software Publishers Association, U.S. K–12 schools spent $4 billion on PC technology in 1995–96, a rise of 53% over the $2.6 billion spent in 1993–94. Figure 1-4 shows how

1-2

Projected worldwide growth of consumer PC shipment value.
Source: Link Resource.

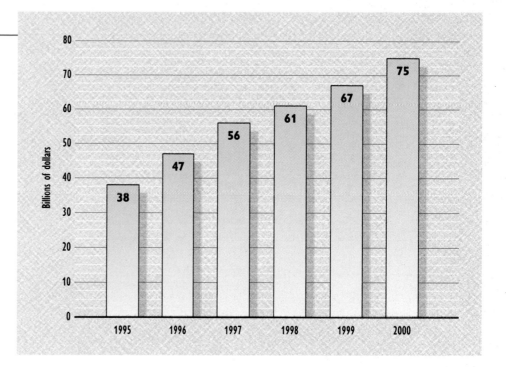

1-3

Growth of the Internet.
Source: Market Vision.

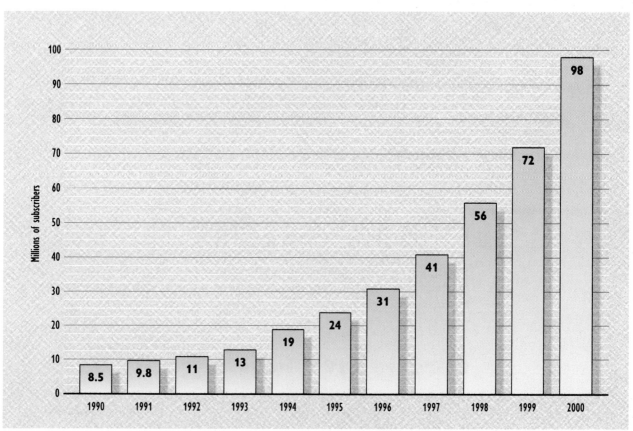

1-4

World multimedia market growth.
Source: Frost & Sullivan.

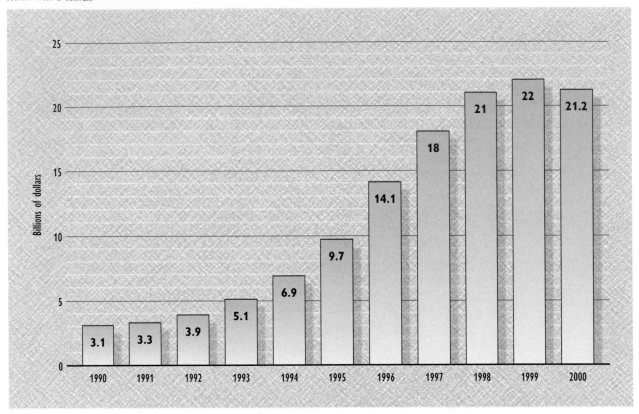

the market for multimedia literacy training materials will grow as multimedia know-how becomes a basic skill for the workforce of the twenty-first century.

For more statistics on the information technology industry, go to Dataquest's online service at http://www.dataquest.com. Once you subscribe, you can request up-to-the-minute statistics about trends in multimedia, networking, videoconferencing, and a wide range of personal computer products and services. Dataquest charges a small fee for each chart or graph you download.

HOW IS MULTIMEDIA CHANGING THE WORLD?

Multimedia is redefining the communication system that forms a significant part of the infrastructure of our society. A large number of corporate mergers and alliances are combining the telephone, television, and personal computer into a mass market multimedia utility.

Mergers and Alliances

Multimedia is fueling an unprecedented number of mergers among companies jockeying for position in this fast-paced field. There were 1,563 high-tech mergers in 1995, up from 879 in 1994. The total value of the transactions was $82.8 billion, up from $69.2 billion a year earlier. According to a Broadview Associations LLP survey, 64% of companies are considering more mergers and partnerships (*Information Week* 1/29/96: 28). For example, Microsoft and the satellite TV broadcast company DirecTV are forming an alliance to offer digital information and entertainment services that can be displayed on a TV set or a computer screen. Microsoft will produce the system software and tools for content developers to get the new service started by early 1997 (*New York Times* 3/12/96: C2). Microsoft has also teamed up with NBC to create a new service called MSNBC—on cable TV as well as on the Web at http://www.msnbc.com. It uses the brand power of a TV network to transition people to become online users and make the online service become a regular part of the way people use television (*Broadcasting & Cable* 5/6/96: 43). Compaq Computer and Thomson Consumer Electronics are joining forces to produce devices that combine the functions of PCs and televisions. Compaq is the biggest PC seller, and Thomson is the largest U.S. maker of TV sets (*Investor's Business Daily* 5/23/96: A3). Oracle and Bell Atlantic are providing interactive TV service in the Washington, D.C., area. Oracle's database technology controls video servers that simultaneously transmit hundreds of movies to residential customers. Called Stargazer, the Oracle/Bell Atlantic alliance is the largest interactive video trial to date. Stargazer is expected to be commercially available to 10 million households by the end of the century (*New York Times* 1/10/94: C4).

Multimedia alliances are not limited to the United States. America Online, in partnership with the Japanese trading company Mitsui and the business publishing company Nihon Keizai Shimbun (Nikkei), is establishing an online service in Japan offering a broad range of Japanese-language material (*Financial Times* 5/9/96: 17). Nintendo, Microsoft, and Japan's Nomure Research Institute are collaborating to deliver a high-speed online service that will beam content such as sports news, online shopping, and entertainment via a TV broadcasting satellite system (*Financial Times* 6/27/96: 15). Deutsche Telekom, France Telecom, and Sprint have formed an alliance called Global One to provide worldwide voice, data, and video services for corporate clients. Global One will be competing against Uniworld—formed by AT&T and four European telecom operators—and Concert, formed by British Telecommunications and MCI (*Financial Times* 2/1/96: 16). Microsoft has joined forces with Nippon Telegraph and Telephone Corporation to allow Japanese customers to receive multimedia services over telephone and computer networks (*Atlanta Journal-Constitution* 3/24/94: D3).

The Canadian Broadcasting Company, in partnership with Bell Canada, Telesat Canada, Newbridge Networks, Oracle, and Televitesse System, is developing a news service that will scan television and other sources according to user specifications, then save articles for later viewing on a personal computer. The target market for the Personal News Network will be companies and government agencies that want news in selected fields (*Montreal Le Devoir* 4/2/96: B2). Bell Canada has also partnered with 3WB to create new commercial services for the Internet, using radio networks that provide businesses a multimedia presence on the Net. Customers will receive the Internet radio using software provided free by 3WB (*Toronto Financial Post* 3/15/96: 6). Electronic Arts, the largest producer of video game software, has purchased Johannesburg-based software distributor Vision Software, which is building import operations in Kenya and four central African countries (*New York Times* 4/9/96: C5).

Telecommuting

Multimedia is changing our place of work. According to a Deloitte & Touche report, **telecommuting** (working from home using computers, modems, and fax machines) accounted for 45% of all new jobs from 1987 to 1992 (*Atlanta Constitution* 1/2/94: E2). A survey by Work/Family Directions found that 20 to 40% of employees would like to telecommute (*Wall Street Journal* 12/14/93: B1). More than half of U.S. businesses permitted telecommuting in 1996, with 1.5 million companies having telecommuting policies in place (*USA Today* 6/18/96: E7). The California earthquakes made many new converts to telecommuting, given the significant long-term damage to traffic routes around Los Angeles (*Investor's Business Daily* 1/27/94: 4). In addition to reducing traffic congestion, an Arthur D. Little study points out how telecommuting can cut pollution. For example, a 10 to 20% reduction in trips would save 3.5 billion gallons of gas per year (*Atlanta Constitution* 12/2/93: A19). Telecommuting has also had an impact on the clothing industry, causing suit sales to plummet as more people work from home (*St. Petersburg Times* 1/3/94: 19).

Microsoft gives away telecommuting software for free. Microsoft NetMeeting enables real-time voice and data communications over the Internet. Two or more people can share applications, transfer files, view and illustrate a shared whiteboard, and chat with each other—all over standard phone connections. Microsoft NetMeeting can be downloaded from the Web at no charge (other than the cost of download time) at http://www.microsoft.com/ie/conf.

Home Shopping

Multimedia is changing how the world shops. Instead of wearing yourself out trekking from store to store, trying to find the size and style you like and then having to wait in line to pay for it, teleshopping services let you shop from home. A Yankelovich Partners survey found that 60% of respondents have tried either online or television shopping. Most cited convenient hours and a secure environment as the reasons they liked the service. Electronic home-shopping sales have surged to more than $3 billion annually and are forecast to rise anywhere from $30 billion to $250 billion in the next 10 years (*Miami Herald* 1/18/94: C1).

Levi Strauss & Company uses computers to let women order "Personal Pair" jeans made to exact specifications. There are 8,448 combinations of hip, waist, inseam, and rise measurements, far too many for a traditional store to stock. As this book goes to press, however, Levi is making jeans only for women who visit a participating store to be measured in person. Maybe by the time you read this, women will be able to order their own personal jeans online at the Levi Web site at http://www.levi.com.

To prepare for writing about teleshopping, the author did all of his Christmas shopping online. The friends and relatives receiving these gifts remarked how appropriate and uniquely suited the gifts were. That is because the author used search engines at the Internet shopping malls to find gifts that matched precisely the needs and desires of his friends. Chapter 3 provides the Web addresses of these Internet shopping malls.

Business and Advertising

Multimedia is changing the face of business. Online shopping and banking are creating a cashless society by eliminating the need for printed money. Brokerage firm Charles Schwab says 20% of its business already comes from electronic stock and mutual fund orders. Schwab is expanding that to include electronic payment capability, and predicts that online orders will represent 30 to 40% of order entry in the next four to five years (*St. Petersburg Times* 5/23/96: E6).

Advertising is paying for Web services, much like advertising covers the cost of television broadcasts so you can watch TV "for free." For example, commercial ads pay for the popular search engine Yahoo at http://www.yahoo.com. Advertising pays for the Internet's amazing PointCast Network (PCN) at http://www.pointcast.com. Soon Internet set-top boxes will enable you to go to a product's Web site simply by clicking on the product with your television's remote control.

Electronic Publishing

Multimedia is changing how we read newspapers by eliminating the need for the paper and offering all the features of multimedia, including full-text search, graphics, audio, and video. According to The Kelsey Group, more than 2,700 newspapers are experimenting with electronic ventures, compared to only 42 in 1989; contributing to the need for these experiments is the fact that half of young people aged 18 to 24 do not read newspapers at all (*US News & World Report* 5/16/94: 60). Table 1-1 lists a few of the newspapers you can read on the Web.

Table 1-1
A Few of the Newspapers
on the World Wide Web

Newspaper	Web Address
New York Times	http://www.nytimes.com
Raleigh News & Observer	http://www.nando.net
San Francisco Chronicle	http://www.sfgate.com
San Jose Mercury News	http://www.sjmercury.com
USA Today	http://www.usatoday.com
Virginian-Pilot	http://www.infi.net/pilot/vpls.html

Dow Jones publishes an electronic version of its flagship *Wall Street Journal* and also offers an online service called Personal Journal that delivers selected stories based on customer demand (*Miami Herald* 12/9/93: C3). Imagine what a timesaver this is. Suppose you are an educator and you want the latest news in education, but you have little interest in sports. Instead of having a newspaper delivered that is 2% education and 40% sports, you get a news feed of all the educational articles from all of the "papers." Executives at Mercury Center, the electronic extension of the *San Jose Mercury News,* predict that reader loyalty will increase because electronic publishing gives a newspaper the tools to focus on small parts of the market, offering topics that may not interest a general audience (*New York Times* 2/7/94: C1).

American Cybercasting Corporation is developing teacher guides that integrate electronic newspapers into school curricula. For more information go to http://americast.com.

Teaching and Learning

Electronic publishing is not the only way multimedia is changing how we teach and learn. Eiser (1992) describes how multimedia has proven so effective in education that the states of California and Texas have adopted videodiscs instead of textbooks, investing former textbook budgets in multimedia technology. After studying hundreds of controlled experiments in which computers were used in college and high-school courses, elementary education, and adult high-school equivalency programs, Kulik (1985, 1986, 1991, and 1994) reports overall learning gains averaging more than a letter grade higher (effect size = .32), and significant reductions in the time required for students to learn (averaging 34% in college and 24% in adult education). Chapter 4 surveys some of these applications and analyzes how computers are changing the nature of education.

Mass Market Use of Information Services

The most strategic use of multimedia may be helping bring the public into the Information Age. In a society that depends so much on processing information, what could be more important? Multimedia relieves information overload and techno stress by engaging more of the senses. If one medium is not getting the message across, multimedia will engage more of the senses to make the communication more effective. Multimedia makes user interfaces easier, thereby providing much wider access to information services and making the whole market grow exponentially. This is why *Fortune* magazine (2/21/94: 101) quotes Microsoft chairman Bill Gates's prediction that by the end of the decade, most of his company's revenues will come from home sales. As this book goes to press, less than 4% of Microsoft sales are home based. Imagine how different the information society will be when more than half of its computing is done from home instead of at work or school. You can read about Bill Gates's vision for the future in his book *The Road Ahead* (Gates, 1995), which comes with a CD-ROM containing the full text of the book plus hundreds of multimedia hyperlinks, a special interview with Bill Gates, and video demonstrations of future technology.

The Internet is competing with television for people's free time. A survey conducted by the Emerging Technologies Research Group shows Internet users spending an average of 6.6 hours a week on the Net, time previously spent watching TV, listening to the radio, or making long-distance phone calls. The average session was 68 minutes (*Tampa Tribune* 1/12/96: B&F1). A Nielsen study reported similar results, concluding that Internet users spend more time online than TV viewers spend with their VCRs. In the U.S. and Canada alone, 24 million people are already on the Internet. The Nielsen study also found that women comprise about one-third of all Internet users, far more than previously thought (*Dow Jones News* 10/30/95).

WHO NEEDS TO KNOW ABOUT MULTIMEDIA?

Ask yourself a few historical questions:

- Who needed to know how to read books after the printing press was invented?
- Who needed to know how to drive cars after highways got built?
- Who needed to know how to call someone when telephones were invented?

Now ask:

- Who needs to know how to use a multimedia computer to access the Information Superhighway?

Anyone who plans to learn, teach, work, play, govern, serve, buy, or sell in the information society needs to know about multimedia. Just imagine the consequences of not knowing about it. For example, suppose you are a journalist who cannot create a hypermedia document and transmit it across a network; how long do you think you will be employable? What about paramedics who cannot upload a picture of a wound and get expert advice on how to treat it? Or architects and designers who cannot use computers to simulate and troubleshoot products before they are built? Or merchandisers who do not know how to advertise products on the network? Or teachers who cannot use multimedia to bring their classrooms to life? Or businesspeople who cannot access corporate data when it is needed to make the right decision? Or governments without the technology needed to detect and deter aggression?

To state the need succinctly: Everyone who plans to function productively in twenty-first-century society needs to know about multimedia.

WHAT IS A MULTIMEDIA PC?

MPC stands for **Multimedia PC** and was established in 1991 as a standard by the Multimedia PC Working Group, an independent special-interest group of the Software Publishers Association (SPA). The MPC standard specified the minimum hardware requirements for multimedia. Critics felt the MPC specification was not powerful enough. In the meantime, technological advances and price decreases enabled people to afford more-powerful computers. In 1993 the SPA announced the Multimedia PC Level 2 specification, MPC2, which required a more robust setup. In 1995 the MPC3 spec was announced, once again raising the standard for multimedia PCs. By the time you read this, it is possible that an MPC4 spec will have been announced; to find out, visit the SPA Web site at http://www.spa.org.

Table 1-2 compares the MPC, MPC2, and MPC3 specifications. In order to understand them, some terms need to be defined.

Table 1-2 MPC Specifications

	PC Multimedia PC	PC2 Multimedia PC	PC3 CERTIFIED Multimedia PC
RAM	2 MB	4 MB (8 recommended)	8 MB
Processor	16 MHz 386SX	25 MHz 486SX	75 MHz Pentium
Hard Drive	30 MB	160 MB	540 MB
CD-ROM Drive	150 KB/sec (single speed), maximum average seek time 1 second, 64 KB on-board buffer recommended	300 KB/sec (double speed), maximum average seek time 400 milliseconds, CD-ROM XA ready, multisession capable, 64 KB buffer recommended	600 KB/sec (quad speed), average access time 250 milliseconds, CD-ROM XA ready, multisession capable, on-board read-ahead buffering required
Audio	8-bit digital sound, 8-note synthesizer, MIDI playback	16-bit digital sound, 8-note synthesizer, MIDI playback	16-bit digital sound, wavetable, MIDI playback
Video Display	640 x 480, 16 colors (256 colors recommended)	640 x 480, 65,536 colors	640 x 480, 65,536 colors
Video Playback	N/A	N/A	MPEG 1 (hardware or software) with OM-1 compliance

RAM and MB

RAM stands for random access memory; it is the main memory at the heart of a computer in which multimedia programs execute. RAM is measured in megabytes (MB). *Mega* means million, and *byte* is the unit of measure for computer memory. A byte can hold a single character, and a megabyte can hold a million characters. Although some programs can run in smaller amounts of RAM, anyone serious about multimedia should have at least 8 MB. Windows 95 users should have at least 16 MB.

Processor and MHz

The **processor** is the brain in your computer where calculations and decisions get made. Processor speed is measured in **MHz**, which stands for megahertz. *Mega* means million, and *hertz* is one cycle per second.

386SX, 486SX, and **Pentium** are three of the processors manufactured by Intel and its licensees. Figure 1-5 shows how the relative power of the various processors is a function of their model number and processor speed. The more powerful the processor, the faster the multimedia computer will respond.

Hard Drive

A **hard drive** is a magnetic storage device on which computer programs and data are stored. Like RAM, hard drives are measured in megabytes. The larger the hard drive, the more programs and data the computer can store. If you plan to record digital video onto your hard drive, it needs to be as large as you can afford to make it; even the 540 MB recommendation in the MPC3 specification will seem small when you record digital video.

CD-ROM

CD-ROM stands for compact disc—read-only memory. A CD-ROM can store about 680 MB of data. That is enough to hold the text of 200 Bibles. Because compact discs are inexpensive to produce yet provide so much storage, CD-ROM has become the medium of choice for publishing multimedia applications.

The speed of a CD-ROM is measured in how many thousands of characters (bytes) it can read per second. In computer spec sheets, the character *K*, which stands for *kilo* (the Greek word for thousand), is used to represent 1,000 characters, or 1 kilobyte. The first CD-ROM drives could transfer data at a rate of 150 KB per second. Double-speed CD-ROM drives can transfer data at twice that speed, or 300 KB per second. Quadruple-speed drives transfer data at 600 KB per second. Even faster drives are available, including so-called 6×, 8×, and 10× speed drives, which read data at 900, 1200, and 1500 KB per second, respectively.

CD-ROM XA stands for CD-ROM extended architecture. It is a CD-ROM enhancement that permits pictures to be narrated via concurrent audio and video. CD-ROM XA can hold more audio than regular audio CDs, because the extended architecture defines audio formats that require less storage per second. Although these XA audio modes may work fine for speech, they do not produce music as faithfully as regular audio CDs.

1-5

Intel's iCOMP index for i386 through Pentium Pro processors. For comparison purposes, the Pentium 120 is assigned an iCOMP2 value of 100. i386 and i486 comparison ratings were interpolated from iCOMP1 data. For more information, go to http://www.intel.com/procs/perf/icomp.

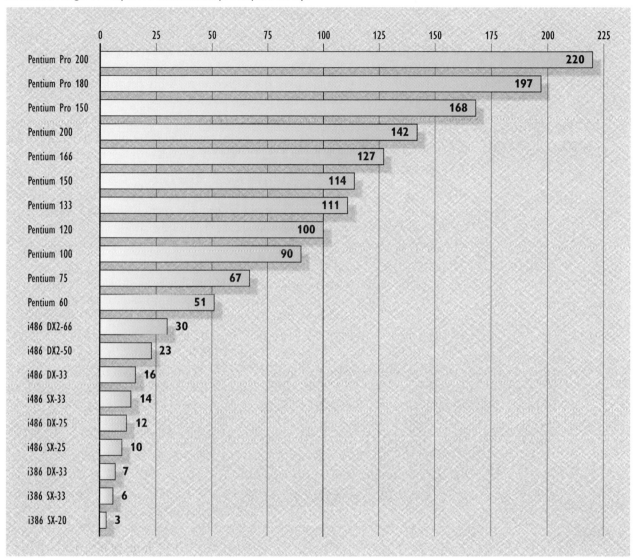

Multisession refers to a CD-ROM drive that can play back CDs that have been recorded on more than once. For example, Kodak offers a service called Photo CD that lets you have pictures placed on a CD. If you take more pictures later, you can have them added to that CD in another recording session. But only a multisession CD-ROM drive can access the pictures from the subsequent session.

Also recorded in the multisession format is the **CD Plus**, on which a regular CD Audio session has been augmented by multimedia materials in another session. You can play back a CD Plus on a regular CD Audio player if you just want to hear the music, or you can install it on a multimedia PC and navigate through hypertext, buttons, pictures, and videos recorded in subsequent sessions. The CD Plus format is also known as **CD Extra** and **Enhanced CD**.

8-Bit and 16-Bit Sound

The term **bit** stands for binary digit. A bit can have one of two values: 0 or 1. When sound is recorded by a multimedia computer, it is represented by a stream of bits that describe the vibrations in the sound wave. The more bits that are used to sample the wave, the higher the dynamic range of the music you hear.

The MPC standard called for 8-bit sound, which produces a dynamic range of 50dB (decibals). The MPC2 and MPC3 standards use 16-bit sound, which increases the dynamic range to 98dB. The greater the dynamic range, the more faithfully the volume levels in the music play back. Because 16-bit recordings have higher fidelity than 8-bit recordings, 16-bit audio sounds better.

Synthesizer, Wavetable, and MIDI Playback

MIDI stands for Musical Instrument Digital Interface. MIDI is the most economical way for multimedia computers to make music, because instead of recording the entire waveform like a digital audio recording does, MIDI encodes only the performance information (such as note on, note off, louder, softer) needed for a synthesizer to play the music.

MIDI setups often involve external equipment, such as music keyboards and sound modules that play the music. This external equipment is costly, however. To let you play back MIDI without needing external devices, the MPC specification requires a MIDI synthesizer driver for your waveform audio board. This enables MIDI playback through your sound board without external MIDI equipment.

The synthesizer driver will rarely sound as good as the external equipment would, however. Enter the wavetable, which the MPC3 spec requires. A wavetable is a list of numbers that describe the desired waveshape of a sound. Every sound has a characteristic waveshape that determines the timbre or kind of sound you hear. You will learn more about waveshapes in Chapter 2. The wavetable helps MIDI do a better job of creating waveshapes that produce the desired sounds.

640 x 480 Screen Size

If you look closely at an image on a computer screen, you will see that the computer makes pictures by turning little dots on and off. **640 × 480** refers to this grid of dots, meaning that there are 640 dots across and 480 dots down the screen.

Pixels and Megapixels

The little dots on the screen are more properly referred to as **pixels**; the term *pixel* stands for picture element. **Megapixel** means 1 million pixels.

64 KB Buffer

KB stands for kilobyte, which means 1,000 bytes. The **64 KB buffer** in the MPC specification is used to speed access to data coming off the CD-ROM. The buffer works like a staging area where data from the CD-ROM gets held until the computer needs it. A computer can access data much more quickly from the buffer than from a CD-ROM.

Bandwidth

Bandwidth refers to the total amount of data that can be transferred in a given amount of time. The more bandwidth you have, the more data can be transferred.

MPEG 1

MPEG is the format that is emerging as the new digital video standard for the United States and most of the world. MPEG 1 is the noninterlaced version of MPEG designed for playback from ordinary CD-ROM players. You will learn about the other versions of MPEG in Chapter 15.

WHAT IS THE INTERNET?

The **Internet** is a worldwide connection of nearly 10 million computers and 45,000 networks that follow the Internet Protocol (IP). The Internet Protocol was invented for the U.S. Department of Defense Advanced Research Projects Agency (ARPA). The goal was to create a network that would continue to function if a bomb destroyed one or more of the network's nodes; information would get rerouted automatically so it could still reach its address. If you want more background, Bruce Sterling's fascinating history of the Internet is found on the *Multiliteracy CD*; to read it, go to the Demonstrations section, select Textbook Examples, and click the History of the Internet button. Figure 1-6 should help you visualize the web formed by the interconnections of computers on the Internet.

Every computer on the Internet has a unique IP address. An IP address consists of four numbers separated by periods. The numbers range from 0 to 255. The smallest address is 0.0.0.0 and the largest is 255.255.255.255. The number of IP addresses this scheme allows is 256^4 which is 4,294,967,296. This provides room for adding more computers as the network grows.

1-6

This image is a visualization study of inbound traffic measured in billions of bytes on the NSFNET T1 backbone for September 1991. The traffic volume range is depicted from purple (0 bytes) to white (100 billion bytes). The NSFNET is one of the most important parts of the Internet in the United States.

Source: Rendered by Donna Cox and Robert Patterson, National Center for Supercomputing Applications/University of Illinois. The data was collected by Merit Network, Inc.

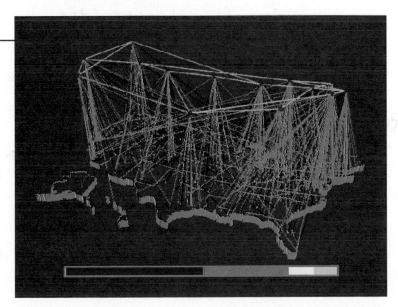

To make IP addresses easier for people to remember, a domain name system (DNS) permits the use of alphabetic characters instead of numbers. For example, the Library of Congress can be reached at the IP address 140.147.248.7 or via the domain name www.loc.gov. Domain names have the format:

`hostname.subdomain.first-level-domain`

In the United States, first-level domains normally consist of one of the following:

.edu	Educational
.com	Commercial
.mil	Military
.net	Network support centers
.org	Other organizations

In the rest of the world, first-level domains are usually country codes, such as *fr* for France. The subdomain refers to the network to which a computer is connected, and the host name refers to the computer itself. For example, in the domain name *www.louvre.fr,* which is the World Wide Web server at the famous Louvre museum in Paris, the first-level domain *fr* indicates that the server is located in France, the subdomain *louvre* tells you that the server is on the Louvre's network, and the host name *www* identifies this computer as the Louvre's World Wide Web server.

WHAT IS THE WORLD WIDE WEB?

The **World Wide Web** (WWW) is a networked hypertext system that allows documents to be shared over the Internet. Developed in Geneva at the European Particle Physics Center (CERN), the Web lets researchers all over the world collaborate on the same documents without needing to travel anywhere.

In 1993 the University of Illinois supercomputer center made available for free a Web browser called Mosaic. The graphical user interface (GUI) in Mosaic made the Web very easy to use, and usage spread rapidly throughout the Internet. Today there are more than 4 million documents on the WWW, and virtually every company, government agency, and educational institution has established a presence on the Web. The most popular Web browsers are Netscape Navigator and Microsoft Internet Explorer.

Hypertext documents on the WWW are known as Web pages. Web pages can contain images as well as text. Any word or image can be linked to any resource on the Web, including pictures, sounds, videos, animations, software, other Web pages, datasets, and multimedia applications. As you will experience in the World Wide Web tutorial in Part Ten of this book, the ease with which Web pages are produced can enable everyone to become a provider, not just a consumer, of multimedia on the Internet.

In the July 1996 issue of *Technology Review,* there is a fascinating interview with Tim Berners-Lee, the person credited with inventing the World Wide Web. You can find the interview online at http://web.mit.edu/afs/athena/org/t/techreview/www/articles/july96/bernerslee.html.

E X E R C I S E S

1. Give examples of how multimedia has affected (a) the nation as a whole, (b) your local community, and (c) your personal life.

2. In your chosen career or profession, would telecommuting be appropriate? How would it help or hinder your work?

3. This chapter described how multimedia is changing the world through mergers and alliances, telecommuting, home shopping, electronic publishing, and computer-based learning. How else do you see multimedia changing the world?

4. Compare the advantages and disadvantages of home shopping as you see them. What impact does home shopping have on traditional stores and shopping malls?

5. Think of an example showing how a computer helped you learn something. What was the subject matter? What role did the computer play? Did you learn better because of the computer? Why or why not?

6. Of all the different kinds of occupations you can think of, which ones need multimedia the most? The least? What is your chosen occupation? Why will you need to know about multimedia to do well in your line of work?

7. The MPC is an evolving standard. In this chapter you saw how the original MPC standard evolved into the MPC3 standard. What new features and capabilities do you think future MPC standards will include? To find out whether newer MPC standards have been announced, go to http://www.spa.org.

8. Rate your own computer or the one you use at school on the basis of the MPC standards provided in Table 1-2. In what ways does your computer surpass the standards? How does it need to be upgraded to meet the standards?

9. Find out the domain name of the computer network at your school or place of work. If you have an e-mail address on that network, the domain name will be the part of your e-mail address after the @ sign. For example, if your e-mail address is santa.claus@toymakers.northpole.com, the domain name is toymakers.northpole.com.

2 Taxonomy of Multimedia Objects

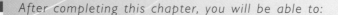

After completing this chapter, you will be able to:

- **Define and recognize linked objects in a multimedia application**

- **Understand the present-day limits of creating those objects**

- **Think about what new kinds of objects there may be in the future as multimedia technology progresses**

- **Consider whether the digitization of media is making communication better or worse, and understand the appropriate role of technology**

THE definition of multimedia in the previous chapter emphasizes the important role that links play in giving users a way to interact and navigate. This chapter defines the objects of those links by providing a taxonomy of multimedia. There are six kinds of objects: text, graphics, sound, video, animation, and software. The roles each kind plays in a multimedia system are described here.

TEXT

Although it is possible to have multimedia without text, most multimedia systems use text because it is such an effective way to communicate ideas and provide instructions to users. There are four kinds of text: printed, scanned, electronic, and hypertext.

Printed Text

Printed text, like the words in this paragraph, appears on paper. Suppose you want to use printed text as the basis for a multimedia document. In order for a multimedia computer to read printed text, you need to transform the text into machine-readable form. The most obvious way to do this is to type the text into a word processor or text editor, but that is tedious and time-consuming. A faster way would be to scan the text.

Scanned Text

Low-cost scanners that can read printed text and convert it into machine-readable form are widely available. There are three basic kinds of scanners: flatbed, handheld,

2-1

A newspaper article from *USA Today*.
Copyright © 1994 USA TODAY. Reprinted with permission.

2-2

The newspaper article being scanned with a handheld scanner.

and page-fed. Flatbed scanners are more expensive because of the motors and pulleys that move the scanner over the paper. Handheld scanners cost less because you move the scanner over the paper manually, thereby avoiding the cost of the flatbed enclosure and mechanism. Page-fed scanners have a slot into which you insert the page you want scanned. Compaq markets a Scanner Keyboard, which is a computer keyboard with a page-fed scanner built in. Regardless of the kind of scanner you have, advances in the optical character recognition (OCR) software that comes with scanners have increased scanning accuracy.

For example, consider the newspaper article in Figure 2-1. Figure 2-2 shows it being scanned by a handheld scanner. You can see the results of the scan in Figure 2-3. Notice how a couple of characters have a caret (^) in front of them. The scanning software marks characters with a caret when it is not sure whether it has accurately recognized them. If you compare Figure 2-3 to the original text in Figure 2-1, however, you will see that every character is correct.

The author used a handheld scanner extensively while writing this book. Instead of typing quotes from books and magazines, the author simply swiped the scanner over the quotes and flowed the scanned text into this document. As this book goes to press, the best handheld scanner, called ScanMan, is manufactured by Logitech. ScanMan comes with industry leader Caere Corporation's OmniPage OCR software. For the latest information, visit http://www.logitech.com and http://www.caere.com.

2-3

The results of the scan. The caret (^) marks characters about which the scanner was unsure.

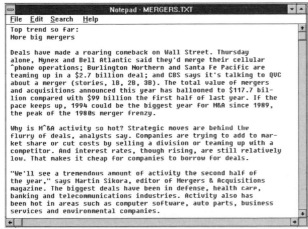

Electronic Text

A tremendous number of texts are available in machine-readable form, because almost everyone who writes books or publishes manuscripts today does so with word processing and electronic publishing equipment. Because they can be read by a computer and transmitted electronically over networks, such texts are referred to as electronic texts. For example, this book was written with Microsoft Word for Windows 95. In addition to being printed on the paper you are reading now, this book can also be used in its electronic form as the basis for multimedia documents. In fact, as you have already seen, large parts of it have been included on the *Multiliteracy CD* bundled with this book.

Electronic text was also used extensively in writing this book. Internet news feeds and other networked resources provided a rich store of information that would otherwise have taken years to research. You will learn how to access this information in the online resources section in Chapter 17.

Hypertext

The prefix *hyper* may be the most important word in this book, because it refers to the process of linking, which makes multimedia interactive. The word *hypertext* was coined by Ted Nelson (1965). Hypertext refers to text that has been linked. When you view a hypertext and click a word that has been linked, your computer launches the object of that link. Any one of the objects listed in this taxonomy of multimedia can be the object of such a link. The links give the text an added dimension, which is why it is called hyper.

To experience the power of hypertext, use the *Multiliteracy CD* to view this taxonomy as a hypertext. To do this, go to the Demonstrations section, select Textbook Examples, and click the Hypertext button. Notice how you can click the headings and subheadings to reveal more text, and even click individual words of the text to view figures and graphs. Imagine what it would be like if this entire book were available in such a form. Perhaps someday, when CD-ROMs become more popular than books, it will be.

GRAPHICS

It has often been said that a picture is worth a thousand words. However, that is true only when you can show the picture you want when you need it. Multimedia lets you do this when graphics are the object of a link. Graphics often appear as backdrops behind text to create a pictorial framework for the text. Pictures can also serve as icons, intermixed with text, representing options that can be selected; or pictures can appear full-screen in place of text, with parts of the picture serving as triggers which, when selected, launch other multimedia objects or events.

Bitmaps

A **bitmap** is a picture stored as a set of pixels that correspond to the grid of dots on a computer screen. To display the picture, the computer sets each dot on the screen to the color specified for it in the bitmap. You can create bitmaps with any graphics editor, such as the Paintbrush program that comes with Windows, or

Table 2-1   The Most Common Computer Graphics Formats

Filename Extension	Intended Purpose
.bmp	Windows bitmap; the BMP file is the most efficient format to use with Windows
.dib	Windows device-independent bitmap; used to transfer bitmaps from one device or process to another
.gif	Graphics Interchange Format; invented by CompuServe for use on computer networks, GIF is the prevalent graphics format for images on the World Wide Web
.pcd	Kodak's Photo CD graphics file format; contains five different sizes of each picture, from "wallet" size to "poster" size
.mac	Macintosh MacPaint format
.jpg	JPEG image, named for the standards committee that formed it: the Joint Photographic Experts Group; intended to become a platform-independent graphics format
.pic	PC Paint graphics format
.pcx	Zsoft Paintbrush graphics format; popular in the DOS world
.tga	Truevision Targa format; Targa is a video capture card
.tif	Tagged Image File Format; known as "the variable standard" because there are so many kinds of TIFF subformats
.wpg	WordPerfect graphics format

commercial drawing programs such as Adobe Photoshop or CorelDRAW. In the section on multimedia tools, you will learn how to use Paint Shop Pro to capture into a bitmap any graphic displayed on your computer screen from any software program, including frames from live video feeds.

Over the years many different graphics formats have been invented for storing images on computers. Table 2-1 lists the most common formats and identifies their intended purpose.

Clip Art

Creating graphics by hand is time-consuming. To save time there are extensive libraries of clip art that you can use in multimedia productions. After you purchase a clip-art library, you can usually use the images in it royalty free, but make sure you read the license carefully because restrictions may apply.

The *Multiliteracy CD* that comes with this book contains bitmaps from several commercial clip-art libraries. Their publishers provided these samples in return for our advertising their libraries in this book. You can inspect these clip-art libraries by going to the Demonstrations section, selecting Textbook Examples, and clicking the Clip Art button.

BeachWare and Jasmine publish a series of clip-art CD-ROMs that are very useful in multimedia production. For example, Figure 2-4 shows some of the images from BeachWare's *Nature Photo Collection* CD. Figure 2-5 pictures background images that consist of textures appropriate for the backdrop of a multimedia screen. Figure 2-6 shows some of the photographic images in the clip-art libraries. For the latest product information, go to http://www.beachware.com and http://www.jasmine.com.

2-4

The Paint Shop Pro Browser lets you browse images like the ones on the *Nature Photo Collection* CD-ROM from BeachWare.

2-6

Collage of clip art from the *Scenic Stills* and *Working Stills* CD-ROMs from Jasmine Multimedia.

2-5

Some of the textures on the *Multiware* CD-ROM from BeachWare and the *Scenic Stills* CD-ROM from Jasmine Multimedia.

Pixar One Twenty-Eight is a clip-art library of 128 high-quality photographic textures on CD-ROM. Pixar developed them for use in its own signature images and films. The textures include bricks, woods, metals, ground covers, animal skins, stones, sidings, fabrics, and roofs. The textures are beautifully photographed and use a patented Pixar tiling technology that allows them to be combined seamlessly. A Windows program called Textile comes on the Pixar CD-ROM. Textile lets you seamlessly tile images into an area of any size. The Pixar CD also includes a tiling plug-in for the popular Adobe Photoshop graphics editor. The images are stored in TIFF format in 24-bit and 8-bit color.

Aris Entertainment publishes a series of clip art and audio clips called *MediaClips*. *MediaClips: Business Backgrounds* is a CD-ROM full of images, audio tracks, and sound effects. *MediaClips: Money, Money, Money* contains images of international coins and currency and videos of money hot off the press. *MediaClips: Jets & Props* is a two-disc set of images of civilian and military aircraft, with rock sound tracks to complement jets, and music with a foreign flair to accompany the props. Several pictures from *Jets & Props* are used in the History of Flight tutorial in Part Six of this book, courtesy of Aris Entertainment. *MediaClips: World View* contains 100 photos of the world from above as well as images from NASA space explorations, plus 100 sound tracks of New Age piano music. *MediaClips: Majestic Places* contains photographs of many of the world's most spectacular vistas, including Mt. Everest and Mt. McKinley, with original contemporary music. *MediaClips: Wild Places* has stunning photographs of deserts, rocks, forests, and seascapes, with music composed to fit each picture. *MediaClips: Island Designs* includes vintage aloha and batik designs as well as playful and rare Hawaiian shirt patterns from the 1930s through the 1950s teamed with 100 sound tracks of early Hawaiian music. *MediaClips: Full Bloom* contains a variety of floral images, accompanied by piano audio clips. *MediaClips: Americana* features American scenes, from the purple mountains to the fruited plains, and from big cities to small towns. *MediaClips: Animal Kingdom* features prides and gaggles, flocks and herds. *MediaClips: New York, NY* features the sights and sounds of the Big Apple, from the subways to the World Trade Center.

There is also a good photo site on the Web at http://www.photodisc.com, where you will find a large collection of royalty-free, digital stock photography. You can order CD-ROMs full of clip art online, or you can search, purchase, and download single images using the integrated CyberCash payment system. There is also a free image offer at the www.photodisc.com site, where any image is yours to keep, just for visiting.

2-7

Both sides of the K-Mart digital imaging service order form.

Digitized Pictures

Video capture cards let you connect a video camera, VCR, videodisc player, or live video feed to your computer and grab frames instantly into bitmaps that can be used in multimedia applications. Think of the pictorial breadth this technology provides: Since video digitizers accept a video signal as input, they can digitize anything a video camera can see. Any photograph, slide, or picture from any book or magazine can be digitized in full color and linked into your multimedia application. Because copyright law prohibits unlawful copying and distribution, however, make sure you study the copyright and fair use guidelines presented in Chapter 16.

Snappy Video Snapshot is an image capture module that connects to the printer port on the back of a desktop or laptop PC. Snappy can capture images up to 1,500 × 1,125 pixels with up to 16 million colors. Since you do not have to put anything inside your computer, Snappy is much easier to install than a video capture card. You should be aware, however, that Snappy does not capture movies like video capture cards do; Snappy just does what its name implies, which is to "snap" still pictures from the output of a video camera or other video source. There is a Snappy demo on the *Multiliteracy CD*. To run the demo, go to the Demonstrations section, select Software, and click the Snappy button. For more information, see the Snappy Web site at http://www.play.com.

If you do not have a capture board or a Snappy, you can shoot a roll of film and take it to a mass market retail store like K-Mart, where it only costs $3.99 extra to get a diskette made along with your pictures (up to 27 exposures; for 36 exposures, it costs $5.99 extra). The diskette has software that lets you view the pictures on your PC and export the images in different graphics formats. As illustrated in Figure 2-7, the K-Mart digitizing service is based on Konica's PictureShow technology.

2-8

A hyperpicture from the *Multiliteracy CD*.

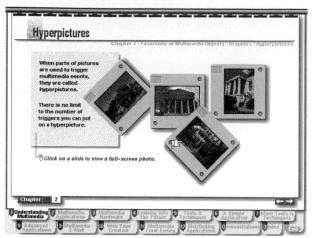

Hyperpictures

Just as words can serve as triggers in a hypertext, so also can parts of pictures. When parts of pictures are used to trigger multimedia events, they are called **hyperpictures**.

Figure 2-8 shows an example of a hyperpicture found on the *Multiliteracy CD*. Try the hyperpicture now by going to the Demonstrations section, selecting Textbook Examples, and clicking the Hyperpictures button. Notice how the cursor changes shape as you move the mouse over a hot spot on the hyperpicture. Click the hot spots to trigger the linked objects.

As you will see when you learn how to make hyperpictures in the multimedia tools part of this book, there is practically no limit to the number of triggers you can put on a hyperpicture.

SOUND

There are three types of sound objects that can be used in multimedia productions: waveform audio, compact disc audio, and MIDI sound tracks.

Waveform Audio

Just as video digitizers can be used to grab any picture a camera can see, **waveform audio** digitizers can record any sound you can hear. Every sound has a waveform that describes its frequency, amplitude, and harmonic content. Waveform audio digitizers capture sound by sampling this waveform thousands of times per second; the samples are stored on a computer's hard disk in a file that usually has a *.wav* filename extension, which stands for waveform. Figure 2-9 shows a waveform in

2-9

Waveform in the process of being sampled; the vertical lines show the points at which samples are taken.

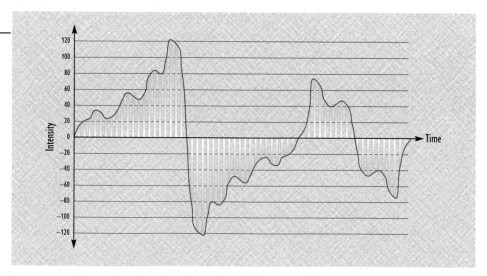

2-10

Samples taken from the waveform in Figure 2-9.

0	33	80	−122	−56	−21	40	−43
15	47	96	−96	−47	−15	43	−40
21	56	122	−80	−33	0	47	−46
24	52	117	−84	−26	10	42	−66
34	48	85	−78	−24	35	18	−74
32	55	0	−55	−32	74	−18	−35
24	78	−85	−48	−34	66	−42	−10
26	84	−117	−52	−24	46	−47	0

the process of being sampled, and Figure 2-10 shows the samples from the corresponding *.wav* file.

There are several waveform audio recordings on the *Multiliteracy CD.* To hear them, go to the Demonstrations section, select Textbook Examples, and click the Waveform Audio button. These clips were provided courtesy of Aris Entertainment from their *MediaClips* clip-art libraries.

For users looking for a CD-ROM full of prerecorded waveform audio sound effects, Applied Optical Media Corporation publishes *WAV Sound Effects,* which contains 1,500 individual sounds.

CD Audio

We are fortunate that virtually all recorded music is available on audio compact discs in computer addressable form. Audio CDs can hold up to 75 minutes of high-fidelity recorded sound. The sampling rate is 44,100 samples per second, which is fast enough to record any sound audible to humans. The samples are 16 bits, producing a dynamic range of 98dB, which is discrete enough to record faithfully a quiet whisper or a loud scream.

The addressing used in CD-ROM drives permits multimedia computers to randomly access any $\frac{1}{75}$ second of sound on the CD. As you will see in the CD Audio examples and exercises in the multimedia tools section of this book, the split-second addressing not only permits you to use any audio CD for background music, but also allows you to access themes and melodies for music instruction, down to the individual notes in a composition.

CD Plus, CD Extra, and Enhanced CD

CD Plus, also known as CD Extra and Enhanced CD, is a music CD that can also function as a CD-ROM, with computer data included on the music disc. If you put the CD Plus into a conventional audio CD player, you hear the music as usual. Insert the CD Plus into a multimedia PC, and the computer programming provides you with dazzling computer graphics, navigation, and interactivity.

As this book goes to press, there are about 60 CD Plus titles on the market. The Recording Industry Association of America (RIAA) is promoting CD Plus as the next audio industry standard, and Sony predicts that within a few years most new music CDs will be CD Extras. For more information visit Intersound's Web site at http://www.intersoundmusic.com, and see Malcolm Humes's excellent article about CD Plus at http://www.emf.net/~mal/cdplus.html.

MIDI

MIDI stands for Musical Instrument Digital Interface. It provides a very efficient way of recording the performance information required to play music. For example, there are MIDI codes for turning notes on and off, making them loud or soft, changing their timbre or tone quality, and bending them or adding other special effects. Compared with the amount of storage required for waveform audio recordings, MIDI takes up so little space that it was included as one of the basic elements in the MPC standard. MIDI files have a *.mid* filename extension. They can be randomly accessed down to an accuracy of $1/128$ second.

The Demonstrations section of the *Multiliteracy CD* contains several examples of MIDI. To access them, select Textbook Examples, then click the MIDI button. The MIDI clips were provided courtesy of Midisoft Corporation.

Hyperaudio

Sound tracks are played over time. Many multimedia creation tools allow you to time the occurrence of objects to sync points in the music. When audio is used to trigger multimedia objects, it is referred to as **hyperaudio**.

The *Multiliteracy CD* contains an example of hyperaudio. To try it, go to the Demonstrations section, select Textbook Examples, and click the Hyperaudio button. You will hear a weather report sound through your waveform audio board, while satellite forecast images appear in synchronization with the audio. Timing cues in the audio trigger the satellite images, which always appear at the right time.

VIDEO

Video provides a rich and lively resource for multimedia applications. There are four types of video that you can use as the objects of links in multimedia applications: live video feeds, videotape, videodisc, and digital video.

Live Video Feeds

Live video feeds provide interesting real-time objects of multimedia links. Any television channel or live camera feed can be the object of a link. Suppose you are teaching civics and you want to illustrate how a bill works its way through Congress. C-SPAN, the Cable-Satellite Public Affairs Network, operates one channel that covers proceedings on the floor of the House of Representatives, and another channel devoted to the Senate; it also broadcasts interviews and call-in shows, congressional hearings, speeches, and press conferences.

If you teach a subject in which current events are important, your multimedia software can put you just a mouse click away from CNN, the 24-hour news channel that summarizes the news every 30 minutes. Or suppose you are a plant supervisor needing to inspect what is happening on one of your assembly lines; a mouse click can instantly display a live video feed on your multimedia computer screen.

The Demonstrations section of the *Multiliteracy CD* has an example of a live video feed. If your computer has a video overlay card with a video source connected, you can access it by selecting Textbook Examples, then clicking the Live Video Feed button.

Videotape

The most widespread video medium is videotape. Almost everyone owns a VCR, and nearly every shopping center has a video store that rents movies on videotape. Corporations use videotape to provide just-in-time training, and public libraries have collections of instructional videotapes.

Videotapes can be the object of multimedia links. This medium is limited by two factors, however. First, videotapes are linear. The information is stored on them in a serial fashion, and in order to access it you may have to wait a long time for the tape to fast-forward or rewind to the spot you want; this can take as long as three minutes. Second, most videotape players are not computer controllable. This means that you must manually press the *play, stop, fast forward,* and *rewind* buttons yourself to use videotape in a multimedia presentation. Happily, the new generation of Sony Hi8 videotape players is computer controllable, and there is a Windows driver for them. The Sony product is called Vbox; it uses Sony's VISCA protocol to translate computer commands into codes that control a wide range of Sony video products, including camcorders, VCRs, and monitors. There is a Microsoft Windows driver that can control up to seven Vboxes at once.

Videodisc

There are two industrywide formats for videodiscs: CAV and CLV. CAV discs can store up to 54,000 still frames or 30 minutes of motion video with a stereo sound track. The frames are addressed by specifying numbers from 1 to 54,000. The CAV format lets you display still frames as well as play motion sequences.

CLV discs can store up to an hour of video on each disc side, which is twice as much video as CAV discs hold. But unless you have an expensive high-end player such as the Pioneer LD-V8000, you cannot show still frames from CLV discs.

Because of its fast random access and minimal consumption of the multimedia computer's resources, videodisc has emerged as one of the most popular means of providing video to multimedia applications in education, government, and industrial training. Although it used to be very expensive to produce videodiscs, you can now have them pressed overnight for as little as $300 per disc. In quantities of 1,000 or more, duplication fees are less than $10 per disc. Optical Disc Corporation operates recording centers in major cities.

Digital Video

Digital video is the most promising and exciting video storage medium. Like waveform audio, digital video is stored in files on a hard disk or CD-ROM. Because the video is digital, it can be served over computer networks, avoiding the need for videotapes and videodisc players. Digital video can be randomly accessed by frame, letting you play specific clips.

High-speed Pentium processors can play full-screen video without needing any special hardware installed. Slower computers need to have digital video cards installed to play movies full-screen. Otherwise, the video plays back in a window about one-quarter the size of the screen.

The Demonstrations section of the *Multiliteracy CD* contains some digital video clips. To view them, select Textbook Examples, then click the Digital Video button.

Hypervideo

Like sound tracks, video clips are played over time. Many multimedia creation tools allow you to time the occurrence of objects to sync points in the video. When video is used to trigger other multimedia events, it is referred to as **hypervideo**.

There is a hypervideo in the Demonstrations section of the *Multiliteracy CD*. As the video plays, it triggers the close captioning beneath it. To play the hypervideo, select Textbook Examples, then click the Hypervideo button.

ANIMATION

In multimedia, **animation** is the use of a computer to create movement on the screen. There are four kinds of animation: frame, vector, computational, and morph.

Frame Animation

Frame animation makes objects move by displaying a series of predrawn pictures, called frames, in which the objects appear in different locations on the screen. If you think about how a traditional movie plays in a theater, you can understand how frame animation works. In a movie, a series of frames moves through the film projector at about 24 frames per second. You see movement on the screen because each frame contains a picture of what the screen should look like at the moment that frame appears. Why 24 frames per second? Because that is the threshold beneath which you would notice flicker or jerkiness on the screen. You will learn how to do frame animation in Chapter 44.

Vector Animation

A vector is a line that has a beginning, a direction, and a length. **Vector animation** makes objects move by varying these three parameters for the line segments that define the object. Autodesk is the industry leader in vector-based animation software.

Computational Animation

Suppose you want to move a word across the screen. There are two ways to do that. You could create a series of frames that show the word inching its way across the screen, with each frame representing one moment in time as the word moves. But this would be inefficient, because the frames consume precious memory, and it takes a lot longer for an artist to draw the frames. In **computational animation**, you move objects across the screen simply by varying their x,y coordinates. The x coordinate specifies the horizontal position of the object, that is, how far across the screen. The y coordinate specifies the vertical position, that is, how far down the screen.

2-11

David morphs into the *Pieta*, then into *The Virgin of the Rocks*, and finally into the *Mona Lisa*.

Morphing

Morphing means to transition one shape into another by displaying a series of frames that creates a smooth movement as the first shape transforms itself into the other shape. For example, Figure 2-11 shows *David* morphing into the *Mona Lisa*. There is an example of a morph on the *Multiliteracy CD*. To run it, go to the Demonstrations section, select Textbook Examples, and click the Morph button. It would take a lot of time and patience to create a morph like this by hand. Morphing software creates the transitional frames automatically. Morphing is discussed in more depth in Chapter 5 in the section on cinematic special effects.

SOFTWARE AND DATA

One of the most powerful concepts in multimedia is the seamless integration you can achieve by creating links to software applications and datasets. The Demonstrations section of the *Multiliteracy CD* provides many examples. For example, the Morph button launches the morph software; the Authorware button launches Authorware; and the Paint Shop Pro button launches Paint Shop. The links between these applications and their buttons enable other software to serve as objects on the screens of the *Multiliteracy CD*.

When you learn how to create your own multimedia applications in the tutorial part of this book, Chapter 21 will show you how to create links to other software applications. You will also learn how to pass parameters that can make the software bring up a specific dataset or start on a certain screen.

FINDING MULTIMEDIA RESOURCES
ON THE WORLD WIDE WEB

The World Wide Web is a rich resource for finding multimedia objects of all types. In Chapter 47 you will learn strategies for locating objects via key word or subject-oriented searching. Web searches provide quick and easy access to millions of text documents, statistical datasets, pictures, sound tracks, musical scores, movies, animations, multimedia utilities, Web page creation tools, and software applications of all types. You will learn how to download these objects to your PC for use in your multimedia applications. You will also learn the proper bibliographic form for citing online resources in term papers and scholarly publications.

E X E R C I S E S

1. Visit your local computer lab and scan a newspaper article into your word processor. Compare the scanned text to the original. How accurate was the scan? What hardware did you use to do the scan? What software? What problems do you see in scanner technology?

2. Get a friend with a camera to take your picture. Have your friend zoom in close, taking the picture portrait style. Take the film to K-Mart and get it developed with the option to have a diskette returned along with your slides or prints. Run the software on the disk you get back from K-Mart, and see if your photo looks OK. You will use this photo in the Web page tutorial in Part Ten of this book.

3. Printed books do not have hypertext ability. Do you believe that hypertext makes documents so powerful as to render printed books obsolete? If so, what kinds? All books, or just certain kinds? For example, is hypertext more important in an encyclopedia than in a novel?

4. Digital audio and video make it possible to digitize anything you can see or hear and edit it seamlessly, without leaving a trace. For example, a *New York Newsday* cover photograph showed ice skaters Nancy Kerrigan and Tonya Harding practicing together when in fact they were not (*New York Times* 2/17/94: A12). Will this capability make it increasingly difficult for courts to accept audio recordings and videotapes as evidence?

5. We live in a time of transition from analog to digital video formats. How long do you think it will be before the average multimedia computer can show full-screen, full-motion digital video without requiring additional hardware?

6. As multimedia technology progresses, the list of objects in the taxonomy this chapter presented will increase. Can you think of any new kinds of objects that have already been invented? How about the future? Dream up and describe a new multimedia object that future technology will support.

Part Two

Survey of Multimedia Applications

3DO believes that consumers have demonstrated a strong preference for interactive rather than passive forms of entertainment. In 1991, for example, U.S. consumers spent approximately $7 billion on interactive coin-operated arcade games, more than they spent on tickets to movies (approximately $5 billion).

— Information Workstation Group, Multimedia Opportunities, page 268

Imagine if our kids' test scores were as high as their Nintendo scores.

— Computer Curriculum Corporation advertisement

*Tell me and I will forget; show me and I may remember;
involve me and I will understand.*

— Chinese proverb

The purpose of this multimedia application survey is to make you aware of the tremendous growth and development of multimedia throughout business, education, government, industry, and entertainment. The applications are illustrated with full-color pictures to give you an idea of what they are like. Demonstrations of many of these applications have been included on the *Multiliteracy CD.*

Perusing these application summaries may give you ideas for multimedia titles you would like to develop. If you have an idea for an application that you do not find mentioned here, chances are it has not yet been developed, and there may be an opportunity for you to be the first to market it. On the other hand, if you find titles described here that are similar to your idea, you will know that the market is already developing, and examining these applications will help you gauge how your idea measures up against the competition. To find out if a CD-ROM title has already been developed, you can search for it in an extensive online catalog of CD-ROM titles at http://www.educorp.com and at http://www.nsiweb.com/cdrom.

3

Business and Industry

After completing this chapter, you will be able to:

- Understand how multimedia is transforming business and industry into a global economy

- Consider the appropriate uses of point-of-sale kiosks, videoconferencing, and just-in-time training systems

- Examine how these technologies are being used in your local community

- Question whether digital video will replace the VCR as the primary means of distributing video recordings

- Experience what it is like to shop for merchandise on the World Wide Web

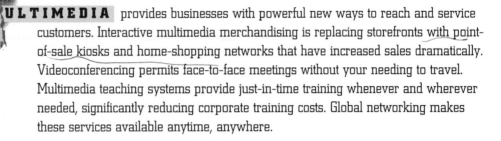

ULTIMEDIA provides businesses with powerful new ways to reach and service customers. Interactive multimedia merchandising is replacing storefronts with point-of-sale kiosks and home-shopping networks that have increased sales dramatically. Videoconferencing permits face-to-face meetings without your needing to travel. Multimedia teaching systems provide just-in-time training whenever and wherever needed, significantly reducing corporate training costs. Global networking makes these services available anytime, anywhere.

INTERACTIVE MULTIMEDIA MERCHANDISING

Anyone who shops has been frustrated by the time and effort required to locate a product you want in the style, color, and size you need. How often have you been told that what you want is out of stock? This section discusses how multimedia computers are being used in specific businesses to solve this problem. These businesses provide interactive merchandising systems that can help you find the product you want in the size you need, and that permit you to do comparison shopping without having to spend all day visiting different stores.

Florsheim Shoes

If you are tall like the author, and have big feet, Florsheim's merchandising kiosk is a godsend. It lets you shop for shoes by style, size, and color by touching the screen and following voice instructions. The kiosk includes a keyboard that lets you enter your name, address, and credit card number, and the system then arranges for drop-shipping the shoes by UPS overnight.

According to Computer Technology Research (CTR), "The Florsheim stores with kiosks report a 20% overall increase in shoe sales, not only through the automated system but also by freeing store salesmen [and women] to handle more customers faster and more expeditiously." In addition to locating kiosks in more than 400 Florsheim stores, there are also about a hundred kiosks in Sears department stores, which extends the market for Florsheim shoes. You can also shop Florsheim Online at http://www.florsheim.com.

MusicWriter's NoteStation

The music printing industry is taking advantage of multimedia computers to solve one of the greatest problems facing music retailers: stocking sheet music. With hundreds of thousands of songs to stock, the logistical problems of maintaining inventory result in such high overhead that conventional music stores actually lose money selling sheet music.

MusicWriter's NoteStation uses multimedia to solve this problem. It is a point-of-sale touch-screen kiosk that lets you search for music by title, artist, composer, style, or catalog number. You can purchase the music either printed out on staff paper or written to disk as a MIDI file. You can even change the key if you need it printed for a singer who performs in a different range.

Warner Brothers in partnership with Thorn-EMI has created this kiosk using IBM multimedia computers. New music is shipped to the kiosks monthly on CD-ROM. In addition to selling more sheet music, thousands of dollars per month of additional sales have been attributed to the increased traffic in stores that have the kiosks. Figure 3-1 shows how this laser-printed music is of true publication quality.

To find the NoteStation kiosk nearest you, visit MusicWriter's Web site at http://www.musicwriter .com, where you can also search the database of songs.

3-1

Sample output from MusicWriter's NoteStation.

Video Merchandising

Olmstead (1993) describes how kiosks are already boosting retail sales in video stores. Advanced Multimedia Solutions has based a kiosk on the best-selling paperback *Video Movie Guide* by Mick Martin and Marsha Porter. Users can locate movies by genre, cast, director, year, and those that are Oscar winners. Customers can also read reviews of 12,800 movies, 1,300 of which include photos of the box covers. The kiosk's hard drive is updated quarterly via CD-ROM. Unique's Video Viewfinder increases sales by keeping a profile of customer preferences. If the company's point-of-sale system, VideoTrace, shows that a selected title is not on the retailer's shelf, the kiosk recommends three movies in stock that the user would be likely to enjoy based on previous selections.

The most animated kiosk comes from the Switzerland-based VStor Company. Its BrowseStation uses Intel's DVI (Digital Video Interactive) technology to display clips of the hottest movies. Users can navigate through the demos, select movies, and use a credit card, ATM account, or membership card to pay their bill. Then a robot arm retrieves the videotapes from the kiosk's collection of up to 700 tapes and delivers the tapes through a small opening at the base, just like a vending machine. Eventually, the Information Superhighway and video dial tone technology (discussed in Chapter 15) will enable all of this to be done from home, with no need for videotapes. Blockbuster is marketing videos on the Web at http://www.blockbuster.com.

Virtual Shopping

The Information Superhighway provides consumers with convenient shopping in any store connected to an online service. As Bovè (1994) reports, this benefits not only the shopper, but also the manufacturer. Online shopping bypasses the traditional distributor to put an information-rich virtual storefront right where a preferred customer is waiting. By enabling the manufacturer to compile and analyze customer habits and buying trends, the network boosts sales, letting vendors market specific products directly to the consumers most likely to buy them.

Consider the Galleria 21 virtual shopping mall at London's Heathrow Airport. A touch-screen kiosk provides online access to dozens of stores, including Royal Doulton, Bally, Waterford Crystal, Burberry's, and The Scotch House. Galleria 21 guarantees speedy delivery of purchases almost anywhere in the world. Galleria 21 is multilingual, accepts a wide variety of credit cards, and recognizes worldwide monetary standards. It will eventually expand beyond Heathrow to become an international electronic shopping network.

You can already shop from home through Prodigy, America Online, and CompuServe, which are upgrading their existing shopping services with better graphics and audio. As more people discover the benefits of virtual shopping, the number of stores on the network will increase dramatically. Because this will increase the time needed for the consumer to do a thorough job of comparison shopping, famous HyperCard developer Bill Atkinson is working to develop "intelligent agents" that can do this for you. His company, General Magic, plans to market agents you can train to go out on the network and do your bidding, not only finding the best deals on retail products, but planning itineraries, making airline and restaurant reservations, and getting seats at your favorite Broadway shows. General Magic's partners in this project include Apple Computer, Motorola, Nippon Telegraph & Telephone, Sony, Matsushita, Philips, Fujitsu, and Toshiba. Another partner, AT&T, plans to make this a worldwide service (*Wall Street Journal* 3/14/94: A4). For the latest information, visit General Magic's Web site at http://www.genmagic.com.

Hundreds of stores have established sites on the World Wide Web. Anyone with a Web browser such as Netscape Navigator, Mosaic, or Microsoft Internet Explorer can visit these stores online. Table 3-1 lists the Web addresses of some Internet shopping services and describes what they do. There is a narrated tour of www.dreamshop.com on the *Multiliteracy CD*. To find out what it is like to shop there, go to the Demonstrations section, select Textbook Examples, and click Virtual Shopping.

There is an extensive list of Internet shopping sites on the Web at http://www.yahoo.com/Business_and_Economy/Companies/Shopping_Centers/Online_Malls.

Table 3-1   World Wide Web Online Shopping Locations

World Wide Web Address	What You'll Find There
http://www.internet-mall.com	1,700 companies organized according to floors: First Floor, Media; Second Floor, Personal Items; Third Floor, Computer Hardware and Software; Fourth Floor, Services; Fifth Floor, Clothes and Sporting Goods; Sixth Floor, Furniture and Housewares; Top Floor, Food Court and The Garage
http://www.dreamshop.com	Eddie Bauer, The Horchow Collections, The Sharper Image, The Bombay Company, Time Warner Viewer's Edge, Editor's Choice Book-of-the-Month Club, Spiegel, and more
http://i-shop.iworld.com	Wide range of information technology products, including network connections, Internet providers, World Wide Web products, digital cameras, video products, and more
http://www.isn.com	Internet Shopping Network (ISN) for computer products, software, and multimedia accessories
http://www.wal-mart.com	Online access to the world's largest retail store chain

DESKTOP VIDEOCONFERENCING

Due to the high cost of transportation and the large amount of employee time spent traveling to meetings, videoconferencing is on the rise. A **videoconferencing** terminal can be created by attaching a video camera to a multimedia PC with a network connection. The typical desktop videoconferencing system consists of a video digitizing and compression board, an ISDN (Integrated Services Digital Network) communications board, a monitor-top video camera, a microphone, and a speaker. Eventually, video lenses the size of pens will be integrated into laptop computers that can be used as portable videoconferencing terminals.

PictureTel Corporation offers upgrade kits that provide anyone with Windows and an ISDN (digital telephone) connection the capability to turn their computer into a videoconferencing system. For less than $6,000, the package includes two add-in boards, a video camera, and a speakerphone and handset. The conferencing software includes shared whiteboard and file-transfer features, and it is available in English, French, Spanish, German, and Japanese.

3-2

A videoconference in progress with IBM's Person to Person.

More than 50 countries have videoconferencing equipment, and in North America alone there are more than 10,000 videoconferencing rooms. Sprint has teamed with Kinko's to make videoconferencing available to everyone through the nation's Kinko stores. The Kinko's network uses equipment from PictureTel including the System 1000 that will accommodate multiperson videoconferences and PictureTel Live, which lets customers not only see others on a Kinko PC, but also share files and work simultaneously on shared documents and databases. For the latest information, point your Web browser at http://www.kinkos.com/products/catalog/video.

Figure 3-2 shows a videoconference in progress, using IBM's Person to Person. The multipoint capability of Person to Person lets up to eight people participate simultaneously. Available in both Windows and OS/2 versions, Person to Person supports a "chatline" feature that lets users type messages for instant display to one another. A drawing board lets users read and mark up a text file, spreadsheet, or database. Person to Person users can also capture images from a scanner or VCR for transmission to other participants. Jack Lowry, operations manager at General Machinery, recounts how computer integration has lowered his company's new-product cycle time from two years to 10 months. "Every time we look at Person to Person, we have a new application for it. It started off as a utility for plant floor people to contact engineering. Now I am seeking to extend Person to Person to my sister divisions and possibly to our customers and suppliers" (Hilferty, 1994).

Not everyone can afford expensive videoconferencing equipment and high-speed dedicated communications lines. A lower-cost alternative on the Internet is CU-SeeMe (pronounced "see you see me"), which is one of the more creative product names coined in this decade. *CU* stands for Carnegie-Mellon University, where the CU-SeeMe videoconferencing technology was invented. Anyone with a multimedia PC that has a video overlay card installed can get on the Internet and establish a real-time videoconference via the CU-SeeMe software. Fetterman (1996) reports success using a $100 black-and-white QuickCam by Connectix; the QuickCam connects to the computer's serial port, eliminating the need for a video overlay card. For information on how to get the CU-SeeMe software, go to http://www.cu-seeme.com. During the holiday season, Santa Claus has been known to visit this site and let users make a CU-SeeMe connection with him. There is a list of CU-SeeMe sites on the Web at: http://www.yahoo.com/Computers_and_Internet/Multimedia/Videoconferencing/CU_seeme.

MULTIMEDIA TRAVEL SYSTEMS

Travel is a natural subject for multimedia because the more you can show customers about where they will travel, what their accommodations will be like, and what they will be able to do at their destination, the more likely the person will enjoy the trip and want to use your service again. That is the goal of SABREvision, a service of American Airlines deployed at more than a thousand travel agencies. The screen displays maps of destinations, photos of hotel lobbies and rooms, and local attractions.

FINANCIAL SERVICES

Anyone who invests in the stock market knows what a dramatic effect current events have on the day-to-day value of volatile stocks. This is why the financial services industry is using multimedia to provide on-screen windows that display broadcast videos including the Financial News Network (FNN), Cable News Network (CNN), Reuters News, Dow Jones News, and Knight-Ridder services. Brokers can buy or sell quickly when news breaks. Figure 3-3 shows a TV station playing in one window while a user works with a database in another window.

The PointCast Network (PCN) is an online "information television" application that you can customize to put a stock market ticker on your computer screen. You can customize the ticker to show the precise stocks you are interested in, and PCN provides you with news stories telling how the companies are doing. Lots of other PCN services are available, including local and national news, weather, and sports. You can download the PCN software for free from http://www.pointcast.com.

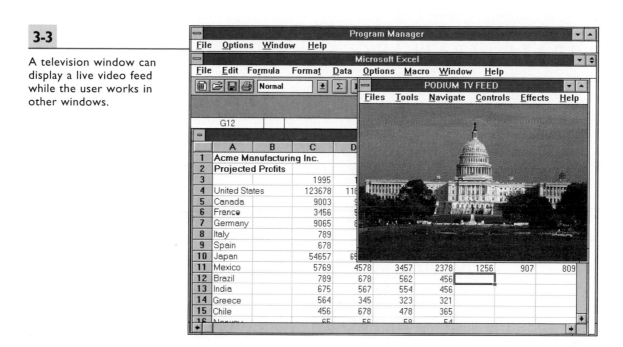

3-3

A television window can display a live video feed while the user works in other windows.

The Securities and Exchange Commission (SEC) has a Web site providing access to corporate filings made with federal agencies one day after they are filed with the agency. Located at http://www.sec.gov, the SEC site also contains policy initiatives, speeches, and enforcement actions.

REAL ESTATE

Another natural for multimedia is the real estate industry. Visiting properties for sale consumes a tremendous amount of time for brokers and buyers alike. Multimedia computers enable buyers to visit hundreds of properties virtually, view on-screen photos of homes, inspect floor plans, see street maps, and study neighborhood demographics to minimize the number of actual visits required.

Developed by Denmark's largest real estate chain, HomeVision is a good example of a real estate marketing system. As buyers use a multimedia PC to browse through potential houses, the system collects input such as type of housing, size, and monthly payment parameters and responds with a local map, outside and inside images of the property, and floor plans. Computer Technology Research (page 53) observes, "Without HomeVision customers would see about 15 houses before a buy decision; however, the multimedia system reduced this figure to seven or eight per customer. The company claims a 50% increase in sales and reduction of sales overhead as a result." For more information point your Web browser at http://www.homevision.com.

House Hunter is intelligent agent software that uses General Magic's Telescript technology to watch for new house listings that fit your profile. You simply specify the type of house, locale, and price range you're looking for. House Hunter monitors the Coldwell Banker real estate listings for houses that fit your profile and sends you an e-mail alert when such a listing appears. For more information go to http://www.genmagic.com.

Another online realty service is the HomeQuest Realty Network, where you can view homes for sale and even take a virtual tour online. HomeQuest Realty is at http://www.virtualcenter.com/homequest.

CORPORATE TRAINING

Corporate America spends a fortune on training. The American Society for Training and Development estimates that as much as $210 billion is spent on employee training each year; 78% of this amount is the cost of participant time and expenses incurred while attending training sessions. Analyzing these costs, Dennis (1994) notes that "Even a small reduction in participant time could make a large impact; for instance, a 5% reduction in training time could save employee time worth $8 billion a year."

Many corporations have used multimedia to reduce training costs and improve employee productivity. For example, Figure 3-4 shows how Omaha-based transportation giant Union Pacific's Harriman Dispatching Center controls the operation of more than 700 trains daily across 23,000 miles of track. Cantwell (1993) notes that Union Pacific used multimedia to reduce training costs by 35% while increasing the speed at which trainees learn by 30% and boosting retention by 40%. The Union Pacific courseware was developed with Allen Communication's Quest authoring system, which is discussed and demonstrated in Chapter 9. Figure 3-5 shows a sample screen from the Union Pacific management training courseware.

Arnold (1993) describes how trainers at AT&T use multimedia to prepare employees to handle blackouts. For obvious reasons, the field managers will not let technicians train on live equipment. So AT&T has used multimedia to simulate a live situation. Figures 3-6 through 3-8 show how AT&T has designed their screen displays. On the right of the screen is a text window in which printed instructions appear. On the left is a presentation window in which graphics, animation, and video appear. Beneath that is a smaller window that displays the active part of the tool. Technicians train on dozens of tasks and subtasks until they master the learning objectives. This mastery learning strategy has saved AT&T considerable costs by eliminating the need to fly 2,000 technicians to corporate headquarters for training.

3-4

The Harriman Dispatching Center controls 700 trains on 23,000 miles of track.

3-5

Union Pacific employees use multimedia computers to work through a simulation that teaches the basics of business finance—profit and loss, supply and demand.

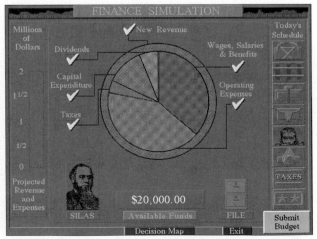

Large libraries of multimedia training materials are available. For example, the Industrial Training Corporation publishes the ACTIV training system shown in Figure 3-9. ACTIV titles include lesson material on air compressor repair, electric motors, eye and face protection, forklift safety, hazardous waste, industrial hydraulic power, industrial lubrication, industrial pneumatic power, mechanical seals, pipefitting, respiratory protection, and valve repair. The Instrument Society of America publishes a series of interactive videodisc titles covering analyzers, control valves, digital instrumentation, electronic maintenance, industrial measurement, process control calibration, control safety, pneumatic maintenance, and troubleshooting. Interactive Media Communications publishes an interactive videodisc *The Laboratory Safety Training Program.* It helps meet training requirements mandated by the OSHA Laboratory Standard "Occupational Exposure to Hazardous Chemicals in Laboratories."

3-6

Measuring battery string float voltage in AT&T's Regen Hut application.

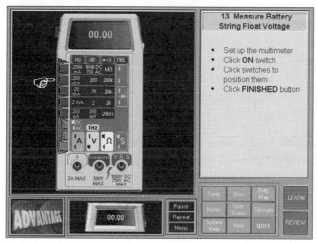

3-7

Calibrating rectifier meters in AT&T's Regen Hut application.

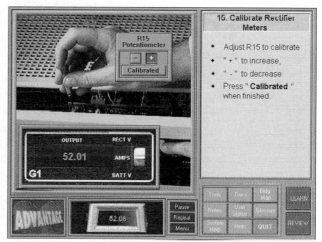

3-8

Preparing for the discharge test in AT&T's Regen Hut application.

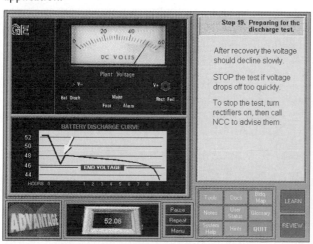

3-9

The ACTIV training system.

JUST-IN-TIME TRAINING

Instruction called **just-in-time training** is required when something goes wrong and a worker must find out how to handle it quickly. Corporate downsizing has greatly increased the need for just-in-time training. With fewer employees on staff, chances are greater that a given worker will not know how to deal with a situation that specialists might have handled before losing their jobs due to downsizing. Forecasting a rapid increase in training costs, Tynan (1993) tells how rightsizing piles new responsibilities onto existing staff and requires hiring temporary staff that need just-in-time training. For example, CTR (page 57) reports on how Owens-Corning Fiberglass uses an interactive multimedia system to help factory workers diagnose and fix production line problems. After the computer performs the diagnosis based on input from workers, appropriate video sequences with instructional commentary show the workers how to correct the problem.

The Electric Power Research Institute has developed a similar system called Sa. Vant. Users describe problems in power plant turbines through the keyboard or a microphone, and Sa. Vant troubleshoots them, providing a diagnosis, associated wiring diagrams, photographs, and videos showing users how to fix the problem.

IBM claims an $800,000 annual savings from a just-in-time training system that guides employees step-by-step through factory processes at its Poughkeepsie, New York, assembly plant. And Tynan (1993) reports that Xerox has a Generic Fault Analysis course that features schematic diagrams. "Trainees move an electronic version of a multimeter—a diagnostic tool that measures ohms and amperage—to different parts of the schematic, which then displays typical readings." He further reports how Alyeska, which operates the trans-Alaska pipeline, uses multimedia to prepare workers for dealing with emergencies such as leaks or fires so they know what valves to open or close and what alarms to sound.

PILOT TRAINING

Every major airline is using multimedia for pilot training. It saves costs by making training more efficient and reducing the amount of time pilots spend in expensive flight simulators. CTR (page 65) notes how SAS Airlines used multimedia to reduce the time needed to train pilots by 35%. The SAS flight training system includes images of cockpit instrumentation, computer-generated instrument readings, and digitized audio clips that let pilots practice flight procedures before training on full-scale flight simulators.

ADVERTISING AND ELECTRONIC BROCHURES

The more you engage a potential customer with an advertisement, the greater the chance of making a sale. That is why multimedia provides such an effective way of advertising. Explaining why other forms of advertising are passive, Goldstein and Wittenstein (1993) note, "With multimedia, users have the ability to actively participate in the way they learn and make decisions. They can design their own car package, get company history, view customer's testimonials or celebrity endorsements, explore a piece of equipment, stopping at any point to receive related branching information, or navigate to any part of the presentation easily and logically."

The electronic brochure is a promotional and marketing tool that usually consists of a single diskette or CD-ROM sent to targeted audiences. General Motors, Ford, Chrysler, General Electric, and Corning Glassware have marketed products this way. While the Direct Marketing Association considers a 1% return successful with paper brochures, electronic brochures draw a 12% response. CTR (page 50) reports how a follow-up survey by the Netherlands Foreign Investment Agency to 10,000 CD-ROMs they distributed (encouraging companies to locate in Holland) in anticipation of Europe 1992 indicated that 85% of the recipients looked at the CD. Paper direct-mail examination, on the other hand, typically ranges from 2 to 4%.

Chrysler Corporation made an electronic brochure entitled *The Jeep and Eagle Adventure* (see Figure 3-10). It is distributed on diskette and costs $6.95. The disk has seven main parts: Models, Motion, Capability, Environment, Safety, Specs, and Pricing Option. Waltz (1993) describes the heart of the disk as "an interactive price worksheet that calculates total cost and monthly payments—taking trade-ins, rebates and interest rates into account." Figures 3-11 through 3-13 show the PhotoQuest wildlife photography adventure game that comes on the Chrysler disk. The user must locate a specific animal and snap its picture with enough time remaining to get back home. Chrysler included the game to encourage people to share the CD with friends; PhotoQuest also provides new ways to show off the cars' features. For example, there are places where the game advises the player to switch into four-wheel drive. The Demonstrations section of the *Multiliteracy CD* contains a demo of the Chrysler disk. You can try it by selecting Applications, then clicking the Jeep/Eagle button.

Corporations are also beginning to offer shareholders annual reports on CD-ROM. An executive at Oracle Corporation notes, "The magic of CD-ROM is that you can make a little show of it" (*New York Times* 3/5/94: 21).

3-10

The main menu of *The Jeep and Eagle Adventure*, a promotional electronic brochure from Chrysler Corporation.

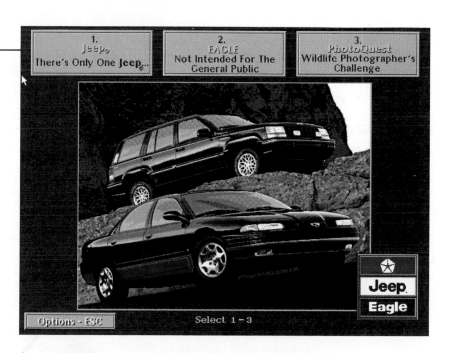

3-11

The Jeep and Eagle Adventure includes the interactive game PhotoQuest in which players are given a photo assignment that requires driving to remote locations to find and photograph specific animals.

3-12

You, the player, get clues from a guide and a phone. You then use the map to navigate a Grand Cherokee to where the animal was last sighted. Once you find the animal, snap a photograph with the "camera" and complete the game.

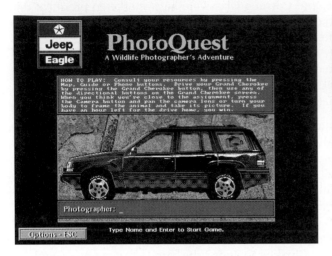

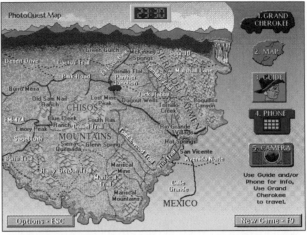

3-13

The player uses the directional buttons at the bottom of the screen to "drive" a Grand Cherokee to various locations.

MASS MARKET APPLICATIONS

Multimedia is wide open for entrepreneurs who can make a lot of money dreaming up ways to use it in mass market applications. For example, nearly everyone is concerned about their appearance, and choosing hairstyles has mass market appeal. Figure 3-14 shows how New Image Industries has made clever use of multimedia to help you decide what hairstyle suits you best. The Styles On Video system uses a multimedia computer with a video capture card and a camera to digitize your head onto the computer screen. Then the operator uses the digitizing tablet and stylus pen shown in Figure 3-15 to remove your hair. The system proceeds to put other hairstyles on your head to show what you would look like in different fashions and hair colors, as shown in Figure 3-16. Then the system creates a videotape that you can study privately or show friends to get their opinion on

3-14

A Styles On Video system in action in a hair salon.

3-15

The Styles On Video system consists of a multimedia computer with video camera, digital video capture card, VCR, pen, and digitizing tablet.

3-16

Styles On Video lets you explore your hairstyle fantasies.

which style you should choose. According to the vendor, Styles On Video is the breakthrough business opportunity of the '90s. You can find out where the nearest Styles On Video imaging salon is in your area by pointing your Web browser at http://www.webcreations.com/styles.

E X E R C I S E S

1. Have you ever used a point-of-sale kiosk? Where? Did it have multimedia? Compare the way it functioned to traditional shopping; did the kiosk complement, replace, or make traditional shopping unnecessary?

2. Find a point-of-sale kiosk in your local community. Describe its look and feel. Observe people using it and describe any problems or advantages you observe.

3. What are the obstacles to digital video replacing the VCR as the primary means of distributing video recordings? If your home has access to a digital video service, how has the service impacted the use of your VCR? Do you rent more or fewer videotapes from your local video store? Why?

4. Visit your local Kinko's and ask to see their videoconferencing facilities. Do you think videoconferencing will become a viable business at Kinko's? For whom and for what purpose? Would you use it in your line of work, or for personal things? Why?

5. Visit some local realtors and find out whether they use multimedia to sell homes. If so, ask what is the benefit; if not, find out why they do not use multimedia.

6. Visit a local business and find out whether they have ever used multimedia computers for just-in-time training. How is just-in-time training used in your chosen profession?

7. Have you ever received an electronic brochure? What about? Was it effective? Examine the Chrysler Jeep/Eagle brochure on the *Multiliteracy CD*. Do you find it well designed? Effective? What would you add or change to sell more vehicles?

8. If you have access to the World Wide Web, use the Web's Yahoo search engine to find out how many new online shopping services have been created since this book was printed. You will find the list of online malls at http://www.yahoo.com/Business_and_Economy/Companies/Shopping_Centers/ Online_Malls. As this book goes to press, about 650 malls are listed there.

4

Education

After completing this chapter, you will be able to:

- Describe how multimedia computers provide a powerful environment for achieving the goals of the cognitive movement in education

- Understand how multimedia computers are being used across the curriculum in a wide range of subjects

- Sample state-of-the-art applications on the enclosed *Multiliteracy CD*

- Assess how up-to-date your local schools are in adopting these technologies

- Question whether technology will make any major difference in the structure of schooling

S ARTICULATED by Brown, Collins, and Duguid (1989), skills and knowledge are too often taught out of context, as ends in and of themselves. To overcome this, teachers are using multimedia to bring into the classroom real-life examples of situations that provide the contextual framework so important for learning. Brown calls this use of multimedia **situated learning**. Multimedia gives teachers instant access to thousands of slides, videos, sound tracks, and lesson plans. These materials can be called up instantly, either for classroom use or as a networked resource for student exploration, discovery, reflection, and cooperative learning. Among educational researchers, the capability to demonstrate vividly and convincingly the real-world applicability of knowledge has become known as **anchored instruction** (The Cognition and Technology Group at Vanderbilt, 1990).

The benefits of multimedia are well documented by Professor James Kulik (1985, 1986, 1991, and 1994) and his associates at the University of Michigan. During the past 20 years, Kulik has analyzed hundreds of controlled experiments on the effectiveness of computer-based learning. Although the term *multimedia* did not exist then, many of the studies used graphics, sound, and video in a manner now referred to as multimedia. Overall, the findings indicate that average learning time has been reduced significantly (sometimes by as much as 80%), and achievement levels are more than a standard deviation higher (a full letter grade in school) than when multimedia is not used.

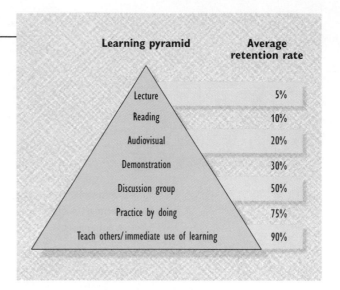

4-1

The learning pyramid.
Source: National Training Laboratories
(NTL) Institute, Bethel, Maine.

Learning pyramid	Average retention rate
Lecture	5%
Reading	10%
Audiovisual	20%
Demonstration	30%
Discussion group	50%
Practice by doing	75%
Teach others/immediate use of learning	90%

The Kulik studies are classified according to grade levels. The Information Superhighway is linking universities, colleges, schools, and homes into a continuum that is helping to break down the distinctions between these grade levels. The Internet is enabling students of all ages to collaborate on worldwide projects, share discoveries, and develop strategies for acquiring knowledge in a social context. As the learning pyramid in Figure 4-1 shows, the more actively involved students are in the teaching and learning process, the more knowledge gets retained.

COGNITIVE VERSUS BEHAVIORAL PSYCHOLOGY

Much of what happens in the traditional classroom was influenced heavily by the behaviorist movement, which dominated American psychology from about 1920 to 1970. Chief among the behaviorists was Skinner (1938, 1953), who saw that human behavior is powerfully shaped by its consequences. Moreover, Skinner felt that psychology was essentially about behavior and that behavior was largely determined by its outcomes. Although Skinnerian methods have been effective in learning how to train animals and helping human beings modify their behavior, the behaviorists fell short of what is most important in education for most educators. To educate, you must do more than modify behavior. To educate, you must help the student learn how to develop strategies for learning. Such is the goal of the cognitive movement in education as defined by Bruning (1995: 1):

> *Cognitive psychology* is a theoretical perspective that focuses on the realms of human perception, thought, and memory. It portrays learners as active processors of information—a metaphor borrowed from the computer world—and assigns critical roles to the knowledge and perspective students bring to their learning. What learners do to enrich information, in the view of cognitive psychology, determines the level of understanding they ultimately achieve.

It is appropriate that Bruning borrows from the computer world in his definition of cognitive psychology. As you will see in the educational applications surveyed in this chapter, multimedia computers provide a powerful environment for helping achieve the goals of the cognitive movement in education. As articulated by Piaget (1969), students learn better when they can invent knowledge through inquiry and experimentation instead of acquiring facts presented by a teacher in class. It is difficult for a teacher to provide this kind of environment for each student in a traditional classroom. Since there is only one teacher for many students, it is physically impossible for the teacher to support each student's individual needs. Multimedia computers help by providing students with a world of interconnected knowledge to explore. The screen-capture and downloading tools you will learn in the tutorial section of this book enable students to collect what they discover and construct a framework for organizing and understanding. Thus, the student becomes an active processor of the information, and knowledge is the by-product.

Since the learner is portrayed as an active processor who explores, discovers, reflects, and constructs knowledge, the trend to teach from this perspective is known as the *constructivist* movement in education. As Bruning (1995: 216) explains, "The aim of teaching, from a constructivist perspective, is not so much to transmit information, but rather to encourage *knowledge formation* and development of metacognitive processes for judging, organizing, and acquiring new information." Several theorists have embellished this theme. Rumelhart (1981), following Piaget, introduced the notion of *schemata*, which are mental frameworks for comprehension that function as *scaffolding* for organizing experience. At first, the teacher provides instructional scaffolding that helps the student construct knowledge. Gradually, the teacher provides less scaffolding until the student is able to construct knowledge independently. For example, in the History of Flight tutorial in Part Six of this book, a lot of scaffolding is provided at first as an aid to learning how to develop a multimedia application; gradually, the scaffolding is removed until the student is able to create new multimedia works independently. Skinner and the behaviorists used related techniques known as *prompting* and *fading*. A hierarchy of sequential prompts firms up and reinforces a student's skill, and fading removes the prompts gradually until the student can perform a task independently.

Vygotsky (1978) emphasized the role of social interactions in knowledge construction. Social constructivism turns attention to children's interactions with parents, peers, and teachers in homes, neighborhoods, and schools. Vygotsky introduced the concept of the *zone of proximal development,* which is the difference between the difficulty level of a problem a student can cope with independently and the level that can be accomplished with help from others. In the zone of proximal development, a student and an expert work together on problems that the student alone could not work on successfully.

A challenge for software designers is to create programs that can function as the expert in the zone where learning and development take place. Software that succeeds can help transform the traditional teacher-centered classroom into a more learner-centered environment. Table 4-1 compares the teacher-dominated and cognitive perspectives. As you review the software surveyed in this chapter, keep this comparison in mind and reflect on the role multimedia computers can and should play in the contemporary classroom.

Table 4-1 Comparison of the Teacher-Dominated
and Cognitive Perspectives on Education

Teacher-Dominated Perspective	Cognitive Perspective
Teacher centered	Learner centered
Teachers present knowledge	Students discover and construct knowledge
Students learn meaning	Students create meaning
Learner as memorizer	Learner as processor
Learn facts	Develop learning strategies
Rote memory	Active memory
Teacher structures learning	Social interaction provides instructional scaffolding
Repetitive	Constructive
Knowledge is acquired	Knowledge is created
Teacher provides resources	Students find resources
Individual study	Cooperative learning and peer interaction
Sequential instruction	Adaptive learning
Teacher manages student learning	Students learn to manage their own learning
Students learn others' thinking	Students develop and reflect on their own thinking
Isolationist	Contextualist
Extrinsic motivation	Intrinsic motivation
Reactive teachers	Proactive teachers
Knowledge transmission	Knowledge formation
Teacher dominates	Teacher observes, coaches, and facilitates
Mechanistic	Organismic
Behavioralist	Constructivist

ART

The ability to display more than 16 million colors lets computers exhibit artwork
in true colors that rival those on the printed page. But unlike books, in which the
pictures are static and unconnected, multimedia computers offer art educators all
the advantages of hypermedia. For example, consider Softkey's *Leonardo 2.0.*
Figure 4-2 shows how the user has instant access to every painting, invention, and
writing of this Renaissance master. The biography chronicles the events that shaped
da Vinci's life and contains hyperlinks that transport you to articles, paintings,
videos, and models of his inventions. Figure 4-3 shows how the timeline correlates
events in da Vinci's life to world history.

4-2

The database in Softkey's *Leonardo 2.0.*

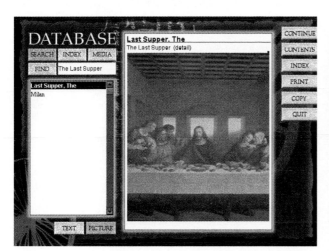

4-3

The timeline in Softkey's *Leonardo 2.0.* The highlighted words are hyperlinks.

Now that graphics are available worldwide on the Internet, museums all over the world are making artwork accessible on the Information Superhighway. The Spring 1994 newsletter of The Getty Center for Education in the Arts discusses the role of the Internet in discipline-based art education:

> Imagine a national network devoted to discipline-based art education (DBAE) in its myriad, evolving applications. This network would open communications between teachers, administrators, school board members, scholars, policy makers, students, artists, community arts groups, art associations, and parents. It would provide access to new ideas, products, and research; innovative programs; opportunities for collaboration; current literature; discussions of ideas; and training techniques. Through print or electronic media it would offer forums for sharing, exchanging, informing, testing, discussing, learning, surveying, or advocating among an expanding community of practitioners, scholars, and advocates.

Getty has been working diligently to make this dream come true. To experience the wealth of resources available for art educators, point your Web browser at http://www.artsednet.getty.edu.

BIOLOGY

Biology teachers are taking advantage of multimedia's ability to bring classrooms to life with animations, full-motion video clips, and stereo sound. Multimedia curriculum resources include animals, dissection, genetics, heredity, and cell biology.

Animals

How We Classify Animals teaches taxonomy. Distributed by the Society for Visual Education (SVE), this multimedia CD begins by explaining the two broad groups of animals (vertebrates and invertebrates). Students examine the different types and categories of animal life such as sponges, animals with stinging cells, worms,

National Geographic's *Mammals: A Multimedia Encyclopedia.*

The result of pressing the Range Map button in *Mammals: A Multimedia Encyclopedia.*

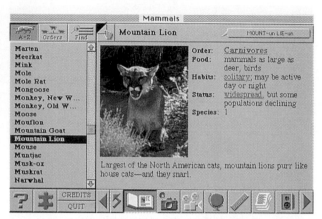

jointed animals, soft-bodied animals, spiny-skinned animals, fish, amphibians, birds, and mammals. A HyperStax interface allows for fully interactive browsing and testing options with a scorekeeper. The teacher's guide features activities that make connections among a wide range of content areas, including language arts, health and nutrition, social studies, art, and critical thinking. For more info go to http://www.SVEmedia.com.

Shown in Figure 4-4, *Mammals: A Multimedia Encyclopedia* is a multimedia CD from the National Geographic Society that covers more than 200 mammals, from aardvark to zorilla. There are 45 full-motion video clips, 150 authentic animal vocalizations, 700 captioned full-screen photographs, fact boxes, and range maps you access with your mouse. For example, Figure 4-5 shows the result of pressing the Range Map button for the mountain lion. Essays about the animals provide the equivalent of 600 pages of text.

Oceans Below is a simulated CD-ROM scuba diving adventure by Amazing Media. After checking your gear on the deck of the ship, reading a small guidebook that turns into a slide show on topics like altered depth perception and ocean conservation, and selecting one of 17 dives (see Figure 4-6), you can view a fish chart like the plastic sheets real divers use (see Figure 4-7). Then, as you dive, the world beneath the waves emerges. You explore the depths with your mouse as many colorful images of sea creatures appear. For example, clicking on a picture of a lionfish lets you watch a video of it—within the frame of a face mask (see Figure 4-8)—and listen to a description.

Dissection

The Curry School of Education has a frog dissection tutorial on the World Wide Web. The tutorial contains highly interactive activities in which the student clicks on a picture of a frog to mark the beginning and end of an incision. If the student is wrong, feedback is provided. When the student gets the answer right, the incision is made, and another picture shows the results. You can do the frog dissection tutorial at http://curry.edschool.virginia.edu/~insttech/frog.

4-6

The world map takes you to any one of 17 exciting dives in Amazing Media's *Oceans Below.*

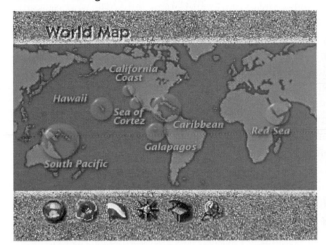

4-7

Narrated sea life charts identify the fish you encounter in *Oceans Below.*

4-8

Full-motion videos play inside the frame of a face mask in *Oceans Below.*

Genetics and Heredity

Exploring Genetics and Heredity is a multimedia CD from Clearvue that uses narrated diagrams and microphotographs to explain DNA structure, meiosis, mitosis, the nature and regulation of genetic material, and the basic patterns of heredity, including an extensive presentation of Mendel's law. Clearvue also publishes three separate CDs entitled *Genetics, Heredity,* and *Evolution,* treating these topics in more detail. For more info go to http://www.clearvue.com.

Virtual FlyLab (VFL) is an interactive Web site for genetics instruction. Developed by Dr. Robert Desharnais at California State University at Los Angeles, VFL enables students to conduct genetic experiments by "breeding" fruit flies over the Web and observing the patterns of inheritance in the offspring. Students can also formulate hypotheses and conduct statistical tests. Virtual FlyLab is on the Web at http://vflylab.calstatela.edu/edesktop/VirtApps/VflyLab/IntroVflyLab.html.

Cell Biology

Clearvue's *Cell Biology* consists of two multimedia CDs that cover biological concepts and cellular processes. *Part I: Cell Structure & Function, Cell Cycle, Mitosis & Cell Division, Meiosis* compares prokaryotic and eucaryotic cells and presents the structure and function of organelles in plant cells. After outlining the phases of the cell cycle, stages of mitosis, and cell division, the CD introduces the basic mechanism of meiosis and examines the sequence of events, sources of genetic variability, cytology of meiotic cell devision, and the differences and similarities between mitosis and meiosis. *Part II: Membranes, Cell Motility* describes how lipid and protein molecules assemble to form cellular membranes and introduces the fluid mosaic model and supporting evidence, as well as major pathways for the transport of molecules through membranes. Cell motility is examined with respect to microtubules and microfilaments.

National Association of Biology Teachers Web Site

You can find out more about how multimedia computers are being used in biology teaching at the National Association of Biology Teachers Web site at http://www.gene.com/ae/RC/NABT. Figure 4-9 shows how there is a teacher's lounge where you can discuss the latest trends with other biology teachers. The teacher/scientist network lets you team with scientists on important projects such as the Human Genome Project. The search engine lets you perform key word searches of all the documents in the NABT site.

4-9

Buttons you can click at the National Association of Biology Teachers Web site.

CHEMISTRY

Illman (1994) reviews the work of several chemistry teachers who are using multimedia tools to make presentations in classrooms, publish electronic journals, illustrate the periodic table, develop animations of ions and molecules, and make multimedia chemistry instruction available on the Internet. Illman predicts that multimedia PCs will become widespread in teaching chemistry due to the wide range of problems MPCs solve.

For example, one of the most perplexing problems in teaching chemistry is that students do not get enough time in the laboratory to conduct experiments. Many schools cannot provide the quantity or quality of lab experience needed for a good education in chemistry. Students are no longer permitted to handle some important chemicals that have been found to cause cancer. Other experiments are too dangerous, expensive, or time-consuming. Enter the multimedia CD-ROM *Exploring Chemistry*. Published by Falcon Software (http://www.falconsoftware.com/falconweb), *Exploring Chemistry* is a comprehensive introductory chemistry course covering both inorganic and organic topics. Its 150 lessons provide 180

4-10

The grain dust explosion lasts only a quarter of a second; students view it in stages by stepping through each frame of video.

hours of instruction. The interactive lab design by Professors Stanley G. Smith and Loretta L. Jones (1993) uses full-motion video to let students conduct lab experiments repeatedly until the students master the material. Two of the experiments are on the *Multiliteracy CD;* one is of a grain dust explosion, and the other deals with equilibrium.

To try the grain dust explosion, go to the Demonstrations section, select Applications, and click the Exploring Chemistry: Dust Explosion button. As you can see, this experiment is much too dangerous to let students try in real life. Figure 4-10 shows how the step frame option lets you view the explosion as it develops; each frame represents a thirtieth of a second.

The equilibrium experiment can be found by going to the Demonstrations section, selecting Applications, and clicking the Exploring Chemistry: Equilibrium button. Figures 4-11 and 4-12 demonstrate how you mix a variety of chemicals, observe the reactions, and learn from the results. The two chemicals used in the experiment, potassium chromate and potassium dichromate, have been widely used in chemistry education. Recently, they have been found to be carcinogens, so the only safe way to teach about them is through simulations like this. The simulations are so realistic that when you click a chemical with your mouse and see a hand pour the chemical into the beaker, it is as if your own hand poured it in.

Active technologies on the World Wide Web are helping solve another problem in teaching chemistry: visualizing the structure of chemical models. In a textbook

4-11

Students mix chemicals to find the one that changes potassium chromate into potassium dichromate.

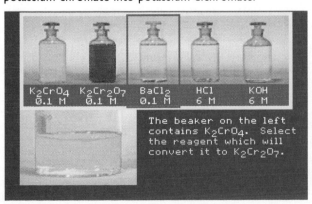

4-12

The result of entering a wrong answer in the equilibrium experiment.

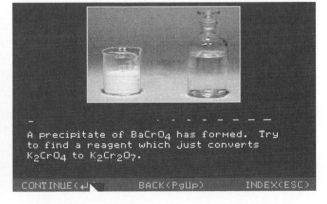

4-13

Java rotations of a model of a benzene molecule. Rotating the chemical model leads the user to discover that the centers of the six carbon atoms and six hydrogen atoms in benzene are coplanar.

Benzene

students are limited to a static photo that shows only one position. On the Web, using active technologies such as Sun's Java, Macromedia's Shockwave, or Microsoft's ActiveX, students can rotate chemical models by clicking and dragging with a mouse. For example, Figure 4-13 shows different stages in the rotation of a model of a benzene molecule on a Java Web page. To try this and other chemical models on the Web, point your Java-enabled browser at http://www.udel.edu/fth/java/MoleculeViewer.

Speaking of textbooks, there is now a multimedia alternative to the best-selling introductory chemistry text *Chemistry and Chemical Reactivity*. Professor John Kotz, primary author of the text, has created a multimedia CD-ROM entitled *Saunders Interactive General Chemistry CD-ROM*, which is distributed by Saunders College Publishing. The CD includes more than 600 custom-designed screens with thousands of full-color photos and illustrations, 150 video clips with narration and sound effects, 200 animations, and more than 100 3-D molecular model rotations generated with CAChe Scientific software, which enables students to manipulate the models in real time. The multimedia materials contain content-sensitive hyperlinks to the complete textbook. Virtual Minilabs let students perform experiments on-screen, manipulate variables, and observe results. The CD-ROM comes packaged with a printed workbook in which students record their observations.

CIVICS

Instead of teaching civics with textbooks that only describe it, multimedia lets teachers bring civics to life with multimedia CD-ROMs, live video feeds from Congress, and online access to government agencies and offices, including the White House (http://www.whitehouse.gov).

Capitol Hill is a CD-ROM from The Software Toolworks that provides a behind-the-scenes look at the inner workings of Congress. The CD explains the origins of the two-party system and what the various congressional committees do. There is even a Capitol tour conducted by C-SPAN commentator Mike Michaelson. After you find out who's who in government, a multiple-choice game tests what you have learned.

To provide more of a historical perspective, Compton's NewMedia publishes *U.S. Civics*, a guide to U.S. history from the 1700s to the present. Biographies, government structure, reference manuals, and sample tests round out this educational database.

A highly motivating teaching resource is *The '92 Vote* by ABC News Interactive. This CD-ROM is presented in the form of a multimedia news magazine. It contains one hour of ABC News video, another hour of supplemental audio, dozens of full-color pictures, and text from ABC News journalists. Students use hypermedia tools to research the people and events of the 1992 campaign from the primaries through Inauguration Day. Resources include biographies of the major personalities and news stories on the convention, debates, election night, and inauguration. By the time you read this, *The '96 Vote* should be in press.

ECONOMICS

A big problem in teaching economics is the static nature of the charts and graphs printed in economics textbooks. Students need to be able to manipulate the data and view changes interactively to gain an understanding of complex economics concepts.

McGraw-Hill is addressing this problem with two multimedia CD-ROMs for the best-selling McConnell *Economics* textbook. The first CD is entitled *Microeconomics*. It covers supply and demand, elasticities, cost, pure competition, monopoly, and tax incidence. The second CD is called *Macroeconomics*. Topics include national accounts, the aggregate expenditure model, aggregate demand and supply, the Federal Reserve and monetary policy, inflation/unemployment, and money, banking, and money creation.

If you compare Figures 4-14 and 4-15, you can see how the *Economics* CD-ROM brings economics to life. Figure 4-14 is one of the graphs in the textbook. The student sees only one view and cannot change anything. Figure 4-15 is the same graph on the *Microeconomics* CD. Buttons enable the student to shift the production possibilities and view the results in a table of data that updates automatically when the student changes the graph.

The Production Possibilities graph is on the *Multiliteracy CD*. To try it yourself, go to the Demonstrations section, select Applications, click the Economics button, and play with the six buttons that shift the curve.

4-14

How the Production Possibilities curve appears in the *Economics* textbook. The student cannot interact with it.

4-15

The multimedia version of the Production Possibilities curve lets the student manipulate the graph and study changes in the data.

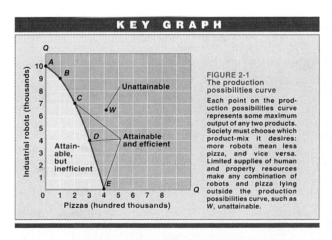

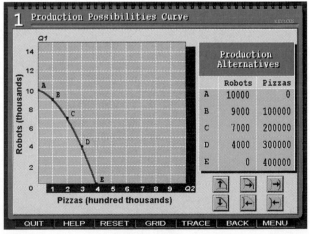

FOREIGN LANGUAGES

When abroad, try conversing in a foreign language you supposedly learned in school and you will quickly grasp the importance of multimedia in foreign-language instruction. Although books can teach grammar and vocabulary, they cannot interact with you the way people converse. Enter multimedia.

Multimedia computers are a natural for teaching language. Digital audio provides pronunciation capabilities, and full-motion video can put students in real-life situations. Exploiting these factors, Syracuse Language Systems has teamed with Random House to publish the award-winning *Living Language Multimedia* series on CD-ROM. The series includes four products:

- *All-In-One Language Fun* contains instruction in Spanish, French, German, Japanese, and English—all on one CD. Designed for ages three to 12, the CD teaches hundreds of words and phrases through multimedia versions of familiar games, including bingo, jigsaw puzzles, Concentration, Simon says, and more. Digital audio of native speakers' voices helps users learn how to pronounce the words.

- *TriplePlay Plus* takes an important leap forward. It uses speech recognition software licensed from Dragon Systems to listen to, analyze, and help improve your pronunciation. *TriplePlay Plus* is available in English, French, German, Hebrew, Italian, Japanese, and Spanish versions. Figure 4-16 shows how interactive comic strips depict everyday situations to build comprehension and conversation skills at a slow or natural rate of speech.

- *Let's Talk* uses Dragon speech recognition to teach on one CD more than 2,200 words in each of four languages: French, German, Italian, and Spanish. Native speakers provide the model, and a "recognition meter" shows how well your pronunciation matched it.

- *Your Way* is a language course based on branching conversations in six everyday settings: social engagements, dining out, hotels and accommodations, around town, travel, and medical needs. For example, Figure 4-17 shows a situation in a restaurant. Challenging games, extensive reference sections, and a multimedia glossary add to the richness of *Your Way*.

4-16

An interactive comic strip in *TriplePlay Plus* from Syracuse Language Systems.

4-17

A conversational situation presented by *Your Way* from Syracuse Language Systems.

The Syracuse CDs have won many awards, including the 1996 Newsweek Editors' Choice Award and a series of Consumer Electronics Show, Technology & Learning, and NewMedia INVISION awards. Highly praised is the use of speech recognition to teach pronunciation. According to Syracuse president Martin Rothenberg, "Using the Automatic Speech Recognition games in *TriplePlay Plus*, language learners can develop a natural-sounding accent and confidence in their speaking skills. Learners will immediately know if they are saying words and phrases correctly, and will be able to practice and improve as they play. The games are also designed so that a native-speaker's voice is always available as a pronunciation model." Except for the specially designed dynamic microphone packaged with the software, no additional hardware is required. Syracuse Language Systems has a Web site at http://www.syrlang.com.

Heinle & Heinle publishes *Nouvelles Dimensions,* an instructional program for listening comprehension in French developed by linguist Dr. James Noblitt. It is based on video materials produced by Bernard Petit, a professor of French at SUNY Brockport. Petit uses a handheld video camera to get authentic samples of French as it is spoken by French people in everyday life. He focuses on situations and speech samples that are useful for the learner. On the computer screen, students can view scenes of French daily life: greetings, ordering food, statements of personal preferences, and introduction of family members. Since what is seen and heard can be controlled through the computer keyboard and mouse, viewers interact with the program, proceeding at their own pace as they practice, take tests, and complete writing exercises. Figure 4-18 shows an example of how the student learns to hear key words in a conversational context. The user may click the Show Text button to see the script, or call up a map, or use the accompanying word processor and dictionary. The interactive format provides user control of instructional support.

Nouvelles Dimensions offers several advantages over simply viewing a videotape. Students may control the pace of instruction, repeating at will any segment that is not clear. Comprehension aids, such as pop-up help screens, may be used for guidance in the analysis of unfamiliar vocabulary or grammar. Maps and a learner's dictionary are available for more-extended exploration. An online word processor that permits direct access to the reference materials provides a means for using what has been learned. Students enjoy the authentic feel of the material and the interactive control. The computer permits an analysis of gestures and facial expressions, on a frame-by-frame basis if necessary, that enhances the

4-18

In *Nouvelles Dimensions* the student learns to hear key words in a conversational context.

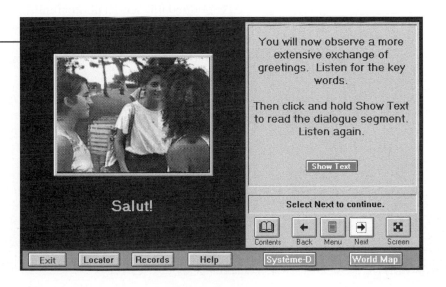

Nouvelles Dimensions
facilitates learning by doing.

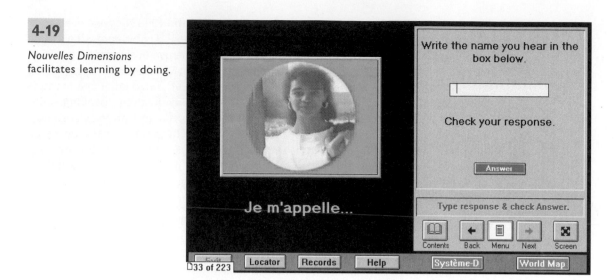

understanding of communicative intent. By adding visual context and reference material to language study, the program can help the learner master techniques for aural comprehension, such as listening for key words. Figure 4-19 shows one example of how *Nouvelles Dimensions* facilitates learning by doing. The learner listens for the person's name, types it in the response box, then clicks the Answer button to confirm the entry. Samples from speakers of all ages and backgrounds assist in ear training. According to Dr. Noblitt, instructors like having an enriched environment for learning essential skills outside the classroom. There is a demonstration of *Nouvelles Dimensions* in the Demonstrations section of the *Multiliteracy CD*. To view it, select Applications, then click the Nouvelles Dimensions button.

GEOGRAPHY

The highly visual nature of geography makes it a natural for multimedia. *Picture Atlas of the World* is a CD-ROM from the National Geographic Society. Covering both physical and cultural geography, it includes world, continental, and regional maps, in addition to high-resolution interactive political and topographical maps. More than 1,200 captioned full-screen photographs, 50 video clips, and dozens of vocal and musical audio clips bring both physical and cultural geography to life. Essays give detailed information about each country along with screens showing vital statistics. Animations, illustrations, and diagrams enliven map projections and show the earth's rotation.

The Software Toolworks publishes the CD-ROMs *U.S. Atlas* and *World Atlas.* They use multimedia to play state songs and national anthems, display flags, and show topographical and statistical maps. An important feature is the way users can add to the database, make personal notes, mark maps, and print stunning graphic reports.

One cleverly designed CD is Brøderbund Software's *Where in the World Is Carmen Sandiego?* Carmen and her gang of villains are stealing the treasures of the world. Sixty countries are involved, with hundreds of animations and thousands of audio

4-20

On-screen tools in *Where in the World Is Carmen Sandiego?* include the videophone (left), Dataminder (bottom center), and Note Pad (bottom right).

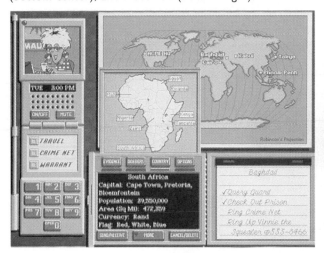

4-21

Dramatic photographs place players in 45 countries around the world.

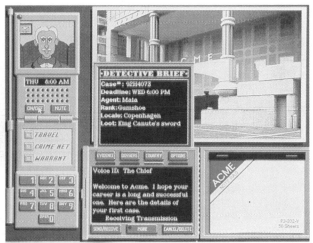

clues, including 500 digitized in foreign languages. The student uses Funk & Wagnall's *World Almanac* to help solve the crime, doing research to find out where to go next to find the criminal and the loot. Figure 4-20 shows the high-tech on-screen tools. Clues include languages spoken, landmarks, and cultural sites. As you can see in Figure 4-21, places are illustrated with pictures from *National Geographic* and accompanied by songs from the Smithsonian. Thus, *Carmen* teaches geography in the context of world culture. The latest release offers an immersive environment in which the student can take a 360-degree walking tour, creating the illusion that the student actually is in the place being explored.

Although *Carmen* is so popular that hundreds of middle schools have held Carmen Sandiego Geography Days, some teachers have trouble figuring out how to integrate programs like *Carmen* into teaching, because it shifts the focus from teacher-centered to student-centered instruction. As Neuwirth (1994) explains, "this game cannot be used in a classroom setting. It is not a very didactic tool as the teacher is not given any time for talking to the student during the game." To learn more about *Carmen* and other award-winning Brøderbund products, go to http://www.broderbund.com.

National Parks of America by Multicom is more utilitarian. Figures 4-22 through 4-24 show how this multimedia CD uses the metaphor of a map to let you navigate to any park in the country and virtually tour it before deciding whether to plan an actual trip there. There are more than 900 photographs by renowned nature photographer David Muench. The CD lets you locate and select any one of 230 parks by name or geographic location or by specific criteria such as camping or hiking. You can research park background information or just tour through dramatic videos and the magnificent beauty of Muench's photographs, as shown in Figure 4-24.

4-22

This map appears when you start the *National Parks of America* CD-ROM. Clicking the buttons lets you navigate down through Regional and State menus to individual parks.

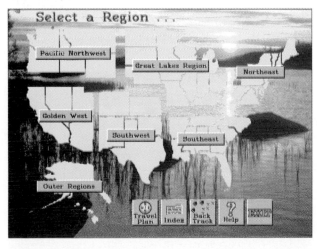

4-23

At the state level, *National Parks of America* lets you view a map that locates each park in the state.

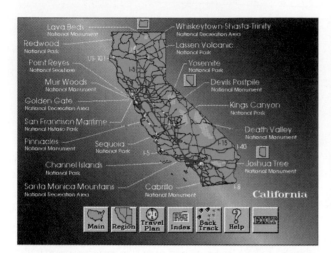

4-24

At the park level, *National Parks of America* lets you access detailed information about each park and view spectacular photos.

Environmental Systems Research Institute's *ArcView* is a geographic information system (GIS) that lets you create and query geographically oriented databases. Using the combined power of the computer, geography, data, and their imaginations, students can develop hypotheses and test scenarios to develop an understanding of the world. For example, Figure 4-25 shows how you can query what countries produced more energy than they consumed in a certain year. Figure 4-26 shows a satellite plot of irrigated fields in part of Kansas. *ArcView* ships with six CD-ROM databases covering different aspects of the United States and the world. In addition, you can create your own databases and import data from dBase or plain text data files. *ArcView*'s Web site is http://www.esri.com.

National Geographic is online at http://www.nationalgeographic.com. The site provides access to back issues of *National Geographic* magazine, plus additional materials that add interactive elements to the magazine's articles and the *National Geographic Explorer* television documentary series.

4-25

An *ArcView* plot answers the question of who produced more energy than they consumed in 1989.

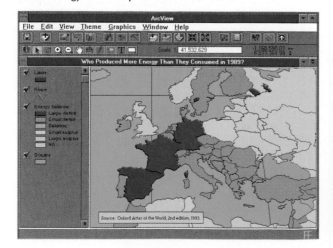

4-26

ArcView plots the irrigated fields southwest of Garden City, Kansas.

HISTORY

There are many ways multimedia brings history to life. As you are about to see, almost all recorded video history of the twentieth century is available on interactive videodiscs; history textbooks on CD-ROMs have video and audio clips with full-text search; multimedia has inspired the creation of new history resources on CD-ROM for which no prior book exists; and the Internet provides online access to source documents, newsletters, and discussion groups.

Videodisc

Instead of attending a traditional lecture in which the instructor occasionally scribbles something on a blackboard for students to take note of, imagine a classroom in which the teacher has access to every major video clip of recorded history. Thanks to a monumental effort by CEL, the most extensive indexed video archive is now available in the form of *The Video Encyclopedia of the 20th Century.* It contains 83 hours of full-motion video on 42 videodiscs. There are 2,338 video chapters, each supported with historical text. Students can compare and link people, events, and time periods. Companion software facilitates the search for subject matter. With a multimedia authoring tool, students can assemble and edit video clips, add narration, and create their own video documentaries.

CEL also publishes a single videodisc version of the series. It allows teachers to access a summary of the materials without having to keep track of 42 videodiscs. One of the great hopes for the Information Superhighway is to make all of this video available digitally on demand to every classroom, thereby avoiding the need to juggle videodiscs.

History Textbooks

D.C. Heath and the Voyager Company have developed multimedia CD-ROM versions of established history textbooks. D.C. Heath has published the American history text *The Enduring Vision, Interactive Edition.* In addition to the text and photographs of the printed version, the CD-ROM includes 3,000 pages of historic documents, U.S. Census data from 1790 to 1990, and audio and video recordings that include footage of President Franklin D. Roosevelt's war message to Congress.

Who Built America? is a CD-ROM by Voyager. Developed by history professor Roy Rosenzweig at George Mason University, it covers the period from the centennial celebration of 1876 to the Great War of 1914. In addition to the text of the printed version, the CD contains historic documents, audio recordings, videos including *The Great Train Robbery,* and more than a thousand pictures.

Dorling Kindersley has created a multimedia CD version of its *Eyewitness Encyclopedia of World History.* The CD covers 10 historical eras from the earliest records of human habitation to Nelson Mandela's election as president of South Africa. Equal treatment is given to Europe, Asia, Africa, the Americas, and Oceania. Online references include Everyday Life, Culture, Inventions, and a Who's Who that provides biographies of historically important personalities.

Multimedia History Titles

Several history titles have been developed on CD-ROM without first appearing as a book. ABC News Interactive publishes an exciting series of interactive videodiscs that includes *Communism and the Cold War, Martin Luther King Jr., In the Holy Land,* and *Powers of the U.S. Government.*

The National Geographic Society has published on CD-ROM *The Presidents: A Picture History of Our Nation,* which describes the personal and political lives of U.S. leaders. This encyclopedic reference tool for home, library, and classroom features historic moments on video, famous speeches, a historical perspective and commentary on each president, more than a thousand captioned photographs, election maps and essays, a political party index, a multimedia timeline that provides a social and historical context for each president, and photo essays on the presidency. The CD also has a narrated tutorial, a pop-up glossary, a game, and the ability to print captions, essays, and speeches.

Vital Links is an ambitious effort by Davidson/Addison-Wesley to provide an environment for students to explore and research historical topics. Instead of presenting information in narrative form, students use tools to access photos, illustrations, maps, songs, and movies. Writing, painting, spreadsheet, graphing, and presentation tools enable students to record their own narrative. Parham (1996) finds that "*Vital Links* is unique in offering students the chance to play the part of professional historians by organizing an era's images into a meaningful story."

There is a demonstration of *Vital Links* on the *Multiliteracy CD.* To try it, go to the Demonstrations section, select Applications, and click the Vital Links button.

Wars

Quanta Press and Compton's NewMedia publish a series of war CD-ROMs. Titles include the *Civil War, World War II, Korea,* and *Vietnam.* In April 1991 Time Warner Interactive released *Desert Storm: The War in the Persian Gulf,* advertising it as "the first electronic magazine with over 6,000 screens of selectable documentation covering the Gulf War." Users follow the evolution of a Gulf War story from its origins to the actual article as it eventually appeared in *Time* magazine. The CD includes *Time* correspondents' files, exclusive audio reports, 300 full-color photographs, and every story report in its original, unedited form, organized chronologically and indexed by subject. There is a glossary of high-tech weapons and a photo gallery, as well as exclusive audio reports, including "as-it's happening" correspondent analyses and interviews. An active timeline of the war lets the user see and hear a synopsis of each week's key events.

Compton's NewMedia offers a competing product, *Desert Storm with Coalition Command,* which comes with a game that lets you deploy ground forces from a sophisticated command post, set policies for providing information to the media, and get vital feedback through direct hotlines to the White House and Pentagon.

FlagTower's *World War II* is a multimedia CD-ROM that presents the Second World War from the British perspective. The CD provides a broad perspective on the war from Germany in the 1920s through postwar reorganization efforts, with explorations of the war's six theaters, in-depth examinations of the impact of the Treaty of Versailles, and a powerful collection of first-person accounts of the Holocaust.

The Assassination of JFK

A CD-ROM that fosters debate is the award-winning *The JFK Assassination: A Visual Investigation.* Published by Medio, it includes more than 20 minutes of narrated overview, video clips from five films documenting the assassination, and computer animations showing conflicting bullet angles. Also included is the complete text of the *Warren Commission Report,* Jim Marrs's best-selling book *Crossfire,* and *The J.F.K. Assassination: A Complete Book of Facts.* Figures 4-27 through 4-30 show how you review the evidence and decide whether there was a conspiracy and who was involved in it. There is a demo of *The JFK Assassination* on the *Multiliteracy CD.* To try it, go to the Demonstrations section, select Applications, and click the Assassination of JFK button.

4-27

The main menu in *The JFK Assassination* introduces you to the background leading up to the assassination, lets you visit the scene in Dealey Plaza, and presents Text, Analysis, and Films & Photos buttons to help you determine whether there was a conspiracy.

4-28

The Films & Photos screen from *The JFK Assassination* lets you view the Nix, Hughes, Zapruder, and Muchmore films.

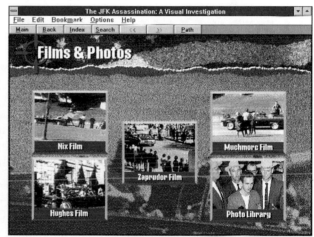

4-29

Autopsy photo from *The JFK Assassination* refuting the *Warren Commission Report.*

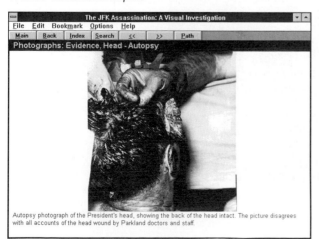

Autopsy photograph of the President's head, showing the back of the head intact. The picture disagrees with all accounts of the head wound by Parkland doctors and staff.

4-30

Evidence of forgery on *The JFK Assassination* CD-ROM.

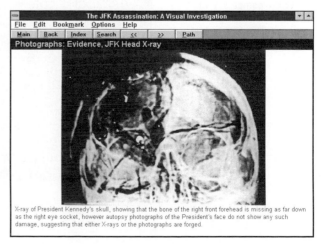

X-ray of President Kennedy's skull, showing that the bone of the right front forehead is missing as far down as the right eye socket, however autopsy photographs of the President's face do not show any such damage, suggesting that either X-rays or the photographs are forged.

Internet Resources for Historians

DeLoughry (1994) tells how the H-Net (history network) project at the University of Illinois at Chicago has set up 20 Internet mailing lists that have attracted more than 4,500 subscribers in 47 countries. The H-Net Web address is http://h-net.msu.edu. HNSOURCE at the University of Kansas provides historians easy access to historical texts and data located all over the network. The HNSOURCE Web address is http://history.cc.ukans.edu/history/WWW_history_main.html. The *Historical Text Archives* at Mississippi State University provide Internet users with such historical documents as the *Instruments of Surrender* signed by Japanese leaders at the end of World War II and *Up from Slavery,* the autobiography of Booker T. Washington. The Web address is http://www.msstate.edu/Archives/History.

Also on the Web is CROMOHS, the Cyber Review of Modern Historiography, which is an electronic journal that provides Web access to research on the principles and methodologies of historical research. The CROMOHS Web site is at http://www.unifi.it/riviste/cromohs.

MATHEMATICS

Mathematics is one of the most highly developed multimedia application areas. Due to the computational nature of mathematics, computers can model the content, monitor student progress, and help students master educational objectives. The National Council of Teachers of Mathematics (NCTM) has issued a set of guidelines that rely heavily on computers as an agent for change in the way mathematics is taught. The NCTM guidelines encourage the teaching of math in real-world contexts in which students investigate problems that have meaning.

For example, Scott Foresman teamed with ABC to produce *Wide World of Mathematics,* in which video footage from ABC News and ABC Sports broadcasts is used to demonstrate how mathematics is used every day, in virtually every field of endeavor. Figure 4-31 shows the Middle School topics, which are available

4-31

The Middle School topics in Scott Foresman's *Wide World of Mathematics.*

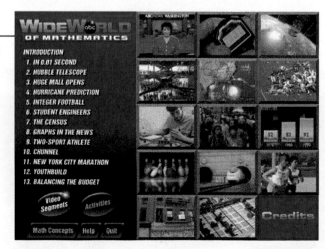

on videotape, videodisc, and CD-ROM. Well-known runner Marty Liqouri takes students step-by-step over the New York City marathon course, using mathematics to compute the length of the course, the runners' rate of travel at different checkpoints, and the combined weight of the runners as they cross the Verazzano-Narrows Bridge. The Hubble space telescope provides a real-world setting for a treatment of very large and very small numbers. The construction of the Chunnel that connects France and England beneath the English Channel introduces dimensions and units. Hurricane Andrew situates prediction techniques with footage from forecasters at the National Hurricane Center. An NFL football game uses a playing field as a number line on which students learn addition and subtraction. To get a copy of a preview of the *Wide World of Mathematics,* call (800) 554-4411 and ask for the videotape demo (code number 37520-X) or the CD-ROM demo (code number 37521-8).

Multimedia is also being used to give a fresh look to classic math software such as Davidson's classic *Math Blaster,* for which there are two new CD-ROMs. *Math Blaster: Episode 1—In Search of Spot* uses dazzling graphics, digitized speech, sound effects, and music to present more than 50,000 problems in addition, subtraction, multiplication, division, fractions, decimals, percentages, number patterns, and estimation. *Math Blaster: Episode 2—Secret of the Lost City* builds on the skills learned in episode 1 by presenting problems that contain two and three operands, up to three-digit numbers, whole and negative numbers, decimals, fractions, and percentages. *Math Blaster Mystery—The Great Brain Robbery* builds prealgebra and word-problem skills as students explore a mysterious mansion. *Alge-Blaster 3* teaches algebra for grades 7 through adult.

Academic Systems markets a series of mathematics CD-ROMs that link students to the instructor's PC, so the teacher can monitor each student's progress and step in for individual assistance when needed. California State University at Northridge reports a higher percentage (70%) of students are passing math than before (only 50% pass without the programs). "Before this I've always felt I never met a technology that didn't ultimately just cost me more money," says CSU Northridge's VP for academic affairs (*Wall Street Journal* 4/3/96: B6). For more information visit http://www.academic.com.

For more information on the NCTM standards, point your Web browser at the Eisenhower National Clearinghouse at http://www.enc.org. IBM publishes a booklet that keys math software to the standards. The title is *A Directory of Educational Objectives and IBM Elementary Mathematics Courseware.* To peruse this and other IBM K–12 support services, visit http://www.solutions.ibm .com/k12.

MUSIC

The music industry has been so totally transformed by multimedia technology that the America 2000 accreditation guidelines require that every music student learn about computer music applications, including music recording, editing, arranging, and printing. Midisoft's *Music Mentor* is an example of the powerful new learning environment multimedia provides. Instead of studying static musical examples printed on staff paper in textbooks, students learn about musical style

4-32

Music Mentor delivers tutorials in a wide range of musical styles.

4-33

Graphical tape-recorder controls make the Personal Studio that comes with Midisoft's *Music Mentor* easy to use.

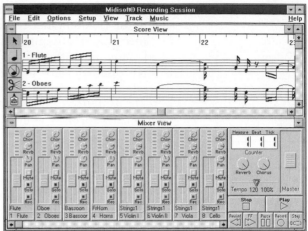

from the interactive tutorials in *Music Mentor,* as shown in Figure 4-32. At any time students can switch to the *Music Mentor*'s Personal Studio, which copies the musical example being studied to the dynamically active computer screen shown in Figure 4-33. Students can experiment by varying the melody, rhythm, orchestration, tempo, and accompaniment. For example, while using *Music Mentor* to study the variations in the second movement of Haydn's Surprise Symphony, students can switch to Personal Studio and create a variation of their own.

Midisoft also publishes *Studio for Windows,* which is very easy to use because of its graphical tape-recorder controls. Anyone who knows how to work a tape recorder can use this program to record and play MIDI sequences. It even notates automatically anything you play on a MIDI keyboard. *Studio* is great for teaching class piano; music teachers can record each one of their students on a different track, complete with orchestral accompaniment, which is highly motivating for students when they rehearse. The latest version of *Studio* lets you record and edit waveform audio, including vocals played in sync with the MIDI tracks.

There is a demonstration copy of *Studio for Windows* on the *Multiliteracy CD.* To try it, go to the Demonstrations section, select Applications, and click the Studio for Windows button. For more information about Midisoft products, go to http://www.midisoft.com.

In *Play Blues Guitar,* published by Play Music, Inc., the student enters a virtual music studio in which blues guitarist Keith Wyatt teaches how to play several blues styles. There are music videos of each piece performed on stage. Hypertext study guides provide historical backgrounds and stylistic explanations. Then Wyatt brings you into his studio and gives lessons on how to play the style. Figure 4-34 shows the guitar model on which the notes to play appear as dots on the fretboard, providing the student with a powerful tool for learning the comps and riffs. The student can speed up or slow the tempo and watch as indicators light up on the fretboard, showing what notes to play in time with the music. There is a demonstration of *Play Blues Guitar* on the *Multiliteracy CD.* To play the demo, go to the Demonstrations section, select Applications, and click on the Blues Guitar button. Play Music also publishes a basic guitar course

4-34

The guitar model in *Play Blues Guitar.*
Copyright © 1995 Play Music, Inc.

4-35

Discovering Music CD-ROM.
Copyright © 1995 Voyetra.

4-36

Jazz: A Multimedia History.

called *Play Guitar,* and intermediate guitar lessons called *Play Rock Guitar.* Play Music has a Web site at http://www.playmusic.com.

Voyetra's *Discovering Music* is a highly produced suite of music software for learning music history, recording music, printing scores, and improvising with an automatic accompaniment program. Figure 4-35 shows the main menu. The CD-ROM containing all this costs just $49, demonstrating how multimedia technology has enabled companies like Voyetra to make highly produced music applications available at mass market consumer prices.

The success of the hit CD title *Multimedia Beethoven* from Microsoft has led to more interactive music titles, including *Multimedia Mozart, Multimedia Stravinsky,* and *Multimedia Vivaldi.* These CDs let you interact with musical scores through annotated program notes, learn about musical style, review historical notes, see musical notation, and learn about musical instruments. For example, *Multimedia Beethoven* contains pages from Beethoven's sketch books, which show how Beethoven would rewrite a melody dozens of times until he got it right.

Microsoft also publishes *Musical Instruments,* a CD-ROM based on the *Eyewitness* book by Dorling Kindersley. The CD contains more than 200 articles, 500 photos, and 1,500 audio recordings. There are four pathways through the material: Families of Instruments, Musical Ensembles (focusing on musical styles ranging from chamber music to rock and roll), Instruments of the World (including rare and exotic instruments and plenty of musical samples), and the A–Z of Instruments (an alphabetical index).

Music education titles include jazz as well as classical music. Compton's NewMedia publishes the CD-ROM title *Jazz: A Multimedia History,* shown in Figure 4-36. The CD takes users on a musical journey from the origins of jazz to the vibrant, electric sounds of today. Students learn about the fathers of jazz, including Duke Ellington, Charlie Parker, and Louis Armstrong, as well as modern jazz innovators, such as Miles Davis, Herbie Hancock, and Weather Report. The CD explains how early jazz was formulated and how it has evolved through the ages, teaching the user how to appreciate and interpret the nuances of jazz. Sigma Designs publishes a complete *Dizzie Gillespie* concert in MPEG format on a multimedia CD. The concert is fantastic.

Coda Music Technology achieved a breakthrough with its Vivace intelligent accompaniment software. Vivace listens to and follows a soloist's tempo changes, providing a way for students to practice playing with an ensemble when human performers are not available. Music schools around the world are using Vivace to provide a more realistic practice experience for soloists. An extensive library of instrumental and vocal music accompaniments is available for Vivace, which comes bundled with the Sound Blaster AWE-32 sound card that plays the accompaniments.

Music Resources on the World Wide Web

Music resources are also coming to the Information Superhighway. The music library at Indiana University has assumed the task of indexing all the music resources on the Web. The index is located at http://www.music.indiana.edu/ misc/music_resources.html. By pointing your Web browser at this excellent index, you can navigate through a wealth of musical treasures. For example, Classics World (http://www.classicalmus.com) lets you browse the latest releases of classical music on CD-ROM. At the Classical Music MIDI Archives (http:// www.prs.net/midi.html), you can download and play MIDI files for thousands of classical music compositions. Thousands of other MIDI files are at the MIDI Files Archive (http://www.dzp.pp.se/midi/). The artist-specific index (http:// www.music.indiana.edu/misc/artists.html) lists hundreds of performing musicians who have established Web sites.

PHYSICS

Physics teachers are using multimedia to help achieve the goals of the National Science Education Standards, which call for providing students with opportunities to get involved in the active process of learning science. Escalada, Grabhorn, and Zollman (1996) used multimedia computers to develop visualization techniques that allow students to collect, analyze, and model motion data. Students use a video capture card to record experiments. Video Analyzer software makes it possible to collect two-dimensional spatial and temporal data, and a Visual Space-Time program combines parts of successive video images into a space/time diagram. These techniques enable students to make connections between concrete, everyday experiences and the abstract principles of physics.

4-37

The *Physics Infomall* CD-ROM.

Pictured in Figure 4-37, *Physics Infomall* is a CD-ROM that contains the text and graphics from 19 physics textbooks and 3,900 articles from *Physics Today, The Physics Teacher,* and *The American Journal of Physics.* The brainchild of University of Nebraska physicist Robert Fuller, *Physics Infomall* provides a rich resource for physics teachers and students to research and explore. As Fuller explains, most students and physicists use books only to find examples of problems they are working on. The *Physics Infomall* fulfills Fuller's dream of providing students with a compact, searchable CD-ROM resource from which physics examples can be cut and pasted and manipulated at will. Distributed by The Learning Team, *Physics Infomall* includes a Problems Place containing 3,000 problems and solutions, and a Demo and Lab Shop containing more than a thousand demos and laboratory exercises.

The Video Encyclopedia of Physics Demonstrations shown in Figure 4-38 is published by The Education Group. It consists of 25 videodiscs that present 600 demonstrations of basic physical principles. Most segments have narration (written scripts are included), and many segments feature slow-motion photography or computer animations. Topics include mechanics, waves, sound, fluid dynamics, heat, thermodynamics, electricity, magnetism, optics, and modern physics. An extensive 1,500-page companion explains how to use the videos. In his very positive review of this package, Beichner (1993) describes how the series can be used to assign homework in which students use data from the videos: "For example, a series of balls of varying diameters and masses are dropped from nearly 4 meters. By stepping through the video a frame at a time, position measurements can be

4-38

The Video Encyclopedia of Physics Demonstrations.

made as the balls fall. Time is included on each frame." The series is also available in middle school and primary school versions.

There is a video clip on the *Multiliteracy CD* that shows examples from *The Video Encyclopedia of Physics Demonstrations.* To view it, go to the Demonstrations section, select Applications, and click the Video Encyclopedia of Physics Demonstrations button.

SCIENCE

Science teachers are using the Internet to provide students with collaborative learning experiences, access to scientific databases, and virtual visits to science laboratories. Reporting on the New Jersey Networking Infrastructure in Education project, Friedman, Baron, and Addison (1996) cite several compelling examples of science study via the Internet. Students gather samples from local pond water, measure chemical characteristics, examine organisms, and share observations with peers over the Internet. An ocean weather database that tracks ships at sea enables students to calculate the speed and direction of oceangoing vessels and predict arrival times. Students visit the Plasma Physics Laboratory at Princeton University to access data from fusion experiments as quickly as Princeton scientists. Table 4-2 lists the Web sites you can visit to learn more about these projects. For

Table 4-2 Web Sites for Science Study via the Internet

Type	Topic	URL
Collaboration	Pond water	http://njnie.dl.stevens-tech.edu/curriculum/water.html
Collaboration	Temperature	http://njnie.dl.stevens-tech.edu/curriculum/temp/intro.html
Databases	Ships at sea	http://njnie.dl.stevens-tech.edu/curriculum/oceans/stowaway.html
Databases	Sunspots	http://www.users.interport.net/~jbaron/solar.html
Science labs	Fusion	http://ippex.pppl.gov/ippex/
Science labs	DNA research	http://morgan.rutgers.edu

the latest information about the New Jersey Networking Infrastructure in Education project, go to http://k12science.stevens-tech.edu.

Interactive videodiscs and multimedia CDs complement these online materials. Science 2000 is a comprehensive seventh-grade science curriculum published on interactive videodisc by Decision Development Corporation. Consistent with the most advanced science frameworks and employing the latest in educational technology, Science 2000 takes an activity-based, thematic approach to teaching science. Within its flexible and open-ended structure, students actively investigate and explore science. They gain a better understanding of a world increasingly shaped by science and technology, plus an insight into the importance of science in solving some of today's critical environmental and health issues. Organized into four units, each of which takes approximately nine weeks to complete, the curriculum in Science 2000 is connected by central themes and is oriented toward solving problems. Multiple disciplines—life, health, social, earth, physical and environmental sciences, math, anthropology, and language arts—are brought into play as students research real-life situations.

Videodiscovery publishes a series of innovative videodiscs for teaching science. There are two volumes of *Science Forums* that challenge students in sixth through ninth grades to grapple with real-world problems. Using a town-meeting format, the forums present role-playing scenarios that focus on science, technology, and societal problems. For example, Figure 4-39 is from a forum on fossil fuel and the greenhouse effect. Students consider whether fossil fuel users should be taxed according to the amount of carbon dioxide that the fuels release into the atmosphere, with the tax revenue used to pay for the greenhouse effects of global warming.

Also from Videodiscovery is the videodisc *Science Sleuths,* in which students solve wacky dilemmas using the research methods and tools of actual scientists. There are 24 open-ended mysteries, ranging from exploding grain silos to crashing computers. Through careful observation and research, students must develop a rational explanation and report their findings. For example, Figure 4-40 is from Chapter B3, "The Misplaced Fossil." An amateur paleontologist found a dinosaur bone from the Cretaceous Age (65–140 million years ago) in a Tertiary Stratum

4-39

Carbon dioxide turns the earth into a giant greenhouse by absorbing heat and trapping it inside the atmosphere. From *Science Forums,* volume I, "Fossil Fuel & the Greenhouse Effect."

4-40

A paleontologist shows the fault line in which a dinosaur bone was found. From the case of the misplaced fossil in *Science Sleuths.*

dating back to only 10 million years ago, and the student must explain the mystery of how it got there. Beautifully produced student manuals and instructor guides accompany the Videodiscovery discs, which can be controlled either by multimedia computers or laser bar-code readers.

Falcon Software's *Environmental Science: Field Laboratory CD-ROM* contains seven modules: stream pollution, minerals for society, energy from coal, radiation, legal control of the environment, streams and floods, and geology of homesite selection. Students learn how to define a problem, sample data, model phenomena, and draw conclusions. For more information go to http://www.falconsoftware.com/falconweb.

ELEMENTARY EDUCATION

So many new titles are appearing in elementary education that a company named KidSoft has established a Web site devoted to updating teachers, kids, and parents about the latest educational and entertainment software for kids. Shown in Figure 4-41, the KidSoft site tells how to get demos of software by subject or age group in full color and with sound. Figure 4-42 shows how the online catalog lets you search for products by category, subject, age group, or title. KidSoft repackages and bundles Macintosh and Windows titles from leading software publishers such as Accolade, Sierra, Knowledge Adventure, MECC, and Compton's. The KidSoft line sells at a suggested retail price of $12.99. KidSoft titles are also sold in stores including Toys R Us, Egghead, and Circuit City.

The KidSoft Web site is at http://www.kidsoft.com. KidSoft is also available via America Online, providing families with demos and product information for quality software in the KidSoft SuperStore (key word: KidSoft Store), as well as games and activities for kids in AOL's Kids Only area (key word: KidSoft). Kidsoft publishes a free printed catalog that you can get by calling (800) 354-6150.

4-41	4-42

The home page of the Kidsoft Web site at http://www.kidsoft.com.

The KidSoft Web site includes demos of software organized according to category, age group, and title.

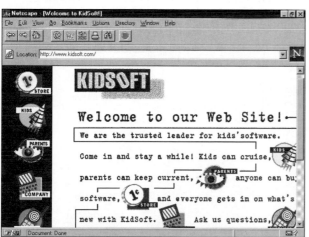

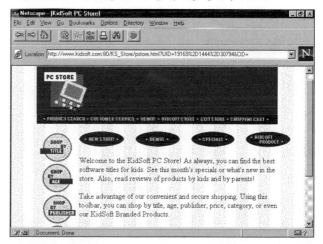

One of the more innovative CD-ROM titles advertised in the KidSoft catalog is *Mario Is Missing!* A geography game published by The Software Toolworks, the CD features the Super Mario Brothers made popular in the Nintendo games. Inspired by Brøderbund's *Carmen Sandiego,* it encourages kids to read and decipher clues as they travel the world on missions of law and order. The evil Bowser imprisons Mario and sends his terrible turtles, the Koopas, to trash historical landmarks and loot priceless artifacts around the globe. So the student must search San Francisco, Bombay, Tokyo, Athens, and 21 other cities in an effort to recover the stolen goods. In the process students learn compass and map-reading skills. Commenting on the strengths of this program's design, Cook (1994) notes, "Teachers will find Mario an entertaining method for getting kids to feel comfortable with geography and map-reading skills. More important, though, the design of this program discourages guessing, encouraging kids instead to read for comprehension, solve problems, and make use of other critical thinking skills."

Shown in Figure 4-43, Macmillan's best-selling *Dictionary for Children* is also available on a multimedia CD-ROM. With 12,000 word entries, 1,000 illustrations, and 400 sound effects, it has a spelling bee and hangman games, and a tour guide named Zak who helps kids learn how to pronounce words. Zak, who is a real ham, is likely to give you his personal reaction when you're looking up a word. Figure 4-44 shows a sample screen in which the student has looked up the word *apple.* The four icons along the right of the screen let the student look up other words, compile a word list, play games, and get help. The *Dictionary* also has word etymologies and language notes.

The National Geographic Kids network (Kids Net) combines online computer activity with real-life interactions and experimentation. Electronic mail engages children in cooperative learning across the Internet. For example, consider the Acid Rain Project. Students designed acid rain collectors and inspected tombstones for acid rain damage. After compiling and analyzing the data, students shared results through e-mail. The result provided a comparison of acid rain damage throughout the United States and Canada. For more information go to http://k12.cnidr.org:90/stories.tools.html.

Another online collaborative network is organized by the KIDLINK Society. Since 1990 KIDLINK has united 60,000 children aged 10 to 15 from 85 countries. Online

4-43

The title screen from Macmillan's best-selling *Dictionary for Children.*

4-44

The result of looking up the word *apple* in the *Dictionary for Children.*

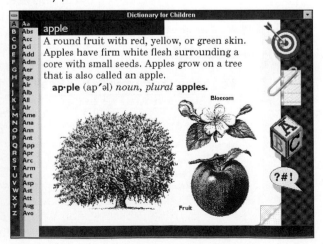

discussions use Internet chat forums. Kids can connect at any time to join conversations on a wide range of subjects. For more information go to http://www.kidlink.org.

READING AND WRITING

Multimedia computers enhance the teaching and learning of reading and writing by providing an environment that motivates students to read and makes it easy for students to begin writing at an early age. The software discussed here demonstrates how the computer addresses a variety of learning styles, puts students in control, encourages exploration and peer tutoring, and fosters the development of modern communication skills.

CD-ROMs that present stories for children in a hypermedia format are becoming very popular. The CDs display full-color illustrations and let the child click items on the screen to have words spoken, defined, or used in sentences, to trigger sound effects and animations, and to link to related materials. The only technical drawback is that although the CDs are highly interactive, the child cannot slow down the pace of the audio.

Just Grandma and Me was the first title to appear in the *Living Books* series by Brøderbund. Based on the best-selling book by Mercer Mayer, the CD contains 12 pages of lively animations, music, sound effects, narration, and talking characters who teach early reading and storytelling skills. Its purpose is to enable children ages three to eight to explore the printed words, as well as the pictures, and to soon learn words, phrases, and complete sentences. Full Spanish and Japanese translations are included. To try a sample from *Just Grandma and Me*, go to the Demonstrations section of the *Multiliteracy CD*, select Applications, and click the Just Grandma and Me button. The demo will read the first page of the book to you, as illustrated in Figure 4-45. Be sure to choose the play option as well, which lets you explore that page with your mouse. Almost every object on the page is active. For example, try clicking the trees, mailbox, fence, door, windows, leaves, cow, sky, ball, flowers, and the words on the screen. You can even run the demo in Spanish, Japanese, or English.

Arthur's Teacher Trouble, the second in Brøderbund's *Living Books* series, is based on the best-selling book by Marc Brown. This interactive, animated storybook features lively animations, original music, realistic sounds, and hundreds of words written, spoken, and even spelled out loud. By putting the child in control of exploring the printed words and the pictures, the CD engages kids in this "whole language" approach to learning. A full Spanish translation is included. To try a sample from *Arthur's Teacher Trouble*, go to the Demonstrations section of the *Multiliteracy CD*, select Applications, and click the Arthur's Teacher Trouble button. The demo will read the first page of the book to you, as illustrated in Figure 4-46. As with *Just Grandma and Me*, be sure to try the play option as well. Active items include objects on the bulletin board, the window shades, the door, each student, and different parts of the professor's body.

One criticism of the *Living Books* has been that the animations take students on tangents that do not contribute to the story. More recent *Living Books* titles such as *The Tortoise and the Hare* and *New Kid on the Block* are linking the animations closer to the story, so the animations lead to better comprehension. *Dr. Seuss' ABC* has been so popular that *Living Books* plans to follow it with another Dr. Seuss classic, *Green Eggs and Ham*. The *Living Books* have won more than 45 awards, including Best Overall Educational Program from the Software Publishers

4-45

The first page of *Just Grandma and Me*.

4-46

The first page of *Arthur's Teacher Trouble*.

Association, Parent's Choice from the Parent's Choice Foundation, and Best Early Childhood Software from the High/Scope Educational Research Foundation. For more information about the *Living Books* and other Brøderbund products, go to http://www.broderbund.com.

From The Learning Company, *Reader Rabbit's Reading Development Library* is a multilevel series for use in grades 1 through 3. For each grade a multimedia CD presents four storybook classics. Three characters tell the story from different points of view to help children see things from many perspectives and develop critical thinking and listening skills. In *Reader Rabbit's Reading Development Library 4,* children can write letters to the storybook characters and receive personalized responses.

Figure 4-47 shows a sample screen from *Reader Rabbit's Interactive Reading Journey*. Designed for beginning readers aged four to seven, it has a record and playback

4-47

The Learning Company's *Reader Rabbit's Interactive Reading Journey*, which PC Data named the top-selling educational CD of 1995.

feature that motivates children to improve oral reading skill as they record themselves reading a storybook and then play back what they've read. There are 40 carefully leveled interactive storybooks and more than 100 skill-building lessons in phonics and word recognition, covering a year's worth of classroom teaching. The package comes with a multimedia CD, 40 printed storybooks, and a microphone on a stand.

MECC adds a new dimension to reading by making it possible for kids to write their own stories. MECC's best-selling *Story Book Weaver Deluxe* lets kids choose from hundreds of scenes, add characters, and weave stories accompanied by sounds and music. Another MECC product, *My Own Stories*, lets kids write, illustrate, and publish stories about themselves and their friends. Both of these MECC products can be downloaded from the *Club KidSoft* CD-ROM discussed previously in the section on elementary education.

Prentice-Hall's *Writer's Solution* includes a writing lab CD-ROM in which students work through interactive writing tutorials that use video clips, music, and graphic organizers. Students work online in a notebook from prewriting to revising to publishing, saving all their work in an electronic portfolio for assessment.

Moxley (1994) analyzes how word processing environments enhance the reproductive, contextual, and selective functions of writing. He concludes that "Computer word processing advances each of these functions far more than paper and pencil writing can. If children are to have the fullest opportunity to use these functions in developing their writing, they need to use computer word processing from the very beginning of their writing" (Moxley, p. 35).

An Internet resource for young writers is the Alphabet Superhighway, which is being created under the Department of Education's READ*WRITE*NOW! initiative. Students learn to create, locate, and communicate information through mentoring, guided discovery, competitions, and other online activities. The goal is to raise reading and writing achievement in the United States. At the heart of the Alphabet Superhighway are Knowledge Neighborhoods, where general topics such as space, earth, peoples, cultures, and technology can be browsed, and CyberCenters, where information about specific topics can be accessed. CyberLands contain cross-cultural information on topics of interest to elementary and secondary students, including popular music, clothing, food, and hanging out. To browse the pilot version of the Alphabet Superhighway, go to http://www.ash.udel.edu. To involve your class, club, or organization in building exhibits or writing "cyberzines," visit the ASH home page and then send an e-mail message to highway@eecis.udel.edu.

PRESCHOOL

Computers are used in preschool as objects of study and to help youngsters developmentally. If children have a positive experience with computers at an early age, the computer phobia older students experience can be diminished or avoided altogether. Cartoon characters are often used to make computers attractive to children. For example, *Our House* is a CD-ROM from Context that features characters from the *Family Circus* comic strip. The CD offers children a fascinating view into a hypothetical American home by showing how everyday objects in each room are used, and comparing modern conveniences to the home life of generations gone by.

Mixed-Up Mother Goose is a CD-ROM from Sierra Online. Winner of the 1990 Software Publishers Award for Best Early Education Program, it presents 16 Mother Goose rhymes with certain pieces missing. Kids learn logic and problem-solving skills while having fun finding the missing pieces.

Figure 4-48 shows *Tuneland,* a CD-ROM by 7th Level. Created with financial backing from Wall Street investor Michael Milken, *Tuneland* is a fully animated cartoon with singing, dancing characters, and voice-over narration by comedian Howie Mandel. Kids explore the beautifully animated barnyard fantasy screens while interacting with dozens of characters, including Mandel, who plays the part of a teddy bear

4-48

An animated barnyard scene from the *Tuneland* CD. Almost every object in the scene is active. For example, you click on the rope to see the monkey swing; the bucket to see the frog do a swan dive; the pig to make him sing "Oh, Susanna"; or the hen to see the whole gang do a square dance.

4-49

The cartoon character Milo stars in *Word Tales*.

4-50

Children must match the correct initial letter to the words presented by *Word Tales*.

that tells jokes and performs hilarious comedy gags. Songs include "Three Blind Mice," "This Old Man," and "The Itsy Bitsy Spider." The goal is to get kids interacting inside a cartoon, involve them with the story and the singing, and make them comfortable with their computer. The CD comes with a *Tuneland* coloring book that contains the words to all the songs.

Word Tales is a CD-ROM from Time Warner Interactive that uses animated activities to teach young children word recognition and initial letter sounds. Figure 4-49 shows how the CD features an animated character named Milo, who teaches children the sounds of letters and how the letters combine to form words. In the first part of the game, children match the correct initial letter to a word, as shown in Figure 4-50, causing an animated scene that contains several items beginning with that letter to appear. Kids are rewarded with an arcade game when they successfully complete each word tale. The arcade games engage the child through animated characters, music, and positive reinforcement. For a demo of *Word Tales*, go to the Demonstrations section of the *Multiliteracy CD*, select Applications, and click the Word Tales button.

E X E R C I S E S

1. What percentage of your teachers used multimedia in the classroom when you were in elementary school? What percentage of teachers do you believe will be using multimedia computers as a classroom teaching aid by the year 2010?

2. During your time as a student, what was the best software package you used in each of the following software categories: - *picks*

   zoombinis!

   - Tutorial
   - Problem solving
   - Drill and practice
   - Cooperative learning

   - Testing
   - Presentation
   - Simulation *Oreg.Trail*
   - Group discussion

3. Of the applications demonstrated on the *Multiliteracy CD,* which one is best, and which one is worst? Why do you feel that way about them?

4. If you have not already run the chemistry equilibrium experiment on the *Multiliteracy CD,* do so now. Do you think mixing the chemicals on the computer screen is just as effective as physically handling the chemicals yourself? Does having the computer do it save you time and help you learn more, or would physically handling the chemicals enable you to learn more?

5. If you have not already run the demo of the interactive story *Just Grandma and Me* on the *Multiliteracy CD,* do so now. Do you find it truly interactive? In what ways is the computer used well? How could the interaction be improved? What issues does this raise for the teaching of reading and reading comprehension?

6. The *Nouvelle Dimensions* language-teaching sample on the *Multiliteracy CD* attempts to teach French by immersing the user into everyday French cultural experiences. To what extent did you find this successful and effective? Are multimedia computers capable of achieving language immersion so realistically that you can learn to converse as well as if you were actually living in the foreign country?

7. How do you believe multimedia technology will affect the future of schooling? For example, do you believe that if the Information Superhighway could serve all the nation's educational software to children at home, there would be no further need for schools as we know them? Are there any aspects of schooling that technology cannot replace?

8. Of the subjects covered in this chapter (art, biology, chemistry, civics, economics, foreign languages, geography, history, mathematics, music, physics, science, elementary education, reading and writing, and preschool), which ones have been influenced most by technology? Have any disciplines been so transformed that the computer has become an integral part of working in that area?

9. How heavily has your state invested in multimedia technology? Should more states divert textbook budgets toward multimedia hardware and software purchases?

10. If you would like to learn more about cognitive psychology and the constructivist movement in education, see Bruning's textbook *Cognitive Psychology and Instruction* (Englewood Cliffs, N.J.: Merrill/Prentice-Hall, 1995, ISBN 0-02-315911-1). The introduction provides an excellent overview, history, and comparison of the behavioral and constructivist movements in education. Another excellent text is Mark and Cindy Grabe's *Integrating Technology for Meaningful Teaching* (Boston: Houghton Mifflin, 1996, ISBN 0-395-67305-4). Chapter 2 is devoted to cognitive learning and technology tools.

5 Entertainment

After completing this chapter, you will be able to:

- **Understand how multimedia is transforming the entertainment industry by moving from passive to interactive art forms**

- **Recognize how multimedia techniques are being used to create cinematic special effects**

- **Question the ethics of digital cinema**

- **Understand how realistic and violent video arcade games have become**

- **Recognize how virtual reality is making interactive environments more immersing and persuasive**

M UCH of the innovation in multimedia sound and graphics originates in the entertainment industry. There is intense competition among cinematographers and video game producers to deliver the most dazzling and engaging special effects. Interactive movies are appearing on multimedia CD-ROMs, which allow the user to influence the story or play a role in it. Research and development in virtual reality are providing new visualization, mobility, and tracking devices that immerse the user so completely that the simulated experience seems real.

CINEMA

Moviemakers are investing heavily in the development of multimedia software to make movies more engaging. Producers use multimedia computers to create realistic special effects through digital imaging, rendering, animation, morphing, superimposition, replacement, and surround sound. Examples of some of these techniques are described in this section. Remember, however, that although multimedia computers may have been used to produce a movie, unless you can interact with it, watching the movie is not a multimedia experience.

Morphing

One of the more interesting multimedia effects is called **morphing**, a computer graphics technique in which one image is transformed into another in a seamless, uninterrupted segment. Duncan (1991) describes how morphing was used in the

5-1

Morph 2.5 is used by many Hollywood special-effects artists.

5-2

The *Mona Lisa* comes to life with Morph 2.5.

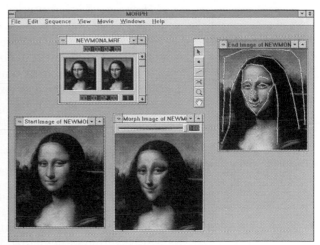

Arnold Schwarzenegger hit movie *Terminator II* to create the model 1000 terminator, a liquid metal machine that could imitate any form with which it came into contact. *Terminator II* went on to win Academy Awards for best visual effects, makeup, sound, and sound effects.

Morphing was used to convey a theme of racial harmony in Michael Jackson's music video *Black and White*. Duncan (1992) tells how 13 young people of varied racial and ethnic backgrounds were transformed into one another in a segment lasting only a minute.

Figure 5-1 shows Morph 2.5 from Gryphon Software Corporation. Morph 2.5 lets you create dynamic morphs from two separate images or exaggerate a single image using the caricaturing feature. Figure 5-2 shows how you use the Curve tool to define the area to be morphed.

The *Multiliteracy CD* illustrates how Morph 2.5 creates movies in which you can view your morphs. To view the morph movie, go to the Demonstrations section, select Software, and click the Morph Movie button. Then pull down the Morph File menu and choose Open, then Movie, then *Madonna.avi*. To find out more about Morph, go to http://www.gryphonsw.com.

Superimposition

When Gabe (Sylvester Stallone) failed in his attempt to rescue Sarah (Michelle Joyner) in the movie *Cliffhanger,* she fell thousands of feet to her death. Or so it seemed. In reality, Sarah fell only 35 feet into a stunt bag. Kaufman (1993) tells how an IBM Power Visualization System (PVS) superimposed her fall into the stunt bag over dramatic photographs of the Dolomites. Developed originally for high-end scientific visualization, the PVS is a rendering, compositing, editing, and viewing tool powerful enough to display composited shots at 30 frames per second (fps).

Animation

The dinosaurs in the Spielberg film *Jurassic Park* took animation to a new level. To tap the talent of stop-motion animators and translate it into the digital domain, a clever interface called the Dinosaur Input Device (DID) was created. As skilled animators moved mechanical dinosaurs to create realistic body movements, the DID created a wireframe model which was converted to a SoftImage file that could be refined through computer animation. Duncan (1993) describes how the mechanical models ensured that the dinosaur's spine, neck, tail, legs, and arms moved correctly, while the computer animated the fingers, toes, and mouth. Once the DID and SoftImage animations were completed, computer animators at Industrial Light & Magic (ILM) did the final rendering, adding breathing effects and the organic wobble of the dinosaur skin. ILM even made computer-generated rain stream off the back of the tyrannosaurus rex to establish realism in one rainy scene.

Toy Story is a Disney film produced by Pixar, which is probably the most innovative 3-D animation company in the world. If you have not seen *Toy Story*, treat yourself by viewing it. While you watch the film, remember that every single frame was computer generated. At the end of the movie, view the credits. You will be impressed by the number of technicians involved and the new job positions created. Table 5-1 contains some interesting statistics about the production of *Toy Story*. Disney also publishes the CD-ROM *Toy Story Animated Story Book*. Designed for children ages three to nine, the CD follows the movie's story line and features educational games on basic skills taught in the context of the story.

Digital Recasting

A series of modern Diet Coke commercials featured the classic black-and-white film stars Humphrey Bogart, Louis Armstrong, and James Cagney playing in full color alongside contemporary stars such as Elton John and Paula Abdul. How can Bogart, Armstrong, and Cagney star in a modern commercial? Were look-alikes found to play the parts of the classic actors? Or were the original films colorized and modern actors somehow superimposed onto them?

Hubbard (1992) explains how digital video techniques were used to create the Diet Coke commercials. First, the classic films were digitized. Then traditional and electronic rotoscoping techniques were used to extract the classic actors from their original environments. Next, the commercials were composited in layers, with a background layer of people seated and dancing, middle layers in which the archival characters interact with the modern actors, and a foreground layer in which people cross in front of the rotoscoped classic actors to impart a sense of reality. Finally, the original actors were colorized, and finishing touches were added, like putting Louis Armstrong's reflection alongside Elton John's on the top of the piano. Digital video editing permitted all of this to be done without any loss of quality. Traditional editing would have required many generations of videotape, with each video transfer progressively degrading the picture quality.

Table 5-1 *Toy Story* Statistics

Object Type	Number
Number of bytes required to store the film information	1 trillion (1 terabyte)
Minutes of completed animation produced each week	3.5
Months it took to write the shader for Andy's hair (it took the longest)	9
"Built-in" lights on Buzz	10
Least number of minutes required to render a frame of film	45
Most number of hours required to render a frame of film	20
Number of characters	76
Minutes of computer animation	77
Number of Sun Workstations in Pixar's Renderfarm operating on a 24-hour basis	110
Texture maps for Buzz (plus an additional 450 to show scuffs and dirt)	189
Gigabytes required to store final frames	500
Number of avars (variables which an animator can control) for Buzz	700
Number of avars for Woody	712
Number of avars for Woody's face	212
Number of avars for Woody's mouth	58
Number of avars for Sid's backpack	128
Number of leaves on the trees in Andy's neighborhood	1.2 million
Number of shaders written for the production	1,300
Final number of shots in the film	1,561
Number of frames of computer animation in the film	110,064
Number of texture maps created for the film (most are painted digitally, but some are photographed and scanned; the carpet in Sid's house was taken from *The Shining*)	2,000
Number of storyboards drawn	25,000
Number of lines in model program required to describe Buzz	34,864
Number of lines in model program required to describe Woody	52,865
Number of machine hours required to render frames	800,000
Number of lines of code needed to create the film's models	4.5 million

VIDEO GAMES

Video games have come a long way since Pong and PacMan. Advances in computer graphics have replaced stick figures and cartoonlike drawings with actual photographs of scenes and characters digitized on multimedia computers. Digital audio has made video games more realistic by providing instant access to recordings of the actual sounds made by characters and objects in the game. New input devices use lasers and 3-D mice to let the user interact more intimately with objects on the screen.

The best place to see the new technology is in video arcades. As the technology progresses, the innovations that emerge first in the arcades become available in portable versions you can play at home. Unfortunately, some of the most violent and offensive games become mass market hits. As this book goes to press, the best-selling video game, *Mortal Kombat,* contains such graphic violence that it provoked a public outcry in favor of government intervention and rating systems for video games. Although *Mortal Kombat* has controls parents can set to limit the level of violence in the game, most kids are more computer literate than their parents and have already figured out how to make the games more violent. Chapter 16 questions whether graphically violent and sexually exploitative games increase the likelihood that young people will engage in similar behaviors in real life. The latest information about *Mortal Kombat* is on the Web at http://www.yahoo.com/Recreation/Games/Video_Games/Titles/Mortal_Kombat.

INTERACTIVE MOVIES

Interactive movies played on multimedia computers let the viewer influence how the story unfolds. Three titles are discussed here: *Iron Helix, Voyeur,* and *Myst.*

5-3

Iron Helix.

Iron Helix

The multimedia CD-ROM *Iron Helix* by Drew Pictures shown in Figure 5-3 is a science fiction thriller that immerses you in a fast-paced virtual reality filled with danger and intrigue. Figure 5-4 shows how you control a robot probe to search a deserted six-story starship on an automated course of destruction. You must prevent intergalactic war and the spread of a deadly virus by destroying the doomsday weapon shown in Figure 5-5, code-named Iron Helix. You navigate through dozens of corridors and rooms, searching for ways to stop the looming annihilation while eluding the ship's deadly defender robot. The photorealistic look of the rooms was achieved by applying textures and shadows painted in Adobe Photoshop to models created in Macromedia's Swivel 3D and rendered with Electric Image's Electric Image Animation System.

There is a demonstration of *Iron Helix* on the *Multiliteracy CD.* To try it, go to the Demonstrations section, select Applications, and click the Iron Helix button. The demo will repeat until you click the mouse

5-4

Controlling the space probe in *Iron Helix*.

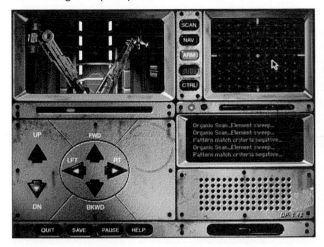 

5-5

The doomsday weapon code-named Iron Helix.

5-6

Voyeur, the first CD-I interactive movie.

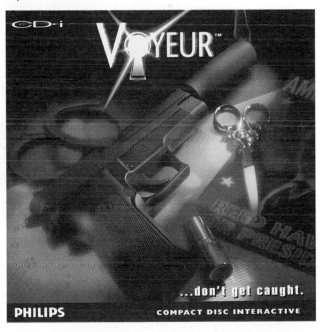

to end it. *Iron Helix,* which is available in Windows and Macintosh versions, is distributed by Spectrum Holobyte.

Voyeur

Voyeur is a CD-I from Philips. Shown in Figure 5-6, it is the first interactive movie shot specifically for CD-I. (*CD-I* stands for compact disc–interactive and is discussed in Chapter 10.) Intended for adults, *Voyeur* is "R" rated. The plot revolves around Reed Hawke, ex-astronaut and millionaire head of Hawke Industries. Set to run for president, he calls his family together one weekend to prepare for what

5-7

Scenes from *Voyeur*.

lies ahead. Unknown to Reed, one member of the family still suffers a long-forgotten wound and is prepared to reveal the dark family secret that will destroy Reed. Reed will do whatever it takes, including murder, to ensure silence. It is your job as voyeur to spy on Reed and those around him to collect enough evidence to stop his bid for the Oval Office. As Figure 5-7 shows, you "videotape" the needed evidence from digital video clips. *Voyeur* plays on soap opera and murder mystery appeal. You must play it several times to see all of the plot twists and dirty deeds. It comes with a lock-out system code intended to prevent young players from viewing the risqué scenes.

5-8

Brøderbund's *Myst* has surpassed 2 million copies sold.

Myst

The photorealism in Brøderbund's *Myst* has taken interactive movies to a new level. After you've been mysteriously transported to the ancient island of Myst shown in Figure 5-8, you learn that your presence there is not an accident. You must travel through several 3-D photorealistic worlds to untangle a web of treachery and deceit. Live actors appear superimposed on stunningly rendered 3-D scenes, such as the graphic shown in Figure 5-9.

Myst has a fully developed story line. The island was created by Artrus, who discovered the secret of writing books that create worlds and transport you from one world to another. But a plot against Artrus has apparently left his island and his worlds deserted. Your challenge is to uncover the story of *Myst* and find Artrus and his family.

Filled with clever puzzles and unexpected twists and turns, *Myst* is a thinking game that requires 40 to 60 hours to complete. The user points and clicks with a mouse to solve the puzzle. The only directions explain merely how to move around. You can find out more about *Myst* on the Web at http://www.myst.com.

5-9

Screen from the
Channelwood Age in *Myst*.

INTERACTIVE MUSIC CD-ROMS

Audio CDs that only play music are beginning to pale by comparison to the new generation of interactive music CD-ROMs. Peter Gabriel's *Xplora1* is a CD Plus designed to play music in an ordinary CD audio player, but insert it into the CD-ROM drive of a multimedia PC, and an amazing world of interactive material awaits you. You can even remix a song. Even more highly produced is the double CD-ROM album *All This Time*, in which Sting takes you on a fantastic journey of his life and his music. Unlike Gabriel's CD Plus, the Sting CD-ROM is mute if you put it into a conventional CD audio player. Designed for Windows 95, *All This Time* presents you with a unique 360-degree scrolling landscape full of environments to explore. You meet Sting's musical influences, sit in on jam sessions, and discuss the creative process involved in creating the 15 full songs presented on the CD. Sting appears in video clips throughout *All This Time*, giving you his perspective on his life and career.

VIRTUAL REALITY

Virtual reality (VR) refers to the use of a computer to immerse the user into a simulated experience so authentic it seems real. VR systems often use special hardware to enhance the experience, including visual displays (monitors, head-mounted viewing goggles, periscope booms, and direct eye scanning), tracking devices (data gloves, joysticks, body suits, or infrared tracking), and mobility devices (motion platforms, treadmills, stationary bicycles, trackballs, and flying mice that let you move in a 3-D space). It is possible to have a virtual experience without any special hardware, however. An example is the *Exploring Ancient Architecture* CD-ROM by Medio shown in Figures 5-10 and 5-11. It lets you use a multimedia PC to walk through the ruins of seven ancient architectural marvels as if the buildings were completely intact. As Brill (1994: 20) explains, "Ultimately, a virtual experience is defined through the participatory relationship of interaction and immersion between the user and the computerized environment."

5-10

Exploring Ancient Architechure by Medio Multimedia, Inc.

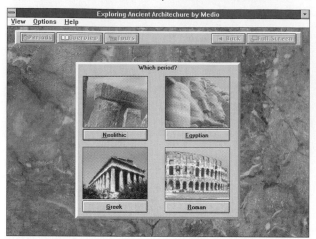

5-11

Exploring the Temple of Khons.

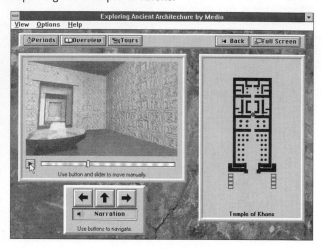

There is a demo of *Exploring Ancient Architecture* on the *Multiliteracy CD.* To try it, go to the Demonstrations section, select Applications, and click the Exploring Ancient Architecture button.

One of the most participatory VR systems is the Cybertron by Straylight. Figure 5-12 shows how the user maneuvers by bodily pivoting and tilting the gyro mechanism. Straylight uses quadraphonic CD audio and 3-D imaging to enhance the experience. For example, Figure 5-13 shows a scene from Straylight's PhotoVR, a photorealistic VR engine that lets users explore highly realistic 3-D virtual environments. PhotoVR imports 3-D designs created with CAD (computer-aided design) programs and lets the user move around the 3-D environment in real time. At present, PhotoVR can deliver 8 frames per second for changing the user's direction of view, and 3 to 4 frames per second for motion within a scene. By the end of the decade, more-powerful PhotoVR engines will provide full-motion video speeds.

5-12

The Cybertron gyroscopic virtual reality system.

5-13

3-D graphic produced with PhotoVR technology.

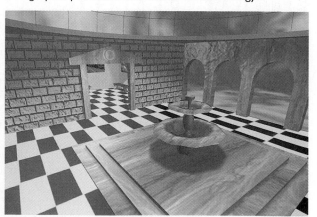

5-14

The CrystalEyes VR hardware consists of one pair of interactive stereo eyewear, one emitter, and an ultrasound speaker array with controller.

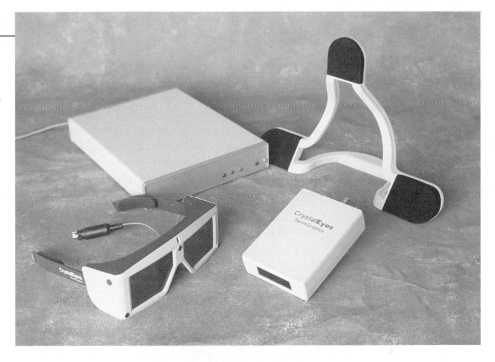

5-15

Stereoscopic images produced by CrystalEyes VR.

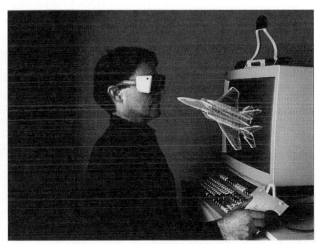

Figure 5-14 shows CrystalEyes VR hardware from StereoGraphics that lets you interact with stereoscopic images as depicted in Figure 5-15. As you move your head from side to side, closer to or farther away from the monitor, the image on the display changes its perspective, giving the convincing illusion that the image is a real object. The tracking mechanism is an ultrasound array of three speakers atop the monitor that sends signals along a line of sight to microphones inside the eyewear. Thus, the user's hands are free to interact with other peripherals, such as the computer keyboard or mouse. For the latest information on CrystalEyes and SimulEyes, visit the StereoGraphics home page at http://www.infolane.com/infolane/stereog/sghp.html.

The entertainment industry is using VR to create virtual actors. Known as VActors, virtual actors appear on-screen as animated characters whose actions are controlled by humans wearing VR sensors. Special input devices track the actor's face, body, and hand movements. SimGraphics Engineering has created VActors for Nintendo to use in trade shows, live TV interviews, videodiscs, and mall tours. SimGraphics has also created VActors for Interplay Productions (*Mario Teaches Typing* CD-ROM), Fugi Television (touring exhibition), Hewlett-Packard (corporate video), and NHK (a high-definition television commercial). A VActor named Ratz the Cat is performed by comedian Paul Brophy on the British television shows *Live and Kicking* and *Children's BBC*. For more information on VActor technology, see http://www.cs.city.ac.uk/homes/ivor/envisn.html.

Virtual reality has also brought Mark Twain to life in the form of *Twain-VR,* created by Color Concepts & Images. The creation of Lake Tahoe–based multimedia producer Gary Jesch, in collaboration with Twain impressionist McAvoy Layne and co-producer Susan Margolis, virtual Mark Twain is spookily similar to the man himself in appearance, in his words and experiences, and in the way he sounds. For more information about Mark Twain and other virtual characters, visit http://www.greatbasin.net/~chops.

Tracking body movements is a tricky problem addressed by Ascension Technology Corporation's Flock of Birds tracking devices, which provide real-time, simultaneous tracking of up to 30 receivers over medium and long ranges. The Flock is typically used for head, hand, and body motion tracking in applications ranging from flight simulation and virtual reality to medical instrument localization and motion capture for character animation. The Flock can transmit up to 144 position and orientation measurements per second. For more information about the Flock, visit http://world.std.com/~ascen.

There is a virtual reality Web site at http://vr-atlantis.com, where you can find out about all of the commercially available VR systems and learn where the nearest VR theme park is in your locale.

CYBER SPORTS

Cyber sports is the use of virtual reality to provide computer users with a realistic sports experience. Two new interactive VR devices let you swing and "hit" balls at your PC. Both are produced by Sport Sciences and can be purchased in retail stores. Sports Sciences has a Web site at http://sports-sci.com.

Batter Up

Pictured in Figure 5-16, *Batter Up* is an electronic 24-inch foam rubber–covered bat that you connect to your PC, Sega Genesis, or Nintendo game system. Alexander and Long (1995) describe what it is like to use *Batter Up:*

> The bat behaves just like a real bat. You watch the screen as the pitcher winds and delivers. The ball appears to come toward you and you knock it out of the park with a lamp-smashing swing. You can time your swing to hit infielders, or check your swing for a ball. You can bat left or right. And when you miss, the crowd groans.

5-16

Batter Up is an electronic 24-inch foam rubber–covered bat used to create a virtual reality batting experience.

PC Golf

Shown in Figure 5-17, *PC Golf* is a 26-inch golf club that enables you to play Picture Perfect Golf from Enteractive Entertainment, or Links 386 Pro from Access Software. Alexander and Long (1995) describe how *PC Golf* works:

> As you swing the club, IR [infrared] beams in the club head emit beams that the base unit senses and measures. The club head speed, angle, and path are measured. These data are streamed to your PC via RS232 [your PC's serial port] and fed to the game.

According to Alexander and Long, *PC Golf* is not bad for driving, okay for chipping, and poor for putting because you can hit a putt as hard as you want and, so long as the putt is lined up with the hole, the ball will go in.

5-17

PC Golf is a 26-inch golf club used to create virtual golfing experiences.

E X E R C I S E S

1. Attend the latest box office hit movie, or view the latest soft drink commercials. Watch for multimedia techniques. Try to find examples of digital imaging, rendering, animation, morphing, superimposition, replacement, and surround sound. How could the movie or commercial have been improved through more use of multimedia?

2. Try an interactive movie by either purchasing it from your local software store or renting it from your local video store. Just how interactive was the movie? How immersing was it? Did you really feel like you were an essential part of the movie? Were you able to influence the movie's outcome? Do you prefer this kind of involvement to just watching a traditional movie?

3. Digital editing techniques permit actors to play in scenes they have never visited physically. Singers are having their voices digitized so they can continue to record new songs after their singing voice wanes. Comment on the ethics of this. Will digitized actors and voices create problems for younger artists who cannot find work if older actors can continue to play long after they would have been forced into retirement without multimedia?

4. When the VCR was invented, it did not sell very well until videotapes of movies too sexually explicit and violent for TV became available. Will the success of multimedia similarly depend on the sale of violent and sexually explicit interactive titles, or could the industry survive if titles that provoke violent and sexually exploitative behavior were taken off the market?

5. Point your Web browser at http://vr-atlantis.com and choose "Where to experience VR" to find out where the nearest VR theme park is in your locale. Visit the theme park and try some VR. Describe the experience. Did you feel like you were actually "in" the situation in which the VR tried to immerse you? How "real" did the simulated experience feel?

6

Government and Politics

After completing this chapter, you will be able to:

- Realize how multimedia can be used to improve access to state and local government

- Assess how your state is using multimedia, and determine whether the way it is using multimedia is good or bad for its citizens

- Understand how the city of Atlanta used multimedia to win its bid to host the 1996 Olympic Games

- Question whether multimedia makes too much information available too quickly to the public during wartime

- Realize how politicians are using the World Wide Web for virtual campaigning

- Find out how to check up on your congressional representatives to see how well they are representing your views on important votes

GOVERNMENT officials have turned increasingly to multimedia for solutions to problems inherent in governance. Multimedia kiosks make services more widely available and enable municipalities to respond more quickly to emergencies and disasters. Videoconferencing and the Internet provide ways for politicians to reach, canvass, and broaden their constituencies. Countries that want to be competitive in the new global economy are quickening the pace of the development of their national Information Superhighways. Governments are using the Internet to find out more about what is happening around the world and to document it for the United Nations. Since human nature unfortunately dictates that peacekeeping will inevitably break down, the military uses multimedia to wage war effectively.

PUBLIC SERVICE KIOSKS

CITY-INFO kiosks have been installed throughout Vienna, Austria, to offer citizens and travelers the ability to find information on addresses, points of interest, shops, restaurants, public transportation, hours of operation, guided tours, and the cost and location of tickets, buses, museums, and events. Set up in public areas like train stations, monuments, and other frequently visited places, the kiosks were designed to be easily recognizable yet blend in with their

6-1

An indoor designer model of the CITY-INFO kiosk. There is also an outdoor vandal-proof model.

6-2

The main menu of the CITY-INFO kiosk.

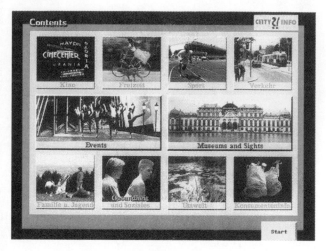

surroundings. The kiosks are connected to a network that updates them simultaneously. Figure 6-1 shows a traveler using a CITY-INFO kiosk, and Figure 6-2 shows its main menu. In their careful analysis of user reaction to the CITY-INFO kiosks, Professors Hitz and Werthner (1993) from the University of Vienna reported these results:

> It can be stated that the system is judged extremely positive (93%) . . . Typical users are young (43% under the age of 25), male (70%), tourists (55%) and well educated (32% high school, 34% university). They strongly recommend the usage of such a system (62% very much) . . . It is interesting that more than half would like to access such information via their [own] equipment and also 52% are willing to pay for such a service.

North Communications has deployed municipal kiosks in the cities of Sacramento, Phoenix, New York, and Brisbane, Australia; and state government kiosks in California, Nebraska, Kansas, Hawaii, Arizona, New Mexico, and Texas. North has also set up federal government kiosks for Medicare, Social Security, veterans' benefits, and the U.S. Postal Service. As illustrated in Figure 6-3, North's family of Info/Media applications covers motor vehicle services, employment services, public information products, legislative access, and court automation.

For example, North developed a Quick Court kiosk for the Supreme Court of the State of Arizona. Now deployed throughout the state in court lobbies and libraries, the Quick Court kiosks provide information to litigants, produce legal documents for use in court cases, and increase public access to the courts. The kiosks use text, graphics, and an on-screen narrator to

6-3

Info/Media products available from North Communications. For the latest information, visit http://www.infonorth.com.

6-4

A regional map showing Oregon Employment Division kiosk locations.

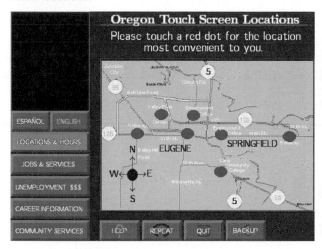

6-5

The result of pressing one of the red dots shown in Figure 6-4.

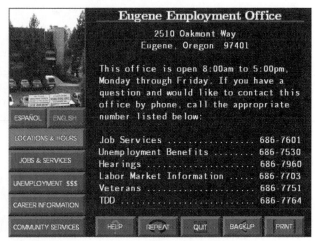

6-6

Oregon kiosk users can select the cities in which they are interested in finding jobs.

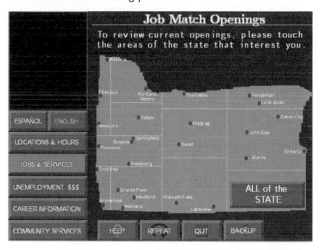

help litigants handle divorces, child support, name changes, affidavits, small claims, and landlord/tenant disputes.

The *Multiliteracy CD* contains a video that illustrates how kiosks can help state governments better serve their constituencies. To view the video, go to the Demonstrations section, select Textbook Examples, and click Info/Texas Kiosk. For the latest information about North Communications touch-screen kiosk applications, visit http://www.infonorth.com.

The State of Oregon's Employment Division uses multimedia kiosks in shopping malls, grocery stores, libraries, and community colleges to provide up-to-the-minute information about job openings that can be accessed simply by touching the screen. When the kiosk is not in use, it attracts users by playing video scenes of Oregon accompanied by lively stereo music. Referring to the kiosks in a press conference, then governor of Oregon Barbara Roberts stated, "We are going to change state government. We must be more efficient, and we must be smarter in how we deliver our services to the people in the state."

Figures 6-4 through 6-6 show screens from the Oregon kiosk. The purple buttons are active all the time and jump straight to the submenu of the button selected. All screens and videos are also available in Spanish by touching the ESPAÑOL button.

ELECTRONIC TOWN MEETINGS

CNN talk show host Larry King and CNN's TalkBack Live host Susan Rook are champions of the electronic town meeting, in which telephones are used to provide interactivity during television broadcasts. Since the number of people who can call in is limited by the length of the broadcast, interactive discussion groups on the Internet are being used to provide more people an opportunity to discuss their views. The Internet makes the meetings virtual, since they are no longer bounded by time or place. TalkBack Live has a Web site at http://CNN.com/CNN/Programs/TalkBack.

The Internet is also becoming popular as a polling device on commercial television networks. Polls are traditionally taken by asking viewers to call different phone numbers to register their response to a given question. Pollsters now advertise Internet addresses, which enable viewers to respond over the Information Superhighway. Many television shows are followed up by discussion sessions on computer networks, where the issues can be debated in more depth.

INTERNET AND THE NATIONAL INFORMATION HIGHWAYS

Governments are spending billions of dollars to hasten the construction of their nations' information highways. The global connection of these highways into a worldwide network is referred to as the Internet. As this book goes to press, more than 70 countries are already connected, with more than 45,000 networks online on the Internet.

For the reasons mentioned earlier, any country that does not go online and become proficient in using the Internet will become disenfranchised and seriously impede its ability to compete in the global economy.

SAFEGUARDING NATIONAL INTERESTS

As president of the United States, George Bush criticized the CIA for being so slow to issue reports that the White House learned more about world developments by watching commercial TV. The government now uses multimedia computers to provide officials with live TV feeds from news channels such as CNN, which appear in windows on the screen alongside other applications. In Chapter 59 you will learn how to get live TV feeds on your computer screen.

The government is also using the Internet to solve crimes. For example, the FBI posted a message on the Internet's NASA Network Information Center, asking for help in solving the Unabomber case, which involved a series of bombings targeting the computer industry, universities, and the aircraft and airline industries. The Web address is http://naic.nasa.gov (*Wall Street Journal* 12/31/93: 10).

WARFARE

The Gulf War demonstrated how effectively multimedia can wage war. Imagine yourself in control of a smart bomb. You are seated at a multimedia computer, aiming a laser that steers the bomb. In a window you view a live video feed from a camera in the smart bomb, showing precisely where it is headed. Your multimedia computer provides such fine control that you can fly the bomb into an air duct to penetrate an otherwise highly fortified building.

Although the accuracy of aerial multimedia weaponry lessens the need for ground forces, army combat is still a reality. When casualties occur, multimedia medicine steps in. For example, consider a group of army doctors at an EVAC hospital, facing a tough decision. Shrapnel has mutilated an artery and a vein in a soldier's leg. Conventional field medicine recommends amputation. Instead, doctors photograph the wound with a Kodak digital camera that has a SCSI (pronounced "skuzzy") port for plug-and-play capability. The images and patient history are uploaded via satellite to the Walter Reed Army Medical Center in Bethesda, Maryland, where specialists guide the field doctors through delicate reconstructive surgery that saves the leg. Information on Kodak digital cameras is on the Web at http://www.kodak.com.

Not all warfare uses conventional weapons. A more subtle form of **information warfare** is emerging. According to Central Intelligence Agency Director John Deutch, the trend toward increased corporate reliance on telecommunications and networks is making the U.S. more vulnerable to information warfare tactics. "The electron, in my judgment, is the ultimate precision-guided munition. Virtually any single 'bad actor' can acquire the hardware and software needed to attack some of our critical information-based infrastructures . . . We have evidence that a number of countries around the world are developing the doctrine, strategies and tools to conduct information attacks" (*Wall Street Journal* 6/26/96: B6). Deputy U.S. Attorney General Jamie Gorelick warns that "an electronic Pearl Harbor" is a very real danger. About 250,000 intrusions into Defense Department computer systems are attempted each year, with about a 65% success rate (*BNA Daily Report for Executives* 7/17/96: A22).

For more information about the use of information technologies in advanced defense applications, go to the Defense Advanced Research Projects Agency (DARPA) Information Technology Office on the Web at http://www.ito.darpa.mil.

OLYMPIC BIDDING

A big problem faced by the city of Atlanta at the outset of its bidding in 1988 for the 1996 Summer Olympics was lack of recognition as an international city. At that time only about 15 of the 90 voting members of the International Olympics Committee had ever been to Atlanta, which was known more for *Gone With the Wind* and similar visions of the Old South. Based on recommendations by Dr. Pat Crecine, then president of Georgia Tech, Atlanta used a multimedia campaign to promote a modern image of the city and project through realistic computer graphics what the planned stadium and other proposed facilities would be like. For example, Figure 6-7 shows the proposed Olympic dormitory complex, and Figure 6-8 shows the computer-generated "Golden Athlete" who carries the Olympic torch into the proposed Olympic stadium. As Gamble-Risley (1992) described the experience:

> Just sit down and prepare yourself to take a magnificent journey as you rush from space toward the Earth, plunge past fluffy clouds and down over snow-capped mountains, rivers and forest until you soar over Georgia and come to the city of Atlanta. After you've flown into the city, you'll come to a futuristic-looking stadium

6-7

A computer graphics rendering of the proposed Olympic dormitory.

6-8

The computer-generated "Golden Athlete" carries the Olympic torch.

6-9

The Atlanta Vision kiosk uses a multiscreen panoramic presentation system.

6-10

Frederick Dyer and the 360-degree panoramic view upon which the Olympic rings float.

where you'll glide down corridors into an office, and exit out a window where you'll view the future site of the Olympic village . . . From there, the tour is literally placed in the hands of the user who uses a trackball to take control over the adventure and can essentially go sight seeing around the city.

Since winning the bid, Atlanta's multimedia presentation has evolved into a system called Atlanta Vision. Figure 6-9 shows how the system allows the observer to tour all of Georgia via a GIS (Geographical Information System) database system showcasing economic development opportunities and other highlights of the state.

Frederick Dyer and Mike Sinclair, co-directors of the Georgia Tech Multimedia Lab during Atlanta's quest for the Olympics, created 360-degree panoramic views by taking pictures from a helicopter with a motordrive 35mm camera. After digitizing the frames, the lab developed techniques for computer-correcting the resulting images for various distortions and then electronically composited them, resulting in images like the one shown in Figure 6-10. The presentation system is supported by the Georgia Power Company. A number of new multimedia ventures for Sports Technology, Coca Cola, and others have been developed from the original technology. For more information contact Mike Sinclair directly at the Georgia Tech Interactive Media Technology Center. His e-mail address is mike.sinclair@oip.gatech.edu. Fred Dyer is fred@peachnet.edu.

POLITICS

On the Web at http://www.PoliticsNow.com is a place to find out what is happening in politics and make your voice heard online. PoliticsNow provides the latest political news from ABC News, the *Washington Post,* the *National Journal, Newsweek,* and the *Los Angeles Times* on the race for the White House to the battle for control of Congress. Created by the merger of ElectionLine and PoliticsUSA, PoliticsNow offers The Buzz, Money Talks, Medium Cool, and Poll Track. Check the Record lets you find out how your representative in Congress is representing you.

PoliticsNow provides opportunities to make your voice heard, talk with others about issues that concern you, and reach out and communicate directly with decision makers in politics and government. Chat rooms of the Caucus, the Congress Alert, and Petition provide ways for you to speak out and reach out.

VIRTUAL CAMPAIGNING

According to Buchanan (1994), the Internet played a significant role in Landon Curt Noll's election to the Sunnyvale (California) City Council. Noll recruited a third of his volunteer campaign organization directly from the Internet, on which voters asked why he was running for office and what he hoped to accomplish. Overall, Noll estimates he reached 50,000 voters through the Internet. As one of his first acts as city councilman, Noll pushed through a proposal to put the Sunnyvale city hall on the Internet. According to Noll, "The best way to look at government access is to say no one communication is going to fit everything. That's why government—if we really want to get citizens involved—has to find and use all the means of communication that people feel comfortable with."

The Internet has become so important in getting elected to public office that almost every political candidate has a Web site. For an index of political candidate Web sites, point your browser at http://www.yahoo.com/Government/Politics/Elections.

CONSUMER INFORMATION

Quanta Press publishes a CD-ROM entitled *Consumer Information* which contains a wealth of information from the United States Government Consumer Information Center in Pueblo, Colorado. Topics include government information on a wide variety of topics: how to start your own business, how to make small home repairs, government forms, personal health safety, condom safety, veterans' affairs, cancer rates, how to attract birds to your yard, endangered species, basic facts about trademarks, patents, résumés, your right to federal records, children's books, the importance of play, education, coping with drugs in schools, what to do when parents divorce, consumer fraud, finance, credit card fraud, managing money, tax preparation, home canning, eating for life, food additives, microwave safety, nutrition for the elderly, choosing a nursing home, medicare, asbestos hazards, chronic fatigue syndrome, home buying and moving, stripping paint from wood, tips for finding the right job, consumer rights, company addresses

6-11

"Carpal Tunnel Syndrome" is one of thousands of articles on the *Consumer Information* CD-ROM.

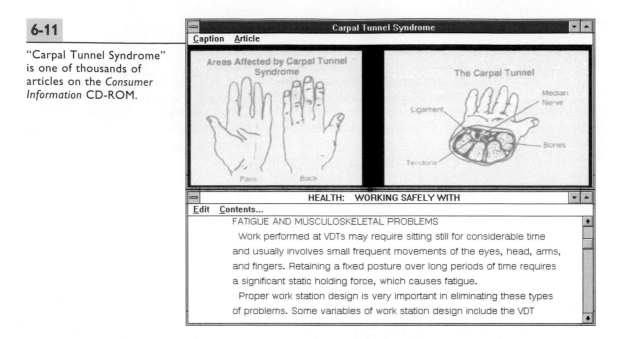

for complaints, and lists of government offices in each state. There is also a retirement guide, a guide to buying insurance, and the complete text of the Americans with Disabilities Act.

For example, Figure 6-11 shows a sample article from *Consumer Information* on carpal tunnel syndrome, which afflicts people who type on computer keyboards too much. Clicking the camera icon displays pictures that illustrate the article.

You can also access consumer information on the Web at http:// www.pueblo.gsa.gov.

OTHER GOVERNMENT SERVICES

FinanceNet

FinanceNet is an independent public Internet network that was established by Vice President Gore's National Performance Review in Washington, D.C. Operated by the National Science Foundation, FinanceNet is the information clearinghouse of the Joint Financial Management Improvement Program. FinanceNet reaches across geopolitical boundaries to link financial management staff worldwide to catalyze continuous improvements in employee productivity and taxpayer resources. FinanceNet is on the Web at http://www.financenet.gov.

Small-Business Assistance

The U.S. Business Advisor offers small businesses online access to guides and government forms needed to comply with regulations or apply for government-backed loans or other federal assistance. The goal is to provide small businesses with one-stop access to federal agencies that regulate and assist business. The Web site is http://www.business.gov (*Wall Street Journal* 2/14/96: B2).

Patent Searches

The U.S. government has a Web site where you can do patent searches online. Go to http://www.uspto.gov and select "Search U.S. Patent Bibliographic Data". This service is maintained by the Center for Networked Information Discovery and Retreival (CNIDR), in cooperation with the U.S. Patent and Trademark Office (USPTO).

Internal Revenue Service

The IRS has a Web site at http://www.irs.ustreas.gov. You can find out about the tax code, download tax forms, and file your income tax return over the telephone.

EXERCISES

1. How is multimedia used by your state government? For example, do multimedia kiosks help tourists find their way around your largest cities? Is there an employment kiosk to help the unemployed find jobs? Is multimedia used to make disaster relief available to those who need it? Does your state use multimedia to deliver driver's license tests?

2. Think of three more ways multimedia could be used to improve government services to your community. Describe how you would want them implemented.

3. The city of Atlanta used multimedia to help win its bid to host the Olympic Games. How could your local government use multimedia to promote your cities and strengthen their economy?

4. President George Bush used to complain that he learned more from watching CNN on TV than he did from the CIA. So could terrorists. To what extent should news coverage of nationally sensitive information and events be curtailed? For example, during their amphibious landing on the beach in Somalia, soldiers complained that television lights betrayed their positions. Should wars be televised?

5. Use your Web browser to visit http://www.PoliticsNow.com and use Check the Record to find out whether your congressional representatives are voting the way you want them to. Send e-mail to express your views. Point-and-click e-mail addresses of every member of Congress are available at:

    http://www.yahoo.com/Government/Legislative_Branch/Congressional_E_Mail_Addresses

Kiosks in schools - /info, advocates (sp. ed laws etc.)
(print paperwork

- video center. - PPTs - kids meet
w/ local officials via Hartford
- interactive town meetings - plug in + real time
video via compt. / senior ctrs. / apts. / website -
etc.
p. 97

Medicine and Nursing

After completing this chapter, you will be able to:

- Recognize the breadth of multimedia applications in health care for medical training, emergency preparedness, and virtual surgery

- Understand how health care professionals in your community should be using multimedia computers to prepare for emergency situations

- Find out whether your local health care professionals are taking advantage of online resources, videoconferencing, and interactive diagnostic programs

WHEN life depends on something, people get serious about it. So it is with multimedia and health care. This chapter surveys applications that promise to provide you with better diagnosis when you get sick, more-efficient treatment, life skills to keep you healthy, and, in an emergency, health care professionals who either know what to do about the situation or who can use a multimedia computer to find out what to do before it's too late.

MEDICAL TRAINING

From the $39.95 *The Doctors Book of Home Remedies* by Compton's NewMedia to the $22,000 *American Heart Association Advanced Cardiac Life Support* training system by Actronics, multimedia computers are providing patients, doctors, and nurses with interactive health care training and medical references. Stewart Publishing's (1995) *Interactive Healthcare Directories* lists nearly 500 videodiscs, more than 200 CD-ROMs, and over 400 computer-assisted instruction programs. Topics include AIDS education, anatomical studies of various body physiologies, intravenous therapy procedures, emergency care, and the handling of shotgun wounds to the abdomen.

Aiming at the mass market, the Mayo Clinic is publishing CD-ROMs that bring health care home. For example, do you know the warning signs of heart or vascular disease? More than 70 million Americans have it. Do you understand your options for tests and treatment? You can learn these things and more from *The Total Heart* CD-ROM by the Mayo Clinic. Instructional 3-D animations and full-text searching through the extensive Mayo Clinic database add a new dimension to cardiac health. Figure 7-1 shows buttons along the right side of the screen that let the user select different sections of the CD. The material being studied appears in the big window next to the buttons.

7-1

A screen from *The Total Heart* CD-ROM.

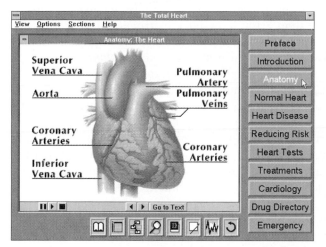

7-2

A screen from the Mayo Clinic's *Family Health Book* CD-ROM.

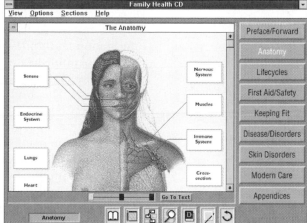

7-3

A diagram of the human ear from the *Family Health Book*.

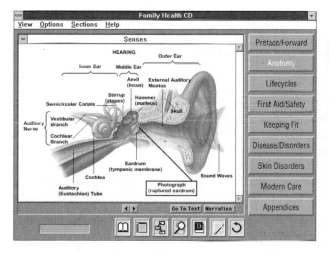

7-4

A user can learn about CT scanning from the *Family Health Book*.

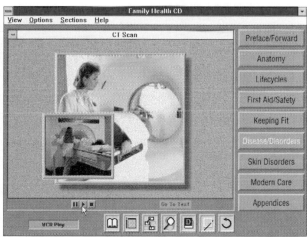

The Mayo Clinic also publishes a CD-ROM version of its best-selling *Family Health Book*. In addition to more than 1,300 pages of text from the printed version, the CD has 45 videos and animations, 500 color illustrations, and 90 minutes of sound and narration. The sections include Anatomy, Lifecycles, First Aid/Safety, Diseases/ Disorders, Skin Disorders, and Modern Care. Figure 7-2 shows how choosing Anatomy presents the user with a picture menu for studying different parts of human anatomy, and Figure 7-3 shows the result of touching the Senses button to study hearing. In Figure 7-4 a user learns how CT (computed tomographic) scanning has revolutionized diagnostic neurology and neurosurgery.

The Interactive Patient is a Web site at Marshall University School of Medicine that simulates an actual patient encounter. This teaching tool for physicians, residents, and medical students offers a case with a chief complaint to the user, who must then interact with the patient by requesting additional history, performing a physical exam, and reviewing laboratory data and X rays. After conducting the examination, the user is encouraged to submit a diagnosis and treatment plan. The system promises to evaluate and provide feedback on all submitted answers. Check it out at http://medicus.marshall.edu/medicus.htm.

The HESC (Health Sciences Consortium) publishes four Interactive Healthcare Directories cataloging more than 2,100 interactive instructional programs that prepare nurses to deal with a broad range of health care topics. For more information see http://www.erols.com/stewpub. The *American Journal of Nursing (AJN)* also publishes a multimedia catalog of interactive nursing programs, including several videodiscs that cover a range of topics from child bearing through bereavement. The *AJN* Web site is at http://www.ajn.org. Other nursing Web sites include the Computers in Nursing home page at http://cin.lrpub.com/cin; the Sigman Theta Tau International Honor Society of Nursing at http://stti-web.iupui.edu/html-docs/text.html; the Nurse Practitioner at http://unhinfo.unh.edu:70/0/unh/acad/health/npract/index.html; and the Nurse Practitioners Support Services at http://www.npl.com/npss.html.

ANATOMY AND PHYSIOLOGY

The *A.D.A.M.* (Animated Dissection of Anatomy for Medicine) CD-ROM by A.D.A.M. Software promotes interactive learning via a comprehensive digital database. The CD combines interactive tools with superbly rendered color images of human anatomy, both male and female. Layer by layer, structure by structure, users can slice through tissue to simulate surgical incisions, zoom in for a closer look at muscles and nerves, rotate views, and explore histology. Sold separately, A.D.A.M. Author is a development tool that lets the user customize applications and program links to additional materials.

Anatomy & Physiology is a double-sided CAV videodisc from Videodiscovery that comes with a two-volume 600-page bar-coded directory. Students can observe the human structure in remarkable detail in the 1,500 3-D animations. Its 3,000 photographs and motion sequences are fully correlated to the nation's best-selling anatomy text. Nine mini-documentaries introduce medical career options and debate various topics. The videodisc also includes the acclaimed Bassett collection of human body dissections.

A fascinating place to visit on the Web is the National Library of Medicine's Visible Human Project at http://www.nlm.nih.gov/research/visible/visible_human.html. The NLM is using body-slicing techniques to create complete, anatomically detailed, 3-D representations of the male and female human body. Transverse CT, MRI, and cryosection images of male and female cadavers are being collected at 1mm intervals. The long-term goal is to produce a system of knowledge structures that will transparently link visual knowledge forms to symbolic knowledge formats such as the names of body parts. You will find a sampler of images from the Visible Human Project at http://www.nlm.nih.gov/research/visible/visible_gallery.html.

The Dynamic Human is a CD-ROM from Wm. C. Brown Publishers containing 3-D anatomical illustrations you can move around, light-up identification for the structures in all 11 body systems, and hundreds of animations showing how your body works. For example, Figure 7-5 shows how you can hear and see the difference between a normal heart and one with a heart murmur. The CD is full of dynamic models like this one, which you can pause at any time or play in slow motion.

7-5

The heart murmur screen from the cardiovascular section of *The Dynamic Human: The 3D Visual Guide to Anatomy and Physiology.*

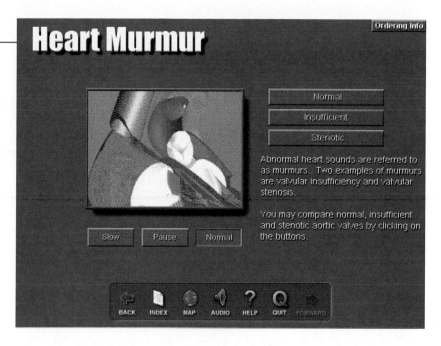

There is a demonstration of the cardiovascular system from *The Dynamic Human* on the *Multiliteracy CD.* To run the demo, go to the Demonstrations section, select Applications, and click the Dynamic Human button.

VIRTUAL SURGERY

Imagine a surgeon using a head-mounted display to rehearse the removal of a brain tumor by moving surgical instruments through a 3-D view of the tumor. Imagine a physician using hand gestures to control tiny robots that swim through your blood vessels and fire lasers to vaporize cholesterol plaques that can cause heart attacks. Imagine being able to take a virtual walk through your body to see how a particular medication acts to prevent an asthmatic attack. According to Merril (1993), all of these scenarios are possible outcomes of current virtual reality research in medical applications. Figures 7-6 and 7-7 show how Merril uses texture mapping to wrap images of actual tissues onto the surface of surgical models.

7-6

Physicians use virtual reality simulations to learn laparoscopic ("belly button") surgery.

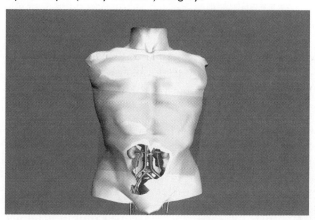

There is a demonstration of virtual surgery on the *Multiliteracy CD.* To view it go to the Demonstrations section, select Textbook Examples, and click Virtual Surgery. This video was provided courtesy of High Techsplanations (HT), Inc., producer of the award-winning TELEOS software. TELEOS is the virtual reality authoring system that HT created for producing surgical training simulations. HT has won many grants and awards for TELEOS and is definitely a company to watch. For more information go to http://www.ht.com.

Texture mapping wraps
images of actual tissues
on the surface of surgical
models.

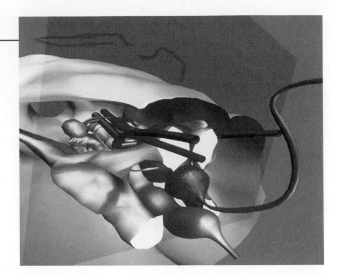

VIDEOCONFERENCING NETWORK

Klinck (1993) describes how the Voluntary Hospitals of America (VHA), the nation's largest alliance of hospitals, is building a videoconferencing network to connect its 900 nonprofit hospitals. Based on VTEL Corporation's PC-based videoconferencing technology, the system will enable health care professionals at different hospitals to use videoconferencing for patient diagnosis and treatment. The equipment can capture videotape transmissions of medical images and clinical procedures, which is ideal for providing continuing medical education to physicians and other health care professionals. Doctors can annotate test results, allowing a more personal and immediate diagnosis. The system also permits the use of stethoscopes, EKG units, X rays, teleradiology systems, sonograms, and other medical devices. In time-sensitive cases, VTEL's system can allow for quick decisions vital to saving a patient's life.

Information about the VHA project and many other health care videoconferencing applications can be found on the Web at http://www.vtel.com/solution/health.

ONLINE RESOURCES

To allow physicians speedy access to the latest clinical research, the American Association for the Advancement of Science publishes the electronic Online Journal of Current Clinical Trials. The Library of Medicine has blessed this new online journal by including it in its MEDLINE database and its *Index Medicus.*

MEDLINE is the primary tool for searching medical information relating to health care administration, biomedical research, medicine, surgery, dentistry, and nursing, dating back to 1966. MEDLINE is online at http://www.healthworks.co.uk. There you can take MEDLINE for a free test drive, but after that you must pay a subscription fee for access.

Jim Clark, founder of Silicon Graphics Inc. (SGI) and Netscape Communications, has created a new Internet business called Healtheon, which will use the World

Wide Web to help companies manage their employee health plans. Clark said: "We are providing a standard health care community interface, using the Internet as a medium, and providing services to health care providers" (*New York Times* 6/18/96: C4). Blue Cross & Blue Shield of Massachusetts has become the first health care provider to sign on with Healtheon (*Wall Street Journal* 6/26/96: B6).

To discover the wealth of online information in medicine and nursing care, point your Web browser at http://www.yahoo.com/Health. The Medical Matrix, an extensive guide to Internet clinical medicine resources, is at http://www.kumc.edu/mmatrix.

E X E R C I S E S

1. Your life or that of a loved one could depend on the extent to which your local health care provider uses multimedia in preparing its staff to handle medical situations correctly. Find out whether your local health care facility knows about Stewart's *Interactive Healthcare Directories,* and ask how many of the interactive video training programs are in place and how many staff members have completed the training.

2. Does your local school of nursing belong to the HESC? Does it have enough multimedia computers to train all of its nursing students on the HESC materials? If your nursing school does not know what HESC is, you've got problems.

3. Is your doctor connected to the Internet? Ask about this during your next appointment. Find out how your doctor uses the network to stay current and learn about new procedures, such as by reading the Online Journal of Clinical Trials.

4. List three ways multimedia computers can help you maintain your personal health today. What other ways do you foresee technology being able to help improve your health in the future?

8

Encyclopedic Resources

After completing this chapter, you will be able to:

- Take advantage of the encyclopedic resources on **CD-ROM** and the Internet

- Appreciate the power of online searching as a research tool

- Understand how the Smithsonian, the Library of Congress, the Louvre, and museums and libraries all over the world have gone online

- Realize when and why the *Encyclopedia Britannica* went online

WEALTH of encyclopedic resources are available on multimedia CD-ROMs and online via networks on the Information Superhighway. CD-ROMs provide the convenience of owning the resource and being able to use it on any multimedia PC. Networks provide access to much more information, which is usually more up-to-date than the CD-ROM.

MULTIMEDIA CD-ROMS

Anyone who has used a printed encyclopedia will appreciate the convenience of multimedia CD-ROMs. Not only does it seem to take forever to find the information you want in a printed encyclopedia, but you also have to check all of the annual updates, which are printed in separate volumes. CD-ROMs not only solve this problem by providing rapid full-text searching, but they also cost less. Thanks to the MPC price wars, the entire multimedia PC costs less than the printed *Encyclopedia Britannica.*

In 1985 Grolier became the first company to publish its printed encyclopedia in a multimedia CD-ROM version. Now the *Grolier Multimedia Encyclopedia* has been supplemented with additional text, expanded audio capabilities, enhanced video clips, narrated animations, and a wider variety of pictures, photographs, and maps. According to *CD-ROM Today,* Grolier has "surged ahead of the competition" (July 1996) and is now "the best" (March 1996). *Learning and Leading with Technology* called Grolier's "the richest home resource among electronic encyclopedias" (March 1996).

Figure 8-1 shows Grolier's main menu, which provides many ways to access the 50,000 entries in the encyclopedia. For example, the Knowledge Tree lets you find articles using a topic hierarchy. The Timeline accesses a database of more than 5,000 historical events. The Interactive Atlas includes more than 1,200 maps,

8-1

The main menu of *The New Grolier Multimedia Encyclopedia.*

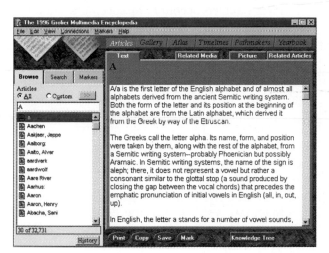

8-2

Grolier's History Dynamic Maps let you travel through time using maps that chart journeys accompanied with sights, sounds, and motion.

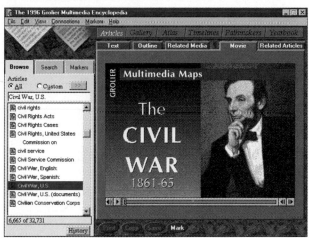

including Thematic Maps, Historical Maps, Exploration Maps, and new City Maps. Each map is linked to key articles. Figure 8-2 shows one of the History Dynamic Maps, in which narrated animations let you march through Civil War battlefields with Generals Grant and Lee, study U.S. territorial growth, and learn about the Gulf War. Figure 8-3 shows a Knowledge Explorer audiovisual essay. Combining photographs, music, and voice narration, there are Knowledge Explorer essays about Africa, the human body, space exploration, music, the animal world, and architecture. Although each essay is fully narrated and self-contained, there are links to the many relevant text articles within the encyclopedia, as well as links to thousands of Web sites that serve as references in the encyclopedia. There is also a Reveal Art feature that provides the insides and outsides of a variety of subjects, just like the overlay transparencies teachers use in the classroom. For example, students can look inside an Indy race car and a Boeing 747 jumbo jet. For the latest information about Grolier products, visit Grolier Online at http://www.grolier.com.

8-3

Grolier's Knowledge Explorer essays combine photographs, music, and voice narration to make learning a multisensory experience.

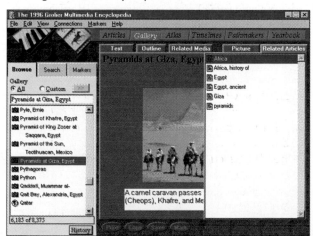

Compton's also publishes a multimedia version of its printed encyclopedia. Shown in Figure 8-4, *Compton's Interactive Encyclopedia* contains the full text and graphics of the 26-volume *Compton's Encyclopedia;* thousands of pictures, drawings, and photos; easy-to-use research paths to retrieve information; an interactive world atlas with links to 121,000 related pictures and articles; enhanced sound and full-motion Video for Windows; and the complete *Merriam-Webster OnLine Dictionary and Thesaurus.*

Compton's thought hard about what tools would make the encyclopedia most useful and provided a rich set of options for browsing and searching. For example, Figure 8-5 shows the InfoPilot, which generates a network of secondary topics related to a main topic. Making one of the secondary topics the main topic causes the InfoPilot to create a new network for that topic. This provides a powerful way of brainstorming ideas.

8-4

Compton's Interactive Encyclopedia.

Figure 8-6 shows how the Timeline tool lets you access information on important people and events in U.S. and world history. There is an Outline view that displays a general outline of history, and a Detail view that offers detailed accounts of specific events. For the latest information on Compton's, visit http://www.comptons.com.

Encarta is a multimedia encyclopedia by Microsoft that includes more than 25,000 articles in 93 categories, a gallery with more than 7,000 photographic images and animations, and seven hours of audio. Users access this information in several ways. First, there is an alphabetical index; second, a category browser lets you narrow down topics by category and subcategory; third, a timeline puts events in chronological order; fourth, an atlas lets you select places by zooming in on a map; last, you can use the Boolean operators (AND, OR, and NOT) to search for specific words or phrases within any article. *Encarta* also lets you set bookmarks, take notes, and copy both textual and multimedia material into personalized files.

In 1994, CD-ROM versions of the *World Book Encyclopedia* and the *Encyclopedia Britannica* appeared on CD-ROM. These flagship encyclopedias delayed moving into an electronic form until market pressures required them to do so. World Book's CD is called the *Information Finder,* which contains the text and tables of the printed encyclopedia and the *World Book Dictionary.* There are 17,000 articles, 1,700 tables, 150,000 index entries, 139,000 dictionary entries, 60,000 cross references, 1,600 reading lists, 3,000 pictures, and 260 maps. An atlas lets you navigate around the world by clicking from map to map. A gallery provides access to the World Book pictures. Timeline lets you move through a graphic chronology of world history beginning at 570,000,000 B.C. InfoTree lets you browse through topics and articles organized by subject. The search engine lets you search by topic or key word.

8-5

The InfoPilot in *Compton's Interactive Encyclopedia* automatically finds articles related to the main topic.

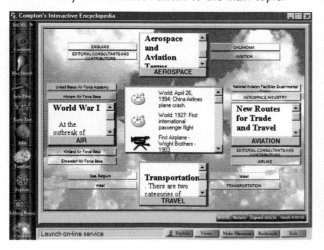

8-6

The Timeline tool in *Compton's Interactive Encyclopedia.*

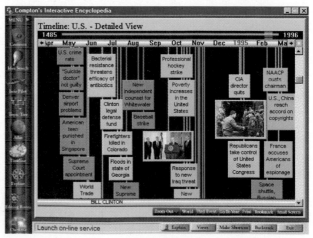

The *Britannica CD* contains all 44 million words of the *Encyclopedia Britannica* plus *Merriam-Webster's Collegiate Dictionary* and *Nations of the World*, and a comprehensive alphabetical index. The *Britannica* search engine lets you type questions in ordinary English, and it rank-orders the responses according to relevance. The *Britannica* can also be searched online, as described in the next section of this chapter. Interestingly, purchasing the CD and the printed encyclopedia together gets you a discounted price on the printed encyclopedia. A librarian once told the author how schools like having the printed encyclopedia, because each student can be researching topics in a different volume, while only one student can be using the CD. The author replied: "That's fine as long as you are willing to restrict Johnny's knowledge to topics beginning with the letter *C*." For more information about the *Britannica CD*, point your Web browser at http://www.eb.com/bookstore/cd.html.

INTERNET RESOURCES

Someday the Information Superhighway may eliminate the need for CD-ROMs by making available all of the necessary databases and programs in the form of a worldwide network, which will function as a public utility that will be as widespread as telephones and televisions are now. All over the world, museums have seized the opportunity to establish a presence on the World Wide Web and provide online access to their collections. This is especially advantageous for persons unable to travel to museums in person. Hundreds of museums are online, so many that you may not know where to start exploring them. Listed below are profiles of some of the more popular museum resources you will find online. Later on, the tutorial in Chapter 47 will provide you with search strategies for finding specific information on the Web. For a list of more than a thousand online museum references, use your Web browser to go to the Yahoo search engine (http://www.yahoo.com) and type in the key word *museum*.

Library of Congress

The Library of Congress operates a Web site that lets you browse historical collections in the National Digital Library, visit Library Reading Rooms, search THOMAS (legislative information), access services of the Law Library of Congress (including the Global Legal Information Network), or locate government information. You can search the Library of Congress online catalog or connect to the Library's Gopher server, which is called LC MARVEL. *MARVEL* is an acronym for Machine-Assisted Realization of the Virtual Electronic Library. Online exhibits include Soviet government documents such as the directive from Lenin ordering the death of anti-Communist farmers; fifteenth-century manuscripts from the Vatican library; sections of the Dead Sea Scrolls along with maps and other images related to the scrolls; and an image bank that chronicles Christopher Columbus's 1492 trip to the Americas. Online access to the Library of Congress is free at http://www.loc.gov.

Smithsonian

The Smithsonian Institution sponsors many Internet services that provide access to materials from its various museums and research arms. For example, the National Air and Space Museum, the National Museum of American Art, and the National

Museum of Natural History are all online. You can search the Smithsonian databases, join discussion groups, and explore information on the Smithsonian's many museums, galleries, research centers, and offices. You can access all of these resources on the Web at http://www.si.edu.

Louvre

The world famous *Musée du Louvre*, the largest museum in western Europe, is online at http://www.louvre.fr. Here you will find an electronic version of the *Louvre* magazine, a schedule of cultural activities, a guide to the collections, the history of the buildings, and thousands of images including the famous *Mona Lisa*.

Encyclopedia Britannica Online

Encyclopedia Britannica Inc. was slow to offer an electronic version of its flagship *Encyclopedia Britannica*. It was frustrating to have such wonderful tools for searching encyclopedic resources but not have the world's finest encyclopedia available online. The desire for online searching led many people to purchase lesser encyclopedias that used the new tools, leading to the loss of market share for the *Britannica*.

Finally, the *Britannica* is available online. The obvious advantage of the online version is that you have access to all the latest information at once, without needing to conduct separate searches through the printed volumes of the *Micropaedia*, the *Macropaedia*, and the annual *Book of the Year*. For information on how to purchase a license to access the online version, go to http://www.britannica.com, where you will find out about a seven-day free trial offer.

EXERCISES

1. Find out whether you can get access to CD-ROM encyclopedias at home, work, or school. What are the titles of the CD-ROM encyclopedias available to you? Where are they located?

2. Select a topic, such as the role Amelia Earhart played in aviation history. Then time how long it takes you to find out information about her and construct an appropriate bibliography from a printed encyclopedia. Now try one of the CD-ROM encyclopedias mentioned in this chapter. How much time did the CD-ROM search save?

3. New technology has benefited researchers considerably. For example, the Xerox machine was invented while the author was a student. No longer did we have to write out by hand the materials we wanted to excerpt from books and magazines in the library; for 10 cents per page, we could make Xerox copies, thereby saving many hours of handwriting time. Today multimedia CD-ROMs and the Information Superhighway provide much more powerful tools. How do you see multimedia computers helping you conduct research? (If you have never used the Information Superhighway, completing the tutorial in Part Eight of this book will help you answer this question.)

4. There is a beautiful bitmap of the *Mona Lisa* online at the Louvre's Web site. Point your Web browser at http://www.louvre.fr and see if you can navigate to the *Mona Lisa:* Choose Les collections, then Peintures, then click on the *Mona Lisa* icon to see her full-screen.

9 Application Development Packages

After completing this chapter, you will be able to:

- **Define the categories of application development packages and recognize the names of the major packages in each category**

- **Know when to use a presentation package, a hypermedia program, an animation package, or a full-fledged authoring tool**

- **Understand the difference between graphical and textual Web page creation tools**

- **Experience what the different packages are like by running product demonstrations on the *Multiliteracy CD***

HERE are five kinds of development software for creating multimedia applications: presentation packages, hypermedia programs, animators, authoring systems, and Web page creation tools. This chapter defines each kind, identifies available products, and provides demonstrations on the *Multiliteracy CD*.

As with most categorizations, there is an overlap among the classifications defined here. For example, some presentation packages provide a limited hypermedia capability; hypermedia programs can create presentations; and full-fledged authoring systems can do just about anything. However, just as you would not normally use a sledgehammer to pound a finishing nail, so also do multimedia tools have their appropriate uses, according to which you will find them classified in this chapter.

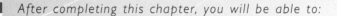

PRESENTATION PACKAGES

Presentation packages try to make it easy for you to produce convincing multimedia shows consisting of slides, audio clips, animations, and full-motion sequences. Vendors often select product titles that imply how their packages can influence an audience; for example, consider the titles—Compel from Asymmetrix, PowerPoint by Microsoft, and Persuasion from Aldus.

Several graphics packages also have presentation capabilities. Lotus Freelance and Harvard Graphics are high-powered graphics packages with presentation capabilities. More recently, word processing giant WordPerfect has entered the multimedia market with WordPerfect Presentations. And Software Publishing has released a new title called ASAP WordPower, intended to help you turn words into presentations "as soon as possible" (ASAP).

PowerPoint

According to Microsoft, there are more than 20 million users of PowerPoint worldwide. PowerPoint addresses the needs of business professionals who need to create compelling graphics and present them effectively. Based on the slide-show metaphor shown in Figure 9-1, PowerPoint has a Slide Sorter that lets you drag slides and position them in the order you want to present them. You can drag and drop slides from one presentation to another, and import charts and spreadsheet data from Microsoft Excel. An AutoContent Wizard helps you figure out what to say, and an Outliner helps organize and reorder thoughts by letting you selectively collapse and expand outline headings.

PowerPoint has an AutoClipArt tool that scans the text on your slides and suggests clip art to enhance your message, drawing from a library of more than 1,100 images. PowerPoint also has a graphing feature to create your own figures, an organization chart creator, and an equation editor to create and display scientific and mathematical equations. A rehearsal feature helps you practice and learn how long a presentation will take, showing how much time you spent on each slide. You can print speaker's notes, audience handouts, and outline pages. There is also a GraphicsLink communications package to send presentations to Genigraphics for next-day delivery of 35mm slides.

According to Microsoft research, 42% of PowerPoint presentations are delivered by projecting the computer graphics onto a large screen; 68% are printed as audience handouts. The rest rely on slides and overhead transparencies. Therefore, PowerPoint's ability to print to film is key to its market penetration. Indeed, PowerPoint swept all of the categories in *CIO* magazine's Readers Choice Awards for presentation graphics.

9-1

The Slide Sorter in PowerPoint.

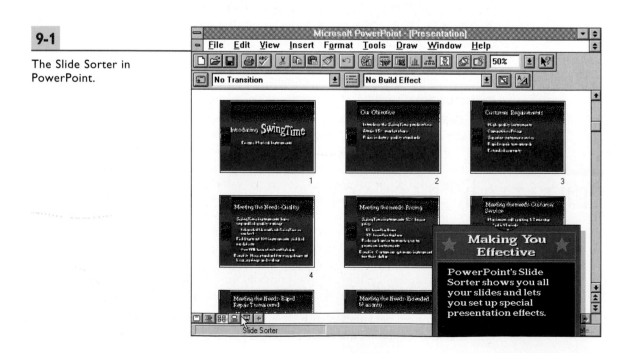

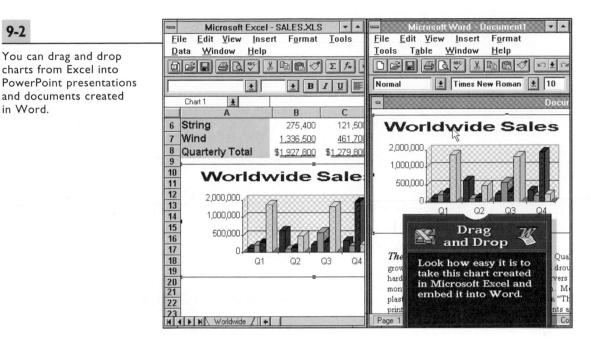

9-2

You can drag and drop charts from Excel into PowerPoint presentations and documents created in Word.

PowerPoint is one of five programs you can purchase bundled together as Microsoft Office Professional. The other four programs include Microsoft's Excel spreadsheet, Access database, Word word processor, and Schedule+ time management package. All five programs look alike and work together. For example, Figure 9-2 shows how you can drag and drop a chart from Excel into a document in Word. When you work on the document in Word and click the chart to edit it, the Excel menu bar appears automatically, without requiring you to switch programs. The Present It button in Word flows text from your word-processed documents into PowerPoint slides.

The *Multiliteracy CD* contains an entertaining demonstration of Microsoft's PowerPoint. To run it go to the Demonstrations section, select Software, and click the PowerPoint button. Be sure to run the part of the demo that shows how PowerPoint functions as part of Microsoft Office. *Note:* This demo was made for the Windows 3.1 version. PowerPoint for Windows 95 has even more features. For the latest information, go to http://www.microsoft.com/mspowerpoint.

Harvard Graphics

Harvard Graphics competes with PowerPoint for market share and claims to have as many users. Published by Software Publishing Corporation, its 5-Minute Coach helps users get started right away with a tutorial that covers creating, enhancing, and managing a presentation. You can view your presentation in outline format with the Outliner, or as a slide show in the Slide Sorter. The QuickLooks feature lets you try different colors, fonts, and perspectives to see how your slides look before you commit to any change. Figure 9-3 shows how the Advisor offers suggestions on layout, color, and fonts.

A chart gallery contains preformatted title, bullet, table, data, and organizational charts. There are 31 professionally designed presentation styles selected after extensive user input. Each style specifies the charting options, color palette, background design, and type font for a presentation. By editing a presentation's master template, you can change the appearance of every slide automatically. Figure 9-4 shows how a slide looks in different styles.

The Harvard Graphics Advisor is always ready to provide tips as you create your presentation.

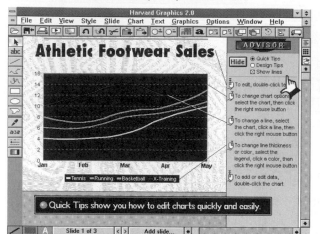

How a slide looks in different styles in Harvard Graphics.

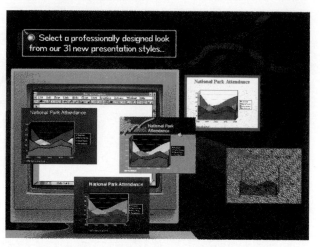

Excerpts and/or illustrations from Harvard Graphics® version 2.0, including text material, are used with the permission of Software Publishing Corporation, which owns the copyright to such product. Harvard Graphics is a registered trademark of Software Publishing Corporation. The Harvard Graphics program is a product of Software Publishing Corporation and has no connection with Harvard University.

Harvard F/X lets you add special effects to text or drawings, and multimedia capabilities let you add music, video, and animation. Its print options enable you to create speaker's notes, handouts, transparencies, and slides on your laser printer, plotter, color printer, or film recorder.

Like PowerPoint, Harvard Graphics has OLE (object linking and embedding) support that lets users drag and drop objects from other applications into a slide. There is also a conferencing capability that lets network users display presentations on up to 64 other computers simultaneously.

The *Multiliteracy CD* contains a demonstration of Harvard Graphics. To run it, go to the Demonstrations section, select Applications, and click the Harvard Graphics button.

ASAP WordPower

Winner of the Editors' Choice Award from *PC Magazine,* Software Publishing's ASAP WordPower is a personal presentation application designed to let users create compelling presentations, reports, and handouts in minutes. Built on SPC's patent-pending Intelligent Formatting, the product helps users prepare complex slides quickly and easily. SPC also publishes ASAP WebShow, a Netscape Navigator 2.0 plug-in that lets you view, download, and print graphically rich reports and presentations created with ASAP WordPower.

There is a demonstration of ASAP WordPower on the *Multiliteracy CD.* To try the demo, go to the Demonstrations section, select Software, and click the ASAP button. The demo lets you run sample presentations and create a little show of your own. To run the samples, pull down the ASAP File menu and select one of the presentations you will find listed in the *ASAP195* directory. The "layouts" presentation gives you a nice overview of the layout possibilities. To create a presentation, you type an outline of your presentation into the Outline window shown in Figure 9-5. Clicking the Preview tab lets you preview the presentation; as shown in Figure 9-6, you can choose different presentation styles and color

9-5

The Outline window in ASAP WordPower lets you type an outline of your presentation.

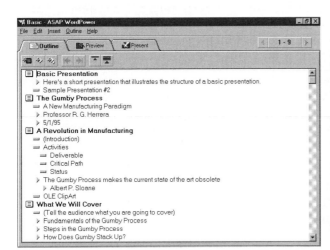

9-6

The ASAP Preview window lets you rehearse your presentation and choose layout styles and color options.

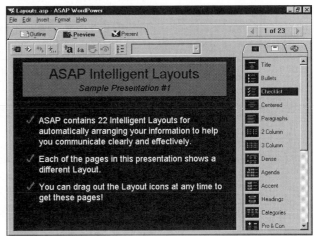

patterns. Clicking the Present option will show the presentation full-screen. Press the ⌷Esc⌷ key to leave the full-screen mode and return to the ASAP editing window. The built-in Help explains other navigation features available in ASAP.

The latest information about ASAP products is on the Web at www.spco.com.

HYPERMEDIA PROGRAMS

Hypermedia programs go beyond the linear slide-show metaphor used in presentation packages to provide an infinite capability to link objects and enable users to navigate among them. The most well-known hypermedia programs are HyperCard for the Macintosh, and ToolBook for Windows.

HyperCard

HyperCard uses the metaphor of a stack of cards. Each screen is thought of as a card you can place anywhere in a stack and link to any other card. You can make simple stacks without learning any programming. You need to learn HyperTalk (HyperCard's programming language) to create more-complex applications.

There are thousands of HyperCard stacks available, many of which are either free or available for a small shareware fee. For more information about HyperCard, point your browser at http://members.aol.com/hcheaven, which is the "HyperCard Heaven" Web site for people who love HyperCard.

ToolBook

ToolBook is published by Asymmetrix. Its purpose is to reduce the amount of time and effort required to create Windows applications. ToolBook is very similar to HyperCard, except that stacks of cards are thought of as books containing pages. You develop applications by creating books full of pages, which can contain text, graphics, and buttons that enable user interaction. Toolbook has a scripting language called OpenScript in which you program interactive and navigational commands that define what the buttons do. You can also attach scripts to hot words in text fields. Particularly useful is a script recorder that will automatically create a script for actions you perform on the screen, such as navigating to a page in a book or creating an animation by moving an object around the screen. ToolBook comes with more than 270 prescripted multimedia objects called widgets that you can copy and paste into your application.

The French-language software *Nouvelles Dimensions* discussed in Chapter 4 is a ToolBook application. There is a demonstration of it on the *Multiliteracy CD*. To sample the kind of application you can create with ToolBook, go to the Demonstrations section, select Applications, and click the Nouvelles Dimensions button.

Asymmetrix is broadening the ToolBook concept by making it possible to deliver interactive learning programs over the Web with ToolBook II, which creates applications based on HTML and Java. The latest ToolBook information is on the Web at http://www.asymetrix.com.

HyperStudio

On the Macintosh, HyperStudio is one of the easiest and most powerful programs for use in schools. Teachers have had a lot of success with students using HyperStudio to create multimedia projects. HyperStudio makes it easy for students to create and edit QuickTime movies, snap pictures with AV Macs, and create projects combining text, sound, graphics, and video.

Although you must have a Mac to author HyperStudio stacks, there is a Windows player that enables HyperStudio applications to run on Multimedia PCs. For more information go to http://www.hyperstudio.com.

ANIMATION AND MULTIMEDIA SEQUENCING

Animation is the use of a computer to create movement of objects on the screen. There are different levels of animation complexity. The simplest form of animation is called **frame animation**, in which the computer displays a stack of predrawn graphics that create a movie when shown in rapid succession. You will learn how to create frame animations in Chapter 44.

More sophisticated are applications that let you define graphic objects and make them move by manipulating real-time parameters that control the object. The morph application that you can run on the *Multiliteracy CD* is one example—to view it, go to the Demonstrations section, select Software, and click the Morph button. The ultimate is the animated movie *Toy Story*, which is discussed in Chapter 5.

Multimedia sequencers are programs that let you show a series of audiovisual events. These events often include animations.

Discussed here are four programs that enable you to create animations and present them as part of a multimedia sequence.

Premiere

Adobe's Premiere is a video editing tool with interactive motion path creation. Premiere has full-featured video capture and editing of 99 video and audio tracks with virtual clips to extend mixing capabilities. There are 75 transitions and 58 filters, plus tools for creating custom transitions and filters. Premiere displays clips "filmstrip style" and lets you zoom in for single-frame editing. Motion control allows any still or moving image to fly along a path with twisting, zooming, rotation, and distortion effects. Premiere comes on a CD-ROM with clip media and video tutorials. For the latest information, visit Adobe's Web site at http://www.adobe.com, where you will find the Premiere product info at http://www.adobe.com/prodindex/premiere/main.html.

Autodesk

Autodesk Animator Studio is a full-featured 2-D animation environment with audio. It consists of four modules:

- The Animator module: Users create and edit digital movies, paint on individual frames of an animation, and combine digitized video segments with text, animations, or other video clips. Paint tools including colors, filters, and transparency effects can be applied either to single frames or as time-based effects across entire animations.

- The Soundlab module: Audio capture, creation, and editing tools integrate sounds and movies for playback as QuickTime or AVI files. You can separate the pitch and tempo of a soundtrack to synchronize audio and video.

- The Scriptor module: Users can build and edit multimedia scripts that use any combination of digital video, animations, still images, and sounds.

- The Player module: This is a stand-alone environment that lets users play back movies, sounds, or scripts. The Player module is free; you can distribute it with your application for no extra charge.

Autodesk Animator Studio includes a Digital Clip Library on CD-ROM, containing more than 400 MB of images, animations, and sound clips that can be edited and distributed royalty free. Autodesk also publishes a 3-D animation environment called 3D Studio. For the latest Autodesk information, visit http://www.autodesk.com.

Director

As illustrated in Figure 9-7, Macromedia's Director is a score-based environment for creating interactive animated applications. Director is the industry leader in multimedia sequencing. Witness groundbreaking applications like Brøderbund's *Living Books* and the Sting CD *All This Time,* which were created with Director.

Director can store up to 32,000 media elements on 48 channels with transitions, sounds, custom palettes, and tempo variations. "Onion skinning" speeds animation development by allowing you to view a graphic while drawing changes in movement on a thin layer above the previous graphic. Following a theatrical metaphor, actors can be cast and scripted to take on a life of their own as objects in an application. The Lingo object-oriented scripting language enables

9-7

Macromedia's Director is the industry-standard multimedia sequencer.

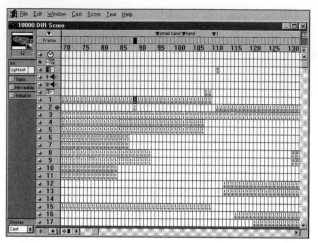

developers to create custom in-house code that plugs in to extend Director's built-in capabilities. Director files can play over the Internet, using Shockwave for Director. For the latest information on Director, visit http://www.macromedia.com.

The *Multiliteracy CD* contains three demos that were created with Director. To run these demos, go to the Demonstrations section, select Applications, and click the Iron Helix button, the Just Grandma and Me button, or the Arthur's Teacher Trouble button. For the latest information on Director, visit http://www.macromedia.com.

Oracle Media Objects

Oracle is competing head-on with Director with aggressive ads like "Save $800 on Macromedia Director; get Oracle Media Objects instead." Oracle Media Objects is an object-oriented multimedia creation environment that can be used to create multimedia titles for CD, the Internet, and interactive TV. True to Oracle's roots as a premier database company, Oracle Media Objects allows easy access and manipulation of relational data. Applications created in Oracle Media Objects can be delivered on CD-ROM and over networks to PCs, Macintoshes, and television set-top boxes. Oracle Media Objects is based on the familiar card-and-stack metaphor.

There is a promotional copy of Oracle Media Objects on the *Multiliteracy CD*. To run the promo, go to the Demonstrations section, select Software, and click the Oracle button. The promo lets you create applications with up to three screens and 100 objects. The latest information on Oracle Media Objects is on the Web at http://www.oracle.com.

AUTHORING SYSTEMS

Full-fledged application development tools that let you present material, ask questions about it, evaluate user input, and branch accordingly are called **authoring systems**. In the past, before graphical user interfaces became popular, authoring was a tedious and time-consuming process, often requiring hundreds of hours of work to create one hour of completed material. Recently, windowed environments have led to the creation of graphically based authoring systems that have reduced considerably the time needed to create a sophisticated application.

Authorware Professional

Macromedia markets Authorware Professional for Windows as "the premier multimedia authoring tool for interactive learning." An advantage Authorware has over most other packages is that it can be used to create applications for both Windows and Macintosh users. This cross-platform capability has given Macromedia a competitive edge in the publishing industry, which wants to create products that will run not only under Windows, but on the installed base of Macintoshes as well.

9-8

The flowline metaphor in Authorware Professional.

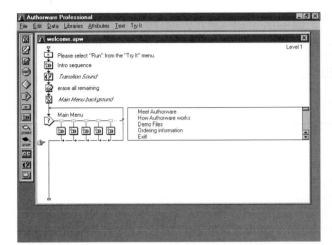

9-9

The Decision icon options dialog in Authorware Professional.

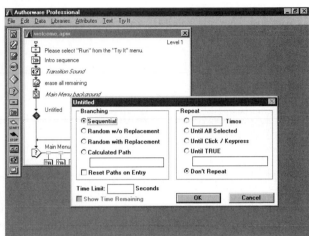

Authorware is rooted in some pretty powerful technology. Its sophisticated judging, sequencing, and instructional management facility builds upon two decades of work by Authorware founder Mike Allen on a computer-assisted instruction (CAI) system called PLATO.

When Authorware merged with Macromind to create Macromedia in 1992, Macromind's Director (discussed earlier) became Authorware's multimedia engine, creating a blockbuster authoring system. Macromedia won publishing contracts with Paramount Publishing, Jostens Learning, HyperMedia Communications, and McGraw-Hill, and they formed strategic alliances with Apple Computer, 3DO, Bell Labs, Bell Atlantic, Brøderbund, Kaleida, and others.

Figure 9-8 shows how Authorware Professional uses a flowline metaphor to create logic structures from 11 design icons. The developer creates an application by selecting icons and dragging them onto the flowline. Double-clicking an icon opens it, allowing the developer to add content. As icons accumulate on the screen, the developer can click the Map icon to group related icons together. Thus, the developer can view the application from a top-down approach, maintaining perspective on how the various program modules interrelate.

Icons control everything from user interactions to the decisions they trigger. For example, Figure 9-9 shows how the Decision icon opens a dialog that lets you choose a sequential presentation of the attached icons, a selection of random icons, or the selection of a calculated path based on the value of a variable.

There is a demonstration of Authorware Professional on the *Multiliteracy CD*. It will introduce you to Authorware Professional, show you how Authorware works, and let you run a sample application about a 35mm camera. To try the Authorware demo, go to the Demonstrations section, select Software, and click the Authorware Professional button.

IconAuthor

Macromedia considers IconAuthor from AimTech to be the primary competition for Authorware Professional. Like Authorware, IconAuthor has a visual programming environment in which you create applications by moving icons into a flowchart that depicts the structure of your project. Then you add content by providing text, graphics, animation, and/or full-motion video to the screens in your application. The *Multiliteracy CD* will let you take IconAuthor for a test drive. You will need 15 MB of free disk space to install the test drive. To install it, go to the Demonstrations section, select Software, and click the IconAuthor button.

The latest information about IconAuthor is on the Web at http://www.aimtech.com. Demos that use IconAuthor's Internet capabilities are found at http://www.aimtech.com/galia.html.

Quest

Macromedia is getting some serious competition from Allen Communication, which has created a Windows version of its award-winning Quest Multimedia Authoring System. During the past decade, corporations and educational institutions have used Quest to create thousands of hours of courseware. Shown in Figure 9-10, Quest Net+ is an object-oriented authoring tool that lets you work at one of two levels: design or frame. At the design level, shown in Figure 9-11, you can experiment and map out the overall structure of your application. The postage-stamp representation of full frames gives the developer an overview of how the screens look and link together. At the frame level, shown in Figure 9-12, you work on the individual frames that make up the application, seeing exactly what the user will see on the screen.

9-10

The Quest for Windows title page.

The Fast Track feature shown in Figure 9-13 lets Quest authors use prebuilt buttons, interactions, screen layouts, and borders. You select a prebuilt object and then add your content, thereby saving the time it would have taken to create the object from scratch. Floating toolbars let you assemble graphics, text, audio, full-motion video, animations, and branching. Every object in Quest is a so-called smart object. A smart object has a life of its own, defined

9-11

At the design level, Quest authors think of the big picture and chart their applications with postage-stamp representations of actual frames.

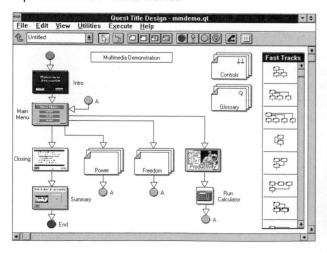

9-12

At the frame level, Quest authors work inside the frame, seeing exactly what the end user will see.

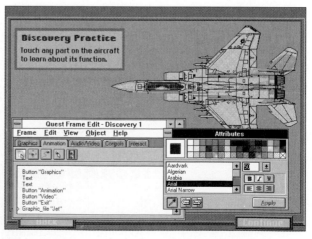

9-13

Quest's Fast Track feature lets authors add their own content to prebuilt screen layouts, menus, templates, borders, buttons, question/answer frames, and interactions.

by the actions and conditions set for it by the developer, who can request data from it and even let the end user manipulate it.

Quest Net+ has Internet capabilities that enable multiple titles or training applications to communicate and exchange data across the network. CMI (computer-managed instruction) objects manage the storage and retrieval of data used for question-and-answer scenarios, tests, and information gathered from kiosks.

There is a demonstration of Quest Net+ on the *Multiliteracy CD*. To take Quest for a test drive, go to the Demonstrations section, select Software, and click the Quest button. The latest Quest information is on the Web at http://www.allencomm.com.

PODIUM

PODIUM is a multimedia application generator, integrator, and telecommunication product invented at the University of Delaware in 1988. Its goal is to make it quick and easy to create and distribute multimedia applications. In the tutorial part of this book, you will experience how easily PODIUM's graphical toolbox enables you to:

- Create presentations and hypermedia programs by combining and linking text, graphics, audio, video, animations, datasets, and software applications residing anywhere on your PC, local-area network, or worldwide on the Internet

- Interact with users, keeping track of what they do and how they respond, and branching accordingly

- Seamlessly integrate any application created with any other multimedia creation tool into a single operating environment

- Create user-friendly front-ends that make software and networks easier to use

- Create multimedia e-mail that you can send to anyone in the world on the Internet, and read multimedia e-mail that other people send you

Because the hands-on section of this book contains beginning and advanced tutorials in PODIUM application creation, PODIUM is not discussed further here. It should be noted, however, that the *Multiliteracy CD* was authored in PODIUM.

By completing the tutorials in the hands-on section, you can learn how to create multimedia applications like the *Multiliteracy CD*. The latest PODIUM information is on the Web at http://www.udel.edu/podium.

WORLD WIDE WEB PAGE CREATION TOOLS

There are two schools of thought on Web page creation tools: graphical versus textual. The graphical camp believes that you should be able to create Web pages in a WYSIWYG (what-you-see-is-what-you-get) environment. You never need to look at the HTML (hypertext markup language) source code behind a Web page because the GUI (graphical user interface) inserts the codes automatically when you edit the Web page. The textual camp believes that you should work directly with the HTML codes for two reasons. First, because Web pages are defined by the HTML codes, being able to edit the HTML codes directly gives you more control over the Web page. Second, since HTML is an evolving language that continually gets new features, graphical tools will always lag behind; working directly with the HTML codes lets you use the latest HTML commands, which may not yet be implemented in the graphical tool.

There are dozens of Web page creation tools. You will find a complete list along with reviews of the tools at http://union.ncsa.uiuc.edu/HyperNews/get/www/htm/editors.html.

This chapter reviews Microsoft's Internet Assistant, which is an example of a graphical tool, and Kenn Nesbitt's WebEdit, which is a textual tool. Then we take a look at three approaches to incorporating active multimedia elements on Web pages: Sun's Java, Macromedia's Shockwave, and Microsoft's ActiveX technologies. The chapter concludes with a discussion of animated GIFs, which provide a simple way for you to add animations to Web pages.

Internet Assistant

Microsoft's Internet Assistant is a free add-on for Microsoft Word that you can download in Macintosh, Windows 3.1, and Windows 95 versions from http://www.microsoft.com/internet/ia. Figure 9-14 shows how the Internet Assistant adds a Web page creation toolbar to Microsoft Word. The philosophy is that if you can create a word-processed document with Word, you can turn that document into a Web page with the Internet Assistant.

The author has used the Internet Assistant to put several of his scholarly publications on the Web. Because these publications were word-processed with Microsoft Word, the author can attest to how easy it was to create Web page versions with the Internet Assistant. Although the Internet Assistant may not let you work with the latest, greatest features of HTML, it certainly provides a quick and easy way to put word-processed documents on the Web in a format that the whole world can access.

For example, you can access one of the author's scholarly papers on the Web at http://www.udel.edu/fth/cms.html. Figures 9-14 and 9-15 compare how the article appears in Microsoft Word and on the Web as viewed with Netscape. The references in the paper are hyperlinked so you can quickly jump to the source materials and examples the paper cites. Imagine how scholarship would be enhanced if all scholarly writings were available in this format on the Web! Researchers and students could learn so much more in an online world of interconnected

9-14

How Microsoft Word appears with a Web page creation toolbar when the Internet Assistant is installed.

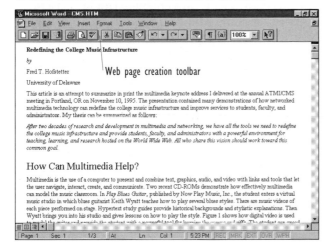

9-15

How the article being edited in Figure 9-14 appears on the Web.

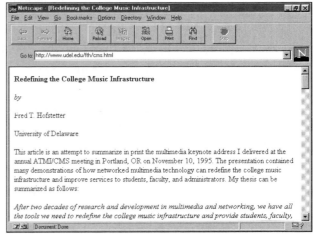

scholarship. Yet many disciplines lag behind, with little scholarly writing mounted on the Web today. The author believes that because the word processors used to write scholarly documents make it easy to create Web page versions of those documents, scholars have no excuse for not mounting their research on the Web and making it accessible to the world.

WebEdit

WebEdit is a textual HTML editor for creating Web pages. As shown in Figure 9-16, WebEdit lets you edit the HTML in one window and view how it will appear on the Web in another. WebEdit is the tool you will learn how to use in the World Wide Web tutorial in Part Ten of this book. Why did the author choose a textual tool like WebEdit instead of a graphical tool like the Internet Assistant for the tutorial? Because WebEdit gives you a better grasp of how HTML works, and it lets you use the latest features of HTML that have not yet been implemented in the Internet Assistant.

9-16

WebEdit lets you edit the HTML source code in the window on the left, and simultaneously view how it will appear on the Web in the window on the right.

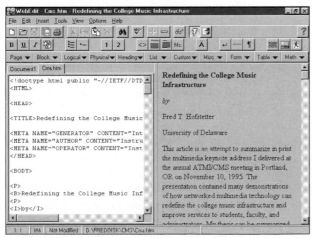

So how do you know when to use a graphical tool like the Internet Assistant? The author's advice is to use the Internet Assistant when you want to create a Web page version of a document word-processed with Microsoft Word, and use a textual tool like WebEdit when you want to create something fancier that uses the latest HTML features that the Internet Assistant may not yet support.

Java and Hot Java

Java is an applet development language invented by Sun Microsystems. An **applet** is a little application that can be downloaded to your computer along with a Web page. The applet can make your computer do things like animate objects on the Web page, make sound, play games, and perform calculations.

Almost anything you can program a computer to do can be downloaded with a Web page in Java, so long as your Web browser is Java enabled. Hot Java is a Java-enabled Web browser from Sun Microsystems. The 32-bit version of Netscape for Windows 95 can do Java, and Netscape is working on Java-enabled Web browsers for other platforms. Microsoft has licensed Java for use in the Internet Explorer.

You can learn more about Java at http://java.sun.com.

Jamba

Jamba is Aimtech's Java authoring software. A Jamba toolbox makes it easy to enhance Web sites with multimedia and interactivity. Jamba objects include picture push buttons, check boxes, list boxes, combo boxes, and hot spots. For more information, go to http://www.aimtech.com.

Shockwave

As you learned earlier in this chapter, Director is the state-of-the-art animation program for multimedia productions. Shockwave is the name of Macromind's Director plug-in for Netscape. Like Java, Shockwave code gets downloaded and runs on your computer when you view a Web page with a Shockwave-enabled viewer. For the latest information on Shockwave, visit Macromind's Web site at http://www.macromind.com.

ActiveX

ActiveX is the name of Microsoft's applet technology, which the Internet Explorer supports. Like Java, ActiveX lets you download little applications that run on your computer to bring a Web page to life. You might wonder why Microsoft licensed Java when Microsoft is pursuing its own ActiveX technology. The reason is because Java got released sooner than ActiveX, and Microsoft licensed Java to calm the fears of customers who worried that they might not have access to Sun's applet technology in Microsoft products.

Applets are an emerging technology that will undergo rapid development over the next few years. For the latest information about Microsoft's applet technologies, visit http://www.microsoft.com/ie/script.

Animated GIFs

There is a simpler way to animate Web pages. Animated GIFs provide an easy way for you to create frame animations without having to learn the complexities of Java programming. As this book goes to press, only Netscape supports animated GIFs; but by the time you read this, other browsers should support animated GIFs as well. GIF stands for Graphics Interchange Format. The GIF file format is the most widely used method of storing bitmaps on the World Wide Web. Animated GIFs are a special kind of GIF file (known as GIF89a) that may contain multiple images intended to be shown in a sequence at specific times and locations on the screen. Netscape supports the GIF89a looping option. When an animated GIF appears on a Web page, Netscape keeps looping the frames in the GIF file, and you see an animation.

Animated GIFs are very efficient; they are downloaded only once, then cached from your hard drive as Netscape loops the images. Some users don't like the constant disk chatter. You can be the judge by trying the animated GIF on the HBO home page at http://www.hbo.com. Another clever use of an animated GIF is found at http://www.microsoft.com/ie/conf, where Microsoft uses animation to show the different options available in its NetMeeting software.

There is a shareware application that you can use to create animated GIFs. The name of the package is GIF Construction Set. You can download it from the Web at http://www.mindworkshop.com/alchemy/gifcon.html. For a tutorial on creating animated GIFs, visit http://webreference.com/dev/gifanim.html.

Multimedia Tour of the Web

You can take a really cool multimedia tour of the Web at http://ftp.digital.com/webmm/fbegin.html. Created by John Faherty of the Digital Equipment Corporation, the purpose of this tour is to demonstrate new Web technology and enable you to assess it. Faherty's tour is a great way to experience what's out there and get what you need to take advantage of it.

EXERCISES

1. What presentation packages does your school or business own? What are the primary reasons for their selection over competing brands?

2. What percentage of the teachers at your school or the executives in your business use multimedia presentation packages? How many of your teachers use the computer to make a presentation, as opposed to just printing slides or transparencies for noncomputer projection?

3. Does your school or business own an authoring system? If so, which one? Why was it selected?

4. What software would you personally use to create a presentation? Why do you prefer it over other brands? What improvements would you like to see the vendor make?

5. Given the features of the presentation packages, hypermedia programs, animators, and authoring systems presented in this chapter, what is your overall impression of the state of the art of multimedia application development? What additional capabilities would you like these tools to have?

6. What are the implications of active technologies on the World Wide Web? How will applet products like Java, Shockwave, and ActiveX influence the creation and distribution of multimedia titles? Will active Web technologies begin to compete with CD-ROM as the preferred publishing medium? What are the potential drawbacks and pitfalls of active Web technologies?

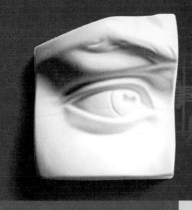

Part Three

Selecting Multimedia Hardware

Buying a multimedia computer may be the most complicated shopping you ever do. Four factors make it difficult. First, because there is no industrywide standard for multimedia, each vendor creates its own brand and produces multimedia applications that work with only its brand. Potential buyers hesitate because they know that getting Brand X will prevent them from running applications made for Brand Y. Second, there are so many options you can add on to a multimedia computer that once you decide which brand to buy, you might still find it confusing to choose multimedia peripherals. Third, it is hard to get a list of all the options that are available, because vendors are interested in showing only those they sell. Finally, once you buy your computer and select the options you want, installing and getting them to work can be a nightmarish experience.

The next four chapters in this book will help you overcome these dilemmas. The good news is that once you finally do get your multimedia computer up and running, you should not have many (hopefully, not any) problems. In other words, most of the difficulty will happen right at the beginning, and if you can persevere through the startup problems, your time and effort will be repaid by the many benefits you will reap from your multimedia computing.

10 Competing Multimedia Standards

After completing this chapter, you will be able to:

- **Understand the competing standards of multimedia and comprehend what is meant by the phrase *multi multimedia***

- **Realize how lack of standardization retards the progress of multimedia development**

- **Consider the level at which standardization would be appropriate**

- **Know which multimedia formats will have the most longevity**

- **Understand the basic architecture of the Microsoft MCI (Media Control Interface)**

H E multimedia computer industry is beset by an unfortunate lack of standardization. Instead of uniting the nation's best minds toward creating a compatible cross-platform system for multimedia, the computer industry is hard at work creating multiple standards and competing products. If this were happening accidentally, one might be more willing to tolerate the situation. Instead, vendors deliberately create disparity to differentiate their products from the competition and to make past purchases obsolete so customers will buy more hardware. In the area of graphics alone, there are more than 30 so-called standards for storing pictures in computer files. When an industry provides 30 different ways of doing something, there is no standard.

Computer industry leaders fail to recognize how self-defeating this lack of standardization is. They should learn a lesson from the musicians. During the early 1980s, the National Association of Music Merchants and the Audio Engineering Society began to discuss how a lack of standards was retarding the market for music synthesizers. Consumers were afraid to buy a keyboard because there was no guarantee that it would be compatible with later models in the same product line, much less with synthesizers made by other vendors. In 1983 the Musical Instrument Digital Interface (MIDI) standard was released, and all of the music merchants endorsed it. Consumers were no longer afraid of obsolescence, and music synthesizer sales mushroomed. Vendors made more money not so much because their market share increased, but because the entire market grew exponentially as a result of standardization.

MULTI MULTIMEDIA

Instead of having one multimedia standard, consumers are faced with a complicated array of competing software and hardware platforms that the author (Hofstetter 1993) describes as "multi multimedia." When you create an application, you must be careful to store your objects in formats that will have the most longevity and compatibility. Otherwise the time and effort you spend will have to be reinvested when the so-called standards change.

Microsoft's MCI

Microsoft's MCI provides Windows users with a strategic approach to coping with this lack of standardization. *MCI* stands for Media Control Interface. The purpose of the MCI is to provide a device-independent means of developing multimedia software. The idea is that vendors who make multimedia hardware supply an MCI translation table for each device. Instead of hard-coding applications to specific devices, developers use MCI commands that get converted automatically by the translation table into the specific instructions needed to control the device. The MCI commands consist of generic multimedia instructions such as PLAY, RECORD, PAUSE, SEEK, SAVE, and STOP.

For example, consider the industrywide problem posed by the differences among videodisc players. Not only do videodisc command sets vary among vendors, but even within a product line manufacturers change the commands on different models. For example, to display a videodisc frame, developers must write different code for each individual brand of videodisc player. If MCI were adopted as an industrywide standard, instead of hard-coding the commands needed to display the videodisc frame on every specific player, developers could simply send the MCI command SEEK TO the frame number. If every videodisc manufacturer provided a device driver with an MCI translation table, the user could use any videodisc player, just as MIDI lets musicians use any keyboard.

Adopting Microsoft's MCI as an industrywide standard would significantly reduce the amount of time lost due to the lack of standardization. Until vendors unite behind a common strategy, the multitude of multimedia will increase, making multimedia more "multi" in the wrong sense of the word. While multimedia has the potential to improve education and communication tremendously, "multi multimedia" retards its development and hinders its widespread adoption.

As this book goes to press, the author believes that Microsoft's MCI is the best solution, which is why Windows was chosen as the multimedia platform for this book. Nevertheless, because a multiliterate person should know about the alternatives, the competing standards are discussed next. You can find out more about Microsoft's multimedia directions at http://www.microsoft.com/mediadev.

Apple's QuickTime

Apple's QuickTime is to the Macintosh what the MCI is to Windows. Like the MCI, QuickTime supports digital audio, MIDI, compact disc, and digital video. Apple's latest release contains many improvements over the original QuickTime. A faster data rate plays digital video more smoothly. Audio compression reduces the amount of storage required to hold digital audio recordings. And, like Windows, QuickTime now supports MPEG (Motion Pictures Experts Group), which is emerging as an industrywide standard for digital video. For the latest information on QuickTime, visit http://www.quicktime.apple.com.

The Macintosh is a very good platform for multimedia. The reason it was not chosen for this book is because there are more than 10 times as many Windows users as there are Mac users. The larger number of developers producing MCI devices will bring more innovations to Windows faster than to the Mac. The author predicts that just as VHS won out over Beta as the mass market videotape standard, so also will Windows emerge as the retail multimedia standard. The Macintosh is the Beta; Windows is the VHS.

As this book goes to press, Microsoft and Apple are having discussions about incorporating QuickTime into the MCI (*Infoworld* 6/24/96). Such a merger would be fantastic; let's hope it happens. There already is a version of QuickTime for Windows, and many cross-platform developers have chosen to produce movies in the QuickTime format for playback on both Windows and Macintosh PCs.

IBM's Ultimedia

Ultimedia is not a typographical error; it is IBM's trademark for multimedia. It is meant to imply that IBM has the ultimate in multimedia. At first the Ultimedia trademark referred to a fairly well-defined product set, but then IBM began using the term to market a more loosely defined "Ultimedia Tools Series." This can be confusing because some of the titles run only under DOS, others under Windows, and still others under OS/2, and the types of files some of these products create are often not compatible with other tools in the series.

IBM has spent a tremendous amount of money trying to establish itself in the field of multimedia. At IBM's Web site (http://www.ibm.com), you can do a search for multimedia and find out about all the different multimedia products IBM is creating, including the award-winning line of IBM ThinkPad laptop computers.

As the lack of standardization across the Ultimedia tools demonstrates, IBM has not adopted a consistent strategy for multimedia as have Apple and Microsoft. Instead of setting a companywide standard, IBM has invested in multiple standards, probably hoping that one of them will become the mass market blockbuster. Once known as the standard setter, IBM has encountered such intense competition that new directions it announces one year turn out to be dead ends a year later. A very good example is the Digital Video Interactive (DVI) technology, which is discussed next.

Intel's DVI and Indeo

Digital Video Interactive (DVI) won Best of Show at COMDEX/Fall '92. Co-developed by Intel and IBM, DVI uses Intel's i750 chip to record and play back digital audio and video full-screen at 30 frames per second. The compression algorithm lets a single CD-ROM hold 72 minutes of video. Initially requiring users to purchase a DVI circuit board called ActionMedia, IBM had plans to integrate the i750 technology onto the motherboard so that all PC buyers would automatically have this capability, and DVI would become ubiquitous.

Then Microsoft announced Video for Windows, which required special hardware only to record the video; any computer with Windows could play it back. Although Video for Windows did not perform as well as DVI, Intel quickly realized that by not requiring playback hardware, Video for Windows would become much more pervasive. So Intel jumped on the Video for Windows bandwagon by creating a Windows MCI driver called Indeo, which stands for Intel Video. The Indeo driver lets you record digital video with Intel's hardware; but then on playback, if the user does not have the Intel board, the video will still play back, albeit with lesser quality, through Video for Windows.

Meanwhile the beautiful full-screen, full-motion DVI technology that won at COMDEX became a dead end. Developers like the author, who spent many months creating native DVI applications, became disenchanted and will be wary the next time IBM and Intel announce a new "standard."

Philips's CD-I

Imagine a home CD player you can hook up to your television set and with which you can use a mouse or a joystick to control interactive software with audio and video coming from the CD. Such was the dream for compact disc–interactive (CD-I). Philips and Sony invented it in 1986, and it came on the market in 1991. There are now more than 150 CD-I titles, ranging from interactive games like *Mad Dog McCree* and the *7th Guest* to a tour of the Louvre and an interactive encyclopedia. You can purchase a CD-I player at your local electronics store for about $400. For another $250, you can get a full-motion digital video add-on adapter that lets you view more than 80 conventional movies now available on CD-I, including *Top Gun* and *Star Trek VI.*

Pearson (1993) tells how CD-I has become portable with the Sony CD-I Viewer and the Philips CDI350 portable players. "Both come with full-color active matrix LCD screens, built-in sound and the ability to operate from battery power, making them complete self-contained presentation systems . . . Both models play CD-I, CD-Bridge discs, Photo CDs and audio CDs."

Many CD-I titles do not make good use of interactive capabilities, however. For example, in his review of Dave Grusin's *The Gershwin Connection,* Rahlmann concludes, "Most of the additional information could have been put on an enhanced audio CD or in liner notes." He recommends that you ignore the visuals and program the CD Audio clips like a normal CD player (*NewMedia* 2/94: 56).

With multimedia computers offering so much more capability, will CD-I really take off? Forecasters remain skeptical. For the latest information on CD-I, go to http://www.philips.com and do a search for CD-I. The product definition of CD-I is at http://www.philips.com/sv/newtech/cdi.html.

COPING WITH MULTI MULTIMEDIA

In hopes of encouraging industrywide standards for multimedia systems, more than 200 multimedia vendors and end-user organizations created the Interactive Multimedia Association (IMA) in 1988. It did not take them long to realize that they are going to have to cope with multi multimedia for a long time. So they changed their focus from hardware to software and are now encouraging software producers to create applications that will run on all the different hardware. This is time-consuming, wasteful, and ultimately self-defeating for the multimedia industry. Developers do not have time to keep rewriting their applications for every new hardware platform. Since time is limited, developers must be cautious. This wait-and-see attitude causes lost opportunities. For example, a company called TCI had to postpone its plans to purchase a million TV set-top converters because of the lack of industry standards for digital compression. Skeptics point to the year-long delay as evidence that the Information Superhighway will take much longer, cost much more, and have far fewer viewers than is generally believed (*Wall Street Journal* 1/21/94: B8).

You have no choice other than to learn to live with the uncertainty. Because of the fast pace of change, you have to jump in quick and get to market fast, before the technology base shifts out from under you. The author recommends that the best strategy right now is to adopt the Windows MCI. Maybe if everyone refuses to purchase multimedia products that are not MCI compliant, we can send the industry the message that multimedia users simply will not tolerate multi multimedia.

E X E R C I S E S

1. Visit your local computer store and find out what multimedia brands it carries. Does it sell Microsoft MCI–based multimedia PCs? Does it carry Apple QuickTime–based Macintoshes? Philips CD-I? IBM Ultimedia? Intel DVI? What other brands does it have? Ask which brand sells best in your community and why.

2. Find out whether the local computer store owner believes in the recommendation this book makes, namely, that the Microsoft Windows MCI standard is the best one to follow, with Apple's QuickTime as the next best choice.

3. To standardize everything about multimedia today would be a mistake. The field is still too young for that, and there must be room for experimentation. On the other hand, certain objects could be standardized now. For example, there are more than 30 "standard" ways of storing bitmaps. The time and effort spent converting images from one format to another could be saved by an industrywide standard for storing bitmaps. Are there other multimedia objects that should be standardized now? List them and state why.

4. Explain how Microsoft's MCI helps developers cope with the multi multimedia dilemma.

5. Visit your local consumer electronics store and ask for a demonstration of CD-I. Do you believe this technology will take off? Why or why not?

11 Multimedia Computer Components

After completing this chapter, you will be able to:

- **Recognize the components of a multimedia PC**

- **Understand the shopping terminology necessary to make intelligent choices when purchasing a multimedia computer**

- **Know the difference between a mouse and a trackball, 8-bit and 16-bit audio, analog and digital video, double- and quad-speed CD-ROM, modems and network cards, flatbed and handheld scanners, and inkjet and laser printers**

- **Understand the datacommunication terminology needed to procure equipment for connecting your multimedia PC to the Internet**

HERE are five categories of components in a multimedia computer: the system unit, multimedia accessories, read/write storage, auxiliary input devices, and communication options. Understanding these components will enable you to follow the multimedia computer checklists provided in Chapter 12.

SYSTEM UNIT

At the heart of every computer is the central processor, which is the "brain" in which computations are performed. The system unit includes the central processor and the electronics required to support it. System units normally ship with a color monitor and a pointing device.

Central Processor

The **central processor** has a numerical name that indicates the basic type and speed of the processor. Processors in MPC-compatible multimedia computers have the numbers 286, 386, 486, or Pentium, which would have been called 586 had the patent office not ruled that the number could not be trademarked. Instead of calling the newest generation of processors the P6 as originally planned, Intel decided to call it the Pentium Pro, because of the mass market popularity of the name *Pentium*. Figure 1-5 in Chapter 1 compares the speed of the most popular central processors. A few of the processor names are followed by the letters *SX*, whereas others have the letters *DX*. SX processors are not rated as fast as DX models.

RAM

RAM stands for random access memory; it is the main memory at the heart of a computer in which multimedia programs execute. RAM is measured in megabytes (MB). *Mega* means million, and *byte* is the unit of measure for computer memory. A byte can hold a single character, and a megabyte can hold a million characters. **Meg** is another abbreviation for megabyte.

Because multimedia objects are big, you need a large amount of RAM to make a multimedia computer work well: 4 MB is the minimum required, but many applications need 8 to run well. Large programs like Windows NT require 16 MB.

Color Display

Color displays are also referred to as color monitors. Measured along the diagonal, they come in screen sizes ranging from 8 to 50 inches or more. The most typical sizes range from 12 to 19 inches. Larger monitors are very expensive and normally are purchased for classrooms or boardrooms, where many people need to be able to see the display.

Independent of the number of inches is the number of **pixels** the computer can display on the monitor. The minimum number for multimedia is 640 pixels across by 480 pixels down the screen. On computer spec sheets, this is expressed as 640×480 (the number across is always printed first, followed by the number down). Other common pixel grids are 800×600, 1024×768, and 1360×1024; these **high-resolution** monitors can also display the more common 640×480 graphics.

Your needs will probably be well met by a 640×480 or an 800×600 monitor. Equally important is the number of colors the system unit can display. Older computers with VGA (video graphics array) can display only 16 colors on a 640×480 grid. For multimedia, you need SVGA (super VGA), which can display 256 simultaneous colors chosen from a palette of more than 16 million colors. By the year 2000, computers with 24-bit color, which can display all 16 million colors simultaneously, will predominate.

Pointing Device

The **mouse** is the most common pointing device on multimedia computers today. In the Windows world, mice have two or three buttons; for most applications, a two-button mouse works fine. Alternatives to mice include mouse pens, which let you write with a stylus instead of dragging a mouse; trackballs, which let you spin a ball instead; and the innovative TrackPoint, which is a tiny joystick mounted in the center of the keyboard on IBM ThinkPad notebook computers. As shown in Figures 11-1 and 11-2, you work the TrackPoint with the tip of your index finger, eliminating the need for a surface on which to run a mouse.

11-1

The tiny joystick in the center of this IBM ThinkPad's computer keyboard substitutes for a mouse.

11-2

A user positions the mouse cursor on the screen with the IBM TrackPoint device.

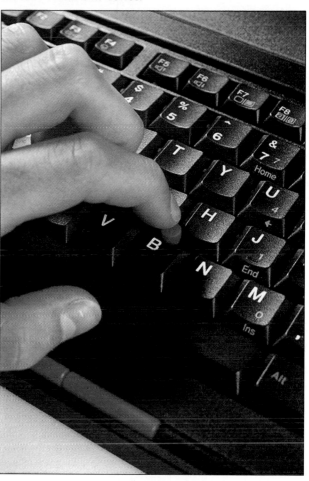

MULTIMEDIA ACCESSORIES

Multimedia accessories give a computer the ability to make sound, play music, and record movies.

CD-ROM

By definition, multimedia personal computers (MPCs) have a CD-ROM drive. If you do not have a CD-ROM drive, you do not have an MPC. CD-ROMs can contain computer data as well as audio sound tracks. Some early CD-ROM drives could read computer data but did not have the audio circuitry needed to make sound. Make sure the CD-ROM you get can play audio as well as read data.

CD-ROM is an evolving technology that keeps improving. The original CD-ROM drives read computer data at a speed of 150 KB per second. Second-generation drives are twice as fast, reading data at 300 KB per second. Called double-speed or 2× speed drives, they can also read multisession CDs, which are discs that have had additional data written onto them in subsequent recording sessions. Quadruple-speed (4×) drives read data at 600 KB per second. Also available are 6×, 8×, and 10× speed drives, which read data at 900, 1200, and 1500 KB per second, respectively.

DVD

As this book goes to press, a new CD-ROM format called DVD (Digital Versatile Disc) is emerging. The DVD can hold seven times more than a conventional CD— 4.7 GB (gigabytes) per layer, as compared to 680 MB for CD. Dual-layer DVDs will be able to hold 8.5 GB on a single side, with 17 GB on a double-sided, dual-layer disc. DVD has the same diameter (120mm) and thickness (1.2mm) as compact disc. The new DVD drives can play the billions of existing music CDs. For more information, including beautiful diagrams that show how DVDs are produced, see http://www.sel.sony.com/SEL/consumer/dvd.

Digital Audio

By definition, MPCs have the ability to record and play back waveform digital audio files. If your system does not have waveform audio, it is not a multimedia computer.

The original MPC standard called for 8-bit sound, which produces a dynamic range of 50dB (decibels). The MPC2 and MPC3 standards use 16-bit sound, which increases the dynamic range to 98dB. The greater the dynamic range, the more faithful the sound reproduction. Any new system you buy should have 16-bit waveform audio. Figure 11-3 shows the Sound Blaster 16-bit audio board used by the author; it is manufactured by Creative Labs.

Audio Speakers

You will need a pair of audio speakers to listen to the sound produced by your multimedia PC. If you get powered speakers with amplifiers built in, you will not need a separate amplifier. Otherwise, you will need an amplifier as well. If your home stereo system amplifier has auxiliary line inputs, you may be able to plug your MPC into them, depending on competition for use of the stereo by other family members.

The author uses the pair of Yamaha MS202 powered speakers shown in Figure 11-4. They sound so good you would swear they were two or three times larger than they really are.

Video Overlay

A video overlay card allows a computer to display common video sources including video cameras, VCRs, and videodiscs while simultaneously displaying computer graphics. The overlay card makes one of

11-3

The Sound Blaster 16-bit waveform audio board.

11-4

Yamaha MS202 powered speakers provide excellent sound reinforcement for a multimedia computer.

the colors in the computer graphics transparent; when that color appears on the screen with the video overlay card activated, the video source shows through.

You must exercise caution when purchasing a video overlay card. There are a lot of competing brands, and they do not all provide the features you may need. You should consider the following features when making a purchase.

MULTIPLE INPUTS

Many cards let you connect only a single video source at a time; if you need to switch among multiple devices, such as a camera, a VCR, and a TV tuner, you will need an overlay card with multiple inputs.

FRAME GRAB

Some cards cannot grab still images and save them as bitmaps; this is a nice feature to have when you are creating a multimedia application.

TV TUNER

Some cards have a TV tuner on board. If you know in advance that you want a TV tuner in your computer, getting it on your video overlay card can save you the slot you will use if you add the tuner later.

VIDEO FOR WINDOWS

Overlay cards do not necessarily enable you to record full-motion video; if you want to make Video for Windows recordings, you need an overlay card that can capture moving video.

MEMORY CONFLICTS

Some overlay cards will not work if a computer has more than 14 MB of RAM. Check this out before you buy.

VIDEO ADAPTER COMPATIBILITY

Some overlay cards may not be compatible with a computer's video adapter, especially if you have one of the latest adapters.

Figure 11-5 shows the WinTV video overlay card used by the author. Manufactured by Hauppauge Computer Works, it has three video inputs and functions as both an overlay card and a digital video recorder. Even though the name of this card is

11-5

The Hauppauge WinTV
video overlay card.

WinTV, the TV tuner is an option that you must specify when you order the card if you want it to have a TV tuner as well. For more information visit http://www.hauppauge.com/hcw/index.htm.

Digital Video

When you purchase a digital video card to make Video for Windows recordings, make sure you get one that comes with a Microsoft MCI overlay driver. Then you can use the card to make Video for Windows recordings and also take advantage of the video overlay features just discussed. Be aware that not all digital video cards provide support for MCI video overlay.

TV Tuner

TV tuner cards give a multimedia computer the ability to tune into both broadcast and cable television channels. Some have video overlay capability on board, whereas others require that you have a video overlay card to which you can connect the video output of your tuner card. If you know in advance that you will want a TV tuner, purchase an overlay card that has a TV tuner built in. The author recommends the Hauppauge WinTV card pictured in Figure 11-5.

MIDI

MIDI stands for Musical Instrument Digital Interface. Because MIDI is a required part of the MPC specification, you do not have a multimedia computer if you do not have MIDI. However, the kind of MIDI required by the MPC is not what musicians would refer to as the "real" MIDI. MIDI was invented to provide a means for music keyboards, synthesizers, and computers to communicate with each other. The "real" MIDI has MIDI IN, OUT, and THRU jacks that let you connect music keyboards, drum machines, and other MIDI devices to your computer. The MPC standard does not require that your computer have MIDI jacks into which you can plug a music keyboard or drum machine. Instead, it requires a driver that plays MIDI sequences through your computer's waveform audio board. Musicians criticize this because it almost always sounds worse than it would if you had an external MIDI device attached.

If you are serious about MIDI, and your computer has a Sound Blaster or compatible waveform audio board, get the MIDI Kit from Midisoft. The MIDI Kit comes with a MIDI adapter cable that plugs into the Sound Blaster's game port. The adapter cable has MIDI IN, MIDI OUT, and joystick connections. The MIDI Kit also includes Recording Session Plus software for recording and arranging MIDI sound tracks, and recording and integrating waveform audio files with MIDI recordings. For more information go to http://www.midisoft.com.

If you have a laptop computer with PC Card slots, you may be interested in the PC Card version of the Roland Sound Canvas. Roland is on the Web at http://www.rolandus.com.

Make sure any MIDI synthesizer or keyboard you purchase follows the General MIDI specification, which standardizes the set of instrumental sounds MIDI devices produce.

Videodisc

Because it requires the installation of a Windows MCI driver and a serial connection to the computer in addition to video and audio cabling, videodisc is always a challenge to install and get working. When you buy a videodisc player, make sure it has a serial port that can be connected to your computer, and make sure there is a Windows MCI driver for it. Some players have a longer seek time than others; the longer the seek time, the longer you will wait to see the video when your application tells it to play. Select a player with a seek time no greater than two seconds, or one second if you can afford the additional expense of the faster player.

As noted earlier, most videodisc players cannot show still frames from CLV videodiscs. If you need that capability, you must purchase a high-end player that can. As this book goes to press, the only player able to still-frame CLV discs is the Pioneer LD-V 8000.

Most videodiscs are pressed in the NTSC video format used in the U.S. and Japan. Users from countries that follow the PAL video format will probably want to purchase videodisc players that can play both NTSC- and PAL-formatted videodiscs. The author sympathizes with people who have to deal with this problem in standards, especially since the NTSC video standard is inferior to PAL.

MPEG

MPEG is the full-screen, full-motion digital video format invented by the Motion Pictures Experts Group. High-end multimedia PCs with Pentium processors faster than 100 MHz are shipping with drivers that can play MPEG without any special hardware; lesser machines require an MPEG board, such as the REALmagic, to play MPEG well.

Recording MPEG requires special hardware. Due to the highly compressed nature of MPEG, a lot of computation is involved in capturing video and compressing it into an MPEG file. The REALmagic Producer is a 32-bit PCI-bus board that captures video and audio in real time, encodes it in AVI-editable MPEG, then transcodes finished work at three times real time into MPEG 1, which is the noninterlaced version of MPEG designed for playback from CD-ROMs. The board comes bundled with Adobe Premier for editing, Caligari Truespace for 3-D graphics, plus a real-time on-screen previewer and a software VCR controller. Call Sigma Designs at (800) 845-8086 for a free information package. Information about the MPEGator capture board is found on the Web at http://darvision.kaist.ac.kr, and the Broadway MPEG board is featured at http://www.b-way.com.

MPEG 2 chipsets are being developed and will probably be on the market by the time you read this. MPEG 2 is the interlaced version of MPEG intended for the all-digital transmission of broadcast-quality TV. With Dolby surround sound and variable bit rates ranging from 3 to 10 megabits per second, MPEG 2 has been adopted by the United States Grand Alliance HDTV (high-definition television) specification, the European Digital Video Broadcasting Group, and a consortium of computer and video companies planning to distribute videos on the new Digital Versatile Disc (DVD). For more information on MPEG, go to http://www.mpeg.org, where you will find the MPEG FAQ as well as many other MPEG resources.

MULTIMEDIA READ/WRITE STORAGE

Multimedia requires a lot of storage if you are into digital audio and video. The storage alternatives are discussed here.

Hard Disk Drive

When you purchase a multimedia computer, you should get as much hard disk built into it as you can afford. No matter how much capacity you get, you will eventually run out as your library of multimedia software grows. The 30 MB hard disk–size requirement in the original MPC standard would not even get you started today. Even the 540 MB requirement of the MPC3 is minimal. Hard disk drive capacities of 1.2 GB and higher begin to look credible for serious users of multimedia. *Note:* 1.2 GB are equivalent to 1200 MB.

SCSI

SCSI (pronounced "skuzzy") stands for Small Computer System Interface. It lets you daisychain up to eight mass storage devices. Although many CD-ROM drives use SCSI, most MPCs do not provide an external SCSI connector to which you can attach additional SCSI devices. If your computer does not come with a SCSI connector, you will probably need to devote a slot to installing a SCSI board. A wide range of SCSI devices is available, including internal and external hard drives, CD-ROM drives, and read/write optical drives.

Iomega Zip Disk and Jaz Disk

Iomega's Zip disk is an attractive storage medium for multimedia developers because the disks are removable. The Zip disk drive comes in a SCSI version or a parallel port version; if you want to be able to move your Zip disk drive easily from one computer to another, the author recommends the parallel port version, although the SCSI runs faster and may be preferred if your computer has SCSI. As illustrated in Figure 11-6, it takes 70 diskettes to hold as much data as one 100 MB Zip disk.

11-6

It takes 70 high-density diskettes to equal the storage capacity of one 3.5-inch Zip disk.

Iomega also manufactures a Jaz drive, which costs about twice as much as a Zip drive but holds up to 10 times more data. Jaz disks come in 540 MB and 1 GB (1,070 MB) formatted capacity. The Jaz drive is a SCSI device. For the latest info, visit http://www.iomega.com.

NOTE Do not confuse the name *Zip disk* with the PKWARE compression utility's ZIP file format. These are totally different uses of the word *zip*.

Recordable CD-ROM

Recordable CD-ROM is called **CD-R**; the *R* stands for recordable, indicating that you can record on the CD. Each CD-ROM can store about 650 MB.

If you purchase a CD-R drive, you should also purchase a gigabyte hard disk to hold the data that will be recorded onto the CD. You may also need a SCSI board for the extra disk drive; check with a knowledgeable vendor for advice. The Iomega Jaz drive is an attractive option because the storage medium is removable, permitting you to work on multiple CD-ROM titles in the same physical drive.

PCMCIA and PC Cards

PCMCIA stands for Personal Computer Memory Card International Association, the name of a standards group that creates specifications for credit card–sized peripherals for personal computers. The group got its name because the first PCMCIA cards were for memory, but PCMCIA is now branching out into modems, network cards, and multimedia cards. For example, Roland manufactures a PCMCIA version of its Sound Canvas MIDI board. To reflect the more general nature of these cards, the industry now calls them PC Cards instead of PCMCIA cards. For more information visit the PCMCIA Web site at http://www.pc-card.com.

LCD PANELS AND PROJECTORS

LCD panels and projectors connect to the VGA video output of a multimedia computer to project the computer display onto a large viewing surface. LCD panels require an overhead projector to provide the light source, whereas LCD projectors have the light source built in. LCD projectors work better than LCD panels, which almost always let unwanted light leak between the panel and the overhead.

Table 11-1 contains LCD evaluation guidelines developed by Connolly (1995) in his comprehensive review of presentation systems for the electronic classroom. The best place to see all the different LCD panels and projectors in action is at the annual Infocomm conference, which has a projection shoot-out in which all the vendors line their projectors up around a huge auditorium where you can walk around and compare how well the different projectors display the same video signal. For more information about Infocomm, go to http://www.usa.net/icia.

Table 11-1 Bruce Connolly's LCD Evaluation Criteria

Performance	Ease of Setup and Use	Portability	Cost
Screen technology ■ Active matrix ■ Passive matrix	Convenience—projectors versus panels	Weight Carrying Case	
Display quality ■ Brightness ■ Detail ■ Contrast	All necessary cables and components included Remote control	**Compatibility**	**Other Considerations**
Image integrity	Controls ■ Logical ■ Legible ■ Self-adjusting	With computer platforms With video standards	Heat dissipation Fan noise
Color reproduction ■ Number of colors ■ Accuracy	Documentation	**Reliability**	Add-ons (i.e., infrared remote, annotation capabilities, etc.)
Audio output capabilities	Bundled presentation software	Overall construction quality Technical support Warranty	

Source: Connolly (1995: 30). Reprinted by permission.

The Beacon Research Group publishes an LCD projection system buyer's guide entitled *Business Consumer Guide,* which compares and prices more than 75 LCD panels and projectors. For more information about the report, which costs $25, call (800) 938-0088.

COMMUNICATION OPTIONS

The datacommunication protocol used on the Internet is called **TCP/IP**, which stands for Transmission Control Protocol/Internet Protocol. Several vendors sell TCP/IP drivers, which add to an MPC's system software a *winsock.dll* file and related network software. The *winsock.dll* allows applications like PODIUM and Netscape to open a socket on the Information Superhighway and let you communicate through it. *Winsock* stands for Windows socket, and *dll* stands for dynamic link library, the expandable software technology that enables vendors to add features easily to a Windows environment. Windows 95 ships with and installs automatically winsock software for virtually any modem or network card on the market today.

Modems

The least expensive way to connect to the Internet is by way of a modem, which communicates over an ordinary telephone line. Modems are either internal or external. Internal modems often take up a slot, whereas external modems connect to the computer's serial port. If you plan to have more than one serial device in use at a time, such as a modem and a videodisc player, you will need a computer with two serial ports.

The faster the modem, the less time it will take to download files to the computer. If long-distance telephone charges are involved, higher-speed modems can save cost as well as time. Modem speeds are measured as a **baud rate**, which tells how many bits per second (bps) can be transmitted. Modems slower than 9600 baud are hardly useful anymore, and modems with speeds as high as 33,600 baud are becoming common.

The best way to connect a modem to the Internet is to use the point-to-point protocol (PPP), which establishes a TCP/IP connection to the Internet. PPP comes built into Windows 95. Windows 3.1 users can get PPP from a variety of sources. For example, PPP comes bundled with Netscape Navigator Personal Edition, which you can buy at computer stores.

When a computer connects to the Internet via PPP, the modem dials up to a port at the local Internet service provider (ISP) network. You must be a registered user of this network before you can connect to it via PPP. If you do not know what ISPs are active in your area, ask a friend who is online, or inquire at your local computer store. There is a list of ISPs by area code on the Web at http://thelist.com.

The following checklist summarizes what you need to establish an Internet connection via modem:

- Internal or external modem installed on your PC
- Telephone line
- PPP software installed on your PC
- PPP account at your local Internet service provider
- Internet browser software, such as Netscape Navigator or Microsoft Internet Explorer

Network Cards

Network cards provide faster ways to access the Internet. If your school or workplace has high-speed Internet cabling, you should consider getting a network card so you can connect to the Internet at high speed.

The most popular network topologies are Ethernet and token ring. Ethernet cards provide access at speeds up to 10 MB per second, depending on how many users are connected to the network. Token ring networks are less prone to slow down as the number of users increases; token ring networks run at 4 MB or 16 MB per second. The faster the connection, the higher the cost. If you plan to purchase a network card, make sure it is compatible with the topology and speed of the network to which you connect.

The following checklist summarizes what you need to establish an Internet connection through a network card:

- Network card installed on your PC
- Local-area network (LAN) or broadband wiring to the Internet
- TCP/IP network connection
- *winsock.dll* installed under Windows
- Internet browser software, such as Netscape Navigator or Microsoft Internet Explorer

Your local network administrator can recommend specific brands of network cards that will work best in your environment.

AUXILIARY INPUT

The auxiliary input devices described here provide convenient ways to digitize preexisting texts and pictures for use with a multimedia computer. The program that converts scanned text into machine-readable characters is known as optical character recognition (OCR) software. OCR software does not necessarily ship with scanners, so if you plan to scan printed text into machine-readable form, make sure you have the necessary OCR software. The best OCR software is industry leader Caere Corporation's OmniPage. For the latest information visit http://www.caere.com.

Handheld Scanners

Handheld scanners have fallen in cost while increasing in reliability. The author used a handheld scanner extensively to scan the quotations that appear in this book. If you are an educator, be sure to ask the vendor if there is an educational discount; most scanner manufacturers have special discounts for educators.

Although personal opinions vary, the author does not believe you need a color handheld scanner. To scan text, all you need is a monochrome scanner, which will cost less than a color scanner. For scanning pictures, color handheld scanners cost as much as camcorders; if you have a video overlay card capable of grabbing frames into bitmaps, you are much better off using a camera to grab the frame instead of hand-scanning it; the hand-scanning software takes much longer to render the image than the frame grab.

For information on the ScanMan family of handheld scanners, visit http://www.logitech.com.

Flatbed Scanners

Flatbed scanners do a nice job of scanning both text and graphics, and the price of color flatbed scanners has fallen steadily. If your budget permits, a flatbed scanner is a good addition for producing multimedia text and image objects. Industry leader Hewlett-Packard's Web site is http://www.hp.com.

Page-Fed Scanners

Page-fed scanners cost less and work as well as flatbed scanners, with the obvious constraint that you can feed only single pages into a page-fed scanner. On flatbed scanners, you can lay an open book down and scan the page without having to make a copy of it first to feed into a page-fed scanner. Compaq sells a computer keyboard called the Scanner Keyboard that has a page-fed scanner built in.

Slide Scanners

Slide scanners have a slot into which you insert a 35mm slide; their purpose is to scan the slide and produce a bitmap image of it. However, the term *slide scanner* gets used loosely. Some slide scanners do the complete job of scanning the slide and producing the bitmap, whereas others merely output a video signal that you still need to digitize.

If you have a video overlay card that can grab frames into bitmaps, the most cost-effective way to scan slides is to purchase the RasterOps Expresso slide scanner. It is the type of "scanner" that produces a video image you still need to digitize. But if you have a video overlay card, you can plug the video output of the Expresso into your overlay card and grab the resulting video frame into a bitmap. Figure 11-7 shows the Expresso in use. For more information go to http://www.rasterops.com. A similar device called the Fotovix comes in both analog and digital versions. The digital version connects to the computer's SCSI port and does not require a video overlay card. For more information go to http://www.tamron.com/fvspcc/prodfv.html.

11-7

The RasterOps Expresso being used to digitize a slide.

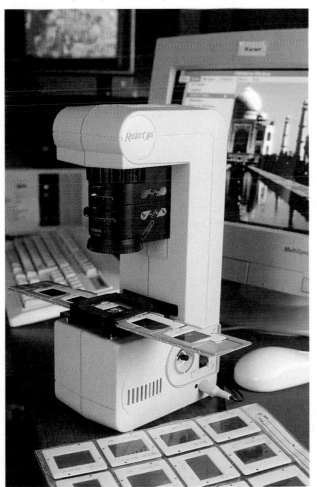

Digital Cameras

Like slide scanners, the term *digital camera* also gets used loosely. A "real" **digital camera** snaps pictures by producing a bitmap that you can read directly into your application, but some so-called digital cameras merely output a video still frame that you then have to digitize with a video capture board. If the camera is not really digital, you are better off buying a Hi8 camcorder. The Hi8 camcorder will cost about the same or less than the so-called digital camera, but you can also shoot full-motion video and use the camcorder with a motion capture board.

Apple's QuickTake 100 is a "real" digital camera that can snap 32 standard-resolution (320×240) or eight high-resolution (640×480) images, which it stores on a megabyte memory chip. To download the images, you connect the camera to your Macintosh or IBM-compatible serial port. Windows file formats that the camera supports include TIFF, BMP, PCX, and JPEG. For more information go to http://www.apple.com.

Kodak's DC40 is another "real" digital camera that comes equipped with auto focus and flash and offers the versatility of normal, macro, wide-angle, and telephoto accessory lenses. The DC40's 4 MB internal memory can store 48 high-resolution (504×756) or 99 snapshot-resolution images. The DC40 is one of the Kodak Digital Science tools that you can learn more about by visiting http://www.kodak.com and doing a search for DC40.

The aspect ratio of the pictures taken by the Kodak DC40 (504 × 756) is not optimal for producing full-screen photos for a 640 × 480 computer screen. In addition to Apple's QuickTake 100, other cameras that snap pictures at 640 × 480 include Epson's PhotoPC, Dycam's 10-C, and the Ritz Dakota DCC 9500. For a more extensive list of digital cameras, go to http://i-shop.iworld.com/1Digital_cameras.html.

Snappy

Snappy Video Snapshot is an image capture module that connects to the printer port on the back of a desktop or laptop PC. Snappy can capture still images from any video source, such as a camcorder, at resolutions up to 1500 × 1125 pixels with 16 million colors. There is a Snappy demo on the *Multiliteracy CD*. To run the demo, go to the Demonstrations section, select Software, and click the Snappy button. For more information see the Snappy Web site at http://www.play.com.

VideoFlex Gooseneck Camera

If you want a high-quality video camera to use conveniently on your desktop for focusing in on small objects you want to digitize, or for use in videoconferencing, Ken-A-Vision's VideoFlex is great. Mounted on a flexible 25-inch gooseneck arm, the VideoFlex camera can be moved to within ¼ inch of an object for maximum magnification, or it can zoom out and take wide-angle shots. For more information call Ken-A-Vision at (816) 353-4787.

PRINTERS

No list of computer accessories would be complete without mentioning printers. Because color is important in multimedia applications, you would ideally like to have a color printer. Happily, the cost of color printers has been declining steadily. If you do not have a color printer, the Windows device drivers automatically convert color bitmaps to grayscale images that look surprisingly good when printed on a monochrome printer.

The quality of output is largely determined by how many dots per inch (dpi) the printer can produce. Printers that print at 300 dpi produce acceptable graphics, but 600 dpi looks a lot better. This book was produced on a printer with 2,400 dpi.

Laser printers produce the best and fastest prints, but they also cost the most. Inkjet printers are an alternative that costs less yet looks almost as good so long as you don't smear the ink before it dries. Some inks run when you get them wet, which is another reason why laser printers are preferred over inkjets.

E X E R C I S E S

1. Define the following terms and explain the role they play in a multimedia computer:
   - Central processor
   - RAM
   - Hard disk
   - Modem

2. Run through the multimedia components discussed in this chapter and make a list of which ones your computer has, which ones it does not have, and, of the latter, which ones you would like it to have.

3. Have you ever used a trackball? If not, go to your local video arcade and play a game that uses one. What advantages does the trackball have over a mouse? What are the disadvantages? Which do you prefer?

4. Does your multimedia PC have MIDI connections (MIDI IN and MIDI OUT), or does it merely do an internal software emulation of MIDI? Have you ever used an application that would have benefitted from MIDI IN or MIDI OUT connections? If so, name the application and describe how MIDI connections would have helped.

5. Do you believe PC Cards will become important in multimedia? Why or why not? Does your computer have PC Card slots?

12 Multimedia Computer Buyer's Checklists

After completing this chapter, you will be able to:

☐ **Use multimedia computer buyer's checklists that clarify what you need to buy and why**

☐ **Assess the multimedia PC you are using now and decide what upgrade(s) it needs next**

☐ **Realize how rapidly prices are falling and how to get the best buys**

THIS chapter contains three checklists. The first one lists the equipment in an affordable, low-budget system that will get you started without a large cash outlay. The second checklist describes a midrange system that is the most strategic buy if you can afford it. The third list is for a multimedia dream machine with all the bells and whistles. Though few readers will ever buy all the components that this chaper enumerates, a checklist is useful because it shows you all the options and lets you consider which items you really need.

The annual *NewMedia Magazine Multimedia Buyers Guide* is very helpful when it actually comes time for you to buy multimedia equipment. Chapter 17 tells you how to apply for a free subscription to *NewMedia*. You can find good comparitive-shopping advice online at *NewMedia*'s Web site at http://www.hyperstand.com.

LOW-BUDGET SYSTEM

System Unit

☐ Pentium 100 MHz central processor

☐ 8 MB RAM

☐ SVGA color display with 16-bit graphics (65,000 colors)

☐ Mouse or other pointing device

Multimedia Accessories

~

10.00

☐ CD-ROM double speed

☐ 16-bit waveform digital audio

☐ Audio speakers (self-powered or with external amp)

Multimedia Read/Write Storage

☐ 1.2 GB hard disk ⌐

Communication Options

☐ 14,400 baud modem with —20.00— 14.4 *Internal*

☐ *winsock.dll* installed under Windows—

Printer

☐ Inkjet printer —98.00 — *color Bubble jet (new)*

MIDRANGE SYSTEM

2175.00 200

860
644
0266

System Unit

☐ High-speed Pentium processor

☐ 16 MB RAM

☐ SVGA color display with 24-bit graphics (16 million colors)

☐ Mouse or other pointing device

Multimedia Accessories

10 B

$35

☐ CD-ROM quad speed

☐ 16-bit waveform digital audio

☐ Audio speakers (self-powered or with external amp)

☐ Video overlay with:

    ☐ Multiple inputs

    ☐ Frame capture

    ☐ Video for Windows capture

☐ Videodisc with two-second maximum seek time

$10-15
$<100

Multimedia Read/Write Storage

☐ 2 GB hard disk

☐ Zip disk (parallel port version)

Communication Options

- [ ] *winsock.dll* installed under Windows with:
- [ ] 28,800 baud modem

  or

- [ ] Network card (ISDN, Ethernet, or token ring) and
- [ ] TCP/IP network connection

Auxiliary Input

- [ ] Handheld scanner
- [ ] Hi8 camcorder

Printer

- [ ] 300 dpi laser printer

HIGH-END SYSTEM

System Unit

~ $275

- [ ] Pentium Pro (P6) central processor
- [ ] 32 MB RAM
- [ ] SVGA color display with 24-bit graphics (16 million colors)
- [ ] Mouse or other pointing device

Multimedia Accessories

$275 —
$35 —
~$40 —

- [ ] DVD-ROM drive
- [ ] 16-bit waveform digital audio
- [ ] Audio speakers (self-powered or with external amp)
- [ ] Video overlay with:
  - [ ] Multiple inputs
  - [ ] Frame capture

$125

  - [ ] TV tuner
  - [ ] Video for Windows capture
- [ ] MIDI IN and MIDI OUT

$99 —
$1000

- [ ] MIDI keyboard
- [ ] General MIDI external synthesizer
- [ ] Videodisc, high-end with CLV still framing
- [ ] MPEG capture board

Multimedia Read/Write Storage

☐ 3 GB hard disk

☐ External SCSI connector

☐ Jaz disk

☐ CD-ROM recordable (CD-R) drive

Drive
3-4 $
disks ~
100.00

Communication Options

☐ *winsock.dll* installed under Windows with:

☐ 33,600 baud modem

or

$50 -

☐ Network card (ISDN, Ethernet, or token ring) and

☐ TCP/IP network connection

Auxiliary Input

☐ Handheld scanner

☐ Flatbed scanner

☐ Slide scanner

100. $

☐ Digital camera

☐ Hi8 camcorder *6 - 700 $*

Printer

$ ~300

☐ 600 dpi color laser printer

HOW TO GET THE BEST BUY

Anyone purchasing a Multimedia PC should realize how fast costs are declining and where to get the best buy. The popularity of multimedia titles has made the MPC a mass market consumer item. Major retailers such as CompUSA, Computer City, Best Buy, Staples, Sears, and Circuit City sell multimedia computers in a broad range of prices.

When you purchase a Multimedia PC, use the checklists in this chapter to help decide what features you want, then visit the retailers and find the best buy you can on the MPC that comes closest to having these features. Make sure it is possible to buy and install any peripherals you may want in addition to those that come with the machine. For example, if you want more RAM than what comes with the machine, make sure the extra RAM is available at a reasonable price, and find out how difficult it will be to install. Check the number of slots and make sure there are empty slots of the type you need for installing extra hardware such as a SCSI board.

E X E R C I S E S

1. Which one of the three checklists provided in this chapter most closely matches your multimedia PC? What features does your MPC have in addition to those listed? What features does it lack?

2. Do you think any of the items listed in the high-end checklist are not needed in a multimedia computer? If so, list the items and explain why they are unnecessary.

3. Take the three checklists to your local computer store and price the equipment. Create an itemized list that shows what each component costs, and compute the total cost of each system.

4. Does your local computer store sell any multimedia peripherals not listed in the high-end checklist? If so, what are they? Do you feel they should be added to the checklist? Why or why not?

13

Configuring a Multimedia Computer

After completing this chapter, you will be able to:

- Connect the audio and video components of a multimedia computer in order to optimize functionality and minimize wiring difficulty

- Use the multimedia hardware preferences of the author as a benchmark against which to compare and contrast other choices

- Save slots by combining multiple features on a single circuit board

- Use a low-cost audio/video switch that can increase the number of devices connected to your computer

 **HEN** the author makes multimedia presentations around the world, his hosts often express amazement at the simplicity of the setup requirements. People expect that it will be complicated to connect all of the video and audio sources to a video projector and sound system, but it is actually quite simple. A clever configuration of multimedia features mixes and switches all of the video and audio sources inside the computer and limits the number of wires emerging from the computer to three: one for SVGA video, and one pair for stereo audio. This chapter shares with you the design that makes this possible.

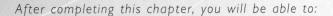

FEATURE CARDS

The author's multimedia computer has a built-in quad-speed CD-ROM drive and the following circuit cards:

- Creative Labs Sound Blaster 16 ASP digital audio board with Musical Instrument Digital Interface (MIDI)

- Hauppauge WinTV video overlay and capture card with TV tuner option

- 3Com EtherLink III network board for connecting to the Internet at high speed

Sometimes multimedia computers contain a separate MIDI board that occupies an additional slot; the author saves a slot by getting the MIDI option on the Sound Blaster card. Similarly, some computers contain a separate TV tuner board; again, the author saves a slot by getting the TV option on his video overlay card.

AUDIO CONNECTIONS

Figure 13-1 shows how some users run their audio outputs into an external mixer, which is in turn connected to loudspeakers. Although this configuration is very straightforward and easy to set up, it has three disadvantages. First, you lose the capability of the computer to switch audio sources on and off. For example, when your multimedia software turns off the sound to a TV channel, you will keep hearing the sound because you wired the audio directly to the mixer. Second,

13-1

Using an external mixer for multimedia sound connections.

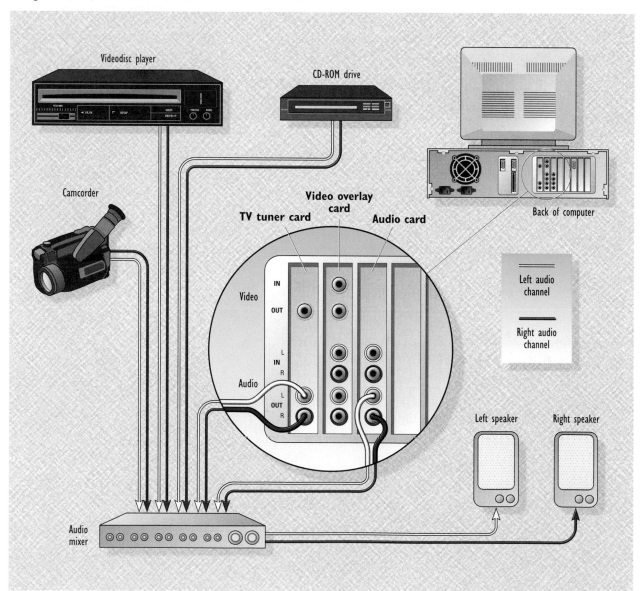

external mixers inevitably introduce noise into the signal, some more than others. Third, it costs more to wire a multimedia computer this way, because you have to buy an external mixer you do not need. Why spend the extra money?

Audio Wiring

Figure 13-2 shows you how to wire your multimedia PC so the audio mixing is done internally. There are four sets of connections in this diagram:

1. Connect the audio outputs of the peripherals (videodisc, camcorder, and TV tuner) to the audio inputs of the video overlay card. Always connect the videodisc to the first set of inputs on the overlay card. Put the camcorder on the second set, and the TV tuner on the third. *Note:* Overlay cards that come with a TV tuner on board already have this third connection made internally.

13-2

Internal audio mixing.

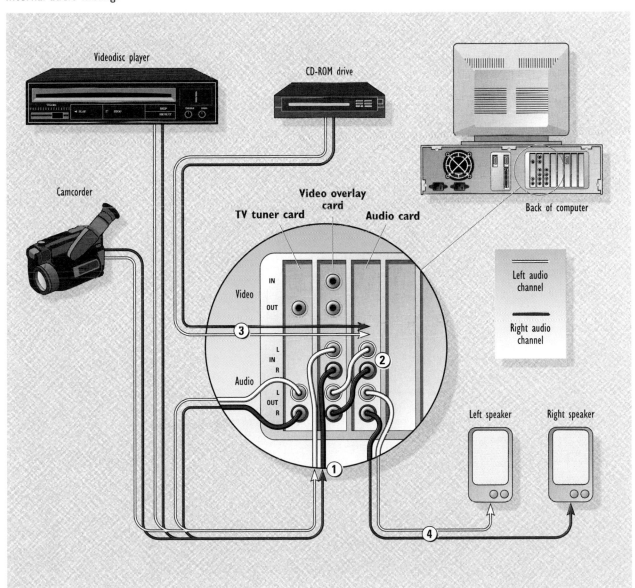

2. Connect the left and right audio outputs of the overlay card to the external input of the waveform audio board.

3. Connect the audio output of the CD-ROM drive to the *internal* input of the waveform audio board. If your computer came with a CD-ROM drive installed, this connection was probably already made. If you try to make this connection yourself, you will need to open up the computer. Make sure your computer and all devices attached to it are *disconnected* from any power sources, and read the sound card and CD-ROM manuals carefully to make sure you connect it right.

4. Connect the stereo output of the waveform audio board to the left and right line inputs of an audio amplifier and speaker system, or to powered speakers that have an audio amplifier built in; Yamaha's MS202 powered speakers do a very nice job at an affordable price.

Audio Mixing

Now you may ask: Since you have eliminated the external mixer, how can you adjust and balance the volume levels of the audio sources? Through software! Figures 13-3 and 13-4 show the mixer programs that come with the Sound Blaster and Turtle Beach audio boards, respectively. The mixer programs let you adjust the relative volumes of each audio input by clicking and dragging on-screen audio controls. The resulting sound is cleaner than when you use an external mixer, and since all of the sound is under the control of the Microsoft MCI, your multimedia software can turn the sound on and off as needed.

13-3

The Sound Blaster mixer screen.

13-4

The Turtle Beach mixer screen.

VIDEO CONNECTIONS

The video connections parallel the audio wiring you just completed. Figure 13-5 shows how you connect the video output from the videodisc player to the first video input of the video overlay card. Plug the video output of the camcorder into the second input, and connect the TV tuner to the third input. *Note:* Video overlay cards that have TV tuners on board already have this third connection made internally.

13-5

Connecting video sources.

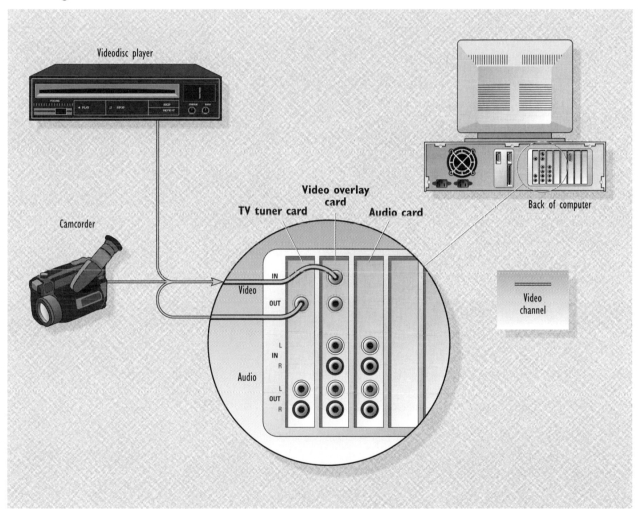

A Low-Cost Audio/Video Switch

Radio Shack makes a low-cost but highly useful switch that comes in handy in the following two situations. First, if your overlay card lacks multiple inputs, but you need to connect more than one video source to it; and, second, when your overlay card has multiple inputs, but you have a greater number of video sources to connect.

Figure 13-6 shows the Radio Shack switch, which costs less than $20. (Its catalog number is 15-1956.) You can connect up to four devices to it, including their video and stereo left and right audio outputs. Then you connect the video and stereo outputs of the switch to the corresponding inputs of your overlay card. To change sources, you simply press one of the four buttons on the switch.

13-6

Radio Shack's Stereo Audio/Video Selector Switch lets you connect up to four devices and select any one of them by simply pressing a button.

EXERCISES

1. Draw a wiring diagram that shows how the multimedia components in your computer are connected. Compare your diagram to the ones in this chapter. How are they alike? How do they differ?

2. Can you improve upon the suggestions made in this chapter? If so, how?

3. How does the mixing screen for your digital audio board compare to the ones illustrated in this chapter? Can you control the volume of your microphone input? Of your CD Audio playback? Of your external line input? Do you have separate left and right volume controls?

Part Four

Looking Into the Future of Multimedia

We must make sure the Information Superhighway is not a toll road for the rich.

— Linda Roberts, Clinton White House Education Adviser, STATE '94 conference

We shouldn't be looking for ways to subject new technologies to old rules.

— Reed Hundt, Federal Communications Commission Chairman,
INET '96 conference

Technology is one of the most difficult areas in which to make predictions, because new inventions occur at such a fast pace that the future changes before it gets here. How can the future change before it gets here? Big companies invest millions of dollars promoting new products, leading the consumer to believe that their products will be the mainstream of the future, but shortly after coming to market, the products get abandoned because the vendors pursue newer technologies that promise bigger profits. This has happened so often during the past decade that almost anyone involved with multimedia has been frustrated by purchasing so-called mainstream technologies that quickly go out-of-date and are abandoned by their manufacturers.

Knowledge is the best strategy for coping with fast-paced change. The more you know about the issues and technologies, the better prepared you will be to make strategic choices. Specifically, you can:

■ Identify the frontiers that multimedia researchers are investigating

■ Study technologies that are emerging

■ Identify societal issues raised by the manner in which multimedia technologies are used

■ Find out about and even contribute to new knowledge in this exciting field

The next four chapters consider these topics.

14

Multimedia Frontiers

After completing this chapter, you will be able to:

- **Understand how researchers invent new uses for multimedia and use multimedia to find new methods for solving problems**

- **Consider what kinds of books can be or should be replaced by CD-ROMs**

- **Know what is meant by the term *rural datafication***

- **Explore how virtual reality will improve the multimedia user interface**

- **Consider whether there are other frontiers of multimedia that ought to be explored**

- **Join and participate in the Electronic Frontier Foundation**

 MULTIMEDIA frontier is a field of technological research and development in which investigators invent new uses for multimedia or determine the extent to which multimedia can solve problems by finding better ways of doing old things. This chapter discusses how multimedia is being used to improve and transform publishing, provide better access to networked information, enhance rural communication, and simplify the user interface.

ELECTRONIC PUBLISHING

How much longer will books, magazines, and newspapers continue to be printed on paper? Anyone who has used hypertext knows how printed manuscripts pale by comparison. Printed manuscripts do not contain links that let you expand the text and navigate to related information; hot words that let you trigger explanatory sound tracks, videos, or animations; or full-text Boolean (AND, OR, NOT) searching that lets you locate quickly the material you need. Printed music does not let you scroll the score back and forth to locate and hear precisely the theme you want to study. Mathemathics and economics textbooks do not allow you to manipulate formulas and visualize your changes through dynamic real-time graphs.

The publishing industry knows this very well. Book publishers realize that their entire way of doing business is undergoing rapid and fundamental change, but they are not sure how it will emerge. Take this book for example. It includes a

14-1

The cover of the
EDUCORP catalog
of CD-ROM titles.

CD-ROM. How much of the text in this book would you have preferred to have on the CD-ROM instead?

Due to the prohibitive costs of producing and printing books, few authors could afford their own four-color separation equipment and printing presses. But what about electronic media? As Chapter 63 demonstrates, you can produce a CD-ROM for much less than a book, and you do not need a publisher to do so. For example, Coupland (1993) discusses eight independent multimedia developers who produced and published their own lucrative CDs. Figure 14-1 shows the kind of mass market retailing that has led to the runaway sales of CD-ROM titles.

THE INFORMATION SUPERHIGHWAY

In 1993 Vice President Al Gore issued a report entitled *The National Information Infrastructure: Agenda for Action.* The report describes how the private sector will build, operate, and maintain the Information Superhighway, while the government will develop policies to ensure that all Americans have access to it, encourage private sector investment in building the network, and create a competitive market for telecommunications and information services. The Electronic Frontier Foundation is concerned about how these policies will control what happens on the network. As Farber (1993) explains:

> In July 1990, the Electronic Frontier Foundation (EFF) was founded by John Perry Barlow and Mitch Kapor (who also founded Lotus Development Corporation) to help civilize the frontier more rapidly. It has the aim of trying to assure freedom of expression in digital media with emphasis on applying the principles embodied in the Constitution and the Bill of Rights to computer-based communication. From the beginning, EFF was determined to become an organization that would combine technical, legal, and public policy expertise. It would then apply these skills to the large number of complex issues and concerns that arise whenever a new communications medium is born. To paraphrase John Perry Barlow, it will take years to civilize the electronic frontier and bring law and order to it. And to quote Mitch Kapor, "There's a new world coming. Let's make sure it has rules we can live with."

You can participate by joining the EFF: Send e-mail to eff-request@eff.org containing the one-line message **Please add me to the mailing list.** Then add a line providing your real name, and one more line stating your e-mail address.

The National Information Infrastructure Advisory Council (NIIAC), which was created by executive order in 1993 by President Clinton, issued a final report in February 1996. *KickStart Initiative: Connecting America's Communities to the Information Superhighway* offers guidance, ideas, tools, and real-world examples of community-based efforts to bring the Information Superhighway to all individuals through schools, libraries, and community centers. The report is on the Web at http://www.benton.org/KickStart. For more information on the NIIAC, go to http://www.uark.edu/~niiac.

RURAL DATAFICATION

Rural America has traditionally lagged behind the rest of the country in gaining access to technological innovations. Telephones, radio, and television came first to big cities. To provide access to the rest of the country, the Department of Commerce made capital funding available through its Public Telecommunications Facilities Program for rural communities to install modern telecommunications equipment. These funds are still available and have recently been used to provide rural communities access to satellites.

Thanks to the efforts of Dr. Michael Staman and his associates, rural America will not experience delayed access to the Information Superhighway. As president of CICNet, a nonprofit regional computer network founded by the schools of the Big Ten, Dr. Staman has received funding from the National Science Foundation to extend Internet connectivity to typically underserved and underutilized communities. Staman refers to this process of extending the Information Superhighway to rural America as **rural datafication**. Rural datafication is a service mark of CICNet. For more information send e-mail to info@cic.net.

AeRie, the Applied Rural Telecommunications Online Clearinghouse, has a resource guide on the Web at http://www.yampa.com/aerie/resource/resource.html. The guide contains examples of how rural communities throughout the world are using telecommunications for economic development. AeRie's home page is at http://www.yampa.com/aerie.

VIRTUAL REALITY

As you are aware from using this book and its CD, multimedia computers can show any picture, play any sound, and link any word of any document or any part of any picture to any object on your computer. What's missing? A better human interface. We need better ways for users to communicate with multimedia computers. As you learned in Chapter 5, researchers in virtual reality have made this an important part of their business, and as new input and output devices get invented, multimedia computers will benefit.

For example, VRML (Virtual Reality Modeling Language) is an object-oriented language that lets you create navigable 3-D spaces for the Web. Figure 14-2 shows how Web page designers can add dimensions, texture, and "lighting" specifications to Web sites. The San Diego Supercomputer Center (SDSC) maintains the VRML Repository at http://www.sdsc.edu/vrml, where you will find more information

14-2

A VRML screen from Len Bullard's tribute to Kate Bush in VRML on the Web at http://fly.HiWAAY.net/ ~cbullard. A static picture does not do this justice; use a VRML-enabled browser to visit this site and use your mouse to explore this exciting 3-D world.

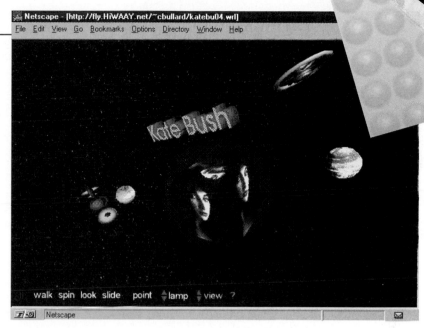

on VRML, viewers and authoring clients, mailing lists, newsgroups, documentation, and sample VRML worlds. The demos contain VRML examples in architecture, art, astronomy, biomedical sciences, chemistry, commercial applications, computer science, entertainment, environmental science, history, maps, mathematics, music, physics, and scientific visualization.

EXERCISES

1. Consider the text of this book and the CD-ROM that accompanies it. What is the role of the book, and what role does the CD play? If you could redesign either the book or the CD or both, how would you present the material they cover? Is either the book or the CD unnecessary?

2. Do you think CDs will ever replace books? Are some kinds of books more likely to be replaced by CDs than others? Give an example of a kind of book that should be replaced by CD and explain why. Then give an example of a book that should not be so replaced and explain why not.

3. To what extent has your local community become "datafied"? Are your schools connected to the Information Superhighway? Do teachers have access to it, or just the administrators? How about students? Is your local library connected? What about homes: Does a cable TV, telephone, or Internet company make Information Superhighway connections available to homes? If so, at what speeds? What online services are provided?

4. View the movie *Lawnmower Man*. Do you believe that multimedia PCs will ever enable users to experience VR immersion to the extent Jobe Smith (Jeff Fahey) did in the movie?

5. If you could invent anything you could think of, what kind of devices would you create for improving your computer's user interface? How would the devices help you communicate with your computer better than you can now? How would they make it easier to use? How would they make the simulated environments you experience seem more real? How would they get you more involved in the interaction?

15 Emerging Technology

After completing this chapter, you will be able to:

- Recognize emerging multimedia technologies

- Understand the role that MPEG, HDTV, and video dial tone technologies will play in the future of digital video

- Realize what ISDN is and how much of the United States has access to it

- Consider the challenge of pen computing and the promise of voice recognition

- Understand what knowbots can do for you on the Information Superhighway

- Recognize the extent to which multimedia is an emerging technology, and question whether multimedia is just a fad or an important life skill.

N E W technologies follow a cycle that includes invention, prototyping, proof of concept, productizing, and manufacture. Throughout this process the inventions are called **emerging technologies**. It often takes many years for an emerging technology to achieve widespread use in the marketplace.

An excellent example of an emerging technology in multimedia is the laser videodisc. Introduced by Pioneer in 1980, videodisc showed great promise. A laser beam would provide split-second access to movies with stereo sound tracks, and still frame capability would enable you to access any one of 54,000 slides within a second. RCA slowed things down somewhat by confusing and disillusioning the public enormously with a stylus-based system that played video off vinyl discs that worked like phonograph records. The stylus negated the random access and still frame capability of the laserdisc. RCA's product fizzled and disappeared from retail stores, while laserdisc emerged as a powerful way to deliver education and training in schools, business, and industry. There is a growing home market as well, witnessed by the large collection of laserdiscs for sale in Sam Goody stores. George Lucas's videodisc release of the *Star Wars* movies, complete with digital surround sound, has made videodisc players popular in home theater systems.

FAD OR FUTURE TREND?

This chapter discusses multimedia technologies that are in the process of emerging. Some of them could get cancelled prior to manufacture, and others may fail in the marketplace. Only technologies that succeed really belong here, because inventions that fail to emerge are by definition not emerging.

Digital Video

There is little doubt that digital video will emerge as the primary way in which movies will be recorded and transmitted in the twenty-first century. The question is, what standard will be followed? Doyle (1994) discusses 15 different algorithms that are in use today. None of them is ideal, and there is still room for someone to invent and patent a better digital video-recording algorithm and make a fortune from it.

As this book goes to press, MPEG appears to be the most likely standard to emerge. MPEG stands for Motion Pictures Experts Group, the name of the ISO standards committee that created it. Endorsed by more than 70 companies including IBM, Apple, JVC, Philips, Sony, and Matsushita, MPEG compresses video by using a discrete cosine transform algorithm to eliminate redundant data in blocks of pixels on the screen. MPEG compresses the video further by recording only changes from frame to frame; this is known as **delta-frame encoding**. MPEG is expected to become the digital video standard for compact discs, cable TV, direct satellite broadcast, and high-definition television (HDTV). Bell Atlantic is already using MPEG in its Stargazer service, and MPEG is the standard for RCA's DirecTV system, as advertised in Figure 15-1. For the DirecTV dealer nearest you, visit http://www.superstar.com/html/dssdlr.htm.

Four versions of MPEG have been worked on:

- **MPEG 1** is the noninterlaced version designed for playback from CD-ROMs.

- **MPEG 2** is the interlaced version intended for the all-digital transmission of broadcast-quality TV. Adopted by the United States Grand Alliance HDTV specification, the European Digital Video Broadcasting Group, and the Digital Versatile Disc (DVD-ROM) consortium, MPEG 2 does surround sound. RCA's DirecTV service uses MPEG 2.

- **MPEG 3** was to be the HDTV version of MPEG, but then it was discovered that the MPEG 2 syntax could fulfill that need by simply scaling the bit rate, obviating the third phase.

15-1

RCA's DirecTV uses MPEG to deliver more than 175 channels of digital TV programming over the nation's first high-power direct broadcast satellite (DBS) service using 18-inch satellite dishes. For more information go to http://www.directv.com.

■ **MPEG 4** is a low bit rate version of MPEG that is being invented for transmitting movies over mobile and wireless communications. For more information on MPEG, go to http://www.mpeg.org, where you will find the MPEG FAQ as well as many other MPEG resources.

HDTV

HDTV stands for high-definition television. It is being developed to replace NTSC as the television standard for the United States. HDTV is based on four technologies:

■ MPEG digital video compression

■ Transmission in packets that will permit any combination of video, audio, and data

■ Progressive scanning for computer interoperability up to 60 frames per second at 1920×1080 pixels

■ CD-quality digital surround sound using Dolby AC-3 audio technology

Even though the broadcast standard is still NTSC, television studios are already recording shows in HDTV so reruns can be broadcast in HDTV when the standard changes. Lucent Technologies is working with Mitsubishi to develop a chipset designed for high-definition television sets that will hit the market in 1998 (*Wall Street Journal* 6/26/96: B6).

ISDN

ISDN stands for Integrated Services Digital Network. It is a digital telephone system being installed by regional Bell companies in most of the United States; as this book goes to press, about 60% of the country can get ISDN. As Fox (1993) reports, "The first national ISDN call was made in November of 1992, connecting 22 sites nationwide, from Reston, Virginia to Los Angeles, California." ISDN services include voice conferencing, voice mail, caller ID, e-mail, fax, shared printers and databases, remote file access and data transfer, and videoconferencing.

ISDN signals are carried over two or more 64 Kbps (64,000 bits per second) circuit-switched channels to carry voice and data, and a lower-speed packet-switched channel that carries control signals. The Basic Rate Interface (BRI) service of ISDN is 144 Kbps, made up of two 64 Kbps data channels and one 16 Kbps control channel. This basic service can carry about 15 times as much information as conventional telephone lines. The Primary Rate Interface (PRI) service uses 23 data channels and a 64 Kbps control channel to boost the data rate to 1,544 Kbps. A second-generation standard, known as **broadband ISDN**, is under development; it uses fiber-optic cables and ATM (asynchronous transfer mode) technology to provide speeds of 155 Mbps and higher.

Video Dial Tones

In 1992 the Federal Communications Commission (FCC) legalized a new way of delivering TV signals. Called **video dial tone**, it allows TV signals to travel over telephone lines. This technology has spurred a furious round of mergers and alliances among phone companies, cable TV operators, and filmmakers wanting to capitalize on it. For example, Baby Bell company US West purchased 25% of

Time Warner (a major owner of cable TV systems around the country), Warner Brothers film studio, and HBO (a pay TV channel).

Many more channels will be available via video dial tone than over cable or broadcast TV. As Lerner (1993) explains, "With current analog technology, in which signals are sent as continuously varying waves, only about 50 channels can be provided. But by digitizing the signal and eliminating redundant bits, 500 channels are possible." Digital transmission also permits a return signal, creating the possibility of two-way interactive TV.

Rosenthal (1993) predicts that by 2008, "Personalized cable systems will offer virtual channels in which video servers furnish material to individual users on a personalized basis." Instead of needing to decide which one of 500 channels to watch, you will get only one channel, but since it will be personalized and interactive, it will always be showing what you want.

Cable Modems

For about $30 per month, cable modems can provide a 10-million bps Internet connection that delivers data hundreds of times faster than plain old telephone service (POTS). Major cable operators including TCI, Time Warner, and Comcast began renting cable modems to customers in 1996. Table 15-1 lists the Web addresses of companies that have cable modems on the market. As this book goes to press, only 10% of cable TV systems are capable of making full use of these modems.

Table 15-1 Cable Modem Companies

Product Name	Vendor Company	World Wide Web Address
Digital ChannelWorks	Digital Equipment Corporation	http://www.digital.com
Remote Link Adapter (RLA)	Hybrid Networks, Inc.	http://www.hybrid.com
CyberSURFER	Motorola	http://www.motorola.com
HomeWorks	Zenith	http://www.ftcnet.com/~dmh/zenith.htm

Set-Top Boxes for the Internet

Imagine watching TV, seeing something that interests you, and clicking to go instantly to the item's Web site. This is just one of the new services that **set-top boxes** will enable by connecting your television to the Internet. The Digital Audio-Visual Council (DAVIC) is developing set-top box standards. More than 200 companies belong to DAVIC, including all the major players in cable television, computing, telecommunications, and multimedia. The goal of DAVIC is to promote broadband digital services by ensuring compatibility and interoperability on a worldwide basis. For more information visit http://www.alpcom.it/davic.

Zenith Electronics is planning a television set that will incorporate a microprocessor and modem with technology that allows viewers to surf the Web via a remote control device (*Wall Street Journal* 5/10/96: B3). By the time you read this, the Zenith product will probably be on the market.

Intercasting in TV's Vertical-Blanking Interval

The vertical-blanking interval is the gap between the frames of a television picture. You see the vertical-blanking interval if your television is out of horizontal adjustment, causing the frames to scroll down the screen. Ever since the invention of television, the vertical-blanking interval has had the capability of carrying additional information, but no one has used it effectively. Until now. Intel has trademarked the term **Intercast**, which means to transmit Web pages and other digital information in the vertical-blanking interval. Partnering with Intel in the Intercast venture are NBC, CNN, Viacom, WGBH, QVC, Comcast, America Online, Asymetrix, En Technology, Netscape, Gateway, and Packard Bell. NBC did its first Intercast during the 1996 Summer Olympic Games, and CNN is doing news Intercasts. For more information go to http://www.intercast.org.

Holography

Most people think of holograms as 3-D photographs. But holograms can also store huge amounts of data. For example, IBM scientists predict that holographic technology will make it possible to store the entire *Encyclopedia Britannica* in a space the size and thickness of a penny. Holographic memory systems can stack data 40 layers deep, as opposed to computer disk and magnetic tape, which line up data on flat, single-layer tracks. The deeper layers can be read by tilting the angle of the laser beam that reads the data (*Investor's Business Daily* 1/20/94: 4).

Pen Computing

Pen computing is an emerging technology that Apple's handheld Newton computer brought to public attention. Referred to as a personal digital assistant (PDA), Newton was supposed to revolutionize business by providing a powerful communication device small enough to put in your pocket. As depicted in Figure 15-2, the need for a bulky keyboard was avoided through using a pen to input characters by writing on the screen.

15-2

The Newton MessagePad recognizes handwriting.

Consumers quickly found, however, that pen computing has a long way to go before it will work well enough for everyday use. Apple claimed that Newton was trainable, that it could learn to recognize your handwriting. But in practice, Newton trained the user, who ended up learning how to write in a format Newton could understand.

Lee and Francis (1994) report how Newton had such a negative impact on the market that "The market for all personal digital assistants (PDAs) has fallen to a level that equals slightly more than half the number of Newton MessagePads that Apple alone sold during a two-month period last year following the Newton's introduction." During those two months, Apple sold 50,000 Newtons.

Nevertheless, pen computing promises to be important as better handwriting recognition software emerges. Witness Microsoft's acquisition of Aha! Software Corporation, maker of pen-based programs and Inkwriter software, which lets users write, edit, and transmit notes in their own handwriting (*New York Times* 4/9/96: C2).

Voice Recognition

With pen computers crying out for a better handwriting algorithm, **voice recognition** is rapidly emerging in a variety of applications such as entertainment and games. For people who either cannot or do not like to type, voice recognition software provides an alternative to keyboarding in word processing programs, as shown in Figure 15-3. Apple's Speech Recognition Manager is a software development kit (SDK) that lets developers incorporate speech recongition into any Macintosh application. Among the first to take advantage of this new technology is Imergy's *Star Trek Omnipedia* CD-ROM, a voice-activated guide to a galaxy of *Star Trek* facts, characters, and movies. Imergy was amazed at how accurate the recognition is, even for phrases like "Denibian Slime Devil." Known as PlainTalk, Apple's Speech Recognition Manager enables the application developer to define how many words are active and to build custom vocabularies or language models. The PlainTalk SDK is available free of charge at http://www.speech.apple.com.

15-3

Voice recognition software enables the user to speak words into a word processor document.

For Windows users, Creative Labs produces a Sound Blaster add-on called Creative VoiceAssist, which you can train to recognize up to 1,024 voice commands. For more information, go to http://www.creaf.com and do a search for voice recognition. Of course, there is a world of difference between a system that can recognize only 1,024 words, and a continuous speech system such as Dragon Systems's DragonDictate for Windows, which can recognize up to 60,000 words. DragonDictate applications include legal dictation, environmental control systems, and word processing by persons with physical disabilities, such as repetitive stress injuries. DragonDictate consumes a lot of RAM—16 MB for the 60,000-word edition. For more information go to http://www.usbusiness.com/talk/dragon.htm.

Internet Phone Services

Anyone with an Internet connection, a full-duplex sound card, and a microphone can use one of the newly emerging Internet phone services. First to market were VocalTec's Internet Phone for Windows, and Electric Magic's NetPhone for Macs. The obvious advantage is cost savings on long-distance phone calls. For example, you can talk with someone overseas without having to pay for a long-distance call; the calling parties connect to their local networks, and the Internet makes the long-distance connection for free. There are several disadvantages, however. If your Internet connection is slow, delays can be significant, leading to jerky, stuttering conversations. This is a problem especially during times of high Internet traffic. If the person you are calling is not logged onto the Net with their phone software running, they cannot answer your call.

Not all sound cards have the full-duplex capability required for Internet phone services. For many years the Sound Blaster was available only in a half-duplex version. With a half-duplex sound card, only one party can talk at a time. Almost all Macintoshes produced since 1990 have full-duplex audio. For more information go to http://www.yahoo.com and search for Internet Voice.

Telecomputing

Withrow (1993) credits George Gilder with coining the phrase **telecomputer** to describe the merging of the telephone, television set, and computer into a single utility device. It will be interesting to watch as these technologies merge and the physical form of the telecomputer takes shape. What do you think it will look like? A black box? A TV? According to *Business Week*, AT&T is betting that the telephone will emerge as the gizmo of choice for accessing the Information Superhighway. AT&T's Project Sage is working on a phone that can be the central controller for routing information to and from household electronic gadgets such as TVs, VCRs, PCs, fax machines, and video cameras (*Business Week* 1/24/94: 37).

Wireless Communications

Wireless communication technologies are enabling users to access telecommunication systems from almost anywhere. No longer must your computer be tethered to the nearest telephone line.

Developing nations are using wireless technologies to avoid the high cost of wiring their countries physically. Cellular networks in Malaysia, Thailand, and the Philippines are expanding so fast that they may leapfrog traditional networks to become the most common form of telephone service. In South America, so many Venezuelans are carrying cellular phones that some restaurants require customers to check them at the door to control the noise level (*St. Petersburg Times* 5/16/94 Business: 2). In Brazil, cellular phones have become such a highway safety hazard that it is illegal to talk on a handheld cellular phone and drive at the same time (*Miami Herald* 5/18/94: C1).

Technology prophet George Gilder envisions wireless systems that will eventually offer worldwide bandwidth on demand, buffering and transmitting information whenever there is room (*Forbes ASAP* 4/11/94: 98). Microsoft chairman Bill Gates is teaming up with Craig McCaw of McCaw Cellular Communications to create such a network, a $9 billion wireless "global Internet." Known as Teledesic, it will use low earth-orbit satellites to provide wireless interactive voice, data, and video services. The system will have 840 refrigerator-sized satellites to connect handheld phones and other electronic devices to telephone networks all over the world (*Wall Street Journal* 3/21/94: A3).

Knowbots

Knowbots are software applications programmed to act as intelligent agents that go out on the network to find things for you. You tell a knowbot what you want, and it worms its way through the Internet, finding all the relevant information, digesting it, and reporting it to you succinctly.

Likening them to robotic librarians, Krol (1996: 418) refers to knowbots as "…software worms that crawl from source to source, looking for answers to your question. As a knowbot looks, it may discover more sources. If it does, it checks the new sources too. When it has exhausted all sources, it comes crawling home with whatever it found." Quarterdeck won Best of Show at COMDEX '95 for a knowbot called WebCompass. You can set WebCompass to go out on the Net automatically at regular intervals and bring back the information you need. For more information go to http://www.quarterdeck.com, where you can download the personal edition of WebCompass for free.

Multimedia

In what sense is multimedia itself an emerging technology? Will the craze fade or evolve into something else, like when the term *multimedia* was invented and people began using it to describe preexisting technology?

The author believes that the ability to use multimedia will emerge as a life skill in the twenty-first century. Citizens who do not know how to use multimedia will become disenfranchised. Cut off from the Information Superhighway, they will end up watching life go by instead of living it fully.

[handwritten top margin: yes, through DSS system]

EXERCISES

1. It seems like it is taking forever for HDTV to come on the market. Did you know about HDTV before you read this book? If so, how did you first find out about it? Have you ever seen an HDTV demonstration? If so, what was your impression of it? If you have never seen high-definition television, contact your local video store and ask where you can see an HDTV demo in your area.

2. Is there a video dial tone service available to homes in your neighborhood? If so, which service? What percentage of homes in your community would you say subscribe to it? What does it cost? What impact has it had on the video stores in your community; are they still in business? Do you think video stores will ultimately go out of business because of video dial tone technology, or will people still prefer to go to the store to pick out videos?

[handwritten: SNET — need a terminal adapter]

3. Contact your local telephone company and find out whether ISDN services are available to homes in your neighborhood. Find out how much it costs to get an ISDN connection. Make sure you ask about ongoing as well as one-time costs. What Internet services are available via ISDN in your neighborhood? Can you get videoconferencing? Does it cost more than lower-bandwidth services?

4. Ask around and find out what percentage of your friends' homes have ISDN installed. Do you think this percentage will increase? Why or why not?

5. Contact your local cable TV company to find out if cable modems are available. If not, register a complaint that your cable company is behind the times. If both cable modems and ISDN are available to you, compare their speeds, costs, and range of services.

6. If you could program a knowbot to go out on the Internet and do your bidding, what would you want the knowbot to do?

7. Do you believe multimedia is just a fad, or is its use emerging as a life skill for the twenty-first century? Give reasons for your belief.

[handwritten notes across bottom of page:]

If SNET cost: 50hrs Conn. 29.95 + $ add. channel hour — Includes Personal Home Page additional email boxes

1) Computers → word process → multimedia app. (CD/disks) etc.

2) Internet

3) Links w/ phone/tv: familiar meets new

1 mo - 50.00 Frstdale $1500 / 800-895-7400

1 yr - 47.50 - 199.00
36 mo - 42.50 - 150.00
60 mo - 40 - 150.00

Non Snet 39.95/month extra for 4.95 + $

16

Societal Issues

After completing this chapter, you will be able to:

- Question the potentially negative impact of multimedia on violence, game addiction, sexual exploitation, pornography, and obscenity

- Understand the regulatory nightmare facing lawmakers on issues of privacy, encryption, censorship, and protectionism

- Realize how fortune seekers have tried to profit from the legal system's lack of experience by patenting basic multimedia technologies that were already widely used

- Consider the copyright law and a teacher's right to fair use of multimedia, and the need to call upon campus copyright officials to get organized, take the lead, and revise their faculty copyright guidelines to permit these fair uses of multimedia

- Understand the issues of entitlement, equity, cost, usability, and universal access, and then question whether the building of the Information Superhighway will create a technological underclass in our society

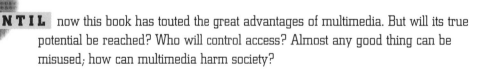

NTIL now this book has touted the great advantages of multimedia. But will its true potential be reached? Who will control access? Almost any good thing can be misused; how can multimedia harm society?

HUMAN IMPACT

A lot of people worry about graphic violence in video games. Is it right to have laser shooting games in video arcades, which can train young people how to aim and fire weapons at people, when the leading cause of death among urban youth is gunshot wounds? Sex CDs let men exploit women severely. With more than 60% of families reporting problems of marital violence, should CD-ROMs in which men can torture women virtually be legal? Research shows that virtual reality is even more addictive than conventional video games. What effect will this have on humankind?

Violence and Game Addiction

In her review of violence in video games, Stefanac (1994) mentions that there were more than 10,000 murders involving handguns in the United States in 1990. During the same year, only 10 such murders occurred in Australia, 13 in Sweden, 22 in Great Britain, and 87 in Japan. In 1991, 55% of those arrested for murder in the United States were under the age of 25. According to federal crime reports, the number of children arrested for murder during the past decade has risen by 55%.

The author suggests that you visit your local arcade and try one of the video games that has laser-targeting firearms. As you hold the weapon, people appear on the screen in front of you. They are not mere "pixellated" computer graphics that only suggest human forms, but real live video recordings of street scenes. You must aim accurately and fire quickly to avoid being shot. Now go outside and walk down the street. Someone appears from around the corner in front of you. What is your basic instinct after playing the game?

Not everyone agrees that video game violence provokes street crime. According to popular-culture professor Christopher Geist (Stefanac 1994):

> People often assume that findings for one medium apply necessarily to the next. Some people are saying that interactive games will have more impact. That's a guess. It could turn out that the interactivity in some of these combat games actually lessens the negative impact; it could serve a cathartic effect. Much more research needs to be done before we start drawing absolute conclusions.

Sex

Sex is very important to most people. Traffic on the Internet reflects this: The newsgroup *alt.sex* has more than 350,000 readers with more than 10 MB of new messages per month; that's the equivalent of three Bibles. But multimedia is being used for more than just distributing erotic stories and pictures. Interactivity is letting users live out their fantasies virtually. For example, *NightWatch* allows the voyeur/player to snoop around a plush singles resort via a bank of security monitors. *Virtual Valerie* lets users roam about and explore Valerie's apartment and have cybersex with her in the bedroom. Linea Jacobson, editor of *CyberArts* (Miller Freeman 1992), has a warning about the dangers of these applications (Stefanac 1994):

> What's wonderful about interactive media is also what's reprehensible about this kind of application: the idea of handing control over to the user. Smut on paper or video is much more benign than interactive stroke books. These products show men that they can have control over women. You can force them to do your bidding and they do it willingly. I am absolutely opposed to censorship, but I think men have to be made aware that this kind of thing can make women feel very uncomfortable.

Pornography and Obscenity

Mike Godwin (1994), online counsel for the Electronic Frontier Foundation, also has concerns about the risks of putting graphic sexual materials on the Internet.

The GIF file format is capable of reproducing over the Net full-color photos of explicit "hardcore" pornography and child pornography. The federal government has been searching and seizing servers that contain such material. These are so popular that Delft University in the Netherlands has had to limit each user to eight downloads per day from its erotic image file server.

The U.S. Supreme Court's 1973 *Miller* ruling gave communities the right to legislate obscenity. To help interpret the laws, Godwin (1994: 58) developed the following four-part test, based on the Supreme Court's 1966 definition of obscenity:

1. Is the work designed to be sexually arousing?

2. Is it arousing in a way that one's local community would consider unhealthy or immoral?

3. Does it picture acts whose depictions are specifically prohibited by state law?

4. Does the work, when taken as a whole, lack sufficient literary, artistic, scientific, or social value?

Distributing such materials over the Internet raises some difficult issues. For example, while an erotic picture might not be immoral in the community where it was uploaded, it may very well be considered obscene in the place it gets downloaded. Internet tools like the Web and the Gopher make it very easy to take things out of context; who can prevent users from circulating an image devoid of the supplementary material that made it legitimate? Moreover, children can easily access materials over the Internet that were intended for adults.

The U.S. child protection laws forbid any pornographic images that use children, whether or not the images meet Godwin's obscenity test. Individuals convicted can be fined up to $100,000 and imprisoned up to 10 years. As the result of a nationwide FBI investigation of online porn, for example, a distributor of child pornography was sentenced to five years in prison for sending sexually explicit photos of children via his America Online account (*Tampa Tribune* 2/24/96: A6).

Canada's best-known computer science school, the University of Waterloo, banned from its campus five Internet bulletin boards dealing with violent sex out of concern that their contents break laws on pornography and obscenity (*Toronto Globe & Mail* 2/5/94: A1).

The Recreational Software Advisory Council (RSAC) has begun to issue Web ratings that allow parents to block Web sites rated as having a high degree of violence, nudity, sex, or objectionable language (*USA Today* 5/29/96: 1D). Web page sponsors fill out an electronic questionnaire to get their sites rated on a scale of 0 (innocuous) to 4 ("X-rated"). Parents can set the level at which content will be blocked and can also block all unrated sites. A password gives parents access to areas blocked from children (*Investor's Business Daily* 5/10/96: A18).

Multi User Domains

In her fascinating book *Life on the Screen,* Sherry Turkle (1995) describes what it is like to participate in Multi User Domains, or **MUDs**, which are virtual spaces in which you can navigate, strategize, and converse with other users. Turkle views MUDs as a new kind of parlor game and a new form of community that lets people generate experiences, relationships, identities, and living spaces that arise only through interaction with technology. One of the dangerous aspects is how men can stalk women in MUDs. For example, Turkle tells of a virtual rape:

> One MUD player had used his skill with the system to seize control of another player's character. In this way the aggressor was able to direct the seized character to submit to a violent sexual encounter. He did all this against the will and over the distraught objections of the player usually "behind" this character, the player to whom this character "belonged." Although some made light of the offender's actions by saying that the episode was just words, in text-based virtual realities such as MUDs, words *are* deeds (Turkle 1995: 15).

Parents need to be aware of the dangers of MUDs, because young people are especially susceptible. Discussing childhood encounters with "netsex," Turkle warns:

> Parents need to be able to talk to their children about where they are going and what they are doing. This same commonsense rule applies to their children's lives on the screen. Parents don't have to become technical experts, but they do need to learn enough about computer networks to discuss with their children what and who is out there and lay down some basic safety rules. The children who do best after a bad experience on the Internet (who are harassed, perhaps even propositioned) are those who can talk to their parents, just as children who best handle bad experiences in real life are those who can talk to an elder without shame or fear of blame (Turkle 1995: 227).

Internet Addiction Disorder

The Internet can be addicting, so much so that **Internet Addiction Disorder** (IAD) has entered the medical lexicon. University of Pittsburgh researcher Kimberly Young maintains that IAD is as real as alcoholism, characterized by loss of control, cravings and withdrawal symptoms, social isolation, marital discord, academic failure, excessive financial debt, and job termination (*Toronto Globe & Mail* 6/15/96: A1). To borrow from the title of Sherry Turkle's book, there is "life on the screen," and certain kinds of people may prefer cyberlife to real life. If you feel yourself becoming addicted, set a time limit for how long you spend on the Internet each day, and try to stay focused on the task at hand. Many Web pages contain enticing ads intended to draw you away from your original purpose. You can reduce the amount of time you spend online if you stay focused on accomplishing your intent instead of surfing off in other directions.

REGULATION

With the broadcast television, cable TV, telephone, and computer network industries all jockeying for position, the Information Superhighway presents a regulatory nightmare. Television broadcasters have requested congressional permission to use some of their allocated spectrum to offer advanced telecommunication services, including sending data to laptops, fax machines, and pagers. TV station owners claim they just want to stay competitive with cable and telephone companies, but opponents say they should have equal opportunity to any extra spectrum (*Wall Street Journal* 2/2/94: B1).

When Senator Ernest Hollings introduced a bill that would open up the local telephone market to competition by lifting the remaining line-of-business restrictions on the seven RBOCs (Regional Bell Operating Companies), long-distance carriers expressed concern over letting RBOCs into the long-distance service area. Spokespersons from AT&T and Sprint testified against the proposed change (*BNA Daily Report for Executives* 2/3/94: A21).

The Clinton administration realized it could get hopelessly tangled in a long series of debates and filibusters with long-distance phone carriers battling to put limits on House and Senate bills that would let the regional Bell telephone companies compete in the long-distance marketplace, cable companies hoping both to offer local phone service and keep local phone companies from providing video services, and TV broadcasters demanding the right to provide data services along with their regular programming (*New York Times* 2/4/94: C1). To prevent this legislative quagmire from holding up progress on the Information Superhighway, Vice President Gore announced the Clinton administration's intent to deregulate the telecommunications industry to a point where any company can offer any services to any set of consumers (*Atlanta Constitution* 12/21/93: C9). According to a survey by the National Consumers League, the public sided with the administration on this issue by a two-thirds majority (*BNA Daily Report for Executives* 2/1/94: A12). On February 8, 1996, President Clinton signed into law the Telecommunications Deregulation Act.

Privacy

Do you realize that many employers claim the legal right to read all of the e-mail and other electronic correspondence that flows through their computer network? While the Federal Electronic Communications Privacy Act of 1986 protects the privacy of messages sent over public networks like MCI Mail and CompuServe, it does not cover a company's internal e-mail (*New York Times* 12/6/93: A8). The author believes this infringes upon freedom of speech and should be changed. Even though your employer pays for the telephone line in your office, your employer cannot listen in on your telephone conversations without having a court order. How then can it be legal to eavesdrop on your electronic conversations? As Neal J. Friedman, a specialist in online computer law, explains: "Employees are under the misapprehension that the First Amendment applies in the workplace—it doesn't. Employees need to know they have no right of privacy and no right of free speech using company resources" (*Computerworld* 2/5/96: 55). Beware of this; do not ever communicate anything electronically that you would not want read by your employer or network administrators.

You should also be aware that when you send e-mail on the Information Superhighway, it passes through one or more **gateways**. Each gateway is a computer that can (and often does for backup and reliability purposes) retain a copy of your communications. Any computer systems analyst with access to that network can read your messages. It is also possible to write sophisticated snooper software that can monitor all of your electronic communications and alert the eavesdropper when your messages contain certain key words or phrases. The Canadian Security Intelligence Service has awarded three contracts to a Montreal firm for a system that can quickly isolate key words and phrases from millions of airborne phone, fax, and radio signals (*CTV National News* 1/31/94: 11:00 P.M.).

Do you write messages in Internet newsgroups? If you do not set the x-no-archive flag on your messages, anyone on the Internet can find your messages via the DejaNews newsgroup search engine at http://www.dejanews.com. Imagine the implications of this kind of technology for job seekers. Sometimes young people do foolish things. Suppose that when you were young, you got on the Internet and wrote immature messages in newsgroups. Later on, when you apply for a job, your potential employer can look you up in DejaNews and obtain an indexed list of everything you have ever written in newsgroups. Is this an invasion of privacy? As you attempt to answer this question, keep in mind that DejaNews did not exist prior to its invention in 1995; suddenly, a search engine appears that makes it possible for anyone to search through newsgroups in which you may have expressed your feelings and orientations on sensitive topics and issues.

Prodigy also has a search engine able to trace all information posted on the company's bulletin boards. Subscribers can peruse more than 17 million notes by subject area or key words, as well as by sender and receiver. Like DejaNews, the Prodigy archives and search capabilities allow prospective employers, merchants, or nosy neighbors to use the Net to develop profiles based on forums you've participated in and what you've contributed over a long period of time (*St. Petersburg Times* 3/11/96: 9).

Encryption and the Clipper Chip

To prevent people from reading electronic correspondence, many firms encrypt their messages. The government is concerned that this prevents law enforcement agencies (who have court orders) from eavesdropping on digital communications. The Clinton administration wants to control the encryption process by requiring that every government computer contain a **Clipper Chip**, which is an encryption device with a "back door" that allows detectives with the proper access to decipher the messages. The Clipper Chip has been denounced by industry groups as well as civil liberties groups concerned about privacy (*New York Times* 2/5/94: A1). The CPSR (Computer Professionals for Social Responsibility) has organized a protest; for more information go to http://www.cpsr.org/dox/home.html.

InfoWorld publisher Bob Metcalfe opposes Clipper Chip technology for technological reasons: "I am against Clipper simply because it will not work, and it will cost an unnecessary amount of tax money to outfit government computers with the chips . . . Smart criminals can easily get around Clipper by using additional encryption. Stupid criminals will continue to do stupid things and get caught" (*Wall Street Journal* 3/22/94: A14).

Pretty Good Privacy (PGP) is an encryption program written by Phil Zimmerman. It is the kind of "additional encryption" to which Metcalfe refers. PGP runs on almost every brand of computer and is the most common way of encrypting e-mail messages. For example, there is a PGP plug-in for the popular Eudora e-mail package. For more information about PGP, go to http://web.mit.edu/network/pgp.html. Also written by Zimmerman is PGPfone, which scrambles phone calls made through a computer modem using a complex algorithm called Blowfish. You can download PGPfone at http://web.mit.edu/network/pgpfone. Both PGP and PGPfone are free.

Censorship

Many people are concerned that in addition to being able to read electronic communications, network administrators also have the ability to censor them. To what extent and under what circumstances should the government act as a censor on the Information Superhighway?

Few would argue that the University of Waterloo erred in banning obscene bulletin boards from its network. But what prevents users from avoiding the ban by distributing the material through e-mail?

In a well-publicized criminal trial in Toronto, the Canadian government exercised its right to ban any publicity about the case, lest prospective jurors become biased and the hearings end in mistrial. So the University of Toronto stopped carrying an Internet bulletin board that disclosed banned information about the case. But that did not stop people from distributing the information through e-mail. It has become virtually impossible to intercept the electronic exchange of such information (*Toronto Globe & Mail* 12/2/93: A4).

There has been a lot of controversy surrounding the Communications Decency Act of 1996 (CDA), which makes it illegal to distribute indecent or offensive materials on the Internet. Ruling that the act violates free speech, a three-judge federal court has blocked enforcement of the CDA, describing it as "a government-imposed content-based restriction on speech," in violation of the Constitution. The full text of the decision is available on the Web at http://www.cdt.org. The Justice Department may appeal to the Supreme Court. President Clinton defended the Communications Decency Act by saying: "I remain convinced, as I was when I signed the bill, that our Constitution allows us to help parents by enforcing this act to prevent objectionable material transmitted through computer networks" (*New York Times* 6/13/96: A1).

Protectionism

Protectionists present the Information Superhighway with yet another stumbling block. Canadian phone company BCE Telecom ran into opposition over its proposed $275 million joint venture with Jones Intercable. Edward Markey, chair of the House Subcommittee on Telecommunications and Finance, said it "raises serious policy issues regarding foreign investment in and control of the U.S. telecommunications infrastructure," and he advocated limiting foreign investment to noncontrolling stakes in American information highways (*Toronto Globe & Mail* 1/21/94: B1).

Nationalism poses yet another obstacle to connectivity. Perceiving the unification of Canada with an information highway as another threat to preserving its regional cultures, Quebec's Internal Department of Communications is considering imposing rules and restrictions on the content of information flowing on the Information Superhighway to Quebec (*Ottawa Citizen* 1/31/94: A4). Saudi Arabia has banned satellite dishes in order to maintain control over the information its citizens can obtain (*St. Petersburg Times* 3/12/94: A8). In 1996 France passed a law requiring any software marketed in France to be presented in French. China is building a centrally administered Internet backbone that will allow government monitoring of e-mail and other online activities (*Wall Street Journal* 1/31/96: A1).

MULTIMEDIA AND THE LAW

Multimedia is putting new pressures on the legal system. Initially slow to learn about new media, the patent office was tricked into granting some patents too broad in scope. Misinterpretations of the copyright law have prevented fair use of multimedia by teachers and students. Lawmakers and enforcers need to be multiliterate so they can bolster the use of new media on the Information Superhighway instead of retarding its progress through lack of understanding. *Note:* This chapter is not intended as a substitute for legal advice. You should consult a lawyer or a campus copyright official before taking action in specific cases, because your circumstances may differ from what is described here.

Patents

The U.S. Patent and Trademark Office granted two multimedia patents so broad in scope that the awardees blatantly announced all other vendors owed them royalties on all past, present, and future products. This created an industrywide protest so severe that one of the vendors withdrew its claim; the patent office overturned the other patent. In both cases, there was so much prior art that for people in the industry these claims were likened to trying to patent sunlight (*Wall Street Journal* 3/25/94: B2).

THE OPTICAL DATA PATENT

The first case involved a patent awarded to Optical Data for the syllabus-based curriculum-outlining method used in the Windows on Science program. The syllabus is so basic to the teaching process that many other products already used it. Kinnaman (1993) describes how Videodiscovery filed a lawsuit seeking a declaratory judgment finding the patent invalid because of prior art and the obviousness of the claims. The Interactive Multimedia Association (IMA) supported the Videodiscovery complaint; as IMA president Philip Dodds politely stated, "Patents such as these, which require nearly every company involved in interactive multimedia and education to license an idea and application that have a long history and are widely known, are not in the best interest of the industry or educators" (Kinnaman 1993).

To stop the flow of negative publicity stemming from the patent, Optical Data Corporation dedicated the patent permanently to the public. According to Optical Data chair William Clark, "It was never our intent to use this patent to inhibit the development of multimedia based interactive teaching methods. A tremendous amount of concern—including a lawsuit by one of our competitors—arose from this patent award. We hope that by voluntarily dedicating this patent to the public, we will end any unfounded fears that Optical Data, or any other company, might try to limit the diversity of interactive, multimedia programs available to educators" (Kinnaman 1994).

But Foremski (1994) reports another company attempting to do just that. Compton's caused an uproar by claiming at COMDEX/Fall '93 that they had been awarded a patent that would require all multimedia developers to pay them royalties. As Compton's CEO Stanley Frank said, "We helped kick start this industry. We now ask to be compensated for our investments. We will do whatever it takes to defend our patent."

THE COMPTON'S PATENT

The Compton's patent is very broad. It covers any type of computer-controlled database system that allows a user to search for mixed media that includes text with graphics, sound, or animation. Compton's did not limit their claims to CD-ROM products; they also claimed rights to any type of database involving interactive TV or the Information Superhighway.

The title of the Compton's patent is *Multimedia search system using a plurality of entry path means which indicate interrelatedness of information.* It claims:

> A computer search system for retrieving information, comprising:
>
> means for storing interrelated textual information and graphical information;
>
> means for interrelating said textual and graphical information;
>
> a plurality of entry path means for searching said stored interrelated textual and graphical information, said entry path means comprising:

textual search entry path means for searching said textual information and for retrieving interrelated graphical information to said searched text;

graphics entry path means for searching said graphical information and for retrieving interrelated textual information to said searched graphical information;

selecting means for providing a menu of said plurality of entry path means for selection;

processing means for executing inquiries provided by a user in order to search said textual and graphical information through said selected entry path means;

indicating means for indicating a pathway that accesses information related in one of said entry path means to information accessible in another one of said entry path means;

accessing means for providing access to said related information in said another entry path means; and

output means for receiving search results from said processing means and said related information from said accessing means and for providing said search results and received information to such user.

Compton's presented all multimedia developers with four patent royalty payment options. Kinnaman (1994) explains how they included "entering into a joint venture with Compton's; distributing products through the company's Affiliated Label Program; licensing Compton's SmarTrieve technology; or paying royalties." Compton's had the audacity to require back royalties of 1% of net receipts from sales before June 30, 1994, and 3% thereafter.

To say the least, developers reacted negatively to Compton's demands. Some suggested that users should burn all Compton's CD-ROMs and refuse to purchase future titles from any company that would try to force such a Machiavellian proviso on the multimedia industry. As a result of public hearings held by the U.S. Patent and Trademark Office to review its handling of software patents, the Compton's patent was rescinded.

The furor over the Optical Data and Compton's patents caused the patent office to initiate reforms that include publicizing patent applications, hiring seven software specialists as examiners, revamping the examiner bonus program so it does not encourage superficial review, and requiring more information about patent applications before decisions are made (*Wall Street Journal* 4/11/94: B6). In fairness to the government, industry leaders like Optical Data and Compton's (who know better) should stop trying to profit from patenting prior art; instead, they should concentrate on improving their products and moving the industry forward.

Copyright

Article I, section 8, of the United States Constitution grants Congress the power "to promote the progress of science and useful arts, by securing for limited times to authors and inventors the exclusive right to their respective writings and discoveries." Congress used this power to pass the Copyright Act of 1976, which defines and allocates rights associated with "original works of authorship fixed in any tangible medium of expression, now known or later developed, or otherwise communicated, either directly or with the aid of a machine or device" (U.S. Constitution, 17 § 102). This means that all of the elements presented in the taxonomy of multimedia in Chapter 2 of this book—including illustrations, text, movies, video clips, documentaries, animations, music, and software—are protected by copyright. There are stiff penalties for copyright offendors. For example, the Software Publishers Association took action in 1993 against 577 organizations for pirating commercial software, resulting in $3.6 million in fines (*Atlanta Journal-Constitution* 2/3/94: C2).

Whenever you plan to publish a multimedia work, whether on a CD-ROM, diskettes, or the Information Superhighway, you must make sure you have the right to use every object in it. Similarly, you should register a copyright for your multimedia creations. On your application's home screen, and on the title page of any printed documentation, print the following copyright notice, replacing *xx* with the current year:

> **Copyright © 19*xx* by *Your Name*. All rights reserved.**

Although this notice legally suffices to protect your copyright, it is also a good idea to register the copyright with the U.S. Copyright Office. If someone infringes your copyright and you take legal action to defend it, copyright registration can help your case. To register a copyright, follow these steps:

1. Go to the U.S. Copyright Office Web page at http://www.loc.gov/copyright and choose "Copyright registration".

2. Choose "Circular 55—Multimedia Works" to display the policies and procedures for multimedia copyright registration. Read the policy to determine what form to use to register your copyright.

3. Go back to http://www.loc.gov/copyright and choose "Copyright Application Forms". Download the form you need.

4. Complete the application form and make a copy to retain in your files.

5. Mail the application along with a copy of the work and the $20 registration fee to the Register of Copyrights, Copyright Office, Library of Congress, Washington, D.C. 20559.

If you want a receipt, have the post office mail your application "return receipt requested." It will take several weeks for the Library of Congress to process your application and send you the registration number.

Fair Use

The **Fair Use** provision of the U.S. Copyright Act allows the use of copyrighted works in reporting news, conducting research, and teaching. The law states:

> Notwithstanding the provisions of section 106 [which grants authors exclusive rights], the fair use of a copyrighted work, including such use by reproduction in copies or phonorecords or by any other means specified by that section, for purposes such as criticism, comment, news reporting, teaching (including multiple copies for classroom use), scholarship, or research, is not an infringement of copyright. In determining whether the use made of a work in any particular case is a fair use the factors to be considered shall include:
>
> 1. the purpose and character of the use, including whether such use is of a commercial nature or is for nonprofit educational purposes;
> 2. the nature of the copyrighted work;
> 3. the amount and substantiality of the portion used in relation to the copyrighted work as a whole; and
> 4. the effect of the use upon the potential market for, or value of, the copyrighted work.

INTERPRETING FAIR USE FOR EDUCATION

To summarize the Fair Use law for education, one may paraphrase its first paragraph as follows: "the fair use of a copyrighted work for . . . teaching (including multiple copies for classroom use) . . . is not an infringement of copyright." The difficulty arises from interpreting the four tests, which are intentionally left vague, as the law goes on to state that "although the courts have considered and ruled upon the fair use doctrine over and over again, no real definition of the concept has ever emerged. Indeed, since the doctrine is an equitable rule of reason, no generally applicable definition is possible, and each case raising the question must be decided on its own facts."

THE CCUMC FAIR USE GUIDELINES FOR EDUCATIONAL MULTIMEDIA

To help educational institutions interpret the Fair Use law with regard to multimedia, the CCUMC (Consortium of College and University Media Centers) spearheaded the creation of the new *Fair Use Guidelines for Educational Multimedia*. The committee that created these guidelines consisted of representatives from print, film, music, and multimedia publishing companies, who spent many months discussing and debating fair use issues with representatives from educational institutions. Professor Lisa Livingston, director of the Instructional Media Division of the City University of New York, chaired the committee, and well-known copyright attorney Ivan Bender was retained to advise on legal issues. As a member of this committee, the author can attest to the rigor of the process.

The CCUMC *Fair Use Guidelines for Educational Multimedia* are on the *Multiliteracy CD*. To read them, go to the Demonstrations section, select Textbook Examples, and click the Fair Use button. The author encourages you to study these guidelines carefully and use them to exercise your right of fair use. Many copyright policies now in effect in colleges and schools are overly restrictive with respect to multimedia. Fair use is the law, and educators have the right to fair use. Encourage your institution to endorse the CCUMC guidelines. By the time this book is printed, the guidelines will probably have been read into the Congressional Record, attached to legislation validating them. Validation of the guidelines will be announced at http://www.cetus.org. See also the Copyright and Fair Use Web site at http://fairuse.stanford.edu.

Ethics

Ethics is a two-way street. If the Information Superhighway is to succeed, users must both behave and be treated ethically and responsibly. Because the Internet is a frontier, new users need a way to find out the rules of the road. In 1990 American University Professor Frank Connolly recognized this need. He led a project at EDUCOM and the AAHE to create *The Bill of Rights and Responsibilities for Electronic Learners*. The goal was to create a computer network policy addressing the rights and responsibilities of individuals, schools, and colleges in the twenty-first century.

Published in 1993, the *Bill of Rights* has four sections. The first section recognizes the right of all individuals to access the Information Superhighway, to find out what kind of information is being collected about them, and to exercise the right of free speech on the Internet. The second section holds individuals accountable for honoring the intellectual property of other users, protecting the integrity and authenticity of information, respecting and valuing each user's right to privacy, and refraining from activities that waste resources or prevent others from using them. Section three gives institutions the right to access the Internet, protect intellectual resources mounted on the Net, and allocate resources. Section four holds institutions accountable for making sure that software has been legally acquired, maintaining security to protect the integrity of individual files, treating personal files as the confidential property of the user, and providing training in the effective use of information technology.

The complete text of *The Bill of Rights and Responsibilities for Electronic Learners* is on the *Multiliteracy CD.* To access it, go to the Demonstrations section, select Textbook Examples, and click the Bill of Rights button. Every user should abide by this *Bill of Rights and Responsibilities.*

EQUITY, COST, AND UNIVERSAL ACCESS

The Clinton administration has promised the public that everyone will have equal access to the Information Superhighway. With estimated costs of building the network as high as $200 billion, however, critics are skeptical.

Entitlement

Wall Street Journal writer Alan Murray warns that Vice President Gore's call for "universal service" on the Information Superhighway is just one more entitlement for the middle class. The current plan proposes expanding on subsidies already inherent in the phone system, but as Columbia University Communications Professor Eli Noam warns, only a small portion (less than $1 billion) of the telephone benefits goes to the truly needy. The rest subsidizes monthly service for the middle class and the affluent (*Wall Street Journal* 1/31/94: A1).

Community-based programs are beginning to provide access to low-income people who otherwise would never be able to afford a PC. For example, East Harlem's Playing to Win program provides six months of computer access for $35 (*Business Week* 4/15/96: 108).

Cost

The Clinton administration has estimated the cost of building the Information Superhighway at between $50 billion and $100 billion over the next 10 to 15 years. But industry analysts say that figure could double, up to $200 billion by the time the network is built (*BNA Special Report: Outlook '94* 1/28/94: S21). In the 1996 State of the Union Address, President Clinton called upon the telecommunications industry to connect every school and library in America by the year 2000.

To pay for this, and to subsidize poor and rural customers, the United States Telephone Association (USTA) wants to raise the average U.S. monthly phone bill by about $10 over the next five years. The proposal assumes an $11 billion cost for wiring schools and libraries, with local phone companies paying about one-third to one-half of that. The rest would come from a surcharge on other services, including cellular. "No single industry should be held responsible for fulfilling this major goal," says USTA's president. "Each has a role and should make a significant contribution to the national education technology mandate" (*Investor's Business Daily* 5/8/96: A7).

A Yankee Group analyst has said that the up-front cost to a cable or phone company for providing a customer with video-on-demand will be $1,000 per household (*New York Times* 1/23/94 Sec. 3: 14). The extra channels available via video dial tones may be used mainly for pay-per-view. As Columbia Professor Eli Noam warns, "The good stuff will inevitably migrate to pay-per-view, so people with just the basics will inevitably get less than they do now. Within 10 years, people will be paying cable bills of $100 to $200 a month because they'll be paying per view for things like baseball and football games that they get for free now" (Lerner 1993).

Usability

Sprint CEO William Esrey questions the potential for consumer services on the Information Superhighway, claiming that the people touted as the prime market are the ones who cannot program a VCR (*Toronto Star* 2/2/94: B1). In 16% of American households, VCRs are permanently blinking "12:00" because no one knows how to set the digital clock, much less program the VCR (*Miami Herald* 2/2/94: C1). Can something as complex as the Information Superhighway be made easier to use than a VCR?

Vendors realize that in order to succeed they must make the Information Superhighway easier to use. In an effort to cater to home users, Microsoft created a new interface that uses familiar scenes—such as a living room—rather than icons. Named "Bob," the new interface was intended to make Windows easy to use; however, public reaction was lukewarm.

Apple tried an online information service called eWorld, which used a village as the metaphor for information services. Individual buildings in the village designated particular categories of information, such as business news, home shopping, and entertainment. Like Microsoft's Bob, Apple's eWorld fizzled, and Apple terminated the service. You can visit "The Unofficial eWorld Farewell Site" at http://edie.cprost.sfu.ca/~rkam/eworld/index3.html.

The challenge remains to make computers easy enough for all citizens to use. Remember that, by definition, half of the people are below average. The person who makes computers easy enough for below-average people to use will be a twenty-first-century hero. As we learned from Microsoft's Bob, the living-room metaphor doesn't work. Neither did Apple's eWorld village metaphor. Maybe you can be the one to invent the right approach for the below-average citizen.

Access

As this book goes to press, only about 20 million Americans are using the Internet. We have a long way to go before achieving universal access. Not even schools are adequately connected yet. As FCC Chairman Reed E. Hundt observed, "There are thousands of buildings in this country, with millions of people in them who have no telephones, no cable television and no reasonable prospect of broadband services. They're called schools" (*New York Times* 12/6/93: C6).

Edward A. Fitzsimmons (1994), special assistant for Education and Training in the Office of Science and Technology Policy in the Executive Office of the President, maintains that the public will get access to the Information Superhighway through HDTV, much like they got access to the nation's telephone system through phones:

> In America the percentage of homes with telephones is 99.9%. This is made possible largely through tariffs which allow a person to pay according to his means. Similar types of subsidies could allow access to two channels on everyone's TV. The technology for these connectors is part of the standards announced for HDTV. When a person buys a TV meeting these standards s/he would be buying into a connection with the world.

Access is a two-way street; not only must users have universal access to information on the Superhighway, but vendors must have open access to put their services on it. The Clinton administration wants to provide open access for all providers of information and entertainment to offer their services over network distribution systems at fair, competitive prices (*New York Times* 1/12/94: A1).

The Technological Underclass

Experts warn that if the Information Superhighway does not have universal access with a user interface that makes it possible for the public to use it effectively, it will create a technological underclass, and communities deprived of computers and telecommunications will end up in poverty (*Star-Ledger* 1/13/94: 41). But there already is a technological underclass, and many of its citizens already live in poverty. The Information Superhighway threatens to amplify this situation unless ways are found to give the disadvantaged equal access. Vice President Gore has promised to create a "regulatory safety net" to make sure everyone will benefit (*Investor's Business Daily* 12/22/93: 1).

But how long will this take? Pacific Telesis, the San Francisco–based regional Bell, will spend about $15 billion over five years to develop a network that can deliver television and high-speed data services throughout California. Phase one called for wiring 1.5 million homes by the end of 1996; phase two will hook up 3.5 million more by the end of the decade. California's remaining 4 million customers would be wired by 2010 (*New York Times* 11/11/93: C4). If it will take until the year 2010 to wire California, how can Vice President Gore promise all citizens equal access? Given the fast pace of the computer industry, 2010 is so far in the future that several new generations of technology will have passed in the meantime. Won't citizens getting wired for today's technology in 2010 be just as disadvantaged then as they are now?

In order to prevent the creation of a technological underclass, universal access needs to happen quickly. Unfortunately, as this part of the book has demonstrated, economic, legislative, and regulatory barriers will make it take decades. In the meantime, the rich will have gotten much richer. As Clinton White House Education Adviser Linda Roberts warned in her keynote address to the Society for Technology and Teacher Education on March 19, 1994, "We must make sure the Information Superhighway is not a toll road for the rich."

Employment

Columnist Jean-Claude Leclerc warns us that plans for the Information Superhighway could lead to a decline in employment and development in inner cities in much the same way that highway systems led to decay when freeways bypassed smaller towns and cities (*Montreal Gazette* 1/31/94: B2). With the crime rate making cities unsafe, who is going to want to go out shopping and risk being mugged or killed when you can use your multimedia computer to cruise the Information Superhighway, browse the contents of dozens of shops in the time it would take you to drive to just one store, and purchase anything in the world at the best price on the network? As home shopping causes traffic in retail stores to plummet, the neighborhoods formerly served by those stores will suffer more unemployment.

Canada's *Blueprint for Delivery of Government Services Using Information Technology* is intended to enable the public to access government information and services through kiosks in shopping malls. However, unions say the plan could make thousands of public servants "road kill" on the Information Superhighway, because cutting jobs is the only way the government could achieve the $2 billion in annual savings forecast in the *Blueprint* (*Ottawa Citizen* 3/23/94: A4).

Multimedia Careers

On a more positive note, multimedia is creating new job opportunities. As the growth charts presented in Chapter 1 demonstrate, multimedia is the fastest-growing industry in the world today. Vivid Studios (1995) has written a book that can help you position yourself for a job in multimedia. The book is entitled *Careers in Multimedia.* You can order it at any bookstore by asking for ISBN 1-56276-311-3. The book covers multimedia industries, projects, work issues, roles, resources, and locations where most jobs are found. Dozens of successful professionals working in multimedia are profiled. Table 16-1 lists careers in multimedia.

Another strategy for finding work in multimedia, or any other field for that matter, is to put your résumé on the Web. Part Ten of this book is a tutorial on creating Web résumés. Once your résumé is online, the Web crawlers will find it and make it accessible to potential employers who search the Net for talent. Several of the author's students have been invited to job interviews in this manner.

Sizing

Traffic on the Information Superhighway is growing very fast. Faster than the bandwidth needed to carry that traffic. The popularity of real-time audio and videoconferencing products has caused Web traffic to increase far beyond what Tim Berners-Lee envisioned when he invented the Web back in 1989.

When the amount of data exceeds the capacity of the routers and switches through which the data flow, a situation known as **Internet brownout** occurs. In an Internet brownout, packets of data sent over the network slow to a crawl and can be lost forever, never getting to their desinations. When your Web browser pops up an alert box telling you that a host is "unreachable," brownout could be the culprit. NetStar's VP for sales and marketing maintains that brownouts have caused the Internet to become "about as reliable these days as the phone system in Russia" (*Business Week* 4/8/96: 82).

The Internet Engineering Task Force (IETF) is working on these problems. Since the World Wide Web is the biggest culprit, the IETF is examining whether there is a way to streamline the transmission of data to and from Web servers. Another proposed solution would meter Internet usage, charging heavy users more and light users less. You can find out more by visiting the IETF at http://www.ietf.cnri.reston.va.us.

Table 16-1 Career Opportunities in Multimedia

■ Advertising	■ Front-ending	■ Presentations	■ Special effects
■ Animation	■ Games	■ Public relations	■ Training
■ CD recording	■ Graphics production	■ Real estate marketing	■ Travel systems
■ Construction planning	■ Instructional design	■ Scientific modeling	■ Video production
■ Content design	■ Interface design	■ Screen design	■ Virtual reality
■ Courtroom trial reenactment	■ Kiosking	■ Scripting and storyboarding	■ WebMaster
■ Electronic publishing	■ Landscape design	■ Simulation	
■ Facilities design	■ Online services	■ Sound tracks	

RCISES

r played the *Mortal Kombat* video game, find a friend who has it and give it a try.
hest level of violence; if you cannot figure out how to do this, ask the kids who play it.
that this kind of graphic violence in video games is good for children to experience?
What do you think should be done about it?

2. Visit your local video arcade and try the latest laser shooting games. Notice how real video footage is used to put you in a situation in which you must kill or be killed. See how realistic the interaction is, and how well you can learn to aim and fire the weapons. Do you believe these games should be available to the kind of crowd attracted to video arcades, especially when gunshot wounds are the leading cause of death among teenagers in our cities? What do you think should be done about this?

3. How do you feel about the use of multimedia for sex? Does virtual sex serve any useful role in our society? How can it be misused? Could it help solve any societal problems?

4. Do you believe software that lets men force women to do their bidding encourages men to believe they can and should have control over women in real life? If so, what should be done about this?

5. As explained earlier in this chapter, a lot of traffic on the Information Superhighway deals with sex. Do you believe this large amount of sexual traffic detracts from the goals and objectives of the Internet? Do you object to the use of public funds to transmit such material? Why or why not?

6. Do you agree that the University of Waterloo was justified in banning obscene bulletin boards from its network? Should obscene bulletin boards be banned from the Information Superhighway as a whole? Are obscene bulletin boards accessible from your connection to the network?

7. Has a government regulation ever prevented you from accessing services you felt you had a right to? For example, when the FCC ruled that cable companies cannot rebroadcast FM signals, the author's community lost its cable access to National Public Radio and several other FM stations. Since we live in an area too remote for good FM reception, we became disconnected from these important stations. And without any warning! Have you had a similar experience? If our government cannot regulate access to a simple FM radio station, how will it ever manage an Information Superhighway?

8. How do you feel about encryption and the Clipper Chip? Since court-ordered wiretaps on the analog telephone lines of criminals will no longer be effective when all of the communication channels go digital, is the government justified in requiring that a "back door" be built into the system through which it can eavesdrop on digital communications? Why or why not?

9. The Clinton administration has promised the public that everyone will have equal access to the Information Superhighway. Do you believe this, or do you feel that its construction will create a technological underclass in our society? What do you see as the major obstacles that must be overcome to provide equal access for everyone?

10. Providing access to every citizen implies that the network is easy enough for everyone to use. The failure of Microsoft's Bob and Apple's eWorld demonstrates that we have not yet found the right way to provide access to the mass public. The challenge is to make computers easy enough for all citizens to use. Since half of the people are by definition below average, this means making computers easy enough for below-average citizens to use. Do you think this is possible? How would you design such a user interface?

17 How to Keep Up

After completing this chapter, you will be able to:

- Know what magazines you should read to keep up with the fast-paced field of multimedia

- Understand how multimedia CDs and networked resources can help you stay current with new technology

- Find out about conferences and exhibits where you can see the latest multimedia hardware and software products

HERE are many reasons why you need to keep up with what is happening in multimedia. Since the ability to use it is emerging as a life skill, you will continually need to develop your multimedia techniques to stay competitive in your profession and live life fully in the information society. As the technology changes and you upgrade your computer, you will need the latest information and advice on what to buy. By subscribing to the periodicals, joining the associations, and attending the conferences listed in this chapter, you will be able to remain current and even contribute your own opinions and ideas about multimedia access to the Information Superhighway.

PERIODICALS

NewMedia

THE MAGAZINE FOR CREATORS OF THE DIGITAL FUTURE

NewMedia magazine is probably the best single source for keeping up with what's new in multimedia. It appears monthly and publishes an annual buyer's guide. *NewMedia* contains dozens of full-color pictures that illustrate the products it describes, and the layout is visually appealing.

To subscribe to *NewMedia*, write to P.O. Box 1771, Riverton, NJ 08077-7331. Phone (415) 573-5170. Fax (415) 573-5131. Be sure to ask about a free subscription, which is available to qualified readers.

NewMedia is also available on the Web at http://www.hyperstand.com, where you will find even more information than what is contained in the printed version.

Internet World

A good source for the latest news about the Information Superhighway, *Internet World* features articles about new trends on the network, advertises Internet addresses of new online resources, and reviews books about the Internet. IWLabs educate users and buyers about important new Internet products and technologies for home and business. *Internet World* presents profiles of the key companies, people, and products that impact the Internet's growth and development. Penetrating analyses probe legal, social, and ethical issues.

Internet World is published monthly by Mecklermedia Corporation, 20 Ketchum Street, Westport, CT 06880. Phone (203) 226-6967. Fax (203) 454-5840. E-mail info@mecklermedia.com. There is an online version at http://www. mecklermedia.com.

T.H.E. Journal

T.H.E. stands for Technological Horizons in Education. *T.H.E. Journal* appears monthly; each issue contains application highlights and dozens of new product announcements. Each year, *T.H.E. Journal* publishes the *Multimedia Source Guide,* which lists hundreds of multimedia products and tells how to order them. Subscribers also receive special multimedia supplements from vendors like IBM, Apple, and Zenith.

T.H.E. Journal is free to qualified individuals in educational institutions and training departments in the United States and Canada. To subscribe, call (714) 730-4011 or fax (714) 730-3739. The mailing address is: 150 El Camino Real, Suite 112, Tustin, CA 92680. There is also an online version at http://www.thejournal.com. The online version lets you download product demos, search back issues, and read articles that did not appear in the printed journal.

Technology & Learning

Technology & Learning is published monthly, except in December and the summer months. Targeted primarily at precollege educators, it reviews software, advertises grants and contests, contains vendor supplements, articulates classroom needs, reviews authoring tools, and has a Q&A section to answer questions about technology and learning. Plus it has great cartoons.

To subscribe call (513) 847-5900. The mailing address is: Peter Li, Inc., 330 Progress Road, Dayton, OH 45449. The online version at http://www.techlearning.com has searchable software reviews.

Wired

Wired is an award-winning monthly magazine that captures the excitement and the substance of the digital revolution. The best writers and designers in the world help you identify the people, companies, and ideas shaping our future.

To subscribe, contact: Wired, 520 Third Street, San Francisco, CA 94107. Phone (800) SO WIRED. Fax (415) 222-6399. E-mail subscription@wired.com.

Syllabus

Syllabus magazine informs educators on how technology can be used to support teaching, learning, and administrative activities. Each issue includes feature articles, case studies, product reviews, and profiles of technology use at the individual, departmental, and institutional level. Regular features cover multimedia, distance learning, the Internet, quantitative tools, publishing, and administrative technology. A variety of multiplatform technologies are covered, including computers, video, multimedia, and telecommunications. Special supplements to *Syllabus* are published on a regular basis, including *Windows on Campus, Computer Science Edition, Engineering Edition,* and *Science and Medicine Edition. Syllabus* is published nine times per year, following the academic calendar.

Syllabus is published by Syllabus Press, 1307 S. Mary Ave., Suite 211, Sunnyvale, CA 94087. Phone (408) 746-2000. Fax (408) 746-2711. Highlights from recent issues are found at http://www.syllabus.com.

Communications Industries Report

Communications Industries Report is the monthly newspaper of the International Communications Industries Association (ICIA). It covers new developments, emerging standards, and analytical reports on video, multimedia, computers, audiovisuals, teleconferencing, industry trends, and government regulations and initiatives.

To subscribe, contact Atwood Convention Publishing at 11600 College Blvd., Overland Park, KS 66210. Phone (913) 469-1110. Fax (913) 469-0806. Web site http://www.usa.net/icia.

Cinefex

If you are interested in cinematic special effects, *Cinefex* is the magazine for you. Since 1980 *Cinefex* has been the bible for special-effects enthusiasts. A profusely illustrated quarterly publication, *Cinefex* covers its subject comprehensively, from miniatures and matte paintings, to exotic makeup and animatronics, to computer-generated imagery and beyond. With each issue the illusions in two or three major films are examined in detail via interviews with key effects artists. Shorter articles unveil technological advances in commercials, music videos, and theme park attractions. The articles identify the multimedia software packages used to create the special effects.

To subscribe, contact Cinefex at P.O. Box 20027, Riverside, CA 92516. Phone (800) 434-3339.

CATALOGS

Directory of Video, Multimedia & Audio-Visual Products

The annual *Directory of Video, Multimedia & Audio-Visual Products* describes more than 3,000 products and services in detail, including photographs, suggested retail price, compatibility, size, weight, and technical specifications. More than 300 manufacturers are represented. There is a glossary of terms, trade names to help you find out who made a certain piece of equipment, and a new, improved index.

The *Directory* is published by the International Communications Industries Association (ICIA), P.O. Box 100, Shawnee Mission, KS 66201. Phone (800) 255-6038. Fax (913) 492-9900. Web site http://www.usa.net/icia.

EDUCORP Online

EDUCORP publishes an extensive catalog of CD-ROM titles. The catalog is available in print and online on the Web.

The online version is at http://www.educorp.com. To get the printed copy, contact EDUCORP Multimedia at 7434 Trade Street, San Francisco, CA. Phone (800) 843-9497. Fax (619) 536-2345.

Multimedia and Videodisc Compendium

The *Multimedia and Videodisc Compendium for Education and Training* is a great way to find out about current videodisc, CD, and multimedia-related software titles. The bound edition appears annually in September, and updates are published each January and July. A QuickSearch Index provides easy access to products by subject, title, company, and other topics in the listing. The *Compendium* provides detailed information on more than 4,200 products for use in education and training. To subscribe contact Emerging Technology Consultants at 2819 Hamline Avenue North, St. Paul, MN 55113-7118. Phone (612) 639-3973. Fax (612) 639-0110.

CD-ROM Online

CD-ROM Online is written for the CD-ROM Multimedia PC user interested in news and reviews of the best CD-ROMs and multimedia products. CD-ROM Online is delivered to your desktop every month, free of charge, via electronic mail. The CD-ROM Online Web site archives back issues as well as the current issue.

To subscribe to go http://www.nsiweb.com/cdrom and choose "Subscribe to CD-ROM Online! (FREE)."

PROFESSIONAL ASSOCIATIONS

AECT

AECT stands for Association for Educational Communications and Technology; it is the leading international organization representing instructional technology professionals working in schools, colleges and universities, and the corporate, government, and military sectors. The mission of the AECT is to provide leadership in educational communications and technology by linking professionals holding a common interest in the use of educational technology and its application to the learning process. The association maintains an active publications program that includes *Tech Trends,* published six times during the academic year; *Educational Technology Research and Development,* a research journal published four times a year; and a large number of books and videotapes.

All members of the AECT receive *Tech Trends* automatically. To join contact AECT at 1025 Vermont Avenue NW, Suite 820, Washington, DC 20005. Phone (202) 347-7834. Fax (202) 347-7839. E-mail aect@aect.org. Web site http://www.aect.org.

SALT

SALT stands for Society for Applied Learning Technology. It holds semiannual conferences and exhibits, and sponsors the publication of research journals. Like the AECT, SALT covers a broad range of applications, with a special focus on industrial and military training applications. Both the AECT and SALT are excellent meetings to attend for anyone dealing with media, regardless of your industry or subject area.

To join SALT, contact their headquarters at 50 Culpeper Street, Warrenton, VA 20186. Phone (540) 347-0055. Fax (540) 349-3169. E-mail salt@lti.org.

ICIA

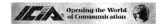

The International Communications Industries Association (ICIA) publishes the aforementioned *Directory of Video, Multimedia & Audio-Visual Products* that lists thousands of products and services. Entries include illustrations, prices, uses, features, specifications, compatibility, and vendor contact information. For ordering information or to join the association, contact ICIA at 11242 Waples Mill Rd., Suite 200, Fairfax, VA 22030. Phone (703) 273-7200. Fax (703) 278-8082. Web site http://www.usa.net/icia.

CONFERENCES AND EXHIBITS

INFOCOMM International

INFOCOMM and INFOCOMM Asia are annual exhibits of audiovisual and new media equipment sponsored by the International Communications Industries Association (ICIA). Cruising the aisles of the INFOCOMM exhibit is an excellent way to see the latest in audiovisual and multimedia presentation technology. For information on upcoming INFOCOMM conferences, contact the ICIA at 11242 Waples Mill Rd., Suite 200, Fairfax, VA 22030. Phone (703) 273-7200. Fax (703) 278-8082. Web site http://www.usa.net/icia.

COMDEX

SOFTBANK COMDEX is the world's leading producer of expositions and conferences for the information technology industry. COMDEX conferences are held all over the world. In the United States, COMDEX is held twice a year, once in the fall and again in the spring. The exhibit is so large that few cities have enough exhibition space to host it. COMDEX/Fall is held in Las Vegas, and COMDEX/Spring is held in Atlanta or Chicago.

COMDEX used to be attended almost exclusively by remarketers looking for products to sell, but now the majority of those attending are end users in search of computing solutions. Vendors invest a small fortune on their COMDEX booths, giveaways, and promotions, and attending COMDEX at least once is an experience anyone working with media will enjoy. For information about COMDEX, contact: SOFTBANK COMDEX Inc., 300 First Avenue, Needham, MA 02194-2722. Phone (617) 433-1500. Fax (617) 449-6953. Web site http://www.comdex.com.

CeBIT

CeBIT is the world's largest computer and communications show, with 600,000 attendees and more than 6,500 company exhibits from 60 countries. It is held annually each March in Hannover, Germany. Regarded as the most important show for introducing products in the German and European markets, the seven-day event features eight USA pavilions, including a USA multimedia pavillion in one of the show's busiest exhibit halls. For information call Hannover Fairs USA at (609) 987-1202 or fax (609) 987-0092.

Ed-Media

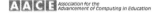

Ed-Media is an international conference on educational multimedia and hypermedia. It includes papers, panels, tutorials, workshops, demonstrations, poster sessions, and tours. Ed-Media is sponsored by the Association for the Advancement of Computing in Education (AACE), P.O. Box 2966, Charlottesville, VA 22902. Phone (804) 973-3987. Fax (804) 978-7449. E-mail AACE@virginia.edu. Web site http://aace.virginia.edu/aace/conf/edmedia.html.

NAB MultiMedia World

NAB MultiMedia World is an annual conference sponsored by the National Association of Broadcasters. It includes multimedia presentations and exhibitions, computers, consumer electronics, telecommunications, publishing, and entertainment. Phone (202) 775-4972. Fax (301) 216-1847. Web site http://www.nab.org.

Interactive Healthcare

Interactive Healthcare is an annual conference dealing with the use of videodisc, CD-ROM, CD-I, and multimedia applications for medicine, nursing, allied health, continuing education, patient education, and health promotion. For information call Stewart Publishing at (703) 354-8155 or fax (703) 354-2177. Web site http://www.erols.com/stewpub.

National Demonstration Laboratory

The National Demonstration Laboratory (NDL), which was established at the Smithsonian Institution in 1987 as the leading demonstration site and clearinghouse on educational multimedia technologies, joined the Academy for Educational Development in 1994 to provide leadership in the application of new media technologies to human development and educational needs in the U.S. and throughout the world. The NDL provides technical assistance, technology awareness workshops, and free public demonstrations by appointment. The NDL collection contains 20 interactive workstations, four Internet workstations, and hundreds of high-quality multimedia applications on a variety of subjects, including language, health, science, math, social science, art, and business training. Individuals may also make an appointment to preview specific applications and multimedia authoring tools during non-demonstration hours. The NDL offers one-, two-, and three-day courses covering both introductory and advanced approaches to multimedia and online communications.

The NDL is located at 1255 23rd Street NW, Washington, D.C. 20037 (Dupont Circle or Foggy Bottom Metro stops). For more information visit the NDL Web site at http://www.aed.org/ndl. The NDL director, Jacqueline Hess, may be reached at (202) 884-8906 or via her e-mail address: jhess@aed.org.

NETWORKED RESOURCES

EDUPAGE

EDUPAGE is a triweekly digest of the week's major news items on information technology. It is available on the Web at http://www.educom.edu, or you can subscribe by sending e-mail to listproc@educom.unc.edu. Leave the subject line blank and, as your message, type:

> Subscribe EDUPAGE *Firstname Lastname*

Replace *Firstname* and *Lastname* with your first and last names.

Electronic Frontier Foundation

The Electronic Frontier Foundation is a professional organization concerned with the legal, social, and political aspects of networks. To subscribe, address an e-mail message to eff-request@eff.org containing the one-line message **Please add me to the mailing list**. Then add a line providing your real name, and one more line stating your e-mail address.

Everybody's Internet Update

Everybody's Internet Update is published monthly by the Electronic Frontier Foundation. Current and back issues are on the Web at http://www.eff.org/pub/Net_info/EFF_Net_Guide/Updates. To receive the updates via e-mail, write to listserv@eff.org. Leave the subject line blank and, as your message, type:

> add net-guide-update

Internet Resources Listserv

The Internet Resources Listserv sends regular updates on new happenings on the Internet. To subscribe, address an e-mail message to listserv@vm1.nodak.edu. Leave the subject line blank and, as your message, type:

> Subscribe news *Firstname Lastname*

Replace *Firstname* and *Lastname* with your first and last names.

Morph's Outpost

Morph's Outpost on the Digital Frontier admits to being on the far side, "where the information superhighway runs into the jungle, and pioneers stop for supplies and sustenance before moving on to blaze new trails," but that makes it captivating to read. Loaded with information, Morph's Outpost contains new product announcements, buyer's guides, marketing tips, new tools, CD-ROM reviews, news on alliances and mergers, and interviews with leading developers. You will surely enjoy the *Adventures of Morph* cartoon strip.

Morph's Outpost is published daily on the World Wide Web at http:// www.morph.com.

Netsurfer Digest

Netsurfer Digest is a great way to keep up with the latest hot spots on the Internet. Netsurfer Digest is on the Web at http://www.netsurf.com/nsd. To receive each new issue via e-mail, you can subscribe by sending e-mail to nsdigest-request@netsurf.com. Leave the subject line blank and, as your message, type:

```
subscribe nsdigest-text
```

Seidman's Online Insider

Another great source of information about the Internet is Seidman's Online Insider, which you will find on the Web at http://www.clark.net:80/pub/robert/home.html. Past issues (all the way back to the premier issue in September 1994) are found there. The Web site is nice because the issues are in HTML with links to all the places Seidman references.

To receive the newsletter via e-mail, send an e-mail message to LISTSERV @PEACH.EASE.LSOFT.COM. Leave the subject line blank and, as your message, type:

```
SUBSCRIBE ONLINE-L Firstname Lastname
```

Replace *Firstname* and *Lastname* with your first and last names.

TERC

TERC, a nonprofit organization founded in 1965, researches, develops, and disseminates innovative programs in science, mathematics, and technology for educators, schools, and other learning environments. TERC is organized into four project-based centers: Mathematics, Research, Science, and Tools for Learning. Some of the recent TERC projects include:

- **The Global Laboratory project:** A worldwide network of student scientists from more than 20 countries involved in collaborative environmental investigations

- **New Directions in Science Playgrounds:** Creating a new type of playground equipment that facilitates the kinesthetic learning of elementary notions of physics in playground activities

- **LabNet:** A telecomputing network of the science teaching community

- **The Hub:** A World Wide Web link to a growing collection of educational resources and services for mathematics, science, and technology educators

You will find TERC online at http://hub.terc.edu.

AAHE Listserv

The American Association for Higher Education (AAHE) has a lively listserv discussion of current topics in educational technology. The AAHE hosts regional and national Teaching and Learning with Technology (TLT) conferences to help colleges and universities make effective use of technology. To join the AAHE listserv, address an e-mail message to LISTPROC@LIST.CREN.NET. Leave the subject line blank and, as your message, type:

> **SUBSCRIBE AAHESGIT** *Firstname Lastname*

Replace *Firstname* and *Lastname* with your first and last names.

INFOBITS

INFOBITS is an electronic service of the Institute for Academic Technology (IAT) at the University of North Carolina at Chapel Hill. Each month the IAT monitors and selects from a number of information technology and ed tech sources and provides brief notes in INFOBITS for electronic dissemination to educators. To subscribe to INFOBITS, address an e-mail message to listserv@unc.edu. Leave the subject line blank and, as your message, type:

> **SUBSCRIBE INFOBITS** *Firstname Lastname*

substituting your own first and last names. INFOBITS is also available online at http://www.iat.unc.edu/infobits/infobits.html.

Distance Education Online Symposium

DEOSNEWS is an online service of the Distance Education Online Symposium (DEOS), headquartered at Pennsylvania State University's College of Education. DEOSNEWS has more than 3,500 subscribers in 63 countries. To subscribe to DEOSNEWS and DEOS-L (a discussion forum), send an e-mail message to LISTSERV@PSUVM.PSU.EDU containing the text:

> **Subscribe DEOSNEWS** *Firstname Lastname*
>
> **Subscribe DEOS-L** *Firstname Lastname*

Replace *Firstname* and *Lastname* with your first and last names.

LISTSERV SEMINARS AND WORKSHOPS

TOURBUS

TOURBUS is a free, virtual tour of the Internet that sends you two e-mail messages a week, telling you about neat Internet sites and tools. To subscribe, address an e-mail message to LISTSERV@LISTSERV.AOL.COM. Leave the subject line blank and, as your message, type:

> **SUBSCRIBE TOURBUS** *Firstname Lastname*

substituting your own first and last names. The TOURBUS messages are archived on the Web at http://csbh.mhv.net/~bobrankin/tourbus.

Atlas

Atlas is a five-week World Wide Web training workshop. The first half of the workshop is distributed via e-mail using a listserver, and the second half is conducted on the Web. Atlas is completely self-paced, so there is no preset starting or ending time. You can find the latest information at http://ua1vm.ua.edu/~crispen/atlas.html.

Roadmap

Roadmap is a free, 27-lesson Internet training workshop. More than 80,000 people in 75 countries have participated in the online version of the Roadmap workshop, and more than 500,000 users have visited the archives. For more information check out the Roadmap home page at http://ua1vm.ua.edu/~crispen/roadmap.html.

EXERCISES

1. Visit your local library and find out whether it subscribes to the periodicals listed in the first part of this chapter. If it does not, ask why not, and then suggest or insist that it should.

2. Several multimedia periodicals offer free subscriptions. If you do not already subscribe to them, apply for your free subscription today, following the instructions provided in the "Periodicals" section of this chapter.

3. Are you aware of good sources for keeping up with multimedia that were not mentioned in this chapter? If so, what are they?

4. Of the many conferences and exhibits listed in this chapter, find out which one will occur nearest you during the coming year, and make plans to attend it. Do you know of other multimedia conferences or exhibits not listed in this chapter?

5. If you ever plan to visit Washington, D.C., be sure to call (202) 884-8906 in advance to make an appointment to visit the National Demonstration Laboratory. If you live within driving distance, ask your teacher to make arrangements to take your class there for a field trip.

Part Five

Multimedia Tools and Techniques

It should be as easy to author in a medium as it is to experience works created in it.
— Ivan Illich, paraphrased by Brenda Laurel, *Edutopia* 1, no.1 (Winter 1993): 6

This part of the book begins the hands-on tutorial that will prepare you to create your own multimedia applications. You will learn how to use a set of everyday multimedia tools and, through practice, develop techniques that will make you proficient in creating applications.

The tutorials in this book teach you how to use the following tools: Paint Shop Pro to capture and format graphics; Video for Windows to record and edit movies and animations; Band-in-a-Box to generate MIDI sequences; WebEdit to create World Wide Web pages; WS_FTP to mount pages on the Web; PKZIP to create self-extracting archives that you can publish on the Web; and a suite of tools in PODIUM for Windows enabling you to record and play back waveform digital audio, make CD Audio and videodisc clips, snap still pictures from a live video source, send and receive multimedia e-mail, and use a multimedia toolbox to link hypertext and hyperpicture triggers on the screen to multimedia objects. Thus, you will learn how to create multimedia applications.

PODIUM is just one of many software packages you can use to create multimedia applications. The many alternatives to PODIUM include presentation packages—such as PowerPoint, Compel, Freelance, Harvard Graphics, ASAP WordPower, Aldus Persuasion, or WordPerfect Presentations—and authoring systems such as Authorware Professional, ToolBook, Quest, TenCore, and IconAuthor. Many of these packages are discussed in Chapter 9.

PODIUM was chosen for this book because it contains a multimedia toolbox that makes it easy for students to complete the tutorial exercises. Users who are familiar with other packages will realize that many of the PODIUM techniques taught in this book can be applied using other sets of tools. What is important here is not the choice of a specific tool, but rather the concepts that are being presented. Later on, the student can apply these techniques using the tools available in different software packages.

18 Screen Design Principles

After completing this chapter, you will understand screen design principles that will prepare you to:

- [ ] **Arrange text in the proper size, color, and font on a multimedia screen**

- [ ] **Choose an appropriate background color and understand how foreground text colors interact with background screen colors**

- [ ] **Arrange pictures on the screen either as background images or design elements for text to flow around**

- [ ] **Make text stand out against a background photo**

- [ ] **Adopt a common look and feel for the screens in your application**

HE hands-on tutorial in this part of the book will enable you to place text anywhere on the screen in any size, color, or font you want. You will learn how to put pictures on the screen, either as backgrounds that appear behind the text, or as design elements around which text flows. Then you will learn how to make your screens interactive by making hypertext links and placing buttons on the screen. Before you begin, it is important to understand a few principles of multimedia screen design that will help you make screens that have a good layout.

Layout

Multimedia screens consist of several design elements, including text, pictures, icons, triggers, and buttons. The relationships among these elements on the screen are called **layout**. When you create a multimedia screen, you should plan its layout so your content gets presented with good balance. Think of dividing the screen into regions, of which some will be pictorial, with others consisting of blocks of text. You must also think about how the user will interact with your screen, and include the appropriate navigational buttons and hypertext links.

Figures 18-1 through 18-6 analyze the screen layouts of some highly successful multimedia applications. Notice how some rely heavily on text, whereas others are more graphical. All of them provide intuitive ways to navigate that make these applications user-friendly.

18-1

Textual screen design.

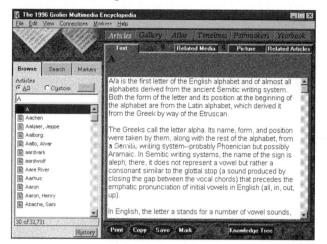

18-2

Layout analysis of Figure 18-1.

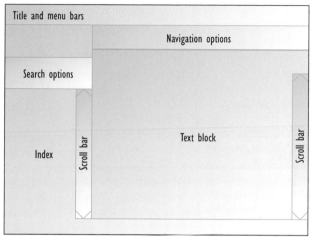

18-3

Graphical screen design.

18-4

Layout analysis of Figure 18-3.

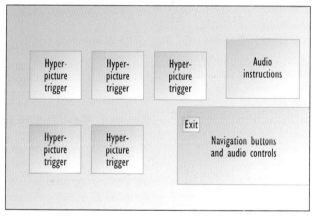

18-5

Mixed screen design.

18-6

Layout analysis of Figure 18-5.

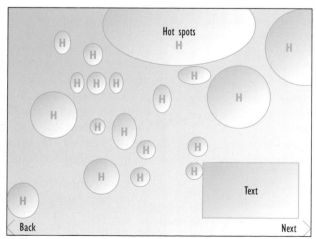

18-7

Standard Windows fonts.

Times New Roman	ABCDEFGabcdefg123456789
Courier New	ABCDEFGabcdefg123456789
Arial	**ABCDEFGabcdefg123456789**
Symbol	ΑΒΧΔΕΦΓαβχδεφγ123456789
Wingdings	✌✍✋👍☛☝☞♋♌♍♎♐📁📄📋⌛⌨🖱

18-8

Comparison of proportional and nonproportional spacing.

Times New Roman

Proportional fonts are pleasing to the eye; their characters are varied in width and easier to read. Use them in text blocks like this, but not for tables:

Sales:	$100,000	$85,000	$43,614
Taxes:	54,521	3,425	6,921
Fees:	231,947	41	324
Total:	$386,468	$88,466	$50,859

Courier New

Nonproportional, or monospaced, fonts are regimented and somewhat graceless, but make vertical alignment much easier:

Sales:	$100,000	$85,000	$43,614
Taxes:	54,521	3,425	6,921
Fees:	231,947	41	324
Total:	$386,468	$88,466	$50,859

Font Selection

The Microsoft Windows TrueType font technology enables you to place any font on the screen in any size and color you want. There are hundreds of different fonts available from vendors such as Adobe and Corel. But be careful when you choose a font for a multimedia application you intend to publish. If the font you choose is not installed on the user's machine, your screen will not appear as intended.

You can rely on all Windows users having the standard fonts listed in Figure 18-7. These fonts are installed with every Windows setup. If your application uses a different font, you must publish that font along with your application. Most fonts are licensed and protected by copyright; make sure you have permission for any fonts you distribute.

Of the five fonts that ship with Windows, all are proportionally spaced except for Courier New. **Proportional spacing** means that wide letters like *m* and *w* take up more space than thin letters like *l* and *i*. Normally, you will want to use a proportional font, because proportional fonts are easier to read than monospaced fonts. However, if you want to make columns of text line up precisely on the screen, such as in a spreadsheet, you will need to use the nonproportional Courier font. Figure 18-8 illustrates the difference between proportional and nonproportional spacing.

An important difference between the Times New Roman and Arial fonts is that Times New Roman has serifs, whereas Arial does not. A **serif** is a line stemming at an angle from the ends of the strokes of a letter. Typefaces without serifs are called **sans serif** fonts. Figure 18-9 compares a few characters from the Times New Roman and Arial fonts, pointing out the serifs in Times New Roman.

18-9

Comparison of Times New Roman and Arial fonts.

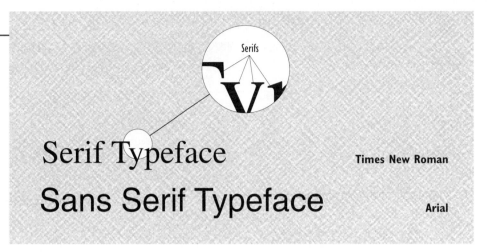

18-10

Comparison of different point sizes.

Text Sizing

Text size is measured in **points**, which tell how high the character is. Windows TrueType fonts can be sized to any standard point size. They can also be stretched and squeezed to create a wide variety of nonstandard sizes. In print media a point is $1/72$ inch. In multimedia a point is about the height of a single pixel on a 640×480 computer screen. Due to different-sized monitors, the actual size of the text will vary somewhat depending on the physical height of the screen. Figure 18-10 illustrates different point sizes.

18-11

Recommended color
combinations and colors
to avoid.

Background Color	Recommended Foregrounds	Foregrounds to Avoid
White	Black, DarkBlue, Red	Yellow, Cyan, LightGray
Blue	White, Yellow, Cyan	Green, Black
Pink	Black, White, Yellow, Blue	Green, Red, Cyan
Red	Yellow, White, Black	Pink, Cyan, Blue, Green
Yellow	Red, Blue, Black	White, Cyan
Green	Black, Red, Blue	Cyan, Pink, Yellow
Cyan	Blue, Black, Red	Green, Yellow, White
LightGray	Black, DarkBlue, DarkPink	Green, Cyan, Yellow
Gray	Yellow, White, Blue	DarkGray, DarkCyan
DarkGray	Cyan, Yellow, Green	Red, Gray
Black	White, Cyan, Green, Yellow	DarkRed, DarkCyan
DarkBlue	Yellow, White, Pink, Green	DarkGreen, Black
DarkPink	Green, Yellow, White	Black, DarkCyan
DarkRed	White, LightGray, Yellow	Black, DarkBlue
Brown	Yellow, Cyan, White	Red, Pink, DarkGreen
DarkGreen	Cyan, White, Yellow	DarkBlue, DarkRed
DarkCyan	White, Yellow, Cyan	Brown, Blue, Gray

Foreground Versus Background Colors

In the next chapter, you will learn how to create colored backgrounds upon which
you will place foreground text in different colors. The choice of the foreground
and background colors is up to you. Some color combinations work better than
others. Figure 18-11 illustrates recommended color combinations as well as colors
to avoid.

Placing Text on Photographic Backgrounds

Exercise care when placing text on photographic backgrounds. Some photos are
so busy that text placed atop them is difficult to read. A drop shadow can improve
the readability of text placed on photographic backgrounds. Figure 18-12 illustrates
text printed on top of a background photo with different amounts of drop shadow.

18-12

A drop shadow can improve
the readability of text
printed on top of a
background photo.

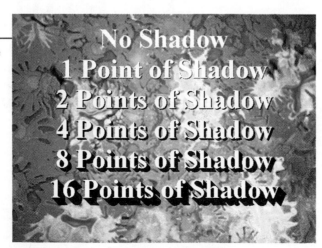

Arranging Text and Pictures on the Screen

Although drop-shadowed text looks cool overlayed on pictures that are not too busy to detract from the readability of the text, you should not overuse text overlay. It is often better to position text above or below a picture, or to flow text around a picture, rather than overlay text on top of an image.

Navigational icons normally work best when they appear lined up in the same region of the screen, instead of being scattered about the screen. Try to position the icons in a logical order. For example, it is logical to place the page-back icon in the lower left corner of the screen, and page-forward in the lower right. Here is a suggested sequence of icons that give the user the option to go back one page, quit, return to the beginning, return to the menu, print the screen, or go forward one page:

It is important that multimedia screens be easy to use. When you plan your layout and decide where you will place pictures and text on your screen, make sure you include navigational buttons, icons, or hypertext to clarify what the navigational options are and where the user should click to navigate.

Because hypertext includes words, your hypertext can be self-documenting. For example, the phrases *Return to the Menu, Next Page, Previous Page, Stop, Print Screen,* and *Quit* can appear in hypertext which, when clicked, makes what they say happen. Iconic navigation is often more effective, takes up less screen space, and works better with international audiences because the icons can be understood regardless of what language the user speaks. For example, instead of the hypertext phrases, you can use icons like these:

Be consistent. If you adopt navigational icons, use them consistently throughout your application. If you use hypertext navigation, be consistent in how you word the directions.

Metaphors

In multimedia screen design, a **metaphor** is a way of thinking about new media in terms of something the user already knows. For example, when a multimedia application launches a series of images that the user will view sequentially, it may help to use the metaphor of a slide show. You might even use the icon of a slide projector to launch the slide show:

In addition to providing buttons to move back and forth through the slides, you could carry the slide projector metaphor a bit further and make a left mouse click show the next slide, and a right click back up a slide, just like the remote control buttons on a 35mm slide projector.

Other metaphors found in multimedia applications include the book (for paging through multimedia screens), a stack of cards (popularized by HyperCard), the tape recorder (for recording and playing back audio clips, as in Microsoft's Media Player), a television tuner (for selecting TV channels on multimedia PCs with TV tuners), and the jukebox (for selecting songs to play). Be creative and inventive in your use of metaphors. Think hard about the content of your application, imagine yourself as a user trying to navigate through it, and adopt a metaphor to help orient the user and make your application intuitive.

Adopting a Common Look and Feel

Avoid the temptation to demonstrate every trick you know when you design a multimedia application. Keep it simple. Do not make every screen look and work a different way. Rather, adopt a common look and feel so the user will be able to navigate intuitively after getting used to how your screens work.

It is frustrating to use an application that mixes metaphors and changes what icons mean on different screens. Be consistent. If users have to relearn how to use your application every time they run it, your design is not intuitive.

Successful designers develop the ability to think like a user and imagine themselves being a first-time user of the application. If you can learn to think like the user, look through the eyes of a novice at the screen you are designing, and imagine how the first-time user will interact with your application, you will become a good multimedia designer. Remember that most users are not as smart as you are. You cannot underestimate the skills of the average user. By definition of the term *average*, half of all users are below average. A successful design takes into account the needs of all potential users.

EXERCISES

1. Suppose you have a photo, two paragraphs of text, a one-line title, and navigational icons for page forward, page back, home, and quit. Sketch three different ways of laying out these design elements on a multimedia screen. Assume that you have the capability to resize the photo, making it as large or as small as you want. Indeed, you will acquire that ability later on in this tutorial.

2. List three different ways you could write a hypertext instruction on the screen which, when clicked, takes the user to the application's home or startup screen.

3. Draw three different ways of providing an icon that moves forward to the next screen of an application.

4. In discussing the role of the metaphor in multimedia applications, this chapter cited the slide projector, the book, the card stack, the tape recorder, the TV tuner, and the jukebox. List three more metaphors and tell how they would be used in a multimedia application. Can you think of a metaphor you have never encountered on a computer screen before?

19 WYSIWYG Text Editing

After completing this chapter, you will be able to:

- Create the folders or directories that store multimedia applications on disk

- Tell people what **WYSIWYG** means

- Create a new multimedia screen and position text on it

- Size, center, edit, shadow, color, and clone text

- Display text in any **TrueType** font installed on your computer

- Change foreground and background colors

- Associate text with mouse clicks, to make text elements appear one-by-one as the user clicks the mouse

EXT is a key element of most multimedia applications, and a good working knowledge of how to enter, edit, and manipulate text is a basic requirement for anyone who wants to become multiliterate. This tutorial begins by showing you how to enter, position, size, color, shadow, clone, and edit text in a multimedia application. You will also learn how to import text from other sources, including word processors and scanners.

Creating a Directory

Before you create a multimedia application, you need to make a directory on your hard disk to put it in. Think of your hard drive as a huge file cabinet that stores information. A directory is like a drawer in the file cabinet. Each multimedia screen you create will be stored in a file that you keep in this directory. Depending on the version of Windows you have, the instructions for creating directories are a little different. Follow the instructions for the version of Windows on your computer.

Movie on CD

Demonstrations
➧ Show Me!
  ➧ Text Editing
    ➧ **Creating a
      Directory in
      Windows 95**

WINDOWS 95

To create a directory with Windows 95, you use the Explorer. To get the Explorer started, you use the Windows 95 Start button. If the Start button is not visible on your screen, hold down the Ctrl key and press Esc, and the Start button will appear. Click the Start button and choose Programs. Figure 19-1 shows how the Explorer is found on the Programs menu. Click on the Explorer to get it running. Figure 19-2 shows how the Explorer provides a visual diagram of how all the files are organized on your computer. For example, if you click the icon that represents your CD-ROM drive, you will see the many directories of the *Multiliteracy CD*

19-1

The Explorer is one of the choices on the Windows 95 Start button's Programs menu.

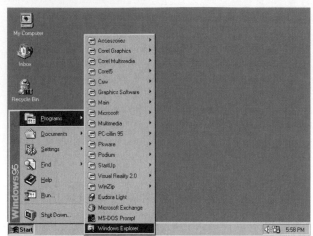

19-2

The Explorer provides a visual overview of all the files and directories on your computer.

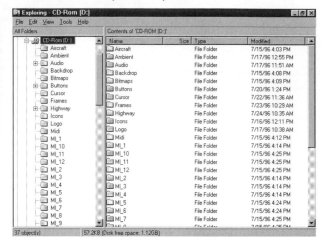

(assuming the *Multiliteracy CD* is currently in the drive). Each directory contains the files needed to present one chapter of this book. Double-click the directory icons to inspect the contents of the individual directories. *Important:* Under Windows 95, directories are usually called folders. In this book, whenever you find the term *directory,* know that under Windows 95, the term *folder* is synonymous.

To create a new directory for your application, follow these steps:

▶ Click the icon that represents the hard disk drive on which you will create the directory for your multimedia application.

▶ Pull down the File menu, select New, and select Folder. Figure 19-3 shows how the new folder will appear with the name *New Folder.*

▶ For this tutorial, you need to make the name of the new folder be *multilit.* Since the name *New Folder* is already selected, you can change the name by simply typing **multilit**

▶ Close the Explorer by clicking on the ⊠ in the upper right corner of the window.

19-3

When you create a new folder, it initially has the name *New Folder.*

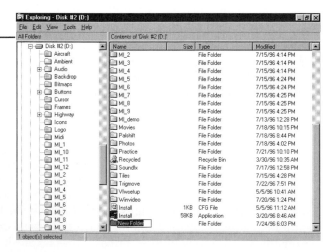

19-4

The File Manager icon appears in the Main group on the Windows desktop.

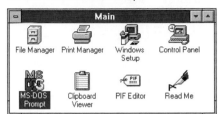

19-5

The Windows File Manager uses a file cabinet metaphor.

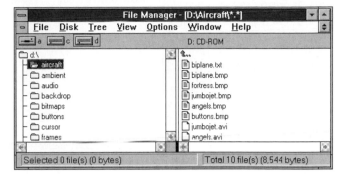

19-6

The Windows File Manager's Create Directory dialog.

Movie on CD

Demonstrations
➡ Show Me!
  ➡ Text Editing
    ➡ **Creating a Directory in Windows 3.1**

WINDOWS 3.1, WINDOWS NT, OR SOFTWINDOWS

To create a directory with Windows 3.1 and compatibles, you use the Windows File Manager. Figure 19-4 shows you how to find the File Manager's icon in the Main group on the Windows desktop. If the Main group is not visible, pull down the Window menu and select Main to bring it up, then double-click the File Manager icon to launch the File Manager. Figure 19-5 shows how the File Manager provides a visual diagram of how all the files are organized on your computer. For example, if you click the icon that represents your CD-ROM drive, you will see the many directories of the *Multiliteracy CD* (assuming this CD is currently in the drive). Each directory contains the files needed to present one chapter of this book. Double-click the directory icons to inspect the contents of the individual directories.

To create a new directory for your application, follow these steps:

▶ Click the icon that represents the hard disk drive in which you will create the directory for your multimedia application.

▶ Pull down the File menu and select Create Directory to bring up the dialog in Figure 19-6.

▶ For this tutorial, you need to create a directory called *multilit*. Assuming your hard drive is C, type **c:\multilit**

▶ Click OK. The directory should now appear in the list of directories displayed by the File Manager. If it does not, scroll to the top of the list on the left side of the File Manager and double-click on the c:\ you will find there.

▶ Close the File Manager by pulling down its File menu and choosing Exit.

19-7

The File Creation dialog
lets you create a new
custom screen.

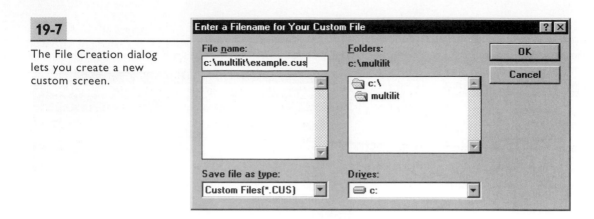

Movie on CD

Demonstrations
➧ Show Me!
  ➧ Text Editing
    ➧ **Starting a**
      New Screen

Starting a New Screen

Now you are ready to create your first multimedia screen! Follow these steps:

▶ If you do not have PODIUM running at the moment, get it started.

▶ If the menu bar at the top of the PODIUM window is not visible, press `F2`, which is PODIUM's full-screen key.

▶ Each time you press `F2`, PODIUM will either expand or contract the size of the PODIUM window. Press `F2` a few times to get used to this.

▶ Pull down the PODIUM Files menu and choose New Custom to make PODIUM display the File Creation dialog shown in Figure 19-7. In the File name field, assuming your hard drive is C, type **c:\multilit\example.cus**

▶ Click OK. PODIUM will create the file *example.cus* and display the custom toolbox. Because there is nothing in the file yet, the screen is blank.

The PODIUM Toolbox

The PODIUM application generator on the *Multiliteracy CD* contains a custom toolbox. It is called a **custom toolbox** because it lets you "customize" the screen. The toolbox makes multimedia application development simple and intuitive—you can design and activate your screen almost by thinking about what you want.

The custom toolbox contains nineteen icons:

Each icon represents a tool. To activate a tool, you click its icon. The cursor assumes the shape of the icon to indicate which tool is active. You mouse around the screen and click the spot where you wish to use the tool. Depending on the tool, PODIUM either opens a dialog or draws a box around the object you clicked, indicating that you can drag it around the screen to reposition or size it.

The toolbox lets you design and create all the elements of a multimedia screen, including the text and graphics that will appear on the screen, the buttons and hot spots that trigger multimedia events, and the order in which these events will be launched when the user clicks the mouse on a button or hot spot.

The toolbox is a window you can move around the screen like any other window. Press F4 to display the toolbox on your screen. To move the toolbox, position the mouse on the title bar (where it says "PODIUM Custom Toolbox"), hold down the left mouse button, and drag the window. Close the toolbox by pressing F4, which is a toggle in PODIUM that makes the toolbox come and go. Practice pressing F4 now. *Note:* When the toolbox is visible, you are an author, creating an application. When the toolbox is closed, you are a user, trying out the application.

As you move the mouse over the icons in the toolbox, PODIUM prints tips in the toolbox title bar. Explore the tips by dragging the mouse over the icons, but do not click anything yet.

Movie on CD

Demonstrations
➡ Show Me!
   ➡ Text Editing
      ➡ **Entering Text**

Entering Text

The copy of PODIUM that comes on the *Multiliteracy CD* is a tutorial edition that lets you create the examples in this book so long as you do not stray too far from the steps in the tutorial. If later you want to make a multimedia application that has your own text in it, you will need to purchase a retail copy of PODIUM, as described in Appendix A.

Follow these steps to learn how to enter text on the multimedia screen:

▶ If the toolbox is not on your screen, press F4 to display it now.

▶ Click the icon represented by the big *T* that stands for text. This is the Text tool. If you move the mouse around the screen, you will notice that the cursor assumes the shape of a text inserter.

▶ Mouse to a spot toward the left of the center of the screen and click the left mouse button; an insert caret begins flashing on the screen.

▶ Type **McGraw-Hill Multimedia Literacy**

▶ Notice how your text appears on the screen immediately, while you type it. This is known as WYSIWYG text entry; *WYSIWYG* stands for what-you-see-is-what-you-get.

▶ Mouse farther down the screen, click the left button, and enter the text **Powerful**

▶ Mouse down a little farther, and enter the text **Tools**

The screen will now appear as shown in Figure 19-8.

19-8

The inserted text appears in the PODIUM window.

Movie on CD

Demonstrations
➡ Show Me!
   ➡ Text Editing
      ➡ **Positioning
         Text**

Positioning Text

The tool that has a hand for an icon moves text around the screen. You can activate the Move tool by clicking on it either with the left or the right mouse button. Clicking the left button makes the tool move text freely to any location on the screen; clicking the right button makes the tool snap text to an invisible grid, allowing you to line things up easily when creating columns or tables of information.

Try the Freehand Move tool first:

▶   Click the hand icon with the left mouse button, and move the cursor around the screen. Notice that the cursor is now in the shape of a hand.

▶   Mouse over *McGraw-Hill Multimedia Literacy,* press and hold down the left mouse button, and drag the text up to the top center of the screen.

▶   Now drag the text to the bottom of the screen. You can put it anywhere you like.

Now try the Grid Move tool. As an example, suppose you want to line up the two words *Powerful* and *Tools* into a column:

▶   Click the hand icon with the right mouse button, and move the cursor around the screen. Notice that the cursor is now in the shape of a hand on a grid.

▶   Click the word *Powerful* and move it where you want to start the column.

▶   Now click the word *Tools* and drag it under the word *Powerful*. Notice how easy it is to line up the words because they snap to an invisible grid.

Movie on CD

Demonstrations
➡ Show Me!
   ➡ Text Editing
      ➡ **Sizing Text**

Sizing Text

The tool with arrows pointing outward in four directions is the Sizer. You can make text be specific point sizes, or you can click and drag the text to any size you want. To size text via the point size method:

▶   Click the Sizer tool, mouse over the text you want to size, and click the left mouse button; the Point Size dialog appears as shown in Figure 19-9.

▶   Select or type the desired point size, and click OK.

19-9

The Point Size dialog.

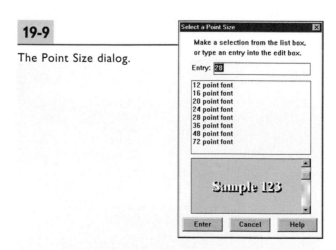

To size text via the click-and-drag method:

▶ Click the Sizer tool, mouse over the text you want to size, hold down the left mouse button, and drag the edges of the sizing box that appears around the text. You can easily make the text any height or width.

Try making the word *Powerful* bigger:

▶ Click the Sizer tool, mouse over the word *Powerful*, hold down the left mouse button, and drag the sizing box. When you release the mouse button, PODIUM redraws the word *Powerful* to fit the size of the box.

Movie on CD

Demonstrations
➡ Show Me!
  ➡ Text Editing
    ➡ **Centering Text**

Centering Text

You will find it difficult to center text exactly using the Move tools. That is why the Centering tool was invented.

Suppose you want to center the text *McGraw-Hill Multimedia Literacy.*

▶ Click the Centering tool, mouse over the text, and click once. *Voila!* The text is centered.

Movie on CD

Demonstrations
➡ Show Me!
  ➡ Text Editing
    ➡ **Editing Text**

Editing Text

Editing text works just like a word processor. Simply click the Text tool, then click the text you want to edit. A flashing caret appears. To insert characters, type what you want. To delete characters, press Backspace or Del . To reposition the caret, press ← or → . You can even drag the mouse over characters to select them, then type something different to replace them. For example, suppose you want to change the word *Powerful* to *Exciting.*

▶ Click the Text tool, then click anywhere on the word *Powerful.*

▶ Drag the mouse over the word *Powerful* to select it; the word *Powerful* will be highlighted as shown in Figure 19-10.

▶ Type **Exciting**

Now change the word *Exciting* back to *Powerful.* Try to do this without looking at the instructions, but if you have trouble, follow these steps:

▶ Click the Text tool, then click anywhere on the word *Exciting.*

19-10

The user has selected the word *Powerful* by dragging the Text tool over it.

▶ Drag the mouse over *Exciting* to select it; the word *Exciting* will be highlighted.

▶ Type **Powerful**

Selecting Fonts

The Font icon looks like a fountain pen. To change the font of any text on the screen:

▶ Click the Font icon, mouse over the text you wish to put in a different font, and click once to open a dialog that lists all the TrueType fonts installed on your computer.

▶ Select the font you want, and the text will change to that font. You can have any number of fonts on the screen simultaneously, although a good designer rarely mixes more than three fonts.

Try changing the font of the word *Tools:*

▶ Click the Font tool, then click the word *Tools*.

Try the different fonts you will find listed in the Font dialog. Which font is your favorite? As you gain experience using fonts, you will find that different typefaces can be used to create visual impact in your application.

Coloring Text

The Color tool appears in the toolbox as a color wheel icon. To change the color of any text on the screen:

▶ Click the Color tool to make PODIUM open a dialog that lists the colors you can select.

▶ Select the color you want; if you do not see the color you want, click the Mix a Color button and mix your own color.

▶ Mouse over the text you want to color, and click to make the text change color.

Try changing the color of the word *Tools:*

▶ Click the Color tool, choose the color you want, and then click the word *Tools*. Try the different colors you will find listed in the Color dialog. In general, you should avoid using more than two or three text colors on the screen at once. Too many colors can be distracting.

Changing the Background Color

You can change the background color with the Backdrop tool. The Backdrop icon appears in the toolbox as a curtain partially opened on a stage, revealing a backdrop behind it. To change the background color:

▶ Click the Backdrop icon: the PODIUM Backdrop dialog appears.

▶ Click the Colors button and select a color.

▶ Click OK to close the dialog; the background will change to the selected color.

Try different background colors. Notice how some color combinations work better than others. On a light background, dark colors have the most impact; on a dark background, light colors stand out. Normally, you should select background colors that are subdued and easy to look at. The author's favorite combination is white text on a dark blue background. Figure 18-11 in the previous chapter shows other recommended color combinations.

Shadowing Text

Varying the amount of drop shadow on your text can make it appear more or less bold against the screen behind it. You can change the amount of drop shadow with the Shadow tool, which appears in the toolbox as a person in a trench coat standing under a streetlight that casts a shadow at night. To change the amount of shadow of any text on the screen:

▶ Click the Shadow tool, and the mouse assumes the shape of the shadow.

▶ Mouse over the text you want to shadow, click once, and PODIUM will open a dialog that lets you choose the amount of shadow you want.

Try putting different amounts of shadow on the text on your screen. Notice how more shadow makes the text stand out. This will be important in the next chapter, which will show you how to put pictures in the background behind text. If the pictures are busy, you will need a lot of drop shadow to bring out your text.

Cloning Text

The Cloning tool is a real timesaver. Suppose you take the time to create a line of text that has a special size, font, and color, and you want another line of text with similar attributes. Instead of having to create a new line of text from scratch, you can clone the existing line, and then simply change its text with the Text tool. To clone text:

▶ Click the Cloning tool, which is pictured in the toolbox as two stick figures side by side. (Watch closely: When you click them, they will smile.)

▶ Mouse over the text you want to clone, hold down the left mouse button, and drag the Cloning box to the location where you want the cloned text to appear on the screen.

For example, you already have the words *Powerful* and *Tools* on your screen. Suppose you want to add the word *Very* to create the phrase *Very Powerful Tools*. And suppose you want the word *Very* to have the same attributes (size, color, font, and shadow) as the word *Powerful*. Instead of specifying the attributes again, you can simply clone the word *Powerful*, and then change the text to *Very*. Here are the steps to follow:

▶ Click the Cloning tool in the toolbox; the clones will smile.

▶ Move the mouse over the word *Powerful* and hold down the left button while you drag the clone up the screen where you want the new word to appear. When you release the mouse button, the cloned word will appear.

▶ Click the Text tool in the toolbox, click the word *Powerful*, and drag the mouse over *Powerful* to select it.

▶ Type **Very** then press [←Enter]. Notice how the word *Very* now has the same attributes as *Powerful*.

19-11

The Text Default Settings
dialog.

Movie on CD

Demonstrations
➡ Show Me!
　➡ Text Editing
　　➡ **Presetting
　　　Text Defaults**

Presetting Text Defaults

It is possible to preset the default settings for text size, color, and shadow. This can save you time when you are entering a lot of text, and you know in advance what size, color, and how much shadow you want. To preset the default text settings:

▶ Click the *right* mouse button on the Text tool icon; the Text Default Settings dialog appears as shown in Figure 19-11.

▶ Click the Color button to change the color.

▶ Click the Font button to change the font.

▶ Click the Shadow button to change the shadow.

▶ Click the Size button to change the text size.

▶ The preview window shows how your text will appear; click OK when you get it the way you want.

In addition, there is a shortcut way to preset the text defaults. PODIUM always sets the text defaults to have the size, color, font, and shadow of the last text edited. If there is any text on the screen that looks like what you want, just click the left mouse button on the Text tool, click anywhere on the text you like, and press ⏎Enter. The next line of text you enter will have the same size, color, font, and shadow.

Movie on CD

Demonstrations
➡ Show Me!
　➡ Text Editing
　　➡ **Building Text**

Building Text

By default, all of the text you entered appears at once on the multimedia screen. Sometimes you do not want to reveal all of the text at once. For example, suppose you are making a presentation, and you want to make the items you are talking about appear one-by-one as you click the mouse button to reveal them. The Mouse Click tool lets you do this by associating the appearance of text fields with mouse clicks. Follow these steps:

▶ To invoke the Mouse Click tool, click the icon that depicts a mouse with a piece of cheese.

▶ Move the cursor over some text and click once. PODIUM opens a dialog that lets you specify which mouse click will make the text appear. Each time the user clicks the mouse, the items associated with that mouse click will appear. You can use this tool to make any number of text fields appear after any mouse click.

For example, suppose you want to make the words *Very Powerful Tools* appear one-by-one as you click the mouse. Here are the steps to follow:

▶ Click the Mouse Click icon in the toolbox.

▶ Click *Very;* the Mouse Click dialog will appear.

▶ In the Mouse Click dialog, choose "mouse click 1".

▶ Click *Powerful* and choose "mouse click 2".

▶ Click *Tools* and choose "mouse click 3".

▶ Press F4 to put the toolbox away and become a user of your application. Notice how the words *Very Powerful Tools* do not appear yet.

▶ Click the mouse, and the word *Very* will appear.

▶ Click again to reveal the word *Powerful,* and click once more to display *Tools.*

In this way, you can make any conceivable combination or pattern of text appear on your screen. It can be more sophisticated. For example, if you assign more than one text field to a given mouse click, multiple fields will appear when you click the mouse. The text need not appear in order from top to bottom; for example, you can make the text at the bottom appear before text at the top.

The Mouse Click tool has many uses. For example, it can make labels appear progressively on a diagram as the user clicks the mouse. It can add detail to a chart by first revealing an outline of your main ideas, and then providing more information with each additional click.

It is also possible to specify a color for clicked text to change to. In other words, each time you click the mouse to reveal more text, previously displayed text can change to a different color, which is called the clicked color. To specify the clicked color, click the *right* mouse button on the Color tool, choose the color you want, then click the left button on the text.

Movie on CD

Demonstrations
➡ Show Me!
  ➡ Text Editing
    ➡ **Undo/Redo**

Undo and Redo

The remainder of this chapter is going to have you play around with some advanced text-editing techniques. Before you start experimenting, you will want to know about Undo and Redo. PODIUM remembers the last 32 things you did to a multimedia screen. Clicking the Undo/Redo icon with the left mouse button lets you undo them, one by one, each time you click. Clicking the Undo/Redo icon with the right mouse button does a redo. Try this now:

▶ Mouse over the Undo/Redo icon; notice how the tip in the title bar says "Undo Tool (right click to redo)".

▶ Click the left button on the Undo/Redo icon to do an undo; the last thing you did gets undone.

▶ Click the left button on Undo/Redo again; the second last thing you did gets undone.

▶ Now do a redo by clicking the right button on Undo/Redo; notice how your most recent undo gets redone.

▶ Click the right button on Undo/Redo again; your screen appears as it did when you started this exercise.

▶ Click the right button on Undo/Redo again; if there is nothing waiting to be redone, PODIUM tells you so.

Word Wrap

Automatic word wrap is one of PODIUM's most popular features. If you type so much text that it won't fit on the line, the text automatically wraps down to the next line on the screen. Try this now. Use the Text tool to start entering text on the screen. Type anything you want, just keep typing past the edge of the screen. Notice how a new line starts automatically when you reach the edge of the screen.

If you want to undo the results of this experiment, click the left button on the Undo/Redo icon.

Blocking Text

By default, the text does not wrap until you reach the edge of the screen. To make the text flow into a predetermined block, you can use the Block tool to draw a block on the screen, and enter your text into the block. Follow these steps:

 ▶ Click the left button on the Block icon.

▶ Draw a block anywhere on the screen by clicking and dragging your mouse. As you drag, the block resizes; make it any size you want.

▶ Click the left button on the Text tool.

▶ Click anywhere inside the block.

▶ Type a bunch of text, and watch how it wraps around inside the block. The block defines the left and right margins of the text you type.

Normally, when you click on a line of text to edit it with the Text tool, the line of text is treated individually. If you want to edit several lines of text as a block, use the Block tool to draw a block around it, then use the Text tool to edit it. A special feature of the Block tool is its ability to collect and reformat blocks of text on the screen. If you draw a larger block around the text, the text will reflow to fill that larger block. You can even collect lines of text that were not originally part of a block by encompassing them in the block you draw.

Using the Clipboard to Copy and Paste Text

The Clipboard icon in the custom toolbox is the Copy/Paste tool. Clicking the Clipboard icon with the left button does a copy, and clicking with the right button does a paste. To copy text, follow these steps:

 ▶ Use the Block tool to draw a block around the text you want to edit, unless you are just going to edit a single line of text, in which case drawing a block is not necessary.

 ▶ Use the Text tool to begin editing the text.

▶ Click and drag over the text you want to copy; the selected text will be highlighted.

 ▶ Click the left button on the Copy/Paste tool (the Clipboard icon); the selected text is now on the Windows Clipboard, which is a temporary holding area.

To paste text, follow these steps:

 ▶ Use the Block tool to draw a block if you want to flow the text into a predefined block on the screen; otherwise, you can skip this step.

 ▶ Click the left button on the Text tool icon, then click the spot on the screen where you want to paste the text.

 ▶ Click the right mouse button on the Copy/Paste tool; the text flows onto the screen from the Clipboard.

Demonstrations
➥ Show Me!
  ➥ Text Editing
    ➥ **Character Map**

Using the Character Map to Insert Special Symbols

Windows has a Character Map that can be used to insert special symbols like ©, ™, ®, μ, ¾, and → into your text. Suppose you want to put a copyright notice on your multimedia screen. Follow these steps:

▶ Get the Windows Character Map running. You will find it on your desktop or in your program list under this icon:

▶ The Character Map appears as shown in Figure 19-12. Use the Font control to select the font you are using in PODIUM.

▶ Click the © symbol, then click the Select button. The © symbol appears in the Characters to copy field.

▶ Click the Copy button to copy the contents of the Characters to copy field onto the Clipboard.

 ▶ In PODIUM, use the Text tool to enter the line of text below. To type the © symbol, click the right button on the Clipboard icon to paste the © symbol from the Clipboard.

Copyright © 1997 by Santa Claus. All rights reserved.

Of course, you should replace *Santa Claus* with your own name, and make sure you use the current year. This style of copyright notice is the international format that reserves rights worldwide.

NOTE If you have Windows 95 and you cannot find the Character Map program *charmap.exe* in the Accessories group on your computer, you can install it as follows. Click the Start button, choose Settings, then choose Control Panel, then Add/Remove Programs, then Windows Setup, then Accessories; then click Details, choose Character Map, click OK to close the Accessories details, and click OK to install the Character Map. After it is installed, you can run the Character Map by clicking the Start button and choosing Programs, then Accessories, then Character Map.

19-12

The Windows Character Map lets you insert special symbols.

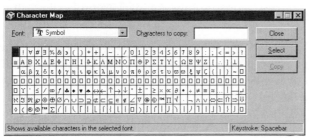

Inspecting Your Custom File

The first edition of this book never told how you can inspect and edit custom files with any text editor. PODIUM users who like this feature wanted it taught in this revised edition. The author is including this information with a word of caution: *Careful!* If you edit custom files with a text editor, you must be careful not to disturb the syntax of the commands in the file. Changing the order of things can cause unpredictable results, especially if you type something that confuses your computer.

With that caveat, you can now be told that the ability to edit the source code of PODIUM's custom files is a feature that experienced authors like a lot. Most multimedia tools keep the content of your files a deep dark secret. There is no way for you to inspect or modify the codes by hand. PODIUM, on the other hand, keeps the files in plain old ASCII text format, which you can inspect and modify with any text editor.

PODIUM is constantly watching the time stamp on the file in the PODIUM window. If the time stamp on that file changes, PODIUM assumes you changed it with a text editor, and PODIUM automatically rereads the file and refreshes the window.

The easiest way to view the source code of a PODIUM file is to follow these steps:

▶ Press F2 to put PODIUM into a window so the menus become visible.

▶ Pull down the Files menu and choose Edit This File.

▶ PODIUM will launch the Windows Notepad and flow the source code of the current custom file into the Notepad.

If you edit the file in the Notepad, do so with care! For example, you will find your lines of text in the file, and you can safely edit them there, but if you start making illogical changes, like deleting the exclamation point with which every link must begin, or removing the @ from the @where command, you will get syntax errors. When PODIUM encounters a syntax error, it tells you the number of the line in which the error occurred and launches the Notepad to let you correct it.

The Anatomy of a PODIUM Custom File

Figure 19-13 shows one way of completing the *multilit\example.cus* screen in this chapter, and Figure 19-14 shows the custom file in the Notepad. By comparing these two figures, you can begin to understand the anatomy of a PODIUM custom file. The beginning of every custom file is the backdrop. The **backdrop** consists of one or more lines that start with an exclamation point. In PODIUM the exclamation point means *link*. When links appear at the very start of the file, they are considered to be links to the backdrop of the file. The backdrop consists of any pictures, icons, graphs, or background colors that appear behind the text.

Every line of text has to be positioned somewhere on the screen. In PODIUM the command that positions text is called @where. In Figure 19-14 you will see that each line of text is preceded by the @where command that tells where it goes on the screen. Other @ commands specify special effects including the color, size, font, and shadow of the text. @where must be first, and it must appear in column 1. If all of the special effects do not fit on the @where line, they can be put on succeeding lines, so long as each line starts with an @ command. The first line

19-13

The *multilit\example.cus* screen created in this chapter.

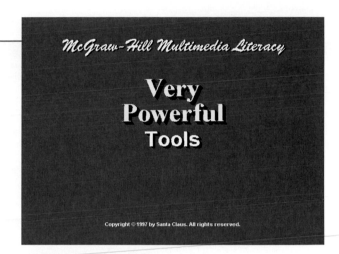

19-14

The *multilit\example.cus* screen displayed in the Windows Notepad.

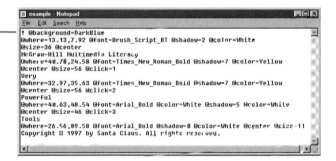

after the @where that does not start with @ is the text that will appear on your PODIUM screen. No @ commands go on the text line; only the text goes there. The text is only one line long. To have another line of text, there must be another @where line preceding it.

Inspecting Any Custom File on the *Multiliteracy CD*

Now that the cat is out of the bag with respect to PODIUM custom files being plain text files, you might as well know that all of the custom files on the *Multiliteracy CD* are plain text files that you can inspect with any text editor. While viewing any custom file on the CD with PODIUM, just press [F2] to put PODIUM in a window, pull down the Files menu, and choose Edit This File. Pat Fox has done a lot of neat things on the *Multiliteracy CD*. If you know how to copy and paste text with a text editor like the Notepad, you can even copy Pat's code and paste it into your own custom files. But you better hold off until you learn more about the different commands that can appear in custom files. To quote from a famous song, "We've only just begun"!

List of Text Commands

Table 19-1 lists the text commands that can appear in PODIUM custom files.

Table 19-1   Text Commands

@ Command	What the Command Does
@background=*n*	Specifies the background color where *n* is a Windows color value. The @background command must appear in the file's backdrop, prior to any @where commands.
@where=*x,y*	Positions text on the screen. *x* and *y* are percentages of the screen; *x* tells how far over from the left, and *y* tells how far down from the top the text will go. @where must be first; the rest of these text commands are optional and can appear in any order after @where.
@color=*n*	Specifies the text color. *n* is a Windows color value. If there is no @color command, the text is white.
@shadow=*n*	Specifies the amount of drop shadow. *n* is an integer telling how many points of shadow there are. If there is no @shadow command, there are three points of shadow.
@size=*n*	Specifies the text size where *n* is the point size.
@size=*l,c*	Specifies a stretched text size where *l* is an integer telling how many lines of text this size would fill the screen vertically; *c* is an integer telling how many characters this size would fill the screen horizontally.
@font=*string*	Specifies the font where *string* is the name of the font. Since the space delimits commands, spaces in a font name must be replaced by underscores, as in @font=Times_New_Roman_Bold.
@click=*n*	Specifies the mouse click upon which the text will appear. If there is no @click command, the text appears without requiring a mouse click.

E X E R C I S E S

Although the multimedia toolbox is easy to use, it still takes time to create a multimedia screen. Suppose you need another screen like the one you created in this chapter, but some of the text needs to change. Instead of re-creating the entire screen, you can use the Save As feature to save the screen under a new filename, and then use the toolbox to edit what you want changed. The exercises below give you practice doing this.

1. If you do not already have the *multilit\example.cus* file on your screen, pull down the PODIUM Files menu, choose Custom, and bring up the *example.cus* screen you created in this chapter. Now pull down the Files menu and choose Save As; the Save As dialog appears. In the File name field, type **c:\multilit\example2.cus** and click OK. Now you have two copies of the same file, one called *example.cus,* and the other one called *example2.cus.* Press F4 to get the toolbox on your screen. Notice how the toolbox title bar tells you which file you are editing. Use the Text tool to make an obvious change to the screen so you can tell it apart from the original. Then pull down the Files menu, choose Custom, and bring up the other copy of your *example.cus* file. Do you see a difference between the two files? Use the Notepad to compare the contents of the two files. How do they differ? *Hint:* To view a file with the Notepad, pull down the Files menu and choose Edit This File.

2. You can use the Save As feature to make a copy of any file you find on the *Multiliteracy CD* that you would like to use as a model for creating a similar file of your own. For example, suppose you like the layout of the text fields in the *custom\copy.cus* file on the *Multiliteracy CD.* Pull down the PODIUM Files menu, choose Custom, and browse to the *custom\copy.cus* file. The file now appears in your PODIUM window. To copy it, pull down the Files menu and choose Save As. In the File name box, type **c:\multilit\copied.cus** and click OK. Press F4 to open the toolbox, and use the Text tool to modify the text fields as you like.

20

Graphics

After completing this chapter, you will be able to:

- **Make any BMP bitmap serve as the backdrop for a multimedia screen**

- **Hang or layer smaller pictures or icons on top of a graphic backdrop**

- **Move graphics and icons to different locations on the screen**

- **Resize pictures hung on a multimedia screen**

- **Use digital chalk to draw on top of an image**

ITH more than 30 graphics standards used in the computer industry, selecting one can be confusing. The most efficient standard to use with Windows is the BMP (bitmap) file format. The names of graphics files that use this format end with a *.bmp* filename extension. This tutorial will use the BMP format.

GIF (pronounced "jiff"), which stands for Graphics Interchange Format, is a popular graphics format used on the World Wide Web. GIF is also supported by PODIUM.

How do you deal with the other formats? In Chapter 31 you will learn how to capture or convert any graphic image into the BMP format.

The tutorial exercises in this chapter continue to use the *example.cus* file you created in Chapter 19. If you do not already have the *example.cus* file on your screen, complete the following steps. *Note:* An instruction to "click" implies using the *left* mouse button.

▶ Pull down the PODIUM Files menu and choose Custom to display the Custom File dialog.

▶ In the File name field, type **c:\multilit\example.cus**

▶ Click OK to bring up the *example.cus* screen.

Movie on CD

Demonstrations
➡ Show Me!
  ➡ Graphics
    ➡ **Backdrops**

Graphic Backdrops

Follow these steps to put a graphic backdrop on your screen:

▶ Press F4 to bring up the PODIUM toolbox. The Backdrop icon in the toolbox resembles a curtain partially opened on a stage, revealing a backdrop behind it.

20-1

The Backdrop dialog lets you set the background for your screen.

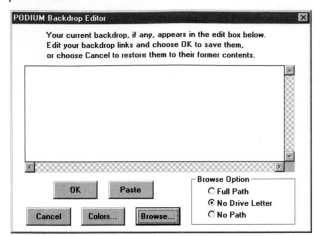

20-2

The Browse dialog lets you browse for bitmaps.

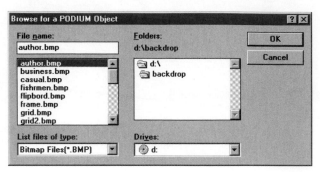

▶ Click the Backdrop icon to set the backdrop. The PODIUM Backdrop dialog shown in Figure 20-1 will appear. If you already know the name of the BMP file you want to use as a backdrop, you can simply type the filename into the edit box. Otherwise, you need to browse for the filename.

▶ Click the Browse button to bring up the Browse dialog shown in Figure 20-2, which lets you browse for files in all your computer's drives and directories.

▶ Pull down the Drives menu and select your CD-ROM drive to browse the *Multiliteracy CD.*

▶ In the list of directories, double-click the letter of your CD-ROM drive to go to the root directory of the CD, then click the directory called *backdrop*.

▶ Notice that several bitmaps are listed in the Files box. Click the first one, *author.bmp*. Notice that its name now appears in the File name field.

▶ Click OK, and *author.bmp* will appear in the Backdrop field.

▶ Click OK again, and PODIUM will load the bitmap and display it as the backdrop behind the text of the *example.cus* file. The backdrop is now a picture of the author working at his multimedia computer.

You can try putting different backdrops behind the text and observe the effects they have. To change the backdrop:

▶ Click the Backdrop tool.

▶ Delete the name of the bitmap currently listed in it.

▶ Browse to a new bitmap.

There are several bitmaps in the *backdrop* directory on the CD. Each one demonstrates a different backdrop technique.

FRAME.BMP

frame.bmp is a frame on which you can overlay text. Use the Move and Sizer tools to move the text into the frame.

LOGO.BMP

logo.bmp is a logo. Logos work very well as backdrops when their colors are subtle. *logo.bmp* uses the author's favorite logo color combination: black on dark blue, which works very well as a backdrop behind white text.

PHOTO.BMP

photo.bmp is a photograph. You need to be careful when using photographs as backdrops. If the photo contains a lot of bright colors, the colors can make the text hard to read. Notice how the photograph in *photo.bmp* consists of fairly subdued colors, which work well in a backdrop.

Photographs placed behind text can be suggestive. For example, a photograph of something you are asking for placed behind the text of a budget request can show your boss what you want. Photos can also make text more comprehensible if the backdrop reflects the intent of the words. Some photos evoke strong feelings, such as the photograph of the Vietnam Memorial that is used as the backdrop on the cover of Compton New Media's *Vietnam* CD-ROM.

Movie on CD

Demonstrations
- Show Me!
  - Graphics
    - **Hanging Pictures**

Hanging Pictures

You may want to place a smaller picture on top of a larger one. For example, you may have a corporate logo you would like to place in the corner of your screen, or you might want to add an Exit button to your backdrop. The Picture Hanger tool lets you do this. It lets you layer as many pictures as you want on top of any backdrop. To hang pictures, follow these steps:

▶ Click the Picture Hanger tool and move the mouse around the screen. Notice how the cursor has assumed the shape of a picture hanger.

▶ To place a logo in the upper left corner of your *example.cus* screen, mouse to the spot where you want the logo to appear, and click once to bring up the Picture Hanger dialog shown in Figure 20-3.

▶ Press the Browse button, then navigate to the *logo* directory on the *Multiliteracy CD*.

▶ Click on one of the BMP files, then click OK; the filename now appears in the Picture Hanger field.

▶ Click OK and watch the logo appear on your screen.

▶ Notice that the *logo* directory contains many logos. For practice, choose two more logos and hang them on the screen.

20-3

The Picture Hanger dialog lets you hang pictures anywhere on the screen.

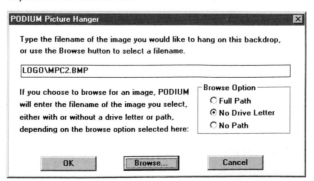

Demonstrations
➡ Show Me!
  ➡ Graphics
    ➡ **Positioning Graphics**

Positioning Graphics

Once a picture is hung on the screen, you can use the Freehand Move tool to position it anywhere on the screen. Follow these steps:

▶ Click the hand icon; the cursor assumes the shape of a hand.

▶ Mouse over the picture you want to move, press and hold down the left mouse button, then drag the picture to its new location.

Recall that if you click the hand icon with the *left* mouse button, you will get the Freehand Move tool that lets you move pictures freely to any location on the screen. If you click the hand icon with the *right* mouse button, you will get the Grid Move tool that snaps pictures to an invisible grid, allowing you to line things up easily, such as when you create columns or rows of icons. See if you can use the Grid Move tool to line up the logos on the screen.

Demonstrations
➡ Show Me!
  ➡ Graphics
    ➡ **Resizing Graphics**

Resizing Graphics

The Sizer tool, with which you learned to size text in a previous chapter, also resizes bitmaps hung on the screen. You can make graphics larger or smaller than their original size. Be aware, however, that graphics can become pixellated (jagged) if you try to make them too big. The best use of the graphics Sizer is to make images smaller, such as when you want to make a picture appear as a little icon on the screen. To resize a picture hung on the screen, follow these steps:

▶ Click the Sizer tool; as you move the mouse around the screen, the cursor has the shape of the Sizer icon.

▶ Move the mouse over the picture you want to resize, and hold down the mouse button; do not release the mouse button until you are done resizing the picture.

▶ Drag the mouse to make the picture be the size you want; then release the mouse button.

If you experiment with the Sizer tool, you will find that it can stretch and squeeze pictures in any direction. You can make wide pictures thin, and tall pictures short. You will distort the picture, however, if you make too large a change to the aspect ratio between the picture's width and height.

Digital Chalk

PODIUM has a feature called **digital chalk**. Anytime the user holds down both mouse buttons simultaneously, the cursor turns into a piece of chalk you can draw with on the screen. While drawing with chalk, the C (color) key is active. Each time you press C while drawing with the chalk, the color changes. If you hold down C continuously, you can draw a rainbow. E is the erase key. Pressing E after you draw with chalk will erase what you just drew.

What you draw with chalk does not become part of your bitmap or alter the images on your hard drive in any way. Its purpose is to allow users to point things out during multimedia presentations. You can use the chalk on any image, including live video feeds from cameras, VCRs, and television stations.

Inspecting Your Custom File

If you would like to see what PODIUM did to your *example.cus* file when you used the graphics tools in this chapter, follow these steps:

▶ Press F2 to put PODIUM into a window so the menus become visible.

▶ If your *example.cus* file is not already in the PODIUM window, pull down the Files menu, choose Custom, type **c:\multilit\example.cus** and press ←Enter.

▶ Pull down the Files menu and choose Edit This File; PODIUM launches the Windows Notepad and flows the source code of the current custom file into the Notepad.

At the very top of the file, you will notice several lines that begin with exclamation points. This is the backdrop part of the file. The backdrop consists of any background color or background picture, followed by the pictures you hung onto the background.

Figure 20-4 shows how Pat Fox completed this chapter, and Figure 20-5 shows her custom file. The first part of the file has lines that begin with exclamation points; these are the pictures in the backdrop of her file.

20-4

The *multilit\example.cus* screen created in this chapter.

20-5

The *multilit\example.cus* screen displayed in the Windows Notepad.

```
example2 - Notepad                                    _ □ ✕
File   Edit   Search   Help
! BACKDROP\PHOTO.RMP
! LOGO\MPC2.BMP @origin=76.25,56.88
! LOGO\IBM_ULT1.BMP @origin=5.78,57.08 @stretch=27.97,65.00
! LOGO\COMPEND.BMP @origin=27.66,72.71
@where=13.13,0.83 @font=Brush_Script_BT @shadow=2 @color=White
@size=36 @center
McGraw-Hill Multimedia Literacy
@where=42.03,8.96 @font=Times_New_Roman_Bold @shadow=7 @color=Yellow
@center @size=48 @click=1
Very
@where=35.63,17.92 @font=Times_New_Roman_Bold @shadow=7 @color=Yellow
@center @size=48 @click=2
Powerful
@where=41.72,28.96 @font=Arial_Bold @color=White @shadow=5 @color=White
@center @size=40 @click=3
Tools
@where=26.56,89.58 @font=Arial_Bold @shadow=0 @color=White @center @size=11
Copyright © 1997 by Santa Claus. All rights reserved.
```

List of Graphics Positioning Commands

The graphics positioning commands use pairs of numbers that represent the *x,y* coordinates on the screen. The *x* coordinate tells how far over from the left, and the *y* coordinate indicates how far down from the top of the screen. In PODIUM the *x,y* coordinates are always expressed as percentages of the screen. That way, when multimedia computers get higher-resolution monitors, your custom screens will still display properly. Table 20-1 explains the graphics positioning commands used in this chapter.

Table 20-1   Graphics Positioning Commands

@ Command	What the Command Does
@origin=*x,y*	Specifies the *x,y* location of the upper left corner of a picture; pictures with no @origin appear as full-screen backdrops.
@stretch=*x,y*	Specifies the *x,y* location of the lower right corner of a picture. This tells how far to stretch a picture that has an @origin; if a picture has an @origin but no @stretch, the picture appears in its original size.

E X E R C I S E S

1. Use PODIUM to bring up *multilit\example.cus* on your screen. Press F4 and use the Picture Hanger tool to layer onto the screen every one of the icons in the *icon* directory on the *Multiliteracy CD*. Now use the Grid Move tool to arrange the icons into a big square. Try your hand at making other patterns.

2. Use the Sizer tool to change the size of the icons. For example, try making one of the icons bigger. How large can you make it before it becomes so pixellated (jagged) that it is no longer usable? Now make the icon smaller. How small can you make it and still see what it is?

21 Triggering

After completing this chapter, you will be able to:

- [ ] **Use the Link tool to create hypertext and connect the hypertext to one or more multimedia objects on your computer**

- [ ] **Use the Trigger tool to create hyperpictures and connect the hyperpictures to multimedia objects**

- [ ] **Position icons anywhere on the screen and link them to any multimedia object**

- [ ] **Edit the links to hypertext and hyperpictures, changing what will happen when the user clicks the mouse**

- [ ] **Make the backdrop of a multimedia screen trigger an audio file**

- [ ] **Launch any executable or batch file as an object in a multimedia application**

- [ ] **Delete objects from multimedia screens**

 **RIGGERS** let you make multimedia applications interactive by linking objects to words or pictures on the screen. The custom toolbox allows you to link any object on your computer or network to any text field or picture or part of a picture. When you mouse over a trigger, the cursor changes shape to indicate that you are on a hot spot; if you then click the mouse, PODIUM launches the links.

Movie on CD

Demonstrations
➤ Show Me!
   ➤ Triggering
      ➤ **Hypertext**

Hypertext

As you learned in Part One, linked text is called **hypertext**. To make hypertext, follow these steps:

▶ Pull down the PODIUM Files menu and select New Custom to bring up the Custom File Name dialog.

▶ In the File name field, assuming your hard drive is C, type **c:\multilit\linkdemo.cus** then click OK.

 ▶ Use the Backdrop tool to give this multimedia screen the *backdrop\rooster.bmp* background.

 ▶ Use the Text tool to put this text on the backdrop: **Speak to me!**

21-1

The Link dialog.

21-2

The cursor changes shape when you mouse over a hot spot.

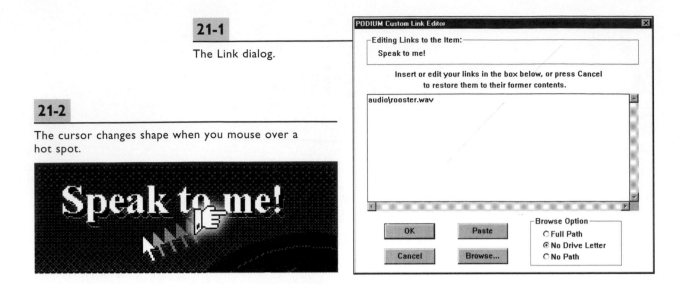

To make the text hyper, follow these steps:

▶ Click the Link icon, which appears in the toolbox as two links in a chain.

▶ Mouse over the *Speak to me!* text you wish to link and click once; the Link dialog in Figure 21-1 will appear.

▶ Click inside the big edit box to position the cursor, then type **audio\rooster.wav**

▶ Press F4 to put the toolbox away and become a user of your application.

Mouse over the words *Speak to me!* Figure 21-2 shows how the cursor changes shape as it passes over the hot spot. If you click the hot spot, you will hear the rooster crow.

You can link more than one object to a line of hypertext. Follow these steps:

▶ Press F4 to bring up the toolbox.

▶ Use the Text tool to enter the text **Show me some pictures!**

▶ Use the Link tool to connect the text to the three pictures:

```
bitmaps\egg.bmp
bitmaps\chick.bmp
bitmaps\rooster.bmp
```

▶ Press F4 to become a user again, and mouse over the words *Show me some pictures!* The first picture will appear.

▶ Click the left button again; the second picture will appear.

▶ Click once more to see the third picture.

▶ Click the right button to have PODIUM back up and show the previous picture.

▶ Keep clicking the left button until you run out of pictures; PODIUM then returns you to the screen from which you triggered them.

Movie on CD

Demonstrations
➥ Show Me!
  ➥ Triggering
    ➥ **Multiple**
       Objects

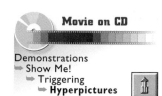

Demonstrations
 ➥ Show Me!
  ➥ Triggering
   ➥ **Hyperpictures**

Hyperpictures

When pictures have links, they are called **hyperpictures**. To put a link on a picture, follow these steps:

▶ Click the Trigger tool, which appears in the toolbox as an upward-pointing arrow on a launch pad. The cursor assumes the shape of the launcher.

▶ Mouse to the beginning of the trigger you want to create, hold down the left mouse button, then drag the Trigger box so that it encompasses the part of the picture you want to serve as a trigger.

▶ Release the mouse button; a dialog will appear in which you can type your links, paste them from the Clipboard, or browse for them. This box enables you to link any part of any picture to any combination of multimedia events, PODIUM objects, or application programs.

For example, suppose you would like the beak of the rooster in the backdrop of your *linkdemo.cus* screen to trigger the sound of a rooster crowing. Follow these steps:

▶ If the toolbox is not open, press F4 to display it on your screen.

▶ Click the Trigger tool, then mouse over to the upper left corner of the area you want to make your trigger. *Do not* click the mouse yet.

▶ Hold down the left mouse button, and—while holding it down—drag the mouse to the lower right corner of the trigger; a box will appear, showing the location of your trigger.

▶ Release the mouse button; PODIUM will display the Link dialog.

▶ Click once inside the big Link box to set the cursor.

▶ Type **audio\rooster.wav** then click OK.

▶ Press F4 to put the toolbox away and become a user again.

▶ Mouse over the rooster's beak, then click. The cock crows! Click the beak to your heart's content. Notice how you do not have to wait for the cock to finish crowing; each click immediately restarts the sound effect.

There is no limit to the number of triggers you can put on your screen. To highlight the triggers, press F11. F11 is a toggle; pressing it again restores the screen to normal. To reposition a trigger, use the Move tools. To resize a trigger, use the Sizer tool. To delete a trigger, click once on the trash can, then click the trigger. *Note:* If you try to create overlapping triggers, PODIUM will warn you that can be confusing and will advise you not to make triggers that overlap.

Demonstrations
 ➥ Show Me!
  ➥ Triggering
   ➥ **Hyper Icons**

Hyper Icons

You can use the Picture Hanger tool to position icons on the multimedia screen, then use the Link tool to link the icons to any object or event. For example, to put a hyper Weather icon on the multimedia screen, you would follow these steps:

▶ If you do not already have your toolbox open, press F4 to display it on your screen.

▶ Click the Picture Hanger tool, then mouse to the location on the screen where you would like the Weather icon to appear.

▶ Click the mouse, and the Picture Hanger dialog will appear.

▶ Use the Browse button to navigate to the *icons* directory on the *Multiliteracy CD,* then select *weather.bmp.*

▶ Click OK to close the Browse dialog, then click OK to close the Picture Hanger dialog.

▶ Use the Trigger tool to draw a trigger around the Weather icon. When the Link dialog appears, enter this link: **bitmaps\forecast.bmp**

▶ Click OK to close the dialog, then press F4 to close the toolbox and become a user of your application.

▶ Mouse over the Weather icon to see how the cursor changes shape, indicating that it is over a trigger.

▶ Click the Weather icon; PODIUM will display a weather satellite map.

Movie on CD

Demonstrations
➥ Show Me!
  ➥ Triggering
    ➥ **Editing Links**

Editing Links

Use the toolbox to change the links you make to hypertext or hyperpictures by following these steps:

▶ Click the Link icon, which appears in the toolbox as two links in a chain, and mouse over the hypertext or hyperpicture trigger whose links you want to edit.

▶ Click the mouse; PODIUM will display a dialog in which you can edit the links.

For example, suppose you want to change the order in which the pictures appear when you click *Show me some pictures!* Click the Link icon, mouse over the text *Show me some pictures,* and click to bring up the Link dialog.

Now you can change the order of the pictures.

NOTE   When editing text in a dialog, you can use Windows control keys to cut, copy, and paste. Highlight the text you want to cut or copy by dragging the mouse over it, then press Ctrl-C to copy the text or Ctrl-X to cut the text. After positioning the cursor where you want to paste the text, press Ctrl-V to paste it.

Movie on CD

Demonstrations
➥ Show Me!
  ➥ Triggering
    ➥ **Triggering
      from the
      Backdrop**

Triggering Multimedia Objects from the Backdrop

So far, you have learned how to trigger items by having the user click objects on the screen. Another way to trigger multimedia objects is to put them in the backdrop of the screen. When the backdrop appears, it will trigger the multimedia objects associated with it.

For example, there are some waveform audio instructions in the *Multiliteracy CD* file *instruct.wav.* Suppose you want a multimedia screen to trigger those instructions so that whenever the user brings up the screen, the instructions will sound, telling the user what to do. To accomplish this, click the Backdrop tool, and insert the following line at the very top of your backdrop:

```
audio\instruct.wav
```

Backdrops can contain a wide range of multimedia events, including CD Audio, MIDI sound tracks, waveform audio recordings, and videodisc images or motion sequences.

Applications As Objects

PODIUM can launch any application on the computer. Any executable file *(.exe)*, batch file *(.bat)*, or Windows PIF file *(.pif)* can be the object of a link. PODIUM launches the file seamlessly, and when the application finishes its task, PODIUM continues processing at the spot from which you launched the application.

For example, suppose you want an icon on the screen that will launch the Windows Notepad. Follow these steps:

▶ Use the Picture Hanger tool to put the Notepad icon—located in the *icons* directory of the *Multiliteracy CD*—on your screen.

▶ Use the Trigger tool to draw a trigger around the Notepad icon and link it to *notepad.exe*.

▶ Press F4 to close the toolbox, then click the Notepad icon.

See how it launches the Notepad?

You can even pass parameters to linked applications. To do this, use the PODIUM @os= feature (*os* stands for operating system). PODIUM passes to the operating system anything typed after an @os=. For example, suppose you have the Microsoft Access database application on your computer, and you want to link it to an item on the screen that will make Access run a macro to graph some data. You might, for example, enter the following into a Link box:

```
@os=d:\access\msaccess.exe mydata.mdb /excl /x graph
```

Databases, spreadsheets, authoring tools, or presentation packages can be the objects of PODIUM links, as can multimedia applications made with ToolBook, Linkway, Authorware, IconAuthor, PowerPoint, Compel, Freelance, Harvard Graphics, Aldus Persuasion, or WordPerfect Presentations. Simply follow the equal sign of the @os= with the command line that would launch the application from the Windows Run dialog that you will find on the Windows 95 Start button menu or the Windows 3.1 Program Manager File menu.

Movie on CD

Demonstrations
→ Show Me!
→ Triggering
→ **Deleting Objects**

Deleting Objects

In addition to letting you create hypertext and hyperpictures, the toolbox also lets you delete them. The Delete tool appears in the toolbox as a trash can. To delete an object:

▶ Click the Delete icon; the cursor assumes the shape of a trash can.

▶ Mouse over the object you want to delete and click once. A dialog will identify the item to be deleted and ask you to confirm that you really want to delete it.

To delete many objects at once, use the Block tool to draw a block around the objects you want to delete, then click the Delete icon and click anywhere inside the block. PODIUM will ask if you really want to delete the items inside the block.

Inspecting Your Custom File

To see what PODIUM did to your *linkdemo.cus* file when you used the Trigger and
Link tools in this chapter, follow these steps:

▶ Press ⬚F2⬚ to put PODIUM into a window so the menus become visible.

▶ If your *linkdemo.cus* file is not already in the PODIUM window, pull down the
   Files menu, choose Custom, type **c:\multilit\linkdemo.cus** and press
   ⬚←Enter⬚.

▶ Pull down the Files menu and choose Edit This File; PODIUM launches the
   Windows Notepad and flows the source code of the current custom file into
   the Notepad.

At the very top of the file, you will notice several lines that begin with exclamation
points. Just like in previous chapters, this is the backdrop part of the file. Anything
linked to the backdrop happens immediately when the file begins.

Figure 21-3 shows how Pat Fox completed this chapter, and Figure 21-4 shows her
custom file. You will notice two new constructs that did not appear before. First,
there are some triggers in the file. In PODIUM custom files, triggers have the form:

```
x1,y1 x2,y2
! Links to the trigger
! go here, signified by
! exclamation points
```

As always, *x,y* coordinates are expressed as percentages of the screen. *x1,y1* is the
upper left corner of the trigger, and *x2,y2* is the lower right corner. Immediately
following the trigger must be one or more lines beginning with exclamation points,
which are the links that will be triggered when the user clicks on your trigger.

The second thing you will notice is how PODIUM encodes hypertext links,
which appear as lines beginning with exclamation points immediately after the
line of text.

21-3

The *multilit\linkdemo.cus*
screen created in this
chapter.

21-4

The *multilit\linkdemo.cus* screen displayed in the Windows Notepad.

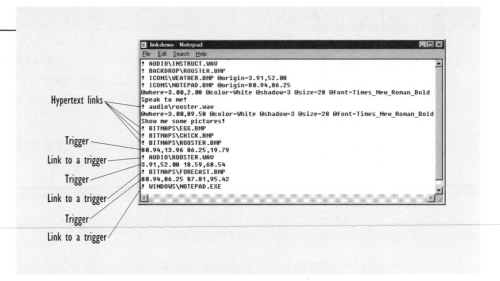

Hypertext links

Trigger

Link to a trigger

Trigger

Link to a trigger

Trigger

Link to a trigger

List of Triggering Commands

Table 21-1 lists @ commands that can appear in the links to hypertext and hyperpicture triggers. Remember that every link must begin with an exclamation point.

Table 21-1 Triggering Commands

@ Command	What the Command Does
@os=*string*	Passes the *string* to the operating system. Everything on the line after the @os= is considered to be part of the *string*, so do not put anything else on this line except the command string you want sent to the operating system. *os* stands for operating system.
@wait=*n*	Makes your computer wait *n* seconds before moving automatically to the next item in the list of links. This provides a very powerful multimedia sequencing ability. *n* can be an integer or a decimal number.
@time=*n*	When @time=*n* appears after the filename of a picture, it specifies how long it should take for the picture to dissolve onto the screen.
@method=*effect*	When @method=*effect* appears after the filename of a picture, it specifies how the picture should dissolve onto the screen. *effect* can be replace, stripes, split, or diag. The default is replace.
@direction=*how*	When @direction=*how* appears after the filename of a picture, it specifies the direction in which the picture should dissolve onto the screen. *how* can be up or down. The default is down.
@from=*n*	When @from=*n* follows a multimedia object that consists of a stream of audio or video, *n* specifies the starting position.
@to=*n*	When @to=*n* follows a multimedia object that consists of a stream of audio or video, *n* specifies the stopping position.

E X E R C I S E S

1. When you click *Show me some pictures!* on the *linkdemo.cus* screen, you see three stages in the development of a chicken: egg, chick, and hen. When the egg, chick, and hen pictures are on your screen, you can use the PODIUM Effects menu to specify different dissolve patterns, directions, and timings that add interest to the images. Try these effects.

> *NOTE* The dissolves work only when you have PODIUM full-screen. To pull down the Effects menu when PODIUM is full-screen, press [Alt]-[E]. *E* stands for effects.

2. Reverse the order of the three images you see when you click *Show me some pictures! Hint:* To edit the links to *Show me some pictures!*, click the Link tool, then click *Show me some pictures!* A Link box will appear that displays the links and lets you edit them.

3. Click the Undo/Redo tool to undo the changes you just made in the second exercise. Then press [F4] to put the toolbox away, and click *Show me some pictures!* to make sure the egg, chick, and hen appear in the proper order. If they do not, edit the links to *Show me some pictures!* until this works properly.

22

Waveform Audio Recording

After completing this chapter, you will be able to:

- **Record and edit waveform audio files via the digital audio hardware in your multimedia PC**

- **Experience how the sampling rate and bits-per-sample settings affect the quality and size of the waveform audio file**

- **Create "sound under stills" by timing the appearance of bitmaps to sounds in waveform audio recordings**

- **Create ambient sound to give a sense of realism to your multimedia screens**

Y DEFINITION, every multimedia PC has the capability to record and play back waveform audio. In this chapter you will learn how to record waveform audio, trigger its playback, and time the appearance of bitmaps to sync points in the audio.

PODIUM's Waveform Audio Tool

PODIUM has a Waveform Audio tool that lets you record and edit waveform audio. To access this tool, pull down the Tools menu and select Waveform Audio. The Waveform Audio tool will appear as shown in Figure 22-1.

22-1

The Waveform Audio tool.

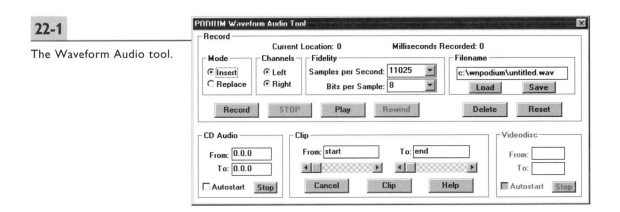

Movie on CD

Demonstrations
➡ Show Me!
 ➡ Waveform Audio
  ➡ **Recording**

Making Your First Recording

To make your first recording with PODIUM's Waveform Audio tool, follow these steps:

▶ Get your microphone ready and click the Record button.

▶ Speak or sing into the microphone, then click STOP.

▶ To hear your recording play back, click Play.

▶ To rewind your recording, click Rewind.

▶ To save a waveform audio recording, type the full path and filename you want to save it as in the Filename field. Make sure the filename extension is *.wav* to indicate that the file is a waveform audio recording. For example, to save the file as *myvoice.wav* in the *c:\multilit* directory, you would type **c:\multilit\myvoice.wav** in the Filename field, and then click the Save button.

Movie on CD

Demonstrations
➡ Show Me!
 ➡ Waveform Audio
  ➡ **Editing**

Editing Waveform Audio Recordings

Sometimes you will want to edit your waveform audio recordings. For example, it is common to have some audio at the beginning and the end of your recording that you do not want to keep. The Clip control group in PODIUM's Waveform Audio tool lets you cut audio sections out of your recording.

▶ Drag the scroll boxes or type numbers into the From and To fields to select the audio segment you want to clip.

▶ Click Play to hear the section of the clip to make sure it is what you want to cut out.

▶ Click the Delete button.

PODIUM measures the length of a recording in milliseconds; 1 second of sound contains 1,000 milliseconds. For example, to cut out the first 1.5 seconds of your recording:

▶ Set the From field to 0 and the To field to 1500.

▶ Click the Delete button.

Now when you play the clip, you will find that the first 1.5 seconds are gone.

You can also insert new audio into an existing sound track:

▶ Use the From field to position the audio at the insertion point.

▶ Click the Insert button in the Mode control group.

▶ Click the Record button.

You can also replace parts of the audio with new recordings:

▶ Set the From and To fields to select the clip you want to replace.

▶ Click the Replace button.

▶ Click Record to replace the clip with your new recording.

Adjusting the Quality of Waveform Audio Recordings

PODIUM lets you adjust two parameters that govern the quality of a waveform audio recording: **sampling rate** and **bits per sample**. Be aware that the higher you set these parameters, the larger your waveform audio file will be. If the settings are dimmed, click the Reset button to activate them. PODIUM will warn you that clicking Reset causes any recording you have not saved to be lost, and you will get a chance to save your recording first.

SAMPLING RATE

If you pull down the Samples per Second menu in the Fidelity control group, you will see how you can change the sampling rate, which determines the frequency response of the recorded sound. To record frequencies faithfully, your sampling rate must be at least two times greater than the highest frequency you want to record. The higher you set the sampling rate, however, the larger your waveform audio file will be.

Since disk space is a limited resource, it is recommended that you first record at the lowest setting—11,025 samples per second. If that does not provide adequate sound quality, try increasing the setting to 22,050. The highest setting, 44,100, is the sampling rate of CD Audio. This setting will give you the highest-quality recording, but unless you really need it, you should avoid consuming so much disk space. To help you grasp the relationship between sampling rate and sound quality, Table 22-1 compares different sampling rates to real-world audio devices of differing fidelities.

Table 22-1   The Relationship Between Sound Quality and Sampling Rate

Samples per Second	Sonic Equivalent
6,000	Telephone
15,000	AM radio
37,500	FM radio
40,000	Phonograph record
44,100	Compact disc

BITS PER SAMPLE

Table 22-2 illustrates how the number of bits per sample determines the dynamic range, which determines how much of a volume change you will hear between the loudest and softest sounds in a recording. Waveform audio devices typically give you a choice of 8 or 16 bits per sample. The original MPC standard required that multimedia computers be capable of recording at 8 bits per sample, whereas the MPC2 and MPC3 standards require 16.

The greater the number of bits per sample, the more disk space your audio recording will consume. Try recording first at 8 bits per sample. Only if that does not provide adequate sound quality should you increase the setting to 16 bits. To help you grasp the relationship between bits per sample and sound quality, Table 22-3 shows the dynamic range equivalents of some real-world sound sources.

Table 22-2   The Relationship Between Bits per Sample and Dynamic Range

Bits per Sample	Dynamic Range	Bits per Sample	Dynamic Range
1	8dB	10	62dB
2	14dB	11	68dB
3	20dB	12	74dB
4	26dB	13	80dB
5	32dB	14	86dB
6	38dB	15	92dB
7	44dB	16	98dB
8	50dB	17	104dB
9	56dB	18	110dB

Table 22-3   Bits-per-Sample Equivalents of Traditional Sound Sources

Sound Source	Bits per Sample Equivalent
AM radio	6
Telephone	8
FM radio	9
Phonograph record	10
Reel-to-reel tape	11
Compact disc	16

Movie on CD

Demonstrations
➡ Show Me!
   ➡ Waveform Audio
   ➡ **Sound Under
      Stills**

Sound Under Stills

Do you remember filmstrip projectors that could synchronize slides with a sound track? That technique is known as **sound under stills**. PODIUM makes it easy for you to create sound under stills.

In Chapter 21, you created a screen called *linkdemo.cus.* You can practice creating sound under stills using this screen. Follow these steps:

▶   If *linkdemo.cus* is not already on your screen, pull down the PODIUM Files menu, select Custom, and choose *linkdemo.cus.*

▶   Click *Show me some pictures!* and make sure it triggers the three bitmaps you linked to it:

bitmaps\egg.bmp
bitmaps\chick.bmp
bitmaps\rooster.bmp

If the pictures do not appear, you need to complete the exercises in Chapter 21 before continuing.

To create a sound track and synchronize it with the three pictures, so the pictures appear on cue at the right time in the sound track, follow these steps:

▶ Pull down the Tools menu and select the Waveform Audio tool.

▶ Use this tool to record the commentary printed below. Make sure to hold the microphone close to your mouth and speak loudly (but do not shout):

Roosters grow through several interesting stages. Here you see how they get born: in eggs! Then they hatch out into little chicks. Eventually, they grow up and look like this. And then they start to crow!

▶ Click Play to hear what you recorded.

▶ If you do not like it, click Reset and record it again.

▶ When you are satisfied with the recording, type the following name into the Filename field: **c:\multilit\growth.wav**

▶ Click the Save button to save the file.

▶ Click Rewind and watch the Current Location counter as you play it back once more. Write down the duration in seconds of the audio that accompanies each slide.

▶ Click Cancel to put the tool away.

▶ Press F4 to bring up the custom toolbox.

 ▶ Click the Link tool, then click the text *Show me some pictures!*

A Link box showing the three pictures you linked earlier will appear.

▶ Put the cursor at the very top of the box and press ⏎Enter to create a blank space.

▶ Type the name of the waveform audio recording you just created, followed by **@wait=0**

▶ Type **@wait=** after each of the next two images, followed by the number of seconds each part of that audio took when you auditioned the recording. Do not be concerned about being 100% accurate here, because you can always adjust the timing later. Your links should now read something like this:

```
! multilit\growth.wav @wait-0
! bitmaps\egg.bmp @wait=6
! bitmaps\chick.bmp @wait=5
! bitmaps\rooster.bmp @wait=7
! audio\rooster.wav
```

▶ Click OK to close the Link box, then press F4 to put the toolbox away.

▶ Click the words *Show me some pictures!* to try your sound under stills. If it works perfectly the first time, congratulate yourself heartily! Otherwise, use the Link tool to go back into the Link box and adjust the timings.

Ambient Sound

Ambient sound is a multimedia technique in which a waveform audio file keeps repeating to create the aural illusion that the user is in the place or situation where the sound was recorded. PODIUM has an @ambient command that makes it easy for you to have ambient sound on any multimedia screen. Follow these steps:

If your custom toolbox is not open, press F4 to get it on the screen.

▶ Click the Backdrop icon; the Backdrop dialog appears.

▶ Delete any waveform audio file that might already appear in the backdrop.

▶ Anyplace in the backdrop, put the following command: **@ambient=**_filename_ where _filename_ is one of the following files from the _Multiliteracy CD_:

```
ambient\traffic.wav
ambient\aircraft.wav
ambient\shopping.wav
```

▶ Click OK and press F4 to close the toolbox; the ambient sound will start.

▶ In addition to the ambient sound recordings that Pat Fox has provided in the _ambient_ directory of the _Multiliteracy CD_, you can use any waveform audio filename in the @ambient command. If you cannot find the sounds you want prerecorded, feel free to record your own ambient sound.

Sound Effects on the _Multiliteracy CD_

You will find a sound-effects library in the _soundfx_ directory on the _Multiliteracy CD_. The sound effects were donated by the vendors acknowledged in the clip media section of the _Multiliteracy CD_. You may make free use of these sound effects in your multimedia productions. If you need more sound effects, contact the vendors you will find by going to the Demonstrations section, selecting Textbook Examples, choosing Waveform Audio, and clicking the Vendors button.

List of Audio Commands

You may have noticed places on the _Multiliteracy CD_ where there are buttons which, when clicked, make the audio stop. This is accomplished by linking @quiet commands to the buttons. PODIUM has three @quiet commands that you can link to any trigger or button that you want audio to stop on. Table 22-4 lists the PODIUM audio commands.

Table 22-4 Audio Commands

@ Command	What the Command Does
@QuietWave	Stops any waveform audio file that may be playing.
@QuietMIDI	Stops any MIDI file that may be playing.
@QuietCD	Stops any CD Audio that may be playing.
@wait=*n*	When the @wait command appears after the name of a waveform audio file, it makes the computer wait *n* seconds before continuing on to the next object in the list of links.
@wait=end	Makes PODIUM wait until the end of a waveform audio file before continuing on to the next item in the list.
@wait=0	Makes PODIUM continue without waiting at all.

EXERCISES

1. Use the PODIUM Waveform Audio tool to record 10 seconds of your voice at 8 bits and then at 16 bits per sample. Save the first recording as *c:\multilit\8bit.wav,* and save the second recording as *c:\multilit\16bit.wav.* Use the PODIUM Files/Audio/Waveform menu to play each file. Can you hear a difference between the two recordings? Use the Windows 95 Explorer or the Windows 3.1 File Manager to inspect the size of these files. How much larger is the 16-bit recording?

2. Use the same process to record some music. If you cannot connect your music source to the line input of your sound card, record it through the microphone. Does the 16-bit setting make more of a difference for recorded music than it does for your voice recording?

3. Try recording music at different sampling rates. Can you hear how the higher sampling rates result in a brighter recording? Lower sampling rates cannot record high frequencies, effectively filtering them out.

4. Record some ambient sound from your home or business. Use the @ambient command to make the sound play repeatedly as part of the backdrop of your custom file. Do you agree that ambient sound adds a sense of realism to a multimedia screen?

23 The History of Flight Picture Menu

After completing this chapter, you will be able to:

◼ **Create a directory for a simple application dealing with the History of Flight**

◼ **Create the opening or "home" screen for the History of Flight application**

◼ **Title the home screen and give it a backdrop**

◼ **Position the text on the History of Flight home screen**

◼ **Use ambient sound to provide a sense of realism for the home screen**

HE simplest way to design a multimedia application is to have it begin with a screen that provides the user with a menu. When the user chooses an item from the menu, the application launches the object(s) linked to it. Then the application returns to the menu, and the user can make another choice.

The *Multiliteracy CD* contains a History of Flight bitmap. Figure 23-1 shows the four buttons on the bitmap that represent different eras in aviation history: biplanes from the 1920s, military aircraft from World War II, jet age Blue Angels, and a

23-1

The History of Flight bitmap has four buttons that feature different eras.

Photos by David K. Brunn. Copyright © 1994 Aris Multimedia Entertainment, Inc.

contemporary Boeing 747 jumbo jet. In this chapter you will learn how to make the History of Flight bitmap serve as your application's main menu. In subsequent chapters you will learn how to link objects that describe and illustrate each era.

Creating the *flight* Directory

When you begin to develop a new application, you must create a directory for it on your hard disk. Since this application deals with the history of flight, you will create a directory called *flight*. The way to create a directory depends on the version of Windows you have. Follow the instructions for your version of Windows:

WINDOWS 95

▶ Use the Windows 95 Start button to get the Windows Explorer started. If you cannot find the Start button, hold down the Ctrl key and press Esc to make the Start button appear. The Explorer is on the Start button's Programs menu.

▶ In the Explorer, click the icon that represents the hard disk drive on which you will create the History of Flight application.

▶ Pull down the File menu, select New, and select Folder. Figure 23-2 shows how the new folder will appear with the name *New Folder*.

▶ Make the name of the new folder be *flight*. Since the name *New Folder* is already selected, you can change the name by simply typing **flight**

▶ Close the Explorer by clicking on the ✕ in the upper right corner of the window.

23-2

A new folder created with Windows 95.

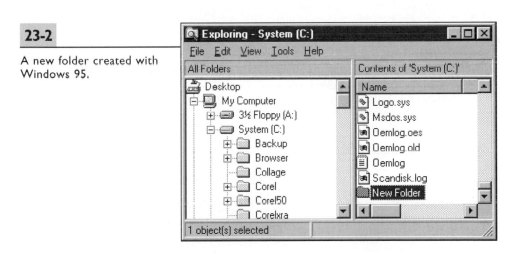

WINDOWS 3.1, WINDOWS NT, OR SOFTWINDOWS

▶ On the Windows desktop, double-click the File Manager icon to launch the File Manager.

▶ Pull down the File menu and choose Create Directory to bring up the Create Directory dialog.

▶ In the Name field, if your hard drive is C, type **c:\flight** and click OK. If your hard drive is not C, replace the *C* with the appropriate drive letter. From now on, this tutorial will always refer to your hard disk as drive C.

▶ Close the File Manager.

Creating the Home Screen

Start PODIUM if it is not already running.

▶ Pull down the PODIUM Files menu and choose New Custom to invoke the File
Creation dialog.

▶ In the File name field, type **c:\flight\history.cus** then click OK.

PODIUM will create a blank screen called *history.cus* and display the custom
toolbox on it. This will serve as the "home" screen around which this application
revolves. Follow the steps in the next section to build this screen into the main
menu of the History of Flight application.

Making the Backdrop

The *aircraft* directory on the *Multiliteracy CD* contains a bitmap called *buttons.bmp*
which contains the four buttons shown in Figure 23-1. Use the browse feature of
the Backdrop tool to put it on your home screen by following these steps:

▶ Click the Backdrop icon.

▶ Click the Browse button to bring up the Browse dialog shown in Figure 23-3.
Use the controls on the right side of the Browse dialog to navigate to the
aircraft directory on your CD-ROM drive. To change drives, pull down the
Drives menu and click on a drive. To change directories on that drive, double-
click the name of the directory.

▶ Click *buttons.bmp* when it appears in the box on the left side of the Browse
dialog as shown in Figure 23-4.

▶ Click OK in the Browse dialog. The name *buttons.bmp* will appear in the
Backdrop dialog.

▶ Click OK in the Backdrop dialog. PODIUM will load *buttons.bmp* and display it
as the backdrop on your screen.

23-3

Use the controls in the right half of the Browse dialog
to make *d:\aircraft* the current directory.

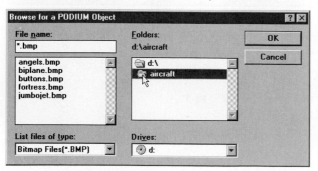

23-4

Click once on the filename *buttons.bmp* to put it in the
File name field.

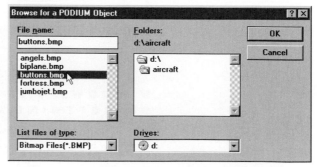

Titling the Home Screen

The next step is very important. Because this is a special tutorial version of the PODIUM software, the text on each screen must match what this tutorial tells you to enter. If the text does not match, PODIUM will think you are trying to create some other application, and you will get a polite message explaining that you need to purchase a retail copy to do that.

▶ Click the Text icon in the PODIUM toolbox to select the Text tool, and use it to enter the following two lines of text. Position the first line at the upper left section of the screen, and place the second line below the first. You must type these in the order in which they are given here to avoid getting the PODIUM "retail" message:

```
The History of Flight:
From Props to Jets
```

▶ Then type the following line at the bottom of the screen:

```
Click an Airplane to Study an Era of Flight
```

Arranging the Text

Use the custom toolbox to arrange the text and make it look good on the screen. Screen design is a matter of personal taste. Figure 23-5 shows one way of arranging this screen. Here are some suggestions of how to arrange the text on your screen:

▶ Use the Sizer tool to make the first line bigger than the others.

▶ Use the Move tools to move each line where you want it on the screen.

▶ Use the Centering tool to center all three lines on the screen.

▶ Use the Color tool to make the second line yellow.

▶ Use the Shadow tool to increase the amount of drop shadow.

23-5

The History of Flight home screen with titles and instructions.

Photos by David K. Brunn. Copyright © 1994 Aris Multimedia Entertainment, Inc.

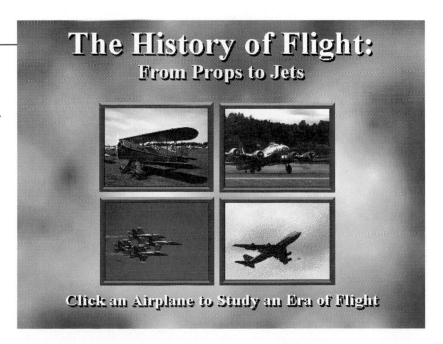

▶   Use the Font tool to change the font if you want.

▶   Use the Move tools to position the text on the screen. The first two lines *(The History of Flight: From Props to Jets)* are the title, so position them above the aircraft buttons. Put the line *Click an Airplane to Study an Era of Flight* below the buttons.

Creating the Ambient Sound

There is a waveform audio file in the *ambient* directory of the *Multiliteracy CD* that makes airport sounds. The name of the file is *airport.wav*. To make this be the ambient sound for the History of Flight application, follow these steps:

▶   Click the Backdrop icon; the Backdrop dialog appears.

▶   In the edit box, position the cursor at the end of your existing backdrop, press ⌐Enter to start a new line, and type the following command:

`@ambient=ambient\airport.wav`

▶   Click OK to close the Backdrop dialog.

▶   Press F4 to put the toolbox away. The ambient sound should start playing. *Note:* Ambient sound does not play when the toolbox is opened; you must close the toolbox to hear the ambient sound.

24

1920s
Barnstorming

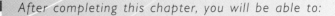

After completing this chapter, you will be able to:

- **Link the Biplane button to a multimedia screen that presents the 1920s barnstorming era in the History of Flight**

- **Create the text and graphics on the Biplane screen, following a detailed list of instructions**

- **Provide realism with the ambient sound of a biplane in flight**

- **Link a biplane in motion using either a videodisc or Video for Windows**

H E home screen you just created serves as a menu. When the user clicks one of the four aircraft buttons, the application branches to materials that describe the corresponding period in aviation history. In this chapter you will create a trigger on the Biplane button and link it to materials describing the barnstorming era of the 1920s.

Making the Link

▶ Click the Trigger icon (the one that looks like a rocket sitting on a launch pad). When you move the cursor around the home screen, it should assume the shape of the Trigger tool. *Do not* click the mouse yet.

▶ Move the mouse carefully to position the tip of the cursor in the upper left corner of the Biplane button.

▶ Hold down the left button as you drag the mouse to the lower right corner of the Biplane button. A box showing the location of the trigger will appear.

▶ Release the button; PODIUM displays the Link dialog.

▶ Click once inside the big Link box to set the cursor.

▶ Type **flight\biplane.cus** then click OK.

NOTE If you make a mistake, you can click the Undo/Redo icon in the toolbox and repeat these six steps.

Triggering the Link

▶ Press F4 to put the toolbox away and become a user of your application. Notice how the cursor changes shape as you mouse over the Biplane button, indicating that you have placed a trigger there.

▶ Click the Biplane button to trigger its link. PODIUM tells you that the *flight\biplane.cus* file linked to this trigger does not yet exist, and asks if you want to create it.

▶ Click OK. PODIUM will then create the *flight\biplane.cus* file, display it on your screen, and open the toolbox for you. The display is blank, because you have not put anything on it yet.

Making the Biplane Backdrop

The *aircraft* directory on the *Multiliteracy CD* contains a bitmap called *biplane.bmp* which will make a nice backdrop for the Biplane screen. Use the browse feature of the Backdrop tool to put this bitmap on your screen. Try to do this without reading any instructions, but if you need help, follow these steps:

▶ Click the Backdrop icon.

▶ Click the Browse button to bring up the Browse dialog. Use the controls on the right side of the Browse dialog to navigate to the *aircraft* directory on the CD-ROM drive. To change drives, pull down the Drives menu and click on a drive. To change directories on that drive, double-click the name of the directory.

▶ Click *biplane.bmp* when it appears in the box on the left side of the Browse dialog.

▶ Click OK in the Browse dialog; the name *biplane.bmp* will appear in the Backdrop dialog.

▶ Click OK in the Backdrop dialog. PODIUM will load *biplane.bmp* and display it as the backdrop on your screen.

Entering the Biplane Text

▶ Use the Text tool to put the following lines of text on the screen; you *must* enter these lines in the order in which they are listed here to avoid getting the PODIUM "retail" message:

`Barnstorming Biplanes`

`Biplanes were popularized by barnstormers who`
`used them to dazzle onlookers during the 1920s.`

`Pictured here is the Waco Taperwing,`
`a very acrobatic biplane.`

`In the 1940s, biplanes were used heavily to`
`train civilian pilots during World War II.`

`Click anywhere to continue.`

24-1

The completed *biplane.cus* screen.

Photo by David K. Brunn. Copyright © 1994 Aris Multimedia Entertainment, Inc.

Barnstorming Biplanes

Biplanes were popularized by barnstormers who used them to dazzle onlookers during the 1920s.

Pictured here is the Waco Taperwing, a very acrobatic biplane.

In the 1940s, biplanes were used heavily to train civilian pilots during World War II.

Click anywhere to continue.

Adjusting the Text

▷ Use the Sizer, Shadow, Color, Font, and Move tools in the toolbox to arrange the text on the screen as you wish. Figure 24-1 shows one way of arranging this screen.

Creating the Ambient Sound

There is a waveform audio file called *biplane.wav* in the *ambient* directory of the *Multiliteracy CD*. Use the Backdrop tool to make *biplane.wav* be the ambient sound for your Biplane screen. Try to do this on your own, but if you need help, follow these steps:

▷ Click the Backdrop icon; the Backdrop dialog appears.

▷ In the edit box, position the cursor at the end of your existing backdrop, press ←Enter to start a new line, and type the following command:

```
@ambient=ambient\biplane.wav
```

▷ Click OK to close the Backdrop dialog.

▷ Press F4 to put the toolbox away. The ambient sound should start playing. *Note:* Ambient sound does not play when the toolbox is opened; you must close the toolbox to hear the ambient sound.

Rehearsing the Link

▷ If the toolbox is opened, press F4 to close it and become a user of your application.

▷ Click anywhere on the Biplane screen to return to the History of Flight menu; you will hear the ambient airport sound in the background.

▷ Click the Biplane button; the Biplane screen will appear, and you will hear the ambient biplane sound.

24-2

The Link dialog.

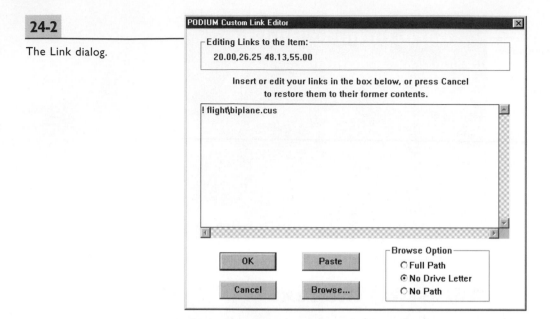

Linking the Motion Sequence

To bring your application to life, you can add a full-motion video clip of a barnstorming biplane in action! Follow these steps:

▶ Display the History of Flight menu *(flight\history.cus)* on your screen.

 ▶ Press ⬚F4⬚ to open the toolbox, then click the Link icon.

▶ Click the Biplane button to bring up the Link dialog shown in Figure 24-2. Notice that the Link box already contains the *flight\biplane.cus* link.

▶ Click once inside the Link box and position the cursor at the end of the *flight\biplane.cus* link. Press ⬚←Enter⬚ to move the cursor down to a new line.

▶ If you have a videodisc player with the videodisc *To Fly!*, type

14600 15850

Otherwise, type

```
aircraft\biplane.avi
```

▶ Click OK to close the Link dialog.

Testing the Motion Sequence

▶ Press ⬚F4⬚ to close the toolbox.

▶ Click the Biplane button—the *flight\biplane.cus* file should appear as before.

▶ Click again—you should now see and hear the biplane in action as the full-motion video clip plays.

▶ Click once more to return to the menu.

If this worked, congratulate yourself—you are well on your way to becoming a multimedia application developer. If you had trouble, try repeating the previous steps. With practice, you can master this process.

25 The Flying Fortress

After completing this chapter, you will be able to:

- **Link the Flying Fortress button to a multimedia screen that presents the World War II era**

- **Create the text and graphics on the Flying Fortress screen with a little less hand-holding than in the previous chapter**

- **Provide realism with the ambient sound of a Flying Fortress in flight**

- **Link a video clip showing the history of aircraft development during World War II**

HIS chapter is very similar to the one you just completed. In fact, all four of the historical aircraft chapters in this beginning-level tutorial have the same design. The goal is to make you so familiar with the process of linking buttons to multimedia materials that you can do it without referring to the instructions. Accordingly, each chapter will provide less hand-holding than the previous chapter until you can make these linkages on your own. Then, in Part Eight, you will learn how to implement more-complex designs.

The second button on the History of Flight menu pictures the Boeing-17G "Flying Fortress," one of the most famous World War II aircraft. This chapter shows you how to create a trigger on the Flying Fortress button and link it to materials describing World War II aircraft.

To get started, follow these steps:

▶ If you do not have the History of Flight menu on your screen, pull down the PODIUM Files menu, select Custom Files, and navigate to *flight\history.cus.*

▶ Press F4 to bring up the custom toolbox.

Making the Link

▶ Click the Trigger icon.

▶ Position the tip of the cursor in the upper left corner of the Flying Fortress button.

▶ Hold down the left button and drag the mouse to the lower right corner of the Flying Fortress button. A box showing the location of the trigger will appear.

▶ Release the button; PODIUM displays the Link dialog.

▶ Click once inside the Link box to set the cursor.

▶ Type **flight\fortress.cus** then click OK.

Triggering the Link

▶ Press F4 to put the toolbox away and become a user of your application. Notice how the cursor changes shape as you mouse over the Flying Fortress button, indicating that you have placed a trigger there.

▶ Click the Flying Fortress button to trigger its link. PODIUM tells you that the *flight\fortress.cus* file linked to this trigger does not yet exist, and PODIUM asks if you want to create the new file.

▶ Click OK. PODIUM will then create the *flight\fortress.cus* file, display it on your screen, and open the toolbox for you. The display is blank, because you have not put anything on it yet.

Making the Flying Fortress Backdrop

The *aircraft* directory on the *Multiliteracy CD* contains a bitmap called *fortress.bmp*. Use the Backdrop tool to put it on your screen. By now you should be able to do this without reading any instructions, but if you need help, follow these steps:

▶ Click the Backdrop icon.

▶ Click the Browse button to bring up the Browse dialog. Use the controls on the right side of the Browse dialog to navigate to the *aircraft* directory on the CD-ROM drive. To change drives, pull down the Drives menu and click on a drive. To change directories on that drive, double-click the name of the directory.

▶ Click *fortress.bmp* when it appears in the box on the left side of the Browse dialog.

▶ Click OK in the Browse dialog. The name *fortress.bmp* will appear in the Backdrop dialog.

▶ Click OK in the Backdrop dialog. PODIUM will load *fortress.bmp* and display it as the backdrop on your screen.

Entering the Flying Fortress Text

▶ Use the Text tool to put the following lines of text on the screen; you *must* enter these lines in the order in which they are listed here to avoid getting the PODIUM "retail" message:

```
World War II Aircraft
```

```
The Allies relied on aircraft to help
win World War II.
```

```
Pictured here is the famous Boeing B-17
bomber, which was nicknamed the Flying
Fortress due to its heavy armament.
```

```
Click anywhere to continue.
```

25-1

The completed *fortress.cus* screen.

Photo by David K. Brunn. Copyright © 1994 Aris Multimedia Entertainment, Inc.

Adjusting the Text

▶ Use the Sizer, Shadow, Color, Font, and Move tools in the toolbox to arrange the text on the screen as you wish. Figure 25-1 shows one way of arranging this screen.

Creating the Ambient Sound

There is a waveform audio file called *fortress.wav* in the *ambient* directory of the *Multiliteracy CD*. Use the Backdrop tool to make *fortress.wav* be the ambient sound for your Flying Fortress screen. By now, you should be able to do this on your own, but if you need help, follow these steps:

▶ Click the Backdrop icon; the Backdrop dialog appears.

▶ In the edit box, position the cursor at the end of your existing backdrop, press ⏎Enter to start a new line, and type the following command:

`@ambient=ambient\fortress.wav`

▶ Click OK to close the Backdrop dialog.

▶ Press F4 to put the toolbox away; the ambient sound should start playing.

Rehearsing the Link

▶ If the toolbox is open, press F4 to close it and become a user of your application.

▶ Click anywhere on the Flying Fortress screen to return to the History of Flight menu.

▶ Click the Flying Fortress button; the Flying Fortress screen will appear, and you will hear the ambient sound.

25-2

The Link dialog.

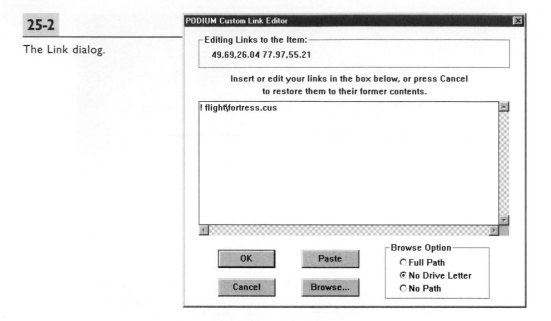

Linking the Motion Sequence

Many aircraft participated in the Allied fight to win World War II. You can add a full-motion video clip to chronicle the history of the development of these airplanes. Follow these steps:

▶ Display the History of Flight menu *(flight\history.cus)* on your screen.

 ▶ Press F4 to open the toolbox, then click the Link icon.

▶ Click once on the Flying Fortress button to bring up the Link dialog shown in Figure 25-2. Notice that the Link box already contains the *flight\fortress.cus* link.

▶ Click once inside the Link box and position the cursor at the end of the *flight\fortress.cus* link. Press ←Enter to move the cursor down to a new line.

▶ If you have a videodisc player with the videodisc *To Fly!*, type:

17918 18145

Otherwise, type

    aircraft\fortress.avi

▶ Click OK to close the Link dialog.

Testing the Motion Sequence

▶ Press F4 to close the toolbox.

▶ Click the Flying Fortress button—your *flight\fortress.cus* file should appear as before.

▶ Click again—you should now see and hear the military aircraft in action as the full-motion video clip plays.

▶ Click once more to return to the menu.

26

The Blue Angels

After completing this chapter, you will be able to:

- **Link the Blue Angels button to a multimedia screen that presents this famous U.S. Navy Flight Demonstration Squadron**

- **Create the text and graphics on the Blue Angels screen with very little hand-holding**

- **Provide realism with the ambient sound of the Blue Angels in flight**

- **Link a spectacular video of the Blue Angels in flight**

HIS chapter provides less hand-holding than the previous ones. If you have trouble, go back to the previous chapter for more-detailed instructions. The only difference is in the filenames of the multimedia objects.

The third button on the History of Flight menu depicts the Blue Angels, McDonnell Douglas F/A-18 Hornets, acrobatic jet aircraft that made their debut in 1978. This chapter shows you how to create a trigger on the Blue Angels button and link it to materials describing these fascinating jets.

▶ If you do not have the History of Flight menu on your screen, pull down the PODIUM Files menu, select Custom Files, and navigate to *flight\history.cus.*

▶ Press F4 to bring up the custom toolbox.

Making the Link

▶ Use the Trigger tool to create a link that covers the Blue Angels button.

▶ When the Link dialog appears, click once inside the Link box to set the cursor.

▶ Type **flight\angels.cus** then click OK.

Triggering the Link

▶ Press F4 to put the toolbox away and become a user of your application.

▶ Click the Blue Angels button to trigger its link. PODIUM tells you that the *flight\angels.cus* file you linked to this trigger does not yet exist, and asks if you want to create it.

▶ Click OK.

Making the Blue Angels Backdrop

The *aircraft* directory on the *Multiliteracy CD* contains a bitmap called *angels.bmp*.

 ▶ Use the Backdrop tool to put this bitmap on your screen.

Entering the Blue Angels Text

 ▶ Use the Text tool to put the following lines of text on the screen in the order in which they are listed here.

```
Blue Angels

Pictured here is the U.S. Navy Blue Angels
Flight Demonstration Squadron.

The Blue Angels are
McDonnell Douglas F/A-18 Hornets.

Click anywhere to continue.
```

Adjusting the Text

Use the Sizer, Shadow, Color, Font, and Move tools in the toolbox to arrange the text on top of the backdrop as you wish. Figure 26-1 shows one way of arranging this screen.

26-1

The completed *angels.cus* screen.

Photo by David K. Brunn. Copyright © 1994 Aris Multimedia Entertainment, Inc.

Creating the Ambient Sound

There is a waveform audio file called *angels.wav* in the *ambient* directory of the *Multiliteracy CD*. Use the Backdrop tool to make *angels.wav* be the ambient sound for your Blue Angels screen.

Hint: The ambient command has the syntax

```
@ambient=path\filename.wav
```

Rehearsing the Link

▶ Press ⌐F4⌐ to close the toolbox and become a user of your application.

▶ Click anywhere on the Blue Angels screen to return to the History of Flight menu.

▶ Click the Blue Angels button; the Blue Angels screen will appear.

Linking the Motion Sequence

Your next task is to link the Blue Angels button to a beautiful full-motion sequence of the Blue Angels in flight. If you have the videodisc *To Fly!*, this video clip is in frames 19267 to 20867; otherwise, you can use the digital video clip *aircraft\angels.avi*.

▶ Display the History of Flight menu *(flight\history.cus)* on your screen.

 ▶ Press ⌐F4⌐ to open the toolbox, then click the Link icon. Use the Link tool to add the Blue Angels video to the materials that are linked to the Blue Angels button. Try to link the video clip without looking at the instructions, but if you need help, follow these steps:

 ▶ Click the Link icon in the toolbox, then click the Blue Angels button to bring up the Link dialog. It will already contain your *flight\angels.cus* link.

▶ Click once inside the Link box and position the cursor at the end of the *flight\angels.cus* link. Press ⌐←Enter⌐ to move the cursor down to a new line.

▶ If you have a videodisc player with the videodisc *To Fly!*, type

19267 20867

Otherwise, type:

```
aircraft\angels.avi
```

▶ Click OK to close the Link dialog.

Testing the Motion Sequence

▶ Press ⌐F4⌐ to close the toolbox.

▶ Click the Blue Angels button—your *flight\angels.cus* file should appear as before.

▶ Click again—you should now see and hear the Blue Angels in action as the full-motion video clip plays.

▶ Click once more to return to the menu.

27 Jumbo Jets

After completing this chapter, you will be able to:

- Link the Boeing 747 button to a multimedia screen that introduces the age of passenger air travel by jumbo jet

- Create the text and graphics on the Jumbo Jet screen without any hand-holding

- Provide realism with the ambient sound of a jumbo jet in flight

- Link the Jumbo Jet button to a dramatic video of a Boeing 747 takeoff

HIS chapter is the supreme test of your ability to create multimedia linkages, because it has no hand-holding! If you have trouble, refer to the previous chapters. The process is exactly the same; only the filenames and the historical information differ.

Creating the Jumbo Jet Link

▶ Display the History of Flight menu. The fourth button on it has a picture of a Boeing 747 jumbo jet, the first wide-body commercial passenger jet.

 ▶ Use the Trigger tool to link the Jumbo Jet button to *flight\jumbojet.cus* and then click the Jumbo Jet button to trigger the link. When PODIUM asks if you want to create the *flight\jumbojet.cus* file, click OK.

Making the Jumbo Jet Backdrop

 ▶ The *aircraft* directory on the *Multiliteracy CD* contains a bitmap called *jumbojet.bmp*. Use the Backdrop tool to put this bitmap on your screen.

Entering the Jumbo Jet Text

 ▶ Use the Text tool to put the following lines of text on the screen in the order listed here.

Jumbo Jets

The Boeing 747 passenger jet pictured
here is the largest aircraft in
commercial service.

27-1

The completed *jumbojet.cus* screen.

Photo by David K. Brunn. Copyright © 1994 Aris Multimedia Entertainment, Inc.

```
Nicknamed the jumbo jet, it was the
first wide-body passenger jet.
It started flying in 1970.

Click anywhere to continue.
```

Adjusting the Text

▶ Use the Sizer, Shadow, Color, Font, and Move tools in the toolbox to arrange the text on top of the backdrop as you wish. Figure 27-1 shows one way of arranging this screen.

Creating the Ambient Sound

There is a waveform audio file called *jumbojet.wav* in the *ambient* directory of the *Multiliteracy CD*. Use the Backdrop tool to make *jumbojet.wav* be the ambient sound for your Jumbo Jet screen.

Rehearsing the Link

▶ Press F4 to close the toolbox and become a user of your application.

▶ Click anywhere on the Jumbo Jet screen to return to the History of Flight menu.

▶ Click the Jumbo Jet button; the Jumbo Jet screen will appear.

Linking the Motion Sequence

Your next task is to link a dramatic takeoff of a Boeing 747 jumbo jet to the Jumbo Jet button. If you have the videodisc *To Fly!,* this video clip is in frames 22300 to 23175; otherwise, you can use the digital video clip *aircraft\jumbojet.avi.*

▶   Bring up the History of Flight menu.

 ▶   Press F4 to open the toolbox, then use the Link tool to add the jumbo jet video to the materials that are linked to the Jumbo Jet button.

Testing the Motion Sequence

▶   Press F4 to close the toolbox.

▶   Click the Jumbo Jet button—your *flight\jumbojet.cus* file should appear as before.

▶   Click again—you should now see and hear the Boeing 747 take off as the full-motion video clip plays.

Self-Assessment

If you were able to complete this linkage without looking at any of the instructions provided in previous chapters, you really should congratulate yourself. You are well on your way to developing the skills needed to create multimedia applications.

28 Providing a Graceful Way to Exit

After completing this chapter, you will be able to:

- Hang an Exit sign on the History of Flight home screen

- Place a trigger on the Exit sign

- Link the Exit sign trigger to the @quit command

- Link other navigation commands to triggers in an application

ALTHOUGH users can always pull down the Files menu and choose Quit to leave your application, it is better to provide a more graceful way to exit. This chapter shows how to hang an Exit sign on a multimedia screen.

If you do not already have the History of Flight home screen in your PODIUM window, pull down the PODIUM Files menu, choose Custom, navigate to the *flight* directory, and select *history.cus*.

Creating the Exit Sign

In the *icons* directory on the *Multiliteracy CD* is an Exit sign called *exit2fly.bmp*. Use the Picture Hanger tool to hang the Exit sign on your History of Flight home screen. Then use the Move tool to locate the Exit sign wherever you want it on the screen. Figure 28-1 shows one way of positioning the Exit sign. If you need help, follow these steps:

28-1

Positioning the Exit sign on the History of Flight screen.

Photo by David K. Brunn. Copyright © 1994 Aris Multimedia Entertainment, Inc.

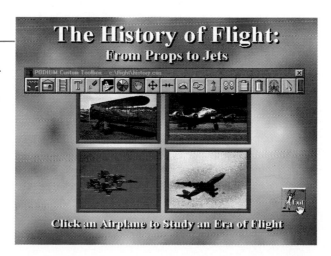

▶ Press ⌐F4⌐ to open the custom toolbox.

▶ Click the Picture Hanger icon.

▶ Move the mouse to the spot on the screen where you want the Exit sign, and click the left mouse button; the Picture Hanger dialog appears.

▶ Click once inside the big edit box to position the cursor, and type **icons\exit2fly.bmp**

▶ Click OK to close the Picture Hanger dialog; the Exit sign appears on-screen.

▶ Use the Move tool to reposition the Exit sign as you wish.

Activating the Exit Sign

▶ If the PODIUM toolbox is not open, press ⌐F4⌐.

▶ Click the Link icon and then click the Exit sign; PODIUM creates a trigger around the Exit sign, and the Link dialog appears.

▶ Click once inside the Link box and type the following command:

`@quit`

▶ Click OK to close the Link dialog.

Testing the Exit Sign

Press ⌐F4⌐ to close the toolbox, and click the Exit sign. PODIUM will ask if you really want to exit. Click No, unless you want to quit.

Customizing the Navigation

In addition to @quit, PODIUM has the following navigation options:

```
@next
@back
@done
@home
```

Just as you linked @quit to the Exit sign, you can link any of these options to any hypertext or hyperpicture on the screen. You can even design your own icons. To get you started, the *icons* directory on the CD contains the following navigation icons:

Next ☞	*next.bmp*
☜ Back	*back.bmp*
Menu	*menu.bmp*
Home ⌂	*home.bmp*
Quit	*quit.bmp*

Disabling the Default Navigation

You will probably want to disable PODIUM's default mouse-click navigation when you design your own navigation. When the default navigation is turned off, the user must click one of your buttons or triggers to navigate.

To disable PODIUM's default navigation, click the right mouse button on the Expand icon at the right end of the PODIUM toolbox to display the advanced tools, and click the Navigate icon. Navigate is a toggle; each time you choose it, PODIUM will turn default navigation on or off. When the Navigate icon appears bright, that means it is on.

List of Navigation Commands

Table 28-1 lists the PODIUM navigation commands.

Table 28-1   Navigation Commands

@ Command	What the Command Does
@quit	Terminates the application. Before terminating, PODIUM asks if the user really wants to quit.
@done	Returns to the screen from which the current screen was launched. The @done command is ineffective on an application's home screen.
@home	Returns to the application's home screen.
@next	Proceeds to the next item in a list of links.
@back	Returns to the previous item in a list of links.
@navigate	When the @navigate command appears in the backdrop of a custom file, PODIUM's default navigation is turned off, and the user can navigate only via hypertext links and buttons built into the application.
@reread	Causes PODIUM to reread, and then restart, the current custom screen.

Part Seven

More Multimedia Tools and Techniques

Now that you have completed the History of Flight tutorial, it is time to learn more multimedia tools and techniques that you can use to create advanced applications. By agreement with each tool's publisher, all of the software you will need is provided on the *Multiliteracy CD*. Some of the tools are shareware, and if you continue using them after you finish this tutorial, you must purchase a retail license. Other tools have been donated freely, and you can use them without charge.

Specific tools you will learn include:

- A suite of Video for Windows tools, which enable you to record and edit movies and create animations

- Paint Shop Pro, which multimedia developers use to capture and manipulate graphics images

- Band-in-a-Box, which is a very popular tool for creating MIDI music sequences

- Several more PODIUM tools that enable you to:
  - Hang movies on the screen
  - Record CD Audio direct to your hard disk drive
  - Create videodisc clips
  - Provide "flying help" to make your applications easy to use
  - Create buttons that appear to push in when clicked
  - Make scrolling text windows
  - Create input fields to interact with users
  - Program logic to make applications more intelligent
  - Use timers to trigger events automatically
  - Change the shape of multimedia cursors
  - Create animation that makes objects move across the screen

After you learn how to use these tools, you will be ready to create advanced multimedia applications in Part Eight of this book.

29 Digital Video Recording and Editing

■ **Prepare your disk drive for direct-to-disk digital video recording**

■ **Record and edit digital video using Microsoft's Video for Windows**

■ **Conserve disk space by compressing the digital video recording**

■ **Understand how digital video recording works and realize why movies play back better on faster computers**

HIS chapter is a tutorial on recording and editing digital video clips with Microsoft's Video for Windows. After you complete this tutorial, the next chapter will teach you how to cut digital video windows into your multimedia screens. Figure 29-1 shows an artist's impression of how your computer's microprocessor plays digital video.

If you do not have a video capture card with Video for Windows installed, you will not be able to make an actual recording; however, you will still be able to complete the digital-video-editing tutorial—all of the software you will need is on the *Multiliteracy CD.*

29-1

An artistic impression of how microcomputers play digital video recordings.

Artwork provided courtesy of Intel, Inc.

An important advantage of Video for Windows over other kinds of digital video is that it can be played back without requiring the user to have any special hardware. Therefore, even if you do not have a video capture card, you will still be able to edit and make clips from the digital video recordings on the enclosed CD-ROM.

How Digital Video Works

To make a digital video recording, you must first connect an analog video source, such as a camera, VCR, or videodisc player, to your video capture card. When you tell Video for Windows to start recording, the video capture card converts this analog video signal into digital information. Because the digital video stream contains an enormous amount of data that is too large for today's computers to store and play back in real time, it gets highly compressed to save space, down to as little as $\frac{1}{200}$ of its original size. One or more of the video compression schemes explained in Table 29-1 may be used.

Table 29-1 Video Compression Schemes

Method	How It Works
YUV subsampling	Divides the screen into little squares and averages color values of the pixels in each square.
Delta frame encoding	Shrinks data by storing only the information that changes between frames; for example, if the background scene does not change, there is no need to store the scene again.
Run-length encoding	Detects a "run" of identical pixels and encodes how many occur instead of recording each individual pixel.

Table 29-2 Video Playback Frame Rates for Different Microprocessors

Processor	Full-Screen (fps)*	1/4 Screen (fps)	1/16 Screen (fps)
i386 SX-25	0	5	10
i386 DX-33	0	10	20
i486 SX-25	5	15	30
i486 DX2-66	10	30	30
Pentium 75	20	30	30
Pentium 130	30	30	30

*fps = frames per second

On playback the computer's microprocessor must read the encoded information, decode it, and route the video to the screen and the sound track to the waveform audio board. Because some computers are slower than others, Video for Windows uses a clever scheme in which audio frames are interleaved with the video. The sound track plays uninterrupted because the audio always takes priority. Then the computer shows as many frames of video as it has time to process. If it is too late to show a given frame, Video for Windows just skips it and goes on to the next frame.

Because the audio has priority, you get the aural illusion of uninterrupted playback, even though video frames may get dropped in the process, resulting in a jerky motion on the screen. Table 29-2 shows how many frames per second (fps) different processors can display depending on the size of the playback window. The faster the processor, the smoother the motion.

Installing the Video for Windows Utilities

Microsoft granted permission for us to include the Video for Windows utilities on the *Multiliteracy CD*. To install them, follow these steps:

▶ If you have Windows 3.1, pull down the Program Manager's File menu and choose Run.

▶ If you have Windows 95, click the Start button and choose Run.

▶ Run the *setup.exe* program you will find in the *winvideo* directory on the *Multiliteracy CD.*

▶ When the setup program asks whether you want to install the playback module only or the playback module plus the tools, choose Video Playback and Video Tools.

▶ Follow the rest of the instructions to install Video for Windows.

The Video for Windows utilities VidEdit and VidCap have now been installed on your computer. There is one more program that you must install by hand, namely, BitEdit. Follow these steps:

▶ Copy the following files from the *winvideo* directory on the *Multiliteracy CD* into the *winvideo* directory on your hard drive:

```
bitedit.exe
bitedit.hlp
paledit.exe
paledit.hlp
```

▶ Get the Windows 3.1 File Manager or the Windows 95 Explorer running. Browse to the *winvideo* directory on your hard drive. Position the windows on your desktop so you can see the Video for Windows group alongside the directory listing of the *winvideo* directory.

▶ Click and drag the *bitedit.exe* icon from the directory listing into your Video for Windows group.

You should now see the BitEdit icon in your Video for Windows group. If so, you have just learned a quick way to create a startup icon for any Windows application.

Preparing Your Hard Drive

Before you can record video to your hard disk drive, you must make sure there is enough space to hold the recording. A rule of thumb is to have 15 MB of free disk space for every minute of video you plan to record. This will get compressed later on to save space, but you need enough free disk space to hold the raw video at first.

To complete the exercises in this chapter, you should have at least 20 MB of free disk space. If you do not have that much available, free some now.

You may need to defragment your hard disk drive. You can try recording first without defragmenting, but if your computer drops frames while recording, you will need to defragment. Your computer may have come with its own defragmenting software; consult your operating manual for instructions. If not, the Norton Utilities from Symantec contain a program called Speedisk that does this. (*Note:* The defragmentation utility built into DOS 6.0 is a copy of Speedisk that Microsoft licensed from Symantec.)

Running the VidCap Program

Figure 29-2 shows the Video for Windows group. Use the Windows 3.1 Program Manager or the Windows 95 My Computer to get this group on your screen.

In the Video for Windows group, double-click the VidCap icon to launch the video capture program. The window shown in Figure 29-3 will appear.

29-2

The Video for Windows group.

29-3

The VidCap window.

NOTE If you do not have a video capture card in your computer, you will not actually be able to capture video during this tutorial, but you will be able to edit video when this tutorial gets to the video-editing part.

Movie on CD

Demonstrations
➡ Show Me!
  ➡ Digital Video Recording and Editing
    ➡ **Setting the Capture File**

Setting the Capture File

The first step in making a digital video recording is to set the capture file. Pull down the File menu and select Set Capture File. Assuming your hard drive is C, in the File Name field type **c:\vidcap.avi**

The first time you do this, *vidcap.avi* will not exist, so Windows will display the Set File Size dialog shown in Figure 29-4. It tells you how much space is available and asks how large you want to make the capture file. Make it at least 10 MB, but leave at least 10 MB free on your hard disk so Windows has room to operate.

29-4

The VidCap Set File Size dialog.

Previewing the Video and Checking the Audio

Make sure the video output of your video source is connected to the video input of your video capture card. Check to see that the audio output of your video source is connected to the audio input of your waveform audio board. Then turn on your video source and make it play.

Click the Overlay Window button in the VidCap button bar. If your video capture card supports overlay, you should see your video source in the capture window and you should hear the audio play. If you have problems, check the following:

- Is your video source connected to the video input on your video capture card?

- Is the audio output of your video source connected to the audio input of your waveform audio board?

- Pull down the VidCap Options menu and select Video Source; make sure the options match your setup.

Movie on CD

Demonstrations
⮕ Show Me!
  ⮕ Digital Video
    Recording and
    Editing
    ⮕ **Grabbing a
      Palette**

Grabbing a Palette

Video for Windows uses palettized graphics to make the colors in the video match as closely as possible the colors in the video. To grab a palette, follow these steps:

▶ Pull down the Capture menu and see if the Palette option is active. If it is dimmed, skip these five steps.

▶ If the Palette option is active, select it; the Capture Palette dialog shown in Figure 29-5 will appear.

29-5

The VidCap Capture
Palette dialog.

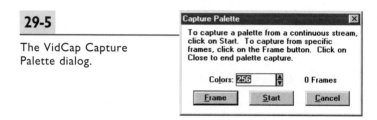

▶ Position your video source to display the beginning of the sequence you intend to record, then click the Frame button in the Capture Palette dialog. This makes Windows grab a custom palette for capturing your video in true color.

▶ If your video contains scene changes with markedly different colors, you can click the Frame button on those scenes as well. For most purposes, however, just the opening scene will suffice.

▶ Click the Close button, and Windows will build the palette map for your capture.

Movie on CD

Demonstrations
⮕ Show Me!
  ⮕ Digital Video
    Recording and
    Editing
    ⮕ **Setting the
      Capture
      Options**

Setting the Capture Options

▶ Pull down the Capture menu and choose Video to make the Capture Video Sequence dialog shown in Figure 29-6 appear.

▶ Set the frame rate to 10 frames per second, and set the capture method to Directly to Disk.

NOTE   You can experiment with different settings later; for your first capture, follow these instructions precisely.

▶ If you want to set a time limit on your recording, check the Enable Capture Time Limit box, and set the number of seconds in the Seconds field. Keep this first capture short, to less than 30 seconds; you can try longer captures later.

29-6

In the Capture Video Sequence dialog, set the frame rate to 10 fps, and set the capture method to Directly to Disk.

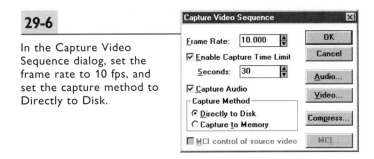

▶ Click the Audio button and make sure the Audio is set to 8 bit, mono, 11 KHz (**KHz** stands for kilohertz, which means thousands of cycles per second; 11 KHz is the sampling rate).

▶ Click the Video button and make sure the Image Dimensions are set for ¼ screen size, and that the Image Format is 8-bit palettized.

▶ Click OK. Windows will prepare everything for you to start capturing the video.

29-7

VidCap displays this box when it is ready to start capturing.

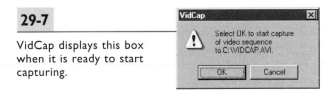

Movie on CD

Demonstrations
➥ Show Me!
  ➥ Digital Video
     Recording and
     Editing
    ➥ **Capturing
        Video**

Capturing the Video

When VidCap has everything set up for you, it will display the dialog shown in Figure 29-7. Cue your video source to the spot where you want to start the capture. Click OK in the dialog to make VidCap start recording, and then start your video source.

If you set a time limit for the recording, VidCap will stop recording automatically when it reaches that limit. Otherwise, you must press Esc to stop recording. Keep this first recording short, initially capturing no more than 10 seconds.

In the status bar at the bottom of the window, VidCap will report statistics telling how many seconds it recorded and how many frames got dropped. Ideally, the number of frames dropped will be zero. If your computer drops frames, you have problems. Here is what you can do about them:

▪ If you did not defragment your hard disk, you should delete your capture file, defragment the hard disk, and re-create the capture file. Fragmentation can cause VidCap to drop frames.

▪ Try lowering the capture size from ¼ to ⅛ of the screen; your processor may not be fast enough to record the larger screen size.

▪ Try lowering the frame rate; again, your processor may not be fast enough to grab frames so often.

Movie on CD

Demonstrations
➥ Show Me!
    ➥ Digital Video
       Recording and
       Editing
       ➥ **Editing Video**

Editing the Video

▶ Pull down the VidCap File menu and select Edit Captured Video. The VidEdit window shown in Figure 29-8 will appear.

▶ Click the Play button to play back the video you recorded. You should see the video and hear the audio; if you do not, something went wrong. If you do not hear audio, you probably did not have the audio output of your video source connected to the audio input of your waveform audio board, in which case you will need to exit VidEdit, correct the error, and redo the capture.

The VidEdit program lets you cut, copy, and paste segments of video, much like you can cut, copy, and paste text with a word processor. For example, click the Play button and listen carefully to the start of your recorded video. It probably contains frames you would like to cut out. You can do this with the slider and the Mark In and Mark Out buttons.

▶ Use your mouse to drag the slider to the very start of your video (it is probably there already, but check to make sure).

▶ Click the Mark In button to mark the beginning of the cut point.

▶ Click the Play button to start the video, and click the Mark Out button when the movie gets to the end of the part you want to cut out.

▶ Drag the slider to the Mark Out spot you just set, click Play, and listen carefully. Does it start exactly where you want? If not, you marked too much or too little to cut. Adjust your Mark Out point by dragging the slider to the new cut point and clicking the Mark Out button. Repeat this step until you have the cut point marked exactly where you want it.

▶ Pull down the Edit menu and choose Cut. Press the Play button, and you will find that the segment you marked has been cut out of the video.

▶ If there is video at the end of the recording that you want to cut, you can repeat this process by setting the Mark In and Mark Out points at the end of the clip. With practice, you will get very good at this. Later on, you can experiment with pasting sequences you have cut into different places in the video to make things happen in a different order than when you recorded them.

29-8

The VidEdit window lets you edit recorded video, compress it, and save it.

Movie on CD

Demonstrations
➡ Show Me!
  ➡ Digital Video
    Recording and
    Editing
    ➡ **Compressing
      Video**

Compressing the Video

VidEdit compresses the video when you save it. To save and compress the video, follow these steps:

▶ Pull down the File menu and choose Save As; the Save Video File dialog shown in Figure 29-9 appears.

▶ In the File Name field, type the filename under which you want the compressed video to be saved. For your first capture, assuming your hard drive is C, call the file **C:\multilit\movie.avi**

29-9

The VidEdit Save Video File dialog has a button that lets you set the compression options.

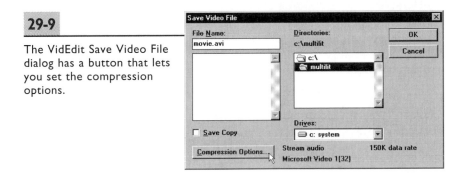

NOTE You should not use the same name as your capture file; rather, use the name you want the file to have in your application. Make sure you give it an *.avi* filename extension; *AVI* stands for Audio Video Interleave, which refers to the method Video for Windows uses to synchronize audio and video data streams.

▶ Click the Compression Options button to open the Compression Options dialog shown in Figure 29-10.

▶ Pull down the Target menu and select CD-ROM 150 KB/Sec.

29-10

The VidEdit Compression Options dialog lets you choose your targeted playback medium and the compression method.

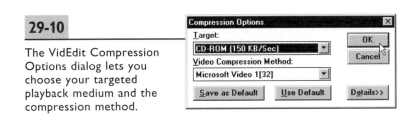

This selection assumes you plan to publish your application eventually on compact disc. On the other hand, if you know you will always be playing back this video from a hard drive, you can choose one of the hard drive targets. The hard drive setting will make your video play back more smoothly from a hard drive, but from a CD-ROM it will be very jerky, and the audio might not even play correctly.

Depending on the brand of audio capture board you have, different options may appear when you pull down the Video Compression Method menu. If you have an Intel Indeo driver installed and the Indeo option appears, choose Indeo; otherwise, choose Microsoft Video 1.

▶ To save these settings so that you won't need to change them next time, click the Save as Default button.

▶ Click OK to close the Compression Options dialog, and click OK in the Save Video File dialog. A status bar will appear, showing you how far along VidEdit is in the compression process as it saves the file.

Rehearsing the Video

To test your video recording, start PODIUM, pull down the Files menu, choose the Motion option, select Video for Windows, and choose the file you just saved. If it plays back in PODIUM, you succeeded; congratulations!

Now you can make the file the object of any link on any PODIUM screen. For example, suppose you want to link the movie to a hypertext on your *linkdemo.cus* screen:

▶ Pull down the Files menu, choose Custom, and select *linkdemo.cus* to open the *linkdemo* screen.

 ▶ Press F4 to open the toolbox, then use the Text tool to put the following line of text on your screen:

Click here to play a movie!

 ▶ Click the Link tool, then click the text *Click here to play a movie!* When the Link box appears, type the following line into it:

multilit\movie.avi

▶ Click OK to close the Link box, press F4 to put the toolbox away, and click the hypertext *Click here to play a movie!* The movie will play back in the center of a blue screen, which is the PODIUM default. In the next chapter, you will learn how to make movie objects, which let you position movies anywhere on a multimedia screen.

E X E R C I S E S

1. There is a movie in the *video* directory on the *Multiliteracy CD* called *clipvid*. When you play it, you will notice that it has material at the start and at the end that should be cut. Use VidEdit to do that. Save the resulting file in your *multilit* directory under the name *edited.avi*.

2. Use VidCap to record a 10-second video clip. Pull down the VidCap File menu and save the clip in your *multilit* directory under the name *rawvideo.avi*. Use the File Manager to find out how large the file is. Now use VidEdit to compress the file. How large is the file now? By what percentage did VidEdit reduce the file in size?

3. Although Video for Windows cannot yet record and play full-screen video, you can create the illusion of full-screen video. Suppose you have a person talking while seated at a desk in an office. Put your camera on a tripod about 20 feet away from the person and zoom in so the person fills the viewfinder. Without moving the camera, zoom out all the way and start shooting video. Zoom in very slowly until the viewfinder is close up on the person again. Record the motion video of the person talking. Use VidCap to record the person talking, and use VidEdit to compress the recording. Now comes the tricky part. You must grab a full screen of video from the moment the camera was zoomed out, so that when you use PODIUM to cut the person talking into the full screen, you will get a seamless matchup, making it seem like a full-screen video is playing. It may take some time to get this right, but once you develop this technique, you can use it for any scene in which a partial screen foreground object moves against a full-screen background.

30

Movie Objects

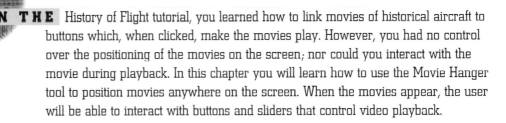

After completing this chapter, you will be able to:

☐ **Cut digital video windows into any multimedia screen**

☐ **Position movies on the screen**

☐ **Use buttons and sliders to control the playback of a movie**

☐ **Place several movies on the screen at once**

☐ **Provide multiple views of the same movie**

☐ **Post messages to movies and query the movie status**

 N THE History of Flight tutorial, you learned how to link movies of historical aircraft to buttons which, when clicked, make the movies play. However, you had no control over the positioning of the movies on the screen; nor could you interact with the movie during playback. In this chapter you will learn how to use the Movie Hanger tool to position movies anywhere on the screen. When the movies appear, the user will be able to interact with buttons and sliders that control video playback.

Creating the *movies.cus* Screen

To complete the exercises in this chapter, you need to create a new multimedia screen called *movies.cus* in the *multilit* directory on your computer's hard drive. Follow these steps:

▶ If PODIUM is not running, start PODIUM now.

▶ Press F2 to put PODIUM into a window and reveal the menu bar.

▶ Pull down the Files menu and select New Custom to create a new screen.

▶ In the File name box, assuming your hard drive is C, type **c:\multilit\movies.cus**

▶ Press ←Enter; PODIUM creates the new screen and opens the custom toolbox for you.

▶ Use the Backdrop tool to give the screen a dark blue background.

▶ Use the Text tool to write the following text at the top of the screen:

Multimedia Literacy Movie Hanger Practice

Now you are ready to hang your first movie on the screen. Read on.

Demonstrations
➡ Show Me!
  ➡ Movie Objects
    ➡ **Movie Hanger Tool**

The Movie Hanger Tool

The Movie Hanger tool appears in the custom toolbox as a piece of film. To hang a movie on the screen, you click the left mouse button on the Movie Hanger icon, mouse to the position on the screen where you want the upper left corner of the movie to appear, and click the left mouse button. A dialog appears that lets you set different options and browse for the movie you want. Movies can be in the Microsoft Video for Windows file format *(.avi)*, Apple's QuickTime format *(.mov)*, or the industry standard MPEG format *(.mpg)*. On the *Multiliteracy CD,* there is a directory full of Video for Windows movies for you to hang on the screen. The name of this directory is *movies.* To hang a movie on the screen, follow these steps:

▶ Click the left mouse button on the Movie Hanger icon; as you move the mouse about the screen, notice how the cursor has the shape of a piece of film.

▶ Position the mouse where you want the upper left corner of the movie to go. For this example, move the mouse about a third of the way down from the top of the screen and about a third of the way over from the left.

▶ Click the left mouse button; the Movie Hanger dialog appears as shown in Figure 30-1.

30-1

The Movie Hanger dialog.

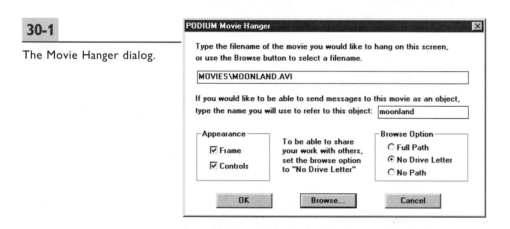

▶ Click the Browse button and browse to the *movies* directory on the *Multiliteracy CD.* You will find several movies listed there.

▶ For this example choose *moonland.avi* and close the browser. The filename field in the Movie Hanger dialog now reads *movies\moonland.avi.*

▶ Beneath the filename field, the dialog provides a place for you to specify a name for the movie object, in case you want to pass messages to it. For this example type **moonland** as the name for the movie object.

▶ In the Appearance group, the boxes for putting a frame around the movie and providing user controls are already checked; leave those options checked.

▶ Click OK; the movie appears on-screen.

▶ Later on, if you ever want to change the parameters of a movie, just click on the movie with the Movie Hanger tool, and the Movie Hanger dialog will reappear.

Movie on CD

Positioning Movies

Once you have a movie on the screen, it is easy to move it around using the Move tool. Follow these steps:

▶ Click the left mouse button on the hand icon to do a freehand move, or click the right button to move on a grid.

▶ As you move the mouse around the screen, the cursor appears as a hand that you can move things with.

▶ Position the hand cursor on the movie, hold down the left mouse button, and drag the movie anyplace you want it on the screen.

Controlling Movies

Figure 30-2 shows the movie controls along with callouts that describe what the controls do. Try out the controls now. Make sure you can perform each of these tasks:

▶ Click the Play button to start the movie. If you let the movie play all the way to the end, the movie will automatically rewind.

▶ Click the Stop button to stop the movie.

▶ Drag the slider knob to reposition the movie. If the movie is playing when you drag the knob, the movie will continue to play after you release the knob.

▶ Click once inside the slider to the *left* of the knob to step *backward* one frame.

▶ Click once inside the slider to the *right* of the knob to step *forward* one frame.

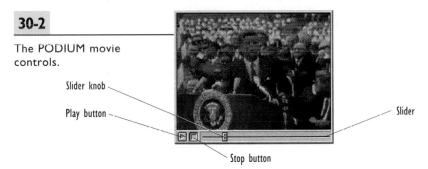

30-2

The PODIUM movie controls.

Slider knob

Play button

Slider

Stop button

Multiple Movies

If your movies are in the Video for Windows or QuickTime format, you can have multiple movies opened on the screen at once. You just have to be careful to avoid the palette shifts that can occur when movies have different palettes. In PODIUM, if you put a bitmap in the backdrop of the screen, any movies hung on top of the bitmap will automatically adjust to the palette of the bitmap, thereby avoiding an unsightly palette shift. Therefore, whenever you hang multiple movies on the screen, you should first put a bitmap into the screen's backdrop. Follow these steps:

▶ Use the Backdrop tool to make the backdrop be *backdrop\space.bmp*.

▶ Use the Move tool to reposition the movie to the left half of the screen.

▶ Use the Movie Hanger tool to place another movie onto the screen; this time, choose *movies\kennedy.avi*. If you have trouble, follow the steps in the preceding section on the Movie Hanger tool.

Experiment by playing and stopping each movie. If your computer is fast enough, you can even play both movies at once, although you will hear the audio for only one movie at a time.

Multiple Views on the Same Movie

Very powerful for instructional purposes is the ability to provide multiple views on the same movie. This enables the user to view and compare different frames. For example, to provide multiple views of the movie *moonland.avi*, follow these steps:

▶ Use the Delete tool to delete the second movie you hung on your screen.

▶ The only movie on your screen now should be *movies\moonland.avi*.

▶ Click the Movie Hanger tool, move the mouse to position the Movie Hanger cursor slightly to the right of the first movie, and click; the Movie Hanger dialog appears.

▶ In the filename box at the top of the dialog, type **movies\moonland.avi** to create another view of this movie.

▶ In the object name box, type **moonland2**

▶ Leave the two check boxes checked.

▶ Press OK to close the dialog.

Two views of the same movie now appear on your screen. Use the controls to position each view to different frames of the movie. Think about how powerful this is for comparing time-sensitive events that occur in a movie.

Posting Messages to Movie Objects

An advanced concept is the notion of posting messages to movie objects. Recall how the Movie Hanger dialog has a field in which you can provide an optional name for the object. This name is used to post messages to the object.

The @post command has the form @post(*object_name*)=*message* where *object_name* is the name you gave the object in the Movie Hanger dialog, and *message* is the string of characters you want to send the object. You can put @post commands in any PODIUM link. Movie objects recognize the following messages:

```
Play
Stop
Step
StepBack
Seek(position)
```

In the Seek message, *position* is the number of the frame you want to seek.

The intended purpose of these @post commands is to provide a way for you to interact with movies when you choose not to include the built-in movie controls. In other words, if you do not check the Controls box in the Movie Hanger dialog when you create the movie, you can control the movie by posting messages to it. There is an example of this on the *Multiliteracy CD*, where custom buttons are used to control a movie. To try this example, go to the Demonstrations section,

Table 30-1 Movie Object Query Questions and the Results They Return

Query Question	Result Returned by the Query
Playing	1 (if playing) or 0 (if not playing)
Length	Length of the movie in frames
Location	Current frame location of the movie

select Textbook Examples, and click Movie Messages. To inspect the custom file and the @post commands, press F2 to put PODIUM into a window, then pull down the Files menu and choose Edit This File.

Querying the Status of Movie Objects

You can query the status of movie objects via the @query command. The @query command has the form @query(*object_name,question,var_name*) where *object_name* is the name you gave the movie in the Movie Hanger dialog, *question* is the question you have about the object, and *var_name* is the name of the variable into which you want the results of the query to be placed. For movie objects, Table 30-1 lists the possible questions and the results they return.

Inspecting Your Custom File

If you pull down the PODIUM Files menu and choose Edit This File to inspect the contents of a custom file on which you have hung a movie, you will see how movie objects appear in a custom file. For example, Figure 30-3 shows the contents of the custom file that gets created when you complete the exercise at the start of this chapter. Movie objects always begin with the command @object and have the form:

```
@object(movie,name) @source=filename @left=x @top=y @right=x
@bottom=y
@frame @controls
```

where *name* is the name of the movie object, *filename* is its path/filename, *x* and *y* are positioning values expressed as percentages of the screen, *@frame* is an optional command that causes a frame to be drawn around the video, and *@controls* is an optional command that causes Play and Stop buttons and a slider control to appear at the bottom of the movie.

30-3

Contents of the
c:\multilit\movies.cus file
created in this chapter.

```
movies - Notepad
File  Edit  Search  Help
! BACKDROP\SPACE.BMP
@where-7.34,6.25 @size=20 @font=Times_New_Roman_Bold @shadow=3 @color=[33]
Multimedia Literacy Movie Hanger Practice
@object(Movie,moonland) @source=MOVIES\MOONLAND.AVI @left=32.00 @top=28.00
@Frame @Controls
```

List of Movie Commands

Table 30-2 lists the PODIUM movie commands.

Table 30-2   Movie Commands

Movie Command	What the Movie Command Does
@object(movie,*name*)	Signals the start of a movie object in a custom file. @object must occur in column 1 at the beginning of the line. *name* is the object's name to be used when posting messages or querying the movie object.
@source=*filename*	Specifies the path/filename of the movie. Supported file types include AVI, MOV, and MPG.
@left=*x*	Positions the left edge of the movie; *x* is a percentage from 0 to 100 and can be an integer or a decimal number.
@top=*y*	Positions the top edge of the movie; *y* is a percentage from 0 to 100 and can be an integer or a decimal number.
@right=*x* @bottom=*y*	@right and @bottom are used to position the lower right corner of MPEG movie objects, which can be resized.
@frame	When present, causes a three-dimensional frame to be drawn around the movie object.
@controls	When present, causes a slider control with Play and Stop buttons to be provided at the bottom of the movie object.

E X E R C I S E S

1. In the *movies* directory on the *Multiliteracy CD,* you will find a movie called *exercise.avi.* Create a new custom screen called *multilit\twoviews.cus* on which you provide the user with two views of this movie, and explain how to use the buttons and sliders to compare different frames in the movie side-by-side.

2. In the *movies* directory on the *Multiliteracy CD,* you will find two movies called *palette1.avi* and *palette2.avi.* These movies have different palettes. Create a new custom screen called *multilit\palshift.cus,* use the Backdrop tool to give the screen a plain blue background, and hang these two movies on it. Close the toolbox, and click the Play button on each movie. Unless your computer has 24-bit graphics, you will see the palettes shift as the most recently clicked movie's palette predominates.

3. Use PODIUM to bring up the *multilit\palshift.cus* file you created in the previous exercise. In the *movies* directory on the *Multiliteracy CD,* you will find a bitmap called *flowers.bmp.* Use the Backdrop tool to make this bitmap be the backdrop. Click the Play button on each movie. Notice how the palette shift you saw in the previous exercise does not recur as PODIUM automatically adjusts the palettes of the movies to match the palette of the bitmap in the backdrop.

31

Image Capture and Manipulation

After completing this chapter, you will be able to:

- Use Paint Shop Pro to capture screens and import graphics from any software application

- Convert graphics from one file format into another, such as from TIFF into BMP

- Compress bitmaps to conserve space on your hard disk drive

- Control palette shifts that occur between images with different palettes

- Know when to resize or resample a picture with Paint Shop Pro

Shop Pro is a Windows program for image capture, creation, viewing, and manipulation. Features include painting, photo retouching, image enhancement and editing, color enhancement, image browsing, batch conversion, and TWAIN scanner support. Included are 20 standard image-processing filters and 12 deformations. Also supported are Adobe-style image-processing plug-in filters. Over 30 file formats are supported, including JPEG, TIFF, Kodak Photo CD, BMP, and GIF.

Paint Shop Pro is **shareware**, which is software that you can try out before you buy. The *Multiliteracy CD* contains a shareware copy of Paint Shop Pro that you can try for 30 days free of charge. If you continue to use the program after 30 days, you must pay for it. The Paint Shop Pro license costs only $54.99, and as you will see from its many uses in this book, it is well worth the price. Appendix B contains the Paint Shop Pro order form.

By the time you read this, a more advanced version of Paint Shop Pro will be available. You can download the new version from the Web at http://www.jasc.com. For the tutorial printed here, however, you should use the version on the *Multiliteracy CD* so the software matches the instructions in the tutorial. Then, once you master the basics, you can proceed to more-sophisticated versions of Paint Shop Pro.

Installing Paint Shop Pro

The shareware version of Paint Shop Pro is on the *Multiliteracy CD* in the *psp* directory. To install it, follow these steps:

▶ If you have Windows 95, click the Start button and choose Run; the Run dialog appears.

▶ If you have Windows 3.1 or Windows NT, pull down the Program Manager File menu and choose Run; the Run dialog appears.

▶ In the Run dialog, assuming your CD-ROM drive is D, type the following (if your CD-ROM drive is not D, use the letter of your CD-ROM):

   d:\psp\setup.exe

▶ Press ⏎Enter, and the Paint Shop Pro setup program will begin.

▶ The setup program will suggest a drive and directory of *c:\psp* on which to install Paint Shop Pro. Click OK.

▶ After the files get installed, the setup program will ask if you would like to add the Paint Shop Pro icons to the Program Manager. Click Yes.

Movie on CD

Demonstrations
➡ Show Me!
  ➡ Image Capture
    and Manipulation
    ➡ **Running
       Paint Shop
       Pro**

Running Paint Shop Pro the First Time

If you do not already have Paint Shop Pro running, get it started now. Figure 31-1 shows how Paint Shop Pro will appear the first time you run it. There are dozens of tools and icons. As you move the mouse over the icons, the status bar at the bottom of the window tells you what each tool does.

The first time you run Paint Shop Pro, you must set up the hot key that you will use to capture graphics. Follow these steps:

▶ Pull down the Capture menu.

▶ Choose Hot Key Setup; the Capture Setup dialog appears as shown in Figure 31-2.

31-1

How Paint Shop Pro appears the first time you run it.

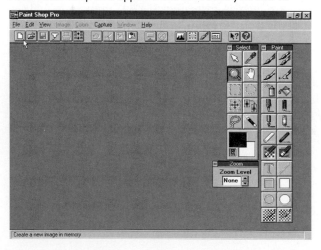

31-2

The Capture Setup dialog with settings that make the hot key be Ctrl-Alt-F12.

▶ Set the hot key to something you never use in any other application; the author recommends you set the hot key to Ctrl-Alt-F12, which is the hot key this tutorial will use.

▶ Click OK. Now you are ready to learn how to capture graphics with Paint Shop Pro.

Demonstrations
➥ Show Me!
  ➥ Image Capture and Manipulation
    ➥ **Capturing Graphics**

Capturing Graphics with Paint Shop Pro

You can use Paint Shop Pro to capture any part of any graphic from any software program running on your computer. To capture graphics with Paint Shop Pro, follow these steps:

▶ Get the program running from which you want to capture a graphic. For example, suppose you want to capture the tiger from the title screen of the *Multiliteracy CD*. Start up the *Multiliteracy CD* to get the tiger on your screen.

▶ Get Paint Shop Pro running, if it is not running already.

▶ Hold down the Alt key, and keep pressing Tab until Paint Shop Pro appears. Alt-Tab is a special Windows key for switching among programs running simultaneously on your computer.

▶ Pull down Paint Shop Pro's Capture menu and select Area; immediately, Paint Shop Pro will disappear.

▶ If the image you want to capture is not visible on your screen, hold down Alt and keep pressing Tab until the screen you want to capture appears.

▶ Press the capture hot key (Ctrl-Alt-F12); the cursor turns into a crosshair.

▶ Click and drag to select the area of the screen you want to capture; in this example, you want to click and drag to select the tiger. Release the mouse button after you select the tiger.

▶ The captured image will now appear in the Paint Shop Pro window. To save it as a BMP file, pull down the File menu and choose Save As.

▶ In the List Files of Type box, select BMP - OS/2 or Windows Bitmap.

▶ In the Format box, select BMP—RGB Encoded.

▶ Type the name you want the bitmap to have in the File Name field. Make sure you give the filename a *.bmp* filename extension. Since this example is a tiger, you might name the image *c:\multilit\tiger.bmp*.

▶ Click OK to save the file, then pull down the File menu and choose Exit to leave Paint Shop Pro.

▶ To make sure everything has gone well, pull down the PODIUM Files menu, select Bitmaps, select BMP, and load the file. If PODIUM can find and display the file, you succeeded; congratulations!

This procedure can be used to capture graphics from any source, including the Internet. For example, anytime you want to capture a graphic from the World Wide Web, you can use your Web browser to get the graphic you want on your screen, and follow the steps above to make Paint Shop Pro capture it.

Table 31-1 Paint Shop Pro Capture Menu Options

Capture Option	What and How to Capture
Area	Press capture hot key, then click and drag to capture an area of the screen.
Full Screen	Press hot key to capture everything on the screen.
Client Area	Press hot key to capture everything inside the frame of the current window.
Window	Press hot key to capture the current window, including the window frame.
Object	Press hot key, move the mouse around the screen until the object you want to capture is highlighted, then click to capture the object.
Include Cursor	Choose this option if you want the cursor included in the capture; normally, you will not want this.

When you pulled down the Capture menu and selected Area to capture the tiger, you may have noticed a few other choices on the Capture menu. Table 31-1 explains what those choices capture. When you capture an image, make the choice most appropriate to the kind of image you are trying to capture.

Movie on CD

Demonstrations
➡ Show Me!
 ➡ Image Capture
   and Manipulation
  ➡ **Converting
     Graphics**

Converting Graphics with Paint Shop Pro

Sometimes you will need to convert graphics from one file format to another. For example, you might have an image on a Kodak Photo CD that you would like to convert to the Windows BMP format. Or you might have a BMP file that you want to convert to a GIF file for use on the World Wide Web. Happily, you can use Paint Shop Pro to convert files to and from more than 30 graphics formats. To convert a file with Paint Shop Pro, follow these steps:

▶ Pull down the Paint Shop Pro File menu and select Open.

▶ In the Type box, select the type of file you want to convert. If the file type is not listed, you will need to grab the image instead of convert it. The preceding section, "Capturing Graphics with Paint Shop Pro," tells you how to grab files.

▶ Open the file you want to convert. For this example, open *photos\convert.tif*.

▶ When the image appears in the Paint Shop Pro window, pull down the File menu and choose Save As.

▶ In the List Files of Type box, select the file type you want to save the image as.

▶ In the File Sub-Format box, select the desired format.

▶ Select the drive and directory in which you want to save the file.

▶ Type the name you want the image to have in the File Name field. Make sure you give it the proper filename extension, such as *.bmp* for Windows bitmaps or *.gif* for GIF files.

▶ Click OK to save the file. Then pull down the File menu and choose Exit to leave Paint Shop Pro.

Movie on CD

Demonstrations
→Show Me!
 →Image Capture
  and Manipulation
  →**Compressing
   Bitmaps**

Compressing Bitmaps with Paint Shop Pro

No matter how much hard disk space you have, multimedia will require you to use it wisely. Bitmaps can take up a lot of space. For example, a 640 × 480 bitmap with 256 colors has 307,200 pixels. When BMP file headers are added, this consumes more than 310 KB of space on your computer's hard drive.

PODIUM supports the Windows **RLE** (run-length encoding) compressed bitmap format. Run-length encoding is a compression method that reduces the size of a bitmap by recording the number of times a color appears in a row, instead of the entire row of pixels. For example, if 20 pixels in a row are red, the encoding is 20R, instead of RRRRRRRRRRRRRRRRRRRR. The more redundancy there is in a picture, the more RLE encoding can reduce its size. Uncompressed bitmaps of 310 KB typically compress down to 100 KB, sometimes to as little as 30 KB.

You can use Paint Shop Pro to compress bitmaps. Follow these steps:

▶ Open the bitmap with Paint Shop Pro. For this example, open *photos\rgbimage.bmp*.

▶ Choose Save As.

▶ In the List Files of Type box, choose BMP - OS/2 or Windows Bitmap.

▶ In the File Sub-Format box, choose Windows RLE Encoded.

▶ Save the file on your hard drive in the directory of your choice.

Not all graphics editors can read compressed bitmaps. If you try to edit a compressed file with a graphics editor that cannot read it, you will need to use Paint Shop Pro to decompress the file first. To decompress a bitmap:

▶ Open the bitmap with Paint Shop Pro.

▶ Choose Save As.

▶ In the List Files of Type box, choose BMP - OS/2 or Windows Bitmap.

▶ In the File Sub-Format box, choose Windows RGB Encoded.

▶ Save the file.

Movie on CD

Demonstrations
→Show Me!
 →Image Capture
  and Manipulation
  →**Resolving
   Palette Shifts**

Resolving Palette Shifts

Developers must be careful to avoid palette shifts in multimedia applications. Until all users have access to 24-bit color adapters, this is going to be a problem. At present, most multimedia computers have 8-bit adapters that can display only 256 colors at once. These colors are selected from more than 16 million possible colors that your computer monitor can display. Palette shifts occur when you show one 8-bit image after another that has a different palette. What happens is that when the new palette gets read, all of the colors currently on the screen get changed to the new palette.

There are two ways to control palette shifts. One is to resolve them by making all of the images have the same palette. The other way is to hide the palette shift by fading to black in between the images.

You can use Paint Shop Pro to make several images have the same palette. Follow these steps:

▶ Use Paint Shop Pro to open the image that has the palette you want the other images to have.

▶ Pull down the Colors menu and choose Save Palette. If Save Palette is not active, this is probably a 24-bit color image that has no palette. To palettize the image, pull down the Colors menu and choose Decrease Color Depth to 256 Colors.

▶ In the Save Palette dialog, give the palette a name; be sure to give it a *.pal* filename extension.

For each image you want to share the palette just saved, follow these steps:

▶ Use Paint Shop Pro to open the image.

▶ Pull down the Colors menu and choose Load Palette; the Load Palette dialog appears.

▶ Choose the palette you want this image to have.

▶ Paint Shop Pro will apply the palette to the image. Depending on how much difference there is in the colors, you may not notice much of a change here.

▶ Pull down the Paint Shop Pro File menu and choose Save.

Movie on CD

Demonstrations
➡ Show Me!
  ➡ Image Capture
     and Manipulation
     ➡ **Creating an
        Optimum
        Palette**

Creating an Optimum Palette

When you use the Picture Hanger tool to layer pictures on top of a bitmap in the backdrop, PODIUM automatically adjusts the palettes of the layered pictures to the colors in the backdrop's palette so you do not get a palette shift. If the palette of the backdrop does not contain colors that are close enough to those in the layered pictures, however, the pictures may not display properly. You can fix this by creating an optimum palette for the backdrop. An optimum palette is a palette containing the best combination of colors from the backdrop and the pictures you plan to hang on top of the backdrop.

To create an optimum palette, you use the Video for Windows tools that you learned in Chapter 29. Follow these steps:

▶ Get the Video for Windows VidEdit program running.

▶ For each bitmap you want included in the optimum palette, follow these steps:

  ▪ Pull down the VidEdit Files menu and choose Insert; the Insert File dialog appears.

  ▪ Set the List Files of Type field to Microsoft Windows DIB (*DIB* stands for device-independent bitmap).

  ▪ In the File Name field, type the name of the bitmap, or you can browse for the filename using the dialog's browser controls.

  ▪ Whenever VidEdit asks if you want to stretch the bitmap to the same size as the others, click Yes.

▶ Pull down the Video menu and choose Create Palette; the Create Palette dialog appears. Click the All Frames button, and set the number of colors to 236 *(not 256)*. Then click OK to create the palette. (*Note:* The reason why you say 236 colors instead of 256 is to leave room for the 20 Windows colors, which you will add later.)

► When the Palette Created dialog appears, click OK. The optimum palette is now on the Windows Clipboard.

► Close VidEdit. When VidEdit asks if you want to save the temporary movie you created, click No.

► Get the Video for Windows BitEdit program running.

► Use BitEdit to open the backdrop bitmap.

► Pull down the Edit menu and choose Paste Palette. This applies the optimum palette to the backdrop bitmap.

► Pull down the Options menu and choose Show Palette; this launches the PalEdit program to display the palette.

► Pull down the Palette menu and choose Make Identity Palette. This adds the 20 Windows colors to the palette. The first 10 colors are in the first 10 palette slots, and the other 10 are in the last 10 palette slots.

► Close the PalEdit window.

► In the BitEdit window, pull down the File menu and save the file.

► Close BitEdit.

► If you already have PODIUM running, pull down the PODIUM Controls menu and choose Erase Picture Buffers; otherwise, you can skip this step.

 ► Use PODIUM's Backdrop tool to make the backdrop be the bitmap you just saved with BitEdit. Then use the Picture Hanger tool to hang the other bitmaps on top of it. If all went well, you will observe a marked improvement in the appearance of the pictures.

Fading to Black to Avoid Palette Shifts Between Pictures

In PODIUM, there is a special effect called @blackout that you can use to hide palette shifts between images. Suppose you have three images that appear one after the other in a slide bank, such as:

```
! image1.bmp
! image2.bmp
! image3.bmp
```

As the user clicks the mouse, the slides appear, one after the other. Palette shifts cause unwanted color changes between the pictures, however. To hide the palette shifts, use the @blackout command, as follows:

```
! image1.bmp @blackout
! image2.bmp @blackout
! image3.bmp @blackout
```

You can also put @blackout after images in the backdrops of your custom files if the backdrops cause palette shifts between files. You should realize, however, that when you use the @blackout command, you negate the smooth screen transitions that the PODIUM dissolve methods create between slides.

You can observe the effects of palette shifts and the @blackout command on the *Multiliteracy CD*. Go to the Demonstrations section, select Textbook Examples, and click the Palette Shift button. Clicking "Slide Bank with Palette Shifts" will take you through a bank of slides that have different palettes. Click the left mouse button to move through the slides. Unless your computer has 24-bit graphics, you will see palette shifts between the images.

Now choose "Slide Bank with Blackouts" and click through the slides again. The blackouts hide the palette shifts, but the screen goes black in between the slides.

Now choose "Slide Bank with Palettes Resolved" and click through the slides. This time you will see no palette shifts, and there will be smooth dissolves between the slides. That is because Paint Shop Pro was used to give these slides a common palette.

How to Resize and Resample Images with Paint Shop Pro

It is easy to resize images with Paint Shop Pro. Follow these steps:

▶ Use Paint Shop Pro to open the image you want to resize.

▶ Pull down the Image menu and choose Resize; the Resize dialog appears as shown in Figure 31-3.

31-3

The Paint Shop Pro
Resize dialog.

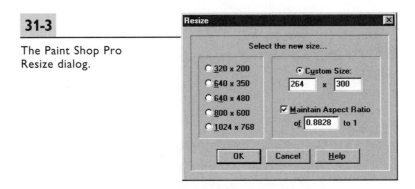

▶ Select the size you want the image to have. Check the Maintain Aspect Ratio box if you want the aspect ratio of the resized image to be the same as the original.

▶ Pull down the File menu and choose Save to save the image, or choose Save As to save the image under a different filename.

Resizing images can have unwanted effects, however. For example, if you enlarge an image too much, it will appear pixellated due to the jagged edges created when the pixels get enlarged. When this happens, try resampling the image instead of resizing it. To resample an image, follow these steps:

▶ Use Paint Shop Pro to open the image you want to resample.

▶ Pull down the Colors menu, choose Increase Color Depth, and increase the image to 16 million colors if it is not already in 16 million colors.

▶ Pull down the Image menu and choose Resample; the Resample dialog appears.

▶ Select the size you want the image to be. Check the Maintain Aspect Ratio box if you want the aspect ratio of the resized image to be the same as the original.

▶ Pull down the Colors menu, choose Decrease Color Depth, and decrease the image to 256 colors if your application is using palettized graphics.

31-4

An original photo with *x,y* dimensions of 160 by 120.

31-5

How the photo in Figure 31-4 appears when resized to full-screen.

31-6

How the photo in Figure 31-4 appears when resampled to full-screen.

▶ Pull down the File menu and choose Save to save the image, or choose Save As to save the image under a different filename.

Resampling works considerably better than resizing when you are enlarging an image. For example, consider the wallet-sized photo in Figure 31-4. When this was resized to fill the screen, it appeared pixellated, as illustrated in Figure 31-5. However, when it was resampled to fill the screen, it looked much better, as shown in Figure 31-6.

NOTE Your computer does *not* need to have a 24-bit, 16-million-color graphics adapter to increase Paint Shop Pro's color depth to 16 million colors. You can complete all of these exercises with an 8-bit, 256-color graphics adapter.

Color Adjustments

If you pull down Paint Shop Pro's Colors menu and choose Adjust, you will see how you can make several different kinds of color adjustments to an image. For example, if an image is too dark, you can increase its brightness or change its contrast. You can adjust highlights, midtones, and shadows. You can change RGB (red, green, blue) color values or adjust colors by hue, saturation, and luminance. You can even do a gamma adjustment to make the color intensities in the image match the luminance curve of your computer monitor. Excellent help is available on each of these features in Paint Shop Pro. Just select the feature and click the Help button in that feature's dialog box. Another nice feature is that Paint Shop Pro gives you a preview window in which you can view the effect of the adjustment before you apply it permanently to an image.

The best way to learn how the different color adjustments affect an image and interact with each other is to experiment. With practice, you will develop skill at enhancing images. The *photos* directory on the *Multiliteracy CD* contains several photographic images you can practice on.

Image Deformations

After all this talk about making images look good, it may seem contradictory to talk about deforming them, but Paint Shop Pro has several deformation routines that

31-7

Paint Shop Pro's
Deformation Browser.

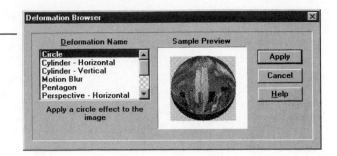

you can use to create special effects in your images. To deform an image, follow
these steps:

▶ Open the image with Paint Shop Pro.

▶ If the image is not already 16 million colors, pull down the Colors menu,
choose Increase Color Depth, and increase the colors to 16 million. The
deformation routines work only on 16-million-color images.

▶ Pull down the Image menu and choose Deformation Browser; the Deformation
Browser appears as shown in Figure 31-7.

▶ In the Deformation list box, choose different deformations and observe what
they do to your image.

▶ When you find a deformation you want to try, click the Apply button; a dialog
will appear to let you fine-tune the effect.

▶ When you are finished and you want to save the result, pull down the Colors
menu, choose Decrease Color Depth, and decrease the colors to 256 if you
are using palettized graphics.

▶ Pull down the File menu and choose Save As to save the image under the
filename you want it to have.

Image Filters

To provide you with even more special effects, Paint Shop Pro has image filters. To
use an image filter on an image, follow these steps:

▶ Open the image with Paint Shop Pro.

▶ If the image is not already 16 million colors, pull down the Colors menu,
choose Increase Color Depth, and increase the colors to 16 million. The filters
work only on 16-million-color images.

▶ Pull down the Image menu and choose Filter Browser; the Filter Browser
appears as shown in Figure 31-8.

31-8

Paint Shop Pro's Filter
Browser.

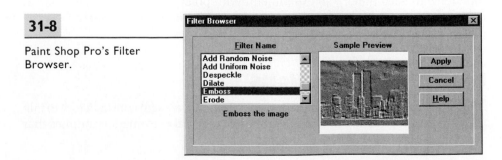

▶ In the Filter list box, choose different filters and observe what they do to your image.

▶ When you find a filter you want to try, click the Apply button; a dialog will appear to let you fine-tune the effect.

▶ When you are finished and you want to save the result, pull down the Colors menu, choose Decrease Color Depth, and decrease the colors to 256 if you are using palettized graphics.

▶ Pull down the File menu and choose Save As to save the image under the filename you want it to have.

Kai's Power Tools

As if Paint Shop Pro did not already do enough, you can extend it further by installing plug-ins, such as Kai's Power Tools, which include the Gradient Designer, Fractal Explorer, Texture Explorer, and the Seamless Welder. One of Kai's plug-ins comes with the shareware version of Paint Shop Pro as a demo. It is a really cool filter called Diffuse More. To try it out, follow these steps:

▶ Open the image with Paint Shop Pro.

▶ If the image is not already 16 million colors, pull down the Colors menu, choose Increase Color Depth, and increase the colors to 16 million.

▶ Pull down the Image menu, and choose Plug-Ins / KPT 2.0 Filters / Diffuse More.

▶ When you are finished and you want to save the result, pull down the Colors menu, choose Decrease Color Depth, and decrease the colors to 256 if you are using palettized graphics.

▶ Pull down the File menu and choose Save As to save the image under the filename you want it to have.

Figures 31-9 and 31-10 compare before and after views of an image that was run through the Diffuse More filter. To learn more about Kai's Power Tools, see the Paint Shop Pro help system for details and how to order.

31-9

An original, untouched photo.

31-10

How Figure 31-9 appears after being run through the Kai's Power Tools Diffuse More filter.

1. If you have access to the World Wide Web, get on the Web and browse to a screen with an image you would like to capture. Otherwise, get PODIUM running and browse to one of the screens on the *Multiliteracy CD* that shows images you like. Get Paint Shop Pro running. Pull down the Capture menu and try all the different capture methods you find there. Which method is most appropriate for capturing images from a multimedia screen? Which method works best for capturing tiny objects on a screen?

2. Use Paint Shop Pro to grab a screen of your choice and save it as an uncompressed BMP file. Use the Windows 95 Explorer or the Windows 3.1 File Manager to inspect the size of the file, and make a note of how large it is. Now use Paint Shop Pro to compress the bitmap by saving it as an RLE-encoded BMP. How large is it now? By what percentage did Paint Shop Pro compress the file?

3. The *photos* directory on the *Multiliteracy CD* contains an image that is too dark. The name of the image is *toodark.bmp*. Use Paint Shop Pro to enhance the image. *Hint:* To achieve the best result, you must not only brighten this image, but also increase its contrast. Brightness and contrast are two image parameters that interact with each other; with experience, you will learn how to make good contrast and brightness adjustments.

4. The *palshift* directory on the *Multiliteracy CD* contains three images that have different palettes. Copy these three images to the *multilit* directory on your hard drive. Then use PODIUM to get the *multilit\linkdemo.cus* file on the screen, and create a link that triggers these three slides. The link will contain the following:

```
! multilit\scene1.bmp
! multilit\scene2.bmp
! multilit\scene3.bmp
```

Trigger the link and click through the slides. You will see the palette shifts, unless your computer has 24-bit graphics. Use Paint Shop Pro to save the palette from *multilit\scene1.bmp* and then load that palette into *multilit\scene2.bmp* and *multilit\scene3.bmp*. Save all the files. Now use PODIUM to click through the slides again. If you still see palette shifts, pull down the PODIUM Controls menu and choose Erase Picture Buffers. If you still see palette shifts, something went wrong; review the steps in the palette shift part of this chapter and try this exercise again.

32

CD Audio Clipmaking

After completing this chapter, you will be able to:

- **Create CD Audio clips by using the CD Audio Clipmaker to locate start and stop points in the music**

- **Copy the clips to the Windows Clipboard, from which you can paste the clips into any link or trigger on a multimedia screen**

- **Create play lists that can instruct your CD-ROM drive to play clips from any audio CD in any order**

- **Record CD Audio clips to your hard disk drive as waveform audio files**

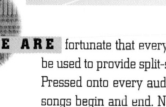 **E ARE** fortunate that every piece of music recorded on an audio compact disc (CD) can be used to provide split-second access to high-fidelity music in multimedia applications. Pressed onto every audio CD is a table of contents that indicates where the different songs begin and end. Not only can you play any song, but you can also extract clips from songs. The clips can be as small as $1/75$ of a second! This split-second accuracy lets you specify the precise start and stop location for CD Audio clips.

CD Audio has a distinct advantage over waveform audio recordings. Whereas waveform audio playback puts a large burden on the central processor, the CD-ROM drive has its own processor that can play music from an audio CD without putting any strain on your PC. Because the music plays independently of the central processor, you can use a multimedia application to start your favorite CD, then go about other computing tasks such as word processing or spreadsheets while the CD continues to play, providing background music.

In this chapter you will learn how to make clips from any audio compact disc and copy the clips to the Windows Clipboard, from which you can paste the clips into any link in your multimedia application. You will also learn how to make play lists and record audio from CDs onto your hard disk drive.

NOTE   In order to complete this chapter, you will need an audio CD. There is no compact disc audio on the *Multiliteracy CD*.

Installing PODIUM on Your Hard Disk Drive

Before you can complete the exercises in this chapter, you must install PODIUM on your hard disk drive. This will require about 2.5 MB of space on your hard drive. The reason why you must install PODIUM on your hard disk drive is because you will be putting an audio CD into your CD-ROM drive to play the music. While the audio CD is in your CD-ROM drive, your computer will not be able to access the copy of PODIUM that is on the *Multiliteracy CD.* To install PODIUM on your hard disk drive, follow these steps:

▶ If you have Windows 95, click the Start button and choose Run.

▶ Otherwise, pull down the Program Manager File menu and choose Run.

▶ Assuming your CD-ROM drive is D, type the following command into the Run dialog, and then press ⏎Enter:

`d:\wnpodium\install.exe`

▶ The installer will ask you to confirm the letter of the drive on which you want to install PODIUM (probably C), and then PODIUM will be installed on your hard disk drive.

▶ This process will place another PODIUM icon on your screen called Hard Drive MLPODIUM. When you want to run PODIUM from your hard drive, click the Hard Drive MLPODIUM icon. *MLPODIUM* stands for Multimedia Literacy PODIUM.

NOTE If you have a retail copy of PODIUM already installed on your hard disk drive, you can use that version of PODIUM to do the exercises in this chapter, instead of installing MLPODIUM on your hard drive.

Movie on CD

Demonstrations
➡ Show Me!
  ➡ CD Audio
    Clipmaking
    ➡ **Running the**
      CD Audio
      Clipmaker

Running the CD Audio Clipmaker

▶ Get PODIUM running from your hard disk drive.

▶ Insert the audio CD of your choice into your CD-ROM drive.

▶ To run the CD Audio Clipmaker, pull down the PODIUM Tools menu and choose CD Audio. This will bring up the dialog shown in Figure 32-1.

32-1

The CD Audio Clipmaker dialog.

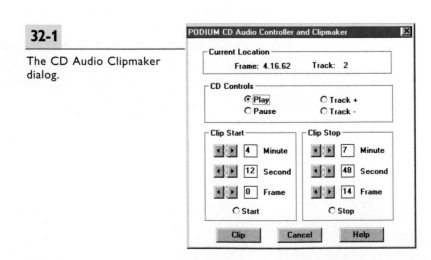

▶ Click the Play button; the CD will begin to play.

▶ To stop the CD, click the Pause button.

▶ To try different tracks on the CD, press the Track+ and Track– buttons.

LOCATING THE CLIP START POINT

To make a clip, begin by setting the start point:

▶ Click on the arrows in the Clip Start control group to adjust the minute, second, and frame address.

▶ Click the Start button to rehearse the clip.

▶ Repeat these steps until the clip starts where you want it.

The minute, second, and frame addressing of audio CDs is called **Red Book** addressing. There are 75 frames per second. The CD Audio Clipmaker lets you adjust the Red Book address with an accuracy of $\frac{1}{75}$ of a second, which lets you pinpoint the exact spot where you want the clip to start.

SETTING THE CLIP STOP LOCATION

To set the clip stop location, follow these steps:

▶ Adjust the minute, second, and frame address in the Clip Stop control group to set the stop point.

▶ Click the Start button to rehearse the clip and make sure the music stops where you want.

COPYING THE CLIP TO THE WINDOWS CLIPBOARD

To copy the clip to the Windows Clipboard, click the Clip button at the bottom of the dialog, and PODIUM will tell you what got written to your Clipboard in a message similar to the one shown in Figure 32-2.

32-2

PODIUM writes the Red Book address of your CD Audio clip to the Windows Clipboard.

LINKING THE CLIP TO YOUR MULTIMEDIA SCREEN

It is very easy to link the clip to any item on your multimedia screen. Follow these steps:

▶ If you do not already have the *linkdemo.cus* screen in your PODIUM window, display it by pulling down the Files menu and choosing Custom.

 ▶ Press F4 to open the toolbox, and use the Text tool to put the following line of text on your screen:

`Click here to hear a CD!`

 ▶ Click the Link tool, then click the text *Click here to hear a CD!*

32-3

Clicking the Paste button copies the clip from the Windows Clipboard into the Link box.

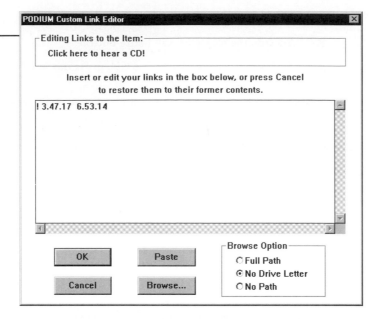

▶ When the Link box appears, click the Paste button. As Figure 32-3 shows, the CD Audio clip gets copied into the Link box from the Clipboard.

▶ Click OK to put the Link box away.

▶ Press F4 to put the toolbox away, then click the text *Click here to hear a CD!* As soon as you click, your CD should begin to play.

NOTE When you copy clips like this from the Clipboard, you are copying only the addresses where the clips are located on the CD, not the music itself. For the music to play, the CD must be inserted in the CD-ROM drive.

Play Lists

PODIUM has a @wait=end feature that makes it possible for you to construct play lists for compact discs. A play list is a list of songs that you want to hear one after the other. To create a play list, follow these steps:

▶ If you do not already have the *linkdemo.cus* screen in your PODIUM window, display it by pulling down the Files menu and choosing Custom.

 ▶ Press F4 to open the toolbox, and use the Text tool to put the following line of text on your screen:

Click here for a play list!

 ▶ Click the Link tool, then click the text *Click here for a play list!* When the Link box appears, enter the start and stop locations of each clip you want in the play list, followed by @wait=end. For example, to play four of the songs on Paul Winston's *Winter into Spring* CD, you would type the following links:

```
0.2.0     6.40.23   @wait=end @doc=January Stars
19.21.60  22.15.68  @wait=end @doc=Reflection
36.45.15  44.52.2   @wait=end @doc=The Venice Dreamer
22.15.68  32.32.23  @wait=end @doc=Ocean Waves
```

NOTE @doc= is a PODIUM command that stands for documentation. Anything you type after the command @doc= gets ignored by PODIUM. When typing a play list, @doc= is a handy way to document song titles.

▶ Click OK to close the List box, then select *Click here for a play list!* Your play list will begin.

▶ If you do not want to wait until the end of a song, press [Spacebar] to move on to the next one.

There is no limit to the number of songs you can put in a play list. Any song can appear anyplace in the list, any number of times. For example, you could make your favorite song appear more often than the other ones. Songs you do not like would not play at all. In effect, you can be your own disc jockey!

Movie on CD

Demonstrations
➡ Show Me!
  ➡ CD Audio
    Clipmaking
    ➡ **Direct to**
      Disk
      Recording

Recording CD Audio to Your Hard Drive

Although compact disc technology is wonderful, it does have drawbacks. If you want music from different CDs to play during your application, you have to keep switching CDs, because only one CD can be in the CD-ROM drive at a time. And if you publish your application, the user will need to have all of the CDs as well.

When you learned how to use the Waveform Audio recording tool in the previous chapter, you may have noticed the CD Audio control group in the lower left corner of the Waveform Audio dialog. The controls in the CD Audio group let you make waveform audio recordings from CDs. You can then play back the music from your hard drive, without needing to switch CDs during your application.

To record music from a CD onto your hard drive, follow these steps:

▶ Use the CD Audio Clipmaker to set the start and stop locations of the clip you want.

▶ Close the CD Audio Clipmaker and click the Waveform Audio tool. The start and stop locations are copied automatically from the CD Audio Clipmaker into the From and To locations of the CD Audio section of the Waveform Audio dialog.

▶ To record the clip onto your hard drive, click Autostart, then click Record.

▶ When the clip stops, click the Stop button.

▶ Rewind the music and click Play to play it back.

▶ If the quality of the recording does not suit you, click the Reset button, then increase the settings in the Fidelity group. But be mindful that the higher the settings, the larger the recorded waveform audio file will be.

NOTE If the CD Audio won't record, the CD Audio option is probably turned off in the recording section of your computer's audio mixer program. Run the mixer program and turn the CD Audio recording option on.

EXERCISES

In this exercise you will use a jukebox metaphor to create a screen that lets you select songs from your favorite audio CD. Follow these steps:

▷ Pull down the PODIUM Files menu, choose New Custom, and create a new file called *multilit\jukebox.cus*. Use the Text tool to enter the following line of text on it:

    Compact Disc Jukebox

▷ Use the Backdrop tool to make the file *backdrop\jukebox.bmp* be the backdrop; notice how this backdrop has blanks in it for the titles of songs in the jukebox.

▷ Press F4 to close the toolbox, and press F2 to put PODIUM into a window.

▷ Put your favorite audio CD into the CD-ROM drive.

▷ Pull down the Tools menu and use the CD Audio Clipmaker to set the start and stop frame numbers of the clips for the songs you want put into the jukebox.

▷ Close the CD Audio Clipmaker, press F4 to open the toolbox again, and use the Text tool to put the song titles from the audio CD into the blanks on the jukebox backdrop.

▷ Use the Trigger tool to put triggers on each of the song titles in the jukebox, linking each one to the corresponding clip on the CD. To document the song titles, put a @doc= command at the end of each link.

To play a song, click its title in the jukebox. You do not have to wait for the song to finish before starting a new song. To start a new song before the old one stops, just click the new song's title.

33

MIDI
Sequencing

After completing this chapter, you will be able to:

- **Use the popular program Band-in-a-Box to generate royalty-free MIDI sound tracks for use in your multimedia applications**

- **Create a classic 12-bar blues with Band-in-a-Box**

- **Make a MIDI play list that will automatically play MIDI files in any order you prescribe**

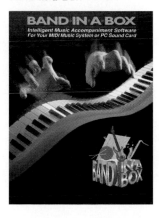

MIDI sequencer is a music software program that lets you record, play, and edit sequences of notes. Because MIDI has become an essential tool for musicians, there are many excellent MIDI sequencers on the market today. Most of them require that you compose the music you put into them, which takes more musical knowledge than the average person has. However, there is a program called Band-in-a-Box (see Figure 33-1) that has automatic accompaniment options you can use to create royalty-free sound tracks for use in your multimedia applications. *PC Magazine* had this to say about Band-in-a-Box:

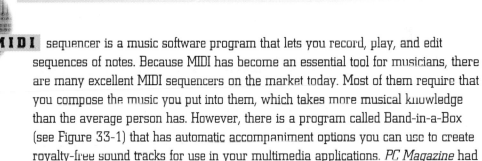

33-1

Band-in-a-Box cover.

> This amazing little program creates "music-minus one" accompaniments for virtually any song, any style . . . Band-in-a-Box understands repeats, choruses and verses and even varies the accompaniment, just as human musicians would. Band-in-a-Box is software that repeatedly surprises and delights you, especially in its jazz styles.
>
> – *PC Magazine* Technical Excellence Awards, January 1991

This chapter contains a tutorial on using Band-in-a-Box to create MIDI sequences. By agreement with the publishers of Band-in-a-Box, the enclosed CD-ROM includes a demonstration copy that lets you do everything except save the MIDI sequences you create with it. To save MIDI sequences, you must order a retail copy from PG Music. For the latest information about Band-in-a-Box, point your Web browser at http://www.islandnet.com/~pgmusic/index.html.

Launching Band-in-a-Box

There is a button in the Demonstrations section of the *Multiliteracy CD*, under Software Demonstrations, that launches Band-in-a-Box. Click this button to bring up the Band-in-a-Box screen shown in Figure 33-2.

33-2

Band-in-a-Box.

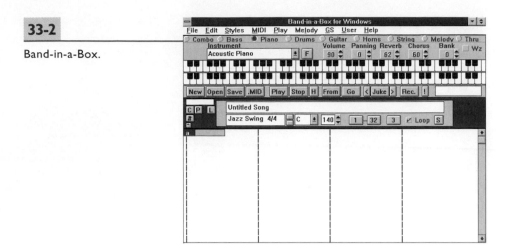

NOTE   If the Band-in-a-Box screen does not appear or does not work properly, it is possible
that your computer's memory has become segmented. If this happens, shut down
Windows and reboot your computer. Restart PODIUM—everything should work fine.

How Band-in-a-Box Works

Here is how Band-in-a-Box works: You enter the basic chord pattern for the kind
of music you want, then specify the number of refrains, choose a musical style,
and click Play. Like magic, Band-in-a-Box creates the sequence for you. You can
change the settings to make any changes you want, then export the music as a
MID (MIDI) file. Any user who has a multimedia PC can play back the MID file. As
noted earlier, MID files are small and efficient. Since music generated by Band-in-
a-Box is royalty free, this is an economical way for you to create sound tracks for
your applications.

Demonstrations
➥ Show Me!
  ➥ MIDI Sequencing

Creating a 12-Bar Blues

You will now learn how to use Band-in-a-Box to make a royalty-free 12-bar blues.
The twelve-bar blues is based on a repeating chord pattern that lasts for 12
measures. The chord pattern is as follows, where each chord lasts for one measure:

         C C F C F F C C G F C G

To enter this chord pattern into Band-in-a-Box, simply type each letter in the
pattern, pressing ⎡←Enter⎤ twice after each one, to space the letters on the bar lines
in the Band-in-a-Box screen, as shown in Figure 33-3.

Setting the Length and Number of Choruses

Toward the center of the screen you will see a chorus setting that looks like this:

33-3

How the screen appears after you enter the 12-bar blues chord pattern.

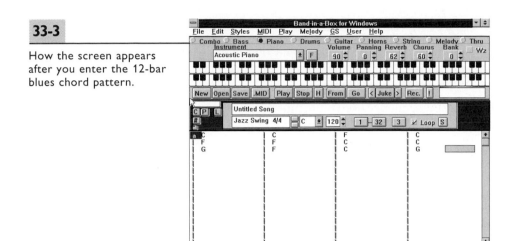

The default number of bars in a Band-in-a-Box chorus is 32. You need to change the 32 to a 12 because you are making a 12-bar blues. Follow these steps:

▶ Click once on **32**; Band-in-a-Box will ask you to click the last bar of your chorus.

▶ Click the last chord you entered and the chorus setting will change to read:

▶ Next to the chorus setting is a single number, which tells Band-in-a-Box how many choruses you want to generate. Click this number, and you will get a dialog that lets you choose from 1 to 10 choruses.

▶ For now, set the number of choruses to 4; you can adjust this later to suit your needs.

Choosing a Style

▶ Pull down the Styles menu to see the large number of styles available in Band-in-a-Box. There are even more styles in the retail version.

▶ Select the Blues Shuffle style, as shown in Figure 33-4.

33-4

Choosing a style in Band-in-a-Box.

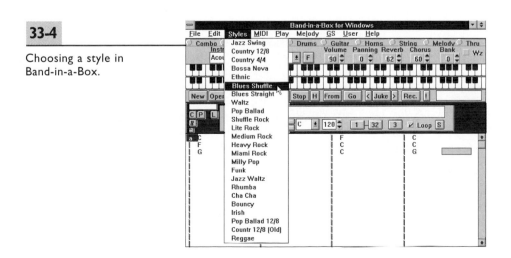

Playing the Blues

Now comes the fun part: click the Play button to hear your blues! Listen carefully when Band-in-a-Box plays choruses two, three, and four. It automatically creates variations as the music plays.

To make the sequence even more interesting, musicians often jazz it up by putting sevenths and ninths on the chords. For example, you might try:

C   C   Fm7   C   Fm9   Fm9   C   C   G7   F7   C   G7

Saving the Blues

The instructions in this section for saving the blues will not work in the demonstration copy of Band-in-a-Box that comes with this book. As explained at the beginning of this chapter, you need a retail copy to save your songs. Once you have a retail copy, you can save the blues by following these steps:

▶ Pull down the Band-in-a-Box File menu and click Make a Standard MIDI File.

▶ The File Destination dialog will appear; click the File on Disk button.

▶ In the File Name dialog, type **multilit\blues.mid** to save the file in your *multilit* directory.

In case you want to load and edit your work at some later date, you should also save your creation as a Band-in-a-Box file. To do this use the Save option on the Band-in-a-Box File menu.

E X E R C I S E S

1. Make a MIDI play list by opening the *linkdemo.cus* file and adding the line of text **Play a List of MIDI Songs**. Use the Link tool to link the following list of songs to that text:

    midi\swing.mid @wait=end
    midi\gigue.mid @wait=end
    midi\minuet.mid @wait=end
    midi\toccata.mid @wait=end

These MIDI files were provided courtesy of Midisoft Corporation.

Click the text *Play a List of MIDI Songs* to play back the MIDI songs. If you grow tired of listening to one song, just press (Spacebar) to skip to the next song.

2. A basic chord pattern called the **harmonic cycle** forms the basis of a lot of popular and classical music. The basic chord pattern (in the key of C) is:

    C   F   G7   C

Enter this pattern into Band-in-a-Box (the same way you did the chords in the 12-bar blues) and experiment playing the harmonic cycle with different styles selected. Which combination is your favorite?

34

Videodisc Clipmaking

After completing this chapter, you will be able to:

- **Browse videodiscs with a Clipmaker tool that helps you find the start and stop locations of video clips**

- **Understand the differences between CAV and CLV videodiscs**

- **Use the Windows Clipboard to copy clips from the videodisc Clipmaker tool and paste them into the links of your multimedia application**

- **Make videodisc slides appear as backdrops to your multimedia screens**

- **Create videodisc special effects**

M A K I N G clips from videodiscs is a lot like making CD Audio clips from compact discs. In addition to containing a stereo sound track like CDs, videodiscs hold video; hence the name **videodisc**. Videodiscs have no built-in table of contents like compact discs, however. Instead, you must rely on printed indexes that normally come with a videodisc, or you need to browse the disc to find the frames you want.

In this chapter you will learn how to use a videodisc browser and Clipmaker, which lets you browse any videodisc, play the video and sound that is on it, scan forward and backward, and turn audio tracks on and off. The Clipmaker also allows you to copy the start and stop locations of the clips you make to your Windows Clipboard, from which you can paste the clips into your multimedia application.

Although you can use any videodisc to work through this chapter, the exercises are specifically designed for use with the videodisc *To Fly!,* which is published by Lumivision and costs $34.95. To order a copy, call (800) 776-5864. This videodisc was chosen for two reasons. First, it is one of the most popular and widely available discs; second, because it is often used in product demonstrations, its purchase for use with this book will serve other purposes as well.

Videodisc Formats

Videodiscs come in two formats: CAV and CLV. **CAV** stands for constant angular velocity, which refers to the fact that the tracks are circular, and the laser beam can focus on one track and constantly display it as the disc spins inside a videodisc player. That is why you still see a picture when you click the Stop button on a CAV disc. The videodisc *To Fly!* is a CAV disc.

Each CAV videodisc can contain up to 54,000 frames per side. The frames are numbered from 1 through 54000. PODIUM recognizes numbers in this range as videodisc frame numbers. When you play a videodisc at normal speed, it plays back 30 frames per second; thus, each side of a CAV videodisc can hold up to 30 minutes of full-motion video, including a stereo sound track.

CLV stands for constant linear velocity. CLV discs hold more video (up to an hour per side) because the track is spiral instead of concentric. Because they hold so much video, CLV discs are often referred to as long-play videodiscs. There is a tradeoff, however: Unless you have the high-end Pioneer 8000 videodisc player, you cannot show still frames from CLV videodiscs. When you click Stop, the picture stops.

Running the Videodisc Clipmaker

▶   To run the Videodisc Clipmaker, pull down the PODIUM Tools menu and choose Videodisc. The Videodisc Clipmaker shown in Figure 34-1 will appear.

34-1

The Videodisc Clipmaker lets you browse and make clips from videodiscs.

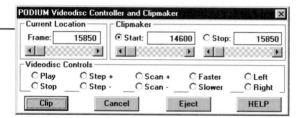

▶   Notice that there are buttons you can use to play and stop your videodisc, step forward and backward one frame at a time, and scan forward or backward at different speeds. Whenever the videodisc is paused, PODIUM will show the frame you are on in the upper left corner of the dialog.

▶   Play awhile with the Play, Stop, Step, and Scan buttons to get used to how they work.

Locating the Clip Start and Stop Points

To make a clip, you must first locate the point where you want the clip to begin. There are two ways to do this. You can drag the slider in the Current Location group of the Videodisc Clipmaker to make the videodisc player access different parts of the disc. Or you can click the Stop button, type a specific frame number into the Current Location Frame field, and click the Play button to make the player go immediately to that frame. When you locate the start point, type its frame number into the Start field in the Clipmaker group.

Now find the point where you want the clip to stop, and type its frame number into the Stop field in the Clipmaker group. Click the Start button in the Clipmaker group to rehearse your clip. You can adjust the frame numbers if the clip starts or stops too soon or too late.

Linking the Videodisc Clip

When you have found the clip you want, click the Clip button to copy it to the Windows Clipboard, from which you can paste it into any one of the links on your multimedia screen. For example, suppose you want to link a videodisc clip that shows what it is like to fly in a hot-air balloon. You will find that clip on the videodisc *To Fly!* in frames 2900 to 3850.

▶ Type those frame numbers into the Start and Stop fields of the Clipmaker, then click Start to rehearse the clip.

▶ When you get what you want in the clip, click the Clip button; PODIUM will tell you what got written to the Windows Clipboard.

▶ Click Cancel to close the Videodisc Clipmaker.

▶ Bring up the *multilit\linkdemo.cus* file.

 ▶ Press F4 to open the toolbox, and use the Text tool to enter a line of text that says **The Balloonist Begins the Ascent.**

 ▶ Use the Link tool to make that line hypertext. When the Link box appears on the screen, click the Paste button. This will paste the videodisc frame numbers from the Clipboard into the Link box.

▶ Click OK to close the Link box.

▶ Press F4 to put the toolbox away, then click the hypertext *The Balloonist Begins the Ascent.* Your clip will play exactly as you set it in the Videodisc Clipmaker.

Showing Videodisc Slides

You can also link multimedia screens to still frames on the videodisc. For example, suppose you want to show a videodisc slide of the Blue Angels. Follow these steps:

 ▶ Use the Text tool to put another line of text on the screen that says **Blue Angels**

 ▶ Use the Link tool to make that line hypertext; in the Link box, type the single number **20309**

▶ Click OK to close the Link box.

▶ Press F4 to put the toolbox away, then click the hypertext *Blue Angels.* You will see a videodisc still frame of the Blue Angels.

Using Videodisc Slides as Backdrops

It is easy to use a videodisc image as a backdrop to a multimedia screen. Simply click the Backdrop tool and enter the frame number of the slide you want to use as the backdrop. If you also have a bitmap in the backdrop, you will not see video unless you use an @under command and the bitmap contains your video overlay card's transparent color. Most overlay cards use pink as the transparent color. This is how you underlay a videodisc slide beneath a bitmap:

```
20309 @under
backdrop\vidframe.bmp
```

Videodisc Special Effects

You can create many special effects with videodisc slides and motion sequences. Table 34-1 provides a few examples.

Videodisc motion sequences are asynchronous; that is, their timing does not depend on the timing of any other events. When you use @wait= after a motion sequence, PODIUM will begin counting time from the beginning of the motion. If the wait is longer than the motion sequence, PODIUM will hold the last frame of the motion sequence on the screen until the wait time has elapsed. If the wait is shorter, PODIUM will move to the next object when the time passes. If the @wait= command is followed by the word *end*, PODIUM will wait for the end of the motion sequence and then continue.

Occasionally, you will see a period (.) used in place of @wait=key; the period is a shorthand way of saying @wait=key, which makes PODIUM wait until the user presses a key or clicks the left mouse button.

Table 34-1   Videodisc Special Effects

What to Link	What It Makes the Videodisc Do
3333 @wait=key 4444	Go to a frame, wait for a key, go to another frame.
3333 . 4444	This does the same with a period.
1000 1100 @channel=B	Play the right channel only.
1000 1100 @channel=none	Play with no volume.
1000 1100 @volume=25	Play at 25% volume.
1000 1100 @speed=25	Play at slow speed.
1000 1100 @speed=300	Play at lightning speed.
2222 @wait=4 100 500	Search frame 2222, wait 4 seconds, play from frames 100 to 500.
100 @wait=0 200 @wait=0 300 @wait=0 400	Show 4 frames as fast as possible.
100 200 @wait=4 500 600	Motion, wait 4 seconds, motion.
100 200 500 600	Motion, motion.
100 200 500 600 700	Motion, motion, slide.
100 200 500 . 600 700	Motion, slide, motion.
100 . 200 . 500 . 600 . 700	Slide bank.
backdrop.bmp @wait=0 100 @target=30,40,60,70	Cut a videodisc frame into a bitmap from 30% over and 40% down (upper left coordinates) to 60% over and 70% down (lower right coordinates) on the screen.

E X E R C I S E S

1. Add a line of text to the *linkdemo.cus* screen that says **Aircraft Slide Bank**. Use the Videodisc Clipmaker to locate at least four different kinds of aircraft on the videodisc *To Fly!* Make note of their frame numbers. Use the Link tool to link these frames to the text *Aircraft Slide Bank*. Make sure you type a period after each slide's frame number; otherwise, you will get a motion sequence instead of a still frame. Press F4 to put the toolbox away, then click *Aircraft Slide Bank*. The first slide should appear. Click the left mouse button to move forward to the next slide. (Each left mouse click will take you one slide forward; clicking the right mouse button will back up a slide.)

2. Replace the periods in between the videodisc frames you linked in the first exercise with @wait= special effects. To save time, keep the @wait values small, such as @wait=2 or @wait=4. Press F4 to put the toolbox away, then click *Aircraft Slide Bank* to observe how the slides advance automatically at a rate determined by the @wait= values.

3. Use the *aircraft\planes.wav* file to provide a sound track for the aircraft slide bank. Use the Link tool to edit the links to the text *Aircraft Slide Bank* and enter the filename **aircraft\planes.wav** at the very top of the slide bank. Follow it with **@wait=0**. Press F4 to put the toolbox away, and click *Aircraft Slide Bank* to hear the waveform audio play while the videodisc slides advance.

35

Flying Help

After completing this chapter, you will be able to:

- **Explain what is meant by the term** *flying help*

- **Create flying help for any hypertext link or trigger on a multimedia screen**

- **Make applications that are self-helping and easy to use**

LYING help is a way to make applications easy to use. You can attach flying help to any hypertext link or trigger on the screen. When the user mouses over the hot spot and hesitates, the flying help pops up to provide the user with helpful information.

There is flying help on the *Multiliteracy CD*. By now, you have probably already experienced it. For example, Figure 35-1 shows that if you put the mouse over the nose of the tiger on the title screen of the *Multiliteracy CD* and hesitate, a flying help appears, telling you that if you click there, the tiger will roar.

35-1

Flying help associated with the tiger's nose on the title screen of the *Multiliteracy CD*.

Demonstrations
➡ Show Me!
    ➡ **Flying Help**

Creating Flying Help with the @HotTip Command

The technical name for flying help in PODIUM is *hot tip.* You create flying help with the @HotTip= command. It is easy to provide flying help for any hypertext link or trigger. To create a flying help, follow these steps:

▶ Use the Link tool to click the hypertext or the trigger for which you want to create a flying help; the Link dialog appears.

▶ Add a line to the Link box that begins with **@HotTip=**

▶ After the equal sign in the @HotTip= command, type whatever you want the user to be told when the flying help appears.

▶ Click OK to close the Link box, and press F4 to put the toolbox away.

▶ Move the mouse over the trigger and wait a couple of seconds without moving or touching anything. The flying help will appear.

Modifying the Flying Help Delay Time

By default, the flying help will appear after the user delays on a hot spot for 1.5 seconds. You can change the delay time with the @HotTipWait command. The syntax is @HotTipWait=n where n is the number of seconds to wait before the flying help appears; n can be an integer or a decimal number.

The best place to put the @HotTipWait command is in the backdrop of your custom file. That will make the delay you specify apply to every hot tip in the file. For example, suppose you want the flying help to appear sooner, waiting only half of a second for the user to click. Use the Backdrop tool to add this line to the backdrop of your custom file:

```
@HotTipWait=0.5
```

To test this, put the toolbox away and mouse over a hot spot that has a flying help linked to it. After you hesitate for half of a second, the flying help will appear.

Changing the Flying Help Color

By default, the background color of the flying help popout is light green. You can use the @HotTipColor command to change the popout color to any one of the standard Windows colors. The syntax is @HotTipColor=*color* where *color* can be black, blue, lightblue, darkblue, brown, cyan, darkcyan, gray, lightgray, darkgray, green, lightgreen, darkgreen, pink, darkpink, red, darkred, white, offwhite, or yellow. Lightblue is a nice color for flying help, but the author likes lightgreen best, which is why that is the default. Use Yellow if you want your flying help to be shocking.

The best place to put the @HotTipColor command is in the backdrop of your custom file. For example, suppose you want the flying help to be yellow. Use the Backdrop tool to add this line to the backdrop of your custom file:

```
@HotTipColor=yellow
```

To test this, put the toolbox away and mouse over a hot spot that has a flying help linked to it. The flying help will appear with a yellow background.

Letting Users Turn Flying Help On or Off

It is possible that some users may find the flying help irritating. For example, experienced users might not want the flying help to pop out on their screen. You can use the @HotTipOn and @HotTipOff commands to provide a way for users to turn the hot tips on and off. Simply create a button or a hypertext that says something like *Turn Flying Help Off* and link to that button the single command:

```
@HotTipOff
```

Similarly, to provide a way for users to turn the flying help back on again, create a button or a hypertext that says something like *Turn Flying Help On* and link to that button the command:

```
@HotTipOn
```

List of Flying Help Commands

Table 35-1 lists the flying help commands and summarizes what they can do.

Table 35-1   Flying Help Commands

Flying Help Command	What the Flying Help Command Does
@HotTip=*string*	Causes the contents of *string* to pop out on the screen when the user hesitates over the hot spot to which the hot tip is linked.
@HotTipWait=*n*	Changes the flying help delay time from the default wait of 1.5 seconds; *n* can be an integer or a decimal number.
@HotTipColor=*color*	Changes the background color of the flying help popout box. The *color* can be black, blue, lightblue, darkblue, brown, cyan, darkcyan, gray, lightgray, darkgray, green, lightgreen, darkgreen, pink, darkpink, red, darkred, white, offwhite, or yellow.
@HotTipOn	Turns flying help on; this is the default.
@HotTipOff	Turns flying help off; prevents flying help from popping out on the screen.

E X E R C I S E S

1. Use the @HotTip= command to add flying help to the History of Flight application you created in Part Six of this book. To each trigger on the menu of the History of Flight home screen in the file *(multilit\history.cus)*, create a hot tip that says something like *Click here to learn about the history of the biplane.* Test each hot tip to make sure it works.

2. In the backdrop of the History of Flight home screen *(multilit\history.cus)*, use the @HotTipColor command to change the color of the popouts to your favorite color. The possible color choices are listed in Table 35-1. Test the hot tips to make sure the color change works.

3. In the backdrop of the History of Flight home screen *(multilit\history.cus)*, use the @HotTipWait command to make the hot tips appear a little sooner than the default 1.5 seconds. Test the hot tips to make sure the delay time works.

36 Drawing Points, Lines, Curves, and Shapes

After completing this chapter, you will be able to:

- **Expand the custom toolbox to reveal the drawing tools**
- **Draw points on the screen**
- **Change the point shape**
- **Draw lines on the screen**
- **Change the line thickness**
- **Draw curves and polycurves**
- **Draw opaque and filled shapes on the screen**
- **Change the fill color and the outline color**

SO FAR, when you wanted to place a graphic on the screen, you used the Backdrop tool or the Picture Hanger tool to bring up an image that had been created in advance. This works well for pictures, but if all you want is a simple line, curve, box, or circle, it is quicker to draw directly on the screen. This chapter teaches you how to use the drawing tools to draw simple graphics directly onto the screen.

Creating the *drawing.cus* Screen

To complete the exercises in this chapter, you need to create a new multimedia screen called *drawing.cus* in the *multilit* directory on your computer's hard drive. Follow these steps:

▶ If PODIUM is not running, start PODIUM now.

▶ Press F2 to put PODIUM into a window and reveal the menu bar.

▶ Pull down the Files menu and select New Custom to create a new screen.

▶ In the File name box, assuming your hard drive is C, type:

`c:\multilit\drawing.cus`

▶ Press ←Enter; PODIUM creates the new screen and opens the custom toolbox for you.

 ▶ Use the Backdrop tool to give the screen a dark blue background.

▶ Use the Text tool to write the following text at the top of the screen:

`Multimedia Literacy Drawing Practice`

Now you are ready to draw your first graphic on the screen. Read on.

Expanding the Toolbox for Drawing and Graphing

In order to draw, you must first expand the toolbox to reveal the drawing tools. To expand the toolbox, you click the left mouse button on the Expand icon at the right edge of the toolbox. Click the Expand icon now. PODIUM will expand the toolbox to reveal the set of drawing and graphing tools shown in Figure 36-1.

36-1

The drawing tools appear in the second row of the expanded toolbox.

Movie on CD

Demonstrations
➡ Show Me!
  ➡ Drawing
    ➡ **Points, Lines, and Curves**

Drawing Points, Lines, and Curves

Follow the steps below to draw points, lines, and curves on the screen. They will appear in the default color, shape, and thickness. After you practice drawing this way, the next part of this chapter will show how to change the defaults. If you practice a lot and your screen gets too busy, use the Delete tool to delete the unwanted graphics. To delete many graphics at once, use the Block tool to draw a block around the graphics, then use the Delete tool to delete them all at once.

DRAWING POINTS

 ▶ To draw points, click on the Point Drawing icon.

▶ As you mouse around the screen, you will see how the cursor appears in the shape of the point of a pencil.

▶ Click on the screen to draw a point in the default shape, thickness, and color. You can change the defaults by clicking on the Point Shape, Drawing Thickness, and Drawing Color icons, as described later in this chapter.

▶ To draw continuously, you can drag the Point Drawing icon across the screen. This enters many points into your custom file, however, and slower computers may take too long to plot them all. It is much more efficient to use the Line, Curve, and Polycurve tools described later.

DRAWING LINES

The Line tool is a click-and-drag tool. To draw a line, follow these steps:

 ▶ Click the Line icon; the cursor takes the shape of the point of a pencil.

▶ Move the mouse to the point at which you want to start drawing the line.

▶ Click and hold down the mouse button as you drag the mouse to the point where you want the line to stop.

▶ Release the mouse button to finish drawing the line.

DRAWING CURVES

The Curve tool is a three-stage click-and-drag tool. To draw a curve, follow these steps:

▶ Click the left mouse button on the Curve tool icon.

▶ Mouse to the point on the screen where you want the curve to start.

▶ Click and hold down the mouse button as you drag the mouse to the point at which you want the curve to stop, then release the mouse button.

▶ Move the mouse to set the shaping point of the curve; as you move the mouse, you will see the shape of the curve change.

▶ Click when the curve has the shape you want.

DRAWING POLYCURVES

The Polycurve tool is a five-stage click-and-drag tool. To draw a polycurve, follow these steps:

▶ Click the left mouse button on the Polycurve icon.

▶ Mouse to the point on the screen where you want the polycurve to start.

▶ Click and hold down the mouse button as you drag the mouse to the point at which you want the curve to stop, then release the mouse button.

▶ To shape the curve, do this three times:

▪ Move the mouse to set a shaping point of the curve; as you move the mouse, you will see the shape of the curve change.

▪ Click when the curve has the shape you want.

Movie on CD

Demonstrations
➡ Show Me!
  ➡ Drawing
    ➡ Shape,
       Thickness,
       and Color

Changing the Default Shape, Thickness, and Color

Before you draw an object on the screen, you can preset its point shape, thickness, and color. Follow these steps:

POINT SHAPE

Points drawn by PODIUM can be circular, elliptical, diamond, or square shaped. To set the shape before you draw a point, click the Point Shape icon. A dialog will let you choose the shape you want.

DRAWING THICKNESS

Objects drawn by PODIUM can have different degrees of thickness. To set the thickness, click the Drawing Thickness icon. A dialog will let you specify the thickness.

COLOR

Objects drawn by PODIUM have either one or two colors. To set the color, click the Color icon. A dialog will display the current color palette. Click the left mouse button to set the primary color, and click the right button to set the border color. Points, lines, and curves get drawn in the primary color. Shapes, which are taught next in this tutorial, have both a border color and a primary color.

Demonstrations
➡ Show Me!
  ➡ Drawing
    ➡ **Rectangles,**
      Ellipses, and
      Polygons

Drawing Rectangles, Ellipses, and Polygons

The toolbox lets you draw several kinds of rectangles. For each kind, the instructions are similar. In the text below, detailed steps are provided for the transparent rectangle. Then special features of the other rectangles are described.

TRANSPARENT RECTANGLE

All of the rectangle tools are click-and-drag tools. To draw a transparent rectangle, follow these steps:

▶ Click the left mouse button on the Transparent Rectangle icon.

▶ As you move the mouse about the screen, you will notice that the cursor has the shape of a crosshair for drawing.

▶ Mouse to the point on the screen where you want to begin drawing the rectangle.

▶ Click and drag to create and shape the rectangle; then release the mouse button.

▶ The rectangle will be drawn in the border color.

There are some special options you can use while drawing rectangles:

■ For a perfect square, hold down Shift as you begin drawing.

■ To center the rectangle on the point where you begin drawing, hold down Alt as you begin drawing.

■ For a perfect square centered on the point where you begin drawing, hold down both Shift and Alt as you begin drawing.

■ To create a three-dimensional rectangle that uses the primary color on top and the border color on the bottom with a black outline around the rectangle, hold down Ctrl as you begin drawing.

FILLED RECTANGLE

The Filled Rectangle tool works just like the Transparent Rectangle tool except that the rectangle is filled with the primary color.

ROUNDED TRANSPARENT RECTANGLE

The Rounded Transparent Rectangle tool works just like the Transparent Rectangle tool except that the corners of the rectangle are rounded.

ROUNDED FILLED RECTANGLE

The Rounded Filled Rectangle tool works just like the Transparent Rectangle tool except that the corners of the rectangle are rounded, and the rectangle is filled with the primary color.

ELLIPSE

The Ellipse tool is a click-and-drag tool. To draw an ellipse, follow these steps:

▶ Click the Ellipse icon to select the tool.

▶ Mouse to the point on the screen where you want to begin drawing the ellipse.

▶ Click and drag to create and shape the ellipse; then release the mouse button.

There are some special options you can use while drawing ellipses:

- For a perfect circle, hold down (Shift) as you begin drawing.

- To center the ellipse on the point where you begin drawing, hold down (Alt) as you begin drawing.

- For a perfect circle centered on the point where you begin drawing, hold down both (Shift) and (Alt) as you begin drawing.

FILLED ELLIPSE

 The Filled Ellipse tool works just like the Ellipse tool except that the ellipse is filled with the primary color.

POLYGON

The Polygon tool is a multistage click-and-drag tool. Polygons can have up to 12 sides in PODIUM. To draw a polygon, follow these steps:

▶ Click the Polygon icon to select the tool.

▶ Click and hold down the mouse button on the point where you want the polygon to start.

▶ Keep holding down the mouse button while you drag to draw the first side of the polygon, then release the mouse button.

▶ Move the mouse and click once on the point where you want the side to stop. Repeat this step for each side of the polygon.

▶ To stop drawing, either double-click the left mouse button, or click once with the right mouse button.

FILLED POLYGON

 The Filled Polygon tool works just like the Polygon tool except that the polygon is filled with the primary color.

Inspecting Your Custom File

If you pull down the PODIUM Files menu and choose Edit This File to inspect the contents of a custom file in which you have drawn graphics, you will see how the graphics commands appear as part of the backdrop of the file. For example, Figure 36-2 shows a screen that consists of several graphic objects, and Figure 36-3

36-2

A multimedia screen with graphics drawn onto it.

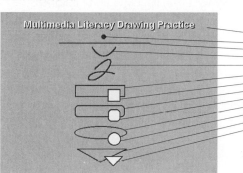

36-3

The custom file for the screen drawn in Figure 36-2.

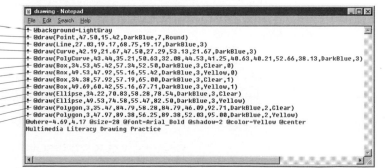

shows its custom file. For each object drawn on the screen, there is a @draw command in the custom file.

List of Drawing Commands

Table 36-1 documents the drawing commands that PODIUM puts into your custom file when you use the drawing tools.

Table 36-1   Drawing Commands

Command Syntax What the Command Does

@draw(Point,*x,y,color,size,shape*)

> Draws a point at position *x,y* on the screen in the color, size, and shape indicated. *x* and *y* are percentages of the screen; *x* tells how far over from the left, and *y* tells how far down from the top to draw the point. *color* can be the name of one of the Windows colors, or a palette reference of the form [*n*], or an RGB color of the form [*r,g,b*]. *size* is an integer telling how large the point should be. *shape* is a string that can have the value Round, Oval, Square, or Diamond.

@draw(Line,*x1,y1,x2,y2,color,thickness*)

> Draws a line in the *color* and *thickness* indicated from the point *x1,y1* to the point *x2,y2*. These points are expressed as percentages of the screen.

@draw(Curve,*x1,y1,x2,y2,x3,y3,color,thickness*)

> Draws a curve of the *color* and *thickness* indicated from the point *x1,y1* to *x3,y3* passing through *x2,y2*. Mathematically, this is a third-degree canonic polynomial.

@draw(PolyCurve,*x1,y1,x2,y2,x3,y3,x4,y4,x5,y5,color,thickness*)

> Draws a curve of the *color* and *thickness* indicated from the point *x1,y1* to *x5,y5* passing through *x2,y2* and *x3,y3* and *x4,y4*. Mathematically, this is a fifth-degree canonic polynomial.

@draw(Box,*x1,y1,x2,y2,BorderColor,BorderThickness,FillColor,bRoundedEdges*)

> Draws a rectangle of the color and thickness indicated. If the *FillColor* is Clear, the box is transparent. If *bRoundedEdges* is 1, the corners of the box will be rounded; if *bRoundedEdges* is 0, the corners will be rectangular.

@draw(Frame,*x1,y1,x2,y2,TopColor,BottomColor,BorderColor,TopThickness,BottomThickness,BorderThickness*)

> Draws a clear frame that lets the backdrop show through; this is used in making three-dimensional buttons.

@draw(Ellipse,*x1,y1,x2,y2,BorderColor,BorderThickness,FillColor*)

> Draws an ellipse bounded by the rectangle *x1,y1,x2,y2*. If the *FillColor* is Clear, the ellipse is transparent; otherwise, the ellipse gets filled by the *FillColor*.

@draw(Polygon,*nPoints,x1,y1,...,BorderColor,BorderThickness,FillColor*)

> Draws a polygon containing the number of points indicated by the variable *nPoints*. The number of *x,y* pairs following *nPoints* must match the number of points indicated by *nPoints*. If the *FillColor* is Clear, the polygon will be transparent; otherwise, it will be filled by the *FillColor*.

@draw(FloodFill,*x,y,FillColor*)

> The FloodFill inspects the color at point *x,y* and changes the color of that point and all points contiguous to it of the same color with the *FillColor*.

EXERCISES

1. Use PODIUM to view the *multilit\drawing.cus* file you created while working through this chapter. Pull down the Files menu and choose Edit This File to view the custom file in the Windows Notepad. Compare the @draw commands in the Notepad to the graphics drawn on your screen. Can you locate the @draw command for each graphic on the screen?

2. You can edit the @draw commands in the Notepad to make subtle changes in the graphics drawn on the screen. For example, for each line drawn on the screen, there will be a line in the custom file that has the form:

   ```
   @draw(Line,x1,y1,x2,y2,color,thickness)
   ```

   Use the Notepad to modify the thickness, save the Notepad file, and view the change with PODIUM. Can you see how the thickness changes on your multimedia screen when you modify the thickness setting in the Notepad file?

37 Button Objects

After completing this chapter, you will be able to:

- Create buttons that appear to press in when clicked

- Make rectangular, elliptical, and polygonal buttons

- Fill buttons with bitmaps to give buttons a custom look and feel

- Create invisible buttons

- Edit button objects

- Post messages and query the status of buttons

S E V E R A L aspects of button objects are important in multimedia applications. First, buttons provide an easy way to present users with options that get triggered when the user clicks the button. Any multimedia event or combination of events can be linked to a button. Second, buttons are design elements that appear on the screen. By filling buttons with bitmaps, you can give your application a custom look and feel. Third, buttons have states (active, inactive, pressed, visible, and invisible) that you can query to find out the current state of a button. You can set states by posting messages to a button.

In this chapter you will learn how to create button objects, fill buttons with bitmaps, link things to buttons, and communicate with buttons through @post and @query commands.

Creating the *buttons.cus* Screen

To complete the exercises in this chapter, you need to create a new multimedia screen called *buttons.cus* in the *multilit* directory on your computer's hard drive. Follow these steps:

▶ If PODIUM is not running, start PODIUM now.

▶ Press F2 to put PODIUM into a window and reveal the menu bar.

▶ Pull down the Files menu and select New Custom to create a new screen.

▶ In the File name box, assuming your hard drive is C, type:

`c:\multilit\buttons.cus`

▶ Press ←Enter; PODIUM creates the new screen and opens the custom toolbox for you.

▶ Use the Backdrop tool to give the screen a dark blue background.

▶ Use the Text tool to write the following text at the top of the screen:

Multimedia Literacy Buttons Practice

Now you are ready to draw your first button on the screen. Read on.

Movie on CD

Demonstrations
→ Show Me!
→ Button Objects
→ **Creating Buttons**

Using the Shape Tools to Create Buttons

In the previous chapter, you learned how to use the shape tools to draw rectangles, ellipses, and polygons. You use the same tools to create buttons. Instead of single-clicking on the tool's icon in the toolbox, however, you double-click to make the tool capable of creating a button. For example, suppose you want to make a rectangular button on the screen. Follow these steps:

▶ Double-click the Filled Rectangle tool icon in the custom toolbox.

▶ Mouse around the screen to the spot where you want to start drawing a button; as you move the mouse, the cursor has the shape of a button maker.

▶ Click and drag as if you were drawing a plain old rectangle; when you release the mouse button after you draw the rectangle, the Button Object Editor dialog appears as shown in Figure 37-1.

▶ Every button object must have a name; in the Name field, type **my_first_button** as the name of this button; note that button names cannot contain spaces.

▶ Every button object must have at least one link. In the Link box, type the following command:

@feedback=You just clicked my first button!

▶ If you wanted to adjust the thickness of the button's borders, you could play with the controls in the Thickness group. Similarly, to change the default appearance of the button, you could modify the controls in the Active, Inactive, and Pressed groups. This tutorial will show how to do that later. For now, just click OK to create the button.

To try out the button and see how it works, close the custom toolbox to become a user of your application. Mouse over the button to see how the cursor changes shape over a hot spot. Click the button; the feedback you typed into the Link box appears.

37-1

The Button Object Editor dialog.

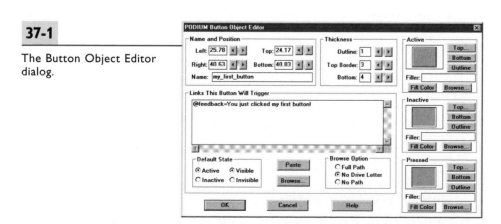

Demonstrations
➡ Show Me!
　➡ Button Objects
　　➡ **Centering Buttons Around Text**

Centering Buttons Around Text

You often see buttons that have a word or two inside them, describing what will happen when the button is clicked. For example, suppose you want to create a Quit button that has the word *Quit* inside of it. Follow these steps to create a button that is centered perfectly around the word *Quit*.

▶ Use the Text tool to print the word **Quit** on the screen in the font, color, and size of your choice.

▶ Double-click the Filled Rectangle tool; the cursor takes on the shape of a button maker.

▶ Without clicking, position the mouse over the center of the word *Quit*.

▶ Hold down Alt to make the button center itself around the spot the mouse is on.

▶ While holding down Alt, click and drag to create a button that encompasses the word *Quit*. *Note:* You can release Alt after you start drawing the button, or you can hold it down the whole time, as you wish.

▶ When you release the mouse button after you draw the rectangle, the Button Object Editor dialog appears.

▶ In the Name field, type **Quit_button** or any other name you would like this object to have.

▶ In the Link box, type **@quit**

▶ If you would like to put in some flying help for this button, add another line in the Link box, such as: **@HotTip=Click here to quit.**

▶ Click OK to close the Button Object Editor dialog.

Close the toolbox to become a user of your application. Test the Quit button. It should work like a charm.

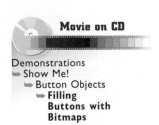

Demonstrations
➡ Show Me!
　➡ Button Objects
　　➡ **Filling Buttons with Bitmaps**

Filling Buttons with Bitmaps

A special feature of the Button Object Editor is the way it lets you change the appearance of the button. Besides changing the thickness and color of the button's border, outline, and interior, you can even fill buttons with bitmaps. By specifying different bitmaps for the Active, Inactive, and Pressed states of a button, you can give your application a slick look and feel, just like professional Windows programs.

The *buttons* directory on the *Multiliteracy CD* contains bitmaps for several common Windows functions. Table 37-1 lists the bitmap filenames for each button. You have already seen these buttons in use throughout the *Multiliteracy CD*. Now you will learn how to create slick buttons for use in your own applications. For example, suppose you want to create a Calculator button that will bring up a calculator when the user clicks it. Follow these steps:

 ▶ The shape of the calculator button is rectangular. Double-click the Filled Rectangle tool.

▶ Mouse to the spot on the screen where you want to create the button.

▶ Click and drag to create a rectangle about the size of the icons in the toolbox; you will fine-tune the size of the button later.

▶ When you release the mouse button, the Button Object Editor appears.

▶ In the Name field, type **calc_button**

Table 37-1 Button Bitmaps on the *Multiliteracy CD**

Purpose	Shape	Directory	Active	Inactive	Pressed
Calculator	Square	*buttons\square*	*calc.bmp*	*icalc.bmp*	*pcalc.bmp*
Notepad	Square	*buttons\square*	*notepad.bmp*	*inotepad.bmp*	*pnotepad.bmp*
Home	Square	*buttons\square*	*home.bmp*	*ihome.bmp*	*phome.bmp*
Done	Square	*buttons\square*	*done.bmp*	*idone.bmp*	*pdone.bmp*
Next	Square	*buttons\square*	*next.bmp*	*inext.bmp*	*pnext.bmp*
Back	Square	*buttons\square*	*back.bmp*	*iback.bmp*	*pback.bmp*
Quit	Square	*buttons\square*	*quit.bmp*	*iquit.bmp*	*pquit.bmp*
Page Up	Square	*buttons\square*	*pgup.bmp*	*ipgup.bmp*	*ppgup.bmp*
Page Down	Square	*buttons\square*	*pgdown.bmp*	*ipgdown.bmp*	*ppgdown.bmp*
Print	Square	*buttons\square*	*print.bmp*	*iprint.bmp*	*pprint.bmp*
Play	Square	*buttons\square*	*play.bmp*	*iplay.bmp*	*pplay.bmp*
Stop	Square	*buttons\square*	*stop.bmp*	*istop.bmp*	*pstop.bmp*
Home	Round	*buttons\round*	*home.bmp*	*ihome.bmp*	*phome.bmp*
Done	Round	*buttons\round*	*done.bmp*	*idone.bmp*	*pdone.bmp*
Next	Round	*buttons\round*	*next.bmp*	*inext.bmp*	*pnext.bmp*
Back	Round	*buttons\round*	*back.bmp*	*iback.bmp*	*pback.bmp*
Quit	Round	*buttons\round*	*quit.bmp*	*iquit.bmp*	*pquit.bmp*
Print	Round	*buttons\round*	*print.bmp*	*iprint.bmp*	*pprint.bmp*
Play	Round	*buttons\round*	*play.bmp*	*iplay.bmp*	*pplay.bmp*
Stop	Round	*buttons\round*	*stop.bmp*	*istop.bmp*	*pstop.bmp*

*Even more buttons are found in the *buttons* directory.

▶ In the Link box, type **calc.exe**

▶ In the group named Active, click the Browse button, browse to the *Multiliteracy CD buttons\square* directory, and select the file *calc.bmp* to make the calculator bitmap fill the button.

▶ In the Name and Position group, click the arrows next to the Right and Bottom fields to expand or contract the size of the frame around the Calculator button so the frame exactly encompasses the calculator.

▶ In the group named Inactive, click the Browse button, browse to the *Multiliteracy CD buttons\square* directory, and select the file *icalc.bmp* to make the inactive calculator fill the button.

▶ In the group named Pressed, click the Browse button, browse to the *Multiliteracy CD buttons\square* directory, and select the file *pcalc.bmp* to make the pressed calculator fill the button.

Editing Button Objects

Buttons can be sized, moved, centered, cloned, mouse clicked, and deleted with the Sizer, Move, Centering, Cloning, Mouse Click, and Delete tools in the custom

toolbox. To edit the links in a button object, click the button with the Link tool. This will bring up the Button Object Editor. Clicking a button object with the Color tool will similarly bring up the Button Object Editor.

To move text along with a button object that you drew around the text, use the Block tool to draw a block around the button and the text, then use a Move tool to reposition the block.

Posting Messages to Buttons

The @post command has the form @post(*object_name*)=*message* where *object_name* is the name you gave the object in the Button Object Editor dialog,

37-2

The message posting example in the file *mldemo\post_but.cus* on the *Multiliteracy CD*.

and *message* is the string of characters you want to send to the object. You can put @post commands in any PODIUM link. Button objects recognize the following messages:

```
Active
Inactive
Visible
Invisible
MoveTo x,y
```

The *Multiliteracy CD* has an example of posting messages to a button object. To view it, go to the Demonstrations section, select Textbook Examples, and click Posting Messages to Button Objects. As illustrated in Figure 37-2, you can activate or deactivate the button, make the button visible or invisible, and move the button to the left, right, or center of the screen. To see the @post commands that make this button do its thing, press F2 to put PODIUM into a window, pull down the Files menu, and choose Edit This File to inspect the file with the Notepad.

Querying the Status of Buttons

You can query the status of button objects via the @query command. The @query command has the form @query(*object_name,question,var_name[,var_name2]*) where *object_name* is the name you gave the button in the Button Object Editor dialog, *question* is the question you have about the object, and *var_name* is the name of the variable into which you want the results of the query to be placed. For queries that return two variables, *var_name2* holds the second return. For button objects, Table 37-2 lists the possible questions and the results they return.

Using Invisible Buttons with Irregular Shapes

Although the examples in this chapter have dealt primarily with rectangular buttons, do not forget that you can make buttons that have irregular (polygonal) shapes. For example, suppose you have a map of the United States and you want to make a button that encompasses the state of Ohio. You would make a polygon-shaped button to do that, using the Polygon Button tool to draw an outline around the state of Ohio. Because the border of the state of Ohio will already be drawn on the map, you would click the Invisible option in the Button Object Editor to prevent the button's outline from getting drawn on top of the map.

Table 37-2   Button Object Query Questions and the Results They Return

Query Question	Result Returned by the Query
IsActive	1 (if active) or 0 (if not active)
IsVisible	1 (if visible) or 0 (if not visible)
Where	Returns two variables—x and y—giving the button's origin in percentage screen coordinates

NOTE   Polygon-shaped buttons have a limit of 12 sides per button. If you have a shape that requires more sides to encompass, just make another polygonal button to handle the other sides.

Disabling the Default Navigation

Remember that unless you disable PODIUM's default navigation options, things may happen when the user clicks outside the buttons on your multimedia screen. If you are using button objects to provide navigation options, you will probably want to disable PODIUM's default navigation. To disable the default navigation, click the right mouse button on the Expand icon at the right end of the PODIUM toolbox to display the advanced tools, and click the Navigate icon. Navigate is a toggle; each time you choose it, PODIUM will turn default navigation on or off. When the Navigate icon appears bright, that means it is on.

Inspecting Your Custom File

If you pull down the PODIUM Files menu and choose Edit This File to inspect the contents of your *multilit\buttons.cus* file, you will see how button objects appear in a custom file. Button objects always begin with the command @object and have the form:

```
@object(button,name) @points(x1,y1,x2,y2...)
@shape=BOXorELLIPSEorPOLYGON @edges=ROUNDED @Click=number
@TopThickness=number @BottomThickness=number
@OutlineThickness=number
@ActiveTopColor=color @ActiveBottomColor=color
@ActiveFill=color_or_bmp
@InactiveTopColor=color @InactiveBottomColor=color
@InactiveFill=color_or_bmp
@PressedTopColor=color @PressedBottomColor=color
@PressedFill=color_or_bmp
@ActiveOutlineColor=color @InactiveOutlineColor=color
@PressedOutlineColor=color
@DefaultState=ACTIVEorINACTIVE @DefaultVisibility=VISIBLEorINVISIBLE
! one or more links
! must go here
```

The *@object* command must be first, and each line of the object must be left justified. The only required parameters are the *@object*, the *@points*, and the links; the other parameters have defaults. *@BottomColor* and *@BottomThickness* apply to rectangular buttons only.

List of Button Object Commands

Table 37-3 lists the button object commands and summarizes what they can do.

Table 37-3   Button Object Commands

Button Object Command	What the Button Object Command Does
@object(button,*name*)	*name* is the name you assign the button object.
@points(*x1,y1,x2,y2...*)	*x1,y1,x2,y2...* is a list of points that define the shape of the object; the points are expressed as percentages of the screen.
@shape=*type*	The type of shape can be BOX or ELLIPSE or POLYGON.
@edges=ROUNDED	Makes rectangular buttons have rounded edges.
@click=*number*	Specifies the mouse click after which the button will appear; if this is missing, the button appears immediately.
@TopThickness=*number* @BottomThickness=*number* @OutlineThickness=*number*	*number* specifies how many pixels thick this will be.
@ActiveTopColor=*color* @ActiveBottomColor=*color* @InactiveTopColor=*color* @InactiveBottomColor=*color* @PressedTopColor=*color* @PressedBottomColor=*color* @ActiveOutlineColor=*color* @InactiveOutlineColor=*color* @PressedOutlineColor=*color*	*color* is a Windows color value that sets the color of these elements.
@ActiveFill=*color_or_bmp* @InactiveFill=*color_or_bmp* @PressedFill=*color_or_bmp*	If a Windows *color* value is specified, the *color* fills the button. If a bitmap filename is specified, the bitmap fills the button.
@DefaultState=*state*	The *state* can be ACTIVE or INACTIVE.
@DefaultVisibility=*type*	The visibility *type* can be VISIBLE or INVISIBLE.

EXERCISES

The *buttons* directory on the *Multiliteracy CD* contains active, inactive, and pressed bitmaps that you can use to create a three-dimensional Print button that looks neat on the screen. To provide users of your History of Flight application an opportunity to print information about each airplane, you can put a Print button on each of your historical aircraft screens. The exercises below help you do that.

1. Use PODIUM to get your *multilit\biplane.cus* file on the screen. Near the bottom of the screen, create a filled rectangular button that is about the size of the icons in the custom toolbox. In the Name field, type **print_button**. In the Link box, type this command:

    @PrintScreen

The filenames of the Print buttons to set as the "filler" for each state of the button are:

Button State	Rectangular Print Button Filename
Active	buttons\square\print.bmp
Inactive	buttons\square\iprint.bmp
Pressed	buttons\square\pprint.bmp

After you create the button, give it a try. If you have a printer installed under Windows, the screen will print. If your printer is a color printer, the screen will print in color; otherwise, the print will be black-and-white.

2. The button you just created took some time to make. You do not want to have to go through all that work again to put Print buttons on the remaining screens in your History of Flight application. To avoid having to repeat all that work, you can use the Notepad to copy the button from one screen to another. To copy a button from one screen to another, follow these steps:

▶ With the button you want to copy in your PODIUM window, pull down the Files menu and choose Edit This File; the Notepad will appear.

▶ Drag the mouse in the Notepad to select the button you want to copy. Make sure you copy all of the button, from the @object command that starts it, through the links that end it. Be careful not to select anything else. Then pull down the Notepad's Edit menu and choose Copy. Close the Notepad.

▶ Use PODIUM to navigate to the screen to which you want to copy the button. In the History of Flight application, the screens you need to copy the button to are *multilit\fortress.cus, multilit\angels.cus,* and *multilit\jumbojet.cus.*

▶ Pull down the Files menu and choose Edit This File; the Notepad will appear to let you edit the file.

▶ Scroll down to the bottom of the Notepad, position the cursor at the very end of the last line in the file, and press ⏎Enter to start a new line. Do not type anything; just leave the cursor there.

▶ Pull down the Notepad's Edit menu and choose Paste; the button flows from the Clipboard into the Notepad file.

▶ Make sure you do not have any blank lines or stray characters before or after the button object.

▶ Pull down the Notepad's File menu and choose Save.

▶ Close the Notepad.

▶ PODIUM automatically rereads the file, and your button appears on the screen.

▶ If you caused a syntax error in the PODIUM file, PODIUM will tell you what line the error is in and bring up the Notepad for you to correct the error.

Repeat these steps for each historical aircraft in the History of Flight application.

38

Text Objects

After completing this chapter, you will be able to:

☐ **Create text objects that display a plain text file as part of your multimedia screen**

☐ **Provide a scroll bar for the user to control a text object**

☐ **Provide buttons for the user to page through and print a text object**

☐ **Control text objects by posting messages**

☐ **Edit text objects**

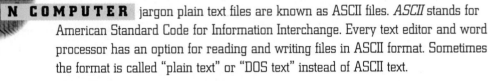

N COMPUTER jargon plain text files are known as ASCII files. *ASCII* stands for American Standard Code for Information Interchange. Every text editor and word processor has an option for reading and writing files in ASCII format. Sometimes the format is called "plain text" or "DOS text" instead of ASCII text.

This chapter shows you how to create text objects that let you display and page through ASCII text files in windows on your multimedia screens. You can have multiple text objects on the screen simultaneously, and the text can be displayed in any size, color, font, and shadow.

Creating the *textflow.cus* Screen

To complete the exercises in this chapter, you need to create a new multimedia screen called *textflow.cus* in the *multilit* directory on your computer's hard drive. Follow these steps:

▶ If PODIUM is not running, start PODIUM now.

▶ Press F2 to put PODIUM into a window and reveal the menu bar.

▶ Pull down the Files menu and select New Custom to create a new screen.

▶ In the File name box, assuming your hard drive is C, type:

`c:\multilit\textflow.cus`

▶ Press ←Enter; PODIUM creates the new screen and opens the custom toolbox for you.

▶ Use the Backdrop tool to give the screen a dark blue background.

▶ Use the Text tool to write the following text at the top of the screen:

`Multimedia Literacy Text Object Practice`

Now you are ready to create your first text object on the screen. Read on.

Movie on CD

Demonstrations
➡ Show Me!
　➡ **Creating Text Objects**

Creating Text Objects

You create text objects with the Text tool. Instead of single-clicking as you do to create normal text, you double-click the Text tool to create a text object. For example, suppose you want to create a text object that contains information about the history of the biplane. There is an ASCII text file about the biplane on the *Multiliteracy CD* in the *aircraft* directory. Its filename is *biplane.txt*. To display *aircraft\biplane.txt* as a text object, follow these steps:

▶ Double-click the Text tool.

▶ As you mouse around the screen, the cursor has the shape of a Text Object tool. Position the cursor where you want the upper left corner of the text object to begin. For this example put the cursor about 10% over from the left of the screen and about 20% down from the top.

▶ The Text Object tool is a click-and-drag tool. You click and drag to draw the rectangle into which you want the text object to flow. For this example click and drag to draw a box that extends about 90% across and 90% down the screen.

▶ When you release the mouse button, the Text Object dialog appears, as shown in Figure 38-1.

▶ In the Name field, you enter the name you will use to refer to this text object when you post messages and query it. For this example, type **biplane_text** into the Name field.

▶ In the Source field, you enter the path\filename of the ASCII file that will provide the text for this text object. The best way to enter the filename is to click the Browse button and browse for it. For this example click the Browse button, browse to the *aircraft* directory on the *Multiliteracy CD*, and select *biplane.txt.*

38-1

How to fill out the Text Object dialog to display the history of the biplane.

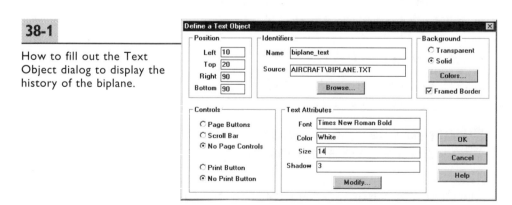

▶ Click the Scroll Bar button; this will provide a way for the user to page through the text.

▶ In the Size field, make the point size be 14.

▶ Click OK; the text object flows onto your screen.

▶ Close the toolbox, and use the scroll bar to page through the text object. Clicking the arrows at the ends of the scroll bar moves one line at a time. Clicking the scroll bar between the slider and bottom arrow pages the text down, and clicking between the slider and the top arrow pages up. You can also drag the slider.

Redefining Text Objects

You can redefine a text object by clicking on it with the Text Object tool. For example, suppose you want to make the font a little smaller. Follow these steps:

▶ Open the custom toolbox and double-click the Text tool icon.

▶ Click anywhere on the text object you want to redefine; the Text Object dialog appears.

▶ Change the options you want to modify. In this example make the font size be 12.

▶ Click OK to close the Text Object dialog.

Using Buttons Instead of Scroll Bars

You probably noticed already that the Text Object dialog gives you the choice of using buttons instead of a scroll bar to control the text object. There is also a Print Button option that places a Print button underneath the text object. If you want to try these options, use the Text Object tool to click anywhere on the text object, and turn the button options on. Close the toolbox and play with the buttons. The buttons are button objects that work just like the ones you learned how to make in Chapter 37. The buttons make the text object page and print by passing messages, which you will learn toward the end of this chapter.

Manipulating Text Objects

In addition to redefining text objects via the Text Object dialog, you can also manipulate them with tools in the custom toolbox. To reposition a text object, you can move it with one of the Move tools. You can resize a text object by dragging the Sizer tool over it. To center a text object, click on it with the Centering tool. To delete a text object, click it with the Delete tool.

Proportional Versus Monospaced Fonts

If the text in a text object consists of columns of information that have been evenly spaced to appear lined up on the screen, you must use a monospaced (nonproportional) font to display the text so the spacing will be even. The monospaced font on every Windows computer is the Courier New font; select Courier New when a text object contains preformatted text.

38-2

Comparison of proportional and monospaced fonts.

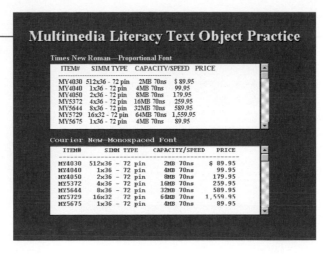

Figure 38-2 compares how preformatted text will appear when you select Courier New versus the Times New Roman font. Notice how the preformatted columns line up perfectly in the monospaced Courier New font, but incorrectly in the proportionately spaced Times New Roman font.

Creating Backgrounds for Text Objects

To change the color of the background in a text object, you click on it with the Text Object tool to make the Text Object dialog appear as shown in Figure 38-1. In the Background group, click the Solid button, and then click the Colors button to make the Color Selector dialog appear. Choose the color you want, and click OK to close the Color Selector dialog. Then click OK to close the Text Object dialog. The color you chose will appear as the background behind the text object.

Posting Messages to Text Objects

The @post command has the form @post(*object_name*)=*message* where *object_name* is the name you gave the object in the Text Object dialog, and *message* is the string of characters you want to send the object. You can put @post commands in any PODIUM link. Text objects recognize the following messages:

```
PageUp
PageDown
Print
```

The *Multiliteracy CD* has an example of posting messages to a text object. To view it, go to the Demonstrations section, select Textbook Examples, and click Posting Messages to Text Objects. As illustrated in Figure 38-3, you can click the PageDown button to page forward, or click the PageUp button to page backward. If your computer has a printer attached, you can click the Print button to print the text object. To see the @post commands that the buttons send to the text object, press F2 to put PODIUM into a window, pull down the Files menu, and choose Edit This File to inspect the file with the Notepad.

38-3

The text object example in the file *practice\post_txt.cus* on the *Multiliteracy CD*.

Querying the Status of Text Objects

You can query the status of text objects via the @query command. The @query command has the form @query(*object_name,question,var_name*) where *object_name* is the name you gave the object in the Text Object dialog, *question* is the question you have about the object, and *var_name* is the name of the variable into which you want the results of the query to be placed. For text objects Table 38-1 lists the possible questions and the results they return.

Inspecting Your Custom File

If you pull down the PODIUM Files menu and choose Edit This File to inspect the contents of your *multilit\textflow.cus* file, you will see how text objects appear in a custom file. Text objects always begin with the command @object and have the form:

```
@object(text,name) @source=source @left=percent @right=percent
@top=percent @bottom=percent @font=string @color=color
@size=point_size @background=color @frame
@PageUpButton=name @PageDownButton=name @PrintButton=name @ScrollBar
```

Replace *source* with the filename or network address (such as a URL) that you want to have serve as the source of the text that will flow into the text object. *@PageUpButton, @PageDownButton,* and *@PrintButton* indicate the names of button objects that get created if you select the Paging and Printing options in the Text Object dialog. Likewise, *@ScrollBar* indicates that you chose the scroll bar option when you created the text object. You can change the default bitmaps

Table 38-1 Text Object Query Questions and the Results They Return

Query Question	Result Returned by the Query
CanPageUp	1 if there is a previous page this object can page up to; otherwise it returns 0.
CanPageDown	1 if there is a previous page this object can page down to; otherwise it returns 0.

PODIUM uses to create paging buttons by editing PODIUM's button bitmaps. The filenames are listed in Table 38-2.

Table 38-2
Filenames of the Default Paging Buttons

Filename	Button State
wnpodium\BUTPUA.BMP	PageUp Active
wnpodium\BUTPUI.BMP	PageUp Inactive
wnpodium\BUTPUP.BMP	PageUp Pressed
wnpodium\BUTPDA.BMP	PageDown Active
wnpodium\BUTPDI.BMP	PageDown Inactive
wnpodium\BUTPDP.BMP	PageDown Pressed
wnpodium\BUTPRA.BMP	Print Active
wnpodium\BUTPRI.BMP	Print Inactive
wnpodium\BUTPRP.BMP	Print Pressed

List of Text Object Commands

Table 38-3 lists the text object commands and summarizes what they can do.

Table 38-3   Text Object Commands

Text Object Command	What the Text Object Command Does
@object(text,*name*)	*name* is the name you assign the button object.
@source=*source*	*source* is the path/filename of the ASCII source file that will stream into this text object.
@left=*percent* @right=*percent* @top=*percent* @bottom=*percent*	*percent* is a number between 0 and 100 indicating a screen coordinate expressed as a percentage of the screen. *percent* can be an integer or a decimal number.
@font=*string*	*string* is the Windows font name.
@color=*color*	*color* is a Windows color value that sets the color of the text printed in the text object.
@size=*point_size*	*point_size* is an integer that specifies the point size of the text.
@background=*color*	*color* is a Windows color value that sets the text object's background color.
@frame	@frame is an optional parameter that causes a frame to be drawn around the text object.
@PageUpButton=*name* @PageDownButton=*name* @PrintButton=*name*	*name* is the name of the button object associated with this text object.
@ScrollBar	@ScrollBar is an optional parameter; when present, it causes a scroll bar to be created alongside the right margin of the text object.

1. There is a file on the *Multiliteracy CD* that contains preformatted text. The name of the file is *practice\preform.txt*. Use PODIUM to get your *multilit\textflow.cus* file on the screen, and use the toolbox to delete the text objects and buttons on it now. Then use the Text Object tool to create two text objects on the screen, one above the other, as shown in Figure 38-2. Make both of the objects use the same source file, namely, *practice\preform.txt*. Give the first object the name **Proportional** and name the second object **Monospaced**. Use a 14-point font for both text objects. Give both text objects scroll bars. Lay out the screen as shown in Figure 38-2, which serves as the "answer" to this exercise. Make the font of the top object be Times New Roman, and make the font of the bottom object be Courier New.

2. Use the Filled Rectangle tool to draw a box behind the two text objects you created in exercise 1. If you have trouble aligning precisely the background rectangle with the text object, use the Notepad to fine-tune the *x,y* coordinates of the @draw commands that create the boxes. Once again, Figure 38-2 serves as the "answer" to this exercise.

39 Logic

After completing this chapter, you will be able to:

- **Assign values to numeric variables**
- **Perform numerical calculations**
- **Print the values of numeric variables**
- **Assign values to string variables**
- **Perform string manipulations**
- **Print the values of string variables**
- **Use variables in if-then-else statements**
- **Collect data**

N COMPUTING, logic is the use of conditional statements that act according to the values of variables. In a multimedia application, you can use logic to make your screens more sensitive to the needs and preferences of the user. You can also use logic to increase the complexity, and hence the pizzazz, of multimedia special effects.

This chapter teaches you how to create and calculate numeric variables, which enable your computer to count things and store the results of mathematical computations. You will also learn how to use string variables, which store alphanumeric characters like the ones printed on this page. After learning how to display the contents of numeric variables and strings on the screen, you will learn how to branch on condition and collect data about what the user does while running your application.

Creating the *logic.cus* Screen

To complete the exercises in this chapter, you need to create a new multimedia screen called *logic.cus* in the *multilit* directory on your computer's hard drive. Follow these steps:

▶ If PODIUM is not running, start PODIUM now.

▶ Press F2 to put PODIUM into a window and reveal the menu bar.

▶ Pull down the Files menu and select New Custom to create a new screen.

▶ In the File name box, assuming your hard drive is C, type:

```
c:\multilit\logic.cus
```

▶ Press ⏎Enter; PODIUM creates the new screen and opens the custom toolbox for you.

▶ Use the Backdrop tool to give the screen a dark blue background.

▶ Use the Text tool to write the following text at the top of the screen:

Multimedia Literacy Logic Practice

Now you are ready to create your first numeric variable. Read on.

Numeric Variables

A **variable** is a memory location in a computer that contains the value of something. Numeric variables are memory locations that contain numeric values. Every numeric variable has a name. When you want to find out the value of a numeric variable, or perform a calculation with a variable, you refer to the variable by its name.

In PODIUM variables are allocated dynamically whenever you need them. There is no need to declare variables in advance. It is as if all possible variables already exist. When you start PODIUM, all numeric variables are initialized to 0. To assign a value to a variable, you can either perform a calculation or read in a dataset. Datasets are covered later in this chapter. In this section you learn about calculations.

THE @CALC STATEMENT

You assign values to numeric variables with the PODIUM @calc statement, which lets you perform numerical computations. Its format is:

```
@calc var_name = expression
```

where *var_name* is the name of a numeric variable, and *expression* is a mathematical expression. For example, suppose you want to add 1 to the variable named *click_counter*. The @calc statement would be:

```
@calc click_counter = click_counter + 1
```

You can display the value of PODIUM variables by putting a ## sign in front of them in your text fields. Consider the following example:

```
You clicked this line ##click_counter times.
```

If the value of *click_counter* is 7, this will appear to the user as:

```
You clicked this line 7 times.
```

PERFORMING SIMPLE CALCULATIONS

You can link @calc statements to any PODIUM hypertext or hypertrigger link. The best way to learn how is to just do it! Follow these steps:

▶ Use the Text tool to create a line of text on the screen that says:

You clicked this line ##click_counter times.

▶ Since the value of all variables is 0, *click_counter* appears as a zero when you press ⏎Enter to enter the line into the custom file.

▶ Use the Link tool to click on the line of text you just entered; the Link dialog appears.

▶ In the Link box, type the following lines:

```
@calc click_counter = click_counter + 1
@reread
```

▶ Click OK to close the Link dialog, and close the toolbox.

▶ Click on the line that says *You clicked this line 0 times.* The @calc statement makes the value of *click_counter* increase, and the 0 changes to a 1.

▶ Click the line again, and again, and again. Each time you click, the value of *click_counter* increases.

Let's create another line that you can click to lower the value of *click_counter.* Follow these steps:

▶ Use the Text tool to create a line of text on the screen that says:

Click here to reduce the value of click_counter.

▶ Use the Link tool to click on the line of text you just entered; the Link dialog appears.

▶ In the Link box, type the following lines:

```
@calc click_counter = click_counter - 1
@reread
```

▶ Click OK to close the Link dialog, and close the toolbox.

▶ Click on the line that says *Click here to reduce the value of click counter.* You will see the value decrease on your screen.

▶ Click the line again, and again, and again. Each time you click, the value of *click_counter* decreases.

▶ Experiment by clicking both lines on the screen, as many times as you want, in any order you want. Observe how the @calc statements change the value of the variable *click_counter.*

MORE-COMPLEX EXPRESSIONS

The @calc statements used in this example were very simple. More-complex expressions can be used. Some examples follow. Notice how spaces are used to separate the different parts of the expressions. You must use spaces to delimit the different elements in your calculations.

```
@calc x = 3 + (x * x)
@calc x = x + sqrt(25)
@calc y = (m * x) + b
```

39-1

The View Data tool lets you inspect the values of all your numeric and string variables.

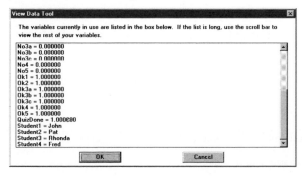

INSPECTING THE VALUES OF VARIABLES WITH THE VIEW DATA TOOL

At any time, you can find out the values of PODIUM variables by pulling down the Tools menu and choosing View Data. Figure 39-1 shows how the View Data tool lets you inspect the values of all your numeric and string variables.

FORMATTING NUMERIC VARIABLES

By default, numeric variables are floating-point values. Sometimes you will want to specify a different format for a variable. For example, if you are creating a column of numbers in dollars and cents, you may specify that you want only two decimal places printed, instead of the double floating-point precision that PODIUM uses when calculating.

To format a numeric variable, you use the @format command, which has the following syntax:

```
@format(var_name,width.precision)
```

var_name is the name of your variable.

width is how wide you want the variable to be overall, in characters, when PODIUM prints it or displays it on the screen. The variable gets padded to the left with blanks if it is not long enough to fill the field. If the variable is too long to fit in the field, PODIUM overrides the width setting, so you never lose data.

precision is how many decimal places you want displayed. PODIUM rounds the number to fit the number of decimal places you specify. For example, if you are working with dollars and cents and you want a variable named Dollars that can hold up to a thousand dollars with two decimal places, your format statement would read:

```
@format(Dollars,6.2)
```

If you use a nonproportional font, such as Courier New Bold, variables formatted this way can be printed beautifully in right-justified columns.

Movie on CD

Demonstrations
➠ Show Me!
  ➠ Logic
    ➠ **String Variables**

String Variables

You create string variables with the @string statement. Its format is:

```
@string var_name = [whatever you want]
```

You can display the value of string variables by putting a $$ sign in front of them in your text fields. Consider the following example:

```
Your name is $$name.
```

If the value of *name* is Thomas, this will appear to the user as:

```
Your name is Thomas.
```

You can link @string statements to any PODIUM hypertext or hypertrigger link. To try an example, follow these steps:

 ▶ Use the Text tool to write the following line of text on the screen:

Click here to make the name be Thomas.

 ▶ Use the Link tool to click on the line of text you just entered; the Link dialog appears.

▶ In the Link box, type the following lines:

@string name = Thomas
@reread

 ▶ Use the Text tool to write the following line of text on the screen:

The value of name is $$name right now.

▶ Put the toolbox away. Notice how the value of *name* has nothing in it.

▶ Click on the line that says *Click here to make the name be Thomas.* Notice how the value of *name* is now Thomas.

 ▶ Use the Text tool to write the following line of text on the screen:

`Click here to make the name be Santa Claus.`

 ▶ Use the Link tool to click on the line of text you just entered; the Link dialog appears.

▶ In the Link box, type the following lines:

```
@string name = Santa Claus
@reread
```

▶ Put the toolbox away and click on the line that says *Click here to make the name be Santa Claus.* Notice how the value of *name* changes to Santa Claus.

▶ Practice clicking the two lines that begin *Click here to make the name be* and observe the effect they have on the line that says *The value of name is.*

CONCATENATING STRINGS

You can use string variables in the @string statement to concatenate (join) strings. For example, suppose the string variable *name* contains the string Thomas. After executing the @string statement:

```
@string name = $$name Mann
```

The value of *name* will now equal Thomas Mann.

HANDLING SPACES IN STRINGS

There is a special case encountered when you concatenate one or more consecutive string variables. For example, suppose *FirstName* equals Thomas and *LastName* equals Mann. After executing the statement:

```
@string name = $$FirstName $$LastName
```

The value of *name* will be ThomasMann, with no space in it. In order to put spaces between strings when you concatenate them this way, put the space(s) inside quote marks. For example, after executing the statement:

```
@string name = $$FirstName " " $$LastName
```

The value of *name* is now Thomas Mann, with a space in it.

HANDLING DOUBLE AND SINGLE QUOTE MARKS IN STRINGS

When PODIUM encounters quote marks in a @string statement, the quote marks are handled as follows. If a double quote mark begins a field, PODIUM looks to see if there is another double quote mark in that field. If there is, PODIUM uses the double quote marks to delimit the field, and only the characters between the double quote marks are included. Similarly with single quote marks: If a single quote begins a field, PODIUM looks to see if there is another single quote mark in that field, and if there is, it ends the field.

The following examples will clarify how PODIUM handles quote marks. In all of these examples, assume that *FirstName* is Thomas, and *LastName* is Mann:

```
@string name = $$FirstName Wonder $$LastName
```

The value of *name* is: ThomasWonderMann

```
@string name = $$FirstName " Wonder " $$LastName
```

The value of *name* is: Thomas Wonder Mann

```
@string name = $$FirstName '" Wonder "' $$LastName
```

The value of *name* is: Thomas "Wonder" Mann

STRINGS IN LINKS

A powerful programming construct in PODIUM is the ability to link to a string. The following syntax is valid in any PODIUM link:

```
! $$string_name
```

where *string_name* is the name of any string variable.

SPECIAL STRING COMMANDS

At the request of PODIUM users who do a lot of string processing, the following special string commands have been provided.

```
@string(truncate,string_name,how_much)
```

This command truncates a string. You replace *string_name* with the name of your string variable, and you replace *how_much* with the number of characters you want the truncated string to contain. For example, suppose the string *name* equals Thomas Mann, and you issue the command **@string(truncate,name,6)**. *name* now equals Thomas.

```
@string(length,string_name,var_name)
```

This command lets you find out how long a string is. You replace *string_name* with the name of your string variable, and you replace *var_name* with the name of a numeric variable. PODIUM will place the length of the string variable in the numeric variable. For example, suppose the string *$$name* equals Thomas Mann, and you issue the command: **@string(length,name,how_long)**. *how_long* now equals 11.

FORMATTING STRING VARIABLES

By default, string variables can be any size or length. To print them on the screen with neat columns that line up, however, you will need to format them. To format a string variable, you use the @format command in the following manner:

```
@format(string_name,length,justify)
```

string_name is the name of the string variable. *length* tells how wide in characters you want the formatted string to be. *justify* can be R for right, or L for left. PODIUM will right- or left-justify the string accordingly.

You will never lose data with PODIUM variables. If the string is too long to fit, PODIUM ignores the formatting and uses the full contents of the string.

Conditionals

PODIUM allows you to use **conditional statements** anyplace in a file where links are permitted. In PODIUM links always begin with an exclamation point. Therefore, anyplace in a PODIUM file where there is an exclamation point in column 1, you can include conditional statements that affect the processing of those links.

The conditionals are @if, @else if, @else, and @endif. Every @if must be terminated with @endif. The @else and @else if conditionals are optional.

CONDITIONAL BACKGROUND AUDIO

For example, suppose you want a custom screen to play audio the first time it appears, but not have audio after that. The following logic would accomplish that in the backdrop of the file:

```
!  picture.bmp @doc=this is the backdrop of the file
!  @if never_played = 0
!     sounds.wav
!     @calc never_played = 1
!  @endif
```

Suppose you wanted different audio to play depending on the value of a variable. The following logic would accomplish that:

```
!  picture.bmp @doc=this is the backdrop of the file
!  @if number_wrong = 0
!     perfect.wav
!  @else if number_wrong = 1
!     onewrong.wav
!  @else if number_wrong < 4
!     fewwrong.wav
!  @else
!     lotwrong.wav
!  @endif
```

CONDITIONAL BRANCHING

Any PODIUM link can be conditional. For example, by putting different custom files after the @if and @else if statements, you can branch on the condition of variables. You can even create compound expressions that test more than one condition. The symbol && means *and*, and the symbol || means *or*. Here is an example of a compound expression in a conditional link:

```
!  @if (number_wrong = 0) && (number_answered = 10)
!     @feedback=Congratulations! You got 10 in a row correct.
!     module10.cus
!  @else if (number_wrong > 5) || (user_gave_up = 1)
!     remedial.cus
!  @else
!     @repeat
!  @endif
```

Data Collection

Data collection enables your multimedia applications to keep records. For example, you can keep track of test scores, how many times the user completed an item, and what screens the user visited in your application.

To save data you simply use a @data= command, which has the following format:

```
@data=[whatever you want to record]
```

The @data= command can contain variables. For example, consider the following statement:

```
@data=The movie played ##MoviesPlayed times.
```

If the value of the variable *MoviesPlayed* is 5, this will record the data:

```
The movie played 5 times.
```

By default, the data gets written to a default data file called *defdata.txt* in your PODIUM working directory. You can specify a different file for the data with the @DataFile command. Its format is:

```
@DataFile=path\filename
```

The *path* can specify any drive connected to your computer or network. For example, if you are connected to a local-area network that has a shared drive called L to which your users have write access, you could use the @DataFile command to direct the data to be recorded on the network with a command such as:

```
@DataFile=L:\records\math101.dat
```

Datasets

Datasets are files that contain the names and values of one or more variables. The @WriteDataset command lets you write datasets, and the @ReadDataset command lets you read them. Recording data with @WriteDataset is quick and easy because all of the variables currently in use get written to the dataset; there is no need to record data individually. Similarly, when you read data with @ReadDataset, all of the data gets read at once.

READING DATASETS

You read datasets with the @ReadDataset command. The syntax is:

```
@ReadDataSet=path\filename
```

where *path* is any drive connected to your computer, and *filename* is the name of the file containing the dataset. The file can be located on your PC, local-area network, or World Wide Web server. The format of the file is very simple. Each line of the file begins with the name of a variable, then one or more blanks, followed by the value of the variable. If the value is all numeric, with no spaces in it, PODIUM creates a numeric variable; otherwise, PODIUM creates a string variable. If you want an all numeric value treated as a string, enclose it inside double quotes marks, such as:

```
"123"
```

Remember that in PODIUM, the names of variables are case sensitive. That is, the variables named *BirthDay* and *birthday* are two different variables.

Printed below is an example dataset called *wnpodium\demo.dat:*

```
name            John Doe
age             21
birthday        April 1
```

The command @ReadDataset=wnpodium\demo.dat causes PODIUM to process @calc and @string commands equivalent to:

```
! @string name = "John Doe"
! @calc age = 21
! @string birthday = "April 1"
```

If a variable contained in the dataset being read is already in use, PODIUM replaces its current value with the value read from the dataset.

WRITING DATASETS

The syntax of the @WriteDataset command is @WriteDataset=*path\filename* which causes PODIUM to write all of the numeric and string variables currently in use to the file denoted by *filename*. If the file denoted by *filename* already exists, PODIUM deletes it and replaces it with the new dataset.

The format of the data file is very simple. Each line of the file begins with the name of a variable, then one or more blanks, followed by the value of the variable.

List of Logic Commands

Table 39-1 summarizes the calculation, string manipulation, conditional, and data-keeping commands covered in this chapter.

Table 39-1   Logic Commands

Command Syntax	What the Command Does
@calc *var_name = expression*	Performs a numerical calculation in which *var_name* is the name of a numeric variable, and *expression* is a mathematical expression.
@format(*var_name,width.precision*)	Formats a numeric variable; *var_name* is the name of the variable, *width* is how many characters wide the variable will be when PODIUM prints it or displays it on the screen, and *precision* is the number of decimal places to be displayed.
@string *var_name = string*	Creates or modifies a string variable. *var_name* is the name of the variable, and *string* is the string of characters to be assigned. *string* can contain numeric or string variables.
@format(*string_name,length,justify*)	Formats a string variable; *string_name* is the name of the string variable, *length* tells how wide in characters the formatted string will be, and *justify* is either R for right, or L for left justification.
@string(truncate,*string_name,how_much*)	Truncates a string. *string_name* is the name of the string variable, and *how_much* is the number of characters the truncated string will contain.
@string(length,*string_name,var_name*)	Finds out how long a string is. *string_name* is the name of the string variable, and *var_name* is the name of the numeric variable in which this command will return the length of the string.
@if *var operator expression* @else if *var operator expression*	*@if* begins a conditional in which *var* is the name of a numeric variable; *operator* is an equal sign (=), less-than sign (<), greater-than sign (>), or not-equal sign (<>); and *expression* is a mathematical expression. The *@if* statement must be followed by one or more links. *@else if* is an optional command that can follow the links to an *@if* statement. *@else if* must be followed by one or more links.
@else	*@else* is an optional command that can follow the links to an *@if* or *@else if* statement. *@else* must be followed by one or more links.
@endif	An *@endif* must follow the last link to signal the end of the conditional statements begun with an *@if*.
@data=*string*	Writes the value of *string* to a data file. *string* can contain numeric and string variables. The default data file is *defdata.txt* in the PODIUM working directory.
@DataFile=*path\filename*	Specifies the data file to which subsequent @data commands will write data.
@ReadDataset=*path\filename*	Reads a dataset in which each record consists of a variable name, followed by one or more spaces, followed by the value of the variable, followed by ⏎Enter.
@WriteDataset=*path\filename*	Writes a dataset consisting of all numeric and string variables currently in use.

1. On the home screen of your History of Flight application *(multilit\history.cus),* use the Text tool to create a line of text that reads:

> `This screen has been accessed ##flight_accesses times.`

Of course, the first time you put this line in, *flight_accesses* will equal 0, so the sentence will say that the screen has been accessed 0 times. Use the Backdrop tool to put the following statements into the file's backdrop:

> `@ReadDataset=multilit\history.dat`
> `@calc flight_accesses = flight_accesses + 1`

In the links to the screen's Quit button, add the following statement (first create a Quit button if this screen does not already have one):

> `@WriteDataset=multilit\history.dat`

Click the Quit button to quit the application, then start it up again. If you completed this exercise successfully, the application will know how many times the History of Flight home screen has been accessed.

2. There is a grammatical flaw in exercise 1. The first time you start the application, the message will state *This screen has been accessed 1 times.* It is poor grammar to say "1 times" because *1* is singular whereas *times* is plural. Correct the grammar by using conditionals to decide whether the statement should say *time* or *times.*

> *HINT*   This is a tricky exercise. You need to replace the word *times* with a string variable, such as *$$time_word.* In the backdrop of the file, after you read the dataset and increase the number of *flight_accesses,* put a conditional statement that uses a @string command to make *time_word* be *time* if *flight_accesses* equals 1, or *times* if *flight_accesses* does not equal 1. To test this, you will need to set *flight_accesses* back to 0 in your dataset. You can use any text editor to do that, such as the Windows Notepad. A quick way to open the Notepad is to pull down the PODIUM Files menu and choose Edit Other File.

40 Input Fields

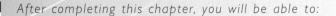

After completing this chapter, you will be able to:

- **Create input fields that let users type information into fields**
- **Query the contents of a field**
- **Perform answer judging to branch on condition of a field's contents**
- **Protect the privacy of what is typed into a field**
- **Perform key-by-key processing on what is typed into a field**

N INPUT FIELD is a blank space on a computer screen into which the user can type information. Input fields expand considerably the way multimedia applications interact with the user. Until now the applications you created in this tutorial limited the user to predetermined choices that appeared as hypertext links or buttons on the screen. The user could not specify something that was not on the screen already. With input fields you will be able to process anything the user can type.

This chapter shows you how to create input fields on the screen, judge what the user types into those fields, and branch accordingly.

Creating the *input.cus* Screen

To complete the exercises in this chapter, you need to create a new multimedia screen called *input.cus* in the *multilit* directory on your computer's hard drive. Follow these steps:

▶ If PODIUM is not running, start PODIUM now.

▶ Press ⟨F2⟩ to put PODIUM into a window and reveal the menu bar.

▶ Pull down the Files menu and select New Custom to create a new screen.

▶ In the File name box, assuming your hard drive is C, type:

`c:\multilit\input.cus`

▶ Press ⟨←Enter⟩; PODIUM creates the new screen and opens the custom toolbox for you.

 ▶ Use the Backdrop tool to give the screen a dark blue background.

▶ Use the Text tool to write the following text at the top of the screen:

Multimedia Literacy Input Practice

Now you are ready to create your first input field. Read on.

Creating Input Fields

You create input fields with the Input tool, which appears as an in-box on the advanced row of the custom toolbox. To reveal the advanced row of the custom toolbox, right-click the Expand icon at the right edge of the toolbox. The expanded toolbox will appear as follows:

Normally, an input field is preceded by some text on the screen that prompts the user for some information. For example, suppose you want to create an input field that asks for the user's name. Follow these steps:

  ▶ Use the Text tool to write the following prompt on the screen:

What is your name?

  ▶ Click the Input tool icon; as you mouse around the screen, the cursor has the shape of the Input tool.

▶ Position the mouse beneath the prompt, where you want the input field to start, and click the left button; the Input Field Editor appears as shown in Figure 40-1.

▶ In the blank where you specify how wide you want the input field to be, type **16** which will let the user type a name up to 16 characters long.

▶ In the blank where you specify the name that you will use to refer to this input field when you query its contents, type **user_name**

▶ Leave the rest of the settings alone; you will learn about them later in this chapter.

▶ Click OK to close the Input Field Editor; then close the custom toolbox.

40-1

The Input Field Editor.

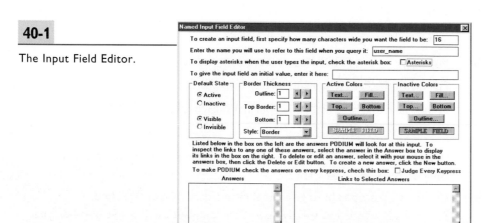

If all went well, the input field has been created on your screen and you can type information into it. If you want to adjust the size of the text in the input field, you can do so by clicking on it with the Sizer tool. To reposition the input field, use the Move tools. To change the color of the text, use the Color tool. To edit other parameters of an input field, click on it with the Input tool to bring up the Input Field Editor.

Movie on CD

Demonstrations
➥ Show Me!
  ➥ Input Fields
    ➥ **Querying the Contents**

Querying the Contents of Input Fields

Now that you have created the input field, it is time to learn how to query its contents. You do that with the @query command. The command syntax is:

@query(*field_name*,contents,*var_name*)

where *field_name* is the name of the field being queried, and *var_name* is the name of a string variable that will hold the contents of the field. To learn how to query the contents of the user_name field that is on your screen now, follow these steps:

▶ Use the Text tool to type the word **Continue** at the bottom of the screen.

▶ Use the Link tool to make the word *Continue* be a hypertext; the Link dialog appears.

▶ In the Link box, type the following four lines:

```
! @query(user_name,content,first_name)
! @string message = "Hello " $$first_name ", it is nice to see you today!"
! @feedback=$$message
! @reread
```

▶ Close the toolbox, type your first name into the input field, and click Continue; a feedback message should appear that uses your name in the sentence that says it is nice to see you today.

There is no limit to the number of input fields that you can have on a screen. In the exercises at the end of this chapter, you will add another input field to the *input.cus* screen you just created.

Answer Judging

Input fields have a powerful answer judging capability. You can specify a list of answers you expect the user might type into an input field, and link to each answer anything you want to make happen if the user types that answer. To learn how to do answer judging, follow these steps:

▶ Pull down the PODIUM Files menu, choose New Custom, and create a new screen on your hard drive called *multilit\judging.cus*.

▶ Use the Text tool to type the following prompt on the screen:

Who is buried in Grant's tomb?

▶ Click the Input icon.

▶ Position the mouse beneath the prompt, where you want the input field to start, and click the left button; the Input Field Editor appears.

▶ In the blank where you specify how wide you want the input field to be, type **16** which will let the user type a name up to 16 characters long.

The Create an Answer
dialog.

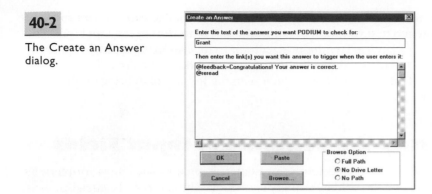

▶ In the blank where you specify the name that you will use to refer to this input field when you query its contents, type **buried_person**

▶ At the bottom of the Input Field Editor, there are boxes that list the answers and the links to the answers to be judged at this input. To create a new answer to be judged at this input, click the New button; the Create an Answer dialog appears as shown in Figure 40-2.

▶ In the field where you type the answer you want PODIUM to check for, type **Grant**

▶ In the Link box, type the following two lines:

@feedback=Congratulations! Your answer is correct.
@reread

▶ Click OK to close the Create an Answer dialog; the answer now appears in the answer box in the Input Field Editor dialog.

▶ Click the New button again to create one more answer to check for; the Create an Answer dialog appears.

▶ In the field where you type the answer you want PODIUM to check for, type **@other**

@other is a key word that will match any answer the user types that is not found in the list of answers.

▶ In the Link box, type the following two lines:

@feedback=No, that is not correct; please try again.
@reread

▶ Click OK to close the Create an Answer dialog; the answer now appears in the answer box.

▶ Click OK to close the Input Field Editor dialog, and close the toolbox.

Try typing different answers to the question *Who is buried in Grant's tomb?* and see what happens. Notice how you get different feedback depending on whether you type *Grant* or someone else's name. Although this is a simple example, you can already sense what power this gives you to judge and process user input. There is no limit to the number of different answers you can check for, and there is no limit to the number or complexity of the links you can use to process the answers.

There is an example of more-sophisticated answer judging on the *Multiliteracy CD*. The question is about a rock, and the correct answer is *metamorphic*. To try this example, go to the Demonstrations secton, select Textbook Examples, and click Answer Judging. At the prompt, try typing **igneous**, **sedimentary**, **metamorfic**, and **metaphoric**. If you would like to try the entire rock tutorial, go to the Demonstrations section, select Textbook Examples, and click History of Rocks Tutorial.

Key-by-Key Processing

When you create or edit an input field, if you check the Judge Every Keypress box, PODIUM will not wait for the user to press ⟨←Enter⟩ before judging the answers. Rather, PODIUM will perform answer judging on every keypress. As soon as what the user types into the field matches one of the answers, PODIUM will trigger the links to that answer.

Posting Messages to Input Fields

You can use @post messages to make input fields become active or inactive, visible or invisible, give a specific field the focus, and change the contents of a field.

The @post command has the form @post(*object_name*)=*message* where *object_name* is the name you gave the object in the Input Field Editor dialog, and *message* is the string of characters you want to send the object. You can put @post commands in any PODIUM link. Input fields recognize the following messages:

```
Active
Inactive
Visible
Invisible
Focus
Content=string
```

When there are multiple input fields on the screen, the user can give different fields the focus by pressing ⟨Tab⟩ to jump forward through the fields, and ⟨Shift⟩-⟨Tab⟩ to jump backward through the fields. You can give a specific field the focus by posting a Focus message to it.

Querying Input Fields

You can query the status of input fields via the @query command. The @query command has the form @query(*object_name,question,var_name*) where *object_name* is the name you gave the input in the Input Field Editor dialog, *question* is the question you have about the object, and *var_name* is the name of the variable into which you want the results of the query to be placed. For input fields, Table 40-1 lists the possible questions and the results they return.

Table 40-1 Input Field Query Questions and the Results They Return

Query Question	Result Returned by the Query
Content	A string holding the contents of the field.
Length	An integer indicating the length of the field.
IsActive	Returns 1 if the field is active, 0 if it is not.
IsVisible	Returns 1 if the field is visible, 0 if it is not.

Inspecting Your Custom File

If you pull down the PODIUM Files menu and choose Edit This File to inspect the contents of your *multilit\judging.cus* file, you will see how input fields appear in a custom file. Input fields always begin with the command @input and have the form:

```
@input=x,y @font=font_name @size=point_size @click=n @length=n
@style=BORDERorBOXorFREEorLINE @asterisk @value=string @shadow=n
@name=string @DefaultState=ACTIVEorINACTIVE
@DefaultVisibility=VISIBLEorINVISIBLE
@ActiveTextColor=color @InactiveTextColor=color
@ActiveOutlineColor=color @InactiveOutlineColor=color
@ActiveTopColor=color @InactiveTopColor=color
@ActiveBottomColor=color @InactiveBottomColor=color
@ActiveFillColor=color @InactiveFillColor=color
@OutlineThickness=n @TopThickness=n @BottomThickness=n @JudgeAlways
@answer=string
! @doc=links to the answers go here
! @doc=each answer must have at least one link
@answer=@other
! @doc=@other is a special keyword that will match anything typed at
! an @doc=input that is not found in an @answer command
```

List of Input Field Commands

Table 40-2 summarizes the input field commands covered in this chapter.

Table 40-2   Input Field Commands

Command Syntax	What the Command Does
@input=*x,y*	Positions the input; *x* and *y* are percentage screen coordinates.
@font=*font_name*	Sets the font to any Windows font specified.
@size=*point_size*	Sets the font size to the integer specified in *point_size*.
@click=*n*	Tells what mouse click the input will appear on.
@length=*n*	Specifies how many characters wide the input will be.
@style=*type*	*type* can be BORDER, BOX, FREE, or LINE.
@asterisk	Makes asterisks appear instead of what the user types.
@value=*string*	Gives the input field an initial value.
@shadow=*n*	Specifies how much shadow the text will have.
@name=*string*	Gives the input field a name for use in @post and @query commands.
@DefaultState=*state*	The default *state* can be ACTIVE or INACTIVE.
@DefaultVisibility=*visibility*	The default *visibility* can be VISIBLE or INVISIBLE.

Table 40-2   *(Continued)*

Command Syntax	What the Command Does
@ActiveTextColor=*color* @InactiveTextColor=*color* @ActiveTopColor=*color* @InactiveTopColor=*color* @ActiveBottomColor=*color* @InactiveBottomColor=*color* @ActiveFillColor=*color* @InactiveFillColor=*color*	Sets the color of the specified element of the input field. *color* is a Windows color value.
@OutlineThickness=*n* @TopThickness=*n* @BottomThickness=*n*	Sets the thickness of the specified element of the input field.
@JudgeAlways	Makes PODIUM judge the input on every keypress.
@answer=*string*	Specifies an answer to be judged. There can more than one @answer command. Each @answer command must be followed immediately by one or more links that get triggered when that answer is entered into the input field.

E X E R C I S E S

1. Use PODIUM to get your *multilit\input.cus* file on the screen. It asks you what is your name. Add another question that asks: **How old are you?** Use the Input tool to create another input field that will hold the age that the user types. Then use the Link tool to edit the Continue button at the bottom of the screen. Add a sentence to the feedback message so it says: **Hello, *name,* it is nice to see you! Today you are *age* years old.**

2. Use PODIUM to get your *multilit\judging.cus* file on the screen. It asks who is buried in Grant's tomb. So far, it checks only for the answer *Grant.* Use the Input tool to check for other answers, such as *Washington,* and link to those answers appropriate feedback messages, such as *Washington is buried in Washington's tomb.* Create the answer *Hoffa* and link it to a feedback message that says, *They haven't found Hoffa's body yet.*

41 Random Number Generation

After completing this chapter, you will be able to:

- **Know when to use random numbers in a multimedia application**

- **Generate a random number with the @random command**

- **Seed the random number generator**

- **Set the range of random numbers to be generated**

- **Specify whether the number generated gets replaced in the random number pool**

RANDOM NUMBER is a value that a computer generates in response to a random number command. Because you do not know the value in advance, the number generated is called a random number.

There are many uses of random numbers in multimedia applications. For example, random numbers can be used to create attract loops that randomly display graphics and make sounds to attract a user to a multimedia kiosk. In training systems, random numbers are used to select test questions from item banks. Random numbers can create variety by changing multimedia design elements such as backdrops and sound effects.

This chapter teaches you how to generate random numbers.

Creating the *random.cus* Screen

To complete the exercises in this chapter, you need to create a new multimedia screen called *random.cus* in the *multilit* directory on your computer's hard drive. Follow these steps:

▶ If PODIUM is not running, start PODIUM now.

▶ Press F2 to put PODIUM into a window and reveal the menu bar.

▶ Pull down the Files menu and select New Custom to create a new screen.

▶ In the File name box, assuming your hard drive is C, type:

`c:\multilit\random.cus`

▶ Press ←Enter; PODIUM creates the new screen and opens the custom toolbox for you.

 ▶ Use the Backdrop tool to give the screen a dark blue background.

▶ Use the Text tool to write the following text at the top of the screen:

Multimedia Literacy Random Number Practice

Now you are ready to generate your first random number. Read on.

The Random Number Assign Command

You generate random numbers with the @random command. The @random command has three subcommands: assign, seed, and range. You assign random numbers with the assign subcommand. The syntax is:

```
@random(assign,var_name)
```

The assign subcommand causes PODIUM to generate a random number and place it in the variable *var_name*. The best way to learn how to use random numbers is to generate some. Follow these steps:

 ▶ Use the Text tool to write the following line of text on your *multilit\random.cus* screen:

The random number is ##number

 ▶ Toward the bottom of the screen, use the Text tool to write the word **Generate**

 ▶ Make the word *Generate* be a hypertext by clicking it with the Link tool; the Link dialog appears.

▶ In the Link box, type:

```
@random(assign,number)
@reread
```

▶ Click OK to close the Link box, and close the toolbox.

Click the word *Generate*. Notice how the value of the random number changes. Click *Generate* again; the number changes again. Each time you click the word *Generate,* you get a new random number.

▶ Quit PODIUM, start it up again, and bring up your *multilit\random.cus* screen. Jot down the first few random numbers it generates when you click *Generate*.

▶ Repeat the previous step; notice how the random numbers are *exactly the same*.

▶ Repeat the previous step again; notice how the random numbers are still the same.

It seems ironic that "random" numbers would be the same each time. Read on to learn how to seed the random number generator to make the list of random numbers be different each time.

Seeding the Random Number Generator

Because of the way computers generate random numbers, you must seed the random number generator if you want the series of numbers to be different each time you run your application. You seed the random number generator with the seed subcommand. The syntax is:

```
@random(seed,value)
```

value is the starting value for generating a series of pseudorandom integers. For each starting value, you will get the same series of pseudorandom integers. If you want the series to be different each time, you can seed the random number generator with the current time by specifying the PODIUM system variable *%%time* as the value for the command:

```
! @random(seed,%%time)
```

The best place to seed the random number generator is in the backdrop of your custom file. Since you probably will want to seed the random number generator just once, you can use an @if statement to prevent the random number generator from getting reseeded each time the file rereads.

 ▶ Use the Backdrop tool to add the following lines to the backdrop of your *multilit\random.cus* file:

```
@if already_seeded = 0
    @random(seed,%%time)
    @calc already_seeded = 1
@endif
```

▶ Quit PODIUM, start it up again, and bring up your *multilit\random.cus* screen. Jot down the first few random numbers it generates when you click *Generate*.

▶ Repeat the previous step; notice how the random numbers are different this time.

Setting the Range of the Random Numbers

When you generate random numbers, you will almost always want to control the range in which the numbers get generated. For example, if you are generating screen coordinates to position a graphic on the screen, you will want the range of random numbers to fall between 0 and 100. If you are selecting test questions from an item pool that consists of 175 test questions, you will want the range of random numbers to fall between 1 and 175.

You set the range of random values with the range subcommand. The syntax is:

```
@random(range,minimum,maximum,replace)
```

Replace *minimum* and *maximum* with the minimum and maximum values for the random numbers to be generated. The value of *replace* indicates whether or not the random numbers get replaced in the random number pool after being generated. If the *replace* parameter is 1, the number generated will get put back into the random number pool, from which it could get randomly selected again; if the *replace* parameter is 0, each number will get randomly generated only once until all the other numbers in the range have also been chosen. Each time PODIUM encounters a random range command, the range settings will be reset immediately to the new values, and the random number pool will be reset.

For example, suppose you want your *multilit\random.cus* file to generate random numbers between 10 and 15. Follow these steps:

 ▶ Click the Backdrop tool to get the Backdrop dialog on the screen.

▶ Position the cusor immediately after the line that reads *@random(seed,%%time)*.

▶ Press ←Enter to create a new line and type **@random(range,10,15,0)**

▶ Quit PODIUM, start it up again, and bring up your *multilit\random.cus* screen. Click *Generate* a dozen times and observe how the random numbers generated are within the range of 10 to 15.

List of Random Number Commands

Table 41-1 lists the PODIUM @random commands.

Table 41-1 Random Number Commands

Command Syntax	What the Command Does
@random(assign, *var_name*)	Generates a random number and places its value in the variable *var_name*.
@random(seed, *value*)	Seeds the random number generator to create a list of pseudorandom numbers beginning with *value;* to make the list of random numbers be different each time, make *value* be *%%time*.
@random(range, *minimum, maximum, replace*)	Specifies the *minimum* and *maximum* values for the random numbers to be generated. If *replace* is 0, numbers generated do not get returned to the random number pool; if *replace* is 1, numbers can get generated again.

E X E R C I S E S

1. Use PODIUM to get your *multilit\random.cus* file on the screen. Create a new line of text that says **Range 1 to 5 with replacement**. Link to that text the following command:

```
@random(range,1,5,1)
```

Make another line of text that says **Range 1 to 5 without replacement**. Link to that text the following command:

```
@random(range,1,5,0)
```

Close the toolbox, click *Range 1 to 5 with replacement,* then click *Generate* a dozen times and jot down the random numbers that get generated. Now click *Range 1 to 5 without replacement,* click *Generate* a dozen times, and jot down the random numbers that get generated. How do the two lists of random numbers compare?

42

Timers

After completing this chapter, you will be able to:

- **Create timers that go off after a specified period of time**
- **Link time-sensitive events to timers**
- **Use timers to create attract loops**

SO FAR the multimedia events you have learned how to create don't happen unless the user clicks or types something to trigger an event. In this chapter you will learn how to set **timers** that can make things happen after a preset period of time. If the user does not navigate elsewhere before a timer goes off, the events linked to the timer get triggered.

Timers are often used to create attract loops. If the user does not interact with your application for a while, an attract loop gets triggered to draw attention to your application. Timers are also used to create sophisticated multimedia sequences that can play any combination of audiovisual events upon entry to a multimedia screen.

Creating the *timer.cus* Screen

To complete the exercises in this chapter, you need to create a new multimedia screen called *timer.cus* in the *multilit* directory on your computer's hard drive. Follow these steps:

▶ If PODIUM is not running, start PODIUM now.

▶ Press F2 to put PODIUM into a window and reveal the menu bar.

▶ Pull down the Files menu and select New Custom to create a new screen.

▶ In the File name box, assuming your hard drive is C, type:

`c:\multilit\timer.cus`

▶ Press ←Enter; PODIUM creates the new screen and opens the custom toolbox for you.

▶ Use the Backdrop tool to give the screen a dark blue background.

▶ Use the Text tool to write the following text at the top of the screen:

`Multimedia Literacy Timer Practice`

Now you are ready to create your first timer. Read on.

Creating Timers

You create timers with the Timer tool, which you will find on the advanced row of the custom toolbox. You also use the Timer tool to edit the timers after you create them. Let's begin with a simple example in which you will create a timer that makes your computer beep every two seconds. Follow these steps:

 ▶ If the advanced row of the custom toolbox is not visible, right-click the Expand icon at the right edge of the toolbox to reveal the row of advanced tools.

 ▶ Click the Timer tool; the Timers Editor dialog appears as shown in Figure 42-1.

42-1

The Timers Editor dialog.

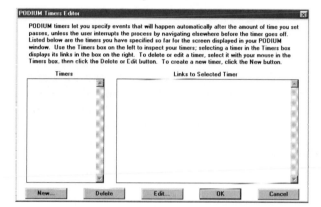

42-2

The Create a Timer dialog.

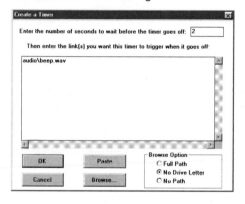

▶ Click New to create a new timer; the Create a Timer dialog appears as shown in Figure 42-2.

▶ Find the field where you type the number of seconds to wait before the timer goes off; in this example, type **2** into that field.

▶ In the Link box, type the links you want this timer to trigger; for this example, type the following line:

```
audio\beep.wav
```

▶ Click OK to close the Link box; the timer appears in the Timers Editor dialog.

▶ Click OK to close the Timers Editor dialog.

▶ Close the PODIUM toolbox.

After two seconds, the timer goes off and triggers the *audio\beep.wav* sound. To make PODIUM reread the file and reset the timer, press F12, which is the reread key; after two seconds, the beep sounds again.

There is no limit to the number of timers you can set. To create another timer, just repeat the previous steps.

Editing and Deleting Timers

To edit a timer, follow these steps:

 ▶ Click the Timer tool; the Timers Editor dialog appears.

▶ In the Timers box, click once on the timer you want to edit; the links to that timer appear in the Links to Selected Timer box.

> ▶ Click the Edit button; the Create a Timer dialog appears, displaying the current settings for this timer.

> ▶ Make any changes you want in the number of seconds or the links, then click OK to close the dialog.

To delete a timer, follow these steps:

> ▶ Click the Timer tool; the Timers Editor dialog appears.

> ▶ In the Timers box, click once on the timer you want to delete; the links to that timer appear in the Links to Selected Timer box.

> ▶ Click the Delete button.

Using Timers for Multimedia Sequencing

Timers provide a way to make a multimedia screen display a sequence of multimedia events. For example, suppose you want a screen to play a series of waveform audio files and hang a picture on the screen in between each audio file. You can make all this happen automatically by setting a timer that uses the @wait command to sequence through the timer's links automatically. There is an example of such a sequence on the *Multiliteracy CD*. To try it, go to the

42-3

The use of a timer for multimedia sequencing.

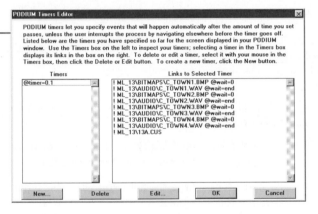

Demonstrations section, select Textbook Examples, and click Timers Demo. Figure 42-3 shows the timer that created this sequence. It goes off after ¹⁄₁₀ of a second to make the sequence begin soon after the screen appears. The @wait=end and @wait=0 commands create the automatic sequencing.

Making Attract Loops

An **attract loop** is a repeating sequence of multimedia events that begins if the user does not interact with an application for a while. The purpose of the attract loop is to attract a user to your application.

You can use timers to make attract loops. Because timers go off only if the user does not click something on the screen, you can set a timer on any screen that you would like to have trigger an attract loop if the user does not do anything before the timer goes off.

There is an example of an attract loop on the *Multiliteracy CD*. To try it, go to the Demonstrations section, select Textbook Examples, and click Attract Loop. If you wait more than five seconds before you click something, a timer goes off and triggers an attract loop called *attract.cus*. The attract loop uses a timer that makes a picture move about the screen in a random pattern. The picture's @origin is determined by variables. The timer goes off after two seconds, uses a @random command to set the values of the variables, and uses a @reread

42-4

The file *practice\begin.cus*, which triggers the attract loop.

42-5

The attract loop *practice\attract.cus*.

command to make the file repeat. This process repeats until the user clicks the mouse, which causes the default navigation to return to the screen from which the attract loop was triggered.

Figure 42-4 shows the contents of the custom file that triggers the attract loop, and Figure 42-5 shows the attract loop file.

Inspecting Your Custom File

If you study the contents of Figures 42-4 and 42-5, you will see how timers have a simple syntax. In a custom file, the timer begins with the command @timer=*n* where *n* is an integer or decimal number that specifies how long to wait before the timer goes off. The timer must be followed by one or more links, which are the lines that begin with an exclamation point. When the timer goes off, it triggers the items linked to it.

Use the Notepad to inspect the timer file *multilit\timer.cus* that you created in this chapter, and you will see how it contains a @timer command followed by the links the timer triggers. Every timer has the following syntax:

```
@timer=n
! @doc=the links to the timer go here.
! @doc=there must be at least one link.
! @doc=immediately following each timer.
```

EXERCISES

1. Use the Waveform Audio tool to record the following sentence:

```
Click one of the airplanes to learn about an era of flight.
```

Save the recording as *flight\clickme.wav*. Get your *flight\history.cus* file on the screen. Use the Timer tool to create a timer that will go off after 10 seconds. Make the link to the timer read as follows:

```
flight\clickme.wav
@UpdateGraphics
@reread
```

Close the toolbox to become a user of your application. If you do not click an airplane within 10 seconds, the timer will go off and play your *clickme.wav* file. The @UpdateGraphics command causes PODIUM to do off-screen buffering for a very smooth screen refresh during the @reread, which makes the file repeat.

43

Cursors

After completing this chapter, you will be able to:

- **Change the shape of the normal cursor**
- **Make different cursors appear over hot spots**
- **Use airplane cursors in the History of Flight application**
- **Create your own custom cursors**

S O F A R you have learned how to customize the backdrop, the graphics, and all of the text printed on your multimedia screens, but one of the most important design elements has been out of your control: the cursor. The cursor is almost always visible on the screen, and being able to customize it enables you to add variety and interest. This chapter teaches you how to create custom cursors that provide a unique look and feel in an application.

Movie on CD

Demonstrations
➡ Show Me!
  ➡ Cursors
    ➡ **Changing the Normal Cursor Shape**

Changing the Shape of the Normal Cursor

The normal cursor is the arrow you see on the screen when the mouse is not positioned over a hot spot. You can change the shape of the normal cursor with the @cursor command. The syntax is @cursor=*filename.bmp,x,y* where *filename.bmp* is the path\filename to a bitmap that contains the cursor. The *x,y* parameters tell PODIUM the pixel location of the cursor's hot spot within the bitmap. If the *x,y* parameters are missing, PODIUM uses the center of the bitmap as the hot spot.

To learn how to use the @cursor command, follow these steps:

▶ Get your *multilit\example.cus* file on the screen.

▶ Use the Backdrop tool to add the following command to the backdrop of the file:

    `@cursor=cursor\fly.bmp`

▶ Close the toolbox and move the mouse around the screen. The cursor has the shape of a fly!

The @cursor command stays in effect until PODIUM encounters a @NormalCursor command, which you use to revert to the default Windows arrow cursor.

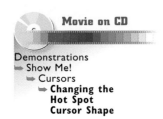

Changing the Shape of the Hot Spot Cursor

You can make each hot spot on the screen display a different cursor via the @HotCursor command. The syntax is @HotCursor=*filename.bmp,x,y* where *filename.bmp* is the path\filename to a bitmap that contains the cursor. The *x,y* parameters tell PODIUM the pixel location of the cursor's hot spot within the bitmap. If the *x,y* parameters are missing, PODIUM uses the center of the bitmap as the hot spot.

To learn how to use the @HotCursor command, follow these steps:

▶ Get your *multilit\example.cus* file on the screen.

▶ Use the Link tool to edit the links to any one of the hot spots on the screen. When the Link box appears, add the following command to hot spot's links:

`@HotCursor=cursor\hotfly.bmp`

▶ Close the toolbox and move the mouse over that hot spot on the screen. Instead of displaying the normal hot cursor shape, the cursor has the shape of a fly with its wings spread.

Imagine the possibilities you have to create different hot cursor shapes. For example, suppose you have a trigger at the right edge of the screen that the user clicks to navigate forward in your application. Using the @HotCursor command, you can display a forward-pointing arrow when the user mouses over that hot spot. Similarly, a trigger at the left edge of the screen that takes the user back to the previous screen can display a backward-pointing hot cursor. A trigger that makes an action stop can display a stop sign hot cursor. A trigger that provides help can display a question mark hot cursor.

Cursor Shapes on the *Multiliteracy CD*

The *cursor* directory on the *Multiliteracy CD* contains many cursors that you can use in your multimedia applications. Table 43-1 lists the cursors you will find in the *cursor* directory.

Creating Custom Cursors

You can use any bitmap editor, such as Paint Shop Pro, to create custom cursors for use with PODIUM. Follow these steps to create a custom cursor with Paint Shop Pro:

▶ Pull down the Paint Shop Pro File menu and choose New; the New Image dialog appears as shown in Figure 43-1.

▶ Cursors are 32 pixels wide by 32 pixels high. Set the width and height parameters in the New Image dialog to 32 × 32.

▶ Set the Image Type to 256 Colors and click OK.

▶ There are three colors in a cursor: black, white, and transparent. When PODIUM reads the bitmap in your @cursor statement, PODIUM treats black pixels as black, white pixels as white, and any other color as transparent. Keeping this in mind, use the Paint Shop Pro drawing tools to draw your cursor.

Table 43-1 Contents of the *cursor* Directory on the *Multiliteracy CD*

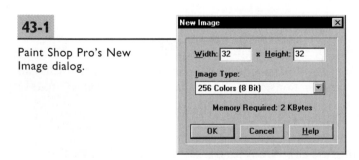

Cursor Theme	Cursor Shape	Cursor Name	Cursor Theme	Cursor Shape	Cursor Name
Airplanes		*biplane.bmp*	Greeting cards		*hotcard.bmp*
Airplanes		*fortress.bmp*	Magic wand		*wand.bmp*
Airplanes		*angels.bmp*	Magic wand		*hotwand.bmp*
Airplanes		*jumbojet.bmp*	Beach		*sun.bmp*
Insects		*fly.bmp*	Beach		*sunburst.bmp*
Insects		*hotfly.bmp*	Stop		*stop.bmp*
Automobiles		*car.bmp*	Home		*home.bmp*
Automobiles		*hotcar.bmp*	Help		*help.bmp*
Greeting cards		*card.bmp*			

43-1

Paint Shop Pro's New Image dialog.

▶ Save the cursor in one of the Windows BMP file formats, either RGB or RLE encoded. The RLE format requires less storage space and loads more quickly than the RGB format.

▶ Test the cursor in PODIUM to make sure it does what you want.

NOTE PODIUM buffers images to make your applications run fast. If you have PODIUM running and you edit a bitmap (such as a cursor) with Paint Shop Pro and then return to PODIUM, you might not see any change in the appearance of the bitmap in PODIUM, because the former version of the bitmap has been buffered inside PODIUM. To clear the PODIUM picture buffers, pull down the PODIUM Controls menu and choose Erase Picture Buffers.

List of Cursor Commands

Table 43-2 lists the PODIUM cursor commands.

Table 43-2 Cursor Commands

Command Syntax	What the Command Does
@cursor=*filename.bmp,x,y*	Changes the normal cursor shape to the bitmap in *filename.bmp*. The *x,y* coordinates are optional. When present, *x,y* defines the hot spot within the cursor. Otherwise, the hot spot is the center of the cursor.
@NormalCursor	Changes the cursor shape back to the default Windows arrow cursor.
@HotCursor=*filename.bmp,x,y*	Changes the hot cursor shape of a specific hot spot. Link the @HotCursor command to the hot spot you want to display the cursor shape in *filename.bmp*. See the @cursor command for documentation of the optional *x,y* coordinates.

E X E R C I S E S

1. Use the Link tool to add @HotCursor= commands to the hot spots on your *flight\history.cus* file. The *cursor* directory contains the following cursor shapes to link to each hot spot:

Hot Spot	Cursor Shape	Cursor Name
Biplane		*biplane.bmp*
Flying Fortress		*fortress.bmp*
Blue Angels		*angels.bmp*
Jumbo jet		*jumbojet.bmp*

Close the toolbox and mouse over each hot spot to make sure it displays the appropriate hot cursor shape.

2. Use Paint Shop Pro, or the bitmap editor of your choice, to create a custom cursor of your own design. The cursor must be a 32 × 32 256-color bitmap; save it in the Windows BMP format. Then use the Backdrop tool to put a @cursor command into the backdrop of your *multilit\example.cus* file, making your custom-drawn bitmap become the cursor on the screen. Close the toolbox, mouse around the screen, and make sure the cursor works properly. Notice how pixels you drew in white appear white, black pixels appear black, and any other color shows transparent.

44

Frame Animation

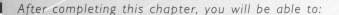

After completing this chapter, you will be able to:

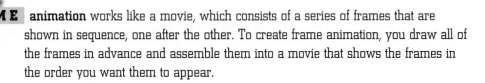

- Use Video for Windows to create frame animation

- Use timers and variables to animate text size and position

- Animate graphics drawn on the screen

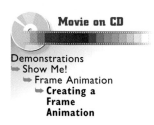

R A M E **animation** works like a movie, which consists of a series of frames that are shown in sequence, one after the other. To create frame animation, you draw all of the frames in advance and assemble them into a movie that shows the frames in the order you want them to appear.

This chapter shows you how to create frame animations with Video for Windows.

Movie on CD

Demonstrations
➡ Show Me!
  ➡ Frame Animation
    ➡ **Creating a**
      Frame
      Animation

Creating a Frame Animation

To make a frame animation, use any graphics package to create the bitmaps to be shown in the animation. Then use VidEdit to create a movie into which you insert each animation frame in order from start to finish. The best way to learn how to do this is to work through an example. The *frames* directory on the *Multiliteracy CD* contains 25 frames of an animation sequence that shows a hand pressing a button. To assemble these frames into an animation sequence, follow these steps:

▶ Get VidEdit running.

▶ Pull down the File menu and choose New.

▶ Pull down the File menu and choose Insert; the Insert File dialog appears as shown in Figure 44-1.

44-1

The VidEdit Insert File dialog.

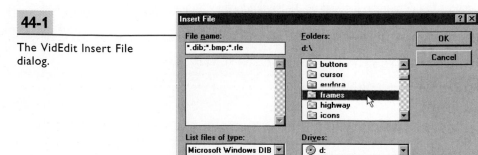

▶ You want to insert bitmaps, so click the List Files of Type arrow and choose Microsoft Windows DIB (*DIB* stands for device-independent bitmap).

Browse to the directory from which you want to insert the frames; in this example, browse to the *frames* directory on the *Multiliteracy CD*.

▶ Select the first frame of the sequence, which in this example is *frame1.bmp,* and click OK. Now you have the world's shortest movie, which consists of just one frame. You won't see the frame unless you reposition the slider to the start of the movie. If you reposition the slider, make sure you slide it back to the end of the movie before proceeding.

▶ Repeat the next three steps for each additional frame in the animation. This example has 24 more frames, so you need to do this 24 times, once for each frame:

⬚ Make sure the slider is positioned at the end of the movie, which is where you want to insert the next frame.

⬚ Pull down the File menu and choose Insert; the Insert File dialog appears.

⬚ Select the next frame in the animation sequence and click OK.

▶ Click the Rewind button, then click the Play button to play the animation. Make sure it plays the frames in the proper sequence.

▶ Pull down the File menu and choose Save; the Save Video dialog appears.

▶ Click the Compression Options button and check your Compression settings; you probably want them set to CD-ROM 150 KB, Microsoft Video 1, at 15 frames per second. Click the Details button and set the key frame to be every 1 frame.

▶ In the File name field, type the filename you want this video to have. Make sure you give it an *.avi* filename extension. For this example, make the filename be **multilit\animated.avi**

Hanging a Frame Animation on a Multimedia Screen

Because the frame animation you just created is a Video for Windows movie, you can use the Movie Hanger tool to hang the animation on any multimedia screen. Let's create a new screen to hang the animation on, so you will have a place to practice the rest of the techniques in this chapter. Follow these steps:

▶ Pull down the PODIUM Files menu, choose New Custom, and create a new screen on your hard drive called *multilit\animated.cus.*

▶ Use the Backdrop tool to make the backdrop be *backdrop\animate.bmp.*

▶ Use the Text tool to write the following line of text near the top of the screen:

`Multimedia Literacy Frame Animation Exercises`

▶ Click the Movie Hanger tool, mouse to the center of the screen, and click; the Movie Hanger dialog appears.

▶ Click the Browse button, browse to your *multilit\animated.avi* movie, and click OK to close the Browse dialog. The filename *multilit\animated.avi* now appears in the File name field of the Movie Hanger dialog.

▶ In the Movie Name field, type **animation1**

▶ Click OK to close the Movie Hanger dialog.

▶ Close the toolbox; the movie appears on your screen.

You can click the Play and Stop buttons and drag the slider to control your animation, just as if it were a movie. In fact, it *is* a movie!

Movie on CD

Demonstrations
➡ Show Me!
  ➡ Frame Animation
    ➡ **Blending
       Animations
       into the
       Screen**

Blending Animations into the Screen

If you study the *multilit\animated.cus* screen you just created, you will notice how the movie does not blend into the screen very well. The frame around the movie makes it appear square, and the controls do not fit the motif of the screen. To blend the animation into the screen, follow these steps:

▶ Open the toolbox and click the Movie Hanger tool.

▶ Click on the animation with the Movie Hanger tool; the Movie Hanger dialog appears, showing the current settings for the animation.

▶ In the Appearance group, click once on the Frame and Controls check boxes to uncheck them.

▶ Click OK to close the Movie Hanger dialog.

▶ Close the toolbox.

Now the animation blends into the screen, with no border around it. You should realize that when you hang movies on top of a bitmap backdrop, the movies are drawn in the same palette as the bitmap. Therefore, when you design applications that blend animations into the screen, you should make the palette of the backdrop be compatible with the colors in the animations.

Press F12 to make PODIUM reread the *multilit\animated.cus* file that is on your screen. Does the animation play? No! Can you make it play right now? No, because you removed the controls that enable users to play it. Suppose you wanted the animation to start playing soon after the screen appears. Follow these steps:

▶ Open the toolbox and right-click the Expand icon to reveal the advanced row of tools.

▶ Click the Timer icon; the Timer dialog appears.

▶ Click New; the Create a Timer dialog appears.

▶ In the number of seconds field, type **.1**

▶ Recall that the name you gave the animation when you hung it on the screen was animation1. In the Link box, type the following link:

`@post(animation1)=play`

▶ Click OK to close the dialogs, and close the toolbox.

▶ Press F12 to make PODIUM reread the screen. When the timer goes off, the @post command will make the animation play.

Suppose you wanted the animation to keep playing repeatedly, restarting automatically when it gets to the end. Follow these steps:

▶ Open the toolbox and click the Timer tool; the Timer dialog appears.

▶ Click once in the Timers box to select the timer that issues the @post command; then click the Edit button.

▶ In the Link box, change the links to read as follows:

```
@query(animation1,length,movie_length)
@query(animation1,location,movie_location)
@if movie_length = movie_location
    @post(animation1)=seek(1)
    @post(animation1)=play
@else if movie_location = 0
    @post(animation1)=play
@endif
@RestartTimers
```

▶ If you study the logic in the Link box, you will see how the movie gets restarted whenever it plays all the way through to the end.

▶ Click OK to close the Timer dialog, and close the toolbox.

Now the animation plays continuously, restarting whenever it reaches the last frame.

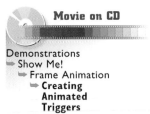

Movie on CD

Demonstrations
➡ Show Me!
  ➡ Frame Animation
    ➡ **Creating Animated Triggers**

Creating Animated Triggers

In highly produced multimedia titles, you often see animated triggers in which things move to create interest on the screen while the user is deciding what to click. You can create animated triggers to give your applications a sophisticated look and feel. To make the animation on your screen into an animated trigger, follow these steps:

▶ Open the toolbox and click the Trigger tool.

▶ Mouse to the upper left corner of the animation where you want the trigger.

▶ Click and drag to draw the trigger around the animation; when you release the mouse button, the Trigger dialog appears.

▶ In the Link box, type the links you want triggered when the user clicks inside the animation. In this example, type the following line into the Link box:

```
@post(animation1)=stop
bitmaps\animate.bmp
```

▶ Click OK to close the Link box, then close the toolbox; the animation begins to play.

▶ Click the animation to trigger what you linked to it.

Movie on CD

Demonstrations
➡ Show Me!
  ➡ Frame Animation
    ➡ **Adding Sound**

Adding a Sound Track to a Frame Animation

The *multilit\animated.avi* movie you made in this chapter has no sound. Suppose you wanted to add a sound track to it. You do that with the VidEdit tool. Follow these steps:

▶ Get VidEdit running.

▶ Pull down the File menu and choose Open; the Open Video File dialog appears. Browse to the movie you want to open and click OK. In this example open the movie *multilit\animated.avi*.

▶ Pull down the File menu and choose Insert; the Insert File dialog appears.

▶ You want to insert a waveform audio file, so click the List Files of Type arrow and choose Microsoft Waveform.

▶ Browse to the directory from which you want to insert the waveform audio; in this example browse to the *frames* directory on the *Multiliteracy CD*.

▶ Select the *animated.wav* file and click OK.

▶ Click the Rewind button and then click Play. The audio has been inserted into the movie.

▶ If the audio is longer than the movie, there will be a gap with no video at the end of the movie. To remove the gap, set the Mark In point at the end of the video, and set the Mark Out point at the end of the audio. Then pull down the Edit menu and choose Delete.

▶ If the audio is shorter than the movie, position the slider at the end of the audio, pull down the File menu, choose Insert, and insert some more audio.

▶ Click the Rewind button and then click Play to audition the movie.

As you can see from this example, it is effective to make the sound track of an animated trigger be the ambient sound you want the user to hear. You should not feel compelled to provide a sound track for every animated trigger you put on the screen, however. Depending on the purpose of the trigger, a silent animation may be more appropriate than one with sound. Plus, if you have more than one animated trigger on-screen at once, you do not want them to be contending for the audio device. In that case, it is better to make the animation silent, and use an @ambient command to provide the ambient sound.

E X E R C I S E S

The following exercises guide you through the steps to create a highly animated screen containing several simultaneously animated triggers. Completing these exercises is guaranteed to result in a screen that will please you.

1. There is a directory called *trigmove* that contains the animations for several moving triggers that you will hang on the screen in these exercises. You need to copy these animations to your hard drive in order to ensure that they can all play back simultaneously on your computer. Follow these steps:

▷ Create a directory on your hard drive called *trigfun*.

▷ Use the Windows File Manager or the Explorer to copy all of the files from the *trigmove* directory on the *Multiliteracy CD* into the *trigfun* directory on your hard drive.

2. Get PODIUM running. Pull down the Files menu and choose New Custom. Create a new screen in your *trigfun* directory called *trigfun.cus*. With the toolbox open, follow these steps:

▷ Use the Backdrop tool to make the backdrop be the bitmap named *trigfun.bmp*, which you will find in the *backdrop* directory on the *Multiliteracy CD*.

▶ Use the Movie Hanger tool to hang the following animations on the screen. Make sure you give the animations the names indicated. Also, make sure you uncheck the Frame and Controls boxes in the Appearance settings for each animation.

Animation Filename	Name to Assign the Animation
trigfun\weather.avi	weather
trigfun\notepad.avi	notepad
trigfun\calc.avi	calculator
trigfun\web.avi	web

▶ Use the Move tools to position the animations on the screen as you like. Figure 44-2 shows one way of arranging them on this particular screen.

44-2

One way to hang the animations on the screen of this exercise.

3. Use the Timer tool to create a timer that will go off soon after the file appears and pass messages to get the animations playing. Use the same logic that the "Blending Animations into the Screen" section of this chapter taught you. Note that you will need to write logic to control four movies at once. If you have trouble, you will find the "answer section" to this exercise in the *animated.cus* file in the *answers* directory on the *Multiliteracy CD*. You can inspect that file with any text editor to have a look at how the @timer gets written for this exercise.

4. To complete this highly animated screen, use the Trigger tool to create triggers around each animation. Link the triggers to the following objects:

Animation Name	Object to Link to the Animation
calculator	*calc.exe*
notepad	*notepad.exe*
web	http://www.yahoo.com
weather	http://www.weather.com

As a final touch, use the Backdrop tool to link an @ambient command to provide ambient sound for this file. The command to link is:

ambient\trigfun.wav

Part Eight

Creating Advanced Multimedia Applications

*If you can **dream** it, you can **do** it.*

    — Adobe Systems Incorporated

You have learned many multimedia tools and techniques in this book. Think about the power they give you over your computer. You can put any text in any size, font, color, and position on the screen and link the text to anything on your computer. You can put any picture anyplace on the screen, make the picture any size, and link the picture to anything you want. You can make digital movies and audio recordings and link or synchronize them with other multimedia objects. You have learned how to use logic to make an application smart, sensing the needs of the user and branching accordingly. Now you are ready to learn some hypermedia design principles that will enable you to harness this power and create an advanced multimedia application.

This part of the book provides you with an overview of hypermedia design principles and techniques. After learning about flowcharting, storyboarding, and scripting, you will use the five multimedia design paradigms to visualize the structure of an advanced application. The *Multiliteracy CD* contains clip-art libraries full of multimedia resources for creating advanced projects. You will learn how to use these materials to get started designing your own applications. Then you will learn how to use online search engines to locate materials that you can download from the Internet. You will also learn the proper bibliographic style for citing material you find on the Internet.

45 Hypermedia Design Principles and Techniques

After completing this chapter, you will be able to:

- ☐ **Know when to use a flowchart, a storyboard, and a script**

- ☐ **Recognize the five basic multimedia design paradigms**

- ☐ **Understand how the linear list design lets the user move back and forth in a sequence of multimedia objects**

- ☐ **Understand how the menu design provides users with a choice of items, and how the hierarchical design provides levels of choices by linking menus to menus**

- ☐ **Realize how the multiple linking in a network design provides the richest form of interactivity**

- ☐ **Visualize how hybrid designs can incorporate lists, menus, hierarchies, and networks**

- ☐ **Define the content of an advanced application and adopt an appropriate navigational metaphor**

 **T IS NOT** unusual for an advanced application to contain hundreds or even thousands of multimedia screens. Your challenge is to present this material in such a way that the user will not get lost or confused. From the get-go, you must have a clear notion of how the material will be organized and how the user will navigate from screen to screen.

This chapter teaches hypermedia design techniques that will help you plan the development of a multimedia application. You will learn to visualize the flow of your application and imagine yourself running through it as a user. You will save time and money by learning to correct problems in the design before costly on-screen development begins.

Design Paradigms

There are five ways to design the flow of a multimedia application: the linear list, the menu, the hierarchy, the network, and the hybrid.

LINEAR LIST

The simplest design is the **linear list** you see in Figure 45-1. As the user clicks the mouse, the application presents the information, one item after the other. Each object in the list can be a text, a graphic, an audio clip, a video, or a compound object consisting of more than one medium playing at once, such as a text overlaid on a graphic accompanied by a sound track. The user can move back and forth through the list, moving forward to new materials or backward to review.

45-1

The linear list design lets the user move forward to see new materials or backward to review.

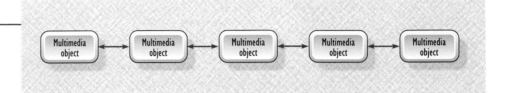

MENU

The second way to design an interaction is to create a **menu** like the one shown in Figure 45-2. The items in the menu can appear as lines of hypertext, graphics in hyperpictures, or a combination of textual and graphical triggers. When the user chooses an item on the menu, the item linked to it appears and stays on the screen until the user clicks the mouse. Then the application returns to the menu, from which the user makes another choice. The home screen in the History of Flight application you created in Part Six used a menu design.

45-2

The menu design presents the user with a set of choices.

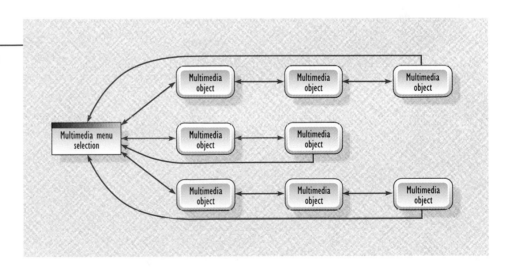

HIERARCHY

The third kind of design is the **hierarchy** shown in Figure 45-3. Each object provides the user with a menu of choices that trigger more menus with more choices. There is no limit to the size or number of menus and submenus you can have in such a hierarchy.

45-3

The hierarchy presents the user with menus of submenus.

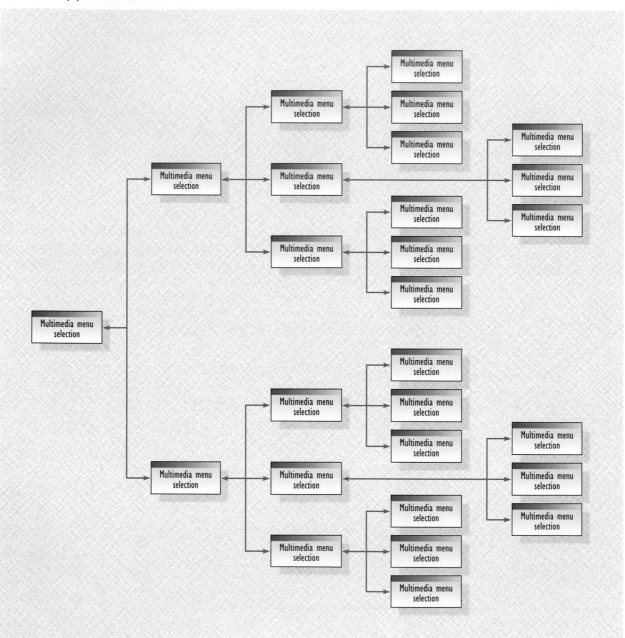

NETWORK

The most complex design is the **network** shown in Figure 45-4, in which objects can be multiply linked in any direction to any object in your application. The *Multiliteracy CD* implements the network design to provide you with a rich set of navigation options.

45-4

The network diagram contains multiply linked items that provide the richest kind of navigation.

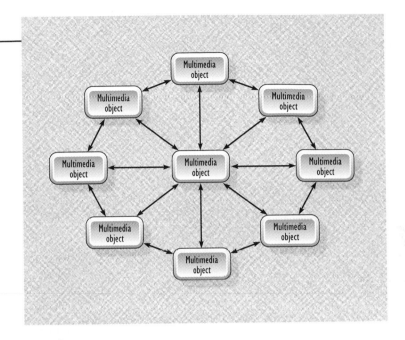

HYBRID

Multimedia applications often use more than one design paradigm, employing lists, menus, hierarchies, and networks where appropriate. For example, a sophisticated network design may trigger a list of images in a slide bank with simple navigation that lets the user move back and forth through the slides. When the user gets to the end of the list, the network design returns to provide richer navigation options. Designs that combine paradigms are called **hybrid**. Figure 45-5 shows an example of a hybrid design.

Content Definition

To develop a good application, you must have a clear idea of what it is going to be about. **Content definition** is the act of specifying what a multimedia application is about. To define an application's content, make an outline of the topics you plan to cover. Think hard about the tasks involved, and make sure you are not leaving out a topic that needs to be covered in order for the user to understand a subsequent topic. The process of hierarchically outlining an application's content is known as **task analysis**.

If you are not an expert in the content area, team with a subject matter expert (SME) who can work with you to make sure the task analysis is not missing an essential step. After you complete the task analysis, pretend you are a user, imagine yourself navigating through your application, and ask yourself whether anything the user needs to know is missing. A good, tight design will never skip an essential piece of information required to prevent the user from getting lost.

d designs employ linear lists, menus, hierarchies, and networks where appropriate.

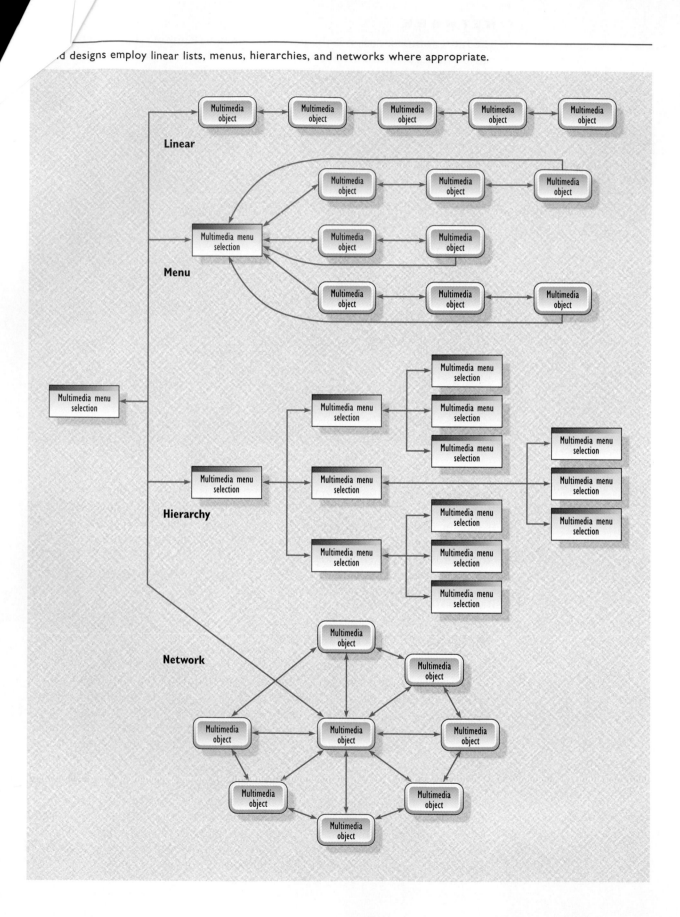

Storyboarding

A **storyboard** is a series of sketches that describe the content of a sequence of multimedia screens. Figure 45-6 shows a sample storyboarding form, which contains a frame for sketching the screen layout, and a space below the frame for making comments. To create a storyboard, you fill out such a form for each screen in an application. Inside the frame, you sketch the design elements that will appear on the screen. In the space below the frame, you write comments describing the screen's function and purpose.

Use the storyboard to reflect on the flow of your application. Spread out the sketches on the floor, tape them to a wall, or tack them onto a bulletin board. Arrange the sketches in their logical sequence—the order in which the user will view them. Seeing your screens all at once can help you visualize the form of your application and help you make design changes before proceeding to the more costly and time-consuming development stage.

45-6

A multimedia storyboarding form.

Module: _____ Strand: _____
Filename: _____
Screen No. _____ of _____
Images: _____
_____
Audio: _____
_____
Video: _____
_____

N A V I G A T I O N
Next: _____
Back: _____
Menu: _____
Help: _____
Notes: _____

Scripting

After you storyboard a project, you are ready to script it. A **script** is a complete specification of the text and narration in a multimedia application. Especially when you are using a team of people to develop an application, it is important to have a written script. Scriptwriting makes the team think through the project thoroughly. A written script helps team members communicate with each other, share comments on the design, and make adjustments prior to beginning the costly development stage. Having a script helps you role-play the application from the viewpoint of a user and identify missing elements.

Flowcharting

Multimedia applications often require users to make decisions. A flowchart is a logic diagram that illustrates the steps involved in an interactive decision-making process. Flowcharts are helpful when designing conditional branching and answer judging in a multimedia application. For example, you might present a test question and ask the user to select the correct answer. Depending on how the user responds, you will either give some positive reinforcement and proceed to the next question, or you will provide remedial feedback explaining why the answer was incorrect. Drawing a flowchart can help you visualize the answer-judging process.

Figure 45-7 shows the shapes designers use to create flowcharts. The most important shapes are the rectangular "process" box and the diamond-shaped "decision" symbol. The flowchart shown in Figure 45-8 uses these symbols to diagram the answer judging in a multiple-choice question. In the process box at the top of the diagram, the user is asked a question. If the user answers correctly, positive feedback will reinforce the correct answer. If the response is incorrect, the computer will provide a hint and repeat the question. If the user fails again, remedial instruction will be provided.

45-7

Flowcharting shapes and symbols.

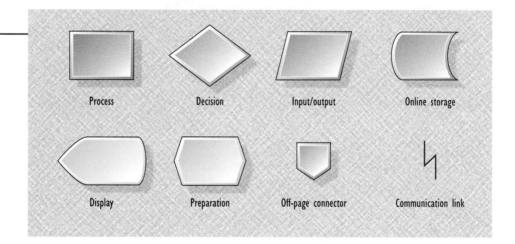

45-8

Flowchart of a multiple-choice question.

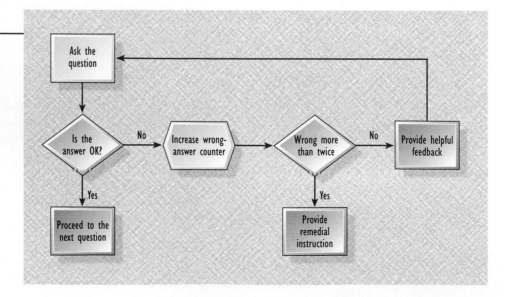

Navigational Metaphor

Designers often adopt a **metaphor** that makes it easy for the user to interact with an application. For example, the multimedia CD-ROM *National Parks of America* by Multicom uses a map metaphor to provide access to more than 230 parks. Novell uses the metaphor of a bookshelf in its user-support server on the Information Superhighway. The *Multiliteracy CD* uses a flipbook metaphor that makes it easy for you to flip to different chapters on the CD.

Visualizing a Structure

Successful designers are so good at visualizing what an application will be like that they can actually run through it in their minds before creating a single screen. With practice, you can develop this ability.

For example, consider the billboard metaphor pictured in Figure 45-9. Think of the billboard as the home screen for a multimedia application about the Internet. Imagine how the words and pictures printed on the billboard could trigger the text, graphics, audio, and video in an application about the Internet. Pause for a few moments and think about how you could design such an application. Then turn the page and study Figure 45-10.

Did you imagine something like the structure shown in Figure 45-10? Notice how the billboard functions as a menu. The first item, "Discover the Information Superhighway," links to a screen that defines the Internet. Clicking the mouse returns the user to the billboard. This is the simplest part of the design. The second menu item, "Explore How It Serves You," launches a submenu listing the kinds of things you can do on the Internet; each submenu item triggers a screen explaining an Internet service. "Test-drive the Internet" lets the user select interesting places to visit on the Information Superhighway and, if a real Internet connection is present, takes the user to those places.

In addition to hypertext, the billboard also contains a few hyperpictures. The Weather icon launches a series of images showing current weather conditions. The images follow a linear list design in which the mouse functions like a remote

45-9

A billboard metaphor for the Information Superhighway application.

of the Information Superhighway application.

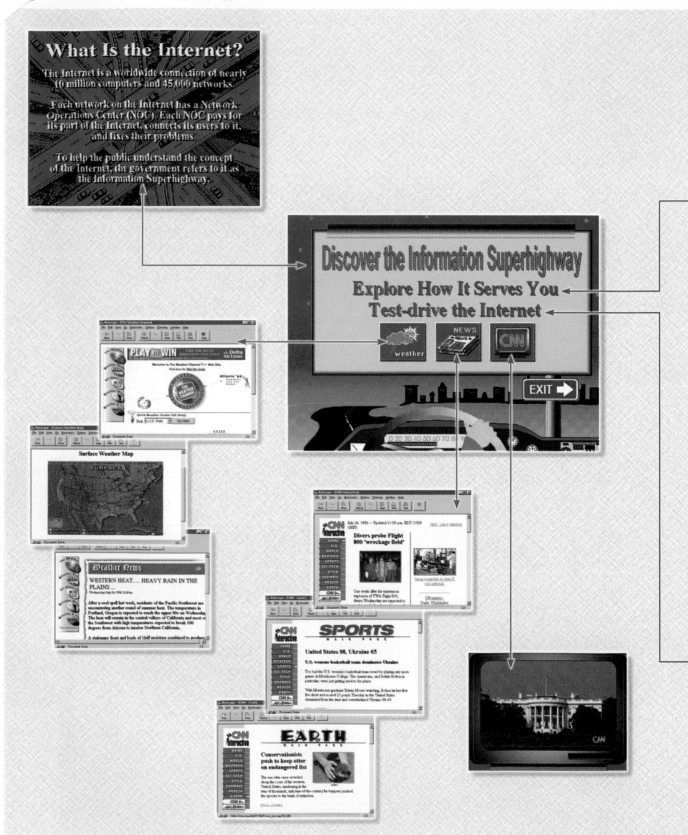

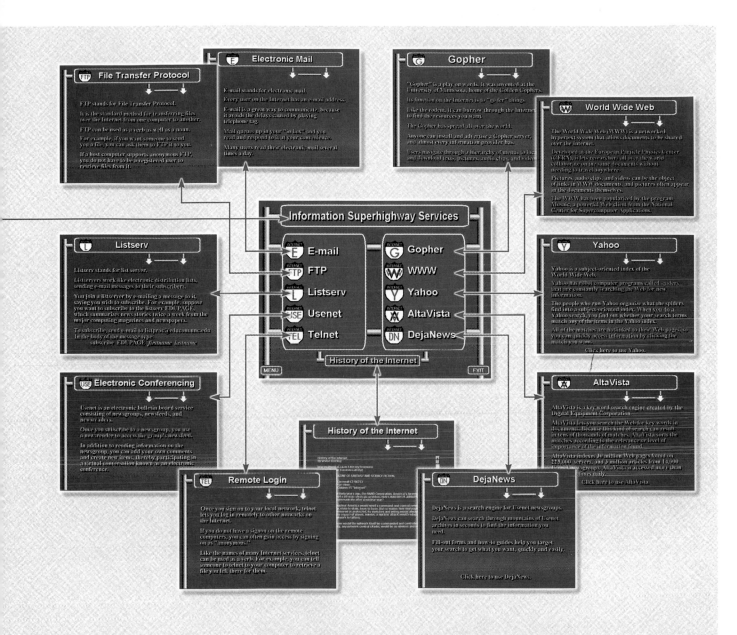

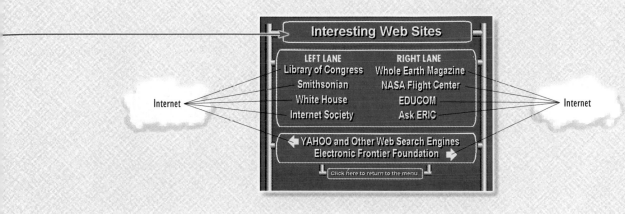

control for a 35mm slide projector; a left mouse click moves the user forward through the list, and a right mouse click moves the user backward. The News icon is linked to an electronic news feed that presents its information as a hierarchy. The Television icon is a live video feed from the CNN newsroom. Users with the necessary hardware will be able to click there to go live to CNN. Finally, the Exit sign provides a graceful way for the user to leave the application.

You can run the Information Superhighway application on the *Multiliteracy CD.* Go to the Demonstrations section, select Textbook Examples, and click the Information Superhighway button. Refer to the diagram in Figure 45-10 as you run the application. As you click the different buttons and hypertext options, keep track of where you are in the diagram. This will help you develop a feel for moving about the hyperspace that gets created when you trigger the links on a multimedia screen.

The Systems Approach

Development projects follow a continuous cycle of design, development, and evaluation that is known as the **systems approach** to instructional design. Figure 45-11 shows an artful depiction of the process from *Designer's Edge* by

45-11

The project development cycle as depicted on the cover of *Designer's Edge* by Allen Communication.

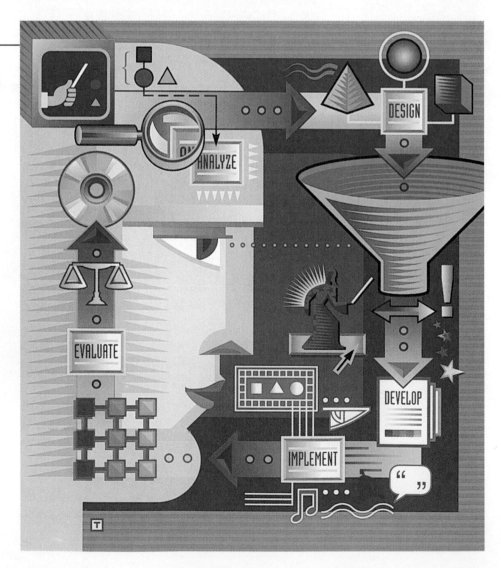

Allen Communication. *Designer's Edge* is an integrated set of preauthoring tools and wizards intended to accelerate the analysis, design, and evaluation of effective technology-based training materials. A visual, task-driven interface walks the user through the entire instructional design process from analysis to evaluation. *Designer's Edge* is a Windows 95 application. There is a demonstration of *Designer's Edge* on the *Multiliteracy CD*. To run the demo, go to the Demonstrations section, select Software, and click *Designer's Edge*. For more information about *Designer's Edge*, go to http://www.allencomm.com.

E X E R C I S E S

1. Draw a diagram showing the structure of the History of Flight application you created in Part Six.

2. What design paradigm(s) does the History of Flight application use? Refer to the diagram you drew in response to the previous question when answering this question.

3. As described in chapter 9, Authorware and IconAuthor use flowcharting symbols as an on-screen aid to program development. Run the Authorware and IconAuthor demos on the *Multiliteracy CD*; go to the Demonstrations section, select Software, and click on either the Authorware button or the IconAuthor button. How do these packages compare with regard to their use of flowcharting symbols? What symbols do both packages have in common? What symbols are different?

4. Discuss the advantages and disadvantages in the use of the flowcharting metaphor in Authorware and IconAuthor. How does flowcharting enhance the development of multimedia applications? Does the flowcharting metaphor hinder the developer in any way? If so, how?

5. Run the *Designer's Edge* demo on the *Multiliteracy CD*. How do you think *Designer's Edge* could help you plan and carry out a multimedia development project? Are there any major omissions from the tools and wizards in *Designer's Edge?*

46 CD-ROM Resources for Creating Advanced Applications

After completing this chapter, you will be able to:

- Locate the libraries for clip art, clip music, and clip video on the *Multiliteracy CD*

- Create multimedia greeting cards to send to your friends and relatives

- Create an interactive kiosk

- Make an electronic brochure

- Create an Information Superhighway application

- Use a flipbook metaphor to make applications easy to use

THE *Multiliteracy CD* contains a selection of clip art, music, and video that you can use to practice creating multimedia applications. This chapter identifies the directories where you will find this material and suggests topics for multimedia applications you can create with it.

Whenever you use the material provided in this chapter, please acknowledge the vendors who graciously provided the clip media for the *Multiliteracy CD* by including a statement such as the following on the title page of your application:

> **This application includes clip art, music, and video provided courtesy of *Company Name*.**

If a copyright notice appears as part of a bitmap on the *Multiliteracy CD,* do not remove that notice when you use the bitmap in your application. The vendors who provided these images did so on the condition that the copyright notice appear on-screen along with the image at all times.

Clip Media on the *Multiliteracy CD*

The clip media on the *Multiliteracy CD* is organized according to five multimedia application topics: greeting cards, kiosks, electronic brochures, Internet services, and flipbook metaphor. Table 46-1 identifies the vendors who graciously donated

Table 46-1 Vendors of Clip Media on the *Multiliteracy CD*

Vendor Name	Type of Media	Address
Ensoniq Corporation	MIDI music	http://www.ensoniq.com 155 Great Valley Parkway, P.O. Box 303, Malvern, PA 19355-0735 (610) 647-3930 (voice) (610) 647-8908 (fax)
Michael Ford Archives	MIDI music	MFArchives@aol.com 103 Daisey Lane, Malvern, PA 19355 (610) 889-9744 (voice/fax)
Voyetra Technologies	MIDI music	http://www.voyetra.com 5 Odell Plaza, Yonkers, NY 10701-1406 (800) 233-9377 (voice) (914) 966-1102 (fax)
Chameleon Music	CD Audio	http://chameleonm@aol.com P.O. Box 339, Agawam, MA 01001 (413) 789-1917 (voice/fax)
BeachWare	Waveform sound effects, photos, backgrounds, textures, and videos	http://www.beachware.com 9419 Mt. Isreal Road, Escondido, CA 92029 (619) 735-8945 (voice/fax)
Jasmine Multimedia Publishing	Photos, backgrounds, waveform music, and videos	http://www.jasmine.com 6746 Valjean Ave., Suite 100, Van Nuys, CA 91406

these clips for use on the *Multiliteracy CD*. These vendors hope that you will contact them when you need to purchase additional clip art or music.

Greeting Cards

You can make multimedia greeting cards with clip art and music on the *Multiliteracy CD*. By adding your own text and waveform audio recording, you can personalize the card to make it appropriate for the friend or relative to whom you send it. Part Nine of this book will show you how to send the card over the Internet as multimedia e-mail. To create a multimedia greeting card, follow these steps:

▶ Create a directory on your hard drive that will contain the greeting card.

▶ Use PODIUM to create a new custom screen in your newly created greeting card directory.

▶ Select an appropriate backdrop from the greeting-card clip-media index provided in Table 46-2, which lists backdrops for birthday cards, get-well cards, Christmas, Valentine's Day, Easter, Mother's Day, Father's Day, Thanksgiving, and general-purpose thank-you cards.

 ▶ If you want some background music, use the Backdrop tool to select an appropriate waveform audio or MIDI file from Table 46-2.

 ▶ Use the Text tool to personalize the card with a salutation such as "Dear Mom." Write your message on the card, and end with a complimentary closing such as "Love, Fred."

▶ Use the Waveform Audio tool to record yourself singing an appropriate song, such as "Happy Birthday." You should be aware that "Happy Birthday" is a copyrighted song. If you include a recording of "Happy Birthday" in an application you plan to publish, you may need to pay a royalty. To find out contact ASCAP at http://www.ascap.com.

Table 46-2 Clip-Media Index for Creating Greeting Cards*

Filename	Purpose	Publisher
media\greeting\bitmaps\birthday.bmp	Birthday, adult	McGraw-Hill
media\greetings\bitmaps\kidsday.bmp	Birthday, juvenile	McGraw-Hill
media\greeting\bitmaps\get_well.bmp	Get-well	McGraw-Hill
media\greeting\bitmaps\xmas.bmp	Christmas	McGraw-Hill
media\greeting\bitmaps\valentin.bmp	Valentine's Day	McGraw-Hill
media\greeting\bitmaps\moms_day.bmp	Mother's Day	McGraw-Hill
media\greeting\bitmaps\dads_day.bmp	Father's Day	McGraw-Hill
media\greeting\bitmaps\easter.bmp	Easter	McGraw-Hill
media\greeting\bitmaps\thankday.bmp	Thanksgiving	McGraw-Hill
media\greeting\bitmaps\thankyou.bmp	Thank you	McGraw-Hill
media\midi\jazz.mid	Jazz mood music	Voyetra
media\midi\playful.mid	Playful music	Voyetra
media\midi\xmas.mid	Christmas mood music	Michael Ford Archives
media\midi\classic.mid	Classical mood music	Ensoniq
media\midi\happy.mid	Happy mood music	Voyetra
media\midi\touchy.mid	Sensitive mood music	Ensoniq

*Even more resources are found in the *media\greetings* directory.

 ► Put a button or a hypertext on the screen that the user can click to trigger your song. If you have a photograph to show along with the singing of the song, your link could take the following form:

```
directory\myphoto.bmp @wait=0
directory\mysong.wav @wait=end
```

► Do whatever else you want to personalize the greeting card.

► Test the card thoroughly to make sure all of the links and special effects work properly.

As mentioned earlier, Part Nine will show you how to send the card over the Internet as multimedia e-mail. If the person to whom you want to send the card is not on the Internet, you can publish the card on diskettes and send the diskettes instead; Part Twelve teaches you how to publish applications on diskettes.

Kiosks (Interactive Restaurant Guide)

A **kiosk** is a multimedia PC used to provide people with information on demand. Although kiosks normally have expensive touch-screen displays housed in tamper-proof cabinets in public places like airports, hotel lobbies, and shopping malls, you can run kiosk applications on low-cost configurations without touch screens and cabinets if the computer will be used in an environment where vandalism is not a risk. The clip-art library on the *Multiliteracy CD* contains backdrops designed for making a kiosk to advertise the restaurants found in your town or city. To create an interactive restaurant guide, follow these steps:

Table 46-3 Clip-Media Index for Creating Restaurant Kiosk*

Filename	Purpose	Publisher
media\kiosk\bitmaps\home.bmp	Home screen	McGraw-Hill
media\kiosk\bitmaps\menu.bmp	Restaurant menu border	McGraw-Hill
media\kiosk\bitmaps\winelist.bmp	Wine list backdrop	Jasmine
media\kiosk\bitmaps\italian.bmp	Italian cuisine backdrop	Jasmine
media\kiosk\bitmaps\french.bmp	French cuisine backdrop	Jasmine
media\kiosk\bitmaps\american.bmp	American cuisine backdrop	Jasmine
media\kiosk\bitmaps\chinese.bmp	Chinese cuisine backdrop	Jasmine
media\kiosk\bitmaps\desserts.bmp	Desserts backdrop	McGraw-Hill
media\kiosk\bitmaps\money.bmp	Money—coins, spare change	McGraw-Hill
media\midi\r&b.mid	Rhythm & blues	Ensoniq
media\midi\softjazz.mid	Soft jazz	Ensoniq
media\midi\funky.mid	Jazz funk	Ensoniq
media\midi\piano.mid	Piano music	Voyetra
media\wave\eating.wav	Ambient restaurant sound	McGraw-Hill
media\wave\cork_pop.wav	Champagne cork popping	BeachWare

*Even more resources are found in the *media\kiosk* directory.

▶ Create a directory on your hard drive that will contain the kiosk application.

▶ Use PODIUM to create a new custom screen in your newly created kiosk directory.

 ▶ Select an appropriate backdrop from the kiosk backgrounds listed in Table 46-3.

 ▶ Use the Text tool to list the cuisines (types of food such as Italian, Chinese, French, or American) you want your kiosk to advertise.

 ▶ Link each cuisine to a new custom screen devoted to that style of food. List the names of the restaurants in your locale serving that kind of food.

▶ To each restaurant listed in the previous step, link a screen telling about the menu choices and prices. If the restaurant serves wine, provide a button that brings up the restaurant's wine list.

▶ Customize your kiosk by including waveform audio recordings telling more about the restaurants. Link these recordings to the backdrop of the screen that should trigger the audio, or put the recordings on a timer that will make the recording start after the user has had a chance to look at the screen for a while.

More-advanced features you might consider including in your restaurant kiosk are listed as follows:

■ Put a timer on each screen to trigger an attract loop. If no one interacts with your kiosk for a minute or so, the attract loop will begin and continue running until a user clicks the mouse or touches the screen of a touch-screen kiosk.

■   Use input fields to let the user specify the kind of restaurant being sought. For example, you might provide input fields for the user to specify the type of cuisine and the maximum price the user is willing to pay for the meal. Depending on what the user enters into the input fields, you would display an appropriate list of restaurants in the area.

Electronic Brochures

In the corporate world, electronic brochures are a hot trend in multimedia. Instead of sending customers a printed brochure, you mail them a diskette or a CD-ROM that presents the material in an interactive format. The rate of response to an electronic brochure is more than 10 times higher than that of a printed brochure. The *Multiliteracy CD* contains materials for creating an electronic brochure out of a company's annual report. To create an electronic brochure, follow these steps:

▶   Create a directory on your hard drive that will contain the electronic brochure.

▶   Use PODIUM to create a new custom screen in your newly created brochure directory.

 ▶   Select an appropriate backdrop from the electronic brochure backgrounds listed in Table 46-4.

 ▶   Use the Text tool to create a table of contents in which the user can click items to go to different sections of the electronic brochure. Table 46-4 lists clip art that will help you create sales reports, growth projections, organizational charts, and attractive forms for framing textual information.

 ▶   To each item in the table of contents, create a link to a new custom screen that will present that item's information.

▶   Use the business clip art and music listed in Table 46-4 to give your electronic brochure the proper look and feel. The *buttons* directory contains professional-looking three-dimensional button shapes that you can use as you see fit.

After you complete an electronic brochure, you can follow the instructions in Part Twelve to distribute it as a multimedia diskette or CD that will engage the user interactively. Plus, if your customers have Internet access, you can e-mail them your annual report, as shown in Part Nine of this book.

Table 46-4   Clip-Media Index for Creating Electronic Brochures*

Filename	Purpose	Publisher
media\brochure\bitmaps\contents.bmp	Table of contents backdrop	McGraw-Hill
media\brochure\bitmaps\sales.bmp	Sales report backdrop	McGraw-Hill
media\brochure\bitmaps\growth.bmp	Growth projection backdrop	McGraw-Hill
media\brochure\bitmaps\orgchart.bmp	Organizational chart backdrop	McGraw-Hill
media\brochure\bitmaps\frame.bmp	Professional text frame	McGraw-Hill
media\midi\upbeat.mid	Upbeat music	Voyetra

*Even more resources are found in the *media\brochure* directory.

Information Superhighway Application

The Internet is a hot topic that almost everyone is interested in. Recall from Chapter 45 the design of an Information Superhighway application based on a billboard metaphor. The screens that tell about different Internet services are illustrated with attractive highway signs that have a three-dimensional look. All of the resources that were used to create the Information Superhighway application are available for your use on the *Multiliteracy CD*. The text that appears on the road signs in the illustrations in Chapter 45 was layered onto the background graphic with the Text tool; the text is not part of the graphic. Therefore, you can easily repurpose those Information Superhighway backdrops by using the Text tool to make the road signs say whatever you want.

Because the Information Superhighway application exists on the *Multiliteracy CD* as a series of PODIUM custom screens, you can use the *.cus* files as multimedia resources for making your own Internet applications. The *.cus* files are listed along with the other Information Superhighway resources in the Internet clip-media index provided in Table 46-5.

Table 46-5   Internet Clip-Media Index*

Filename	Purpose	Publisher
highway\bitmaps\billboard.bmp	Billboard backdrop	McGraw-Hill
highway\bitmaps\highway.bmp	Ribbons of highways backdrop	McGraw-Hill
highway\bitmaps\bigsign1.bmp	Info services menu backdrop	McGraw-Hill
highway\bitmaps\sign.bmp	Single street sign backdrop	McGraw-Hill
highway\bitmaps\bigsign2.bmp	Interesting Web sites backdrop	McGraw-Hill
highway\custom\infohigh.cus	Information Superhighway home screen	McGraw-Hill
highway\custom\internet.cus	What Is the Internet screen	McGraw-Hill
highway\custom\services.cus	Info Highway Services menu custom screen	McGraw-Hill
highway\custom\e-mail.cus	Electronic mail custom screen	McGraw-Hill
highway\custom\ftp.cus	FTP custom screen	McGraw-Hill
highway\custom\listserv.cus	Listserv custom screen	McGraw-Hill
highway\custom\usenet.cus	Usenet custom screen	McGraw-Hill
highway\custom\telnet.cus	Telnet custom screen	McGraw-Hill
highway\custom\gopher.cus	Gopher custom screen	McGraw-Hill
highway\custom\www.cus	World Wide Web custom screen	McGraw-Hill
highway\custom\yahoo.cus	Yahoo custom screen	McGraw-Hill
highway\custom\altavsta.cus	AltaVista custom screen	McGraw-Hill
highway\custom\dejanews.cus	DejaNews custom screen	McGraw-Hill
highway\custom\history.cus	History of the Internet custom screen	McGraw-Hill
ml_demo\history.txt	History of the Internet text file	McGraw-Hill

*Even more resources are found in the *media\highway* directory.

Flipbook Metaphor

You have probably been impressed by the flipbook metaphor used on the *Multiliteracy CD*. Because the flipbook makes it easy to jump to any section of the CD anytime you want, users never get lost in the material on the *Multiliteracy CD*. To enable you to make use of the flipbook metaphor in your applications, the clip-media index in Table 46-6 identifies some of the backgrounds used to create the flipbook screens. Feel free to make use of these design elements in creating your own flipbooks.

Table 46-6   Clip-Media Index for Creating Flipbook Screens*

Filename	Purpose	Publisher
media\flipbook\f1.bmp	First folder	McGraw-Hill
media\flipbook\f1_ch.bmp	First folder, chapter page	McGraw-Hill
media\flipbook\f1_pg.bmp	First folder, information page	McGraw-Hill
media\flipbook\f2.bmp	Second folder	McGraw-Hill
media\flipbook\f2_ch.bmp	Second folder, chapter page	McGraw-Hill
media\flipbook\f2_pg.bmp	Second folder, information page	McGraw-Hill

*Up to seven folders with appropriate chapter and information pages have been provided.

Clip Sound Effects

Table 46-7 lists clip sound effects provided on the *Multiliteracy CD*. You can use these sounds to embellish your applications. A special effect can be achieved by linking a sound effect to a button or hypertext link. When the user clicks, you play the sound effect, then trigger the link. To create such a special effect, put the sound effect at the top of the links, as follows:

```
whatever.wav @wait=end
whatever.cus
```

Table 46-7   Clip Sound Effects*

Filename	Purpose	Publisher
media\soundfx\ding.wav	Ding	BeachWare
media\soundfx\cord.wav	Chord	BeachWare
media\soundfx\swoosh.wav	Swoosh	BeachWare
media\soundfx\gunshot.wav	Gunshot	BeachWare
media\soundfx\cork.wav	Champagne cork popping	BeachWare
media\soundfx\next.wav	Next noise	BeachWare
media\soundfx\back.wav	Back noise	BeachWare
media\soundfx\footstep.wav	Footsteps	Chameleon Music
media\soundfx\typewrit.wav	Typewriter	Chameleon Music

*Even more resources are found in the *media\soundfx* directory.

E X E R C I S E S

1. You probably have a friend who has a multimedia PC. Use the multimedia resources in the greeting-card section of this chapter to make a greeting card to send to your friend. If your friend has an Internet connection, you can use Part Nine of this book to send the card in a multimedia e-mail envelope. Otherwise, you can use Part Twelve to send the card on a multimedia diskette or CD-ROM.

2. Get a copy of the Yellow Pages from your town's phone book. Study the restaurant advertisements, select a few of your favorites, and create a kiosk application advertising them. Demonstrate your kiosk to the restaurant owners or your town's Chamber of Commerce. You might stimulate some interest in creating multimedia kiosks in your town. This could create jobs for multimedia developers such as yourself or others who would like to be paid to work on such a project.

3. Get your organization's annual report. If you are a student, get ahold of a brochure about your school, or ask any businessperson you know for a copy of their annual report. Make an electronic brochure out of it. If the person from whom you obtained the report has an Internet connection, use Part Nine of this book to send the electronic brochure in a multimedia e-mail envelope. Otherwise, use Part Twelve to distribute the report on diskettes.

47 Downloading Multimedia Resources from the Internet

After completing this chapter, you will be able to:

- Use Internet search engines to locate resources in specific application content areas

- Download text and graphics from the Internet

- Download audio and video resources from the Internet

- Use proper bibliographic form when citing sources from which Internet materials were downloaded

- Use good judgment in deciding what is a fair use, and what requires copyright clearance, when downloading materials from the Internet

 **H E** richest source of multimedia materials on the planet is at your fingertips when you are connected to the World Wide Web. Never before have students had such a fantastic resource for scholarship and research. Millions of texts, images, audios, and videos await you on the Web.

This chapter teaches you how to use search engines to find materials that pertain to your application's content area. You will learn how to use Yahoo to perform subject-oriented searches, and AltaVista to perform key word searches on documents. You will be amazed how quickly you can have just the right multimedia resources on your screen.

After you learn how to locate resources on the Internet, this chapter proceeds to teach you how to download multimedia objects to your computer's hard drive. Before using a resource downloaded from the Internet, you need to determine whether your purpose falls within the Fair Use guidelines; if not, you must seek copyright clearance in order to obtain the legal right to use the material. Finally, you will learn the proper bibliographic form for citing electronic information.

Internet Search Engines

Figures 47-1 through 47-5 illustrate several search engines on the Internet that can help you locate resources in your application's content area. You access the search engines by pointing your World Wide Web browser at the addresses listed in Table 47-1. The search engine will provide you with a blank field into which you type one or more search terms or key words that indicate what you seek.

As this book goes to press, the most famous search engines are Yahoo and AltaVista. Yahoo is a good place to begin your search. Yahoo has robot computer programs called spiders that are constantly searching the Web for new information. The people who run Yahoo organize what the spiders find into a subject-oriented index. When you do a Yahoo search, you find out whether your search terms

47-1

The Yahoo search engine.

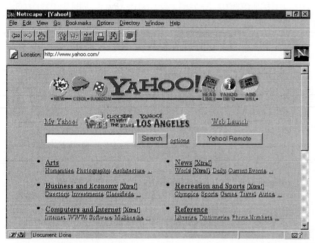

47-2

The AltaVista search engine.

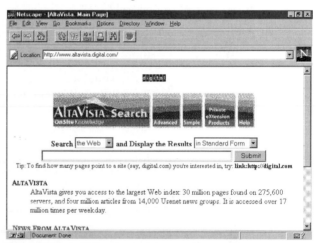

47-3

The Lycos search engine.

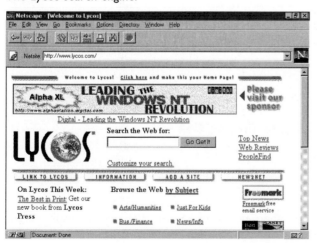

47-4

The WebCrawler search engine.

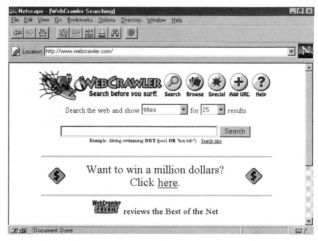

47-5

The Excite search engine.

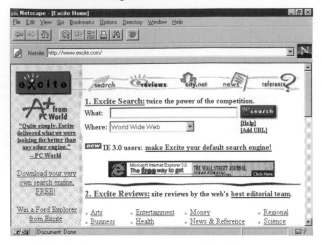

match any of the items in the Yahoo index. All of the items listed are hotlinked to their Web pages, so you can quickly access information by clicking the indexed entry. A nice feature of Yahoo is that if you don't find what you want, Yahoo provides buttons you can click to try other search engines.

AltaVista is a search engine created by the Digital Equipment Corporation. Like Yahoo, AltaVista has spiders that are constantly combing the Web and feeding information into a database. Unlike Yahoo, AltaVista does not organize the Web according to subject areas; rather, AltaVista lets you search for key words in documents, regardless of the "subject" of the documents. AltaVista is therefore likely to produce more "hits" than Yahoo, but the hits may not be as relevant to your subject. AltaVista sorts the hits according to the relevance or level of importance of the information found. As this book goes to press, AltaVista indexes 30 million Web pages found on 225,000 servers, and 3 million articles from 14,000 Usenet newsgroups. According to Digital, AltaVista is accessed more than 10 million times daily.

Search engines are undergoing a lot of research and development on the Internet. By the time you read this, new search engines will have been announced that were not available when this book went to press. You can use Yahoo to find out the latest information about new search engines and what they do. Point your Web browser at http://www.yahoo.com, go to the Yahoo section on Computers and Internet, and do a search for the key word *search*.

Table 47-1 World Wide Web Addresses of Internet Search Engines

Search Engine	Kind of Search	Web Address
Yahoo	Subject-oriented search	http://www.yahoo.com
AltaVista	Searches for key words in documents	http://www.altavista.digital.com
Lycos	Searches Carnegie Mellon University's Worldwide Internet Catalog	http://www.lycos.com
WebCrawler	Global Network Navigator search engine licensed by America Online	http://www.webcrawler.com
Excite	Concept search or key word search	http://www.excite.com

How to Do a Yahoo Search

To perform a Yahoo search, follow these steps:

▶ Point your Web browser at http://www.yahoo.com; the Yahoo home page appears.

▶ If you want to search all of Yahoo, type your key word(s) into the blank search field and click the Search button.

▶ If you want to search within a Yahoo subject area, scroll down through the subjects listed on the Yahoo home page and click on the subject area you want; the Yahoo subject area page appears.

47-6

The advanced search options screen in Yahoo.

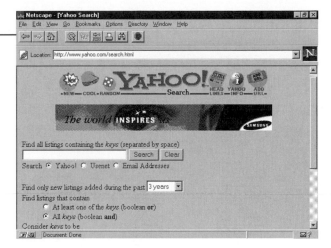

▶ If subtopics are listed on the subject area page, scroll through the subtopics and select the one you want. Repeat this process until you have narrowed the subject area of your search.

▶ When you are ready to conduct a search, type your key word(s) into the blank search field.

▶ Click the option to search all of Yahoo, or just the subject area you have chosen.

▶ Click the Search button; Yahoo will perform the search and display the items that match your key word(s).

▶ Scroll through the matches to see what Yahoo found. All of the matches are hyperlinked; to see an item, click a highlighted word.

▶ If there are more matches to be displayed, you will find "Next 25 matches" printed at the bottom of the search results. Click "Next 25 matches" if you want to see more.

By default, Yahoo combines your search terms with the Boolean **AND** which means that you will get a match only when all of the search terms are found together in an item. If you want a Boolean **OR** done instead, click the word *Options* next to the Search button, and the advanced search screen appears as shown in Figure 47 6. In addition to letting you set the Boolean OR option, the advanced options let you choose whether to search Usenet newsgroups, e-mail addresses, or the Yahoo index. You can specify whether search terms are considered to be substrings, which means that if the search term appears as part of a larger word, you want Yahoo to consider that a match. You can also change the number of entries that Yahoo will return on each Web page of your search results; the default number is 25 entries per page.

How to Do an Advanced Search with AltaVista

To make the most effective use of AltaVista, you need to know how to do an advanced search. To perform an advanced search, follow these steps:

▶ Point your Web browser at http://www.altavista.digital.com; the AltaVista home page appears.

47-7
_____

AltaVista's advanced search
screen.

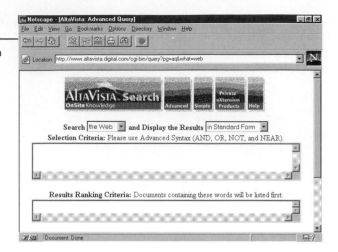

▶ Click the Advanced Search button; the advanced search screen appears as
shown in Figure 47-7.

▶ In the Selection Criteria field, you type your search terms using Advanced
Search Syntax, which allows you to:

▪ Put quote marks around phrases you want treated as search terms; for
example, **"Martin Luther"** will search for the words *Martin* and *Luther*
appearing next to each other

▪ Use the operators AND, OR, NOT, and NEAR; for example, to search for
Martin Luther but not *Martin Luther King,* you would enter **"Martin
Luther" AND NOT "Martin Luther King"**

▪ Use parentheses to group search terms, such as **"Martin Luther King"
AND ("I Have a Dream" OR "Letter from a Birmingham Jail")**

▶ In the Results Ranking Criteria field, you have the option of specifying words
for AltaVista to use in sorting the matches it finds; if you do not want the
matches sorted, leave this field blank.

Almost anything in the world that you want to know is retrievable once you
develop skill at using the Advanced Search Syntax. The exercises at the end of this
chapter will help you develop this skill. For more information about advanced
searching, click "Selection Criteria" on the AltaVista advanced search screen.

Movie on CD

Demonstrations
➡ Show Me!
   ➡ Downloading
   Internet
   Resources
      ➡ **Downloading
      Text**

Downloading Text from the Internet

The quickest way to download text from the Internet is to copy the text onto the
Windows Clipboard, from which you can paste the text into any other window on
your screen. Most Web browsers let you copy text onto the Clipboard. To download
text this way, follow these steps:

▶ Use your Web browser to display the text you want to download.

▶ Drag the mouse over the text you want to copy; the selected text will appear
highlighted. Or, if you want to select all of the text on the Web page, pull down
the browser's Edit menu and choose Select All.

▶ Press the Windows copy key Ctrl-C or pull down the browser's Edit menu
and choose Copy.

▶ If the application into which you want to paste the text is not already running, get it running now.

▶ Position the cursor at the spot in the window to which you want to paste the text.

▶ Press the Windows paste key Ctrl-V or pull down the application's Edit menu and choose Paste.

Most Web browsers permit you to download the HTML source code of the Web page on the screen. To download all of the HTML source code, follow these steps:

▶ Pull down the browser's File menu and choose Save As; the Windows Save As dialog will appear.

▶ Type the path\filename under which you want the HTML to be saved.

▶ Click OK to save the HTML.

If you want to download only part of the HTML, pull down the browser's View menu and choose Document Source. When the HTML source code appears, drag the mouse to select the HTML codes you want and press the Windows copy key Ctrl-C. Then position the cursor where you want to paste the HTML, and press the Windows paste key Ctrl-V.

Movie on CD

Demonstrations
➥ Show Me!
  ➥ Downloading
  Internet
  Resources
    ➥ **Downloading
    Graphics**

Downloading Graphics from the Internet

The quickest way to download a graphic from the Internet is to use your Web browser's option for saving the image to a file. For example, if you are using Netscape, you can usually save a graphic to a file by clicking the graphic with the right mouse button. A popout menu will give you an option to "Save this image as . . ." When you select that option, the Windows Save As dialog appears.

If your Web browser does not have this option, or if the graphics file format used by the Save As option is not the type of image you want, you can grab the graphic with Paint Shop Pro. Many users prefer using Paint Shop Pro because they already learned how to use it in Chapter 31 of this book.

Downloading Audio and Video from the Internet

If your Web browser supports the option to download links, you can download any audio or video file that has been linked to a Web page. For example, if you have Netscape, you can download audio or video files by following these steps:

▶ Click the right mouse button on the hot spot that you normally click with your left button to play the object—the Options menu pops out.

▶ Choose the option Save this link as . . . ; the Save As dialog appears.

▶ Type the path\filename under which you want the link to be saved. Make sure you give the filename the proper extension for the type of object you are saving. For example, if the object is a Video for Windows movie, give it the *.avi* filename extension. If the object is a Windows waveform audio file, give it the *.wav* filename extension.

▶ Press ←Enter or click the Save button to save the file.

Bibliographic Form for Citing Internet Resources

University of Vermont librarians Xia Li and Nancy Crane are working on a book entitled *Electronic Styles: An Expanded Guide to Citing Electronic Information*, which should be in print by the time you read this. Li and Crane provide guidelines for citing information in American Psychological Association (APA) and Modern Language Association (MLA) styles from databases, electronic mail, listservers, newsgroups, Gopher, and the World Wide Web. For the latest information on the availability of the Li and Crane book, visit their Web site at http://www.uvm.edu/ ~xli/reference/estyles.html. The guidelines provided here were taken from the Li and Crane Web site in the section on citing World Wide Web resources in the APA style. You can also view MLA style guidelines at the Li and Crane Web site.

Keep in mind that the goal of citing electronic information is to make it possible for the user to retrieve the information again. When you cite an electronic source, you should make sure that the information you provide allows the work to be retrieved. Check the punctuation and capitalization in the citation's URL. Sometimes it is not possible to determine the original date of publication of a World Wide Web resource. If the date is not available, type **no date** in the space provided for the date of publication.

Here are the Li and Crane guidelines for citing World Wide Web information in the APA style for individual works, parts of works, journal articles, magazine articles, and newspaper articles:

INDIVIDUAL WORKS

Author/editor. (Year). *Title* (edition), [Type of medium]. Producer (optional). Available Protocol (e.g., HTTP): Site/Path/File [Access date].

Example:

Pritzker, T. J. (1992). *An early fragment from central Nepal* [Online]. Available: http://www.ingress.com/~astanart/pritzker/pritzker.html [1995, June 8].

PARTS OF WORKS

Author/editor. (Year). Title. In *Source* (edition), [Type of medium]. Producer (optional). Available Protocol (e.g., HTTP): Site/Path/File [Access date].

Example:

Daniel, R. T. (1995). The history of Western music. In *Britannica online: Macropaedia* [Online]. Available: http://www.eb.com:180/cgi-bin/g:DocF=macro/ 5004/45/0.html [1995, June 14].

JOURNAL ARTICLES

Author. (Year). Title. *Journal Title* [Type of medium], *volume*(issue), paging or indicator of length. Available Protocol (e.g., HTTP): Site/Path/File [Access date].

Examples:

Carriveau, K. L., Jr. [Review of the book *Environmental hazards: Marine pollution*]. *Electronic Green Journal* [Online], *2*(1), 3 paragraphs. Available: gopher:// gopher.uidaho.edu/11/UI_gopher/library/egj03/carriv01.html [1995, June 21].

Inada, K. (1995). A Buddhist response to the nature of human rights. *Journal of Buddhist Ethics* [Online], *2,* 9 paragraphs. Available: http://www.cac.psu.edu/jbe/twocont.html [1995, June 21].

MAGAZINE ARTICLES

Author. (Year, month day). Title. *Magazine Title* [Type of medium], *volume* (if given), paging or indicator of length. Available Protocol (e.g., HTTP): Site/Path/File [Access date].

Example:

Viviano, F. (1995, May/June). The new Mafia order. *Mother Jones Magazine* [Online], 72 paragraphs. Available: http://www.mojones.com/MOTHER_JONES/MJ95/viviano.html [1995, July 17].

NEWSPAPER ARTICLES

Author. (Year, month day). Title. *Newspaper Title* [Type of medium], paging or indicator of length. Available Protocol (e.g., HTTP): Site/Path/File [Access date].

Example:

Johnson, T. (1994, December 5). Indigenous people are now more combative, organized. *Miami Herald* [Online], p. 29SA (22 paragraphs). Available: gopher://summit.fiu.edu/Miami Herald--Summit-Related Articles/12/05/95--Indigenous People Now More Combative, Organized [1995, July 16].

Fair Use Guidelines for Downloading Internet Resources

The CCUMC Fair Use Guidelines for Educational Multimedia appear on the *Multiliteracy CD.* To view them, go to the Demonstrations section, select Textbook Examples, and click Fair Use Guidelines. Each time you download material from the Internet, check whether your use of the material falls within the CCUMC Fair Use guidelines. If you exceed any one of the guidelines, you must obtain written permission from the copyright holder. For example, when the author of this book downloaded the bibliographic style examples from the Li and Crane Web site, he reflected on the intended use of those examples in this book. Since McGraw-Hill prints tens of thousands of copies of this book and profits from selling it, the author sought and obtained written permission from Li and Crane.

You should also be aware that copyright laws and Fair Use guidelines are subject to change. As this book goes to press, certain members of Congress are attempting to challenge the concept of fair use of materials on the Internet. Because it is so easy to copy material from the Internet, and since the copies are exact duplicates of the original, anything published on the Internet is easily prone to illegal copying. However, this certainly is not a good reason to do away with the concept of fair use on the Internet.

As you learned in Chapter 16, Fair Use is a law of the United States of America. This law gives you the legal right to fair use of all media. Stand up for this right and use the CCUMC guidelines to make fair use of multimedia on the Internet. Tell your state's senators and congressional representatives that you vehemently oppose any attempts to make fair use illegal on the Internet.

EXERCISES

1. Perform a Yahoo search on the key words *set-top box*. How many matches did Yahoo find? Were the documents found appropriate to the topic? Now perform an AltaVista search on *set-top box*. How many matches did AltaVista find? Were the documents retrieved by AltaVista more informative than those found by Yahoo? How do you explain why AltaVista found more matches than Yahoo?

2. Use AltaVista to perform the following searches. How many matches does each search find? Can you explain why these particular searches find progressively fewer matches?

   - `"Martin Luther"`
   - `"Martin Luther" AND NOT "Martin Luther King"`
   - `"Martin Luther King" AND ("I Have a Dream" OR "Letter from a Birmingham Jail")`
   - `"Martin Luther King" AND "Letter from a Birmingham Jail"`

3. Choose one of the documents you found in exercise 2 and write a bibliographic citation for it in APA style. Use this chapter's examples of citing Internet resources as a guide to writing your set-top box citation.

4. Get the Windows Notepad running and practice copying text from your Web browser to the Notepad. If your Web browser does not support the copying of text from a Web page, you should get a browser that does, such as Netscape.

5. Point your browser to a Web page that has an image on it. For example, the Yahoo Web page at http://www.yahoo.com always displays the Yahoo logo. Use your Web browser's image save feature to save the image to a file on your hard drive. For example, if you have Netscape, click the image with the right mouse button, then choose "Save this image as." After you save the image, use Paint Shop Pro to view it. How many colors does the image have? How many pixels are there in the x,y dimensions of the image?

6. Repeat exercise 3 except instead of using your Web browser to save the image, use Paint Shop Pro to grab it off the Web page. How do the statistics compare?

7. Write a letter to your U.S. senators and congressional representatives, letting them know whether or not you support the notion of fair use, and whether you oppose any attempt to make fair use illegal on the Internet. Because the concept of fair use on the Internet is being challenged, it is important for you to take a stand on the issue and let your lawmakers know how you feel about it. You can obtain the mailing addresses of all U.S. senators at http://www.senate.gov. Congressional representatives are at http://www.house.gov. The Senate and House agendas and committee assignments can also be reviewed at these sites.

Part Nine

Multimedia
E-mail

Almost all e-mail sent during the twentieth century relied on one medium: text. In a world that depends heavily on photographs, voice, video, and sound to communicate, users have been constrained by text-only e-mail. Telltale signs that e-mail needs more than text are the emoticons used to convey body language that cannot be seen in a text. For example, if you are just kidding about something you write in an e-mail message, and you want to make sure the reader knows you are not serious, you type the emoticon : -) which conveys a smiling face. Sometimes text-only e-mail conjures other media with phrases like "Picture this," "Imagine what it sounds like," or "If you could only see me now." With multimedia e-mail, you can.

This part of the book teaches you how to send and receive multimedia e-mail. You will be happy to realize that you already know how to create a multimedia e-mail message—with the custom toolbox! Anything you create with the custom toolbox, links and all, can be sent as a multimedia e-mail message to anyone in the world with an Internet e-mail address.

To send and receive multimedia e-mail messages, you need to install an e-mail package that can handle multipurpose mail on the Internet. The *Multiliteracy CD* contains such a multipurpose e-mail package called Eudora, which Chapter 48 shows you how to install and use. Then Chapter 49 shows you how to pack a multimedia application into a PODIUM e-mail envelope, which Chapter 50 enables you to send to anyone on the Internet. So that you can receive multimedia e-mail, Chapter 51 shows you how to read (and hear and play) the multimedia messages people send you in reply.

48

Eudora: A MIME-Compliant E-mail Package

After completing this chapter, you will be able to:

- Understand when to use MIME, the Multipurpose Internet Mail Extensions

- Install the freeware version of Eudora from the *Multiliteracy CD*

- Configure Eudora to work with your Internet connection

- Send and receive messages with Eudora

MULTIMEDIA users are fortunate that there is a freeware version of Eudora. Qualcomm permits us to distribute the freeware in hopes that you will eventually buy the retail version. The freeware version of Eudora is called Eudora Light, and the retail version is called Eudora Pro. This chapter shows you how to install and use Eudora Light. After you install Eudora Light, you will be able to pull down the Help menu and choose About Eudora Pro to learn more about the retail version. For the latest information, point your Web browser at http://www.qualcomm.com/quest.

What Is MIME?

MIME stands for Multipurpose Internet Mail Extensions. MIME is a protocol that lets you attach a file to a mail message. When you send the mail message, the attached file goes along with it. When a user receives the message, the attached file gets decoded and stored on the user's PC, where the file can function just like it does on your PC.

In order to send or receive multimedia e-mail messages, you must have a MIME-compliant e-mail package. If you send a multimedia e-mail message to someone who replies they cannot read it, either because they do not have a MIME e-mailer or a copy of PODIUM, recommend that they purchase a copy of this book and complete Part Nine, which is the part you are reading now.

Installing Eudora from the CD-ROM

Eudora is a MIME-compliant e-mailer. To install Eudora Light from the *Multiliteracy CD,* follow these steps:

▶ If you have Windows 3.1:

    ▪ Pull down the Program Manager's File menu and select Run; the Run dialog appears.

▶ If you have Windows 95:

    ▪ Click the Start button and select Run; the Run dialog appears.

▶ Run the *setup.exe* program in the *EUDORA* directory on the *Multiliteracy CD*. For example, if your CD-ROM drive is D, type **d:\eudora\setup.exe** and press [←Enter].

f:\eudora\setup.exe ← me

▶ Follow the setup instructions to install Eudora onto your computer's hard drive.

Configuring Eudora for Your Internet Connection

Before you can send e-mail with Eudora, you need to configure it for your Internet connection. Follow these steps:

Directory
c:\Eudora

▶ Double-click the Eudora icon to get Eudora running on your computer. Eudora appears on your screen as shown in Figure 48-1.

▶ Pull down the Tools menu and choose Options; the Options dialog appears as shown in Figure 48-2.

▶ To see the different options you can change, use the scroll bar to scroll through the menu of options, then click the option you want to change. Start by clicking the first option in the menu, which is called Getting Started. In the POP account field, enter your Internet e-mail address, such as **toymaker@northpole.com**. In the Real Name field, type your real name, such as **Santa Claus**.

▶ There is one other option that you might want to change. With the Option dialog still on-screen, click Checking Mail to reveal the mail-checking options. Notice the check box for "Leave mail on server." If you check that box, your mail will remain on the mail server when Eudora downloads the mail to your PC. If that box is not checked, Eudora will delete your mail from the server

---

48-1

How the Eudora window appears on startup.

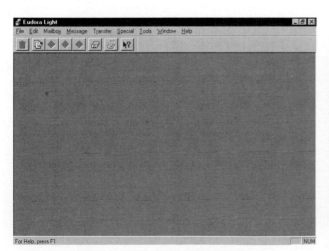

48-2

The Eudora Options dialog. Enter your Internet e-mail address into the POP account field.

after downloading. If you read mail from just one location, such as your PC, you will probably not want that box checked. If you want your messages accessible from multiple locations, such as from your office computer as well as your home PC, you will need to check the box "Leave mail on server."

Sending Simple Messages with Eudora

Movie on CD

Demonstrations
➡ Show Me!
   ➡ Multimedia
      E-mail
      ➡ **Sending**
         Simple
         Messages
         with Eudora

Before attempting to send multimedia e-mail, you should get used to sending ordinary text-based messages with Eudora. Follow these steps:

▶ Pull down the Message menu and choose New Message, or click the New Message icon; a new message window appears as shown in Figure 48-3.

▶ To move from field to field in the message window, you either press (Tab), or click the mouse in the white space next to the field you want to enter.

▶ In the To field, type the e-mail address of the person to whom you want to send a message; the From field will automatically contain your name and e-mail address.

▶ In the Subject field, type a word or phrase that indicates what this message is about.

▶ In the Cc field, if you want to send a copy of this message to someone else, type the e-mail address of the person who should receive a copy; *Cc* stands for carbon copy. *Bcc* stands for blind carbon copy; if you type someone's e-mail address in the Bcc field, that person will get a copy without the knowledge of the person addressed in the To field. Most often, you leave the Bcc field blank.

▶ Leave the Attachments field blank for now. Later on, you will use this field to attach your multimedia e-mail envelope.

▶ Click once beneath the line that appears under the Attachments field; the cursor begins to flash in the main body of the message window. Type the body of the e-mail message. All of the standard Windows text-editing conventions are available to you in this window. For example, if there is text on the Windows Clipboard that you want to paste into your mail message, you can pull down the Edit menu and choose Paste.

48-3

The window in which you compose messages to send people with Eudora.

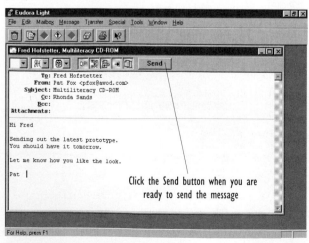

Click the Send button when you are ready to send the message

▶ Read carefully the message you have composed and make any final changes you want before proceeding.

▶ If your computer is not connected to the network at the moment, establish a network connection now. For example, if you are using PPP (the point-to-point protocol used to establish an Internet connection over a modem), get PPP running.

▶ To send the message, click the Send button. While Eudora connects to the Internet, the Progress dialog will appear as shown in Figure 48-4. If Eudora cannot connect, you will get an error message explaining the problem.

48-4

The Progress dialog appears while Eudora connects to the network.

48-5

The Eudora Out Box.

The *S* marks messages that have been sent

The *Q* indicates messages in the queue, waiting to be sent

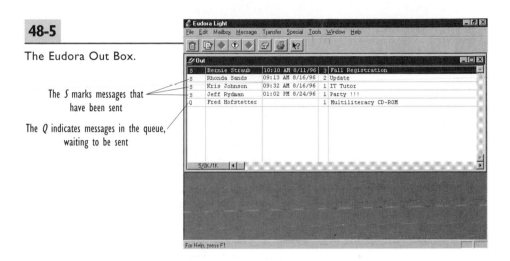

One of the nice features of Eudora is the Out Box, in which you will find copies of the messages you have sent. To review the contents of the Out Box, pull down the Mailbox menu and choose Out. The Out Box appears as shown in Figure 48-5. In the box to the left of each message is a code that indicates with an *S* messages that have been sent, and with a *Q* messages that are in the queue waiting to be sent. To delete a message from the Out Box, click the message once to select it, then press (Delete). To review a message in the Out Box, double-click it.

Movie on CD

Demonstrations
→ Show Me!
  → Multimedia
  E-mail
    → **Receiving**
    Simple
    Messages
    with Eudora

Receiving Simple Messages with Eudora

To read mail with Eudora, follow these steps:

▶ Pull down the Eudora File menu and choose Check Mail.

▶ Eudora will prompt you for your Internet e-mail password; type your password and click OK.

▶ The Progress dialog shown in Figure 48-6 will show you the status as Eudora downloads mail from the e-mail server to your PC.

▶ You can do other things on your computer while the mail downloads. You can even use Eudora to compose more mail messages.

▶ When the mail is downloaded, the New Mail dialog appears as shown in Figure 48-7, and Eudora opens your In Box.

▶ Figure 48-8 shows how the In Box resembles the Out Box. In the first column, a round bullet marks messages that you have not read yet.

48-6

The Eudora Progress dialog shows the number of messages waiting to be downloaded and the percentage of the current message that has been downloaded so far.

48-7

Eudora's New Mail dialog.

48-8

Eudora's In Box resembles the Out Box in look and feel. The round bullet • marks messages that have not been read yet.

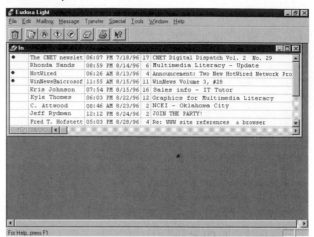

▶ To read a message, double-click it. To respond to a message, press Ctrl-R. To delete a message while reading it, click the trash can icon or press Ctrl-D. To return to your In Box, pull down the Mailbox menu and choose In Box, or press Ctrl-I.

Eudora Function Keys

Table 48-1 lists some of the shortcut keys that can speed up your use of Eudora. To find out about other shortcut keys in Eudora, pull down the Help menu, choose Contents, and click Shortcut Keys.

Table 48-1   Commonly Used Shortcut Keys in Eudora

Shortcut	What the Shortcut Does
Ctrl-D	Deletes the current message
Ctrl-I	Opens the In Box
Ctrl-M	Checks mail; connects to your mail server to see if any messages are waiting for you
Ctrl-N	New message; creates a new message window
Ctrl-R	Replies to a message
Ctrl-C	Copies selected text to the Windows Clipboard
Ctrl-V	Pastes text from the Windows Clipboard to the current cursor location
Ctrl-X	Cuts selected text to the Windows Clipboard

Eudora uses the Windows Multiple Document Interface (MDI) to make it possible for you to have several message windows open at once. The MDI enables you to edit several windows simultaneously and easily cut, copy, and paste information among messages. The exercises below are designed to develop your MDI skills.

1. Get Eudora running and maximize the size of the Eudora window by clicking the maximize button in the Eudora title bar. Then follow these steps:

▶ Pull down the Eudora Message menu and choose New Message, or click the New Message icon. A new message window appears.

▶ Create a message to someone. Do not send the message yet. Instead, click the New Message icon again; another message window appears.

▶ Create another message to somebody else. Do not send the message. Instead, click the message window's minimize button. When the window minimizes, you will see the first message window you created in this exercise.

▶ Click the first message window's minimize button. When the window minimizes, you will be able to see any other windows that might be open in Eudora at the moment. Click their minimize buttons.

▶ Keep clicking the minimize buttons until the only window not minimized is the Eudora main window. Now you will see all of the minimized windows' title bars at the bottom of the Eudora main window. Proceed to exercise 2.

2. Click the expand button on the first message window you created in exercise 1. The first message window expands. Now you should be able to resize the first message window by clicking and dragging the frame around the window. Try that now. If you cannot grab hold of the window frame, you probably maximized instead of expanded the window when you tried to expand it; not to worry, just click on the window's expand button until you are able to resize the message window by clicking and dragging the frame around the window. You should also be able to move the message window around the screen by dragging its title bar; try that now, then proceed to exercise 3.

3. With the first message window still visible on your screen, click the expand button in the second message window; the second message window will expand. Practice resizing it by dragging the edges of the frame around the window, and move it by dragging its title bar. Arrange the two message windows so that message 1 appears in the top half and message 2 appears in the bottom half of the screen. Now practice cutting, copying, and pasting text between the two message windows. For example, drag the mouse over the first sentence of the first message window to highlight the text. Pull down the Edit menu and choose Copy. Click inside the body of the second message and position the cursor at the spot where you want to paste the text you just copied. Pull down the Edit menu and choose Paste.

4. When you are finished editing the messages, establish your Internet connection if you are not already connected, and click the Send button on any one of the messages. Eudora will send all of the messages that are waiting to be sent. This can save cost if you are paying for an Internet connection by the minute or by the hour, because you need to connect only once to send all of the e-mail messages you created, instead of having to stay connected while you create messages one by one.

49 Creating a Multimedia E-mail Message

After completing this chapter, you will be able to:

- **Create a multimedia e-mail message**

- **Use the PODIUM multimedia e-mail tool**

- **Pack a multimedia application into a PODIUM e-mail envelope**

- **Review the packing list in preparation for sending the message**

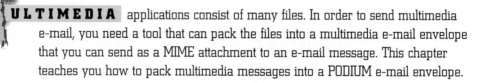 **ULTIMEDIA** applications consist of many files. In order to send multimedia e-mail, you need a tool that can pack the files into a multimedia e-mail envelope that you can send as a MIME attachment to an e-mail message. This chapter teaches you how to pack multimedia messages into a PODIUM e-mail envelope.

Composing the Message

Creating multimedia e-mail with PODIUM is easy, because you use the custom toolbox to compose the message. The tools work just like when you create a multimedia application with PODIUM. Indeed, the only difference between a multimedia application and a multimedia e-mail message is that the e-mail message gets packed into a multimedia e-mail envelope that you can send over the Internet.

Let's compose a short multimedia e-mail message that you can use to learn how to pack a PODIUM e-mail envelope. Follow these steps:

▶ Pull down the PODIUM Files menu, choose New Custom, and create a new custom screen called *multilit\mail.cus.* (multilit.cus)

▶ Use the Backdrop tool to make the backdrop be an ocean scene that you will find on the *Multiliteracy CD* in the file *backdrop\ocean.bmp.*

▶ Use the Text tool to write the following message on top of the ocean scene to whomever you want to receive this message:

Dear *whomever*,

> This is a multimedia e-mail message that was created with the custom toolbox. If you have your speakers turned on, you can already hear the sound of the waves that you see in the background of this screen.

Click here for some music!

I would like you to send me a multimedia reply. Pull down the PODIUM Files menu, choose New Custom, and use the custom toolbox to create your reply. Then pull down the Files menu, choose PODIUM E-mail, and send me your message.

Enjoy!

Your Name

 ▶ Use the Backdrop tool to add the following line to the backdrop of the message:

`ambient\ocean.wav`

 ▶ Use the Transparent Rectangle tool to draw a button around the text that says *Click here for some music!* and link the button to the following link:

`audio\swing.mid`

▶ Close the toolbox and test the link. When you click the text that says *Click here for some music!* you should hear some jazz.

Obviously, this is a very simple example of an e-mail message. Eventually, you will be able to make your e-mail messages contain as many links as you want, including all of the multimedia tools and techniques you have learned. Read on to learn how to use the Multimedia E-mail tool to prepare to send the message over the Internet.

Movie on CD

Demonstrations
⮕ Show Me!
  ⮕ Multimedia E-mail
    ⮕ **Creating a Multimedia E-mail Message**

Using PODIUM's Multimedia E-mail Tool

The Multimedia E-mail tool can pack any application into a PODIUM e-mail envelope that you can send over the Internet. To use the Multimedia E-mail tool, follow these steps:

▶ Use PODIUM to bring up the custom file that serves as the home screen of your multimedia e-mail message. In the example used in this chapter, the home screen is *multilit\mail.cus*.

▶ Pull down the PODIUM Files menu, choose PODIUM E-mail, and select Send Multimedia E-mail; the Multimedia E-mail dialog shown in Figure 49-1 appears.

▶ The name of your e-mail message's home screen appears in the Home Screen field. If the name is not correct, use the Browse button to browse to the correct custom screen.

49-1

The Multimedia E-mail dialog.

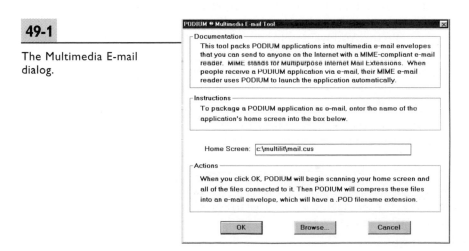

PODIUM • Multimedia E-mail Tool

Documentation
This tool packs PODIUM applications into multimedia e-mail envelopes that you can send to anyone on the Internet with a MIME-compliant e-mail reader. MIME stands for Multipurpose Internet Mail Extensions. When people receive a PODIUM application via e-mail, their MIME e-mail reader uses PODIUM to launch the application automatically.

Instructions
To package a PODIUM application as e-mail, enter the name of the application's home screen into the box below.

Home Screen: `c:\multilit\mail.cus`

Actions
When you click OK, PODIUM will begin scanning your home screen and all of the files connected to it. Then PODIUM will compress these files into an e-mail envelope, which will have a .POD filename extension.

[OK]   [Browse...]   [Cancel]

Packing Your Message into a Multimedia E-mail Envelope

The Multimedia E-mail dialog is self-documenting; read the instructions on the screen before proceeding. The instructions tell how PODIUM will scan your message for all of the files that need to be packed into the multimedia e-mail envelope.

▶ Click OK to begin the scan.

▶ The scan will happen very quickly. During the scan, PODIUM inspects every file that is linked to your e-mail message and builds a packing list of all the files that need to be compressed into the multimedia e-mail envelope.

▶ The status of the scan will be displayed in the Actions window.

▶ When the scan is done, the packing list will appear in the list box shown in Figure 49-2.

49-2

The multimedia e-mail packing list.

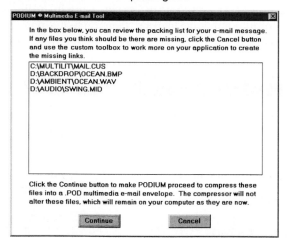

49-3

The Multimedia E-mail dialog's packing screen.

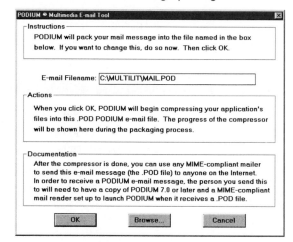

Reviewing the Packing List

You should review the packing list before proceeding. The packing list includes all of the files that are linked to your e-mail message. If the packing list does not include a file that you wanted to send along with this message, click Cancel, and use the custom toolbox to link the missing file to your message before proceeding. Figure 49-2 shows how the packing list should appear for this chapter's example file *multilit\mail.cus*. To complete the multimedia e-mail process, follow these steps:

▶ Read the instructions on the screen; the Multimedia E-mail tool is self-documenting, and the instructions will help you understand how the tool works.

▶ To compress the packing list into a PODIUM e-mail envelope, click the Continue button. The dialog shown in Figure 49-3 appears.

▶ In the E-mail Filename box, PODIUM will propose a filename for the *.pod* file into which your e-mail message will get packed. You can change the filename by editing it or browsing for a previously created *.pod* file. If you enter the name of a previously created *.pod* file, its contents will be replaced by the new message you are compressing. For the *multilit\mail.cus* example in this chapter, leave the filename set to *multilit\mail.pod*.

▶ Once again, read the instructions on the screen so you understand what the tool is about to do for you.

▶ Click OK to create the *.pod* file. Depending on how long your message is, it may take a few seconds or minutes to compress your message. The status of the compressor will be displayed in the Actions window.

▶ When the compressor is done, the All Done dialog shown in Figure 49-3 will appear. Click OK.

Now you have your first multimedia e-mail message all packed and ready to send. The next chapter shows you how to send it over the Internet.

E X E R C I S E S

The following exercises will give you practice creating and reviewing e-mail packing lists for different applications.

1. Use PODIUM to bring up your History of Flight home screen *flight\history.cus*. Pull down the Files menu, choose PODIUM E-mail, and select Send Multimedia E-mail. Click OK to scan the History of Flight application and create an e-mail packing list for it. Review the list and observe how it contains all of the files linked to your History of Flight application. Then click Cancel to terminate the e-mail process (unless you really do want to e-mail your History of Flight application to someone).

2. Use PODIUM to bring up your *multilit\linkdemo.cus* screen. Pull down the Files menu, choose PODIUM E-mail, and select Send Multimedia E-mail. Click OK to scan the *linkdemo.cus* file and create an e-mail packing list for it. How many files are included in the list? Make a note of the number of files contained in the packing list. Then click Cancel to terminate the e-mail process. Proceed to exercise 3.

3. Use the custom toolbox to edit your *multilit\linkdemo.cus* screen. Use the Text tool to add a line of text called **nonexistent link** and use the Link tool to link the following nonexistent filename to it: *multilit\notexist.cus*. Close the toolbox, pull down the Files menu, choose PODIUM E-mail, and select Send Multimedia E-mail. Click OK to scan the *linkdemo.cus* file again. What happens this time? Does PODIUM warn you that your e-mail message contains a nonexistent link? Click Cancel to terminate the e-mail process.

4. Pull down the PODIUM Files menu, choose New Custom, and create the screen *multilit\notexist.cus*. Make the screen say anything you want. Close the toolbox, pull down the Files menu, choose PODIUM E-mail, and select Send Multimedia E-mail. Click OK to scan the *linkdemo.cus* file again. What happens this time? How many files are contained in the packing list? Click Cancel to terminate the e-mail process.

5. Delete the file *multilit\notexist.cus* so these exercises will work properly if you or someone else chooses to work through them again on your computer.

50 Sending Multimedia E-mail with Eudora

After completing this chapter, you will be able to:

- **Create an e-mail message explaining that there is a MIME attachment and telling what to do with it**

- **Attach the multimedia e-mail message**

- **Send the multimedia e-mail message to anyone on the Internet**

SINCE you will be one of the first people in the world sending multimedia e-mail, you will need to provide some instructions when you send mail to novices who have never used MIME before. This chapter shows you how to send multimedia e-mail along with a message that helps novices learn how to read it.

Addressing the E-mail

To prepare for sending someone a multimedia e-mail message, you create an ordinary text-based message explaining that you have attached multimedia e-mail for them to read with PODIUM. To do this with Eudora, follow these steps:

▶ Click the New Message icon; a new message window appears.

▶ In the To field, type the e-mail address of the person to whom you want to send the message.

▶ In the Subject field, type a word or phrase that indicates what this message is about; for this example, type **Multimedia E-mail!**

▶ In the body of the message, type instructions that will help a novice know how to read your e-mail message. Printed below is a sample you can modify to suit your purposes. So you do not have to type all this by hand, you will find these instructions on the *Multiliteracy CD* in the file *eudora\sample.txt.*

This is a multimedia e-mail message that has an attachment encoded in the Internet's MIME format. In order to read the multimedia e-mail attachment, you need a MIME-compliant e-mail package and a copy of the PODIUM multimedia software. If you do not have either of these items, you can get them both on the CD-ROM that comes with the McGraw-Hill textbook *Multimedia Literacy*. The ISBN is 0-07-913107-7. Most bookstores have this book; if not, they can order it for you via the ISBN.

The name of the PODIUM e-mail envelope attached to this message is *mail.pod.* If your MIME mailer does not make PODIUM open the mail message automatically, follow these steps to read the message:
(1) Pull down the PODIUM Files menu and choose Open Mail; the Open dialog appears.

(2) Click the Browse button, browse to the *mail.pod* file, and click OK.

(3) PODIUM will suggest the name of a directory in which to unpack the mail message; you can change the name of the directory if you want. Later on, if you want to delete the mail message, you simply delete this directory. No files will be put in any other place on your computer.

(4) When you click OK, PODIUM will quickly unpack and display the message.

Movie on CD

Demonstrations
➡ Show Me!
　➡ Multimedia
　　E-mail
　　➡ **Attaching a**
　　　Multimedia
　　　E-mail
　　　Message

Attaching the Multimedia E-mail Message

To attach the multimedia e-mail message, follow these steps:

▶ Pull down Eudora's Message menu and choose Attach File; the Windows file browser appears.

▶ Browse to the *.pod* file you want to attach; in the example, the file to attach is *multilit\mail.pod*. Click OK to close the browser.

Figure 50-1 shows how the Attachments field in your message window should now contain the name of your PODIUM e-mail attachment *.pod* file. Your multimedia c-mail message is now ready to send.

50-1

The completed multimedia e-mail message, all ready to send.

The *multilit\mail.pod* file is attached to this e-mail message

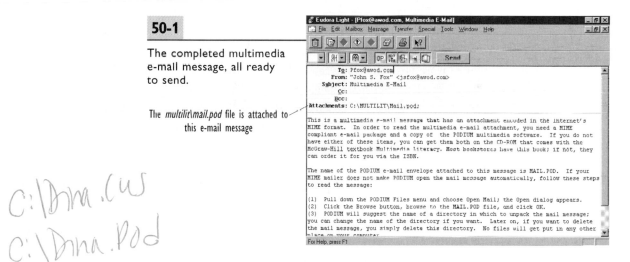

Movie on CD

Demonstrations
➡ Show Me!
　➡ Multimedia
　　E-mail
　　➡ **Sending**
　　　Multimedia
　　　E-mail

Sending the E-mail over the Internet

To send your multimedia e-mail message, follow these steps:

▶ Read carefully the message you have composed and make any final changes you want before proceeding.

▶ If your computer is not connected to the network at the moment, establish a network connection now. For example, if you are using PPP (the point-to-point protocol used to establish an Internet connection over a modem), get PPP running.

▶ To send the message, click the Send button. While Eudora connects to the Internet, the Progress dialog will appear as shown in Figure 50-2. If Eudora cannot connect, you will get an error message explaining the problem.

50-2

The Eudora Progress dialog.

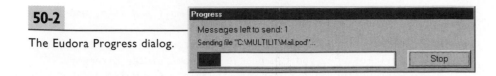

If your message is long and your Internet connection is slow, it may take several minutes to send the message. Since Windows is a multitasking operating system, you can continue working with other applications while Eudora sends your mail. Do not run any applications that could crash your computer, however, because you do not want to interrupt Eudora while your multimedia e-mail is being sent.

E X E R C I S E S

Now that you know how to send multimedia e-mail messages, you can let your imagination run wild. Here are some exercises to get you started:

1. Make a multimedia greeting card that has a picture of something appropriate for the greeting. Use the Waveform Audio tool to create a voice recording of yourself giving a greeting. Put a button on the card that the user can click to listen to the recording and see a recent snapshot of yourself. You will find resources for making multimedia greeting cards in Chapter 46 of this book, and in the *media\greeting* directory of the *Multiliteracy CD. Hint:* The links to the button will go something like this:

```
! bitmaps\whatever.bmp @wait=0
! audio\whatever.wav @wait=end
```

2. No matter what line of work you are in, you can find a reason to mail a multimedia application to someone. For example, teachers can share multimedia lesson plans. Students can e-mail multimedia term papers to their instructors. Job applicants can e-mail résumés linked to working examples of their creative multimedia abilities. Take one of the applications you have developed while working through this book, pack it into a multimedia e-mail envelope, attach it to a multimedia e-mail message, and send the message to the appropriate person.

51

Receiving Multimedia E-mail with Eudora

After completing this chapter, you will be able to:

- **Use Eudora to receive a multimedia e-mail message**

- **Use PODIUM to unpack the multimedia e-mail message**

- **Read the multimedia e-mail message**

- **Save or delete the message**

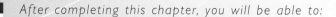

IT IS a lot easier to receive multimedia e-mail messages than it is to send them. All the user needs in order to read a message is a MIME-compliant e-mail package such as Eudora, and the multimedia software needed to view the message, which in this case is PODIUM. This chapter shows how to receive multimedia e-mail messages with Eudora and view them with PODIUM.

Receiving the Packed Multimedia E-mail Message

When you receive multimedia e-mail with a MIME-compliant e-mail package such as Eudora, the multimedia attachment gets downloaded to your computer automatically. The headers at the beginning of the mail message will tell you the filename of the *.pod* file that contains the multimedia files. If you have Eudora Light, you need to get PODIUM started on your own to read the *.pod* file; but if you have Eudora Pro, you can set up Eudora to launch PODIUM automatically when a *.pod* file is received.

To receive a multimedia e-mail message with Eudora, follow these steps:

▶ Pull down the Eudora File menu and choose Check Mail.

▶ Eudora will prompt you for your Internet e-mail password; type your password and click OK.

▶ The Progress dialog will show you the status as Eudora downloads mail from the e-mail server to your PC. If the multimedia attachment is long and your Internet connection is slow, this may take several minutes.

▶ You can do other things on your computer while the mail downloads, but do not run any applications that may crash your computer while Eudora is downloading mail.

51-1

How the message window identifies the name of an attached file.

The *multilit\mail.pod* file is attached to this e-mail message

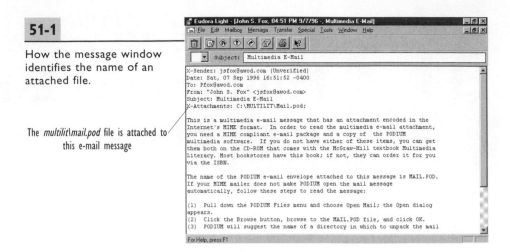

> When the mail is downloaded, Eudora opens your In Box. Double-click the message you want to read.

> Messages that have a MIME file attached have an Attachments header, as shown in Figure 51-1, identifying the drive letter, path, and filename of the attached file.

Movie on CD

Demonstrations
➡ Show Me!
  ➡ Multimedia
     E-mail
     ➡ **Receiving
       Multimedia
       E-mail**

Unpacking the Multimedia E-mail Message

If you have Eudora Pro and you have set it up to auto-launch PODIUM when a *.pod* file is received, the steps below will happen automatically. Otherwise, you need to get PODIUM running and follow these steps:

> Pull down the PODIUM Files menu, choose PODIUM E-mail, and select Read Multimedia E-mail; the browser dialog appears.

> Browse to the *.pod* file that was downloaded to your computer and click OK.

> The PODIUM E-mail Reader dialog appears as shown in Figure 51-2.

The E-mail Reader is self-documenting. Read the instructions, which explain how PODIUM is going to unpack the mail message into a *podmail* directory on your computer. You can change the name of the directory if you want, but this is not recommended. If you leave the directory name the way PODIUM proposes, you are guaranteed that none of the files contained in the incoming message will overwrite any other files on your computer. After you read the instructions, click the Read Mail button.

51-2

PODIUM's Multimedia E-mail Reader.

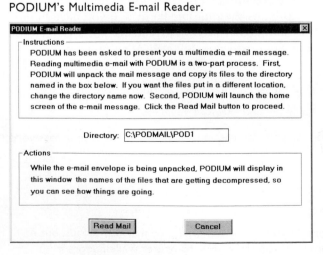

Reading the Multimedia E-mail Message

Reading the multimedia e-mail message is the easiest part. Once the home screen of the mail message appears, you become a PODIUM user and you read the message by clicking on its buttons or hypertext, just like any PODIUM user.

Saving or Deleting the Multimedia E-mail Message

After you read a multimedia mail message, you will face the dilemma of whether to save or delete it. Some of the messages you get will be so beautiful and creative that you will want to keep them forever, but, unfortunately, multimedia takes up a lot of disk space. Happily, there is a strategy that can help you cope with this dilemma.

After you unpack and read a multimedia e-mail message, it resides on your computer in two forms: first, as the *.pod* file that was downloaded to your computer from the Internet and, second, as a multimedia application that got installed into a folder in the *podmail* directory on your computer's hard drive. If you want to free up the maximum amount of space but still keep the message in a retrievable state, you can delete the e-mail message's folder from your *podmail* directory and retain the copy of the *.pod* file. Because the *.pod* file is highly compressed, the application takes up much less space as a *.pod* file. Anytime you want to reread the mail message, all you need to do is use the Read Multimedia E-mail tool to unpack it again.

E X E R C I S E S

Every time you install an application on your computer, you are performing an act of faith that the installation program will not erase or replace critically important files on your computer with outdated or corrupted copies. The PODIUM E-mail tool was designed to guard against this automatically. The exercises below will help you understand how PODIUM prevents users from e-mailing applications that may corrupt your computer.

1. Create a new directory called *testmail* on your hard drive. Use PODIUM to create a new custom file called *testmail\home.cus;* this will be the home screen of the test mail message. Use the Backdrop tool to make the screen have your favorite color. Then use the custom toolbox to write the following line of hypertext on the screen:

History of the Biplane

Use the Link tool to link the following file to the "History of the Biplane" text:

flight\biplane.cus

Test the link to make sure the *biplane.cus* screen appears.

2. With the *testmail\home.cus* file created in exercise 1 on your screen, pull down the Files menu, choose PODIUM E-mail, and select Send Multimedia E-mail. Accept all the defaults, and pack this message into a multimedia e-mail envelope called *testmail\home.pod*.

3. Pretend that someone just sent you the multimedia e-mail message you created in exercise 2 and you want to read it. Pull down the Files menu, choose PODIUM E-mail, select Read Multimedia E-mail, and unpack the *testmail\home.pod* file. Do not change the name of the *podmail* directory into which PODIUM will propose installing the mail message. After the mail message is installed, use the File Manager or the Explorer to inspect the contents of your *podmail* directory. You will find all the files in the *testmail\home.pod* mail message in subdirectories of the *podmail* directory. Now inspect your *flight* directory. Is the *biplane.cus* file still there? Yes, with its original time and date. The original files have not been replaced or altered in any way. Thus, you can see that when you install mail into the *podmail* directory, you will never overwrite or corrupt any of the other files on your computer.

Part Ten

World Wide Web Page Creation

You can do it.

> — Bela Karolyi, 1996 Olympics U.S. women's gymnastic team coach,
> to athlete Kerry Strug

This tutorial on creating a Web page has a topic that will interest almost everyone: creating a résumé that you can use to apply for a job. Creating a résumé on the Web may provide you with a strategic advantage, because you will be able to give prospective employers the World Wide Web address of your résumé. This shows you have network savvy that can benefit an employer in an information society.

On the Web your résumé will be presented in color with hypertext links that make it quick and easy to read your résumé and find information in it. You will be able to print your résumé from the Web; the printed version will be neatly typeset with professional-looking fonts, headings, graphics, and bulleted lists of your qualifications and accomplishments.

You will also learn how to create your **home page**, which is the Web page that serves as your main menu on the Web. By linking things to your home page, you create a hierarchy that makes it easy to go to other Web pages and access resources on the Web. For example, one of the things you will link to your home page is your Web page résumé.

This tutorial also shows how to link your résumé to multimedia samples of your work so prospective employers can review term papers, publications, pictures, sound tracks, animations, movies, spreadsheets, databases, or computer software you have created.

Web Page Design

After completing this chapter, you will be able to:

- Identify the basic elements that constitute a **Web page**

- Explain the uses and general appearance of the elements of a **Web page**

- Begin thinking about the design of your own **Web page** and how to make it engaging and informative

HERE are two primary factors to consider in Web page design: how the page will look and how the user will interact with it. This chapter presents the elements you will use to design your Web page résumé.

52-1

Web page elements in action.

Heading

Image

Links
(The blue underlined text is linked to other Web pages)

Paragraph

List

Horizontal rule

Symbol

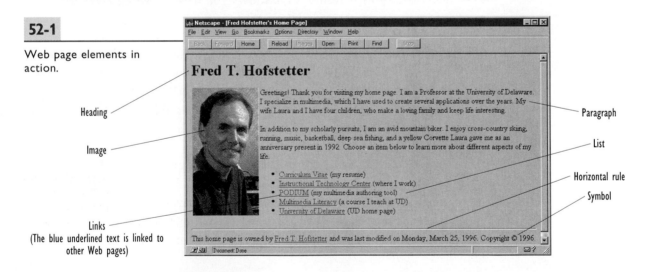

Elements of Your Web Page Résumé

World Wide Web pages consist of elements defined in the HTML language that is used to create Web pages. The résumé that you will create in this tutorial uses the following elements, as illustrated in Figure 52-1:

- Headings
- Paragraphs
- Lists
- Horizontal rules
- Images

- Backgrounds
- Bookmarks
- Links
- Symbols

HEADINGS

There are six heading styles numbered from H1 to H6. The smaller the number, the bigger the heading. H1 is the biggest or most important heading, and H6 is the smallest. Headings can be left justified, centered, or right justified.

PARAGRAPHS

Paragraphs consist of plain text that flows onto the screen in a continuous stream of characters. Paragraph text automatically wraps at the right margin and adapts to changes in window size.

LISTS

Lists can be ordered or unordered. In an ordered list, the items are numbered automatically; in an unordered list, the items are bulleted.

HORIZONTAL RULES

Horizontal rules are a design element used to create dividers between sections of a Web page. Horizontal rules appear with a neat three-dimensional effect. It is possible to vary the length, thickness, and shading of a horizontal rule, but the default settings look pretty good.

IMAGES

Images enhance the visual appeal of Web pages. Images can be left justified, right justified, or centered on the screen. Text can be made to flow around an image.

BACKGROUNDS

Backgrounds can be filled with a solid color (the default is gray), or you can tile a bitmap into the background to create a textured appearance. It is important to choose a background that does not detract from the readability of the text. For this reason, black text on a white background is the most popular color choice on the Web.

BOOKMARKS

To provide the user with a quick way to jump around among the various topics on your Web page, you can insert named bookmarks. For example, you might set a bookmark named "education" at the start of the education section of your résumé. In your résumé's bulleted table of contents, you would link the education bullet to the bookmark named "education" to provide a quick way of jumping to your educational qualifications.

LINKS

Links are the most essential element in web design, because links create webs. Without links, there would be no webs! On World Wide Web pages, links can be textual or pictorial. Any word or picture on the screen can be linked to any resource on the Web. Most links connect you to other Web pages or to bookmarks on the current Web page. As you will learn in Chapter 57, however, any multimedia file or application can be the object of a link on the World Wide Web. For example, your term papers, scholarly publications, software, and multimedia applications can all be mounted on the Web and linked to your résumé so potential employers can review samples of your work.

SYMBOLS

Web pages can contain special symbols such as the Greek characters used in scientific notation, as well as diacritical marks, mathematical functions, operators, delimiters, arrows, and pointers. In this tutorial you will learn how to insert the © copyright symbol on your Web pages.

Designing Your Web Page Résumé

Figure 52-2 diagrams the design of the résumé you will create in this tutorial. The diagram uses two of the design paradigms you studied in Chapter 45. First, it has a *menu* from which users will be able to branch to different parts of your résumé. Second, because it is linked to your home page, it is part of a *hierarchy*.

After you complete this tutorial, you will be able to modify and add to this design, giving your résumé its own unique traits and design elements. For example, you will probably want to customize the bulleted table of contents to reflect your skills and qualifications. For more design tips, see the World Wide Web design guidelines by Barron et al. (1996).

52-2

Diagram of the hypertext links to and from your résumé.

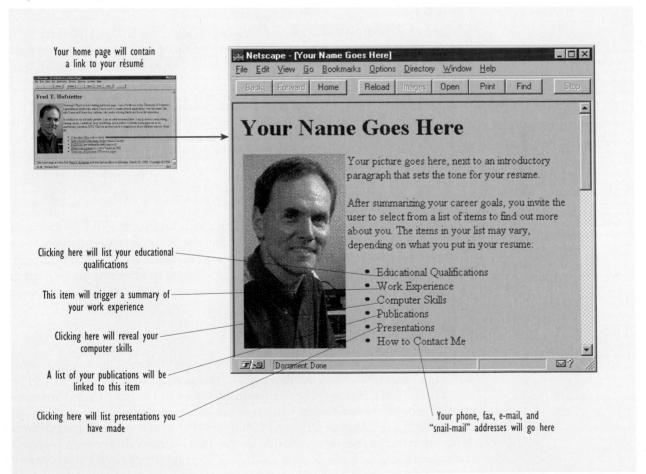

E X E R C I S E S

1. Using the design elements presented in this chapter, draw a diagram for your résumé. Think about the menu choices you will want to provide prospective employers who visit your Web page to find out about your experience and qualifications. Include this menu in your design. Possible menu items include:

- Educational Qualifications
- Work Experience
- Computer Skills
- Grants and Awards
- Honorary Societies

- Professional Association Memberships
- Publications
- Software
- Presentations
- How to Contact Me

2. Because it is possible to link any document, audio, picture, movie, or software application to your Web page, you will be able to link your résumé to examples of your work to prove your worth to a prospective employer. What examples would you like to link to your résumé? Include these links in your résumé design.

53

What Is HTML?

After completing this chapter, you will be able to:

- Explain the concept of a markup language

- Realize that different Web browsers may display the same HTML markup somewhat differently

- Understand the two HTML tag formats

- Define the families of HTML tags

- Understand the HTML tags used in creating a résumé

- Describe how HTML evolved and still is emerging

- Understand the elements of a URL

TML is the markup language used to create hypertext documents for the World Wide Web. *HTML* stands for hypertext markup language. The key to understanding how HTML works is to know what it means to mark up a text.

Understanding Markup

To mark up a text means to insert codes called **tags** into the text. The tags control how the text appears on a Web page. For example, compare Figures 53-1 and 53-2. In Figure 53-1 you see how a text appears on a Web page; notice the different-sized headings, the paragraphs, and the list of bulleted items. In Figure 53-2 you can see the HTML tags that mark up the text. By comparing these two figures, you can begin to understand how the HTML markup controls the appearance of text on the Web. Notice how the HTML tags always appear <inside> brackets.

Be aware that different Web browsers may display the same HTML somewhat differently. For example, the six styles of headings from <H1> through <H6> specify relative differences in heading size, not absolute font sizes. It is up to the Web browser to set the specific font size. Thus your headings may appear with slight size differences when viewed with various Web browsers.

53-1

How the author's home page appears on the Web.

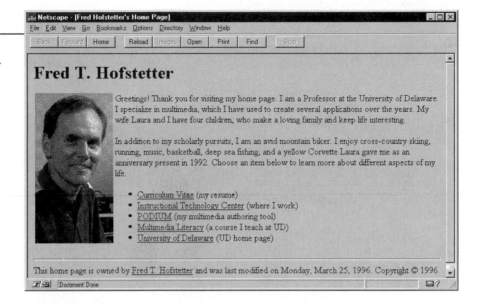

53-2

The HTML source code that creates the author's home page. The codes in brackets are the HTML tags that "mark up" the text.

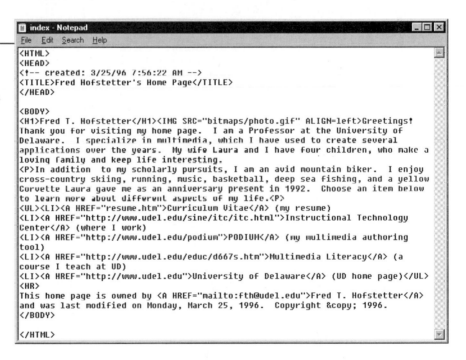

HTML Tag Formats

There are two HTML tag formats: paired tags and single tags.

Paired tags come in pairs, which consist of a start tag and a stop tag. Headings are an example of paired tags. For example, to make the words *Multimedia Literacy* appear in the largest style of heading, you would mark them up as follows:

```
<H1>Multimedia Literacy</H1>
```

<H1> is the start tag, and </H1> is the stop tag. The words between them will appear in heading style H1, which is the largest of the six heading styles. You can tell a start tag from a stop tag because the stop tag always has a slash, as in </H1>.

Single tags function on their own with no stop tag. For example, the tag <HR> makes a line known as a horizontal rule appear on your Web page; there is no stop tag for a horizontal rule.

Families of HTML Tags

Kenn Nesbitt, author of the Web creation software you will study in Chapter 54, groups the HTML tags into families that form the basis for the tools he has created. The following taxonomy is helpful in gaining an appreciation for the broad scope of things you can do with HTML.

- **Page structure tags** provide a framework for the document as a whole. They identify that the document is encoded in HTML and provide titling, framing, and header information that defines the structure of the file.

- **Block-style tags** control the flow of text into blocks on the screen. The most common block style is the paragraph.

- **Logical font-style tags** include styles for abbreviations, acronyms, citations, and quotations.

- **Physical font-style tags** let you create text that is blinking, bold, italic, subscripted, superscripted, or underlined.

- **Heading tags** let you create headings in six different levels or sizes of importance.

- **Lists and miscellaneous tags** let you create ordered lists (i.e., numbered lists), unordered lists (i.e., bulleted lists), menus, directories, horizontal rules (i.e., dividing lines), and line breaks.

- **Form tags** let you create input fields, radio buttons, and selection boxes for gathering information from the user.

- **Table tags** let you define tables that present data in neat rows and columns.

- **Math tags** provide a wide range of special symbols used in scientific notation.

- **Anchor/link tags** let you create bookmarks, hypertext, and hyperpicture triggers and link them to any resource or file on the World Wide Web.

- **Image tags** let you insert figures, center or align pictures with the left or right margin, flow text around images, or place icons inline in the midst of your text.

- **Server side includes (SSI) tags** provide a simpler way of adding database access to your Web pages than the old method of writing CGI (common gateway interface) scripts to interact with database programs on a server.

- **Java tags** provide a means for defining a way to interact with Java applets, which are little applications that get downloaded to your computer along with a Web page.

Tags Used in the Résumé Creation Tutorial

There are more than a hundred HTML tags. It is beyond the scope of this tutorial to teach them all. Rather, this tutorial teaches the basic set of tags you need to create a résumé. After you complete this tutorial, you will be provided with a

Table 53-1   HTML Tags Taught in This Tutorial

Tag	Description
\<HTML\> and \</HTML\>	These tags define the beginning and end of an HTML document. Your Web pages will always begin with the \<HTML\> start tag and end with the \</HTML\> stop tag.
\<HEAD\> and \</HEAD\>	The headers of your HTML file will appear between these tags.
\<TITLE\> and \</TITLE\>	The title of your HTML file goes between these tags, which in turn go between the header tags.
\<BODY\> and \</BODY\>	The body of your HTML file goes between these tags.
\<H1\> and \</H1\>	You will use the H1 heading tags at the beginning of your résumé to make your name appear in the most important heading style.
\<P\> and \</P\>	The \<P\> tag marks the beginning of a new paragraph. The stop tag \</P\> is optional. The \<P\> tag will always begin a new paragraph, whether or not a \</P\> tag marks the end of the paragraph.
\<UL\> and \</UL\>	These unordered list tags will mark the beginning and end of the table of contents in your résumé.
\<LI\>	The list item tag will mark the beginning of each item in your table of contents. There is no end-of-list-item tag.
\<HR\>	The horizontal rule tag makes the neat three-dimensional dividing lines on Web pages.
\<A NAME="name"\>	*A* stands for anchor. The anchor name tag creates names for the bookmarks in your résumé.
\<A HREF="url"\> \</A\>	*HREF* stands for hypertext reference. The anchor HREF tag creates hypertext links to bookmarks and URLs on the Web.
\<IMG SRC="filename"\>	The image tag places pictures on your Web page.
\<BODY BACKGROUND ="filename"\> \</BODY\>	The background body tag tiles an image into the background of your Web page to give your résumé a sophisticated look.

handy way of learning more tags and extending your grasp of HTML. Table 53-1 lists the tags taught in this tutorial.

Versions of HTML

The World Wide Web is an emerging technology, and new HTML tags get invented constantly. As this book goes to press, HTML is in its third version. By the time you read this, HTML will probably have advanced beyond version 3. Happily, new versions of HTML are backward compatible, meaning that Web pages you create with today's version will continue to work with future versions.

Sometimes the hottest new features of HTML are not supported by all browsers. For example, Netscape's latest HTML features may not work in Microsoft's Internet Explorer, and vice versa. The World Wide Web Consortium (W3C) is the standards body that officially registers new features into HTML. All of the major computing vendors and network companies belong to the W3C.

Elements of a URL

Every file on the World Wide Web has a URL. The **URL** is the address of the file on the Web. If you know a file's URL, you can create a link to it and retrieve it from the Web.

Table 53-2   Elements of a URL

Element	Description
protocol	Protocols include http, gopher, ftp, mailto, and news; the most common protocol is http, which stands for hypertext transfer protocol. Every Web page's URL begins with *http*.
server name	The server name is the Internet address of the computer or file server on which the resource resides.
port number	Port numbers rarely appear in URLs because almost every file server is on the Web's default port, which is port 80.
filename	The filename is the name the file has on the server. If the file is in a directory or subdirectory on the server, the filename includes the path to the file as well as the name of the file. If a URL that begins with *http* does not contain a filename, the default filename is *index.html*.
anchor	The anchor is a named bookmark within an HTML file. Anchors are optional. If a URL does not contain an anchor, the browser begins display at the start of the file.

URL stands for universal resource locator. A URL can have several parts, which always appear in this order:

```
protocol
server name
port number (optional)
filename (optional)
anchor (optional)
```

Table 53-2 shows what the different parts of a URL mean.

The following analysis shows how the various parts of a URL are combined into a specific address on the World Wide Web. This example is the URL for the education section of the author's résumé.

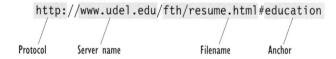

In most cases, a URL simply consists of a protocol, a server name, and a filename, such as http://www.udel.edu/fth/resume.html.

E X E R C I S E S

1. Compare the advantages and disadvantages of the evolutionary nature of HTML. What is good about designing the language so new HTML tags can be added to it? Are there disadvantages to developing a language this way?

2. Think about the taxonomy of HTML tags provided in this chapter. What capabilities do you think the World Wide Web should have that are not enabled by this taxonomy?

54 Creating Your Web Page Résumé

After completing this chapter, you will be able to:

- **Create a directory for your Web pages**

- **Install the WebEdit software and get it running on your PC**

- **Use WebEdit to create the body of an HTML file**

- **Enter your own content into the Web page**

- **Create new paragraphs on a Web page**

- **Make lists on a Web page**

- **Put pictures on a Web page**

- **Tile a background onto a Web page**

- **Create bookmarks on a Web page**

- **Create links to bookmarks**

- **View the Web page with your favorite Web browser**

N O W that you understand how markup languages like HTML work, you can put your new knowledge to work. This chapter takes you through all the steps needed to build your own online résumé with text, graphics, and links to other Web pages.

Creating a Directory for Your Web Pages

When you create a World Wide Web page, you begin by creating the directory in which the Web page will reside. The name of the directory for this tutorial is *website;* you should create the *website* directory now. Follow these steps:

▶ If you have Windows 3.1, pull down the File Manager's File menu, choose Create Directory, type **c:\website** and press ⏎Enter.

▶ If you have Windows 95, click the Start button, choose Programs, open the Explorer, navigate to the root directory of your hard drive, pull down the Explorer's File menu, choose New/Folder, and type **website**

Installing the WebEdit Software

This tutorial shows how to create Web pages with an authoring tool called WebEdit. The *Multiliteracy CD* contains a shareware version of the WebEdit software that you can use free for 30 days. Follow these instructions to install WebEdit from the *Multiliteracy CD:*

▶ If you have Windows 3.1, pull down the Program Manager's File menu and choose Run.

▶ If you have Windows 95, click the Start button and choose Run.

▶ Type the full path to the *setup.exe* program in the *webedit* directory on the *Multiliteracy CD*. For example, if your CD-ROM drive is D, you would type:

  d:\webedit\setup.exe

▶ When the setup program asks whether you want a full or a custom installation, choose full.

▶ After asking you to confirm the name of the WebEdit program group, the setup program will display a note from Kenn Nesbitt, who created WebEdit. After you read Kenn's message, the installation will be complete, and a WebEdit icon will appear on your screen.

Movie on CD

Demonstrations
➥ Show Me!
  ➥ Web Page
     Creation
     ➥ **Setting the**
        WebEdit
        Configuration
        Options

Running the WebEdit Software

Double-click the WebEdit icon to get it running. The WebEdit license will appear. After you read the license, click the Accept button. The 30-day evaluation dialog will appear. Your first time through, click Continue without unlocking. After completing this tutorial, you will probably decide to purchase a license, which will provide you with the code needed to unlock WebEdit and enable more features, such as floating toolbars that make WebEdit even easier to use.

Figure 54-1 shows how the WebEdit window consists of a menu bar, a toolbar, and a document window.

You must first set a few options that this tutorial will use. You need to set these options only the first time you use WebEdit; once set, WebEdit will remember them.

▶ Pull down the Options menu, choose Configure, and select the Previewer tab. Click the Display Preview option. This will make WebEdit split your document window down the middle. The left side is where your HTML source code will appear. The right side is a viewer that shows what your document will look like out on the Web. Do not close the Options dialog yet.

▶ If you have a fast computer, click Automatically Update Previewer. A check mark next to the Automatically Update Previewer option indicates that it is on. If you have a slow computer, leave this option off and instead press the F5 function key whenever you want to update the WebEdit preview window. Do not close the Options dialog yet.

▶ Select the Preferences tab and select Word Wrap to turn on the Word Wrap option. A check mark next to the Word Wrap option indicates that it is on.

54-1

How the WebEdit menu, toolbar, and document window appear when you start WebEdit the first time.

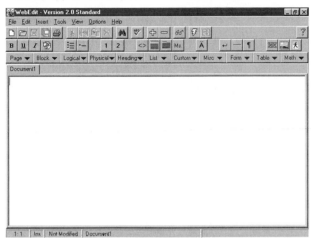

54-2

How your screen should appear after setting the options in WebEdit.

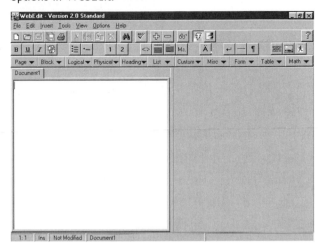

▶ In the Browsers group of the Preferences tab, if you have Microsoft's Interent Explorer, click the number of the version you have. If you have a different browser, such as Netscape, click the Add or Edit Browser button, then type the name and the complete path/filename of your Web browser into the fields provided. If you are not sure of the complete path/filename of your Web browser, click the Browse button and browse for it.

▶ Click OK to close the Options dialog.

▶ Double-click the WebEdit title bar to make WebEdit expand to fill the screen.

▶ Double-click the document title bar to expand the document window.

Your screen should now appear as shown in Figure 54-2. If it does not, carefully repeat these steps to set the options so your copy of WebEdit will be set up to work like the one used in this tutorial. Later on, you will be able to modify the options to suit your personal preferences after you complete this tutorial. It is possible that the positioning of the vertical frame between the HTML and preview windows on your screen will not match that shown in Figure 54-2. Not to worry: You can use the mouse to drag the vertical bar left and right to change the relative size of the source code window and the viewer.

Movie on CD

Demonstrations
➥ Show Me!
➥ Web Page
Creation
➥ **Creating the Minimal HTML**

Entering Minimal HTML

Now that you have WebEdit running, you can create your Web page. Start by clicking the Add Minimal HTML button—the big yellow plus sign on the WebEdit toolbar; this enters what WebEdit calls "minimal HTML" into your HTML window, as shown in Figure 54-3. This "minimal" amount of HTML is a quick way to get started creating a Web page.

Remember that *HTML* means hypertext markup language. If you compare the HTML source code on the left to the preview on the right, you can see how HTML works: The HTML tags that appear inside the brackets are the "markup" that affect how the text between them will appear on your Web page.

54-3

The "minimal HTML" is entered onto a Web page by clicking the WebEdit + icon.

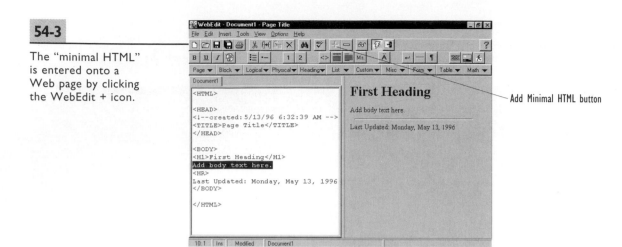

Add Minimal HTML button

Changing the Page Title

Between the title start tag <TITLE> and stop tag </TITLE>, you can see the text *Page Title*. This is the Web page's title that will appear in your Web browser's title bar to identify your Web page. Use the mouse to position the cursor in the HTML window on the words *Page Title* and replace those words with an appropriate title for this Web page. For example, if your name is Santa Claus, you might type **Santa's Résumé** since this Web page will be your résumé. Notice how WebEdit displays the title of your Web page in the WebEdit title bar.

The title is used by many Web search engines, so make sure the title identifies the primary purpose of your Web page by including key words you want search engines to find.

Changing the Heading

Between the heading start tag <H1> and stop tag </H1>, you can see the text *First Heading* that appears as the heading of the document. Use the mouse to position the cursor in the HTML window on the words *First Heading* and replace those words with your own name. Be careful not to disturb the HTML codes <H1> and </H1> which delimit the heading. Your name should now appear as the heading of the Web page, as shown in Figure 54-4.

54-4

What you type between the <TITLE> tags appears in the title bar; what you type between the <H1> tags appears on your Web page in the largest heading style.

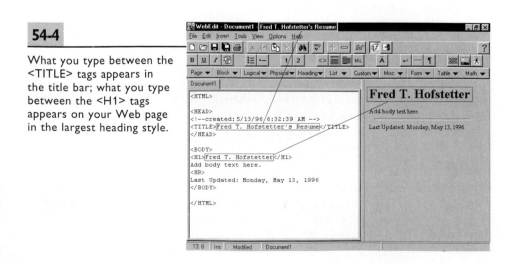

54-5

How the author began his résumé.

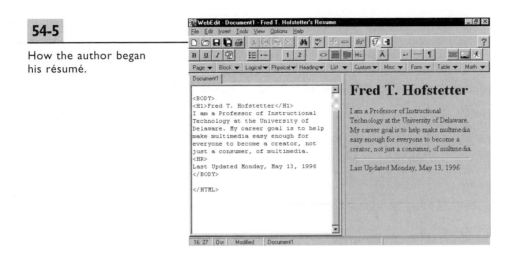

Entering the Body Text

Mouse to the spot in the HTML window where it says *Add body text here.* Use the mouse and keyboard to replace those words with a few sentences about yourself. Don't be bashful: A résumé should begin with a strongly stated summary of your professional qualifications and career goals. Figure 54-5 shows how the author began his résumé.

NOTE   You can drag the vertical frame between the HTML and preview windows left and right to change the relative size of the source code window and the viewer.

Movie on CD

Demonstrations
➡ Show Me!
  ➡ Web Page
    Creation
      ➡ **Creating New
        Paragraphs**

Block ▼

Starting a New Paragraph

To make a new paragraph, position the cursor in the HTML window where you want the new paragraph to start. Then click the Block button and choose Paragraph. In the Paragraph dialog, accept the defaults by clicking OK. Notice how the HTML tag <P> appears in your document; <P> means paragraph. Now type another paragraph that summarizes what is in your résumé. Figure 54-6 shows how the author completed this task.

54-6

How the author completed the second paragraph of his résumé. Notice how the <P> causes a new paragraph to begin, even though there is no line break before it.

Block button

Paragraph tag

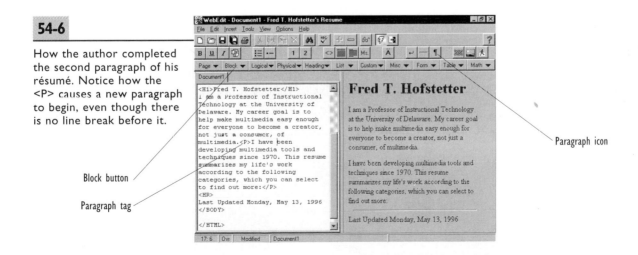

Paragraph icon

Web browsers pay no attention to line breaks and start new paragraphs only if they reach a <P> tag. Thus, you can insert line breaks to make your HTML easier to read and maintain, without having those line breaks appear on your Web page. For example, the following HTML will appear exactly the same when viewed with a Web browser. The example on the right is easier to maintain, because the line breaks make it obvious where the new paragraph begins.

```
My career goal is to help make it        My career goal is to help make it
possible for everyone to become a        possible for everyone to become a
creator, not just a consumer, of         creator, not just a consumer, of
multimedia.<P>I have been developing     multimedia. <P>
multimedia tools and techniques
since 1970.                              I have been developing multimedia
                                         tools and techniques since 1970.
```

 Another way to create a new paragraph in WebEdit is to click the Paragraph icon. This inserts the HTML tags <P></P> and positions the cursor right before the </P>, which is the end-of-paragraph tag. You type the paragraph between these two tags. The </P> tag is optional in HTML. The <P> tag will always begin a new paragraph, whether or not the previous paragraph ends with a </P> tag.

Movie on CD

Demonstrations
➡ Show Me!
  ➡ Web Page
    Creation
    ➡ **Unordered**
      Lists

Creating a List

Position the cursor in the HTML window where your résumé's bulleted table of contents will begin. Click the List button and choose Unordered List. When the List dialog appears, accept the defaults by clicking OK. Notice how the codes <UL></UL> are inserted with the cursor positioned *between* them. Because <UL> signals the start of an unordered list and </UL> stops the list, the cursor must be positioned between the tags to enter the list.

 To enter an item into the list, click the List button and select List Item. The code <LI> appears in your HTML to indicate the start of a list item. Type the list item.

To enter another item into the list, click the List button again, select List Item, and type the item. Notice how the list appears in the preview window as you type it into the HTML window.

Enter as many items as you want to list right now. You can always add more items to your résumé later on. Figure 54-7 shows how the author typed his list. Notice how line breaks in the HTML keep the list items lined up to make the HTML source code easy to maintain.

54-7

How the author typed the bulleted table of contents in his résumé.

Line breaks before each list item help make this HTML source code easy to maintain

Unordered List button   List Item button   List button

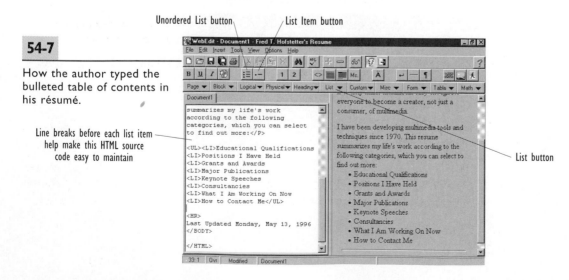

Another way of creating an unordered list is to click the Unordered List button to enter the <UL></UL> into your HTML, and then click the List Item button to enter the <LI> tag that creates a list item.

Horizontal Rules

Notice the nice dividing line that appears after your list in the preview window. That line gets drawn there because of the <HR> tag in your HTML window. If you delete that tag, the divider will disappear. Go ahead and delete the <HR> tag now to make the divider disappear.

 To insert a horizontal rule, click the Misc button and select Horizontal Rule. In the Horizontal Rule dialog, accept the defaults by clicking OK.

Although it is easy to insert horizontal rules in your documents, and the dividers look cool, don't give in to the temptation to overuse them! Horizontal rules are best used to separate major sections of a document.

 Another way to insert horizontal rules is to click the Horizontal Rule button.

Saving the File

 Periodically, you must remember to save your HTML file to prevent accidental loss due to power failure or some other accident. To save the file, click the Save icon or pull down the File menu and choose Save. The first time you try to save a file, you will get the Save As dialog. When you save your résumé the first time, give it the filename **c:\website\resume.htm**

Movie on CD

Demonstrations
→ Show Me!
  → Web Page
    Creation
    → **Creating New**
      Headings

Inserting a New Heading

Every main section of your résumé should begin with a large heading that identifies the section. It is common for Web pages to have a title displayed in the largest size <H1> and then use the next-smaller size <H2> for subheads. For example, when you enter the educational qualifications section of your résumé, follow these steps to give it a heading:

▶ Click the Heading button.

▶ Choose the heading size you want; Heading 1 is the largest, and Heading 6 is the smallest; the Headings dialog will appear.

▶ Pull down the Alignment selection box and choose the kind of alignment you want; headings in a résumé should be either left justified or centered.

▶ Click OK; the heading tags will appear in the HTML window, with the cursor positioned between them.

▶ Type the new heading.

 A quick way of creating left-justified headings of size 1 or size 2 is to click the Level 1 Heading button or the Level 2 Heading button.

 To begin a new paragraph after the heading, click the Paragraph button or the Block button and choose Paragraph. In the Paragraph dialog, accept the defaults by clicking OK. Type the new paragraph.

Creating Bookmark Names

As you create the different sections in your résumé, it will grow too long to fit on the screen all at once. To make it easy for the user to find the different parts of your résumé, you can insert named bookmarks into your HTML. Then you can link each item in your résumé's bulleted table of contents to its corresponding bookmark to make it quick and easy for the user to find that section.

To create a bookmark, use the mouse to position the cursor in the HTML window where you want the bookmark to occur. Then click the Anchor/Link button to make the Anchor/Link dialog appear. In the Name field, type the name you want the bookmark to have. Then click the Anchor button to anchor the bookmark onto your Web page. For example, to create a bookmark called "education" at the start of the education section in your résumé, follow these steps:

▶ Position the cursor at the start of the education section in the HTML window.

▶ Press the Anchor/Link button; the Anchor/Link dialog appears.

▶ In the Name field, type **education** as shown in Figure 54-8.

▶ Click the Anchor button to create the bookmark.

In the HTML window, you will see how WebEdit inserted the following code into your HTML:

```
<A NAME="education">
```

This causes no visible change in the preview window, because bookmarks cannot be seen on a Web page. Figure 54-9 shows how the anchor <A NAME="education"> appears in the HTML window but has no visible effect on the Web page.

54-8

Creating the "education" bookmark in the Name field of the Anchor/Link dialog.

Type the name of the bookmark here

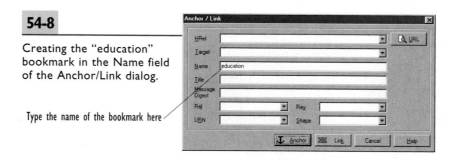

54-9

The "education" bookmark has no visible effect on the Web page.

The "education" bookmark

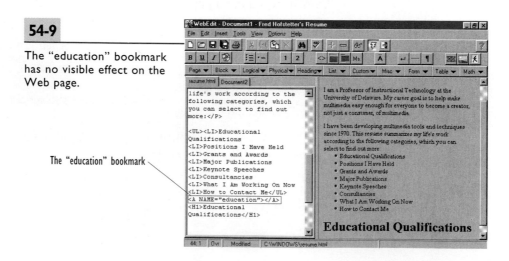

Demonstrations
➡ Show Me!
  ➡ Web Page
    Creation
    ➡ **Bookmark**
      Links

Linking to Bookmark Names

To link to a bookmark, use the mouse to highlight the text that will trigger the link. Click the Anchor/Link button to make the Anchor/Link dialog appear. In the Anchor/Link dialog, click the URL button to make the URL Builder appear. To create a URL for a bookmark, you type the name of the bookmark into the Anchor field, then click OK. The name of the bookmark appears in the HRef field with a hatch mark (#) in front of it. *HRef* stands for hypertext reference; the hatch mark is the URL symbol for a link relative to the current document. To finish the link, click the Anchor button to anchor the link to the hypertext on your Web page.

For example, to link your résumé's bulleted list item *Educational Qualifications* to the "education" bookmark in your résumé, follow these steps:

▶ In the HTML window, position the cursor in the bulleted list right before *Educational Qualifications*.

▶ Drag the mouse over the words *Educational Qualifications* to select them.

▶ Click the Anchor/Link button; the Anchor/Link dialog appears.

▶ In the Anchor/Link dialog, click the URL button; the URL Builder appears.

▶ In the Anchor field, enter the name of the bookmark by typing **education**

▶ Click OK to close the URL Builder; the HRef field now contains the anchor #education.

▶ Click the Anchor button to complete the link.

Now the words *Educational Qualifications* should appear blue in your résumé's bulleted table of contents. The coloration denotes hypertext; clicking the colored text will trigger the link.

Let's test the link. Click the words *Educational Qualifications* in the preview window. If the preview window jumped to the Educational Qualifications section of your résumé, congratulations! If not, repeat these steps, compare your HTML to the samples shown here, and keep trying until you get the bookmark link to work.

Returning to the Table of Contents

Web pages that use bookmarks often provide a way for the user to return to the table of contents. This return-to-contents capability is created with another bookmark. First, you create a bookmark at the start of the bulleted list to which you want the user to return; then you create a return link to that bookmark at the end of each section in your document.

To create a return bookmark for the education section of your résumé, follow these steps:

▶ Position the cursor in the HTML window at the start of the bulleted table of contents.

▶ Create a bookmark named "contents"—try to do this on your own, but if you need help, follow these steps:

  ▪ Click the Anchor/Link button; the Anchor/Link dialog appears.

  ▪ In the Name field, type **contents**

  ▪ Click the Anchor button to create the bookmark.

> Position the cursor in the HTML window at the end of the Educational Qualifications section of your résumé. Insert a new paragraph that contains the text *Resume Contents.*

> Link the words *Resume Contents* to the "contents" bookmark—try to do this on your own, but if you need help, follow these steps:

> ▪ In the HTML window, drag the mouse over the words *Resume Contents* to highlight them.

> ▪ Click the Anchor/Link button; the Anchor/Link dialog appears.

> ▪ In the Anchor/Link dialog, click the URL button; the URL Builder appears.

> ▪ In the Anchor field, type **contents**

> ▪ Click OK to close the URL Builder; the HRef field now contains the anchor #contents.

> ▪ Click the Anchor button to complete the link.

> Test the link to see if it works. Clicking on *Resume Contents* in the preview window should return you to the bulleted table of contents near the top of your résumé.

In the preview window, test your bookmark links. Clicking on *Educational Qualifications* in the bulleted table of contents should jump to the education section of your résumé. At the end of that section, clicking on *Resume Contents* should return you to the table of contents.

Preparing Pictures for a Web Page

Because Web pages can contain images, it would be nice to put a color picture or graphic at the top of your Web page. If you completed the picture-taking exercise at the end of Chapter 2, you will already have a digital photograph of yourself. If not, you can use one of the images in the *Multiliteracy CD* clip-art directory *media\bitmaps. Note:* Some people choose not to include a photo on their résumé to prevent employers from discriminating on the basis of age, sex, color, or ethnicity. If you are concerned about that, use a graphic instead of a personal photo to complete these exercises.

Before you can put a picture into your résumé, you must adjust it a little with Paint Shop Pro. First, you need to size the picture so it will fit nicely on your Web page. Pictures that are too big take a long time to load and take up too much screen space. Second, when you save the image, you should choose the GIF file format. GIF is the file format most often used on the World Wide Web for pictures; all graphical Web browsers support GIF images. Third, you need to save the GIF image in the directory on your hard drive where you are creating your résumé. Follow these steps:

> Get Paint Shop Pro running, pull down the File menu, choose Open, and open the photo.

> Pull down the Image menu and choose Resize; the Resize dialog appears.

> Check the "maintain aspect ratio" box if it is not checked already.

> Click the Custom Size button.

> Type a length of **120** pixels; Paint Shop Pro will set the height automatically.

> Click OK to make the resized picture appear.

If the picture looks distorted, you have probably tried to shrink it too much. With practice, you will develop skill at knowing how far you can reduce a picture before it begins to distort. An alternative to shrinking is to cut a small portion out of the original picture and work with that instead. To cut a portion out of an existing picture, follow these steps:

▶ If the Paint Shop Pro tools window is not visible, pull down the View menu and choose Show Tools.

▶ Click once on the dotted-box icon in the Tools menu (this is the Selection tool).

▶ Drag the mouse over the photo to select the part of the picture you want to copy.

▶ Pull down the Edit menu and choose Copy.

▶ Pull down the Edit menu and choose Paste.

▶ The selected region of the photo now appears in a smaller window.

When you save the file, you must choose the GIF file format, because GIF is the image format used on the World Wide Web. Follow these steps:

▶ Pull down the Paint Shop Pro File menu and choose Save As; the Save As dialog appears.

▶ Set the file type to GIF.

▶ Set the file sub-format to GIF 89a - interlaced; the interlaced format is what permits Web browsers to stripe images onto the screen, which is a nice effect particularly with slow network connections that make pictures take longer to appear.

▶ In the filename field, type the full path to your World Wide Web directory, followed by the name of the file, which we will call *picture.gif*; for example, if your hard drive is C, you would type **c:\website\picture.gif**

Movie on CD

Demonstrations
↦ Show Me!
  ↦ Web Page
    Creation
    ↦ **Pasting a**
      Picture onto
      a Web Page

Pasting Your Picture onto Your Web Page Résumé

To place your picture next to the first paragraph on your Web page, follow these steps:

▶ Position the cursor in the HTML window right before the first paragraph of your résumé, right after the résumé's heading.

▶ Click the Inline Image button; the Image dialog appears as shown in Figure 54-10.

▶ Click the topmost URL button (the one next to the Src field); the URL Builder appears.

▶ If the Anchor field contains anything, clear the Anchor field.

▶ Click the Browse button and browse to your *picture.gif* file.

▶ Click OK; the name of your bitmap appears in the Src field (*Src* stands for source).

▶ To make the text of your résumé flow around the picture, pull down the Alignment control, and choose left.

54-10

The WebEdit Image dialog.

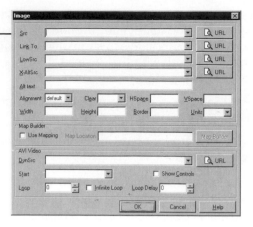

▶ Click OK; the picture appears in your résumé.

In the HTML window, you will find the codes that WebEdit inserted to display the photo:

```
<IMG SRC="picture.gif" ALIGN=left>
```

You may be concerned, however, that in the WebEdit preview window the text does not wrap around your picture. (If it does, you have a more recent version of WebEdit than the one used in this tutorial.) Not to worry: Netscape and most other Web browsers will flow the text of your résumé around the picture. Read on to learn how to preview your résumé with a Web browser.

Viewing Your Résumé with a Web Browser

 To see how your résumé will appear on-screen with a Web browser, click the View Document with Browser button. If the Web browser does not appear, it probably is running but does not have the focus. To make it appear, hold down Alt and press Tab until your Web browser appears. To return to WebEdit, do likewise: Hold down Alt and press Tab until WebEdit appears.

If you ever want to change the Web browser that WebEdit launches, pull down the Options menu, choose Configure, and, on the Preferences tab, click the Add or Edit Browser button.

At this point in the tutorial, you may wish to begin using your Web browser instead of the WebEdit preview window to view your Web page as you create it. To turn off the WebEdit preview window, pull down the WebEdit Options menu, choose Configure, select the Previewer tab, and uncheck the Display Preview option.

Movie on CD

Demonstrations
➡ Show Me!
  ➡ Web Page
    Creation
    ➡ **Tiled**
      Backgrounds

Tiling a Background onto a Web Page

As a final touch, let's add some pizzazz to your résumé. Netscape and most other Web browsers permit you to set a background bitmap that the browser uses to tile the background. **Tiling** means that the bitmap gets drawn repeatedly across and down the screen until the entire window surface has been covered. If the bitmap is designed in such a way as to hide the edges when tiled, you get a seamless appearance in the background tiling.

The *Multiliteracy CD* has a directory that contains a few backgrounds designed for tiling on Web pages. The name of this directory is *tiles*. Follow the steps below to make one of these tiles fill the background of your résumé.

▶ Copy the files in the *tiles* directory to the *website* directory on your hard drive.

▶ Position the cursor near the top of the HTML window, before the heading and after the <HTML> tag that begins the HTML file.

 ▶ Click the Page Structure button and choose Body; the Body dialog appears.

▶ Click the URL button. If the Anchor field contains anything, clear the Anchor field.

▶ Browse to the background tile you want to try; make sure you browse to the copy of the tile in the *website* directory on your hard drive, not the *tiles* directory on your CD-ROM drive.

▶ Click OK; the name of the background tile appears in the Body dialog.

▶ Click OK; WebEdit inserts the following tags into your HTML window:

<BODY BACKGROUND="*filename*.gif"></BODY>

▶ Delete the </BODY> tag so WebEdit won't think this is the end of the body.

▶ Click the View Document with Browser button to see how the tiled background will appear with your Web browser.

Tiles are neat, but be careful that the pattern in your tiling does not obstruct or interfere with the text on the screen. A good tile provides a subtle backdrop texture that enhances readability. Bad tiles interfere and make the text harder to read. To conserve bandwidth, tiles should be small, like the ones in the *tiles* directory.

Remember to Save Your File

 Don't forget to save your file. The filename of your résumé should be *c:\website\resume.htm*.

EXERCISES

1. This chapter got you started creating your Web page résumé. Now you should complete your résumé by adding all the sections you sketched when you designed your résumé at the start of this tutorial. If you have any trouble, refer back to the step-by-step instructions in this chapter for creating new paragraphs, headings, list items, and horizontal rules.

2. Each item in your bulleted table of contents should be linked to its corresponding section in your résumé. Insert bookmark names at the beginning of each new section. Then link each item in the table of contents to the corresponding bookmark name in your résumé. Test the links to make sure they work.

3. At the end of each section in your résumé, provide a way for the user to return to the table of contents.

55

Making a Local Web

After completing this chapter, you will be able to:

- **Create a home page**
- **Identify yourself as the home page owner**
- **Use special symbols on Web pages**
- **Link your résumé to your home page**
- **Link your publications to your résumé**
- **Test the links with a Web browser**
- **Make e-mail links**

 **EBS** are created by links that connect things together. If all of the objects of those links reside on your PC, you have what is known as a **local web**. Because all of the resources are local, you can use a Web browser to surf the local web, with no need for an Internet connection. In this chapter you will learn how to create a local web.

The local web will start with a home page, which is the Web page that serves as your main menu to other Web pages and resources. By linking things to your home page, you create a hierarchy that provides quick access to the documents and resources you want users to have access to. For example, your home page will contain a link to the résumé you created in the previous chapter.

Creating a Home Page

When someone asks "What is your home page?" they want you to respond with the URL (universal resource locator) of the Web page that you consider your home base on the Web. You see a lot of home page URLs that end with filenames like *home.html* or *welcome.html,* but the coolest home page addresses are the short ones that omit the filename. For example, Microsoft's home page is http://www.microsoft.com with no filename specified.

Having a cool home page address with no filename in it indicates you understand that when someone visits a Web site directory without specifying a filename, the server looks to see if the directory contains that Web site's default home filename, which is almost always *index.html.* Since you will want the name of your home page to be cool, this tutorial names it *index.html.* Well, actually *index.htm* since DOS/Windows restricts you to filename extensions of three characters. When we

FTP this file to a UNIX-based file server in the next chapter, we will add the *l* to the end of *index.htm*.

To create a home page that has the name *index.htm,* follow these steps:

▶ Pull down the WebEdit File menu and choose New; the New Page dialog appears.

▶ Choose New Blank Page and click OK. (*Note:* Do not choose the Home Page Wizard; it does a lot of things automatically that you need practice doing yourself right now.)

 ▶ Click the Minimal HTML icon to enter the minimal HTML into the HTML window.

▶ Pull down the File menu and choose Save As; the Save As dialog appears.

▶ Type the full path to your local web directory, followed by *index.htm;* assuming your hard drive is C, you would type **c:\website\index.htm**

Now that you have created the *index.htm* file, you can begin customizing it the way you want your home page to appear. Follow these steps:

▶ Change *First Heading* to read what you want at the start of your home page; for example, if your name is Santa Claus, you might say **Santa's Home Page**

▶ Replace the words *Add body text here* with a paragraph introducing your home page; for example, Figure 55-1 shows the paragraph that begins the author's home page.

Feel free to add any of the HTML elements that you learned while creating your résumé. Here is a summary of what you can do; for more detail, refer to the step-by-step instructions in the previous chapter:

 ▶ To add another paragraph, click the Block button and choose Paragraph, or click the Paragraph button.

 ▶ To add an image, position the cursor where you want the image to appear, and click the Inline Image button.

 ▶ To insert a horizontal rule, click the List button and select Horizontal Rule, or click the Horizontal Rule button.

55-1

The author's home page on the World Wide Web.

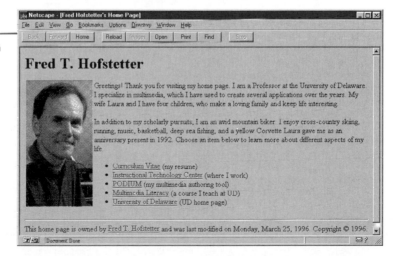

▶ To create a new heading, click the Heading button and select the level of the heading (Heading 1 is most important), or click the Level 1 Heading or Level 2 Heading button to create left-justified headings of size 1 or 2.

▶ To create a list, click the List button and choose Unordered List, or click the Unordered List button.

▶ To enter an item into the list, click the List button and select List Item, or click the List Item button. The code <LI> appears in your HTML to indicate the start of a list item. Type the list item.

Figure 55-1 shows how the author used these elements to design his home page. Yours will probably be more interesting!

Demonstrations
➡ Show Me!
  ➡ Web Page
    Creation
    ➡ **Linking Your
      Home Page
      to Your
      Résumé**

Linking Your Home Page to Your Résumé

Somewhere on your home page, you should advertise the existence of your résumé and provide a way for the user to link to it. As you can see in Figure 55-1, the author did this by including his résumé in a bulleted list of items to choose for more information. To link your home page to your résumé, follow these steps:

▶ In the HTML window, drag the mouse to select the text that you want to link to your résumé.

▶ Click the Anchor/Link button; the Anchor/Link dialog appears.

▶ In the Anchor/Link dialog, click the URL button; the URL Builder appears.

▶ Click the Browse button, browse to your résumé, and click OK; the filename of your résumé appears in the File field of the URL Builder.

▶ Click OK to close the URL Builder; the HRef field now contains the filename of your résumé.

▶ Click the Anchor button to complete the link.

To test the link, click it in the WebEdit preview window or in your Web browser. If the link works, it will take you to your résumé.

Returning to Your Home Page from Your Résumé

Although it is possible for users to return to your home page by clicking their Web browser's Back button, it is customary to provide a return link to your home page. Such a return link often appears at the bottom of a Web page, and sometimes at the end of major sections, if the document is lengthy. The link to your home page will also come in handy for users who might enter your résumé some other way, such as through a search engine or via your résumé's URL.

Try to create such a return link on your own, but if you need help, follow these steps:

▶ In the HTML window, enter the text that will serve as the link back to your home page; the two words *Home Page* will do.

▶ Drag the mouse to select the text you want to link back to your home page.

▶ Click the Anchor/Link button; the Anchor/Link dialog appears.

▶ In the Anchor/Link dialog, click the URL button; the URL Builder appears.

▶ Click the Browse button, browse to your home page, and click OK; the filename of your home page appears in the File field of the URL Builder.

▶ Click OK to close the URL Builder; the HRef field now contains the filename of your résumé.

▶ Click the Anchor button to complete the link.

Test the link by clicking it in the WebEdit preview window. If the link works, you will be taken back to your home page.

Linking Your Home Page to Other URLs

There are more than 4 million documents on the World Wide Web. You can link your home page to any document for which you know the URL. For example, if the place where you work or go to school has a home page, you might want to provide a way for the user to navigate there. Follow these steps:

▶ In the HTML window, drag the mouse to select the text that you want to link to some other Web page.

 ▶ Click the Anchor/Link button; the Anchor/Link dialog appears.

▶ In the HRef field, type the URL of the Web page you want to link; for example, to link to the University of Delaware home page, you would type:

`http://www.udel.edu`

▶ Click the Anchor button to complete the link.

Identifying the Web Page Owner

"Netiquette" (network etiquette) calls for Web pages to end with a few lines of text indicating who owns the page and how to contact the owner. To identify yourself as the owner of your Web page, follow these steps:

▶ Position the cursor in the HTML window right before the </BODY> tag, which you will find near the end of your document.

▶ Click the Paragraph button to begin a new paragraph.

▶ Type **This Web page is owned by** *Your Name*

Movie on CD

Demonstrations
➡ Show Me!
  ➡ Web Page
     Creation
     ➡ **Creating an
        E-mail Link**

Creating an E-mail Link

It is customary for Web page owners to include a link to their e-mail address to make it easy for you to contact them. When you click such a link, an e-mail dialog appears, automatically addressed to the Web page owner.

For example, consider the Web page owner statement you put at the bottom of your home page. Your name appears there. To link your name to your e-mail address, follow these steps:

▶ In the HTML window, drag the mouse over your name to select it.

 ▶ Click the Anchor/Link button; the Anchor/Link dialog appears.

▶ In the HRef field, type **mailto:** followed by your e-mail address. For example, if your e-mail address is santa.claus@northpole.com, you would type **mailto:santa.claus@northpole.com**

▶ Click the Anchor button to complete the link.

Demonstrations
➡ Show Me!
  ➡ Web Page
   Creation
    ➡ **Inserting**
      Special
      Symbols

Inserting Special Symbols

If you want to protect your right to ownership of the contents of your Web page, you should include an international copyright notice, which has the form:

    Copyright © 1996 by Santa Claus. All rights reserved.

The Special Characters feature comes in handy for inserting special symbols such as accent marks on the word *résumé,* or the copyright symbol. To insert a copyright symbol, follow these steps:

▶ Position the mouse in the HTML window where you want to insert the copyright symbol.

▶ Click the Special Characters button; the Special Characters dialog shown in Figure 55-2 appears.

▶ If necessary, click the Special tab, and then click the © symbol.

▶ Notice how the code *&copy* appears in the HTML window, whereas the © symbol appears on your Web page; *&copy* is the code for the copyright symbol.

55-2

The WebEdit Special
Characters dialog.

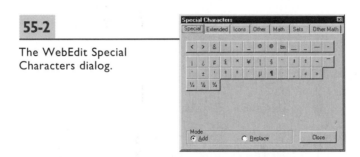

Remember to Save Your File

Don't forget to save your file. The filename of your home page should be *c:\website\index.htm.*

E X E R C I S E S

Prospective employers can be impressed by samples of your work. Especially if you have a well-written term paper or publication, linking that to your résumé can provide an employer with a convincing writing sample.

1. Use WebEdit to create an HTML version of your term paper or publication. If your writing sample is already word processed, you can copy-and-paste the text from your word processer into WebEdit instead of typing it all again, or you can use the Export as HTML feature available in some word processors. Save the new Web page version of your writing sample as an *.htm* file in your *website* directory. Then link it to your résumé. Test the link to make sure it works. Then put a return link at the end of your writing sample to provide an easy way to return to your résumé.

2. If your writing sample is a scholarly work, and one or more of the references in your paper is on the Web, use WebEdit to create hypertext links to the online references. Use your Web browser to test the links and make sure they work.

56

Mounting Files on the World Wide Web

After completing this chapter, you will be able to:

- **Understand the elements of a URL**
- **Explain the purpose of the hypertext transfer protocol**
- **Define what it means to FTP a file**
- **FTP files to a World Wide Web site**
- **Cope with case-sensitive file servers**
- **Create links to URLs**
- **Test links to URLs**
- **Maintain a good directory structure**
- **Define the new profession of WebMaster**

H E N you "mount a file onto the Web," you are transfering it into a directory on a World Wide Web file server. Unless your computer happens to be a Web file server, you need a way to transfer your files to the Web. This chapter provides you with the knowledge and the tools needed to transfer files from your PC to a Web server.

What Is HTTP?

As noted earlier, **HTTP** stands for Hypertext Transfer Protocol. HTTP is very powerful. In addition to transferring the HTML files that define Web pages, HTTP can transfer any type of computer file over the World Wide Web, including images, audio, video, word-processed documents, spreadsheets, databases, animations, multimedia, and computer software.

HTTP is easy to use. For example, suppose you want to put a movie on the Web. All you need to do is FTP the movie to your World Wide Web file server. Then you can use HTTP to serve that movie to anyone in the world who has an Internet connection and a Web browser configured to play that kind of movie.

What Is FTP?

FTP is one of the Internet's most important services. **FTP** stands for File Transfer Protocol, which is how you transfer files over the Internet from one computer to another. FTP is used so much on the Internet that it has become a verb: to "FTP a file" means to transfer the file from one computer to another. FTP is used to mount files on the World Wide Web. To mount a file on the Web, you simply FTP the file to your World Wide Web server.

Installing the Windows Sockets FTP Program

The *Multiliteracy CD* contains an FTP program called WS_FTP LE, which stands for Windows Sockets FTP Limited Edition. WS_FTP LE will work on any computer that has a Windows socket connection. WS_FTP LE may be used without fee by any United States government organization, by individuals for noncommercial home use, and by students, faculty, and staff of academic institutions. All others must contact Ipswitch, Inc., by sending e-mail to info@ipswitch.com or calling (617) 676-5700 for license information. Ipswitch may also be contacted via mail at 81 Hartwell Ave., Lexington, MA 02173 or fax at (617) 676-5710. At the WS_FTP home page http://www.ipswitch.com/pd_wsftp.html, you can learn about WS_FTP Pro, which is the commercial version of WS_FTP. WS_FTP Pro adds advanced features including drag-and-drop file transfers, automated login, and a collection of TCP/IP network utilities. WS_FTP Pro costs $37.50 for a single-user license.

How do you know whether your computer has the Windows socket connection needed to use WS_FTP? If your computer has Windows and you are using a graphical Web browser like Netscape, Mosaic, or the Internet Explorer to surf the Web, you already have a Windows socket connection to the Internet.

If you do not have a Windows socket connection, there are several ways to get one. For example, you can install the personal edition of the Netscape Explorer Complete Internet Access Kit that you can get at any computer store. The Netscape kit comes with PPP, the point-to-point protocol that establishes a Windows socket connection over ordinary phone lines. Or, if you have Windows 95, you can install the Dial-Up Networking feature that comes with Windows 95. Dial-Up Networking also uses PPP.

For more information about getting a Windows socket connection for your PC, contact your local computer store or check your phone book's Yellow Pages for Internet service providers. The director of the computer network at your local college, university, or workplace can provide you with leads and advice pertaining to your locale.

To install the WS_FTP LE program, follow these steps; if your CD-ROM drive is not D, substitute the letter of your CD-ROM drive.

FOR WINDOWS 3.1

▶ In the Program Manager, pull down the File menu and choose Run; the Run dialog appears.

▶ Type **d:\ws_ftp\install.exe** and click OK.

▶ Follow the on-screen instructions to install WS_FTP LE.

FOR WINDOWS 95

▶ Click the Windows 95 Start button and choose Run; the Run dialog appears.

▶ Type **d:\ws_ftp\install.exe** and click OK.

▶ Follow the on-screen instructions to install WS_FTP LE.

How to Create a Session Profile

Double-click the WS_FTP icon to get it running; the Session Profile dialog shown in Figure 56-1 appears. The first time you run WS_FTP, you need to create a new profile for your World Wide Web server. Otherwise, you just select the profile you created in a previous session. To create a new profile, follow these steps:

▶ In the Session Profile dialog, click New; this clears the fields in the Session Profile dialog.

▶ In the Profile Name field, type the name you want the new session profile to be called; for example, if your name is Santa Claus, you might call it **Santa's Web Site**

▶ In the Host Name field, type the domain name of your World Wide Web site, such as **www.santa.com**

▶ In the User ID field, type the user ID by which you are known on your Web server; this will probably be the first part of your e-mail address, up to but not including the @ sign.

▶ If you are not concerned about the security of your password on your local PC, you can type your password into the Password field, but this is not recommended for security reasons; if you do not enter your password here, your server will prompt you for it when you connect later on in this tutorial.

▶ Click Save to save the profile.

56-1

The WS_FTP Session Profile dialog.

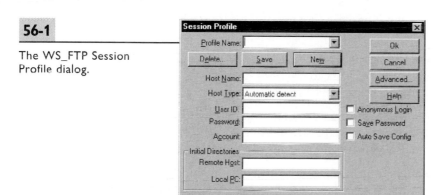

How to FTP HTML Files to the Web

Figure 56-2 shows how the WS_FTP program has graphical controls that make it very easy to FTP a file. All you need is an account on the Web file server to which you want to FTP the file. WS_FTP will connect you to the server and let you transfer files to and from it with ease.

For example, suppose you want to FTP your home page and your résumé from your PC to your World Wide Web account. Follow these steps:

▶ If you are not connected to the network, establish your network connection now.

▶ If WS_FTP is not already running, double-click the WS_FTP icon; the Session Profile dialog appears.

▶ In the WS_FTP Session Profile dialog, pull down the Profile Name selection box and choose your Web site's profile; if your Web site is not listed in the

Movie on CD

Demonstrations
➡ Show Me!
  ➡ Web Page
    Creation
     ➡ **How to FTP
       HTML Files
       to the Web**

The WS_FTP program displays directory listings for your local system and the remote system.

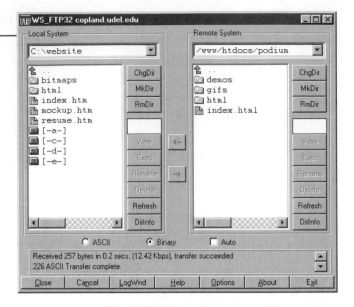

selection box, follow the steps in the previous section of this tutorial for creating an FTP session profile. Click OK to establish the connection and return to your WS_FTP window.

▶ To transfer HTML files to the Web, you must make sure the ASCII button is checked. *ASCII* stands for American Standard Code for Information Interchange; ASCII is the format for plain text files, which is what HTML files are. Click the ASCII button now.

▶ On the Local System side of the WS_FTP window, browse to the directory in which the file you want to transfer resides; in this example, browse to the *website* directory on your hard drive.

▶ On the Remote System side of the WS_FTP window, browse to the directory in which you want to transfer the files; in this example, that will be the main directory of your World Wide Web account.

▶ To transfer your résumé, click once on *resume.htm* on the Local System side of the WS_FTP window; then click the ⟶ button to transfer the file to the Web. After the transfer completes, you will see your *resume.htm* file listed on the Remote System side of the WS_FTP window in your World Wide Web directory.

▶ To transfer your home page, click once on *index.htm* on the Local System side of the WS_FTP window; then click the ⟶ button to transfer the file to the Web. After the transfer completes, you will see your *index.htm* file listed on the Remote System side of the WS_FTP window in your World Wide Web directory.

▶ If your Web server allows the use of long filename extensions, click once on the *index.htm* filename on the Remote System side of the WS-FTP window, click the Rename button, and rename the file **index.html** to make your home page the default file that will appear when users access your Web site without a filename specified.

How to FTP Image Files to the Web

To transfer images to the Web, the process is almost identical; the critical difference is to check the Binary button instead of the ASCII button. Follow these steps:

▶ If WS_FTP is not already running, double-click the WS_FTP icon; when the Session Profile dialog appears, pull down the Profile Name selection box, choose your Web site's profile, and click OK to log on.

▶ Click the Binary button.

▶ Follow these steps for each image on your home page and résumé page:

- Click once on the filename of the image on the Local System side of the WS_FTP window.
- Click the ⊡ button to transfer the file to the Web.
- After the transfer completes, you will see the filename of the image appear on the Remote System side of the WS_FTP window.

▶ To close this FTP session, click the Close button.

▶ To quit the WS_FTP program, click the Exit button.

Coping with Case-Sensitive File Servers

If your Web server is case sensitive, you need to make sure that the filenames you FTP to the server match the case that you gave them in your HTML source code. For example, the UNIX operating system is case sensitive. On a UNIX-based server, if an image is named *PORTRAIT.GIF* and your HTML file attempts to access it as *portrait.gif,* you will get a "File Not Found" error message.

To cope with case-sensitive file servers, always keep the names of your files in all uppercase or all lowercase. Most people use all lowercase.

How to Test Your New Home Page on the Web

A special moment in everyone's life is when you first access your brand-new home page on the World Wide Web. To test your new home page, get your Web browser running. If the browser has a URL location field, click on the field to activate it, then type the URL of your home page and press ⏎Enter. Otherwise, pull down your browser's File menu, choose Open Location, type the URL of your home page, and press ⏎Enter.

Remember how to construct the URL of your home page. If the name of your Web server is www.santa.com and the directory in which your home page is found is called *claus,* the URL of your home page will be:

```
http://www.santa.com/claus/index.html
```

Since *index.html* is the default filename for Web sites, you can also access your home page by its directory name:

```
http://www.santa.com/claus
```

Test all of the links on your home page and on your résumé to make sure they work OK. If you get errors trying to link to files that you know you FTP'd to your Web site but your Web browser cannot find them, you probably strayed from this tutorial's advice about creating directories and being careful to maintain a good directory structure.

Maintaining a Good Directory Structure

You need to be careful how you create directories and subdirectories when you create a local web that you plan to mount on the World Wide Web. Links that you make to local files are made relative to those files. In order for the local web to function properly on the World Wide Web, the directory structure of the local web must be exactly the same as you intend to have out on the World Wide Web.

If you have lots of HTML files, pictures, sounds, and movies that you plan to mount on the World Wide Web, you should keep them organized in a neat directory structure like this:

```
📁 c:\website
   📄 index.htm
   📁 sounds
      📄 ambient.wav
      📄 welcome.wav
   📁 pictures
      📄 logo.gif
      📄 portrait.gif
   📁 movies
      📄 dance.mpg
      📄 effects.mpg
   📁 html
      📄 resume.htm
      📄 article.htm
```

If your files are scattered across multiple directories and multiple drives on your PC, it will be time-consuming and tedious to create that same directory structure on your Web server. It is also more difficult to troubleshoot problems that occur on Web sites that are not well organized.

Setting the File Permission Attributes

After you FTP your files to the Web, you will probably want to set the file permission attributes to let anyone in the world read your files, but allow only you to modify or delete them. If your Web server is UNIX based, the command to type is *chmod 644* (*chmod* is pronounced "shmode" in UNIX land). For example, if your filename is */www/htdocs/fth/index.html,* you would type the following command at your UNIX prompt:

```
chmod 644 /www/htdocs/fth/index.html
```

To chmod all of the files in that directory at once, you can use the wildcard symbol (*) as follows:

```
chmod 644 /www/htdocs/fth/*.*
```

For more information about chmoding files, type **man chmod** at your UNIX prompt.

Becoming a WebMaster

An exciting new profession that has emerged along with the World Wide Web is that of WebMaster. A **WebMaster** is a person in charge of a Web site. The WebMaster keeps track of all the files in the web, maintains a good directory structure, and makes sure the links in the web work properly.

If you found this tutorial easy to complete, you may well have the knack for becoming a WebMaster. To learn more about this new profession, you may be interested in subscribing to *WebMaster* magazine. To apply for a free subscription, go to WebMaster online at http://www.cio.com/WebMaster/wmhome.html.

EXERCISES

1. If you do not have a World Wide Web account on which you can mount your home page, résumé, and associated files, find out how to get one by contacting your local computer store or looking up Internet service providers in your phone book's Yellow Pages. The director of the computer network at your local college, university, or workplace can provide you with leads and advice pertaining to your locale.

2. If you have an Internet account and you completed the tutorial in this chapter, find a few friends who have Web browsers, and send e-mail to your friends, asking them to try out your new home page and résumé. Be sure to include the URL of your home page so your friends know its address on the Web. Be aware that your home page may not appear exactly the same on each of your friends' computers. Depending on the brand of Web browser, the graphics resolution of the computer screen, and the current size of the browser window, your Web page may appear differently. The information will be correct, but the formatting may vary.

3. At the end of your Web page, you identified yourself as the Web page owner and provided a mailto link so that people can get in touch with you. Use your Web browser to get on the Web, go to your home page, and test the mailto link. Click the link and see if you can send an e-mail message to yourself. If you get a message telling you that your browser has not been configured for e-mail, pull down your browser's Options or Preferences menu, find the e-mail settings dialog, and fill in your name and e-mail address. Then click OK and try your e-mail link again.

57 Multimedia and the Web

After completing this chapter, you will be able to:

- ☐ Explain the concept of a helper application
- ☐ Configure helper applications for a Web browser
- ☐ Add links that use helper apps in your résumé
- ☐ Understand the limits of a helper application
- ☐ Share the vision for integrating multimedia elements into "active" Web pages

ECAUSE HTTP can transfer any type of file over the World Wide Web, you have the potential to link your résumé to more than just HTML files. For example, you could link samples of artwork you have created, movies you have made, sound tracks you have recorded, or spreadsheets and databases that demonstrate your information technology skills. These non-HTML file types will be unintelligible to most Web browsers, however. When a Web browser encounters a file it does not know how to handle, it looks for a helper app to handle the file instead.

What Are Helper Apps?

A **helper app** is an application that helps handle a file that your browser cannot deal with on its own. If your Web browser does not have built-in support for that kind of file, the browser will seek assistance from a helper app.

Helper apps are especially useful for multimedia. There are hundreds of multimedia file types, and no browser knows how to handle them all.

Making Links That Use Helper Apps

To demonstrate the creation of a link that uses a helper app, let's make a waveform audio recording that welcomes users to your home page. Follow these steps:

▶ Get PODIUM running, pull down the Tools menu, and choose Waveform Audio.

▶ Click the Record button, record a welcome to your home page, then click the Stop button.

▶ Click the Rewind button, and then click Play to rehearse your welcome message. If you do not like it, click Reset and record it over again.

▶ Click the Stop button.

▶ In the filename field, type the full path to the name under which you want to save this file. Assuming your hard drive is C, type **c:\website\welcome.wav**

▶ Click the Save button to save the file.

▶ Click Cancel to put the tool away.

▶ Pull down the PODIUM Files menu and choose Exit to put PODIUM away.

On your home page, create a link to the audio file you just recorded. Follow these steps:

▶ Use WebEdit to open your home page *(website\index.htm)*.

▶ In the HTML window, create some text that you will want users to click to hear your welcome message.

▶ Drag the mouse to select the text you want to link to your *welcome.wav* file.

 ▶ Click the Anchor/Link button; the Anchor/Link dialog appears.

▶ In the Anchor/Link dialog, click the URL button; the URL Builder appears.

▶ Click the Browse button, browse to your *website\welcome.wav* file, and click OK; the filename of your waveform welcome appears in the File field of the URL Builder.

▶ Click OK to close the URL Builder; the HRef field now contains the filename of your audio welcome.

▶ Click the Anchor button to complete the link.

Use your Web browser to test the new audio link on your home page. Unless you have previously configured a helper to handle waveform audio files, you will probably get an error message such as "Helper Application Not Found." Read on to learn how to configure your Web browser to use a helper app.

Helper Configuration

To enable your browser to use helper apps, you need to configure your browser so it knows what applications to launch for handling different kinds of files. Printed below are instructions for configuring a waveform audio helper application for Netscape. If you have some other browser, the procedure will be similar. For Netscape, follow these steps:

▶ Pull down the Options menu and choose General Preferences; the Preferences dialog appears.

▶ Click the Helpers tab; the helper options appear.

▶ In the File type list box, choose audio/x-wav; the filename extension *.wav* appears in the Extensions field.

▶ Click the Browse button and browse to your Windows directory.

▶ Select the Windows Media Player, which is *mplayer.exe,* and click OK.

Test your home page audio link with your Web browser again. This time, the Media Player should play the audio.

Are Helper Apps Multimedia?

By linking your Web pages to media that gets handled by helper apps, it may seem like your Web pages are being brought to life through multimedia. This kind of linking, however, has an important limitation: The browser has no knowledge of what is happening in the helper application. For example, when a browser launches a helper app to play a movie, the browser does not know whether the movie started OK, how much of the movie has played so far, or whether the user stopped the movie and quit watching it.

In effect, helper apps create a form of mixed media in which a Web page can launch a medium such as a movie; but since the Web page has no knowledge of what is happening in the movie, the kind of synchronization and integration so important in multimedia is absent.

This is one of the reasons why there is so much interest in active Web technologies such as Sun's Hot Java, Macromedia's Shockwave, and Microsoft's ActiveX technologies. These emerging active Web technologies provide the capability to integrate all kinds of media on the Web page without needing helper apps.

Annotated List of HTML Tags

This concludes the World Wide Web tutorial section of this book. If you want to learn more about HTML, there is an excellent help file in WebEdit. If you pull down the WebEdit Help menu, choose Contents, then choose Learning HTML, you will get a menu of excellent resources for expanding your knowledge of HTML. If you choose the Index of Tags option from the Learning HTML menu, you will get a list of new tags from each version of HTML. The list concludes with some vendor-specific tags that are not yet accepted as "official HTML" as this book goes to press. Eventually, they will probably become standard HTML tags. And more new tags will surely be invented.

You may also want to visit the WebEdit site on the World Wide Web and download the latest version of the WebEdit software. The URL for the WebEdit site is http://www.nesbitt.com.

EXERCISES

1. Configure your Web browser to use *mplayer.exe* as the helper app for the following types of files: MIDI, WAV, AVI, and MPG. If you have an application you like better than *mplayer.exe* for one or more of these file types, feel free to use it instead.

2. There is some hot jazz in the *audio\aris_wav* directory on the *Multiliteracy CD*. The name of the file is *ny_jazz1.wav*. Copy that file to the *website* directory on your hard drive. Create a link from your home page to the jazz. For example, you might enter a line of text that says, *I like to listen to hot jazz*. Link the words *hot jazz* to the *ny_jazz1.wav* file in your *website* directory. Then use your Web browser to display your home page and test the *hot jazz* link.

3. If you have a World Wide Web site, FTP the *ny_jazz1.wav* file to your World Wide Web directory. Make sure to set the Binary option when you transfer the file. Also transfer the new version of your home page to your World Wide Web site, making sure to check the ASCII option for transferring an HTML file. Test your home page on the Web to make sure the waveform link works OK.

Part Eleven

Multimedia Front-Ending

Front-ending is the creation or use of software to make it easy for people to perform computing tasks that would otherwise be too complicated or time-consuming for everyday use. This part of the book enables you to apply the concept of front-ending to your PC, your television, the World Wide Web, and the stock market.

After you complete the front-ending tutorials in the next four chapters, you will understand how front-ending can make computers easier to use. Not only will you be able to use front-ending techniques to improve your own multimedia applications, but you will be ready to dream of new ways to design user interfaces to multimedia products and services.

58 Front-End Your PC

After completing this chapter, you will be able to:

- **Design a new desktop for your PC**

- **Make your desktop appear automatically when Windows starts up**

- **Switch at any time from your front-end to the conventional Windows desktop**

- **Create links that pass parameters to start Windows programs the way you want your software to begin**

 ESPITE all the hype about how easy Windows is to use, anyone who has tried to teach Windows to a novice knows that beginners have difficulty with several Windows concepts. For starters, it can be difficult for a novice to get a program running. If the program's icon is not visible on the screen, how does the novice find it? Novices get confused by overlapping windows that hide things, pull-down versus pop-out menus, and the subtleties of left versus right mouse clicks, to say nothing of what happens when Ctrl or Alt is held down simultaneously.

This chapter teaches you how to simplify the user interface by creating a multimedia front-end for your computer.

Designing a New Desktop for Your PC

Think about the design elements on a PC's desktop. They boil down to two basic elements: text and graphics. Everything you see on the screen is either a text or a graphic. There is nothing else to be seen.

Now think about the multimedia toolbox you have learned how to use. You can use the Backdrop tool to make any bitmap become the backdrop on the screen. You can use the Text tool to put any text anyplace on the screen in any color, font, or size. You can use the Picture Hanger tool to hang icons anyplace on the screen.

Thus, you are able to create any conceivable look that you want your new desktop to have.

Then you can use the Link tool, the Trigger tool, and the button-making tools to link any text or graphic on your desktop to anything your computer is capable of doing. This enables you to interact with your desktop any way you want.

58-1

A simple front-end that provides access to a paint program, a notepad, and a calculator.

For example, suppose you want your computer to have a simple desktop that makes three programs available at the click of a mouse: the Windows Paint program, the Notepad, and the Calculator. Follow these steps:

▶ Pull down the PODIUM Files menu, choose New Custom, and create a new screen called *multilit\desktop.cus*.

 ▶ Use the Backdrop tool to make the backdrop be *backdrop\desktop.bmp,* which is one of the backdrop files on the *Multiliteracy CD*.

 ▶ Use the Picture Hanger tool to hang the following three icons on the screen. Figure 58-1 shows one example of how to do this.

icons\paint.bmp
icons\desknote.bmp
icons\calc.bmp

 ▶ Use the Text tool to write any text you want on the screen.

▶ Use the Link tool to click on each icon. When the Link box appears, link the icon to the appropriate filename:

Icon	Link
icons\paint.bmp	*mspaint.exe* (Windows 95)
	pbrush.exe (Windows 3.1)
icons\desknote.bmp	*notepad.exe*
icons\calc.bmp	*calc.exe*

NOTE You do not need to specify a path to these filenames, because the Paint program, the Notepad, and the Calculator are all part of Windows, and Windows knows where to find them.

▶ Close the toolbox and test your new desktop.

Admittedly, this is a simple example designed as an exercise to get you started thinking about the concept of front-ending. The exercises at the end of this chapter will build on this example and make it do more.

Making Front-Ends Appear Automatically on Startup

To make a multimedia front-end appear automatically when the user starts a computer, you create an icon that launches the front-end, test the icon to make sure it works, then drag the icon into your Windows Startup group. After Windows boots, the Startup group launches your icon automatically, and your front-end appears. To make the *multilit\desktop.cus* screen autolaunch when you start Windows, follow these steps:

Movie on CD

Demonstrations
↠ Show Me!
  ↠ Front-Ending
    ↠ **Autolaunching**
       from Windows 3.1

FOR WINDOWS 3.1

▶ Click once inside the PODIUM group to make it the active program group.

▶ Pull down the Program Manager's File menu and choose New; the New Program Object dialog appears.

▶ Click Program Item and click OK; the Program Item Properties dialog appears.

▶ In the Description field, type a one- or two-word title, such as **New Desktop**

▶ In the Command Line field, type the full path to your PODIUM executable file, followed by the name of your front-end's custom file, followed by the suppress-title-page switch and the full-screen switch. Assuming your CD-ROM drive is D and your hard drive is C, here is the command to type:

```
d:\wnpodium\mlpodium.exe c:\multilit\desktop.cus /t /f
```

▶ In the Working Directory field, type **C:\wnpodium**

▶ Click OK; the new icon appears in the PODIUM group.

▶ Double-click the icon to make sure it launches your desktop file properly.

NOTE   Because the full-screen switch is on, F2 will no longer work to put PODIUM into a window. If you need to access the PODIUM menus, do so by holding down Alt and typing the first letter of the menu, such as Alt-F to access the Files menu.

▶ Pull down the Window menu and choose Startup; your Startup group appears on the screen.

▶ Position the Startup group on your screen so you can see the PODIUM icon you just created as well as the Startup group.

▶ Drag the icon from the PODIUM group into the Startup group.

▶ Shut down your computer and restart it. If Windows does not start automatically, get Windows running. Windows will boot up to your Startup screen.

Movie on CD

Demonstrations
↠ Show Me!
  ↠ Front-Ending
    ↠ **Autolaunching**
       from Windows 95

FOR WINDOWS 95

▶ Click the right mouse button on any blank space on the Windows 95 desktop; the options menu pops out.

▶ Choose New, then choose Shortcut; the Create Shortcut dialog appears.

▶ In the Command Line field, type the full path to your PODIUM executable file, followed by the name of your front-end's custom file, followed by the suppress-title-page switch and the full-screen switch. Assuming your CD-ROM drive is D and your hard drive is C, here is the command to type:

```
d:\wnpodium\mlpodium.exe c:\multilit\desktop.cus /t /f
```

▶ Click Next; the Select a Title dialog appears.

▶ Type a name for the shortcut, such as **New Desktop** and click Finish. The new shortcut icon appears on your screen.

▶ Double-click the icon to make sure it launches your desktop file properly.

NOTE   Because the full-screen switch is on, F2 will no longer work to put PODIUM into a window. If you need to access the PODIUM menus, do so by holding down Alt and typing the first letter of the menu, such as Alt-F to access the Files menu.

▶ Your Startup folder is nested a few levels deep inside your Windows 95 directory. To get your Startup folder on the screen, use My Computer to open your Windows 95 folder, then open the Start Menu folder, then open the Programs folder, then open the Startup folder.

▶ Position the Startup folder on your screen so you can see the PODIUM icon you just created as well as the Startup folder.

▶ Drag the PODIUM icon into the Startup folder.

▶ Shut down your computer and restart it. Windows will boot up to your startup screen automatically.

Switching from Custom Front-Ends to the Conventional Windows Desktop

If you made Windows start up a custom front-end automatically and you want to do something on the conventional Windows desktop, follow these steps:

FOR WINDOWS 3.1

▶ Hold down Alt and keep it pressed until these instructions tell you to release it.

▶ Press Tab until the Program Manager is selected.

▶ Release Alt.

▶ To return to your custom front-end, hold down Alt and press Tab until your front-end is selected.

FOR WINDOWS 95

▶ Hold down Ctrl and press Esc.

▶ The Windows 95 Start menu will appear.

▶ Do whatever you want.

▶ To return to your custom front-end, hold down Alt and press Tab until your front-end is selected.

Passing Parameters to Initialize Windows Programs on Startup

When you front-end a PC, you might want to make an icon start up a specific file when the user clicks to start a program. You can make most Windows programs begin on a specific file by passing parameters on the link that launches the program.

To pass parameters to Windows programs in PODIUM, you use the @os= command. For example, suppose you want the Notepad to start up, displaying the text of the History of the Internet from the *Multiliteracy CD*. Assuming the letter of your CD-ROM drive is D, the link to type is:

```
@os=notepad.exe d:\ml_demo\history.txt
```

Making PODIUM Be the Shell in Windows 95

If you have Windows 95, a clever way of making your PODIUM front-end replace the conventional desktop is to make PODIUM be the shell. To do this, you edit the *system.ini* file in your Windows directory. In the [boot] section of the file, you will find a command that says "shell=Explorer.exe". Insert an asterisk right before the word *shell* to disable that command. Then insert a new line right below it that reads as follows, replacing *drive* with the letter of the drive on which you have PODIUM installed, and replacing *path\filename* with the path and filename of your startup custom file:

```
shell=drive:\wnpodium\mlpodium.exe path\filename.cus /f
```

Save the change and reboot your computer; your PODIUM application will totally replace the conventional Windows 95 desktop. To change back to your conventional Windows 95 desktop, press Alt-F to pull down the PODIUM Files menu, choose Edit Other File, and edit your *system.ini* file, making the shell statement be "shell=Explorer.exe". Save the file and reboot your computer; your Windows 95 desktop will reappear.

NOTE Only experienced Windows 95 users should attempt to change their shell. If you own a copy of Personal PODIUM or Retail PODIUM, make the shell be *wnpodium.exe* instead of *mlpodium.exe*.

E X E R C I S E S

1. Use Paint Shop Pro to grab the icon of your Web browser. Save it as a 256-color bitmap, making sure to include the Windows colors in the icon's palette. Use the Picture Hanger tool to put the icon on your *c:\multilit\desktop.cus* screen. Then use the Link tool to link the icon to the complete path\filename of your Web browser. Close the toolbox and test the link by clicking on the icon. Your Web browser should appear. Troubleshoot any problems until you get this to work.

2. Customize the *c:\multilit\desktop.cus* screen to give it the look and feel you want your desktop to have. What are the advantages of your desktop over the conventional Windows desktop? What is easier to do on your desktop? What are the disadvantages of your desktop?

59 Front-End Your Television Tuner

After completing this chapter, you will be able to:

- **Cut a live video window into your computer screen**

- **Resize the video window**

- **Use overlay commands to adjust brightness, color, sharpness, and volume**

- **Tune to specific television channels**

- **Make buttons that launch specific television channels, such as CNN**

IN ORDER to complete the television tutorial in this chapter, you will need an overlay device and a television tuner installed on your multimedia PC. If you do not have the necessary hardware, you can read this chapter to learn about video overlay and television front-ending, but you will not be able to complete the tutorial exercises. It is possible to skip this chapter entirely without missing any concepts needed to understand the rest of the book.

PODIUM communicates with all multimedia devices through the Windows MCI (media control interface). Therefore, this tutorial will work with any overlay device or TV tuner that has an MCI driver installed under Windows. PODIUM has special support for the Hauppauge WinTV Celebrity card. If you are purchasing new hardware for use with this tutorial, get the Hauppauge WinTV Celebrity with the television tuner option. You can phone Hauppauge toll free at (800) 443-6284.

If you get error messages when you try using newly installed video overlay hardware with PODIUM, contact the vendor to make sure you have the latest MCI driver for the device. Some early drivers did not implement fully the MCI commands needed to perform the techniques taught in this chapter.

Video Inputs

To complete the exercises in this chapter, you need to create a new multimedia screen called *overlay.cus* in the *multilit* directory on your computer's hard drive. Follow these steps:

▶ If PODIUM is not running, start PODIUM now.

▶ Press `F2` to put PODIUM into a window and reveal the menu bar.

▶ Pull down the Files menu and select New Custom to create a new screen.

▶ In the File name box, assuming your hard drive is C, type:

    `c:\multilit\overlay.cus`

▶ Press ⏎Enter; PODIUM creates the new screen and opens the custom toolbox for you.

▶ Use the Backdrop tool to give the screen a dark blue background.

▶ Use the Text tool to put the following text at the top of the screen:

    `Multimedia Literacy Video Overlay Practice`

▶ At the bottom left of the screen, type **Video Input 1**

▶ At the bottom center of the screen, type **Video Input 2**

▶ At the bottom right of the screen, type **Video Input 3**

▶ Use the Link tool to link each one of the video input lines to a @vinput command. @vinput stands for video input. The syntax is @vinput=*n* where *n* is the number of the video input. For example, you should link **Video Input 1** to the command:

    `@vinput=1`

Close the toolbox and click *Video Input 1*. You should see whatever video source you have connected to the first video input on your overlay card. Click anywhere to return to your *overlay.cus* screen.

Now click *Video Input 2*. If your computer has a second video input, you should see the video source connected to the second video input. Click anywhere to return to your *overlay.cus* screen.

Click *Video Input 3*. If your computer has a third video input, the video source connected to the third video input will appear. Click anywhere to return to your *overlay.cus* screen.

One of the three video inputs should display the output of your television tuner. On the WinTV card, the television is video input 3.

PODIUM has hot keys that let you quickly display your video inputs. To show video input 1, press Alt -1. For video input 2, press Alt -2. For video input 3, press Alt -3. You can also access the video inputs via the PODIUM Controls menu.

Creating a Live Video Window

Overlay cards display video on the screen by means of a process known as a **chroma key**, whereby one of the colors on the screen becomes transparent. Anyplace the transparent color appears, you see the video input. Most overlay cards use pink as the tranparent color.

CREATING WINTV WINDOWS

PODIUM has special support built in for the WinTV card. To cut a WinTV window into the screen, follow these steps:

▶ Use PODIUM to display the custom screen into which you want to cut the video window. In this example use PODIUM to display your *multilit\overlay.cus* screen.

▶ Open the toolbox and expand it so the drawing tools are visible.

59-1

The Video Overlay Window Creator dialog.

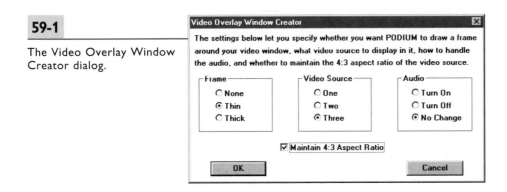

Click once on the Transparent Rectangle tool.

▶ Press the Ⓥ key and keep holding down Ⓥ when you do the next step. *V* stands for video. If you want to maintain the 4:3 aspect ratio of the original video source, press Shift-Ⓥ and keep holding down Shift-Ⓥ when you do the next step.

▶ Click and drag to draw a rectangle on the screen. When you release the mouse button, the Video Overlay Window Creator dialog appears as shown in Figure 59-1.

▶ Set the frame, video source, and audio options as you wish. Then click OK.

Close the toolbox, and the video window should appear on your screen. If you try this with a different brand of TV tuner and you get error messages, your overlay card does not support the MCI commands needed to do this. Pull down the PODIUM Files menu and choose Edit This File to inspect the source code in your *multilit\overlay.cus* file. Near the top of the file, you will see the @overlay command that PODIUM put into your file when you drew the video window. If you are getting error messages as a result of that command, delete the @overlay command and proceed to the next paragraph. If your overlay command works properly, you can skip the next section.

CREATING OVERLAY WINDOWS VIA MCI COMMANDS

If you know the MCI command strings for your overlay device, it is possible to create overlay windows by issuing MCI commands. If you do not know the MCI command strings, contact the vendor of your overlay card and ask for documentation on the MCI command strings your device supports. To create an overlay window using MCI command strings, follow these steps:

▶ Use PODIUM to display the custom screen into which you want to cut the video window. In this example use PODIUM to display your *multilit\overlay.cus* screen.

▶ Open the toolbox and expand it so the drawing tools are visible.

▶ Click the Color tool and set the primary color to be the chroma key (transparent color) of your overlay card.

▶ Click once on the Transparent Rectangle tool.

▶ Click and drag to draw a rectangle on the screen.

 ▶ Click the Backdrop tool; the Backdrop dialog appears.

▶ Into the backdrop, type the @mci commands needed to make your overlay device display the video source into the target rectangle. The syntax of the @mci command is @mci=*string* where *string* is the MCI command string. For example, to create a video window with the WinTV card, you would type the following @mci commands after the @draw command created by the Transparent Rectangle tool:

```
@background=4194368
@draw(Box,30,20,70,60,Black,1,Pink,0)
@mci=put overlay frame at 0 0 253 190
@mci=put overlay destination at 193 96 444 288
@mci=setvideo overlay source to 2
@mci=setvideo overlay on
@mci=setaudio overlay source to 2
@mci=setaudio overlay on
```

NOTE On startup, PODIUM opened the overlay device and called it *overlay*. You need not and should not issue any MCI commands to open or close the *overlay* device. Let PODIUM handle that.

If you do not have a WinTV card, chances are the MCI command strings for your overlay device will not match exactly the ones provided here. In an ideal world, all vendors would follow Microsoft's MCI guidelines precisely, and the overlay commands would be identical for all devices. In today's imperfect world, however, you need to cope with differences among various vendors' overlay commands.

FIXING CHROMA-KEY PROBLEMS

If you follow all of the instructions provided here and video does not appear on your screen, it is possible that your current palette does not contain your overlay card's chroma-key color. This can happen when you have a bitmap on the screen that customizes all 256 colors without including the Windows colors. To fix this problem, use Paint Shop Pro to add the Windows colors to the bitmap's palette. First, increase the color depth to 16 million colors. Then reduce the color depth back to 256 colors, checking the box that says to include the Windows colors. Chapter 31 provides detailed instructions for using Paint Shop Pro.

Editing the Live Video Window

To edit a live video window, pull down the PODIUM Files menu, choose Edit This File, and use the Notepad to edit the coordinates that size and position the live video window. To delete a live video window, use the Notepad to delete the commands that created it.

Overlay Commands

You can use @mci commands to control many video parameters. Brightness, color, contrast, and tint control the appearance of the video. Volume, balance, bass, and treble commands let you control the sound. Consult the list of MCI command strings for your overlay device, and use PODIUM's @mci command to control audiovisual parameters on your computer. If you have the WinTV card, PODIUM has a special set of @overlay commands that simplify this process. Table 59-1 documents the @overlay commands.

Table 59-1   The PODIUM Overlay Commands

Command Syntax	What the Command Does
@overlay(Window,$x1,y1,x2,y2$,Source,FrameType,Audio)	Cuts a video window into the screen, sizing the video to fit the window. The x,y parameters are percentages of the screen. They define the rectangle into which the overlay video will display. *Source* is a number from 1 to 3 (3 is TV on the WinTV card). *FrameType* is 0 for no frame, 1 for a thin buttonlike frame, or 2 for a thicker frame like Video for Windows has. *Audio* is 0 to turn the audio off, 1 to turn it on, or 2 to leave the current state of the audio unchanged.
	Holding down the ⟨V⟩ key while drawing with the Transparent Rectangle tool makes PODIUM create video windows via this command. Just holding down ⟨V⟩ while drawing lets you create a video window of any rectangular shape; the 4:3 aspect ratio does not get enforced. Holding down ⟨Shift⟩-⟨V⟩ preserves the 4:3 aspect ratio; as you drag the mouse to the right, PODIUM will automatically create the bottom dimension to be a 4:3 aspect ratio for proper video display. When you release the mouse button to complete the window, PODIUM will invoke a dialog that lets you set the video source, audio, and frame parameters of the video window.
@overlay(Rectangle,Frame,x,y,*Width,Height*)	Frames the overlay video. The x,y coordinates position the upper left corner of the frame. x and y are percentages relative to the destination window's x,y coordinates. Most often you will set x and y to zero. The *Width* and *Height* parameters are percentages of the screen.
@overlay(Rectangle,Destination,$x1,y1,x2,y2$)	Sets the destination rectangle of the overlay video. The x,y parameters are percentages of the screen. They define the rectangle into which the overlay video will display.
	Note: Whenever you use frame and destination in combination, always give the frame command first; otherwise, sync problems can arise.
@overlay(Rectangle,Source,$x1,y1,x2,y2$)	Sets the source rectangle of the overlay video buffer. The x,y parameters are percentages of the screen. They define the rectangular portion of the video buffer to be displayed.
@overlay(Rectangle,Video,$x1,y1,x2,y2$)	Sets the rectangle of the video source to be displayed in the destination window. The x,y parameters are percentages of the screen.
@overlay(Audio,On-or-Off)	Turns the overlay card's audio on or off.
@overlay(Volume,n)	Sets the volume to n. Some overlay cards are inaudible at settings below 50. The maximum setting is 100.
@overlay(Freeze)	Freezes the overlay on the current video frame.
@overlay(Unfreeze)	Unfreezes the overlay video.
@overlay(Source,Audio-or-Video,n)	Sets the audio or video source to source n; the range of n is from 1 to 3.
@overlay(Bass,n)	Sets the bass level to n. The maximum setting is 100.
@overlay(Treble,n)	Sets the treble level to n. The maximum setting is 100.
@overlay(Balance,n)	Sets the balance to n. The maximum setting is 100; 0 is all left, 100 is all right, and 50 is the center setting.
@overlay(Brightness,n)	Sets the brightness level to n. The maximum setting is 255.
@overlay(Color,n)	Sets the color level to n. The maximum setting is 255.
@overlay(Contrast,n)	Sets the contrast level to n. The maximum setting is 255.
@overlay(Tint,n)	Sets the tint level to n. The maximum setting is 255.

The *Multiliteracy CD* contains a screen that illustrates all of these commands in action. If you have a WinTV card, go to the Demonstrations section, select Textbook Examples, and click Live Video.

Television Tuner Command

To change channels on your television tuner, PODIUM has a @tune command. The syntax is @tune=*n* where *n* is the number of the channel to which you want to tune. If the @tune command does not work with your TV tuner, consult the MCI command string summary for your TV tuner, and use @mci commands to change channels on your tuner.

Movie on CD

Demonstrations
➥ Show Me!
➥ Front-Ending
➥ **Front-End
CNN**

TV Presets: Cable News Network Feed

Because you can tune to any television channel with the @tune command, you can use the custom toolbox to create links to specific television channels. For example, suppose you like to watch CNN and you want an icon you can click to bring up CNN on your screen. Follow these steps:

▶   Use PODIUM to get your *multilit\overlay.cus* file on the screen.

▶   There is a CNN icon in the *icons* directory on the *Multiliteracy CD*. Use the Picture Hanger tool to hang the *icons\cnn.bmp* icon on the screen.

▶   Use the Link tool to make the CNN icon be a hot spot; the Link dialog will appear.

▶   In the Link box, assuming that CNN is channel 23 and your TV tuner is on video input 3, type the following commands:

```
@tune=23
@vinput=3
```

Close the toolbox and click the CNN icon. You should now see and hear CNN full-screen. Click anywhere to return to your *multilit\overlay.cus* screen.

TV Channel Scanner

The WinTV card has a frame grab capability that works under the Windows MCI. By issuing the command:

```
@mci=save overlay filename at x1 y1 x2 y2
```

you can grab the frame currently in the overlay buffer and save it to the file *filename* at a size determined by the rectangle *x1 y1 x2 y2*. The *Multiliteracy CD* contains a TV channel scanner that was built using this frame grab command. If you have a WinTV card, you can run the channel scanner by going to the Demonstrations section, selecting Textbook Examples, and clicking TV Channel Scanner. Depending on the speed of your computer, the scanner will run either fast or slow. Figure 59-2 shows how you can click any one of the frames to view its TV channel full-screen.

To inspect the source code of the TV channel scanner, use the Notepad to look at the file *overlay\scanner.cus* on the *Multiliteracy CD*. You will see how the TV scanner uses variables to create the filenames for each TV channel screen.

59-2

Clicking one of the channels displayed here expands the channel to fill the screen.

E X E R C I S E S

1. If your computer has a video overlay card, pull down the PODIUM Controls menu and select each one of the three Video Input options. If your overlay device has three inputs, all three video input options should work on your computer. Troubleshoot any problems to get the inputs working.

2. If you have a video camera, connect it to one of the inputs on your video overlay card. Imagine yourself as a security guard who must periodically check what is happening on a surveillance camera. Put a timer on your *multilit\overlay.cus* screen that goes off every 30 seconds to display the live video feed from the surveillance camera.

3. Create a custom screen to provide quick and easy access to your favorite television stations. Make a hypertext or icon to click for each channel you select. In the middle of the screen, put a preview window that lets you see what is going on when you select a channel. Then make a full-screen button that lets you view the channel full-screen. *Hint:* The full-screen button needs only one command linked to it, namely, @vinput=*n* where *n* is the number of the video input to which your TV tuner is connected.

4. The television scanner example on the *Multiliteracy CD* in the file *practice\scanner.cus* scans only the first nine channels on your TV. Develop logic that makes the scanner display all of the channels on your TV in blocks of nine. For example, the scanner would begin by displaying channels 2 through 10, then channels 11 through 19, then 20 through 28, and so on, until all of the channels have been scanned. Then the scanner would start over at channel 2 again.

60

Front-End the World Wide Web

After completing this chapter, you will be able to:

☐ **Configure your Internet connection**

☐ **Create links to specific Web sites**

☐ **Download datasets from the Web**

☐ **Upload datasets to the Web**

HERE are several ways to front-end the World Wide Web. First and simplest is to create links to your favorite Web pages. When you trigger the link, your Web browser displays the Web page. A more sophisticated approach is to create World Wide Web templates into which Web pages flow. Instead of viewing the Web page with a browser, you repurpose the data on the Web page and display it on your custom screen. This chapter teaches both approaches and provides you with examples to use in creating your own front-ends.

Configuring Your PODIUM Internet Connection

To create a front-end that launches your Web browser to specific Web pages, you must first configure your PODIUM Internet connection. Follow these steps:

▶ Pull down the PODIUM Controls menu and choose Configuration; the Configuration dialog appears.

▶ In the WWW Browser field, type the full path and filename to your Web browser. For example, if you have Netscape on your C drive and you are using Windows 3.1, you would type:

`c:\netscape\netscape.exe`

If you have Windows 95, you would type:

`c:\Progra~1\Netscape\Naviga~1\Program\netscape.exe`

If you don't know what to type, click the Browse button to search for your Web browser.

▶ Click OK to close the Configuration dialog.

To test the configuration, and to prepare for completing the exercises in this chapter, you need to create a new multimedia screen called *webbing.cus* in the *multilit* directory on your computer's hard drive. Follow these steps:

▶ If PODIUM is not running, start PODIUM now.

▶ Press F2 to put PODIUM into a window and reveal the menu bar.

▶ Pull down the Files menu and select New Custom to create a new screen.

▶ In the File name box, assuming your hard drive is C, type:

`c:\multilit\webbing.cus`

▶ Press ←Enter ; PODIUM creates the new screen and opens the custom toolbox for you.

▶ Use the Backdrop tool to give the screen a dark blue background.

▶ Use the Text tool to put the following text at the top of the screen:

`Multimedia Literacy WWW Practice`

▶ Type the following text an inch or so down the screen:

`PODIUM's Home Page`

▶ Use the Link tool to link *PODIUM's Home Page* to the following URL:

`http://www.udel.edu/podium`

▶ Close the toolbox and click on *PODIUM's Home Page*.

If you configured your WWW setting correctly, your Web browser will be launched and pointed at PODIUM's home page. If this does not work, check the path to your browser by pulling down the Controls menu, and correct the information in the WWW Browser field. Then click *PODIUM's Home Page* again. If your Web browser still does not launch, seek help from a friend or colleague who is Windows savvy.

Weather Forecast Feed

Movie on CD

Demonstrations
➡ Show Me!
  ➡ Front-Ending
    ➡ **Front-End
      the Weather
      Channel**

You can make PODIUM links that launch any site on the World Wide Web. For example, suppose you want an icon to click to see the weather forecast. Follow these steps:

▶ Use the Picture Hanger tool to put the weather icon on the screen. The weather icon is on the *Multiliteracy CD* in the file *icons\weather.bmp*.

▶ Use the Link tool to click the weather icon; the Link dialog appears.

▶ In the Link box, type:

`http://www.weather.com`

▶ Close the toolbox and click the weather icon; PODIUM will launch your Web browser and point it at The Weather Channel, as shown in Figure 60-1.

60-1

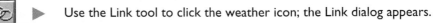

The Weather Channel at http://www.weather.com.

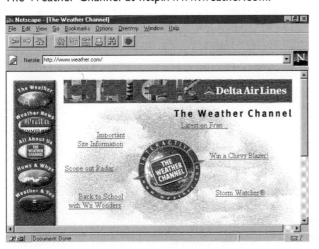

You will need to navigate through The Weather Channel to get to the weather forecast for your town or city. To save time the next time you want a weather forecast, you can customize your weather link to go directly to the forecast for your city. Follow these steps:

▶ With The Weather Channel in your Web browser window, click Current Conditions.

▶ Navigate to your state.

▶ Choose the five-day forecast for the city nearest you.

▶ If the URL of the Web page you are on now is not visible, pull down the Options menu and choose Show Location.

▶ Drag the mouse over the URL to select it; then press [Ctrl]-[C] to copy the URL to the Windows Clipboard.

 ▶ In PODIUM use the Link tool to click the weather icon; the Link box will appear, showing the link to http://www.weather.com. Erase that link. Then click the Paste button to copy the contents of the Clipboard into the Link box. The URL for your city's weather forecast will appear. For example, if you live near Dover, Delaware, the link will read:

```
http://www.weather.com/us/cities/DE_Dover.html
```

Close the toolbox and click the weather icon. The five-day forecast for your city should appear, as illustrated in Figure 60-2. From now on, whenever you want to know the weather forecast for your town, just click the weather icon.

60-2	60-3
A five-day forecast displayed by The Weather Channel at http://www.weather.com/us/cities/DE_Dover.html.	Sample screen from CNN Interactive at http://www.cnn.com.

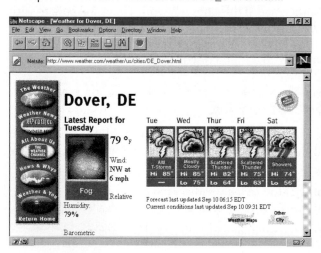

Electronic News Feed

Following the same method, you can create links to any Web site in the world. For example, suppose you want an icon that you can click to read the most recent news headlines. Follow these steps:

 ▶ Use the Picture Hanger tool to put the news icon on the screen. The news icon is on the *Multiliteracy CD* in the file *icons\news.bmp.*

 ▶ Use the Link tool to click the news icon; the Link dialog appears.

▶ In the Link box, type:

http://www.cnn.com

Close the toolbox and click the news icon; your Web browser will display the latest news headlines from CNN Interactive, as illustrated in Figure 60-3. The headlines are hyperlinks; click a headline for the story linked to it.

Front-Ending Remote Systems

PODIUM provides an easy way to create an attractive multimedia front-end to mainframe data. In order to understand how this easy way works, consider the transactional manner in which data gets processed by the mainframe. A user at a computer terminal enters data onto the screen and presses a key that causes a transaction to be sent to the mainframe for processing. The mainframe processes the transaction and returns the result for display on the terminal.

Using TCP/IP Internet protocols, PODIUM can send and receive these transactions with the mainframe and combine the results with sound and graphics to give the mainframe data a multimedia look and feel.

The three essential ingredients are (1) the sending of a message from PODIUM to the mainframe, (2) the mainframe processing of that message, and (3) the return to PODIUM of the mainframe's response.

SENDING A MESSAGE TO THE MAINFRAME

PODIUM sends messages to mainframes via the @post command. The format of the @post command is @post(*address*)=*message* where *address* is the IP address of the mainframe, and *message* is the command string you want the mainframe to process. The *message* normally has two parts. The first part tells the mainframe what program should process the message, and the second part contains the commands and/or data to be processed. You can use PODIUM variables along with the @string and @calc statements to create any conceivable message to send to the mainframe.

MAINFRAME PROCESSING OF THE MESSAGE

When the mainframe receives the message from PODIUM, the mainframe processes the message and sends PODIUM a reply. The reply contains the names and values of the variables that PODIUM will use to process and display the result on a multimedia screen. Depending on how the mainframe has been programmed to return the response, some reprogramming may be required to reformat the data being returned. This reprogramming can either be done on the mainframe itself, or a server can be placed between PODIUM and the mainframe; the server receives the message from PODIUM, makes the request of the mainframe, receives the mainframe response, reformats the response, and sends the response back to PODIUM.

The PODIUM data format is very simple, so any programming that may be needed either on the mainframe or on a server is very easy to do. In many cases, no reprogramming of any kind will be required.

PODIUM RECEIVING THE MAINFRAME'S RESPONSE

The mainframe will return its response to PODIUM according to some data format. PODIUM will take the appropriate action, depending on the kind of formatting the data has. The easiest formatting to work with is a simple list of the names and values of the variables being returned by the mainframe. The stream of data returned by the mainframe consists of the name of the first variable, followed by one or more spaces, followed by the value of the variable, followed by a line feed character; then comes the name of the second variable, followed by one or more spaces, followed by the value of the second variable, followed by a line feed character, and so on, for as many variables as the mainframe wants to return. An example of this format shows how easy it is. Consider a request to a mainframe for a user's checking-account balance. The data returned would be formatted as follows:

```
name          John Doe
balance       $5,225.43
```

In order to cause such a transaction to occur between PODIUM and a mainframe, you tell PODIUM to read the dataset that will be returned as the result of the @post command. The syntax is:

```
@ReadDataset=@post(address)=message
```

It is also possible for PODIUM to read datasets via World Wide Web addresses. Any dataset that has an HTTP address can be read into PODIUM. Here is an example:

```
@ReadDataset=http://www.udel.edu/podium/testdata.dat
```

You may want the data returned from a mainframe to be displayed in PODIUM input fields. This is also very easy to do. When you use PODIUM's custom toolbox to create the input field, simply type the name of the variable into the Initial Value box in the Input Field Editor.

Dynamic Data Exchange

Dynamic Data Exchange (DDE) is an advanced front-ending protocol that enables you to initiate conversations with other applications and exchange data with them. The application that initiates the conversation is known as the DDE client; an application responding to the conversation is called a DDE server. PODIUM supports both the client and the server side of DDE.

As a client, PODIUM can converse with DDE servers via the @DDE subcommands. There are five subcommands: Initiate, Request, Execute, Poke, and Terminate. As a server, PODIUM responds to the DDE topics listed in Table 60-1.

Although it is beyond the scope of this book to provide a tutorial on DDE, advanced users can learn how to use the DDE commands by pulling down the PODIUM Help menu, choosing Index, typing **DDE**, and selecting Dynamic Data Exchange.

Table 60-1   DDE Topics to Which PODIUM Responds

DDE Topic	Function
PODIUM_VERSION	Tells what version of PODIUM is running
PODIUM_SHOW	Makes the PODIUM window visible
PODIUM_HIDE	Hides the PODIUM window, making it invisible
PODIUM_POS	Repositions the PODIUM window
PODIUM_FILE	Makes PODIUM open a specified custom file
PODIUM_ASSIGN	Assigns values to numeric and string variables
PODIUM_QUERY	Queries the values of numeric and string variables
PODIUM_QUIT	Causes PODIUM to exit

EXERCISES

1. Printed in column 1 of the table below is a list of icons that you will find on the *Multiliteracy CD*. The second column provides the URL of a Web site for you to practice linking to each icon. Use the Picture Hanger tool to put each icon on your *multilit\webbing.cus* screen, and use the Link tool to link each icon to its URL. Test the links to make sure they work. If a link does not work, double-check the spelling of the URL in your custom file. If you spelled the URL correctly and the link still does not work, it is possible that its Web site has been discontinued or moved since this book was printed.

Web Site	Icon on the *Multiliteracy CD*	URL of the Icon's Web Site
Microsoft	icons\microsft.bmp	http://www.microsoft.com
Library of Congress	icons\loc.bmp	http://www.loc.gov
Home Vision	icons\homevis.bmp	http://www.homevision.com
Yahoo	icons\yahoo.bmp	http://www.yahoo.com
White House	icons\whithous.bmp	http://www.whitehouse.gov
PODIUM	icons\podium.bmp	http://www.udel.edu/podium
Smithsonian	icons\smithson.bmp	http://www.si.edu
Dream Shop	icons\shopping.bmp	http://www.dreamshop.com

2. Create your own customized WWW front-end. Make a new custom screen with a combination of backdrop, text, buttons, and icons that create the look and feel you want. Link the hypertext, buttons, and icons to your favorite Web sites.

61 Front-End the Stock Market

After completing this chapter, you will be able to:

- **Query the current value of any stock or fund**

- **Find out the ticker symbol for any stock or fund**

- **Create links to your favorite stocks**

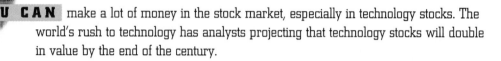

YOU CAN make a lot of money in the stock market, especially in technology stocks. The world's rush to technology has analysts projecting that technology stocks will double in value by the end of the century.

A particularly good opportunity to make money is when hot stocks first go on sale. Hot stocks usually surge in value the first day. Yahoo is a good example. When Yahoo went public, it opened at $12. The first opportunity for outsiders to buy it was for $26. The author bought 500 shares. Yahoo stock proceeded to climb to $43; then it began to fall. The author sold his shares at $36. The profit was $5,000 in less than two hours.

In order to make money in this manner, you need a quick way to query the value of a specific stock. This chapter provides a way to do that.

Querying the Current Value of a Stock

There is a site on the World Wide Web that lets you query the current value of any stock or fund. The URL is http://www.pathfinder.com. Point your browser there, scroll down through the Pathfinder table of contents, and choose Quick Quotes. The Quick Quotes screen will appear as shown in Figure 61-1. To query the current value of a stock, you type the stock's ticker symbol into the query field, then click the Send Query button. For example, Microsoft's ticker symbol is MSFT. Type **msft** into the query field, click the Send Query button, and Quick Quotes will return a screen like the one shown in Figure 61-2. When you are finished looking at Microsoft's stock, click Get Another Quote to return to the Quick Quotes screen.

Finding a Stock's Ticker Symbol

So long as you know a stock's ticker symbol, you can look up its value in Quick Quotes. If you do not know the ticker symbol, Quick Quotes has a Search feature that lets you find the ticker symbol of the company you are looking for. To find a stock's ticker symbol, click the Search feature, which is underneath the Send Query button on the Quick Quotes screen. The Ticker Symbol Finder will appear

61-1

The Quick Quotes screen at the Time Inc. New Media Pathfinder site on the World Wide Web.

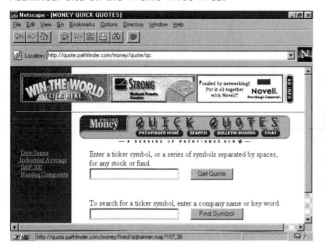

61-2

The result of querying the ticker symbol *msft*.

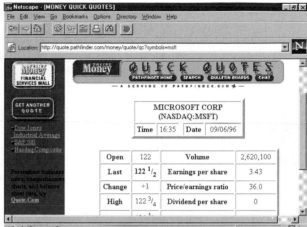

61-3

The Quick Quotes Ticker Symbol Finder.

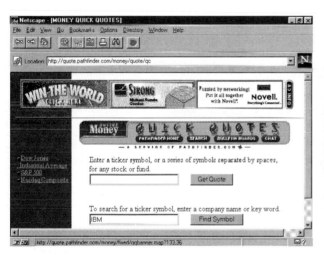

61-4

How the Ticker Symbol Finder returns the search results.

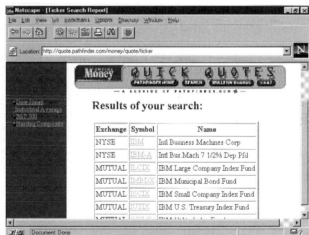

as shown in Figure 61-3. Type a word or word fragment into the search box, click the Find Symbol button, and the Ticker Symbol Finder will return the results of your search as shown in Figure 61-4.

Movie on CD

Demonstrations
➥ Show Me!
  ➥ Front-Ending
    ➥ **Front-End**
      the Stock
      Market

Creating Hot Links to Specific Stocks

It can take time to get your Web browser running, go to the Pathfinder site, browse to the Quick Quote screen, key in the ticker symbol of the stock you want, and get the results you need. You can speed the process by creating links to specific stocks. When you trigger the link, your Web browser automatically gets the Quick Quote you need. Suppose you want a link that will get you a Quick Quote for Microsoft stock. Follow these steps:

▶ Use PODIUM to get the *multilit\webbing.cus* file on your screen.

 ▶ Use the Picture Hanger tool to put the Microsoft icon on your screen. The Microsoft icon is on the *Multiliteracy CD* in the file *icons\microsft.bmp*.

▶ Use the Link tool to click the Microsoft icon; the Link box appears.

▶ In the Link box, type the following URL:

`http://quote.pathfinder.com/money/quote/qc?symbols=msft`

▶ Close the toolbox and click the Microsoft icon. Your Web browser displays the current value of the Microsoft stock.

▶ You can follow this method to query the value of any stock. Simply replace *msft* in the URL with the ticker symbol of the stock you want to query.

E X E R C I S E S

1. Practice front-ending the stock market by putting icons on the screen that are linked to Quick Quotes that display the stock's current value when you click the company's icon. Use the following icons and ticker symbols:

Company	Icon	Ticker Symbol
Apple Computer, Inc.	*icons\apple.bmp*	aapl
Compaq Computer Corporation	*icons\compaq.bmp*	cpq
International Business Machines Corporation	*icons\ibm.bmp*	ibm
Microsoft Corporation	*icons\microsft.bmp*	msft
Netscape Communications Corporation	*icons\netscape.bmp*	nscp

Use the Link tool to link each icon to the following URL, subsituting *ticker_symbol* with the stock's ticker symbol:

`http://quote.pathfinder.com/money/quote/qc?symbols=ticker_symbol`

2. Create your own custom screen to front-end the stocks in your portfolio. Use the Quick Quotes Search feature to find out each stock's ticker symbol. For each stock, create a line of hypertext or a symbol which, when clicked, launches a link in the following format:

`http://quote.pathfinder.com/money/quote/qc?symbols=ticker_symbol`

3. This is an advanced exercise that helps you create an input field that you can use to look up the value of any stock for which you know the ticker symbol. Use the Input tool to create an input field named *ticker*. Make the input field five characters long. Use the Text tool to write the word *Search* next to or underneath the input field, and use the rectangular button maker to draw a button around the word *Search*. The Link box will appear. In the Link box, enter commands that query the value of the input field, and use that value to create a string containing the URL needed to find that stock's value. The links would read as follows:

```
@string stem = http://quote.pathfinder.com/money/quote/qc?symbols=
@query(ticker,content,field_value)
@string sender = $$stem $$field_value
$$sender
```

Close the toolbox, type **msft** into the input field, click the Search button, and Microsoft's Quick Quote should appear. If it does not, troubleshoot what went wrong. When you get this working, write user-friendly instructions on the screen to help other people use your input field to look up stock market quotes.

Note: To invoke the rectangular button maker, double-click the Transparent Rectangle tool.

Part Twelve

Distributing Multimedia Applications

After helping you learn how to create multimedia applications, it is appropriate for this book to conclude by teaching how to distribute them. The final chapters show how to distribute multimedia applications on CD-ROM, diskettes, and the World Wide Web. The author encourages you to take advantage of these methods to share your multimedia works with other users. Multimedia should not be a spectator sport. Everyone should be able to create and contribute, not just sit back and consume.

For those who would like to make money developing multimedia applications, Coupland (1993) tells about eight independent multimedia developers who made huge profits producing their own CDs. If you have an entrepreneurial flare and possess the combination of skills needed to create a multimedia title on your own, it is quite feasible for you to succeed as an independent developer.

It is also possible to partner with a commercial publisher. All of the big-name publishers are looking for multimedia titles to distribute. The trend to include multimedia CD-ROMs along with textbooks presents the opportunity for you to contact the editors of the leading textbooks in your field to find out if there is a project you could work on as a multimedia developer.

Meanwhile, the World Wide Web is making it even more feasible to succeed on your own. In the past you had to spend a lot of money advertising and setting up distribution channels. Today you can simply create a Web page announcing your product and let the Web crawlers find it. When potential customers use WWW search engines to look for materials in your content area, your product will be listed and hotlinked to its Web page.

62

Introduction to Multimedia Publishing

After completing this chapter, you will be able to:

- **Describe three multimedia publishing alternatives and decide which one best suits your application**

- **Understand how the PODIUM Installer works with a configuration file that controls the installation process**

- **Configure installation files for CD-ROM or hard disk playback**

- **Specify the startup screen and the name for the icon that will launch your application**

- **Suppress the PODIUM title screen and make your application run full-screen only**

- **Inspect an *install.cfg* file and understand the installation switch settings**

T IS easy to publish multimedia applications created with PODIUM. All you need is the PODIUM Installer and a copy of Runtime PODIUM.

The PODIUM Installer is free. Its name is *install.exe*. It is found in the root directory of the *Multiliteracy CD*. The PODIUM Installer works with any multimedia publishing medium, including CD-ROM, diskettes, and the World Wide Web.

The PODIUM runtime is called *rtpodium.exe*. You will find it in the *wnpodium* directory on the *Multiliteracy CD*. You are permitted to distribute Runtime PODIUM free of charge if your application is also free and is not being used for commercial purposes; otherwise, you must pay a modest fee for a Runtime PODIUM license, as described in Appendix A.

Multimedia Publishing Alternatives

There are three ways to publish a multimedia application created with PODIUM. First, you can create a multimedia CD-ROM. This is the easiest method, and it is also the most popular. A good example is the *Multiliteracy CD* that came with this book. You may recall how easy it was to install the *Multiliteracy CD* when you started reading this book. Chapter 63 teaches you how to create multimedia CDs that are just as easy to install.

Second, you can publish PODIUM applications on diskettes. PODIUM has a tool that makes diskette publishing easy. If your application is large, it may require too many diskettes, but the diskette method is attractive if your application is small or if you do not have easy access to a CD-R (compact disc—recordable) drive. The diskette method is also a handy way to create a backup of your application, so you have an extra copy on diskette in case an accident occurs on your hard disk drive. Chapter 64 teaches how to publish PODIUM apps on diskettes.

Finally, you can publish PODIUM applications on the World Wide Web. This is a two-step process. First, you pack your PODIUM application into a "zip" file. Chapter 65 shows how to do that. Then you put the zip file into a self-extracting archive on the Web and link the archive to your Web page. To install your application, the user downloads the self-extracting archive and unzips it onto the hard drive. Chapter 66 is a tutorial on World Wide Web publishing.

Movie on CD

Demonstrations
➡ Show Me!
  ➡ **Creating the**
     Install.cfg File

Creating the *install.cfg* File

The PODIUM Installer is customizable. You can configure the Installer to set up applications in different ways. For example, you can make applications appear full-screen or in a window, you can suppress the PODIUM title page, and you can make any screen be the startup screen. To configure the Installer, you create an *install.cfg* file; *cfg* stands for configuration.

Regardless of what method you use to publish a PODIUM application, you will need to create an *install.cfg* file. PODIUM has a tool that makes it easy to create an *install.cfg* file. For example, suppose you want to create an *install.cfg* file for the History of Flight application. Follow these steps:

▶ Pull down the PODIUM Controls menu and choose Installation; the Installation dialog appears as shown in Figure 62-1.

▶ The Filename of PODIUM executable file field will be preset to *rtpodium.exe*. Leave that field alone unless you have a special license to distribute some other version of PODIUM.

▶ In the Title of Application for Startup Icon field, type the name you want the startup icon to have on your user's desktop. Keep this name short; one or two words is best. For the History of Flight application, make the title be:

History of Flight

62-1

The Installation dialog via the PODIUM Controls Menu.

▶ In the Application Startup Home File field, type the path\filename of your application's home screen. Do not enter a drive letter, such as *c:\flight\history.cus;* rather, omit the drive letter, as in **flight\history.cus**

▶ Leave the Path field blank. Although it is possible to set a path here and omit paths from the links in your application, your software will be more transportable if you always put the path on your links and leave the Path field blank.

NOTE   You have heard this before, but it cannot be overemphasized: Do not put drive letters in your links. For example, instead of linking to a file as *c:\flight\history.cus,* enter the link as *flight\history.cus.* The reason why you should not include drive letters is to enable your application to run from any drive the user chooses to install it on.

▶ In the PODIUM "Full Screen" Size list box, leave the setting at Automatic unless you have a particular reason for making the maximum size of the PODIUM window be some other size.

▶ In the Graphics Design Size list box, leave the screen size set to 640 × 480 unless you designed your application for some other screen size.

NOTE   To design an application for a different screen size, you must pull down the PODIUM Controls menu, choose Configuration, and change the design size *before* you begin developing the application. Unless you have a screen size greater than 640 × 480 and *all* of your users have screens at least that big, you should not change the design size settings from the default 640 × 480.

▶ In the Startup Switches group, you will probably want to check Full Screen Only to make your application run at full-screen size, and if your application starts with a title page that you want to have replace the PODIUM title page, you can check the Suppress Title Page switch as well. The other switches should remain unchecked for most applications.

▶ If you are publishing on diskettes or the World Wide Web, you should check the Read/Write Drive button in the Run PODIUM From group. If you are publishing on CD-ROM, you will probably want to check the CD-ROM button, which will make PODIUM run from the CD to save space on the user's hard drive.

▶ Click the Save button and save the *install.cfg* file in the same directory where your application's startup file resides. For the History of Flight application, make the filename be:

```
c:\flight\install.cfg
```

Inspecting the *install.cfg* File

The *install.cfg* file is a plain text file that you can inspect with any text editor. For example, to view the *install.cfg* file in the root directory of the *Multiliteracy CD,* follow these steps:

▶ Pull down the PODIUM Files menu and choose Edit Other File; the blank Notepad appears.

62-2

The *install.cfg* file in the root directory of the *Multiliteracy* CD.

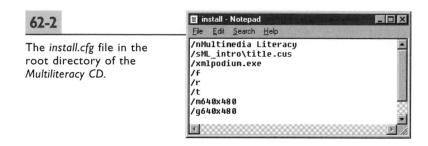

> Pull down the Notepad's File menu, choose Open, and open the *install.cfg* file in the root directory of your CD-ROM drive. Assuming your CD-ROM drive is letter D, the file to open is *d:\install.cfg*.

> The file appears as shown in Figure 62-2.

Each line of the *install.cfg* file is an installation switch. The switches begin with a forward slash (/). The first letter after the slash identifies the switch. Table 62-1 tells what the switch letters mean. A few of the switches have parameters that appear immediately after the switch letter. There are no spaces typed between the switch letter and the parameter.

Although it is possible to edit an *install.cfg* file in the Notepad, it is safer to use the Installation dialog. To edit an *install.cfg* file with the Installation dialog, follow these steps:

> Pull down the PODIUM Controls menu and choose Installation; the Installation dialog appears.

Table 62-1 *install.cfg* Switches

Switch	What the Switch Does
/a	Automatic sequencing switch; makes the application run all by itself by triggering the next link if the user does not click anything. This feature is intended only for self-running demos.
/b	Bitmap resize switch; suppresses the automatic resizing of bitmaps to fill the PODIUM window.
/c	Cursor change switch; suppresses the automatic change of the cursor shape when the user mouses over a hot spot.
/d*param*	Directories switch; *param* is the search path. *Example:* /dc:\;d:\;c:\windows
/f	Full-screen-only switch; the user will not be able to put PODIUM into a window.
/g*param*	Graphics design size; the minimum screen resolution for which the application was designed. *Example:* /g640x480
/h	Hard drive switch; installs the application to the user's hard drive.
/m*param*	Maximum screen size; the size to which PODIUM will expand when the full-screen key F2 is pressed. *Example:* /m640x480
/n*param*	Name switch; specifies the name that will appear as the title of the icon that launches the application. *Example:* /nHistory of Flight
/r	Read-only switch; makes the application run from a CD-ROM instead of install itself to the hard drive.
/s*param*	Startup filename; specifies the name of the file with which the application will begin. The filename should contain a path but not a drive letter. *Example:* /sflight\history.cus
/t	Title screen switch; suppresses the appearance of the PODIUM title screen.
/x*param*	Executable switch; specifies the name of the PODIUM executable file. *Example:* /xrtpodium.exe

▶ Click the Open button and browse to the *install.cfg* file you want to edit; the switch settings appear in the Installation dialog.

▶ Change the settings in the Installation dialog as you like.

▶ Click the Save button to save the *install.cfg* file.

List of *install.cfg* Switches

Table 62-1 lists the *install.cfg* switches and explains what they do. When the user runs the PODIUM install program, the switches control the properties of the icon that gets created to launch your application.

E X E R C I S E S

1. Use the Notepad to inspect the *history\install.cfg* file you created for the History of Flight application. Notice how the /n name switch setting is *History of Flight*. Close the Notepad. Use the Installation dialog via the PODIUM Controls menu to edit the *history\install.cfg* file. Change the title to *Aviation History* and save the file. Use the Notepad to inspect the *history\install.cfg* file. What does the name switch say now?

2. Use the Notepad to inspect the *history\install.cfg* file. Observe how it contains a /f switch to make the application run full-screen. Use the Installation dialog via the PODIUM Controls menu to edit the *history\install.cfg* file. Turn off the Full Screen Only switch and save the file. Use the Notepad to inspect the *history\install.cfg* file. What happened to the /f switch?

63

Creating Multimedia CDs

After completing this chapter, you will be able to:

- **Package your application for publication on CD-ROM**

- **Optimize your screens to run fast from CD-ROM**

- **Decide whether to roll your own CD or use a compact disc service bureau**

Y definition, every multimedia PC has a CD-ROM drive. So it is no surprise that CD-ROM has become the medium of choice for publishing multimedia applications. The production process has become so streamlined that thousands of CD-ROM copies can be pressed quickly and inexpensively. Even the cost of CD-R (CD recordable) drives has fallen to the point at which most developers can afford to buy their own CD-R for making so-called "one-off" copies on writable CDs. The term *one-off* refers to CD-ROMs that get made one at a time on a CD-R drive.

It is incredibly easy to publish a multimedia CD with PODIUM. This chapter describes the process. This is the same process that was used to create the *Multiliteracy CD* that comes with this book.

Packaging Your Application for CD-ROM

There is very little work to do in packaging a PODIUM application for publication on CD-ROM. That is because the CD-ROM simply consists of an exact copy of the directories and files in your application, along with Runtime PODIUM, the PODIUM Installer, and your application's *install.cfg* file.

An ideal way to produce a multimedia CD is to have a spare hard disk drive that is large enough to hold the contents of a CD-ROM. Most computers have a free bay into which you can install an extra disk drive. The cost of hard disk drives has fallen to the point at which it costs very little to add a gigabyte drive that can hold the contents of a CD-ROM. The Iomega Jaz drive is another attractive alternative; because gigabyte Jaz disks are removable, you can be working on several projects simultaneously, with each project residing on a different disk.

NOTE One gigabyte is 1,000 megabytes. A CD-ROM can hold about 650 megabytes. Therefore, gigabyte drives can store the contents of an entire CD-ROM, with room to spare.

If you have a CD-R drive, another option is to use a writable CD. You will not be able to correct problems on the writable CD like you can on a read/write hard disk or Jaz disk; but the cost of writable CDs has fallen to such a reasonable level ($9 as this book goes to press) that it does not cost all that much if you have to make changes and press another one-off.

Whatever medium you target for creating the CD contents, the publication process is the same. Follow these steps:

▶ Your application will consist of one or more directories; create all of your application's directories on the targeted storage device.

▶ Copy all of your application's files into the proper directories on the targeted storage device. Make sure the target has exactly the same directory structure that your application has.

▶ Create a *wnpodium* directory off the root directory of the targeted storage device.

▶ Copy the following three files from the *Multiliteracy CD* into the *wnpodium* directory on the target:

wnpodium\rtpodium.exe	This is the PODIUM executable file
wnpodium\wnpodium.hlp	This is the PODIUM help file
wnpodium\podcover.bmp	This is the title screen graphic

▶ Following the instructions provided in Chapter 62, create an *install.cfg* file for this application. Make sure you check the CD-ROM switch.

▶ Copy the *install.cfg* file to the root directory of the targeted storage device.

▶ Copy the *install.exe* file from the root directory of the *Multiliteracy CD* to the root directory of the targeted storage device.

The targeted storage device now contains an exact copy of what you want to have pressed onto CD-ROM. Before you start making thousands of copies, test the target thoroughly. Run the install program to make sure it works correctly. Test the icon that the install program creates to start the application. Does the icon have the correct name? Does the icon launch the application's home screen? Does the display appear the way you want it? If there are any problems, use the Installation dialog via the Controls menu to change the *install.cfg* file, and test the installation again.

After you get the installation working, run through your application. Try all of the links. Make sure everything works. Test, test, test. You cannot overtest an application before you publish it.

Running the Optimizer

CD-ROM is inherently slower than hard disk. When you run your application from a CD, you may notice delays, especially if your CD-ROM is one of the slower models. PODIUM has an Optimizer that can speed up your application.

Although the Optimizer was created for PODIUM authors who are creating CD-ROMs, it will also speed up applications running from hard disk. Users with fast computers will probably not notice much of a difference, but on slow machines optimization can make quite a difference.

WHAT THE OPTIMIZER DOES

If you have a multimedia screen that consists of several buttons and icons layered onto a bitmap, it can take several seconds to load that screen from a CD-ROM, because each graphic requires a disk access. With the average CD-ROM seek time being around ⅓ second on most players, layered graphics can create a considerable delay. A simple screen with just three or four buttons can take more than a second to display.

PODIUM's Optimizer solves this problem by collecting all of the layered graphics into a single bitmap. Instead of loading each graphic individually, PODIUM loads the optimized bitmap. Everything appears at once.

To speed the application further, the Optimizer also gathers any text, graphs, and drawn objects into the optimized bitmap, so everything pops out on the screen at once. The Optimizer knows not to gather objects that are subject to change, such as a variable that gets plotted on a graph, or a graphic that moves across the screen.

Movie on CD

Demonstrations
➡ Show Me!
　➡ **Optimizing
　　a File**

HOW TO OPTIMIZE A FILE

The Optimizer appears in the advanced row of the toolbox. To optimize a file, follow these steps:

▶ Get the screen you want to optimize into your PODIUM window.

▶ Press ⌷F4⌷ to open the toolbox, and right-click the Expand icon at the right edge of the toolbox; the advanced row of tools appears.

▶ Click the Optimizer icon; the Optimizer dialog appears as shown in Figure 63-1.

▶ In the box at the bottom of the Optimizer dialog, PODIUM will have proposed a filename for the optimized bitmap that is about to be created; change the name now if you want a different filename, then click OK.

▶ PODIUM will warn you if the bitmap already exists. If the preexisting bitmap is not one created from a previous optimization of this file, you should specify a different filename for the optimized bitmap to avoid overwriting one of your application's images.

▶ PODIUM optimizes the file and closes the toolbox.

If you try to open the toolbox on an optimized file, PODIUM will tell you that the file has been optimized and ask if you want to remove the optimization. To remove the optimization, click Yes; otherwise, click No. The toolbox cannot be used to edit an optimized file, so if you click No, the toolbox will close.

63-1

The Optimizer dialog.

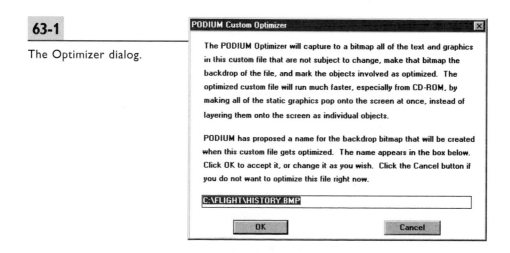

PODIUM Custom Optimizer

The PODIUM Optimizer will capture to a bitmap all of the text and graphics in this custom file that are not subject to change, make that bitmap the backdrop of the file, and mark the objects involved as optimized. The optimized custom file will run much faster, especially from CD-ROM, by making all of the static graphics pop onto the screen at once, instead of layering them onto the screen as individual objects.

PODIUM has proposed a name for the backdrop bitmap that will be created when this custom file gets optimized. The name appears in the box below. Click OK to accept it, or change it as you wish. Click the Cancel button if you do not want to optimize this file right now.

`C:\FLIGHT\HISTORY.BMP`

[OK]　　　　[Cancel]

Rolling Your Own CD

CD-R drives (the *R* stands for recordable) have come down in price considerably. If you plan to get serious about becoming a multimedia developer, it probably will cost you less to buy a CD-R drive than to pay a compact disc service bureau to make one-offs for you. Deciding when to use a service bureau is a simple matter of estimating how many discs you will need to make, finding out how much the service bureau charges to make one-offs, and computing the break-even point at which it would be more cost-effective to buy a CD-R drive and roll your own CDs.

There are trade-offs to consider. Although having your own CD-R drive is convenient, it does take time to make CDs, and CD-R drives can be tricky to install. On the other hand, when you are working against a deadline, a problem arises, and you need to get a new CD made quickly, nothing beats having your own CD-R. Hurtig's (1996) *CD Recorders Buyers Guide* lists a half-dozen CD-R drives that cost less than $1,000. For the latest information on CD-R drives and other multimedia products, visit http://www.hyperstand.com.

Compact Disc Service Bureaus

Having a service bureau press a CD-ROM for you is a straightforward process. You send in your application on a storage medium the service bureau supports, and the bureau produces the CD-ROM for you, making as many copies as you request. The service bureau will tell you what storage media are supported. You will save a lot of time and cost if the bureau supports the medium you used to package your application. As this book goes to press, typical CD-ROM pressing costs are about $1,000 for mastering and setup, and $1.50 per disc. In large quantities, discs cost less than a dollar each.

Because CD-ROM is a read-only medium, it cannot be changed after the CD is pressed; therefore, if you do not have a CD-R machine to make your own one-off, it is wise to pay for the service bureau to make one for you. The one-off will cost $50 to $300, depending on how quickly you need the bureau to make it for you. Test the one-off thoroughly to make sure your application runs from the CD exactly as intended before you pay the price for pressing multiple copies. Ideally, you should try installing and running your application on a machine that has neither PODIUM nor your application on it already.

You can find out more about pressing CDs by contacting Disc Manufacturing, Inc. (DMI). Point your Web browser at http://www.discmfg.com, which tells how to get a demo disc that contains all of DMI's technical papers and takes you on a tour through a virtual museum dedicated to CD technology. You can learn about compact disc technology from the CD-ROM Family Tree and watch how CDs are made in the DMI Plant Tour.

List of Optimizing Commands

There are two optimizing commands that will appear in a custom file after you optimize it. The first line of the file will contain the following command:

```
! @optimized filename.bmp
```

The key word @optimized indicates that the file has been optimized, and *filename* is the name of the optimized bitmap that appears as the backdrop on the screen.

The other command is called @opt. You will find @opt written at the end of each line that has been optimized. When PODIUM runs an optimized file, the lines marked with @opt are ignored, because the @opt lines are handled by the optimized backdrop.

E X E R C I S E S

1. Use PODIUM to get your *multilit\example.cus* file on the screen. If you completed the Multimedia Tools and Techniques tutorial in Part Five of this book, your *multilit\example.cus* file should contain lots of icons and lines of text. Press F12, which is PODIUM's reread key, to make PODIUM redraw the screen. Watch closely and you should be able to see the graphics being drawn one-by-one as each icon's bitmap is read. Now press F4 to open the toolbox, and right-click the Expand icon to reveal the advanced tools. Click the Optimizer icon and optimize the file. Now press F12, and see whether the display plots more quickly. It should be instantaneous now.

2. After completing exercise 1, inspect the *multilit\example.cus* file with the Notepad. Does the @optimized key word appear at the top of the file? What is the name of the optimized bitmap that appears next to the key word @optimized? Search for the key word @opt, which marks the lines of the file that have been optimized. Was anything optimized that you think should not have been? Was anything not optimized that you think should have been?

3. After completing exercise 2, remove the optimization from *multilit\example.cus* by opening the toolbox on it. Click Yes when the toolbox asks if you want to remove the optimization. Inspect the file with the Notepad. Has the @optimized command been removed from the first line of the file? Have all of the @opt commands been removed?

64

Publishing on Diskettes

After completing this chapter, you will be able to:

- **Use the PODIUM Publisher to publish a multimedia application on diskettes**

- **Configure the PODIUM Installer to install a multimedia application from diskettes**

- **Create a packing list for publishing a multimedia application on diskettes**

Not everyone can afford the hardware needed to roll their own CDs. Even if you own a CD-R drive, there will be times when you would like a quick way to publish something on a diskette. For example, you might have an application small enough to fit on a couple of diskettes. Perhaps you want to share an application with someone who does not have a CD-ROM drive.

For these reasons, the PODIUM Publisher was created. This chapter teaches you how to use the PODIUM Publisher to publish multimedia applications on diskettes. The tools you will learn in this chapter are the same tools that are used to distribute the retail version of PODIUM on diskettes.

Movie on CD

Demonstrations
➡ Show Me!
  ➡ **Publishing on Diskettes**

The PODIUM Publisher

To use the PODIUM Publisher to publish an application onto diskettes, follow these steps:

▶ Get several blank formatted diskettes ready. It is important to keep the disks clearly labeled and numbered throughout the publication process. On the stick-on label of the first disk, write the name of your application, followed by *Disk 1*. For example, if you are publishing your History of Flight application, write this on the label:

   `History of Flight`
   `Disk 1`

▶ Use PODIUM to bring up the home screen of the application you want to publish.

▶ Pull down the Tools menu and choose PODIUM Publisher; the Publisher dialog appears as shown in Figure 64-1.

64-1

The PODIUM Publisher dialog.

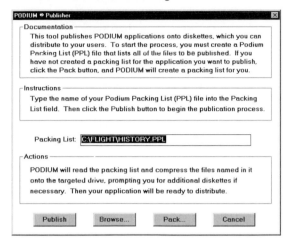

64-2

The PODIUM Packing List Creator dialog.

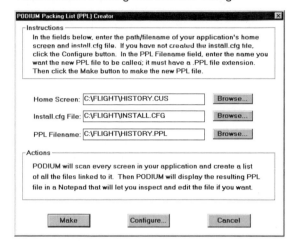

▶ The Publisher dialog prompts you for the name of your application's packing list. If you have not yet created a packing list for this application, or if you want to regenerate the packing list, click the Pack button; the Packing List Creator dialog appears as shown in Figure 64-2.

▶ In the Home Screen field, if the name of your application's home screen is not correct, fix it now. This field must contain the complete path to the home screen's filename, including the drive letter.

▶ In the Install.cfg File field, enter the complete path\filename of your application's *install.cfg* file. If you have not yet created an *install.cfg* file for this application, click the Configure button to create one, and make sure you choose the Read/Write Drive option since you are publishing on diskettes. If you need help, follow the detailed instructions in Chapter 62 for creating an *install.cfg* file.

▶ In the PPL Filename field, enter the name you want this application's packing list to have. The packing list must end with a *.ppl* filename extension; *PPL* stands for PODIUM packing list. Normally, the packing list resides in the same directory as your application's home file, and it has the same filename as your application's home screen. For example, if you are creating a packing list for your History of Flight application, you would normally enter the following *.ppl* filename:

`c:\flight\history.ppl`

▶ Click the Make button to make the PPL file. PODIUM will scan your application and make a packing list of all the files linked to it. The status of the scan will be printed in the Actions window at the bottom of the Packing List Creator dialog.

▶ When the scan is done, PODIUM will give the message: "Your packing list has been created. Would you like to view it in the Notepad?" Click Yes; the Notepad will appear.

▶ In the Notepad, you will find two columns of information. The first column is a list of the files linked to your application. The second column is the destination where those files will be copied onto diskettes when you publish your application.

▶ Before you continue, check the left column of the Notepad. Do you see any obvious mistakes there? Are there filenames without paths? If so, you should not continue publishing, because it is poor netiquette to put files in the root directory of the user's hard drive when you publish an application. You should move those files to one of your application's directories, then start this publication process again.

▶ If the PPL file in the Notepad looks OK, close the Notepad. The name of the PPL file should now appear in the Packing List field of the Publisher dialog. If not, click the Browse button and browse for the PPL file.

▶ Click the Publish button. PODIUM will ask you to insert your first blank, formatted diskette. Do that and click OK. PODIUM will prompt you if more disks are needed.

▶ Label each disk before you put it into the drive. For example, if you are about to put in disk 2 of your History of Flight application, write this on the disk's stick-on label:

```
History of Flight
Disk 2
```

If PODIUM reports any errors during the publication process, you should correct those errors, then repeat the process. Do not distribute diskettes to your users if PODIUM reported errors during the publication process.

Distributing Diskettes to End Users

As always, before you distribute diskettes to your users, you should test the disks and make sure they work OK. Put disk 1 into your computer and use Windows to run the install program on disk 1. Only after you verify that the application installs and runs OK should you consider distributing diskettes.

When you do distribute your application, you should include instructions on how to install the application. Since the installation process is so simple, you can tell the user something like this:

```
To install the History of Flight application, put disk 1 into your
diskette drive and use Windows to run the install program on disk 1.
The Installer will prompt you with additional instructions as needed.
```

If your users are experienced, your instructions can be very brief. On the label of disk 1, you can simply write the following line:

```
Run "install" to install.
```

If your users are novices, you will need to supply more-detailed instructions, explaining how to "run" an install program under Windows 3.1 and under Windows 95. Here is an example:

```
If you have Windows 3.1:
    Pull down the Program Manager's File menu and select Run.
    The Run dialog will appear.

If you have Windows 95:
    Click the Start button and select Run.
    The Run dialog will appear.

Insert disk 1 and type:
    a:install

Press Enter or click OK. Further instructions will appear on-screen.
```

Anatomy of a PODIUM Packing List

PODIUM packing lists are plain old ASCII text files that have the filename extension *.ppl*. You can either create the packing list by hand, or you can use the PODIUM Publisher to create it automatically. Figure 64-3 is a sample packing list that shows how you type your application's filenames into two columns. In column 1, you indicate the "source" directories and filenames in the application; in column 2, you indicate the "target" directories and filenames you want these items to have on the application's distribution diskettes.

Two files must be targeted for the root directory of the application's diskettes: *install.exe* and *install.cfg*. These two files must occur first in the packing list. All of the other files should remain in the directories in which you created them.

Wildcards are permitted in column 1; for example, to copy all of the bitmaps from the History of Flight application, you could type **d:\aircraft*.bmp** instead of listing all of the bitmaps individually.

64-3

A sample PODIUM packing list.

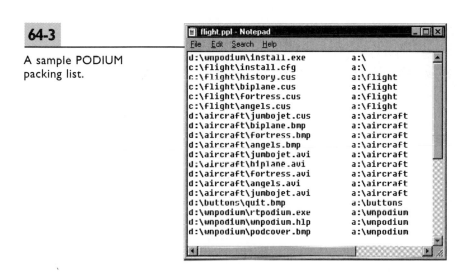

EXERCISES

These exercises are designed to help you develop your PODIUM publishing skills. First you create a tiny application, then you publish it onto diskette. Finally, you test the diskette to make sure the application installs properly.

1. Use PODIUM to create a new custom file called *pubtest.cus* in the *multilit* directory on your hard disk drive. Use the Backdrop tool to make the backdrop be *backdrop\ocean.bmp*. Use the Text tool to enter the following line of text:

> `Click here to listen to the ocean.`

Use the Link tool to link the following waveform audio file to the text just entered: *audio\ocean.wav*. Put the toolbox away and test the link to make sure it works. You should hear the ocean.

2. Get a blank formatted diskette and follow the instructions in this chapter to publish the *multilit\pubtest* application you created in exercise 1. When you create the *install.cfg* file, name the application **Publication Test** and save the *install.cfg* file in your *multilit* directory. When you make the PODIUM packing list, save it in the *multilit* directory under the name *multilit\pubtest.ppl*.

3. When you are done publishing, compare your *multilit\pubtest.ppl* file to the one in Figure 64-4. If they match (except for possible differences in drive letters if your hard drive is not C or your CD-ROM drive is not D), congratulate yourself because you succeeded. If they do not match, repeat these exercises and try to find what went wrong.

64-4

Contents of the
multilit\pubtest.ppl file.

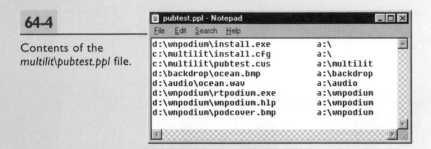

4. Put the disk you published into the diskette drive, and run its install program. Follow the installation instructions that appear on the screen. When you are done, the Publication Test icon should appear on your screen. Double-click the icon to see if it launches the *pubtest.cus* file. If so, you are well on your way to becoming a multimedia publisher. If not, review this chapter and try to figure out what went wrong.

65 Zipping and Unzipping Multimedia Applications

After completing this chapter, you will be able to:

- **Understand why you want to be able to compress and decompress multimedia applications**

- **Recognize PKWARE as the industry leader in compression and decompression technology**

- **Know what it means to zip and unzip a file**

- **Use PKZIP for Windows to zip your multimedia applications**

- **Recognize filenames with** *.zip* **extensions as applications that have been zipped via PKZIP**

- **Unzip files that have been zipped**

MULTIMEDIA applications consist of many files. It is not unusual for an application to contain hundreds or even thousands of files. Imagine what it would be like trying to publish such an application if you had to distribute each file separately. For example, suppose you want users to be able to download your application from the World Wide Web and run it on their multimedia PCs. If users had to download hundreds of individual files, the process would be so time-consuming and cumbersome that no one would bother.

Happily, there is a way to compress and combine all of the files in your application into a single file called a zip file. Zipped files have the filename extension *.zip*. To zip an application means to compress all of its files into a single zip file. To unzip an application means to extract its files from the zip file and restore them to their original condition. This chapter teaches you how to zip and unzip files. Then the next chapter teaches you how to turn zipped files into self-extracting archives that you can publish on the World Wide Web.

NOTE   Do not confuse the *.zip* filename extension with the Iomega Zip drive. Iomega Zip is a trade name, not a file type. You can store any kind of file on a Zip drive, including a zip file.

Installing PKZIP for Windows

The computing industry is fortunate to have an acknowledged leader in compression and decompression technology. PKWARE, Inc., dominates the market with a DOS product called PKZIP and a Windows product called PKZIP for Windows. Zipped files are interchangable between the DOS and Windows versions of PKZIP. This book uses PKZIP for Windows.

The shareware version of PKZIP for Windows is found on the *Multiliteracy CD* in the *pkware* directory. If you decide to use PKZIP for Windows, you must fill out the form printed in Appendix C and mail it to PKWARE with the fee indicated for your intended purpose. For more information, visit PKWARE's Web site at http://www.pkware.com.

To install PKZIP for Windows, follow these steps:

▶ If you have Windows 3.1:

  ▪ Pull down the Program Manager's File menu and select Run. The Run dialog will appear.

▶ If you have Windows 95:

  ▪ Click the Start button and select Run. The Run dialog will appear.

▶ Run the *pkzws201.exe* program in the *pkware* directory on the *Multiliteracy CD*. For example, if your CD-ROM drive is D, type **d:\pkware\pkzws201.exe** and press [←Enter]. The Installation dialog appears as shown in Figure 65-1.

65-1

The PKZIP for Windows Installation dialog.

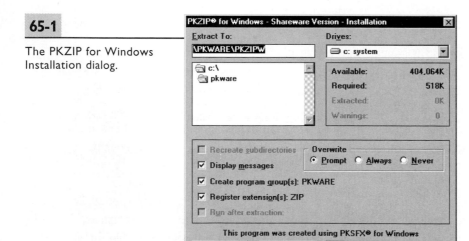

▶ Make sure the Drives setting is showing the letter of the drive on which you want to install PKZIP (probably C); leave all of the other settings alone.

▶ Click the Extract button. The software installs very fast and sets up an icon you can double-click whenever you want to run PKZIP for Windows.

Zipping Applications into Zip Files

The graphical user interface makes it very easy to zip applications with PKZIP for Windows. Follow these steps:

▶ Double-click the PKZIP icon to get PKZIP for Windows running.

▶ Pull down the PKZIP File menu and choose New; the Save As dialog appears.

▶ Type the filename you want your new zip file to have. Make sure you give it a *.zip* filename extension. Then click OK; the Add Files dialog appears as shown in Figure 65-2.

▶ The top left quadrant of the Add Files dialog contains the familiar Windows file browser. Use the controllers to browse to the drives and the directories that contain the files you want to zip, and double-click the filenames you want included in the zip file. As you double-click the files, their names appear in the Files and Directories to Zip box in the lower left quadrant of the dialog.

▶ If you need help in the Add Files dialog, click the Help button; PKZIP for Windows has a thorough help system.

▶ Click the Preferences button; the Zip Preferences dialog appears as shown in Figure 65-3. Leave all the settings alone except for the Path Information group, where you should click the Full path option. This will preserve the directory structure of your application when it gets zipped. Click the Save as default button so you will not have to keep setting the preferences every time you zip a file. Click OK to close the Zip Preferences dialog.

▶ When you are ready to create the zip file, click OK. PKZIP will zip all the files you selected into a single zip file. During the zipping process, the Add Status dialog will appear as shown in Figure 65-4 to let you know what is going on. When PKZIP is finished, a Done button will appear; click the Done button.

▶ A new window will appear, displaying a directory of the contents of the newly created zip file. Scroll through the directory to make sure things look OK. Scroll right if you want to review the PKZIP statistics, telling how much each file got compressed. Then close the window and close PKZIP.

65-2	65-3
The Add Files dialog in PKZIP for Windows.	The Zip Preferences dialog. Click the Full path option in this dialog.

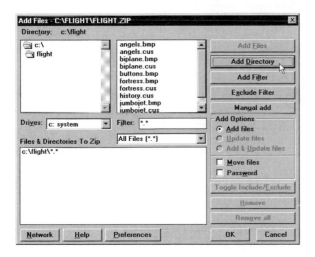

65-4

The Add Status dialog shows the progress of the compressor.

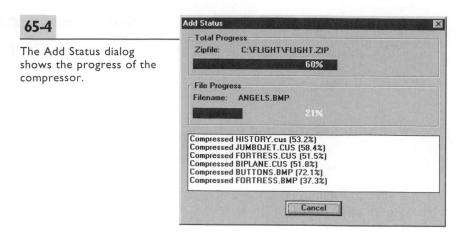

Unzipping Applications from Zip Files

To unzip an application from a zip file, follow these steps:

▶ If the person who distributed the zip file instructed you to install it into a particular directory, use the File Manager or the Explorer to create the directory off the root of your hard drive.

▶ Double-click the PKZIP icon to get PKZIP running.

▶ Pull down the PKZIP File menu and choose Open; the Open dialog appears as shown in Figure 65-5.

▶ Browse to the zip file you want to unzip, and click OK; a window opens to reveal the contents of the zip file.

▶ Pull down the Unzip menu and select Extract Files; the Extract dialog appears as shown in Figure 65-6. If the person who distributed the zip file instructed you to install it into a particular directory, click the Browse button and browse to that directory.

65-5

The PKZIP Open dialog lets you browse for the zip file you want to unzip.

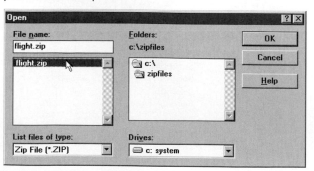

65-6

The PKZIP Extract dialog.

65-7

How to set the options in the Unzip Preferences dialog when you unzip files.

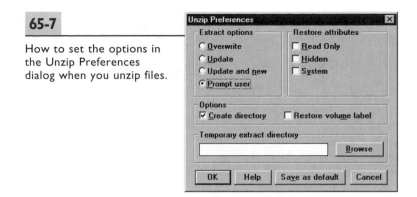

▶ Click the Preferences button and make sure the options are set as shown in Figure 65-7. It is important that the Create directory option be set so the directories will get created, and that the Prompt user option will make PKZIP ask you before it replaces any files on your computer with files of the same name in the zip file. Click OK to close the Unzip Preferences dialog.

▶ Click the Extract button to unzip the files.

▶ Close the window and close PKZIP.

E X E R C I S E S

In addition to combining several files into one zipped file that is easy to distribute, PKZIP compresses the size of the files considerably. For example, there is a text file in the *highway* directory on the *Multiliteracy CD* called *history.txt* that contains Bruce Sterling's excellent History of the Internet. In an uncompressed state on the *Multiliteracy CD*, the size of the *history.txt* file is 21,396 bytes. Use PKZIP for Windows to compress the *history.txt* file into a zip file called *multilit\history.zip* in the *multilit* directory of your hard drive. Then answer these questions:

1. How large is the *multilit\history.zip* file?

2. By what percentage did PKZIP compress the *history.txt* file?

After you answer these questions, you may delete the *c:\history.zip* file.

66 World Wide Web Publishing

After completing this chapter, you will be able to:

- **Zip your multimedia application into a self-extracting archive**

- **Upload the self-extracting archive to the Web**

- **Link the self-extracting archive to a hyperlink on your Web page**

- **Provide installation instructions that make it easy for users to download and install multimedia applications from the Web**

- **Download self-extracting archives from the Web**

H E World Wide Web provides one of the quickest and easiest ways to publish multimedia applications. This chapter shows you how to zip your multimedia applications into self-extracting archives that you can publish on the Web. When a user triggers a link to a self-extracting archive on the Web, the Web browser knows automatically that the archive needs to be downloaded to the user's PC, and a dialog pops out that helps the user download the archive. Then it is a simple matter for the user to execute the archive and install your application.

Creating a Self-Extracting Archive

To create a self-extracting archive for a multimedia application created with PODIUM, follow these steps:

▶ Copy the PODIUM Installer to the main directory of your multimedia application. For example, suppose you are publishing the History of Flight application. Copy the *install.exe* program from the root of the *Multiliteracy CD* to the *flight* directory on your hard drive.

▶ Create an *install.cfg* file in the same directory to which you copied the *install.exe* file in the previous step. Review the steps in Chapter 62 if you are not sure how to create an *install.cfg* file.

▶ Create a directory to put your zip file in. You should *not* put the zip file in your application's directory. Instead, create a directory on your hard drive called *zipfiles*.

▶ Get PKZIP running, pull down the File menu, and choose New. PKZIP will ask you to name the new file; make up a filename that makes sense for your application. For example, if you are publishing the History of Flight application and your hard drive is C, you could name the zip file *c:\zipfiles\flight.zip*. Click OK, and the Add Files dialog appears.

▶ In the Add Files dialog, select all the files in the application you are publishing. Make sure to include the following files that are needed to publish an application created with PODIUM:

install.exe	From your application's primary directory
install.cfg	From your application's primary directory
rtpodium.exe	From the *wnpodium* directory on the *Multiliteracy CD*
wnpodium.hlp	From the *wnpodium* directory on the *Multiliteracy CD*

▶ Before you click OK to zip your application, click the Preferences button and make sure the Full path option is checked.

▶ After the zip file is created, scroll through the window that displays the files that were compressed. Make sure there are no files from the root directory; users get really mad when you write files into the root directory of their computers. All of the files should be in your application's directories.

▶ Close PKZIP.

NOTE The rest of these steps require the use of DOS. PKWARE is working on a Windows version that will make this easier. To find out whether the Windows version is available, check PKWARE's Web site at http://www.pkware.com.

▶ Double-click your computer's DOS icon to get a DOS session running. Change to the directory that contains the zip file you just created. In this example, assuming your hard drive is C, the commands to type are:

```
c:
cd \zipfiles
```

▶ Now you will use PKWARE's *zip2exe* program to create the self-extracting archive. Assuming your CD-ROM drive is D, the command to type is:

```
d:\pkware\zip2exe flight.zip
```

▶ When the *zip2exe* program finishes, you will find a self-extracting archive named *flight.exe* in your *zipfiles* directory. Type **Exit** and press ⏎Enter to end the DOS session.

Linking Self-Extracting Archives to World Wide Web Pages

To link the self-extracting archive to your Web page, follow these steps:

▶ FTP the self-extracting archive to your World Wide Web site. If you are not sure how to do this, review the FTP instructions in Chapter 56.

66-1

Sample Web page instructions for downloading and installing self-extracting archives. Modify the italicized words to adapt these instructions for your projects.

> The *History of Flight* application is very easy to download and install. All of the files you need are contained in a self-extracting archive named *flight.exe* that you download to the root directory of your hard drive. Then you run the *flight.exe* file, which will create two directories on your hard drive. The *flight* directory will contain the application, and the *wnpodium* directory will contain the runtime PODIUM module, plus anything else you might already have in your *wnpodium* directory.
>
> To setup the demo, you use Windows to run the Install program you will find in the *flight* directory. The install program sets up an icon on your Windows desktop that launches the *History of Flight* application.
>
> When you run the self-extracting archive *flight.exe*, make sure you follow these directions:
>
> - Make sure your current drive is the drive on which you want the demo to be installed, because the self-extracting archive will copy the demo to your current drive.
> - When you run the *flight.exe* file, make sure you use the -d option. For example, if your hard drive is C, you would type the command: c:\flight.exe -d
>
> Now you can **download** the *flight.exe* file or **return** to the index.

▶ Use your Web creation software, such as WebEdit, to create a new Web page that contains instructions for the user to follow when downloading and installing your self-extracting archive. Figure 66-1 provides a sample of instructions you should feel free to copy and modify for your projects. The HTML file for these instructions is found on the *Multiliteracy CD* in *html\download.htm*.

In Figure 66-1, you can see how the word *download* is printed in blue. That is the hyperlink to which you should link your self-extracting archive on the Web. Use the WebEdit software to make a link to the archive's URL. For example, if your WWW site is www.northpole.com and your self-extracting archive is called *zipfiles\santa.exe,* the URL would be http://www.northpole.com/zipfiles/santa.exe.

Link the HTML file you just created to the appropriate word or phrase on the Web page that advertises the existence of your multimedia application. Users will click there to bring up the instructions containing the hyperlink that downloads your self-extracting archive.

Downloading Self-Extracting Archives from the World Wide Web

It is easy to download self-extracting archives from the World Wide Web. When you trigger a link to a self-extracting archive, your Web browser knows that the file must be downloaded to your PC in order to run. The best way to learn how to download an application is to just do it. Follow the steps below to download a set of interactive graphs that were created for an economics course at the University of Delaware. By getting on the Web and actually working through this example, you will get a feel for how the downloading process works.

To download and install a self-extracting archive from the World Wide Web, follow these steps:

▶ Browse to the Web page to which the self-extracting archive is linked. In this example, you would point your Web browser at http://www.udel.edu/podium to bring up the PODIUM Web page. Scroll through the table of contents and choose PODIUM Demos to Download. Then choose Interactive Graphs. The screen shown in Figure 66-2 appears.

66-2

The Key Graphs download instructions.

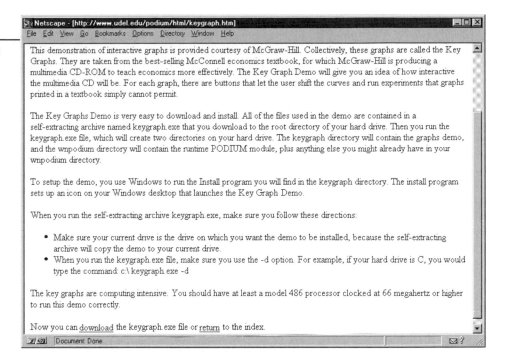

> Read the instructions carefully, especially the part about the -d option that you type when you run the self-extracting archive. The -d option re-creates your application's directories. If the -d option is missing, your files will get copied to the user's current directory instead of to your application's directories.

> When you are ready to download the self-extracting archive, click the blue highlighted word *download*.

> Web browsers know that self-extracting archives need to be downloaded, so the Download dialog appears.

> Before the download starts, you will be asked to specify the drive and directory to which you want to download the file; assuming your hard drive is C, type: **c:**

> Click whatever button your browser provides to begin downloading the file.

> After the download is completed, run the self-extracting archive. In this example the name of the archive is *keygraph.exe*. Assuming your hard drive is C, the command to run is: **c:\keygraph.exe -d**

> Run the install program, which in this example will be found in the *keygraph* directory on your hard drive; after the installation is complete, a PODIUM icon named Key Graph Demo will appear on your screen.

> Double-click the icon and make sure the application runs OK.

> If you want to conserve disk space, you can delete the self-extracting archive from your hard drive, because you do not need it any longer.

Make sure you test thoroughly any self-extracting archive that you put on the Web before you announce it to the world. You will make yourself very unpopular if you cause problems for other users. Scan your computer for viruses before you create your self-extracting archive; you do not want to put any viruses up on the Web. Make sure your self-extracting archive puts the files into the right places. Then run your application, try all of the links, and make sure all the files that need to be there are present. Ideally, you should test this on a computer that does not already have your application installed on it.

Publishing PODIUM Applications Natively on the World Wide Web

PODIUM supports the HTTP protocol on the World Wide Web. This makes it possible to publish PODIUM applications directly onto the Web and run them from the Web, without needing to zip them and without requiring the user to download and install them. Network delay can slow the application, however. Especially during the playing of real-time data streams such as movies, network delay can cause unacceptable interruptions. It is possible to create so-called hybrid applications in which the movies reside on a hard disk or CD-ROM attached to the user's computer, with only the PODIUM files residing on the Web. Someday, the network might get fast enough to provide uninterrupted real-time data streams. It is already possible to run an intranet (as opposed to Internet), wherein you run the World Wide Web protocols on a closed network that can be optimized to provide high-bandwith real-time continuous multimedia data streams.

It is very easy to run PODIUM applications directly off the Web. If you want to give this a try, follow these steps:

▶ On your Web server, create the same directory structure that the application has on your PC.

▶ FTP your application's files to the same directories on your Web server.

▶ To launch an application from the Web, you use the @server command. The @server command makes a Web site act as though it were another hard drive added to the path of your PODIUM application. The syntax of the @server command is @server=*url*. For example, suppose your Web account is www.northpole.com and the startup file of your PODIUM application is *fastcars\corvette.cus*. To launch this application from the Web, you would simply link the following two lines to any PODIUM hypertext or trigger:

```
@server=http://www.northpole.com
fastcars\corvette.cus
```

PODIUM can retrieve any type of file from the Web, including custom files, bitmaps, audio files, movies, executable files, and text files. Any hypertext or trigger can launch a PODIUM application directly from the Web.

When running applications from the World Wide Web, PODIUM buffers and caches files and domain names in order to streamline and hide network delay as much as possible. PODIUM keeps its WWW cache in the PODIUM working directory on your hard drive. PODIUM deletes the cache when you quit PODIUM. The cache is dynamic. PODIUM looks ahead and caches objects in advance when it is obvious what the user is going to do next. It is also possible to preload multimedia objects with the @preload command. The syntax of the @preload command is @preload=*filename* where *filename* is the path\filename of the file you want PODIUM to preload.

Concluding Comment

Because this is the last chapter in the book, it should probably conclude with some profound statement about the future of multimedia. This book is already full of statements attempting to be profound, however, so let's end instead with a quote from a famous old song: "We've only just begun." Now that you're started, enjoy the journey.

E X E R C I S E S

The following exercises will help you develop the ability to create self-extracting archives. First, you make a tiny application called Acid Test. Then you zip it into a self-extracting archive. Next comes the acid test, hence the application's name: You delete the application from your computer and then see if you can restore it by running the self-extracting archive. Once you can successfully complete this exercise, you will be ready to create self-extracting archives for more-complicated applications.

1. Create a new directory on your hard drive called *acidtest*. Use PODIUM to create a new home screen called *acidtest\home.cus*. Use the Text tool to write the following text on the screen:

```
THE ACID TEST
This is a test of zipping an application into a self-extracting archive.
This is screen 1. Click here to see screen 2.
```

Link the last line of the *acidtest\home.cus* file to a nonexistent file called *acidtest\screen2.cus*. Put the toolbox away and trigger the link. Say Yes when PODIUM asks if you want to create the file. Use the Text tool to write the following text on the screen:

```
This is screen 2 of the Acid Test application.
Click anywhere to return to the first screen.
```

Close the toolbox and click to test the links between the two screens of the Acid Test application.

2. Following the procedures outlined in this chapter, zip the Acid Test application into a self-extracting archive. Follow all the steps, which will result in the creation of an archive that contains the *install.exe* and *install.cfg* files along with a copy of Runtime PODIUM. Name the archive *acidtest.exe*.

3. Copy the *acidtest.exe* file to the root directory of your hard drive. Then delete the entire *acidtest* directory.

4. Now comes the "acid test" to see if you can re-create the contents of the *acidtest* directory by running the *acidtest.exe* self-extracting archive. From a DOS prompt, type the following commands:

```
c:
cd \
acidtest.exe -d
```

5. Close the DOS session. Use Windows to run the *install.exe* program in the *acidtest* directory. This should set up an icon for starting the Acid Test application. Double-click the icon and test the links in the application. If this works, you are ready to begin publishing more-complex applications.

Appendix A: How to Purchase PODIUM

You can purchase PODIUM directly from the University of Delaware by mail, fax, or e-mail. Credit-card orders must include the type of credit card, the account number, the expiration date, and the cardholder's signature. Send your orders to:

Instructional Technology Center   Phone: (302) 831-8164
307 Willard Hall Education Building   Fax: (302) 831-2089
University of Delaware   E-mail: podium@udel.edu
Newark, DE 19716

PODIUM Pricing

There are many ways to purchase PODIUM. Individuals who want a copy of PODIUM for their personal use may purchase a Personal PODIUM license at a substantial discount off the normal retail price. Personal PODIUM is a fully functioning copy of the retail product, yet it costs only $149. Educational institutions are permitted to purchase copies for individual employees at the Personal PODIUM price.

Shipping charges are applied to orders outside the United States.

Quantity discounts make PODIUM very affordable for schools and companies. Institutional licensing provides a cost-effective way for institutions that adopt PODIUM to make it "freely" available to all of their employees.

	New Buyers	Upgrades
Personal PODIUM	$ 149	$ 89
Runtime PODIUM	$ 35	$ 25
Retail PODIUM	$ 495	$ 150
2–5 copies	$ 395	$ 125
More than 5	$ 300	$ 100
More than 10	$ 200	$ 75
20-user network license	$ 2,750	$ 500
Each additional 10 users	$ 1,375	$ 250
Institutional license	$ 10,000	$ 2,000

Institutions that use PODIUM for kiosking must pay a runtime license of $89 per kiosk, unless the institution has puchased an institutional license, in which case there is no additional charge for kiosking. Educators and end users who distribute applications for free may include Runtime PODIUM at no extra cost.

Appendix B: **Paint Shop Pro Order Form**

Product	Quantity	Price	Total
Paint Shop Pro		$69.00 each	
Sales tax (Minnesota residents only)		$4.49 each	
Shipping and handling in U.S. & Canada: $5.00			
Shipping and handling outside of U.S. & Canada: Air—$16.00; ground (allow up to 8 weeks)—$5.00			
Total			

☐ Windows 95 CD-ROM ☐ Windows 95 3.5" disk ☐ Windows 3.1 3.5" disk

☐ VISA ☐ MasterCard ☐ Check **(U.S. funds drawn on U.S. bank)**

☐ Purchase order (enclosed) # _____

Card # _____

Exp. date _____ Signature _____

Name			
Company			
Street			
City		State	Zip
Country			
Day phone			

Please return this form when you order.
JASC, Inc.
Attn: Orders
P.O. Box 44997
Eden Prairie, MN 55344

Order Now By Calling
(800) 622-2793
9 A.M.–5 P.M. CST
Fax number: (612) 930-9172, 24 hours

Appendix C: **PKZIP Order Form**

Name: _____ Date: _____

Company: _____

Address: _____

City: _____

State: _____ Zip: _____ Country: _____

Daytime phone: _____ Fax: _____

PKZIP,® PKUNZIP,® and PKSFX® for Windows

INDIVIDUAL USE

☐ Diskette with programs and documentation .... $49 $_____.____

MULTIPLE USE

Site License for the use of PKZIP, PKUNZIP, and PKSFX includes one diskette with programs and documentation.

☐ 2 to 9 computers at $38 each .... # computers _____ × 38 $_____.____
☐ 10 to 24 computers at $30 each .... # computers _____ × 30   _____.____
☐ 25 to 49 computers at $24 each .... # computers _____ × 24   _____.____
☐ 50 to 99 computers at $18 each .... # computers _____ × 18   _____.____
☐ 100 to 199 computers at $14 each .... # computers _____ × 14   _____.____
☐ 200 to 500 computers at $12 each .... # computers _____ × 12   _____.____

Write or call for pricing on quantities over 500.

☐ Extra program disk and documentation with purchase of
  Site Licenses of two or more available at $8 each.   _____ × 8 $_____.____

Shipping and handling (postal) U.S. and Canada: $6.00/item
Outside U.S. and Canada $13.50/item .... $_____.____

Wisconsin residents add applicable state and county sales tax .... $_____.____

TOTAL ENCLOSED U.S. FUNDS ....   US$_____.____

☐ MasterCard   ☐ VISA   Expiration date _____

Card number: _____

Cardholder's signature REQUIRED _____

Send form to:

> **PKWARE, Inc.**   (414) 354-8699 voice
> 9025 N. Deerwood Dr.   (414) 354-8559 fax
> Brown Deer, WI 53223   (414) 354-8670 BBS

TERMS: MasterCard, VISA, check, or money order drawn on a U.S. bank in U.S. funds. Corporate purchase orders (net 30 days) accepted for software from large corporations within the U.S. and Canada. ALL LICENSES ARE PREPAID ONLY. ALL ORDERS OUTSIDE OF THE UNITED STATES AND CANADA MUST BE PREPAID. Please make remittance payable to PKWARE, Inc. Prices and terms subject to change without notice.

PKWARE, PKZIP, PKUNZIP, and PKSFX are registered with the U.S. Patent and Trademark Office. Windows is a registered trademark of Microsoft Corporation.

Glossary

8-bit graphics A computer graphics mode capable of displaying up to 256 different colors simultaneously; 256 is 2 to the eighth power (2^8).

16-bit graphics A computer graphics mode capable of displaying up to 65,536 different colors simultaneously; 65,536 is 2 to the sixteenth power (2^{16}).

24-bit graphics A computer graphics mode capable of displaying up to 16,777,216 different colors simultaneously; 16,777,216 is 2 to the twenty-fourth power (2^{24}).

A/D converter Analog-to-digital converter. A device that uses quantization and sampling to transform a continuous analog waveform into a digital bit stream.

algorithm A sequence of processing steps that perform a particular operation, such as compressing a digital video to store it efficiently and decompressing it upon playback.

AltaVista A full-text key word search engine for the World Wide Web invented by the Digital Equipment Corporation. AltaVista is on the Web at http://www.altavista.digital.com.

ambient sound A multimedia technique in which a waveform audio file keeps repeating to create the aural illusion that the user is in the place or situation where the sound was recorded.

animation In multimedia, animation is the use of a computer to create movement on the screen.

anonymous FTP A method by which computers on the Internet allow public access to certain files. These files can then be examined and downloaded by anybody. See *FTP*.

applet A little application that gets downloaded to your computer along with a Web page.

aspect ratio The relative width-to-height dimensions of a computer display's picture elements (pixels). The typical 640×480 screen has an aspect ratio of 4:3.

avatar An agent representing the user in a virtual reality system.

bandwidth The capacity of a device to process or transmit information. The more information it can handle per second, the greater its bandwidth.

baud rate See *bps*.

bitmap The picture formed by assigning different colors to the pixels on a computer screen; or the computer file that specifies how to color the pixels to create such a picture.

BMP The three-character filename extension for Microsoft Windows bitmaps. See *bitmap*.

bookmark A place in a World Wide Web document that you can jump to by name.

bounce To mix two or more audio tracks into one.

bps Bits per second. A measurement of the speed at which data is transmitted over a communications medium. Also known as *baud rate*.

camcorder A combination of *camera* and *recorder*. A portable device that records video and sound onto videotape.

CAV Constant angular velocity. A type of videodisc that can hold 54,000 still frames per side, or 30 minutes of motion video. See also *CLV*.

CD Audio The use of a compact disc (CD) to play back recorded music. Compact discs can hold up to 75 minutes of audio. Multimedia computers can access the audio in increments as small as $1/75$ of a second.

CD Extra See *CD Plus*.

CD-I Compact disc–interactive. A multimedia delivery platform standard invented by Philips and Sony. The special players required for CD-I discs can also play CD Audio discs.

CD Plus A multisession CD-ROM format in which a regular CD Audio session has been augmented by multimedia materials in another session. You can play back a CD Plus on a regular CD Audio player if you just want to hear the music, or you can install it on a multimedia PC and navigate through hypertext, buttons, pictures, and videos recorded in subsequent sessions. Also known as *Enhanced CD* and *CD Extra*.

CD-ROM Compact disc—read-only memory. The use of a compact disc to store computer data. CD-ROMs can hold up to 680 MB.

CD-ROM XA CD-ROM extended architecture. Increases to as much as 19 hours the amount of audio that can be stored on a compact disc by providing lower-quality recording and playback rates.

chroma key Process whereby overlay cards display video on the screen and one of the colors becomes transparent. Anyplace the transparent color appears, you see the video input.

client A computer seeking information on your behalf from a server on a network.

CLV Constant linear velocity. A videodisc format that permits up to an hour of video to be recorded on each side of the disc. Most videodisc players cannot show still frames from CLV discs. See also *CAV*.

copyright A law that secures for limited times to authors and inventors the exclusive right to their respective writings and discoveries. See *fair use*.

custom toolbox An object-oriented set of multimedia development tools in the PODIUM multimedia application generator.

data rate The speed of data transfer, normally expressed in bits or bytes per second. For example, the data rate of a single-speed CD-ROM is 150,000 bytes per second, or 150 KB; double-speed CD-ROMs are twice as fast at 300 KB per second.

dB Decibel, a measurement of loudness. The higher the rating, the louder the sound. A whisper is 10dB; jet aircraft engines produce 130dB, which can permanently damage hearing.

DCT Discrete cosine transform. A video compression algorithm that eliminates redundant data in blocks of pixels on the screen. It is used in JPEG (stills), MPEG (motion), and CCITT (fax) compression standards.

DejaNews A search engine for Usenet newsgroups on the Internet. DejaNews is at http://www.dejanews.com.

digitizing The process of converting analog audio and video signals into a digital format that can be stored, manipulated, and displayed by a computer. Digitizing is accomplished by A/D converters on scanners and audio/video capture cards. See also *A/D converter*.

directory An index to the files and subdirectories that are stored on a computer storage device.

dissolve A transition effect between two sequential images on the screen. Dissolve patterns include splits, stripes, diagonals, and fades.

DLL Dynamic link library. The expandable software technology that enables vendors to add features easily to the Microsoft Windows environment.

domain name Allows numeric IP addresses (like *140.147.248.7*) to be expressed by names like *www.loc.gov*. See also *IP address*.

DSP Digital signal processor. A chip designed to process digitized sound and video quickly.

Enhanced CD See *CD Plus*.

Ethernet A high-speed network topology that provides access at speeds up to 10 MB per second, depending on how many users are connected to the network. Multiple users on an Ethernet can cause data collisions, which require data to be re-sent, causing the network to slow down. See also *token ring*.

fade A gradual decrease in the brightness of an image or the loudness of a sound.

Fair Use A section of the U.S. copyright law that allows the use of copyrighted works in reporting news, conducting research, and teaching. See the *Fair Use of Educational Multimedia* guidelines in the Demonstrations/Textbook Examples section of the *Multiliteracy CD*.

FAQ Frequently asked question. A list of frequently asked questions and their answers.

File Transfer Protocol See *FTP*.

flowchart A logic diagram that illustrates the steps involved in an interactive decision-making process.

fps Frames per second. A measure of the recording and playback rate of digital videos.

frame animation Makes objects move by displaying a series of predrawn pictures, called frames, in which the objects appear in different locations on the screen.

frame rate The speed at which frames are displayed on the monitor. Broadcast television in North America and Japan is displayed at 30 fps; in Europe it is displayed at 25 fps.

freenet An organization that provides free Internet access to people in a certain area, usually through public libraries.

front-end The creation or use of software to make it easy for people to perform computing tasks that would otherwise be too complicated or time-consuming for everyday use.

FTP File Transfer Protocol. Allows users to send a file from one computer to another over the Internet.

full motion Video played at the broadcast television frame rate. See also *frame rate*.

gateway A computer whose role on a network is to reformat data sent from one computer into a form it can forward to another.

GB See *gigabyte*.

GIF Graphics Interchange Format. Invented by CompuServe for use on computer networks, GIF is the prevalent graphics format for images on the World Wide Web.

gigabyte One billion bytes. A byte can hold a single character; a gigabyte can hold a billion characters. Abbreviated *GB*.

Gopher A menu-based system for accessing Internet resources, including host computers, directories, and files.

Gopherspace The connection of all existing Gopher servers.

GUI Graphical user interface. Allows direct manipulation of on-screen objects and events using icons, menus, toolbars, and dialog controls. Macintosh, Windows, and OS/2 Presentation Manager are examples of GUIs.

hard drive A magnetic storage device on which computer programs and data are stored.

helper app An application that helps a World Wide Web browser handle a file that the browser cannot deal with on its own.

home page The Web page that serves as your main menu or home base on the Web. By linking things to your home page, you create a hierarchy that makes it easy to go to other Web pages and access resources on the Web. See *Web page*.

host The main computer to which a user is connected when accessing the Internet.

hot spots Places on the computer screen which, when selected, trigger the objects or events linked to them.

HTML Hypertext markup language. The coding specification for creating Web pages. An HTML file contains the text you see on a Web page, plus special codes called markup that determine how the text gets displayed and how the user interacts with the Web page.

hyper In multimedia, a prefix used to indicate that a link has given a new dimension to a word (hypertext), video (hypervideo), audio (hyperaudio), or part or all of a picture (hyperpicture).

IAB Internet Architecture Board. The governing body that makes decisions about Internet standards.

IETF Internet Engineering Task Force. A volunteer group that investigates and solves technical problems and makes recommendations to the Internet Architecture Board. See also *IAB*.

IMA Interactive Multimedia Association. The IMA encourages the setting of industrywide standards for multimedia hardware and software.

Information Superhighway A popular term coined by the Clinton administration to refer to the Internet with a metaphor the public could understand. See *Internet*.

input field A blank space on a computer screen into which the user can type information.

internaut A user who navigates the vast expanse of the Internet, much like an astronaut traverses outer space.

Internet The worldwide network of networks that are connected to each other via the Internet Protocol (IP).

Internet address Each computer on the Internet has a named address such as *www.loc.gov* (the Library of Congress Web site). See also *domain name*.

Interner Explorer See *Microsoft Internet Explorer*.

IP address A 32-bit numeric address of a computer on the Internet. An IP address consists of four numbers separated by periods. The numbers range from 0 to 255. The smallest address is 0.0.0.0 and the largest is 255.255.255.255. The number of IP addresses this scheme allows is 256^4, which is 4,294,967,296. See also *domain name*.

ISDN Integrated Services Digital Network. A high-bandwidth digital telecommunications network being installed gradually throughout the United States. This network handles voice, video, and data; it also supports videoconferencing.

ISO International Standards Organization.

IVD Interactive videodisc. A multimedia format in which a computer is connected to a videodisc player to provide interactive video capabilities.

Java An applet technology invented by Sun Microsystems. See *applet*.

JPEG Joint Photographic Experts Group. An ISO (International Standards Organization) body creating a new standard for digitizing still photographic images. The standard (which is also called JPEG) is cooperatively developed by more than 70 companies and institutions worldwide, including Sony, Philips, Matsushita, and Apple. The JPEG standard permits compression ratios ranging from 10:1 to 80:1—but the greater the compression, the lower the quality of the image.

K One thousand, a unit of computer measurement. For example, 150 K means 150,000. (Purists will tell you that the *K* used by computer scientists actually means slightly more than a thousand [1,024 to be precise], but for the measurements used in this book, a thousand is close enough and much easier to compute.)

KB See *kilobyte*.

kilobyte One thousand bytes. A byte can hold a single character; a kilobyte can hold a thousand characters. Abbreviated *KB*.

knowbot An information retrieval tool that you can train to go out on the Internet and find things for you.

layout The relationships among graphic design elements that appear on the screen, including text, pictures, icons, triggers, and buttons.

logic The use of conditional statements that act according to the values of variables. In multimedia, logic is used to make screens more sensitive to user needs and preferences. Logic is also used to increase the complexity, and hence the pizzazz, of multimedia special effects.

login To type your name and password to initiate a session with a host computer.

lossy Compression techniques in which decompressed images do not contain all the original information. JPEG and MPEG are lossy. The opposite is lossless compression. RLE (run-length encoding) is lossless but does not compress as much. See *RLE*.

markup Special codes inserted into a document, informing programs that read the document how to display or handle it. See *HTML*.

MB See *megabyte*.

meg See *megabyte*.

megabyte One million bytes. A byte can hold a single character; a megabyte can hold a million characters. Abbreviated *meg* or *MB*.

megahertz One million cycles per second. Processor speed is measured in megahertz. *Mega* means million, and *hertz* is one cycle per second. Abbreviated *MHz*.

megapixel One million pixels. See *pixel*.

metacognition Knowledge about your own thinking and learning.

metacognitive knowledge Knowledge about how tasks are performed and what makes some tasks more difficult than others.

MHz See *megahertz*.

Microsoft Internet Explorer Microsoft's World Wide Web browser.

MIDI Musical Instrument Digital Interface. The MIDI standard is a protocol by which electronic musical instruments communicate with computers and each other.

MIME Multipurpose Internet Mail Extensions. An Internet protocol that lets you attach a file to a mail message. When a user receives the message, the attached file gets decoded and stored on the user's PC.

modem A datacommunications device that connects a computer to a telephone line and lets the user transfer data at speeds ranging from 1200 bits per second (bps) to 33.6 KB per second.

morph To transition one shape into another by displaying a series of frames that creates a smooth movement as the first shape transforms itself into the other shape.

Mosaic A World Wide Web browser created in 1993 by the University of Illinois supercomputer center. The graphical user interface in Mosaic made the Web very easy to use and led to the Web's becoming the most popular protocol on the Internet.

MPC Multimedia PC. An industrywide specification of the minimum hardware requirements needed for multimedia. For the latest MPC specs, go to http://www.spa.org.

MPEG Motion Pictures Experts Group, an ISO (International Standards Organization) body creating a new standard for digital video. The standard (which is also called MPEG) was cooperatively developed by more than 70 companies and institutions worldwide, including Sony, Philips, Matsushita, and Apple. MPEG is emerging as the digital video standard for compact discs, cable TV, direct satellite broadcast, and high-definition television.

multiliterate Understanding the principles of multimedia, its impact on the world, and how to use it for attaining business, professional, educational, and personal objectives.

multimedia The use of a computer to combine and present text, graphics, audio, and video with links and tools that let the user navigate, interact, create, and communicate.

multisession A type of CD-ROM drive that can play back CDs that have been recorded on more than once.

Netscape Navigator One of the most popular World Wide Web browsers for the Internet.

NIC Network Information Center. Every network on the Internet should have an NIC and a network administrator. Each NIC looks after the needs of the users connected to its network.

NOC Network Operations Center. The organization responsible for the day-to-day operations of a network.

NTSC National Television Standards Committee. The North American TV standard is named after the committee that created it.

overlay To superimpose text and graphics on still or motion video images.

PAL The European television standard that displays 25 frames per second. Used in all European countries except France; see also *SECAM*.

palette A table of colors used to paint pixels on the screen. The typical multimedia computer with SVGA graphics can display a 256-color palette.

PC Card A plug-in credit card–sized PCMCIA peripheral for personal computers. See *PCMCIA*.

PCMCIA Personal Computer Memory Card International Association. The name of a standards group that creates specifications for credit card–sized peripherals for personal computers. See *PC Card*.

Pentium A microprocessor chip manufactured by Intel and its licensees. See *processor*.

pixel Picture element—the tiny dots that make up the computer screen. Each pixel has a specific color and intensity level.

play list A sequence of CD Audio clips, or MIDI or waveform audio files, that play back one after another.

point-to-point protocol Establishes a TCP/IP connection to the Internet through a modem. Abbreviated *PPP*.

PPP See *point-to-point protocol*.

processor The brain in a computer where calculations and decisions get made.

protocol A definition of how computers communicate with each other.

RAM Random access memory. The main memory at the heart of a computer in which multimedia programs execute.

Red Book The CD Audio protocol for recording audio onto compact discs. The minute-second-frame CD Audio addresses defined in the Red Book specification are known as Red Book addresses.

resolution A measurement of the number of pixels on a display. The typical multimedia computer has a resolution of 640 × 480 pixels. See *pixel*.

RGB Red, green, and blue. Each pixel displayed on the screen consists of a certain amount of red, green, and blue. For example, a black pixel has no red, green, or blue, whereas a white pixel has the maximum amount of each.

RLE Run-length encoding. A lossless data compression technique that encodes the number of times a repeated data element recurs instead of recording each occurrence. For example, 12 red pixels in a row would be encoded as 12R instead of RRRRRRRRRRRR.

root directory The primary directory on a hard disk from which all other directories branch. See also *directory*.

sampling The process of measuring and recording the values of an analog signal at evenly spaced time intervals.

sampling rate The number of times an analog signal is sampled each second. For example, CD Audio is recorded at a rate of 44,100 samples per second.

SECAM Sequential Couleur Avec Memoire. The French national standard for color TV that is also used in Russia and eastern Europe. It operates at 25 frames per second.

self-extracting archive A list of files that have been archived into a single executable file that decompresses itself automatically when the user runs the archive.

server A computer on the Internet that provides information on demand to client computers. See also *client*.

shareware Computer software distributed with no up-front cost. Users who try the software and wish to keep using it must pay a fee. Shareware is not free.

SMPTE Society of Motion Picture and Television Engineers. Pronounced "sempty," SMPTE refers to a time code expressed in hours, minutes, seconds, and frames. SMPTE time code is written in the form HH:MM:SS:FF.

socket A portal on the Internet through which an application sends and receives information.

storyboard A time-based outline or script for a video or multimedia production.

subdirectory A directory inside another directory.

surf To browse an electronic medium for information. "Channel surfing" means to flip through the channels on a television set, looking for something that interests you. "Surfing the Internet" means to browse through the interconnected menus of information servers like Gopher and the World Wide Web.

SVGA Super VGA. A screen resolution standard created by the Video Electronics Standards Association (VESA) that delivers a screen resolution of up to 800 × 600 with 256-color graphics.

tag A markup element in an HTML document. Tags are surrounded by brackets, such as the <P> tag that begins a new paragraph. See *HTML* and *markup*.

task analysis The process of hierarchically outlining an application's content.

TCP/IP Transmission Control Protocol/Internet Protocol. Computers connect to the Internet via TCP/IP.

telnet A protocol that allows users to log on to remote host computers on the Internet.

terminal The computer that connects to a host. The terminal can be a personal computer.

timeout A situation in a multimedia program in which the user must respond before a predetermined time limit expires and a default action occurs.

token ring A network topology that passes data in tokens that travel the network in a ring. Token ring networks run at 4 MB or 16 MB per second and are less prone to slow down as the number of users increases. See also *Ethernet*.

unzip To expand a zipped file back to its original uncompressed state. See *zip*.

upload To send a file to your host or to a remote host on the Internet. See also *host*.

URL Universal resource locator. The address of a resource on the World Wide Web.

vector animation A vector is a line that has a beginning, a direction, and a length. Vector animation makes objects move by varying these three parameters for the line segments that define the object.

videodisc An optical disc on which video signals are recorded. Usually 12 inches in diameter, videodiscs are used for entertainment and to provide video in multimedia training applications. Videodiscs come in two formats: CAV and CLV. See also *CAV* and *CLV*.

WAIS Wide-area information servers. An Internet utility that provides full-text search capability.

waveform audio A method of creating sound by digitizing an analog audio waveform and storing the digital samples on a disk in a WAV file, from which the recording can be played back on demand. *WAV* stands for waveform.

wavetable A list of numbers that describe the desired waveshape of a sound.

WebMaster The person in charge of creating and maintaining a World Wide Web site.

Web page An HTML hypertext document on the World Wide Web. See *HTML*.

winsock The name of the dynamic link library (DLL) that enables the Windows operating system to open sockets on the Internet.

World Wide Web A networked hypertext system that allows documents to be shared over the Internet. Developed in Geneva at the European Particle Physics Center (CERN). Abbreviated *WWW*.

WWW See *World Wide Web*.

Yahoo A subject-oriented index of the World Wide Web. Located at http://www.yahoo.com.

zip To compress one or more computer files into a smaller file that contains the same information in a compressed format that occupies less space on a computer.

Bibliography

Alexander, Joanna, and Mark Long. "Cyber Sports." *VR World* (July/August 1995): 12.

Arnold, Kandy. "AT&T Braces for Blackout." *NewMedia* 3, no. 9 (September 1993): 33.

Bangert-Drowns, Robert L., James A. Kulik, and Chen-Lin C. Kulik. "Effectiveness of Computer-Based Education in Secondary Schools." *Journal of Computer-Based Instruction* 12, no. 3 (Summer 1985): 59–68.

Barron, Anne, Brendan Tompkins, and David Tai. "Design Guidelines for the World Wide Web." *Journal of Interactive Instruction Development* (Winter 1996): 13–16.

Beichner, Robert J. "The Video Encyclopedia of Physics Demonstrations." *Educational Technology Review* (Autumn/Winter 1993): 50–51.

Brill, Louis M. "Home VR: Electronic Playgrounds, Living Room Style." *Virtual Reality World* 2, no. 2 (March/April 1994): 18–32.

Brown, J. S., A. Collins, and P. Duguid. "Situated Cognition and the Culture of Learning." *Educational Researcher* 28 (1989): 32–42.

Bruning, Roger H., G. J. Schraw, and R. R. Ronning. *Cognitive Psychology and Instruction.* Englewood Cliffs, N.J.: Merrill/ Prentice-Hall, 1995.

Buchanan, Leigh. "The Virtual Campaign." *CIO* (April 1, 1994): 66–70.

Cantwell, Steve. "Multimedia Transforms Union Pacific's Training Strategy." *Tech Trends* 38, no. 6 (November/ December 1993): 21–22.

Cognition and Technology Group at Vanderbilt, The. "Anchored Instruction and Its Relationship to Situated Cognition." *Educational Researcher* 19 (1990): 2–10.

Computer Technology Research Corporation. *Multimedia Technology.* Charleston: Computer Technology Research Corp., 1992, 1993.

Connolly, Bruce. "Presentation Systems for the Electronic Classroom." *MultiMedia Schools* (May/June 1995), 29–37.

Cook, Nancy. "Mario Is Missing." *Technology & Learning* 14, no. 4 (January 1994): 7–13.

Coupland, Ken. "Declarations of Independents." *NewMedia* (October 1993): 48–54.

DeLoughry, Thomas J. "History, Post-Print." *The Chronicle of Higher Education* (January 12, 1994): A19–20.

Dennis, Verl E. "How Interactive Instruction Saves Time." *Journal of Instruction Delivery Systems* 8, no. 1 (Winter 1994): 25–28.

Doyle, Bob. "Crunch Time for Digital Video." *NewMedia* (March 1994): 47–50.

Duncan, Jody. "A Once and Future War." *Cinefex*, no. 47 (August 1991): 4–59.

———. "Morphing to the Music." *Cinefex*, no. 50 (May 1992): 18–19.

———. "The Beauty in the Beasts." *Cinefex*, no. 55 (August 1993): 44–95.

Eiser, Leslie. "Multimedia Science Programs: Moving Science Education Beyond the Textbook." *Technology & Learning* (March 1992): 16–30.

Escalada, L.T., R. Grabhorn, and D. Zollman. "Applications of Interactive Digital Video in a Physics Classroom. *Journal of Educational Multimedia and Hypermedia* 5, no. 1 (1996): 73–97.

Farber, David. "Cyberspace, the Constitution, and the Electronic Frontier Foundation." *Educators' Tech Exchange* (Summer 1993): 22–27.

Fetterman, David M. "Videoconferencing On-line: Enhancing Communication over the Internet. *Educational Researcher* (May 1996): 23–27.

Fitzsimmons, Edward A. Interview by Barbara Clinton in *Journal of Instruction Delivery Systems* 8, no. 1 (Winter 1994): 4–5.

Foremski, Tom. "Straight Outta Compton's: A Patent Play." *Morph's Outpost* 1, no. 5 (January 1994): 16–17.

Fox, John, Karen Loutsch, and Michelle O'Brien. "ISDN: Linking the Information Highway to the Classroom." *Tech Trends* 38, no. 5 (October 1993): 18–20.

Friedman, E. A., J. D. Baron, and C. J. Addison. "Universal Access to Science Study via Internet. *T.H.E. Journal* (June 1996): 83–86.

Frost & Sullivan. *Desktop Video Markets.* Mountain View, Calif.: Frost & Sullivan, 1993.

Gamble-Risley, Michelle. "Multimedia Makes the 1996 Olympic Team." *Government Technology* 5, no. 9 (September 1992): 1.

Gates, Bill. *The Road Ahead.* New York: Penguin, 1995.

Godwin, Mike. "Sex and the Single Sysadmin: The Risks of Carrying Graphic Sexual Materials." *Internet World* 5, no. 2 (March/April 1994): 56–62.

Goldstein, Jackie, and Mike Wittenstein. "Uses of Interactive Multimedia for Advertising, Marketing, and Sales." *Multimedia Review* 4, no. 2 (Summer 1993): 60–64.

Hilferty, Dan. "General Machinery: Show & Tell on the Plant Floor." *IBM Multimedia Solutions* 4, no. 1 (January/ February 1994): 11–13.

Hitz, Martin, and Hannes Werthner. "Development and Analysis of a Wide Area Multimedia Information System." *Proceedings of the 1993 ACM/SIGAPP Symposium on Applied Computing* (February 1993): 238–46.

Hofstetter, Fred. "Multi Multimedia." *T.H.E. Journal* (February 1993): 6.

Hubbard, Janice. "Reflections of the Dead." *Cinefex*, no. 50 (May 1992): 82–83.

Hurtig, Brent. "CD Recorders Buyers Guide." *New Media* (June 3, 1996), 31–34.

Illman, Deborah. "Multimedia Tools Gain Favor for Chemistry Presentations." *Chemical and Engineering News* 72, no. 19 (May 9, 1994): 34–40.

Information Workstation Group. *Multimedia Opportunities.* Alexandria: Information Workstation Group, 1993. Call (703) 548-4320 to order this 600-page five-year forecast. $1,890 for the first copy; $200 for additional copies ordered at the same time.

Kaufman, Debra. "Effects in the Vertical Realm." *Cinefex*, no. 54 (May 1993): 30–53.

Kinnaman, Daniel E. "Compton's Re-ignites Patent Wars." *Technology & Learning* 14, no. 5 (February 1994): 14.

———. "Videodiscovery Files Complaint Against Optical Data." *Technology & Learning* 14, no. 3 (November/December 1993): 9.

Klinck, Nancy. "Back to School at Work: Training Strategies for the 90s." *Tech Trends* 38, no. 6 (November/December 1993): 32–34.

Krol, Ed, adapted by Bruce Klopfenstein. *The Whole Internet: User's Guide & Catalog,* Academic Edition. Sebastopol, Calif.: O'Reilly & Associates, Inc., 1996: 418.

Kulik, Chen-Lin C., and James A. Kulik. "Effectiveness of Computer-Based Education in Colleges." *AEDS Journal* (Winter/Spring 1986): 81–108.

———. "Effectiveness of Computer-Based Instruction: An Updated Analysis." *Computers in Human Behavior* 7 (1991): 75–94.

Kulik, Chen-Lin C., James A. Kulik, and Barbara J. Shwalb. "The Effectiveness of Computer-Based Adult Education: A Meta-Analysis." *Journal of Educational Computing Research* 2, no. 2 (1986): 235–52.

Kulik, James A. "Meta-Analytic Studies of Findings on Computer-Based Instruction" in Eva L. Baker and Harold F. O'Neil, Jr. (eds.) *Technology Assessment in Education and Training.* Hillsdale, N.J.: Lawrence Erlbaum, in press.

Kulik, James A., Chen-Lin C. Kulik, and Robert L. Bangert-Drowns. "Effectiveness of Computer-Based Education in Elementary Schools." *Computers in Human Behavior* I (1985): 59–74.

Lee, Yvonne, and Bob Francis. "PDA: Shooting Star or Falling Star?" *Infoworld* (May 2, 1994): 1.

Lerner, Eric J. "500 Channels: Wasteland or Wonderland?" *EDUCOM Review* 28, no. 6 (November/December 1993): 26–33.

Merril, Jonathon R. "Surgery on the Cutting-Edge; Virtual Reality Applications in Medical Education." *Virtual Reality World* (November/December 1993): 34–38.

Moxley, Roy A. "Three Functional Advantages of Computer Word Processing for Children's Writing." *Educational Technology Review* (Autumn/Winter 1994), 30–36.

Nelson, Theodor H. "The Hypertext." *Proceedings of the World Documentation Federation,* 1965.

Neuwirth, Konrad. "Where in the World Is Carmen Sandiego?" *Educational Technology Review* (Autumn/Winter 1994): 46–48.

Newson, Gillian. "Virtual Valerie." *NewMedia* 2, no. 11 (November 1992): 42–43.

Olmstead, Jack. "Video Stores Starstruck by Multimedia." *NewMedia* 2, no. 11 (September 1993): 23.

Parham, Charles. "Interacting with the Past." *Technology & Learning* (February 1996): 8–11.

Pearson, LaTresa. "Multimedia Hits the Road." *Presentations* 7, no. 11 (November 1993), 29–39.

———. Releasing the Power of CD-ROM. *Presentations* 8, no. 2 (February 1994): 22–26.

Piaget, J. *The Mechanisms of Perception.* New York: Basic Books, 1969.

Rahlmann, Reed K. "Dave Grusin: The Gershwin Connection." *NewMedia* 4, no. 2 (February 1994): 56–57.

Rosenthal, Steve. "Mega Channels." *NewMedia* 3, no. 9 (September 1993): 36–46.

Rumelhart, D. E. "Schemata: The Building Blocks of Cognition" in J. T. Guthrie (ed.) *Comprehension and Teaching: Research Reviews.* Newark, Del.: International Reading Association, 1981: 3–26.

Skinner, B. F. *The Behavior of Organisms.* New York: Appleton-Century-Crofts, 1938.

———. *Science and Human Behavior.* New York: Macmillan, 1953.

Smith, Stanley G., and Loretta L. Jones. "Multimedia Technology: A Catalyst for Change in Chemical Education." *Pure & Applied Chemistry* 65, no. 2 (1993): 245–9.

Stefanac, Suzanne. "Sex & the New Media." *NewMedia* 3, no. 4 (April 1993): 38–45.

———. "Digital Carnage: Do Violent Interactive Games Promote Real-Life Violence?" *NewMedia* 4, no. 1 (January 1994): 72–77.

Stewart Publishing. *Interactive Healthcare Directories.* Alexandria: Stewart Publishing, Inc., 1995.

Turkle, Sherry. *Life on the Screen: Identity in the Age of the Internet.* New York: Simon and Schuster, 1995.

Tynan, Daniel. "Multimedia Goes on the Job JUST IN TIME" in John Hirschbuhl (ed.) *Computers in Education,* 6th ed. Guilford, Conn.: The Dushkin Publishing Group, Inc., 1993: 188–94.

Vivid Studios. *Careers in Multimedia.* Emeryville, CA: Ziff-Davis Press, 1995.

Vygotsky, L. *Mind in Society: The Development of Higher Psychological Processes.* Cambridge, Mass.: Harvard University Press, 1978.

Waltz, Mitzi. "Four-Wheeling with Two Megs." *NewMedia* 3, no. 11 (November 1993): 39.

Withrow, Frank. Guest editorial in *T.H.E. Journal* 21, no. 2 (September 1993): 10.

Index of PODIUM @ Commands

PODIUM Command Syntax Summary Tables

Title	Table Number	Page(s)
Audio Commands	Table 22-4	243
Button Object Commands	Table 37-3	328
Cursor Commands	Table 43-3	365
Drawing Commands	Table 36-1	320
Flying Help Commands	Table 35-1	314
Graphics Positioning Commands	Table 20-1	228
Input Field Commands	Table 40-2	352–353
Logic Commands	Table 39-1	345
Movie Commands	Table 30-2	284
Navigation Commands	Table 28-1	267
PODIUM Overlay Commands	Table 59-1	469
Random Number Commands	Table 41-1	357
Text Commands	Table 19-1	222
Text Object Commands	Table 38-3	335
Triggering Commands	Table 21-1	235

Index